Advances in Languages and Compilers
for Parallel Processing

TITLES IN THIS SERIES

Optimizing Supercompilers for Supercomputers, Michael Wolfe, 1989

Reconfigurable Processor-Array: A Bit-Sliced Parallel Computer, Andrew Rushton, 1989

Partitioning and Scheduling Parallel Programs for Execution on Multiprocessors, Vivek Sarkar, 1989

Functional Programming for Loosely-coupled Multiprocessors, Paul H. J. Kelly, 1989

Algorithmic Skeletons: Structured Management of Parallel Computation, Murray I. Cole, 1989

Execution Models of Prolog for Parallel Computers, Péter Kacsuk, 1990

Languages and Compilers for Parallel Computing, David Gelernter, Alexandru Nicolau and David Padua (Editors), 1990

Massively Parallel Computing with the DAP, Dennis Parkinson and John Litt (Editors), 1990

Implementation of a General-Purpose Dataflow Multiprocessor, Gregory M. Papadopoulos, 1991

Implementation of Non-Strict Functional Programming Languages, Kenneth R. Traub, 1991

Parallel Processing for Computer Graphics, Stuart Green, 1991

Lazy Functional Languages: Abstract Interpretation and Compilation, Geoffrey Burn, 1991

Advances in Languages and Compilers for Parallel Processing, Alexandru Nicolau, David Gelernter, Thomas Gross and David Padua (Editors), 1991

RESEARCH MONOGRAPHS IN PARALLEL AND DISTRIBUTED COMPUTING

Edited by
Alexandru Nicolau, University of California, Irvine,
David Gelernter, Yale University,
Thomas Gross, Carnegie-Mellon University,
David Padua, University of Illinois at Urbana-Champaign

Advances in Languages and Compilers for Parallel Processing

Pitman, London

The MIT Press, Cambridge, Massachusetts

PITMAN PUBLISHING
128 Long Acre, London WC2E 9AN

© A. Nicolau, D. Gelernter, T. Gross, D. Padua 1991

First published 1991

Available in the Western Hemisphere and Israel from
The MIT Press
Cambridge, Massachusetts (and London, England)

ISSN 0953-7767

British Library Cataloguing in Publication Data
Advances in languages and compilers for parallel
processing.—(Research monographs in parallel
and distributed computing)
  I. Nicolau, Alexandru   II. Padua, David
  III. Series
  004

  ISBN 0-273-08841-6

Library of Congress Cataloging-in-Publication Data
Advances in languages and compilers for parallel processing / edited
  by Alexandru Nicolau.
      p.   cm.—(Research monographs in parallel and distributed
  computing)
    Includes bibliographical references.
    ISBN 0-262-64028-7
    1. Programming languages (Electronic computers)   2. Compilers
  (Computer programs)   3. Parallel processing (Electronic computers)
  I. Nicolau, Alexandru.   II. Series.
  QA76.7.A38   1991
  005.13—dc20

All rights reserved; no part of this publication may be reproduced,
stored in a retrieval system, or transmitted in any form or by any
means, electronic, mechanical, photocopying, recording or otherwise
without the prior written permission of the publishers or a licence
permitting restricted copying in the United Kingdom issued by the
Copyright Licensing Agency Ltd, 90 Tottenham Court Road, London
W1P 0BR. This book may not be lent, resold, hired out or otherwise
disposed of by way of trade in any form of binding or cover other than
that in which it is published, without the prior consent of the
publishers.

Reproduced and printed by photolithography
in Great Britain by Biddles Ltd, Guildford

Foreword

This book contains selected refereed papers representing recent advances in Languages and Compilers for Parallel Computing. Early versions of these papers were presented at the Third Workshop on Languages and Compilers for Parallel Computing held during August 1–3 1990 in Irvine California, under the sponsorship of the Computer Systems Design Research Unit at the University of California at Irvine. The previous workshops in this series were held in Ithaca NY, August 1988, and in Urbana-Champaign, 1989.

The topics of the papers in the book are representative of the various aspects of research in this area and illustrate the great amount of interest parallel computing in general, and parallelizing compilers and languages in particular, are currently generating.

The book is divided into several sections, roughly corresponding to the major efforts in the field. The papers by Eigenmann *et al.*, Foster & Overbeek, and Jagannathan discuss languages and language extensions. Those by Gelernter *et al.* and Gannon *et al.* present two innovative environments for parallel programming. Miller & Netzer describe techniques for debugging parallel programs. Guzzi *et al.*, Eisenbeis *et al.*, Solworth, and Gao *et al.* deal with the very important issue of data organization and management during parallel processing. New compiler techniques for parallelizing loops are described by Banerjee, Ayguadé *et al.*, and Wolf & Lam. Important new results in code scheduling are given by Gross & Ward and Aiken & Nicolau. Innovative approaches to dependency analysis and representation are provided by Kallis & Klappholz, Haghighat & Polychronopoulos, and Pingali *et al.* An interesting insight into the measurement of parallelism implicit in ordinary programs is revealed by Larus. Finally, Mehrotra & Van Rosendale, Quinn *et al.*, Li & Chen, and Dietz *et al.* deal with programming and compiling for distributed and shared memory multiprocessors.

We, the Editors, are very pleased with the breadth and depth of the work presented in these papers. Taken together, these papers are an accurate reflection of the state of research in Languages and Compilers for Parallel Computing in 1990. We hope this book will be as interesting to the reader as it was for us to compile.

Alexandru Nicolau.

Contents

1 **Cedar Fortran and its Restructuring Compiler** 1
  R. Eigenmann
  J. Hoeflinger
  G. Jaxon
  D. Padua
  Center for Supercomputing Research and Development,
  University of Illinois at Urbana-Champaign

2 **Bilingual Parallel Programming** 24
  Ian Foster
  Ross Overbeek
  Mathematics and Computer Science Division, Argonne National Laboratory

3 **Optimizing Analysis for First-Class Tuple-Spaces** 44
  Suresh Jagannathan
  Department of Computer Science, Yale University

4 **The Linda Program Builder** 71
  Shakil Ahmed
  Nicholas Carriero
  David Gelernter
  Department of Computer Science, Yale University

5 **SIGMACS: a Programmable Programming Environment** 88
  Bruce Shei
  Dennis Gannon
  Indiana University

6 **Detecting Data Races in Parallel Program Executions** 109
  Robert H. B. Netzer
  Barton P. Miller
  Computer Sciences Department, University of Wisconsin–Madison

7 **A Strategy for Array Management in Local Memory** 130
  Christine Eisenbeis
  INRIA, Le Chesnay
  William Jalby
  Daniel Windheiser
  François Bodin
  IRISA, Campus Universitaire de Beaulieu, Rennes

8 **On the Performance of Parallel Strips-Based Lists** 152
   Jon A. Solworth
   University of Illinois at Chicago

9 **An Efficient Monolithic Array Constructor** 172
   G. R. Gao
   Advanced Computer Architecture and Program Structures Group, McGill University
   Robert Kim Yates
   Advanced Computer Architecture and Program Structures Group, McGill University
   Jack B. Dennis
   Laboratory for Computer Science, Massachusetts Institute of Technology
   Lenore Restifo Mullin
   Centre de Recherche Informatique de Montréal

10 **Unimodular Transformations of Double Loops** 192
   Utpal Banerjee
   Intel Corporation, Santa Clara

11 **Parallelism Evaluation and Partitioning of Nested Loops for Shared Memory Multiprocessors** 220
   E. Ayguadé
   J. Labarta
   J. Torres
   J. M. Llaberia
   M. Valero
   Departament d'Arquitectura de Computadors, Universitat Politècnica de Catalunya, Facultat d'Informàtica de Barcelona

12 **An Algorithmic Approach to Compound Loop Transformations** 243
   Michael E. Wolf
   Monica S. Lam
   Computer Systems Laboratory, Stanford University

13 **The Suppression of Compensation Code** 260
   Thomas Gross
   School of Computer Science, Carnegie Mellon University
   Michael Ward
   IBM T. J. Watson Research Center, Yorktown Heights, NY

14 **A Realistic Resource-Constrained Software Pipelining Algorithm** 274
   Alexander Aiken
   IBM Almaden Research Center, San Jose
   Alexandru Nicolau
   Dept. Information and Computer Science, University of California, Irvine

15 Handling Unresolvable Array-Access Aliases in Refined C   291
Apostolos D. Kallis
David Klappholz
Department of Electrical Engineering and Computer Science,
Stevens Institute of Technology

16 Symbolic Dependence Analysis for High-Performance Parallelizing Compilers   310
Mohammad Reza Haghighat
Constantine D. Polychronopoulos
Center for Supercomputing Research and Development,
University of Illinois at Urbana-Champaign

17 Parallelism in Numeric and Symbolic Programs   331
J. R. Larus
Computer Sciences Department, University of Wisconsin–Madison

18 An Efficient Implementation of Thread-Specific Data   350
Mark D. Guzzi
Rich Simpson
Don Parce
Encore Computer Corporation, Marlborough MA

19 Programming Distributed Memory Architectures Using Kali   364
Piyush Mehrotra
John Van Rosendale
Institute for Computer Applications in Science and Engineering,
NASA Langley Research Center, Hampton Va

20 Implementing a Data Parallel Language on a Tightly Coupled Multiprocessor   385
Michael J. Quinn
Oregon State University
Philip J. Hatcher
University of New Hampshire
Bradley K. Seevers
Oregon State University

21 Automating the Coordination of Interprocessor Communication   402
Jingke Li
Dept. Computer Science, Portland State University
Marina Chen
Dept. Computer Science, Yale University

22 An Introduction to Static Scheduling for MIMD Architectures   425
Henry G. Dietz
Matthew T. O'Keefe
Abderrazek Zaafrani
School of Electrical Engineering, Purdue University

23 Dependence Flow Graphs: an Algebraic Approach to Program Dependencies 445
Keshav Pingali
Micah Beck
Richard Johnson
Mayan Moudgill
Paul Stodghill
Cornell University

1 Cedar Fortran and its Restructuring Compiler
R. Eigenmann, J. Hoeflinger, G Jaxon, D. Padua

Abstract

The Cedar architecture integrates shared memory into a distributed system of Alliant mini-supercomputers. Nested parallel loops and a hierarchical memory model allow Cedar Fortran to offer a wide range of implementation possibilities for an algorithm, which makes automatic parallelization easy to do, but hard to do well. Techniques from both shared memory and distributed memory programming paradigms are applied to this problem. Early results show that restructuring can speed up kernels and algorithms. We identify improved techniques that may extend these results to full applications.

1 Cedar Fortran within the Cedar System

The hardware and software structure of Cedar was motivated by a desire to achieve a low cost/performance ratio for a wide variety of applications, and to make that performance easily available to the user [28]. The hardware offers a hierarchical memory structure as well as the means to control fine-, medium-, and coarse-grain parallelism. The Cedar Fortran compiler, with support from its runtime library and the Xylem operating system, makes those architectural features available through the direct expression of parallelism within a Fortran context. The compiler includes a restructurer which can automatically translate serial programs into a parallel form.

Cedar combines two complementary approaches to parallel processing. On one hand, it can be viewed as a distributed system with high-bandwidth communication channels. On the other hand, it may be seen as a shared memory machine. A given program may

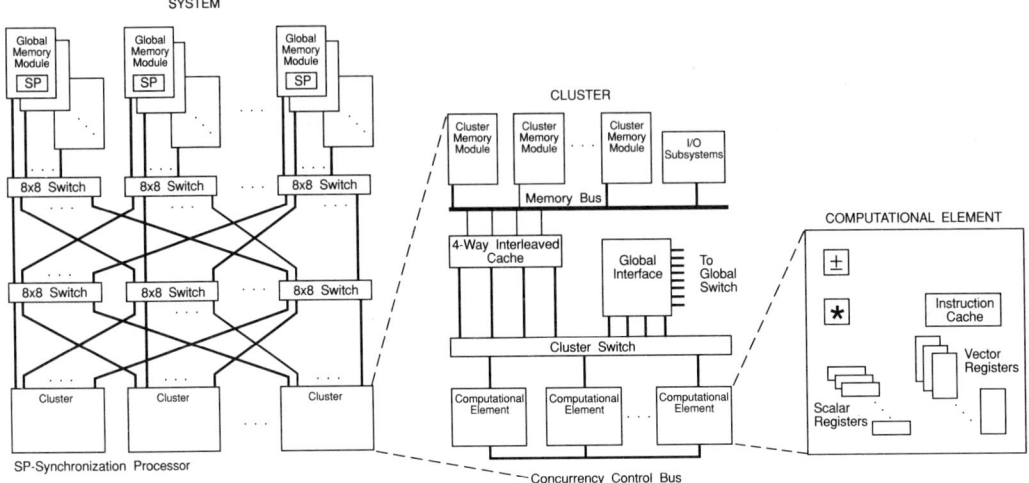

Figure 1: The Cedar Architecture

make use of both programming paradigms as the situation dictates.

The layers of concurrency in Cedar and the various ways parallel activity can be expressed in the Cedar Fortran language present many opportunities to speed up parallel programs. But, this becomes a complexity issue for the Fortran restructurer, which must choose one good translation for a given serial program from among many alternatives.

In this paper, we describe the Cedar architecture, the software environment in which Cedar Fortran runs, and the Cedar Fortran language. We then discuss the issues that this hardware and software environment presents to the Fortran restructurer. Finally, we mention some results and future directions for our research.

1.1 The Cedar Hardware Architecture

The Cedar machine (Figure 1) consists of several processor *clusters* (currently four) connected through a network to a *global memory*.

Each cluster is a modified Alliant FX/8 multiprocessor, containing up to eight vector-pipelined *computational elements* (CEs) that share a *cluster memory* [3]. Access to each cluster's local memory is accelerated by a large data cache shared by all the CEs of that cluster. On each cycle, it can respond to four memory references from different CEs in the cluster. In addition, each CE has a private instruction cache and a virtual-to-physical address translation buffer.

The physical addresses generated by Cedar's CEs have been extended. Addresses beyond the original range are routed to the CE's *global interface* instead of to the cluster's memory cache. The global interface links each CE to global memory through two communication networks. One sends data, the other receives it. Each direction in the network crosses two stages, each stage is made of 8×8 crossbar switches. The switches interconnect in the "perfect shuffle" pattern that forms an Ω-network. The resulting communication bandwidth is close to that of two complete crossbars at a much lower cost [13].

The latency to access a single word in the global memory can still be large, so the global interface includes a pipelined vector-prefetch capability. Using this, a CE may request a block of data from global memory and continue its computations while the prefetch buffer fills up. Once vector data resides in the prefetch buffer it can be accessed at the CE's peak rate. The Cedar Fortran compiler places a prefetch request in the code stream before each use of a global vector; sometimes overlapping other computation. The following table compares the incremental cost of each Cedar memory access mode.

	Relative speeds of Cedar Memory			
	LOCALE			ACCESS MODE
FAST	Register	R	W	
	Global	R		vector read already prefetched
	Cluster	R	W	cache hit
	Global	R		vector read while prefetching
	Cluster	R	W	vector read/write
	Global		W	write
	Cluster	R	W	cache miss
	Cluster		W	test & set
	Global	R		vector read no prefetching
	Global	R		scalar read
	Global		W	test & set
LESS FAST	Global	R	W	synchronization op

Synchronization processors on the global memory boards provide a large set of atomic operations on data stored there. The Cedar synchronization hardware [45, 38] operates on up to two consecutive words of global memory. Many common critical sections are available as indivisible instructions, including the *fetch-next-iteration* step for a multi-cluster parallel loop. This hardware supports fine-grain synchronization among all CEs in every Cedar cluster.

The CEs within each cluster also connect to a *concurrency control unit* (CCU) by a special purpose bus. The CCU can form a group of CEs that will cooperate to execute parallel codes. This has been implemented in software on other machines such as the IBM RP3 [41], Sequent [36], and the Cray X-MP [9], where it is known as *microtasking*. The Alliant FX series hardware support for microtasking includes

self-scheduling of the iterations of a 1-cluster parallel loop: as each CE finishes an iteration, the CCU gives it the next available iteration number,

`AWAIT` and `ADVANCE` instructions to serialize the order of some memory references made from different iterations of a parallel loop, and

barrier synchronization after the last iteration, to ensure that all iterations are done before the program continues.

1.2 The Xylem Operating System

The software that coordinates the clusters is the Xylem Operating System [20], an extension of Unix. Under Xylem, a program executes as a *Xylem process*. A process is made up of one or more independently scheduled *tasks*. Each task is assigned to a particular Cedar cluster for its lifetime. In a task's address space, each page of memory has its own attributes of *locale* (**cluster** or **global** memory) and *visibility* (**private** or **shared** by all tasks of this process). All four combinations of locale and visibility are possible [33].

Pages that are **shared cluster** are handled in a special way. If the page is *read-only*, it is simply copied into the cluster memory of each task that refers to it. If the page is *writable*, the first task using it gets a cluster memory copy; Xylem traps subsequent uses in other tasks so that the program's runtime system can mediate the communications needed to actually share the data.

The **shared** memory of a process is owned by a master address translation table which Xylem keeps in global memory. The individual tasks take registered copies of entries from this table to initialize or restore invalid entries in their private memory maps. Xylem's virtual memory system periodically invalidates a few random entries in each task's memory map. Thus, unused pages gradually lose their registered users. A shared page with no registered referents may be moved to secondary storage: either to the cluster memory of the last referent, or to a disk connected to that cluster.

This design for shared virtual memory adds a hidden cost to programs that make sustained use of shared memory: keeping the private memory maps valid. When amortized over all memory references, this cost is quite low. But, revalidating any single entry takes several hundred microseconds, comparable to entire loops in many applications. This is a source of load imbalance between processors. Self-scheduling of parallel work can compensate for some of this imbalance. But, scheduling across clusters usually increases the map revalidation costs since it increases the number of memory maps involved.

1.3 The Cedar Fortran Runtime Library

Various intrinsic functions, for which it is not practical to generate inline code, are supplied by a runtime library. The library includes a set of Cray-style tasking and synchronization routines [16] that exercise Xylem system services. In particular these support the `CTSK` and `MTSK` family of intrinsics to be described in section 1.4.3.

Chief among the services supplied by the runtime library is a software version of microtasking that can quickly spread work across clusters. In order to use several clusters in parallel, the library runs the program in a Xylem process that contains several extra *helper* tasks ("implicit tasks" in IBM terminology[26]). The helpers run for the duration of the process, waiting for microtask work to be posted. The most important unit of microtask work is a multicluster parallel loop, which we call a *spread loop*. When some task reaches a spread loop, it posts one microtask describing the loop into global memory. We say this task is the *parent* of the microtask. This signals the helper tasks to wake up and join the parent in competing for loop iterations to execute. We implemented three variations of this simple idea in separate libraries, which we call Queued, Simple, and Static.

	Queued	**Simple**	**Static**
Interfaces	MTSKSTART SDOALL XDOALL QUIT QQUIT	SDOALL XDOALL	SDOALL ID=0,n
SDOALL helped by	$0 \to \#helpers$	$0 \to \#helpers$	$n \equiv \#helpers$
Max# microtasks	queue size	1 at a time	1 at a time
Max# parents	process size	$\#nonhelpers$	1
Sync Used	Test&Set Lock	Test&Set Lock	Barrier
Wait Used	spin/dawdle/block	spin	spin
Avg. Latency[1]	9μ/100μ/100m sec	9 μsec	9 μsec
4-way Fork & Join[2]	**320** μsec	**180** μsec	**40** μsec
Scheduling	self-scheduled	self-scheduled	static schedule
Wait Used	spin/dawdle	spin	none
Get Next Iteration[2]	**25** μsec	**<10** μsec	**0**

[1]no other jobs active
[2]minimum times

Figure 2: Comparison of Three Microtasking Libraries

Queued: Like a traditional scheduler, this library queues up microtasking work as it is generated by several parent tasks, or by the nesting of spread loops. In theory, the helpers should stay busy constantly emptying this queue; they do this by *self-dispatching*. This scheme does not guarantee that a particular helper will participate in the execution of any particular loop. The flexible control mechanism needed for this design invited the inclusion of additional features: Loops spread by this library version can be terminated prematurely by a QUIT statement; and parallel subroutine calls can be queued alongside parallel loops by MTSKSTART.

The "queued" library assumes that there is a vast variety of parallel work in progress, so it allows other tasks to take over the cluster when one task must wait. For a short time the library code repeatedly tests the wakeup condition; but it soon surrenders the task's timeslice (via the dawdle system call). Finally, if the wakeup condition is still not satisfied, further execution of the task is blocked until a wakeup signal is posted (Xylem system calls wait_ and clear_xlock). Synchronization delays can be quite high because the task scheduler on each cluster and the microtask schedulers in each process work independently. But since the clusters can stay busy during these delays, overall throughput is usually acceptable.

Under a simple load (e.g., one spread loop running in single-user mode) the "queued" library can avoid much of the overhead and unpredictability introduced by the system calls. But it cannot avoid all costs of the extra features, nor the cost of queueing and dequeueing. The available parallelism is also reduced by the latency time it takes to reactivate the helpers and return them from the `dawdle` or `wait_xlock` system calls that they made while waiting for work.

Simple: So, in the "simple" library version, we restricted or removed features to reduce costs: tasks which must wait never surrender their processor; `QUITs` and `MTSKs` are not supported; and only one loop may be spread at any one time (others are forced into serial execution). We retained the idea that loop iterations are self-scheduled and that helpers are self-dispatched (i.e., helpers are only volunteers). In exchange we experienced lower, and more reproducible, startup and shutdown costs, and improved turnaround time for single applications under light load conditions.

Self-scheduling and self-dispatching distribute a loop's iteration space across the clusters in a fortuitous pattern, that tends to balance the workload. These techniques must be controlled by short *critical* sections of code during which one processor has exclusive use of the microtask description. In both the "simple" and "queued" libraries, the critical sections can be provided by the Cedar synchronization hardware. But as of this report, we have not yet timed library versions using that hardware. Instead we have used traditional locks, supported by an atomic "Test & Set" instruction to protect critical regions. This software method is three times slower than the Cedar hardware, so further improvement is expected.

Static: In some cases, load balancing is not as important as low overhead and absolute repeatability. So we implemented a *statically* dispatched and scheduled `SDOALL`, without critical regions. The "static" library guarantees that every helper task participates in every parallel section. Each helper is assigned a unique index for the life of the process, and also knows the total count of helpers. With these parameters, a compiler can distribute any iteration space or index set in a repeatable pattern. In section 2.7 we describe how repeatability will allow the restructurer to use this form of `SDOALL` for data distribution.

The high performance of the "static" library is vulnerable to scheduling disruptions that arise on one cluster, but require that all helpers be delayed. The average performance of static microtasks deteriorates quickly as other loads are added to the system. However, this library has let us explore Cedar's peak performance.

1.4 The Cedar Fortran Language

The Cedar Fortran language [24] is an extension of Alliant's FX/Fortran [4], which is FORTRAN 77 augmented with vector constructs like those in the Fortran 90 standard [44]. The additions made to Alliant Fortran to form Cedar Fortran are mainly those that express various types of parallel loops, and make use of Cedar's memory system and runtime library facilities.

1.4.1 Cedar Fortran data declarations

Cedar Fortran includes three new statement types that declare the memory attributes (*locale* and *visibility*) of the storage needed for program variables.

```
GLOBAL    variable   [ ,  variable ]  ...
CLUSTER   variable   [ ,  variable ]  ...
PROCESS COMMON  /  name  /  variable  [ ,  variable ]  ...
```

Figure 3: Cedar Fortran data declaration statements

In Cedar Fortran, an ordinary Fortran COMMON declaration statically allocates private storage in the cluster memory of each task, not visible to any other task. A COMMON block may be declared as PROCESS COMMON, which marks its content as shared by all tasks of this Xylem process. By default a PROCESS COMMON block is placed in global memory.

Variables outside common blocks may be declared GLOBAL or CLUSTER. By default, a subprogram's variables are dynamically allocated on a stack. This yields separate storage for each recursive or parallel call. Static allocation (SAVE) is also available, but it must be properly synchronized in the case of parallel calls to the subprogram.

A CLUSTER declaration specifies that the variable will be (stacked) in private cluster memory, inaccessible to other tasks. Declaring a variable GLOBAL means it will be allocated on a stack in shared global memory so that it can be used by every task in the program. By itself, the GLOBAL statement does not enlarge the *scope* of a variable; other subprogram calls only learn the variable's address by ordinary parameter passing mechanisms.

COMMON and PROCESS COMMON block names may also appear in CLUSTER or GLOBAL statements to change their default locale (but not their visibility). For example, a PROCESS COMMON block named in a CLUSTER statement is placed in shared cluster memory as described in section 1.2. Figure 3 summarizes the syntax of these statements.

1.4.2 Concurrent loops

The syntax of a concurrent loop in Cedar Fortran is an extension of the syntax for a FORTRAN 77 DO loop, with "DO" changed to a new keyword that selects a concurrent execution rule. The keywords are: CDOALL, CDOACROSS, SDOALL, SDOACROSS, XDOALL, and XDOACROSS. Figure 4 gives a synopsis of this syntax. Several optional sections have been added to the loop body that are not available in ordinary DO loops:

Local Declarations define variables that are private to each iteration of the loop and inaccessible outside the loop. Several iterations may execute concurrently and refer to their local variables without interfering with each other, since they are really referring to different storage cells.

The **Preamble** is executed once by each participating entity before starting its first iteration of the loop.

SDO and XDO loops offer one further optional part:

$$\left\{ \begin{array}{c} C \\ S \\ X \end{array} \right\} \left\{ \begin{array}{l} \texttt{DOALL} \\ \texttt{DOACROSS} \end{array} \right\} \quad [label] \quad index \quad = \quad start \quad , \quad end \quad [, \quad incr]$$

$$[local\ declarations]$$

$$\left[\begin{array}{l} preamble \\ \texttt{LOOP} \end{array} \right]$$

$$body$$

$$\left[\begin{array}{l} \texttt{ENDLOOP} \\ postamble \end{array} \right] \qquad \text{(only for SDO or XDO loops)}$$

$$\left\{ \begin{array}{l} labeled\ statement \\ \texttt{END} \left\{ \begin{array}{c} C \\ S \\ X \end{array} \right\} \left\{ \begin{array}{l} \texttt{DOALL} \\ \texttt{DOACROSS} \end{array} \right\} \end{array} \right\}$$

Figure 4: Concurrent loop syntax

A **Postamble** is executed once by each participant when it finds no more iterations left to execute.

CEs participate independently in CDO and XDO loops, whereas in an SDO loop, the participants are whole tasks (parents or helpers). Every participant takes at least one iteration. Every iteration is executed by exactly one participant. In each of these types of parallel loop, once all the iterations and postambles have finished, one CE continues executing the code that follows the loop, and the others go idle or go to work for other tasks.

DOALL loops may perform their iterations in any order whatsoever and should not contain any synchronization between iterations. In contrast to this, the iterations of a DOACROSS loop are guaranteed to start in the same order as they would if the loop were serial. This makes it possible to pass synchronization signals from early iterations to later ones, an interaction called *cascade synchronization*, which can be implemented without deadlock.

CDOALL and CDOACROSS loops are executed totally within a single cluster. They use the cluster concurrency bus to activate and coordinate all CEs assigned to the task.

In CDOACROSS loops, the cluster's concurrency control unit (CCU) may be used for cascade synchronization. Cedar Fortran provides intrinsic subroutines AWAIT and ADVANCE that use the CCU to synchronize between iterations.

SDOALL and SDOACROSS loops are examples of *spread loops*. They use global memory and facilities provided by the runtime library to bring the program's *helper tasks* into parallel execution of the loop.

Idle helper tasks always leave one CE awake to watch for microtasking work. When the program's execution reaches a spread loop, a description of the loop is posted in global memory. In each helper task, one CE reads the description and begins executing the preamble and body. To activate the other CEs in each participating task, an SDO loop body should contain some kind of CDO loop.

Any data that flows into or out of a spread loop iteration must reside in shared memory so it is visible from all clusters; read-only data can be copied into each cluster's private memory in the SDO preamble.

The runtime library provides a synchronization point at the end of a spread loop to ensure that all helper tasks finish with their work before the parent task continues.

XDOALL and XDOACROSS are spread loops like SDOALL, except that they do not need an inner CDO to start using all the CEs in a cluster. As each helper task joins the execution of a XDO loop, all of its processors automatically begin executing iterations of the loop. This simplifies the use of the machine in that its division into clusters can be ignored.

Since it is a cross-cluster loop, the data used in a XDO need the same processwide visibility as data in a SDO.

1.4.3 Explicit tasks and microtasks

Cedar Fortran provides two ways of specifying work that may execute separately from the task which starts it. In the CTSK mechanism, a brand new cluster task is added to the process and is given a subroutine to execute. The new task becomes an independent sibling of the task which created it. Each such *cluster task* can be preempted or resumed as needed to synchronize with any other cluster task. The startup and shutdown costs and the resources consumed by this approach confine its use to coarse grain parallelism. The following routines are used to start, wait for, and inquire about cluster tasks:

> *task_id* = CTSKSTART(*processors,* [*cluster_id,*] *subroutine* [*, argument*] ...)
> call CTSKWAIT(*task_id*)
> *logical* = CTSKDONE(*task_id*)

The other mechanism (MTSKs) uses an existing helper task to execute the subroutine as a *microtask*. This avoids most startup costs, and supports medium grain parallelism. Since there is only a fixed number of helper tasks (possibly none), and no preemptive scheduling for microtasks, ordinarily correct synchronization could deadlock. But it is safe to wait for a given microtask to finish. The following routines are used to start, wait for, and inquire about microtasks:

> *work_id* = MTSKSTART(*subroutine , priority* [*, argument*] ...)
> call MTSKWAIT(*work_id*)
> *logical* = MTSKDONE(*work_id*)
> call MTSKWAITALL

2 Program Restructuring for Cedar

Restructurers have a long history, highlighted by Parafrase from the Univ. of Illinois [29], PFC from Rice University [2], Kap from Kuck&Associates Inc. [25], and Vast from Pacific Sierra Research Inc. [10]. These projects began by automatically translating Fortran code into vector form. When traditional vector architectures grew into multiprocessors such as Alliant FX/8 and Cray/YMP, the commercial projects added a capability to generate concurrent code. New projects have started with concurrentization as their prime objective, e.g., Ptran from IBM [1].

Many analysis and transformation techniques now exist [37]. They are used to transform sequential programs into vector/concurrent code that runs significantly faster than the original version. Yet they seldom exploit all the parallelism identified by simulations such as Yew, et al [12]. Thus, a main area of research is to continuously refine the analysis and restructuring techniques [42, 1, 39, 31, 7].

Another main thrust in compiler research attempts to better integrate parallelizing compilers into the software development process. Interactive restructurers are being designed that let users participate in the transformation process [40, 5, 6, 18].

New developments in computer architecture also spur corresponding adaptations in compiler optimization. Recent examples [21, 11, 46, 27] address the Very Long Instruction Word (VLIW), and Distributed-memory multiprocessor architectures. The Cedar project belongs to this general category.

2.1 The Cedar Fortran Restructurer

The Cedar Fortran restructurer builds on previous work in compiler design, but its approach to optimization is also evolving in response to the Cedar architecture. In the Cedar system, the arrangement of data in the memory hierarchy is as important to program performance as the order of computations in a loop nest. Changing the data layout in a large program requires cooperation between the optimizations done in textually separate program segments.

Data placement has been discussed [17, 23, 15] mainly for registers and software-managed cache. There have also been theoretical treatments applicable to local memories [22, 19]. But, current practice in Fortran compilation includes few techniques capable of drastically reorganizing a program's memory map.

Clustering of processors introduces a longer communication delay between clusters than exists within a cluster. It is no longer evident that a DOALL loop can activate arbitrarily many processors quickly enough to be of benefit, or that a DOACROSS loop can signal between clusters at a fine enough granularity to outperform a version where the same loop is distributed into serial DOs and parallel DOALLs.

An understanding of how Cedar's many components really interact on significant programs is now taking shape at the Center for Supercomputing Research & Development. Serial Fortran programs from many application areas are being transformed into Cedar Fortran codes, both manually and automatically. The insights gained by comparing the results of performance experiments run on Cedar using these codes are being incorporated into the restructurer, one component of the Cedar Fortran compiler.

Cedar Fortran's restructurer is built upon Kap, a proprietary Fortran restructurer from Kuck & Associates, Inc. [30]. Kap is a system of analysis and program transformation that can find and express the parallelism in Fortran codes. We have adapted Kap's parallelizing techniques to the Cedar architecture.

The restructurer accepts FORTRAN 77 or FX/Fortran programs that may include GLOBAL, CLUSTER, or PROCESS COMMON declarations (Figure 3) to force particular memory allocation choices. It produces Cedar Fortran source code as output. Substantial revisions of Kap were required to coordinate several optimization techniques across many levels in a loop nest, and to work within Cedar's three levels of data visibility and three tiers of parallel loops.

From the start we found that strategies for concurrentization were an open issue. A compiler that is concurrentizing attempts to enclose as much code as possible into each parallel loop. To do this, the most powerful of the traditional vectorization techniques must be applied to larger sections of code. As more source lines are examined, more techniques must cooperate. Increasing the parallelization problem size also increases compilation time.

2.2 Cedar as a Shared Memory Multiprocessor

```
DO i=1,n                XDOALL i=1,n,strip
   a(i) = b(i)    ⟶       a(i:min(i+strip-1,n)) = b(i:min(i+strip-1,n))
END DO                  END XDOALL
```

Figure 5: Stripmining a parallel loop

Consider the transformation in Figure 5. The restructurer has detected that the iterations of the sequential loop are independent. Following the shared memory model, their execution can spread onto all the independent processors (CEs) of Cedar. The iteration space has been *stripmined* [37, 32] so that each CE executes the vector statement inside the loop, but operates on a separate *strip* of data. For a given loop, accessing a given configuration of data, the optimal strip length depends on the total number of iterations and the number of CEs that participate. Where these quantities are not known, we currently use default values. Runtime computation of the strip size may improve on this.

Regardless of whether the parallel loops correspond directly to original program loops or are created by stripmining, the restructurer must determine how much parallelism will actually be effective. Recall from Figure 2 that involving 4 Cedar clusters in a self-scheduled spread loop takes at least 180 μsecs; 300 μsecs would not be unusual if data addresses must also be communicated. How many loop nests in real programs take significantly longer than that? Figure 6 shows the average execution time of 135 loop nests from the Perfect Benchmark suite [8] when run on one cluster. 65% of these nests took longer than 1 msec on average. This suggests to us that two out of three parallel nests could benefit from being spread across clusters.

The restructurer makes a rough estimate of the average iteration cost by counting up the number of serial and vector statements and weighting them by their relative depth within the nest. Using recent Cedar performance measurements we are now trying to

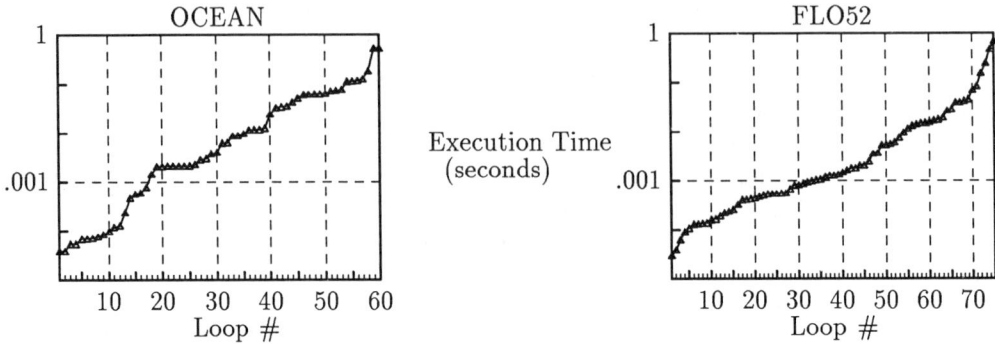

Figure 6: Average loop execution times in Perfect Benchmark codes OCEAN and FLO52

balance the expected performance gain from parallel execution against the cost of parallel loop control.

Often the compiler does not have enough information to make a performance tradeoff and so needs the capability to defer choices until runtime. When the tradeoff depends on the size or location of the loop's data and the loop body is big enough to absorb the added cost of a runtime decision, the technique of *multiversion loops* is useful. This involves generating code for two or more different translations of a single original loop, along with tests to decide which will run fastest.

2.3 Static Use of the Memory Hierarchy

The example in Figure 5 is incomplete. The declaration "GLOBAL a,b,strip,n" is needed to make those variables visible to all the CEs. The Cedar restructurer's *globalization* pass finds the variables that must be visible to all Cedar processors and declares them GLOBAL where possible. Variables used only in serial, vector, or CDO loops, are left in cluster memory. Since the program's execution is confined to one cluster during such loops, this use of private cluster memory still fits the shared memory model.

The restructurer's *localization* pass finds variables that are not shared across iterations of a loop. Suppose we eliminate the common subexpression in the upper bound of the vector indices of Figure 5. Since its value is different in each iteration of the outer loop, the storage we need must be declared locally within each iteration (see section 1.4.2) if the loop is to remain parallel. The resulting loop looks like:

```
GLOBAL a, b, strip, n
XDOALL i=1,n,strip
  INTEGER upper
  upper = min(i+strip-1,n)
  a(i:upper) = b(i:upper)
END XDOALL
```

Localization is related to the transformation called *scalar expansion* [43] where scalars expand into arrays with one element per iteration of the vector loops. Localization requires only one storage cell per processor (instead of one per iteration), and uses scalar access (instead of array element access). Both techniques require that any iteration that uses the variable must first assign to it. The restructurer searches for this usage pattern at every level in a loop nest. It creates temporary storage using a combination of localization and scalar expansion. This can result in local arrays whose dimensions are computed at runtime.

How well does this technique work? Despite its simplicity, this is the most significant accelerator in at least two of the Perfect Benchmark applications. In the MGD code, one loop accounts for 90% of the sequential execution time. It operates mainly on scalar and array data that can be localized by simply recognizing its usage pattern. In the BDNA code there are two loops that together cover 88% of the execution time. They use arrays that can be declared locally.

Two improvements on this technique seem worthwhile: array expansion, and multiple localization. Array expansion would recognize localizable uses of arrays in the original program. Multiple localization would allow a variable to be localized or expanded to break storage conflicts in several levels of one loop nest. So far, the Cedar restructurer recognizes multilevel localizations, but can only parallelize the innermost level.

2.3.1 Scope of the data placement problem

Both the globalization and localization passes cooperate with the code that judges the best execution mode for each loop. But, an inherent difficulty of deciding the static placement of a single data item is that the decision affects the execution time of all parts of the program where the data item is used. Placing an array in global memory may benefit some parallel loops, but slow down some serial loops that cannot take advantage of the vector prefetch facilities. These costs and benefits cannot even be calculated at compiletime in most cases, yet placement must be done for every data item. Data placement choices are also complicated by EQUIVALENCE and COMMON block relations between variables.

Often the placement analysis must span procedure boundaries. The Cedar restructurer provides *in-line expansion* of subroutine calls as an option to reduce the number of routine boundaries, and meet some interprocedural analysis needs.

To further simplify the static placement problem, the compiler makes one data placement choice for all the data whose usage may cross a routine boundary, which we call *interface data*. This includes COMMON blocks and all formal and actual parameters in subroutine and function calls. Where no single choice is satisfactory, the programmer can force the placement of particular variables and also override the default placement of interface data. Some of the remaining data may be globalized in order to form spread loops, but data locked into cluster memory prevents the loops that use it from spreading across clusters.

2.3.2 Toward dynamic data placement

In future work we plan to break the data placement problem into smaller pieces by introducing temporary variables. In regions of the program that do not contain spread loops, global memory references can be redirected to a cluster memory copy of the data. Conversely, in regions where parallel loops cannot be spread due to cluster memory references, a copy of that data in global memory may allow broader parallel activity.

Some portion of the original data must be moved into and out of the new temporary, and this adds memory traffic to the program. The new placement must accelerate many accesses in order to recover the added cost. When used to increase data locality, the potential benefits are substantial, since global scalar reads are among the slowest access methods on Cedar. So far, we have realized these benefits only by manual transformations.

2.4 Static Use of the Processor Hierarchy

An alternative to XDOALL in our example loop can be produced by stripmining the loop once more, producing a hierarchical schedule:

```
GLOBAL a, b, sstrip, cstrip, n
SDOALL i=1,n,sstrip
   INTEGER supper, j
   supper = min(i+sstrip-1,n)
   CDOALL j=i,supper,cstrip
      INTEGER cupper
      cupper = min(j+cstrip-1,supper)
      a(j:cupper) = b(j:cupper)
   END CDOALL
END SDOALL
```

Deciding between the XDOALL and SDOALL/CDOALL versions of the loop in Figure 5 involves trading off flexibility for efficiency. The XDOALL version uses cross-cluster synchronization to give each CE its work, whereas, in the S/CDOALL version, each iteration of the outer loop commits to a large chunk of work, then uses the fast cluster concurrency hardware to divide it among that cluster's CEs. In small kernels with a large number of iterations, the synchronization needed to get the next iteration can dominate. In one such case we observed optimally scheduled S/CDOALLs up to 3 times faster than equivalent XDOALLs.

However, the division of labor across clusters in the S/CDOALL version has a coarser grain than the XDOALL version and does not adapt to a dynamic load imbalance as readily. With larger loop bodies or smaller iteration counts, load imbalances are more likely and here XDOALL yields better average performance. Even under apparently balanced loads, like our example, XDOALL can offer a 10% improvement over the *average* time of an S/CDOALL version.

2.5 Reductions, Recurrences, and Synchronization

The Cedar restructurer recognizes loops that can be parallel if the order of their arithmetic or logical operations is allowed to change. Loops such as dot products, linear recurrences (e.g., `X(i) = X(i-1)*B(i) + C(i)`) and minimum/maximum searches are replaced by calls into a library of Cedar-optimized functions. For example, a dot product can be distributed to all Cedar processors, its partial results being summed up in two steps: within each cluster, then across the clusters. When this transformation was applied in the Conjugate Gradient algorithm [34], it improved performance by 50%.

A Cedar-optimized intrinsic function adjusts its use of the machine depending on the (runtime) size of the computation. Very small computations use only the vector hardware on one CE, larger computations make use of all CEs of a cluster, and the largest computations spread out to other clusters.

To make use of a library routine, the restructurer must often distribute an original loop to isolate those computations done by library code. This adds loop control overhead, reduces the average grain size of parallel activity, and reduces the effectiveness of the machine's registers. The payoff comes from the wealth of algebraic and programming insight that library authors use to reduce operation counts and memory references [14].

Loops where different iterations use the same storage cells can usually be parallelized as `DOACROSS` loops. Uses of the shared locations are serialized by the `AWAIT` and `ADVANCE` functions in the concurrency control hardware, while the rest of the loop executes in parallel. The Cedar restructurer inserts the smallest set of synchronization instructions that will suffice [35].

When considering a `DOACROSS` loop version, the restructurer lowers its estimate of the benefit due to parallel execution by a *synchronization delay* factor. Intuitively this is proportional to the size of the synchronized region divided by the number of processors that may be in it concurrently. To reduce this delay, the Cedar restructurer may reorder the statements of a `DOACROSS` to separate its serial and parallel portions. Further reduction of the synchronization delay seems possible if we split long expressions into their serial and parallel components.

2.6 Central Control Over Optimization Alternatives

Once parallelism has been recognized, there are still many ways that concurrent activity can be scheduled. To find the right match between loop levels and hardware levels, the restructurer considers a whole loop nest at one time. A central coordinator tries out many potential transformations such as how loops in a nest might be interchanged, parallelized or stripmined, and which data must then be placed in global memory. The many sources of parallelism and synchronization in Cedar can make the number of alternatives to consider become quite large, and the number will grow as new transformation techniques are added. Currently, the restructurer uses simple heuristics to identify transformed program versions worth further consideration. A user-settable hard limit (50 by default) keeps the number of candidates in bounds for practical purposes.

We intend to use the results of performance experiments on Cedar to develop more heuristics to cope with the increase in the number of alternatives. We believe that as the number of alternatives increases, so does the number of near-optimal ones. This should allow us to keep the heuristics simple and still be confident of finding a good translation of a loop. We intend to expand the central judgement module to support a program-wide optimization strategy by saving off optimal versions of each nest under different data placement choices. Once all relevant nests have been seen, the placement alternatives can be compared, and a globally optimal set of loop nests can be selected.

2.7 Integrating Shared and Distributed Memory Approaches

In real programs, variables often carry values from one loop nest to the next. If either nest has a spread loop, a shared memory restructurer will place these variables in shared global memory. Private cluster memory is only used when some limits can be set on the scope of a variable.

By contrast, a restructurer for a distributed memory system must partition the array variables and store a strip for each processor in its private memory. Typical approaches to this problem use language extensions that let the user specify data partitions or try all possible partitionings to determine the best.

On Cedar, both approaches are possible. We expect to develop a strategy that distributes data where possible and shares it otherwise.

Data distribution We have found cases in which it is possible to leave data distributed in cluster memory across several spread loop nests, thereby reducing global memory use. The "static" microtask library supports this with a *statically scheduled* SDOALL construct (see section 1.3). Under this scheme, every helper task participates in every loop; they each have a unique index number that identifies their place in the distribution pattern. So between loops, when the helpers are idle, they can still be carrying live data which the parent task has distributed. The data might even be in the cluster cache when the next spread loop needs it.

In experiments with the Conjugate Gradient algorithm for solving a linear system, a few automatable rules for data distribution improved performance to within 80% of the best manually parallelized version. In this experiment, arrays which are not involved in cross-iteration dependences within or between loops are put into cluster memory. Each cluster is assigned a subset of the array's index set. Although only half of the program's memory references were redirected by this transformation, the distributed algorithm on four clusters runs almost 4 times faster than the best single cluster version.

The "distributed system" approach can probably be extended to cover cases where the program needs some communication between data partitions. Between parallel loops, data needed soon by other clusters can be exchanged while at the same time a serial component of the original program executes elsewhere in Cedar. We are currently learning how to partition data spaces automatically, find communication bands, manage code replication and realign indices into partitioned data sets.

To accomplish data distribution within the "shared memory" paradigm, Xylem's virtual memory system offers the possibility of using *shared cluster* memory (see section 1.2). Xylem and the runtime system could cooperate to move pages to cluster memory when they are used in a non-shared way, and to global memory when they begin to be shared. The compiler's role in this scheme is to separate the shared and non-shared execution phases for a particular piece of data, and to group the data used by each cluster into separate memory pages. Since communication is done on demand by the operating system, a program with a large amount of data does not have its working set or cache contents disrupted by massive data movements. On the other hand, data migration done on a page-by-page basis through the Xylem page fault handler is too costly and coarse-grained to be broadly applicable.

2.8 Performance analysis methods

We have begun timing whole applications from the Perfect Benchmarks and other sources on Cedar. We built an automatic instrumentation tool that lets us measure the performance of each loop nest in a program. It reduces the data from all executions of a loop into a few simple statistics (e.g., minimum, average, total). Any of these statistics can then be used as a basis to compare two related experiments. The comparison is made on compound graphs like those shown in Figure 7. Each tic on the x-axis represents a different outer loop within a compilation unit of the program. Of course, each loop nest has a different impact on the overall performance, so we present them sorted in increasing order by their accumulated execution time in the baseline version of the program. Loop nests plotted at the far right cover more of the application's execution time than those to the left.

The y-axis contains two regions. On top we plot the raw statistic for each nest, solid line for the baseline version, dotted for the "sped up" version. At the bottom we report the speedup ratio of that statistic between the two versions. On the right, an arrow reports the overall speedup of the whole program. Plotting the accumulated execution time statistic points us to the most significant loops. The minimum and average time statistics indicate the granularity of the parallel work.

One use of these graphs is to compare speedups under various compiler options, to identify what works best where. If we allow performance tuning via a parallelizing compiler to become an iterative process, we are soon led to compilers that make direct use of performance data. In one experiment we automatically constructed a composite version of the program in which each loop nest is compiled with the options under which it performed best.

Conjugate Gradient Algorithm [34] In one benchmark exercise we solved a banded linear system of 255 equations using the Conjugate Gradient algorithm. Our test data required around 65,000 iterations in the key loops, enough to exploit all the parallelism in Cedar. The kernels were transformed into SDOALL/CDOALL/vector loop nests. Figure 7 shows the speedups for the main kernels of this code. The basis statistic is the *minimum* execution time over several hundred repetitions. This statistic eliminates a few executions inadvertently delayed by other system software.

These runs were made on a half-sized Cedar with 16 CEs, each having 4 stages in its vector pipeline, so 64 calculations can occur in parallel. But the effective parallelism in the shared memory network never exactly matches the processor parallelism. Speedup

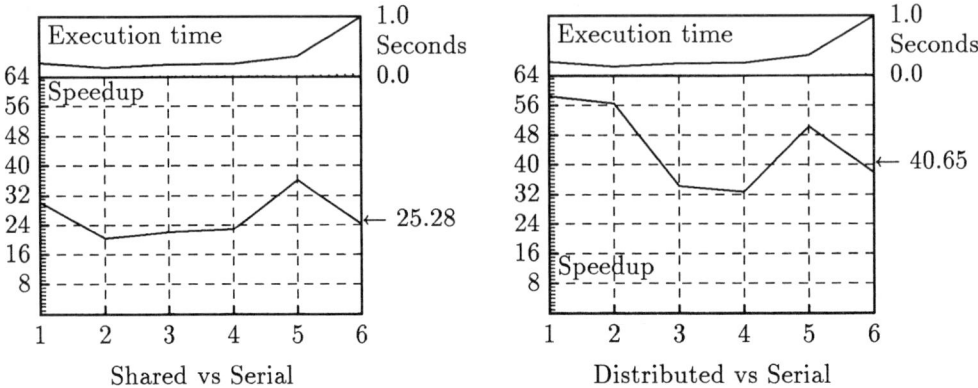

Figure 7: Speed up of Conjugate Gradient algorithm

ratios vary from kernel to kernel because each has a different ratio between the number of memory references and the number of arithmetic operations. The beneficial effects of cache and prefetching, and the detrimental effects of network contention affect each loop differently.

The first curve shows the speedup ratios gained using only the fully automated techniques of the shared memory paradigm described in section 2.2. Loops 1 and 2 are dotproducts. Their speedups indicate that the benefit of computing partial dotproducts in parallel dominates the serial summation of the partial results for this data size. Although the two loops have the same code, their speedups differ due to the different cache precondition in the sequential version.

The second diagram in Figure 7 reports the speedup due to manual application of the data distribution techniques described in section 2.7. The bandwidth of the global network and memory, which limits the shared methods, does not restrict this scheme. The overall speedup is now 40, and individual kernels are becoming processor-bound.

We report these preliminary performance figures only to demonstrate the feasibility of the Cedar transformation techniques when applied to program kernels or algorithms. Such results do not generally hold for the overall performance of whole application codes. Two features of larger codes that limit their performance are the generally smaller iteration counts, and a range of program patterns not easily recognized as parallel by our compiler technology.

2.9 The program development process

We have not made a controlled study comparing the development time for automatically and manually parallelized programs. But we have attacked several applications using both approaches and have come to recognize some benefits of automatic restructuring.

Given that one is starting with a sequential program or an isolated sequential subroutine and no knowledge of its parallel properties, the restructurer's analysis is indispensible. It is useful even when optimization will proceed manually. Many manual optimizations start with a compiler message indicating why a certain loop was not parallelized. Many manual efforts end by simply asserting some new facts about the program to the compiler.

Our source-to-source restructurer produces readable Cedar Fortran, which can be further modified. In our work, these manual improvements are the main source of new compiler technique. For instance, the data partitioning scheme that was manually applied to the Conjugate Gradient algorithm is currently being automated.

It takes longer to become a skilled parallel programmer than it does to write sequential programs and apply a restructuring compiler. But, for best results, a restructuring compiler may need a number of options and directives, which requires the user to know the performance characteristics of the target machine and of the algorithms that make up the application. We think this suggests the parallelizing compiler be integrated well in the program development process, where performance feedback complements facilities to apply automatic as well as manual program transformations.

3 Conclusions

We have presented an overview of the Cedar architecture and its software system including the Xylem operating system, the Cedar Fortran language and runtime library, and the restructuring compiler. These have been integrated into a working multiprocessor system currently in use by a large group of researchers working on architecture, hardware, system software, algorithm libraries, and application programs. Cedar has been available with as many as 16 processors (4 clusters of 4), 32Mbytes of global memory on 16 boards, and 22 million doublewords/sec. of global network bandwidth. This is half of the final machine.

We have elaborated on the project for automatically restructuring FORTRAN 77 programs for parallel execution on Cedar. The hierarchical clustering in Cedar presents new challenges to an automatic restructurer. In the first project phase we have adapted traditional compiler technology to the new issues: Loop iterations are spread across all Cedar processors; any data seen by all processors is placed in shared memory; many variables are easily recognized as locals by their usage pattern. Many kernels from real programs are successfully optimized for a Cedar architecture using this simple strategy. Where such kernels dominate an application, we can achieve good overall performance.

We have compiled the Perfect Benchmark suite and many other "real-world" application codes. To analyze our results we use timing reports broken down by individual loop nests. These direct us to the significant sections in an application program, and from there to the relevant transformation and analysis techniques in the restructurer. We are extending these quantitative methods so we can relate dynamic performance data to static performance estimators actually used in the restructurer.

However, this feedback loop was only recently completed. As Cedar grows and we tune the Cedar-specific parts of the restructurer, we intend to continuously review the following issues: How well does the compiler detect parallelism? What performance is gained by optimizing? How useful is the compiler in program development?

Future Directions

Our experiments have identified several areas where automatic restructuring techniques can be improved, those likely to be important over the long-term include:

- **Data localization and distribution:** The pay off from improving data locality is substantial. More advanced techniques of data localization and data partitioning must be developed. Much work needs be done to balance memory traffic and to find good strategies for migrating data within a hierarchy. While there is much related work in the areas of distributed memory multiprocessors and software-managed cache, it seems the integration of these findings with traditional compiler technology is just beginning. By embracing both distributed and shared memory approaches, the Cedar architecture allows progress in this direction to happen stepwise.

- **Larger grain parallelism found interprocedurally:** The search for large grain parallel threads, beginning with larger outer loops, must be made more aggressive. Furthermore, there is a compelling need to widen the restructurer's horizons beyond the loop nest. Although interprocedural analysis techniques are well known, they are only the first step towards coordinated optimization of whole programs.

- **Parallelizing methodology:** We have also briefly addressed the role of a compiler in the program development process. To the extent that restructuring can be automated, the programming skill needed to exploit parallel supercomputers can be reduced. But existing techniques require the user to be a knowlegeable programmer. The integration of an automatic restructurer in an iterative program development cycle is therefore another important area of research.

Acknowledgement

This work was supported by the U.S. Department of Energy under Grant No. DOE DE-FG02-85ER25001.

References

[1] F. Allen, M. Burke, P. Charles, R. Cytron, and J. Ferrante. An Overview of the PTRAN Analysis System for Multiprocessing. In *International Conference on Supercomputing*, pages 194–211, 1987.

[2] R. Allen, D. Callahan, and K. Kennedy. Automatic decomposition of scientific programs for parallel execution. *14th annual ACM Symposium on Principles of Programming Languages*, pages 63–76, 1987.

[3] Alliant Computer Systems Corporation, 42 Nagog Park, Acton, Massachusetts 01720. *FX/Series Architecture Manual*, 1986. Part Number: 300-00001-B.

[4] Alliant Computer Systems Corporation, 42 Nagog Park, Acton, Massachusetts 01720. *FX/Fortran Language Manual*, 1987. Part Number: 302-00007-A.

[5] B. Appelbe, K. Smith, and C. McDowell. Start/Pat: A Parallel-Programming Toolkit. *IEEE Software*, 6(4):29–38, July 1989.

[6] V. Balasundaram, K. Kennedy, U. Kremer, K. McKinley, and J. Subhlok. The ParaScope editor: An interactive parallel programming tool. In *International Conference on Supercomputing*, pages 540–550, 1989.

[7] U. Banerjee. A Theory of Loop Permutations. In *2nd Workshop on Languages and Compilers for Parallel Computing*, pages 54–74. The MIT Press, 1990.

[8] M. Berry, D. Chen, P. Koss, D. Kuck, L. Pointer, S. Lo, Y. Pang, R. Roloff, A. Sameh, E. Clementi, S. Chin, D. Schneider, G. Fox, P. Messina, D. Walker, C. Hsiung, J. Schwarzmeier, K. Lue, S. Orszag, F. Seidl, O. Johnson, G. Swanson, R. Goodrum, and J. Martin. The perfect club benchmarks: Effective performance evalution of supercomputers. *Int'l. Jour. of Supercomputing Applications*, 1989.

[9] M. Booth and K. Misegades. Microtasking: A New Way to Harness Multiprocessors. *Cray Channels*, pages 24–27, 1986.

[10] B. Brode. Precompilation of Fortran programs to facilitate array processing. *Computer*, 14(9):46–51, Sept. 1981.

[11] D. Callahan and K. Kennedy. Compiling Programs for Distributed-memory Multiprocessors. *Journal of Supercomputing*, 2(2):151–169, Oct. 1988.

[12] D.-K. Chen, H.-M. Su, and P.-C. Yew. The impact of synchronization and granularity on parallel systems. *Proc. of the 17th Int'l. Symp. on Computer Architecture, Seattle, WA*, December 1989.

[13] P.-Y. Chen, D. H. Lawrie, D. A. Padua, and P.-C. Yew. Interconnection Networks Using Shuffles. *IEEE Computer*, 14(12):55–64, Dec. 1981.

[14] S. Chen and D. Kuck. Time and Parallel Processor Bounds for Linear Recurrence Systems. *IEEE Trans. on Computers*, pages 701–717, July 1975.

[15] H. Cheong and A. Veidenbaum. Compiler-directed cache management in multiprocessors. *IEEE Computer Journal*, 23(6):39–47, June 1990.

[16] Cray Research, Inc., 1440 Northland Drive, Mendota Heights, Minnesota 55120. *Multitasking Users Guide*, 1985. SN-0222.

[17] R. Cytron, S. Karlovsky, and K. McAuliffe. Automatic management of programmable caches. *Proc. of 1988 Int'l. Conf. on Parallel Processing, St. Charles, IL*, pages 229–238, August 1988.

[18] J. Davies, P. Petersen, G. Jaxon, and D. Padua. The Delta Program Manipulation System. Extended Abstract with Source Code, 1990.

[19] C. Eisenbeis, W. Jalby, D. Windheiser, and F. Bodin. A Strategy for Array Management in Local Memory. *3rd Workshop on Languages and Compilers for Parallel Programming*, 1990.

[20] P. A. Emrath. Xylem: An Operating System for the Cedar Multiprocessor. *IEEE Software*, 2(4):30–37, July 1985.

[21] J. A. Fisher, J. R. Ellis, J. C. Ruttenberg, and A. Nicolau. Parallel processing: A smart compiler and a dumb machine. In *Proceedings of the SIGPLAN'84 Symposium on Compiler Construction*, pages 37–47, Montreal, Canada, June 1984.

[22] K. Gallivan, W. Jalby, and D. Gannon. On the problem of optimizing data transfers for complex memory systems. *Proc. of 1988 Int'l. Conf. on Supercomputing, St. Malo, France*, pages 238–253, July 1988.

[23] E. H. Gornish, E. D. Granston, and A. V. Veidenbaum. Compiler-directed Data Prefetching in Multiprocessors with Memory Hierarchies. Technical Report 996, Univ. of Illinois at Urbana-Champaign, Center for Supercomp. R&D, May 1990.

[24] M. D. Guzzi, D. A. Padua, J. P. Hoeflinger, and D. H. Lawrie. Cedar Fortran and other Vector and Parallel Fortran dialects. *Journal of Supercomputing*, pages 37–62, Mar. 1990.

[25] C. Huson, T. Macke, J. R. Davies, M. J. Wolfe, and B. Leasure. The KAP/205: An Advanced Source-to-Source Vectorizer for the Cyber 205 Supercomputer. In K. Hwang, S. M. Jacobs, and E. E. Swartzlander, editors, *International Conference on Parallel Processing*, pages 827–832, 1730 Massachusetts Avenue, N.W., Washington D.C, 20036-1903, 1986. IEEE Computer Society Press.

[26] International Business Machines Corporation. *Parallel FORTRAN: Language and Library Reference*, 1988. SC23-0431-0.

[27] K. Kennedy and H. P. Zima. Virtual Shared Memory for Distributed-Memory Machines. In *Workshop on Compiling Techniques and Compiler Construction for Parallel Computers*. British Computer Society, Parallel Processing Specialist Group, Sept. 1989. Keble College, Oxford UK.

[28] D. J. Kuck, E. S. Davidson, D. H. Lawrie, and A. H. Sameh. Parallel Supercomputing Today and the Cedar Approach. *Science*, pages 967–974, Feb. 1986.

[29] D. J. Kuck, R. H. Kuhn, B. Leasure, and M. Wolfe. The Structure of an Advanced Vectorizer for Pipelined Processors. *Proc. of COMPSAC 80, The 4th Int'l. Computer Software and Applications Conf.*, pages 709–715, Oct. 1980.

[30] Kuck&Associates, Inc., Champaign, IL 61820. *KAP User's Guide*, 1988.

[31] Z. Li, P.-C. Yew, and C.-Q. Zhu. An efficient data dependence analysis for parallelizing compilers. *IEEE Trans. Parallel Distributed Syst.*, 1(1):26–34, Jan. 1990.

[32] D. B. Loveman. Program Improvement by Source-to-Source Transformation. *J. ACM*, 24(1):121–145, Jan. 1977.

[33] R. E. McGrath and P. A. Emrath. Using Memory in the Cedar System. In E. Houstis, T. Papatheodorou, and C. Polychronopoulos, editors, *International Conference on Supercomputing*, pages 43–67. Springer-Verlag, June 1987.

[34] U. Meier and R. Eigenmann. Parallelization and Performance of Conjugate Gradient Algorithms on the Cedar hierarchical-memory Multiprocessor. Technical Report 1035, Univ. of Illinois at Urbana-Champaign, Center for Supercomp. R&D, 1990.

[35] S. Midkiff and D. Padua. Compiler Algorithms for Synchronization. *IEEE Trans. on Computers*, C-36(12), Dec. 1987.

[36] A. Osterhaug. *Guide to Parallel Programming on Sequent Computer Systems*. Sequent Computer Systems, Beaverton, Oregon, 1986.

[37] D. A. Padua and M. J. Wolfe. Advanced Compiler Optimizations for Supercomputers. *Commun. ACM*, 29(12):1184–1201, Dec. 1986.

[38] D. Pointer and G. Jaxon. Cedar Synchronization Processor Instruction Set Reference. Technical Report 1017, Univ. of Illinois at Urbana-Champaign, Center for Supercomp. R&D, July 1990.

[39] C. Polychronopoulos, M. Girkar, M. R. Haghighat, C.-L. Lee, B. Leung, and D. Schouten. Parafrase-2: A new generation parallelizing compiler. *Int'l. Jour. of High Speed Computing*, 1(1):45–72, May 1989.

[40] B. Shei and D. Gannon. SIGMACS: A Programmable Programming Environment. *3rd Workshop on Languages and Compilers for Parallel Programming*, 1990.

[41] J. Stone, F. Darema-Rogers, V. Norton, and G. Pfister. *Introduction to the VM/EPEX FORTRAN Preprocessor*. IBM T.J. Watson Research Center, 1985.

[42] M. Wolfe. Loop Skewing: The Wavefront Method Revisited. *Int'l J. Parallel Programming*, 15(4):279–294, Aug. 1986.

[43] M. J. Wolfe. *Optimizing Compilers for Supercomputers*. PhD thesis, University of Illinois, Oct. 1982.

[44] X3J3. *Fortran 90: Draft International Standard Fortran*, June 1990.

[45] C.-Q. Zhu and P.-C. Yew. A Scheme to Enforce Data Dependence on Large Multiprocessor Systems. *IEEE Transactions on Software Engineering*, SE-13(6):726–739, June 1987.

[46] H. P. Zima and M. Gerndt. SUPERB: A tool for semi-automatic MIMD/SIMD parallelization. *Parallel Computing*, 6:1–18, 1988.

2 Bilingual Parallel Programming

I. Foster, R. Overbeek

Abstract

The key idea in bilingual programming is to code the upper levels of applications in a high-level language, while coding selected lower level components in low-level languages. This permits the advantages of a high-level notation to be obtained without the cost in performance usually associated with high-level approaches. In addition, it provides a natural framework for reusing existing code. In this paper, we argue that bilingual programming should be viewed as a logical development of fundamental concepts in programming methodology, rather than as an ad-hoc attempt to deal with transient engineering problems. We suggest that the bilingual approach is particularly attractive on parallel computers, due to the additional complexity of parallel computing. We outline the key features of a particular bilingual approach with which we have had considerable experience, and summarize our experiences developing large parallel applications in computational biology, weather modeling, and automated reasoning.

1 Introduction

Numerous experiments have demonstrated that computationally intensive algorithms support adequate parallelism to exploit the potential of large parallel machines. Yet successful parallel implementations of serious applications are rare. One limiting factor is clearly programming technology. None of the approaches to parallel programming that have been proposed to date — whether parallelizing compilers, language extensions, or new concurrent languages — seem to adequately address the central problems of portability, expressiveness, efficiency, and compatibility with existing software.

In this paper, we advocate an alternative approach to parallel programming based on what we call *bilingual programming*. We argue that this approach provides an effective solution to parallel programming problems.

The key idea in bilingual programming is to construct the upper levels of applications in a high-level language while coding selected low-level components in low-level languages. This approach permits the advantages of a high-level notation (expressiveness, elegance, conciseness) to be obtained without the cost in performance normally associated with high-level approaches. In addition, it provides a natural framework for reusing existing code.

The roots and motivations for bilingual programming predate parallel computers; they grow naturally out of fundamental issues associated with the programming task on *any* computer. Hence, we first review some of the lessons that have been learned during the past thirty years of programming uniprocessors. This background allows us to present the central tenets of bilingual programming as logical developments of fundamental concepts in programming methodology, rather than ad-hoc attempts to address issues that arise with concurrency. We then argue that the additional complexity of parallel programming makes the bilingual approach particularly attractive on parallel computers.

In the latter part of the paper, we introduce a particular bilingual approach with which we have considerable experience. The concurrent programming language Strand is used as the high-level language; lower-level routines are coded in C or Fortran. We summarize our experiences developing large parallel applications in computational biology, weather modeling, and automated reasoning. Finally, we review other approaches to parallel programming in the light of our analysis of the bilingual approach.

2 The Program Development Process

The program development process can be viewed as the formulation and implementation of a set of *design decisions* concerning algorithms and data representations. Research in program development methodologies has identified *stepwise refinement* as a fundamental technique for reducing the number of decisions involved in a design and for localizing the effect of individual decisions [17]. *High-level languages* provide a means of avoiding certain decisions altogether.

Stepwise Refinement. The key idea in stepwise refinement is to tackle a task by repeatedly dividing it into smaller and smaller subtasks. The refinement process starts with an abstract specification for an algorithm and proceeds via a series of refinement steps to obtain an executable program. Each refinement step involves a number of decisions concerning how a particular task and its data are to be implemented. Decisions concerning representational details are deferred for as long as possible.

High-Level Languages. High-level languages reduce programming effort by specifying standardized implementations for commonly-used abstractions. This permits programmers to truncate the development process at an earlier stage than would otherwise be possible. For example, LISP provides list manipulation and memory management facilities; hence, a design that is expressed in terms of a "list" data type requires no further refinement if LISP is used as an implementation language. In contrast, an implementation in a lower-level language would require additional design decisions to produce a representation of lists and an implementation of the associated operations.

Unfortunately, standardized implementation decisions provided by high-level languages are unlikely to be optimal for all situations. A programmer can generally improve performance by making additional design decisions that exploit application-specific knowledge. For example, the abstract data type "list of elements" may be implemented as a singly linked list, a doubly linked list, or an array; each implementation will be effective in different circumstances. No existing high-level language compiler is able to determine which strategy is optimal for all possible situations. Hence, there is necessarily a trade-off between implementation effort and efficiency.

3 Bilingual Programming

When developing programs, we are frequently interested in *minimizing* development and maintenance costs and *maximizing* performance. The cost of a program is closely related to the number of design decisions (implementation commitments) made during development. Each decision leads to a development cost (incurred when the decision is implemented) and a possible maintenance cost (incurred when changing circumstances lead to backtracking on the original decision). Hence, one way of reducing costs is to adopt the standardized implementation decisions offered by a high-level language. Another is to adopt decisions encapsulated in existing code.

The use of a high-level language reduces costs but, as noted previously, can adversely affect performance. Performance optimization requires the substitution of application- and environment-specific design decisions for the standardized decisions encapsulated in high-level languages. Fortunately, it is generally the case that only a small proportion of the total design need be considered when seeking to optimize performance. Hence, it is usually possible to construct a program that provides "almost" optimal performance but that retains a significant portion of its logic in a high-level language. Such a bilingual program retains the advantages of a high-level language program without sacrificing performance.

The bilingual approach can be seen as a logical outgrowth of developments in methodologies and languages. Yet clearly it is not widely used in sequential programming today. We attribute this fact to accidental rather than intrinsic factors. In particular, the lack of standard interfaces between languages has hindered the development of portable bilingual programs. However, given the increasingly dominant role of C, along with the recognized need for new solutions within the context of parallel processing, it seems possible to us that standardized interfaces between higher-level languages and C may appear. In any event, we do advocate such standardization as an important step forward.

4 Bilingual Parallel Programming

The design and development process for parallel programs is in many respects similar to that for sequential programs. However, the need to manage multiple processors introduces additional complexity: Problems concerned with concurrent execution, communication, synchronization, partitioning, mapping, load balancing, and data distribution must be addressed. Low-level solutions to these problems often compromise two highly desirable properties in a parallel program: scalability and portability. Hence, the developer of parallel programs is faced with both additional complexity and pressing reasons for deferring and localizing commitment to the design decisions required to address this complexity. This suggests that high-level languages may have an important role to play.

At the same time, the primary motivation for parallel computation is performance. This point requires emphasis: users develop parallel implementations of algorithms to attain higher performance, and an elegant approach that sacrifices this central objective will not be widely accepted. The effort required to develop a concurrent program can be justified only if an application requires substantial performance, and in most applications performance requires both good algorithms and low-level optimizations. Hence, we expect bilingual programming techniques to be particularly useful on parallel computers.

A high-level language to support parallel programming must provide linguistic support for important concurrent programming concepts: process management, communication, and synchronization. It should encourage portability by allowing programmers to express concurrent algorithms in a machine-independent manner and by minimizing the effort (if any) required to specialize machine-independent programs for a particular computer. Finally, it should encourage the development of scalable applications by supporting separate specification of concurrency on the one hand and partitioning and mapping on the other.

It is presumably possible to design a language that provides these features and also supports the efficient implementation of low-level sequential algorithms. However, we believe that it is advantageous to work with a small, clean high-level language with a simple concurrent semantics. This simplifies understanding, analysis, and transformation of concurrent programs. We have had good success with one particular language with these properties, Strand, and will restrict subsequent discussion to this particular context. (The related language PCN [4] has also proved effective.)

The decision to work with Strand represents an initial design decision that restricts the class of parallel algorithms that can be expressed in two ways. First, we are committed to MIMD rather than SIMD as the architectural model. This represents a personal preference. Second, we are committed to working within the message-passing model on which Strand is based. Space does not permit a detailed justification of this decision. However, we point out that message-passing models have proved adequate for the vast majority of concurrent applications. Furthermore, they tend to simplify application development by reducing opportunities for unexpected interactions between concurrent processes.

5 Bilingual Programming in Practice

We now outline the key features of the Strand approach to bilingual parallel programming. We describe the language used to specify concurrent computations, explain why partitioning and mapping can be specified separately from program logic, and describe various aspects of the interface to low-level languages.

5.1 Specifying Concurrent Computation

The concurrent programming language Strand provides a high-level notation for expressing concurrent computations. It has been implemented on a wide variety of parallel computers. The language is based on four key ideas [9, 10]. *Single-assignment variables* provide an abstract model of communication and synchronization. Every procedure call is executed as a *concurrent process*, providing an inherently concurrent execution model. *Non-deterministic choice* is used to select between alternative process actions. Finally, *separation of sequential code* permits a clean and simple interface to state change and sequencing, and supports reuse of existing code.

Single-Assignment Variables. Processes exchange information via single-assignment variables. A single-assignment variable is initially undefined; it can be assigned at most a single value and subsequently does not change. A process that requires the value of a variable waits until the variable is defined.

A shared single-assignment variable can be used to both communicate values and synchronize actions. For example, consider two processes **producer** and **consumer** that share a variable X:

$$\text{producer}(X), \text{consumer}(X)$$

The variable X may be used to *communicate* a value (e.g., "msg") between the processes. The **producer** procedure may *assign* a value to X and thus send this value to the consumer:

$$\text{producer}(X) :- X := \text{"msg"}.$$

The **consumer** procedure may use this value in subsequent computation, hence receiving the value:

$$\text{consumer}(X) :- X == \text{"msg"} \mid \text{use}(X).$$

The concept of *synchronization* is implicit in this model. In the example, the comparison X == "msg" can be made only if the variable X is defined. Hence, execution of the consumer is delayed until the value is available.

Concurrent Processes. Conceptually, every procedure call is executed as a separate concurrent process. A process is able to execute when its data is available; if the data is available, the process is guaranteed to execute eventually. There is no other constraint on the order in which processes execute. In particular, processes can be executed in parallel.

Non-deterministic Choice. Process actions are defined by sets of guarded rules. Each rule specifies a condition plus an associated set of procedure calls (i.e., new processes) which can be invoked if the condition is satisfied. For example, the following procedure defines a more complex **consumer** process which performs different actions, depending on the message that it receives:

$$\text{consumer}(X) :- X == \text{"msg1"} \mid \text{use}(X).$$
$$\text{consumer}(X) :- X == \text{"msg2"} \mid \text{do\_not\_use}(X).$$

The conditions specified by the rules defining a procedure need not be mutually exclusive. If more than one condition is satisfied, one set of actions is chosen non-deterministically.

Separation of Sequential Code. Single-assignment variables provide an abstract model of communication and synchronization that can be implemented efficiently on parallel computers. However, some algorithms can be expressed particularly naturally in terms of sequencing and state changes. Fortunately, languages such as Fortran and C already provide familiar notations for expressing these concepts. Hence, state change and sequencing can be integrated by providing an interface to these languages. This provides both a separation of concerns and a mechanism for reusing existing code. The interface is discussed in more detail below.

Discussion. Single-assignment variables can be implemented efficiently on both message-passing and shared-memory parallel computers [9]. In addition, the value of a single-assignment variable does not change once it is defined. Hence, the order and location of execution of processes does not change the result computed. This permits decisions concerning partitioning and mapping to be isolated from the rest of the program design process.

5.2 Partitioning and Mapping

A Strand program indicates opportunities for concurrent execution but does not specify how these opportunities are to be exploited. The partitioning of the set of concurrently executing processes into tasks and the mapping of these tasks to the nodes of a particular parallel computer represent separate design decisions that need not be made until after a program has been developed. These decisions affect the efficiency of the final program but not its correctness. Tools provided with Strand systems reduce the effort required to implement these decisions [10, 7]. Hence, programs tend to be easily portable: little or no effort is required to adapt a program for a new parallel computer.

The extent to which programs can be specialized to employ different partitioning and mapping decisions depends in part on the structure of the original code. For example, a program designed to solve a grid problem will probably be developed with a particular domain decomposition in mind, and will explicitly create the process network required to handle this decomposition on a parallel computer. This program has already been substantially specialized by the programmer and requires significant rewriting before an alternative decomposition can be employed.

On the other hand, consider the following program that encodes the top level of a state-space search. A tree is searched by first exploring a fixed number of nodes with a depth first strategy, then splitting any remaining subtree into a number of simpler trees, each to be searched in turn. This program specifies opportunities for concurrent execution in the state-space search (each subtree can be searched concurrently) but says nothing about how processes are to be mapped to processors.

```
search([Prob | Probs],Solns,Solns2) :−            % To search nodes,
    search_subtree(Prob,Solns,Solns1),            %    search one node,
    search(Probs,Solns1,Solns2).                  %    and search rest.
search([ ],Solns,Solns1) :− Solns := Solns1.      % Search done.


search_subtree(Prob,Solns,Solns2) :−              % To search single node,
    process_prob(Prob,NewProb,Solns,Solns1),      %    expand node,
    split_prob(NewProb,Probs),                    %    split subtree.
    search(Probs,Solns1,Solns2).                  %    and continue.
```

This problem can be partitioned and mapped in several different ways: static embedding, dynamic load balancing, and random mapping are all possibilities. Once a design decision has been made, a more specialized program that implements the decision can be obtained from the code shown here. Specializations can easily be performed manually. Alternatively, they can be implemented as automatic source transformations that can be encapsulated in libraries [7].

To reiterate, we find that programs are developed in two distinct stages. During the first stage, only minimal thought is given to issues relating to execution of the program in a parallel processing context; rather, the main effort is to develop a straightforward formulation of the desired algorithm, in which execution sequence has not been over-specified. The second stage introduces decisions concerned with partitioning and mapping; this normally represents a small percentage of the overall time required to implement an application. In many cases, several very different parallel codes can be obtained by making different design decisions in the second stage. Strand provides a context in which these alternatives can be explored and evaluated at little cost.

5.3 Interfacing to Foreign Code

Effective mixed-language programming requires a clean and simple interface between heterogeneous components. This is achieved in Strand with two mechanisms, *user-defined operations* and *user-defined data types*. These are used to encapsulate foreign code and foreign data, respectively.

A user-defined operation invokes a foreign procedure. The Strand compiler ensures that a user-defined operation is scheduled only when data that it requires to execute is available. The foreign procedure can then perform a finite amount of sequential execution. Upon completion, values computed for output arguments are returned to the concurrent component, which may pass them as arguments when invoking other user-defined operations. Note that user-defined operations are not coroutined on a single processor; instead, the execution of each operation is viewed as an indivisible action.

The Strand compiler automatically generates code to perform type conversion between Strand and other foreign representations of simple data types such as integers, reals, and strings. More complex foreign data structures (e.g., arrays) can be encapsulated in a special *user-defined data type*. Strand programs can pass user data from one user process to another but cannot examine their contents. As user data may be migrated from one processor to another, such data cannot contain addresses. This is the only restriction placed on their contents.

The foreign interface imposes a certain discipline on the programmer, as it requires that all communication between user processes be achieved by argument passing; common areas and other forms of global variables cannot (in general) be employed. This restriction has two important benefits. First, individual foreign procedures can be developed and debugged independently. Second, bilingual programs can be executed on both a single processor and multiple processors without modification.

5.4 Integrating Mutable Data

Recall that Strand variables have the single assignment property: their value is initially undefined and, once defined, cannot subsequently be modified. This property is important for several reasons. First, it avoids the race conditions that can arise when several concurrent processes read and write the same variable. Second, it permits a number of important optimizations in a parallel implementation. In particular, it permits non-variable data structures to be copied between processors without concern for the consistency of copies.

In contrast, sequential languages such as C and Fortran presuppose mutable data structures. Indeed, it is the ability to modify large data structures in place that permits these languages to provide succinct and efficient implementations of many algorithms.

We wish to maintain the single-assignment property in the concurrent component of bilingual programs, while permitting updates in foreign procedures. Hence, we require that foreign procedures which modify data structures be disguised to look like programs that use single-assignment variables. This slight of hand can be achieved by imposing the following restrictions on the ways in which foreign procedures are used. The user must be able to demonstrate that a bilingual program satisfies these requirements.

1. *User-defined operations provide a single-assignment interface.* An operation that modifies a data structure (say D) must return as an output argument a *new reference* (D') to that same data structure. This new reference will be regarded in the concurrent component as a new single-assignment data structure.

2. *Data structures are single-threaded.* At most one update operation can be applied to a data structure.

3. *Reads precede updates.* All read operations applied to a data structure must complete before any update operation is applied.

For example, assume that two user operations inc_vector(V,V1) and sum_vector(V,Sum) have been defined to increment and sum the elements of a vector (an integer array, represented as a user data type). The first operation returns a new reference V1 to the input vector V; the second computes the sum of its elements. Then the following set of processes correctly increments the vector V twice before summing its elements to yield S.

inc_vector(V,V1), inc_vector(V1,V2), sum_vector(V2,S)

On the other hand, the following set of processes would be illegal, as V would be updated by two processes.

inc_vector(V,V1), inc_vector(V,V2)

5.5 Enriching the Interface

Strand programs frequently need to deal with complex data types (such as arrays and record structures) constructed by foreign procedures. As these data do not correspond to any primitive Strand type, they will be passed to Strand as user data types. A closer integration of Strand and foreign components of a bilingual program can be achieved by providing operations defining appropriate *abstract data types*. For example, a one-dimensional integer array type may be implemented in Strand as a user data type (used to represent the array) as well as operations to read and write array elements:

- new_array(Size?,Array↑): returns an initialized Array of the designated size.

- size(Array?,Size↑): returns the Size of Array.

- get_int(Index?,Array?,Item↑): returns Item, the contents of element Index in Array.

- set_int(Index?,Array?,Item?,NewArray↑): updates element Index in Array to contain Item, and returns a new reference to the array, NewArray.

These operations allow Strand programs to access arrays created by foreign language procedures directly. For example, the following program creates a new array initialized to zero. Observe that this program obeys the restrictions stated in Section 5.4.

zero(Size,NewArray) :−

   new_array(Size,Array), zero_1(1,Size,Array, NewArray).

zero_1(I,Max,A,NewA) :−

   I ≤ Max | set_int(I,A,0,A1), I1 is I+1, zero_1(I1,Max,A1,NewA).
   zero_1(I,Max,A,NewA) :− I > Max | NewA := A.

6   The Issue of Code Reuse

The overall goal of the bilingual approach is to reduce software development costs. When developing new applications, we advocate that only performance-critical routines be coded in low-level languages. In order to minimize development and maintenance costs, one naturally attempts to maintain as much of the code as possible in the high-level notation.

However, the coding of new applications is not the only or even the dominant form of software development. We are frequently faced with the need to retarget an existing application to parallel environments. The existing code, which may have been heavily optimized, represents a major investment which must be preserved if we are to achieve the overall goal of minimizing software development costs. In such cases, the use of bilingual programming often leads to a situation in which relatively small amounts of high-level language code is used to coordinate large blocks of low-level language code.

We do not view the coordination of existing code and the development of new codes as fundamentally different applications of bilingual programming; the former simply reflects an appropriate recognition of a sizable existing investment. We differ in this respect from advocates of "coordination languages", who suggest that a coordination language should be used to express issues relating to parallelism, while sequential languages are used to express the coordinated components. The difference between the two views is often revealed during maintenance or extensions of existing bilingual programs. We find that for reasons of convenience, extensions are most often implemented in the high-level language, without concern for whether the extension reflects an aspect of parallel computation or an extension to a sequential component.

In summary, bilingual programming is certainly an effective technology for moving sequential applications to a parallel environment. However, we do not believe that it is desirable to view the sequential components and the coordination components as "orthogonal". Rather, we advocate keeping as much of the code as possible in the high-level concurrent language, given the constraints imposed by performance and the existing software investment.

7 Experiences

We have provided a detailed account of some of our experiences developing bilingual parallel codes elsewhere [8]. Here we summarize our results and the conclusions reached.

In collaboration with colleagues, we have developed bilingual programs in computational biology, weather modeling, and automated reasoning. Each of these codes is a substantial application, used by scientists on a daily basis to support their research. In the following table, we characterize a selection of the codes in terms of the foreign language used and their code size.

Program	Language	Foreign (lines)	Strand (lines)
Weather	Fortran	25000	250
Dynamics	Fortran	4000	120
Prover	C	5000	400
SimSearch	C	500	210
Composite	C	1600	600
Alignment	C	1200	1700

The codes cover a wide spectrum of applications and parallel algorithms. *Weather* is a large "dusty deck" numeric modeling code; it was parallelized by using domain decomposition techniques. *Dynamics* is a molecular dynamics code; its performs a state-space search to find configurations of molecules that satisfy certain criteria. The top level of this code is essentially the fragment given in Section 5.2; it was parallelized by using a dynamic load-balancing strategy. *Prover* implements a parallel theorem-proving algorithm based on a software pipeline. *SimSearch* solves a database search problem; a manager/worker structure is used to allocate parts of the database to idle processors. *Composite* solves atmospheric dynamics equations on the sphere by using a finite difference method and two overlapping grids. Finally, *Alignment* implements an algorithm for computing "alignments" of sequences of genetic material from different organisms; it was parallelized by using functional decomposition and dynamic load-balancing techniques.

The first three applications use substantial amounts of pre-existing code. In these examples, the Strand component is used principally to coordinate the execution of the low-level sequential components. In contrast, *SimSearch*, *Composite*, and *Alignment* were developed from scratch as bilingual applications. In the latter two codes, the Strand component implements all but I/O procedures and the most computationally intensive components of the algorithm.

All six applications went through several revisions in the course of their development. In each case, we found that the bulk of the modifications occurred in the high-level component of the code. The existence of a concise, high-level specification greatly simplified the exploration of alternative algorithms.

Our experience suggests that the bilingual approach permits the benefits of a high-level language to be attained without the performance degradation normally associated with high-level approaches. For example, in *SimSearch*, *Weather*, and *Dynamics*, we observed no significant difference in uniprocessor performance between the bilingual code and an equivalent sequential code written entirely in C or Fortran; in *Composite*, the difference was about 2%. Furthermore, good speedups were achieved in most applications. For example, *Weather* achieved a speedup of 10 over the sequential Fortran code on 16 Sequent Symmetry processors. *SimSearch* achieved a speedup of 56 on a 64 processor Symult hypercube. A preliminary version of *Composite* gave a speedup of 13 on 18 Sequent processors.

The bilingual programs that we developed also proved to be highly portable. For example, *SimSearch* was run on eight different parallel computers. Porting was problematic only when low-level sequential code used non-portable constructs or excessive local memory.

We found that linguistic support for concurrent execution encouraged a modular approach to parallel programming and the encapsulation of parallel algorithms in libraries. Library code was frequently reused in other applications. For example, the state-space search code developed in *Dynamics* was used to develop parallel implementations of two different applications, simply by substituting alternative definitions for two low-level procedures. No changes to the concurrent component were required. At a lower level, both *SimSearch* and *Dynamics* used the same scheduler library code.

A final and important point is that we did find that the use of bilingual programming introduced any special difficulties. We attribute this to the simple interface between the sequential and concurrent components. This permitted sequential procedures and concurrent programs to be developed and tested independently. Furthermore, the bilingual program could generally be tested on a single processor.

8 Related Approaches

It is instructive to review other approaches to parallel programming in the light of the analysis of program development methodologies presented in Section 2.

Parallelizing Compilers. For several years, a number of respected researchers have argued that the key to successful exploitation of parallel processors is advanced compilers [6, 12, 14]. They suggest that programmers should write standard Fortran, which compilers would automatically restructure to take advantage of parallel hardware.

This approach has proved successful when applied to fine-grained parallelism: vectorizing and trace-scheduling compilers give excellent results on certain codes. However, we argue that the approach is seriously flawed as a technique for exploiting large-grained parallelism, as it requires that programs be refined in an inappropriate sequence. Some of the refinements used to target a program toward a specific architecture must be achieved at a level well above that of a Fortran program. In particular, the refinement that commits to an implementation based upon processes that communicate via message passing is naturally thought of as occurring before those that commit to specific implementations of abstract data types. The consequence of making these refinements out of sequence is that systematic analysis of the actual code becomes difficult if not impossible. Properties that could have been stated and verified when made about abstract data types before committing to a specific implementation (with the corresponding details introduced by memory management, etc.) become hard to express and verify.

High-Level Languages. Another group of respected researchers has also argued for compilers but in the context of high-level languages [13, 16]. They suggest that programmers should only need to write a high-level, declarative description of an algorithm; the compiler (and run-time system) will produce code appropriate to specific computational environments.

We believe that this argument is also flawed, due to the fact that automated refinement, while not necessarily sacrificing performance theoretically, often does impact performance in practice. Performance is sacrificed because refinements made by a human who understands the peculiarities of an algorithm are almost always capable of attaining greater performance than generalized transformations included in any actual compiler. This is the essence of the point discussed above in Section 2, and illustrated with the "list of elements" example. The refinements required to effectively map processes to processors and to balance load are areas in which completely automatic choice of optimal strategies seems particularly difficult.

Language Extensions and Layering. Most parallel programming to date has used lower-level languages extended with parallel processing constructs [1, 2, 5, 11, 15]. If properly designed, these extensions can maintain portability without sacrificing substantial performance. A number of packages offering such extensions exist; we have been involved in several efforts based on this approach. The principal drawback of the approach is the loss of notational elegance and freedom from detail associated with high-level languages.

Advocates of languages such as C++ argue that layering of software can provide many of the benefits of a high-level language and in addition allow exploitation of the additional options offered by a lower-level language. For example, one can easily envision a set of routines that supports list processing, memory management, and synchronization facilities similar to those provided by Strand. This sort of layering can dramatically reduce complexity. However, experience suggests that the support and maintenance of lower layers introduces significant intellectual overhead. There is a substantial difference between an algorithm coded with C list-processing routines and an equivalent algorithm coded in Strand. Details introduced by the lower-level context must be remembered, and the lack of notational elegance (e.g., the syntax of a list) produces a marked loss of clarity.

Similar arguments are advanced by proponents of high-level languages that support low-level features such as arrays and assignment (e.g., Common LISP). The low-level features permit efficient implementation of low-level algorithms, and hence seem to permit the benefits of the bilingual approach to be achieved in a single language. However, we believe that the introduction of low-level features tends to compromise the semantic elegance of the high-level language. For example, unrestricted use of updates in Strand would prevent the automatic transformation of programs to incorporate load balancing. The use of a distinct high-level language enables a clean separation of concerns between high-level and low-level components.

Coordination Languages. Some of the arguments we have advanced in this paper have also been put forward by advocates of "coordination languages" [3]. Indeed, we are in basic agreement with the essential positions taken by advocates of coordination languages, and we have in the past discussed the use of Strand as a mechanism for coordinating computations written in lower-level notations [8]. However, we have since come to the view that the boundary between the languages should be determined by tradeoffs between implementation cost and performance, rather than by a division between a sequential component and a coordination component.

9 Conclusions

Bilingual programming has a long, if not noble, history. It has been used since the earliest experiments with high-level languages as a mechanism for mitigating the performance penalty associated with notations that offer standardized implementations of common abstract data types. Its value as a programming methodology is a direct consequence of the trade-offs between ease of expression and performance.

We have argued in this paper that bilingual programming should not be viewed as an ad-hoc solution to transient engineering problems but instead as a logical development of fundamental concepts in programming methodologies. The use of a high-level language permits programmers to adopt standardized implementation decisions when performance is not critical. This minimizes development costs and maximizes flexibility. At the same time, access to low-level languages permits the programmer to perform additional refinement steps when necessary. This permits efficient implementation of critical components.

The bilingual approach is applicable in many areas. However, we believe that it is particularly appropriate in parallel programming, where the need to specify not only sequential execution but also partitioning, scheduling, communication, and synchronization introduces additional complexity. High-level concurrent languages can reduce this complexity by providing standard implementations for common concurrent program structures and by permitting separate specification of program logic, partitioning, and scheduling. At the same time, the efficiency provided by low-level languages is particularly important on parallel computers.

We have accumulated considerable experience in bilingual programming using the high-level language Strand and the lower-level languages C and Fortran. We have developed major codes in several application areas using this technology; some of these have been implemented from scratch, while others reuse large amounts of existing code. We have found that the bilingual approach encourages the development of parallel programs that perform well, are portable, and are easy to maintain. We advocate the adoption of bilingual programming as a technology for programming parallel processors.

Acknowledgments

This research was supported by the Applied Mathematical Sciences subprogram of the Office of Energy Research, U.S. Department of Energy, under Contract W-31-109-Eng-38.

References

1. Babb, R., Parallel processing with large grain data flow techniques, *IEEE Computer*, 17, 55–61, 1984.
2. Boyle, J., Butler, R., Disz, T., Glickfeld, B., Lusk, E., Overbeek, R., Patterson, J., and Stevens, R., *Portable Programs for Parallel Processors*, Holt, Rinehart, Winston, 1987.
3. Carriero, N. and Gelernter, D., Coordination languages and their significance. Technical report YALEU/DCS/RR-716, Yale University, 1989.
4. Chandy, M. and Taylor, S., Program composition, *Proc. Supercomputing '89*, Reno, Nevada, 1989.
5. Dongarra, J. and Sorenson, D., Schedule: Tools for developing and analyzing parallel Fortran programs, *The Characteristics of Parallel Algorithms*, MIT Press, 1987.
6. Fischer, J., Ellis, J., Ruttenberg, J., and Nicolau, A., Parallel processing: a smart compiler and a dumb machine, *Proc. SIGPLAN '84 Symp. on Compiler Construction*, ACM, 37–47, 1984.
7. Foster, I., Automatic generation of self-scheduling programs, *IEEE Trans. on Parallel and Distributed Computing* (to appear).
8. Foster, I. and Overbeek, R., Experiences with bilingual parallel programming, *Proc. 5th Distributed Memory Comp. Conf.*, IEEE Press, 1990.
9. Foster, I., Kesselman, C, and Taylor, S., Concurrency: simple concepts and powerful tools, *The Computer Journal*, Dec. 1990.
10. Foster, I. and Taylor, S., *Strand: New Concepts in Parallel Programming*, Prentice-Hall, Englewood Cliffs, N.J., 1990.
11. Halstead, R.H., MultiLisp - A language for concurrent symbolic computation, *ACM Trans. Prog. Lang. and Syst.*, 7(4), 1985, 501-538.
12. Padua, D.A., Kuck, D.J., and Lawrie, D.H., High-speed multiprocessors and compilation techniques, *IEEE Trans. on Computers*, C-29(9), 1980.
13. Peyton Jones, S., *The Implementation of Functional Programming Languages*, Prentice-Hall, 1987.
14. Polychronopoulos, C., *Parallel Programming and Compilers*, Kluwer Academic, Boston, Mass., 1988.
15. Seitz, C., The cosmic cube, *CACM* 28(1), 22-33, 1985.
16. Warren, D.H.D., Or-parallel execution models of Prolog, *TAPSOFT'87, The 1987 Intl Joint Conf. on Theory and Practice of Software Development*, Springer-Verlag, 243–259, 1987.
17. Wirth, N., Program development by stepwise refinement, *CACM,* 14, 1971, 221–227.

3 Optimizing Analysis for First-Class Tuple-Spaces
S. Jagannathan

Abstract

This paper considers the design and optimization of a simple asynchronous parallel language that uses first-class tuple-spaces as its main communication and process creation device. Our proposed kernel language differs from other tuple-space languages insofar tuple-spaces are treated as true first-class objects. Moreover, we develop a formal framework for constructing an optimizing pre-processor for such a language. The semantic analysis is based on an inference engine that statically computes the set of tuples (and their structural attributes) that can occupy any given tuple-space. The inference system is non-trivial insofar as it operates in the presence of higher-order functions and non-flat data structures (*e.g*, lists). The result of the inference procedure can be used to customize the representation of tuple-space objects.

1 Introduction

Communication and synchronization are fundamental concerns in the design of any parallel language: through what medium is information transmitted from one process to another and how is access to this medium regulated?

In this paper, we consider the semantics and implementation of a simple asynchronous (*i.e.*, loosely synchronized) parallel language that uses *distributed data structures* as its

---

[†]Funding for this work was provided in part by National Science Foundation grant CCR-8657615 and in part by Office of Naval Research grant N00014-89-J-1906.

main communication device. A distributed data structure is a shared data object to which many processes may append and remove information. It is a *non-strict* object; thus, it is meaningful for processes to probe its contents even if all of its component elements are not yet available. Processes communicating via distributed data structures do so with minimal coordination and book-keeping: processes may deposit data without being aware of the receivers who will access it; processes may access data without being aware of the producers that generated it. The semantics of a program in which such requests occur is well-defined. Non-strictness implies asynchrony since the generation of information is decoupled from its consumption.

Distributed data structures are found in a number of languages. Non-strict languages based on *futures* (*e.g.*, [10]) support distributed data structures since a complex structure whose elements are futures may be examined and manipulated by many processes simultaneously. The write-once I-structure [1] found in the mostly-functional language Id [16] can also be viewed as a distributed data structure: an expression that attempts to access an empty I-structure blocks; well-defined constraints are imposed on how such structures are filled. Concurrent object-oriented languages (*e.g.*, [11]) that permit an object to receive messages simultaneously from several processes also support a form of distributed data structure since the state of such an object may be visible to many processes concurrently.

The most well-developed use of distributed data structures is in the Linda programming model [4]. The fundamental mechanism by which distributed data structures are built and manipulated in Linda is the *tuple-space*, a data abstraction that resembles a shared associative memory. A tuple-space permits processes to add, read, evaluate and remove shared data. (The main data objects which reside within tuple-space are known as *tuples*.) C.Linda, a dialect of C that supports the tuple-space abstraction, has been used with notable success on a variety of different machines and applications [2,5]. We discuss the semantics of tuple-spaces in the sections following.

A tuple-space is a powerful abstraction because it imposes no pre-defined structural constraints on the elements which occupy it. The tuples which occupy a tuple-space can be assembled into arbitrary kinds of data structures. The elements of these data structure collections can be read by many processes simultaneously. Synchronization is mediated by a unification procedure that attempts to unify a tuple containing unbound variables with an element in a bag of tuples found within a specified tuple-space. Failure to produce a substitution causes the executing process to block.

Although it's a flexible device, its amorphous structure makes its efficient implementation a challenging exercise. Optimizing compilers for C.Linda do exist [6] and the technologies which they employ have been quite successful. Nonetheless, no semantic framework for describing or analyzing these optimizations has yet been developed; our goal in this document is to develop such a framework and to significantly expand on what has been thus far developed only informally. We expect compilers based on these semantic analyses will be simpler to construct and will implement a wider range of optimizations.

The paper is organized as follows. In the next section, we present a kernel language (called $\mathcal{TS}$) whose semantics permit the creation and manipulation of *first-class tuple-spaces*.

Section 3 develops a semantic analysis framework for this language. The analysis is described in terms of an inference engine that statically computes the set of tuples that can occupy any given tuple-space. The inference system is non-trivial insofar as it operates in the presence of higher-order functions and non-flat data structures. The result of the inference procedure is then used to customize the representation of tuple-space objects. Section 4 presents conclusions and scope for further research.

2 A Kernel Language

We first give an informal description of $\mathcal{TS}$ and then discuss the motivation underlying its design. A formal semantics for the language is given in [13].

$\mathcal{TS}$ is defined by the grammar shown in Figure 1. We use x to range over identifiers, s to range over strings, and c to range over natural numbers. E (and its subscripted variants) range over expressions; T (and its subscripted variants) range over the class of expressions allowable inside tuple-space operations.

2.1 Informal Semantics

The basic operators in $\mathcal{TS}$ form a simple higher-order lexically-scoped functional language with sequencing (;), conditionals ($\rightarrow$) and lists (:). In addition to function definition and application, $\mathcal{TS}$ also supports five operations for creating and manipulating tuple-spaces.

2.1.1 Creating Tuple-Spaces

The `make-ts` operator creates a new tuple-space; more precisely, `make-ts` returns a reference to a tuple-space object. A tuple-space is a data abstraction that defines a shared associative memory whose elements are heterogeneous ordered sets of values known as

```
E    ::=         true | false | c | x | s |
                 (λ (x₁ x₂ ...xₙ) E) | (E₁ E₂ ...Eₙ) |
                 [ ] | [E:E] | (hd E) | (tl E) |
                 E_b → E_t ; E_f |
                 (begin E₁ ; E₂ ; ...; Eₙ) |

                 (make-ts)
                 (out E (E₁, E₂, ..., Eₙ))
                 (eval E (E₁, E₂, ..., Eₙ))
                 (rd E (T₁, T₂, ..., Tₙ) E_b)
                 (in E (T₁, T₂, ..., Tₙ) E_b)

T    ::=         E | ?x
```

Figure 1: Grammar for $\mathcal{TS}$.

tuples. The value yielded by make-ts is a *tuple-space*. A tuple-space in $\mathcal{TS}$ is a first-class object that may be built into list structures, passed as an argument to a function or returned as a result of an application.

The value yielded by make-ts can be thought of as a *capability* to a shared associative memory; expressions that have access to this capability can perform read, write and remove operations on this memory. This model suggests a non-hierarchical relation among tuple-space: the elements of a tuple-space are tuples whose component fields are themselves never tuple-space objects. A tuple can contain the address of a tuple-space, never the tuple-space itself.

The lifetime of a tuple-space is a function of the number of objects and variables which refer to it. A tuple-space that is not referenced by any active object[1] or variable may be garbage collected. Thus, in the expression:

((λ (x) (λ (y) y)) (make-ts))

the lifetime of the tuple-space bound to x is precisely the lifetime of x; once the outer application is evaluated, the space allocated for this tuple-space may be reclaimed.

A process can communicate with other processes only via the set of tuple-spaces to which it has access. (We describe how processes are created below.) In other words,

---
[1] An object is "active" if it is be referenced by some other active object.

processes in this computation model cannot communicate via environments or ordinary shared variables; the only shared data object in this model are tuple-spaces.

2.1.2 Access and Manipulation of Tuple-Spaces

A tuple is deposited into a tuple-space using one of two operators. Let `ts` be a tuple-space[2]; then, the expression:

    (out ts (e_1, e_2, ..., e_n))

evaluates each of the e_i to get a value v_i and deposits the tuple,

    [v_1, v_2, ..., v_n]

into the tuple-space denoted by `ts`. A value is either a constant (*e.g.*, an integer, Boolean or string), a list whose elements are all values, a closure[3], or a reference to a tuple-space object. Out is strict in all of its arguments; thus, each of its arguments must evaluate to values before the operation is considered complete. The value of `out` is unspecified; it is executed for effect, not value.

The e_i in the tuple to be generated are ordinary $\mathcal{TS}$ expressions. They may include identifiers, applications, function definitions, or other tuple operations. For example, the expression:

    ((λ (x) (out ts (x, 10))) (make-ts))

deposits a two-field tuple into the tuple-space denoted by `ts`. The first field in this tuple is a reference to a tuple-space; the second field is 10.

Eval is the non-strict counterpart of `out`. If `ts` is a tuple-space, the expression

    (eval ts (e_1 e_2 ... e_n))

deposits a tuple consisting of n processes into `ts`; the ith process is responsible for computing the value of e_i. Each process evaluates within its own private environment. To achieve this, all functions applied within `eval` are transformed into closed combinators that reference no free variables.

Out and `eval` generate tuples into tuple-space. Rd and In read tuples and binding-values from tuple-space. Consider the expression:

    (rd ts (e_1, e_2, ..., e_n) *body*)

Unlike tuple-generator expressions, each of the e_i may be either an ordinary $\mathcal{TS}$ expression *or* an identifier prefixed by a "?". The evaluation of the above expression takes place

---

[2] In the following, we'll blur the distinction between a reference to a tuple-space and the tuple-space itself when the intended meaning is clear from context.

[3] A closure is pair consisting of the values of all free variables defined within the function along with the text of the function body.

in two steps. Every $\mathcal{TS}$ expression is first evaluated to a value. The resulting object is known as a *tuple-template*: it consists of values and identifiers prefixed with "?"; these identifiers are known as *formals*.

This template is pattern-matched against the tuples found in ts. A successful pattern-match results in each of the "?"-prefixed identifiers in the template obtaining as their binding-value the value of the corresponding field in the tuple to which this template was matched. These bindings are then used in the evaluation of *body*. The result of the entire expression is the value yielded by *body*. Free references in *body* not defined by any of the formals are resolved relative to the in or rd's lexical environment.

Assume that the tuples,

[true, 10, *closure of* (λ (x) (1+ x))]

and

[false, 20, *closure of* (λ (x) (1+ x))]

have been deposited into ts. The expression:

(rd ts (true, ?x, ?y) (y x))

yields 11. The tuple-template successfully pattern-matches against the first tuple; as a result of this match, the variable x becomes bound to 10, and the variable y becomes bound to the closure. This template does not match the second tuple because of the different values found in the first field of the template and the tuple.

If the pattern-matching operation fails because there is no tuple with the same value-correspondence of actuals, the operation blocks. It resumes when a tuple of the appropriate structure and/or the requisite binding-values have been deposited. If there are several tuples that match a template, only one is chosen to establish the binding-values of the template's formals.

The in operation is semantically identical to rd except that the tuple chosen for the match is removed from the given tuple-space. Thus, the expression

(in ts (true, ?x, ?y) (y x))

establishes the appropriate bindings and removes the tuple

[true, 10, *closure of* λ (x) (1+ x))]

before evaluating the application constituting its body.

2.2 Why First-Class Tuple-Spaces?

First-class tuple-spaces have been proposed elsewhere [8,12] and have been implemented (to a degree) in certain implementations of Linda [15]. The kernel language developed here extends these proposals by embedding first-class tuple-space into a language that supports higher-order functions and complex structure types. The matching algorithm over tuples is suitably extended to handle tuple-spaces as well.

The motivation for incorporating first-class tuple-spaces is in part technical and in part conceptual. By permitting tuple-spaces to be denoted, we allow the programmer to partition the communication medium as he sees fit. Partitioning of this kind in turn permits the compiler to customize the representation of individual tuple-spaces based on their contents. Of course, a clever optimizing compiler can infer a partitioning scheme even if tuple-spaces were not explicitly denotable. Such a compiler would require the use of a designated field within a tuple to serve the role of a hash key — all tuples containing the same hash key would be placed in the same partition of tuple-space. First-class tuple-spaces simplify the complexity of compile-time analysis in this respect. Moreover, the specification of the optimizations underlying the parameterization of a tuple-space structure becomes amenable to formal description because tuple-spaces themselves constitute a distinguished type: the same analyses underlying the optimization and use of other data types in the base language can be applied to tuple-spaces as well.

Conceptually, first-class tuple-spaces unify the conceptual bridge between the ordinary data objects found in the base language and the processes and passive objects resident within a tuple-space. Without first-class tuple-spaces, it becomes difficult (if not impossible) to denote a well-defined subset of the objects and processes resident in tuple-space using the linguistic mechanisms available within the base language. Modularity is therefore compromised: all tuples are accessible to all expressions; conventional namespace management techniques applicable over objects in the base language cannot be applied to the objects found in tuple-space. Ad hoc conventions are invariably required to impose structure over the global tuple-space. Greater modularity and control over process structure are the primary motivating factors in the design of the kernel language described here; both concerns are addressed by first-class tuple-spaces. To build a set of related processes, we encapsulate the processes within the same tuple-space; data values that need to be accessed by a known collection of processes are deposited within a tuple-space accessible only to these processes.

The absence of any rigid structural constraints on the contents of a tuple-space has other implications as well. Since tuple-spaces contain processes (generated via **eval**) as well as passive data elements (generated via **out**), there is no pre-specified process structure imposed on a $\mathcal{TS}$ program: $\mathcal{TS}$ programs configure themselves automatically and dynamically based on the number of tuple-spaces created and the contents found within them.

An Example

Figure 4 gives a $\mathcal{TS}$ implementation of a pipeline-based version of the Sieve of Erasthosenes prime-number finder algorithm.

The program implements the prime number filtering program as a pipeline in which each pipeline component represents a process dedicated to filtering out all multiples of a particular prime number; each successive component of the pipeline sees only those elements that are not multiples of primes seen earlier in the pipe. Whenever the current last component in the pipeline sees a number that is not a multiple of the prime it represents (*i.e.*, whenever it encounters a new prime), it extends the pipeline by adding a new component process responsible for filtering out multiples of this new prime.

The function **primes** takes as its input two integers, the first indicating the size of the integer sequence to be examined and the second indicating the number of primes desired in that sequence. (We assume that **size** > **n**.) It defines two tuple-spaces: the first is the **primes-list** which holds two-tuples of the form $[i, v]$ where v is true if i is prime and false otherwise. The second tuple-space holds all active pipeline processes.

There are two abstractions used in the program; the first is a stream abstraction shown in figure 2; the second is a cell abstraction shown in figure 3. Streams are implemented as tuple-spaces that processes use to transmit information; new elements can be added to the stream in constant time.

Given the optimizing analysis described in section 3, the cell and stream implementation would be compiled into basically the same code as would have been generated had we used ordinary shared variables accessed, for example, via semaphores. The advantages of using tuple-spaces in this implementation are two-fold: (1) it allows us to retain a well-defined functional core about which we can reason formally; (2) more importantly, different structured-assignment paradigms (*e.g.*, I-structures [1], read-only logic variables [17], accumulators [16], etc.) can be expressed using simple and easily implemented patterns of tuple operations.

Local to each process is an **end-of-pipe?** flag that is true if the process is the last element currently in the pipeline. The "heart" of each process is a loop function that scans down its input sieve. If the first number in the sieve is a multiple of its local prime, the process loops on the remainder of its input; if the number is not, then there are two possibilities. If the process happens to be the current last component in the pipeline, then the number it has just scanned must be a prime; in this case, it records the fact in the **primes-list**, adds a new pipeline element (*i.e.*, deposits a new process in **active-tuples**) whose filter agent is the prime number just scanned, sets its own **end-of-pipe** flag to nil and, finally, recurses. If the function is not part of the last pipeline element, it attaches the scanned number to its output stream (called **outbox**) and recurses; the loop function found in the pipeline element to the right of this component uses this stream as its input sieve.

Tuple-spaces are used in this example in three different ways: (1) they serve as the main stream communication mechanism between different filters; (2) they serve to implement a cell abstraction[4]; and (3) they act a process control device in which new processes are evaluated. Constructing an efficient inter-process communication protocol given the presence of a large, possibly dynamic, number of processes (as in this example) becomes first and foremost an exercise in modularity; first-class tuple-spaces simplify the task considerably.

3 Semantic Analysis

In this section we consider the problem of generating efficient representations of first-class tuple-spaces based on a static analysis of a $\mathcal{TS}$ program. To see why this is a non-trivial problem, consider the following expression:

```
((λ (x)
    (begin
       (out x ("foo"))
       (out x ("bar"))
       (rd  x (?y) y)))
  (make-ts))
```

The argument to the abstraction in the application is a tuple-space; the body of the function effects a mutation on this tuple-space by depositing two tuples (via **out**). The issue at hand is whether we can statically construct a representation for the argument tuple-space based on properties which can be inferred about the tuples deposited within it. Stated another way, we would like to infer a representation for a tuple-space based on the structure of the tuples which inhabit it.

In the above example, it is clear that the only tuples which occupy the tuple-space denoted by **x** are tuples of length one with the sole tuple-field containing a constant. An ideal representation for a tuple-space of this sort is in terms of two semaphores named **foo** and **bar**: the translation of an **out** expression is given in terms of a V operation on its specified semaphore argument; **rd** and **in** expressions implement P operations. A naive implementation (*i.e.*, an implementation insensitive to the structure

---

[4]In this example, the need for a cell abstraction would be obviated given an explicit assignment operation.

```
make-stream =
   (λ ()
        let new-stream = (make-ts)
        in
         (begin
            (out new-stream ("head",0));
            (out new-stream ("tail",0));
            new-stream))

stream-car =
  (λ (stream)
       (rd stream ("head",?index)
           (rd stream (index,?value)
               value)))

stream-cdr! =
  (λ (stream)
       (in stream ("head",?index)
           (begin
              (out stream ("head",(1+ index)));
              stream)))

attach =
  (λ (stream elt)
       (in stream ("tail",index)
           (begin
              (out stream (index,elt));
              (out stream ("tail",(1+ index)));
              stream)))
```

Figure 2: A stream abstraction using first-class tuple-spaces.

```
make-cell =
  (λ ()
      let cell = (make-ts)
      in
        (begin
           (out cell ("state", "empty"));
           cell))

read-cell =
  (λ (cell)
      (rd cell ("value",?v) v))

write-cell =
  (λ (cell v)
      (in cell ("state",?condition)
          condition = "empty" →
            (begin
               (out cell ("state","full"));
               (out cell ("value",v)));
          (in cell ("value",?old-v)
             (out cell ("value",v)))))
```

Figure 3: A cell abstraction using first-class tuple-spaces. We introduce a "state" condition to determine whether an in operation should be performed before writing a new value into the cell.

```
primes =
  (λ (size n)
      let primes-list = (make-ts)
          active-tuples = (make-ts)
          int-stream = (λ (initial-stream stream first last)
                           let loop = (λ (stream m)
                                           (begin
                                              (> m last) → stream;
                                                            (attach stream m);
                                              (loop stream (1+ m))))
                           in
                             (loop initial-stream first))

          pipeline-elt = code for individual pipeline elements given in Figure 5

      in
       (begin
          (out primes-list (1,t));
          (out primes-list (2,t));
          let initial-stream = (make-stream)
          in
           (begin
              (eval active-tuples ((pipeline-elt 2 initial-stream)));
              (eval active-tuples ((int-stream initial-stream 3 size))))
          primes-list))
```

Figure 4: A Sieve of Erasthosenes-based prime-number finder using first-class tuple-spaces.

```
(λ (my-prime sieve)
    let outbox = (make-stream)
        end-of-pipe? = (make-cell)
    in
     (begin
       (write-cell end-of-pipe? true);
       let loop =
        (λ (sieve)
            let next-candidate = (stream-car sieve)
            in
             (multiple? next-candidate my-prime) →
                (begin
                  (out primes-list (next-candidate,false));
                  (loop (stream-cdr! sieve)));
                (begin
                  (read-cell end-of-pipe?) →
                    (begin
                       (out primes-list (next-candidate,true));
                       (eval active-tuples ((pipeline-elt next-candidate
                                                           outbox)));
                       (write-cell end-of-pipe? false);
                       (loop (stream-cdr! sieve)));
                    (begin
                       (attach outbox next-candidate)
                       (loop (stream-cdr! sieve))))))
        in
         (loop sieve))
```

Figure 5: A pipeline element for the primes program.

of the tuples inhabiting a tuple-space) would consider a most general representation for
x, namely one in which x is represented by a hash table or some similar data structure
suitable for general matching. The constants foo and bar would serve as keys into this
structure. Clearly, this is significantly more complex and inefficient than the semaphore-
based representation.

To take another example, consider the expression:

((λ (x y) [x : y]) (make-ts) (make-ts))

Both x and y are bound to tuple-spaces and are used as elements of a list object.
Operations on these tuple-spaces take place indirectly through list access operations. An
optimized representation for these tuple-spaces must be sensitive to this fact. A naive
implementation in terms of a complex hash structure for these tuple-spaces may be
excessively wasteful especially if the tuple-operations performed on these objects require
minimal matching.

In order to construct an optimized representation for tuple-spaces, we need to design
a procedure capable of computing the *types* (or attributes) of all tuples that can occupy
any given tuple-space object. Given such information, it now becomes possible to analyze
various structural properties of the set's elements thereby allowing an optimizer to build
a suitable representation. The construction of such sets is complicated by the fact that
tuple-spaces are first-class objects.

In a system such as C.Linda, an analysis of this sort takes place by considering every
tuple to be an element of the single global tuple-space and proceeding to partition this
set based on obvious constraints (*e.g.*, tuple-length and type). In $\mathcal{TS}$, on the other
hand, not every tuple need reside in every tuple-space. Moreover, the fact that one
can abstract over tuple-spaces, return them from functions or embed them inside data
structures implies that a given tuple may be deposited into more than tuple-space. Naive
examination of the source text will not reveal accurate tuple usage in such cases.

We approach the problem of statically inferring a suitable structure for tuple-space
as a variant of a semantic analysis technique known as *collecting interpretation* [14].
Collecting interpretation is an abstract interpretation [7] that attempts to infer the set
of values a given variable can acquire during the execution of a program. In our case, the
variables of interest are those bound to tuple-spaces, and the values we are interested in
are the values of tuple fields.

Our approach is as follows. We construct an inference system that associates with
every expression a *type*. The type of a tuple-space is defined as a set of *tuple-types* where a
tuple-type defines relevant structural properties of a tuple, *i.e.*, length, kind (*e.g.*, read or
generate), number and position of formals, actuals and constants. The inference system

$$
\begin{array}{lcl}
\tau & ::= & \sigma \mid \iota \mid \phi \mid \tau_1 \times \tau_2 \times \ldots \times \tau_n \rightarrow \tau \mid \textbf{List}[\tau] \mid TS \\
TS & ::= & TS_\perp \mid TS[Tuple] \\
Tuple & ::= & (\mathcal{K}, \mathcal{C}, \mathcal{F}, \mathcal{S}, \textbf{N}) \\
\mathcal{K} & ::= & \text{READ} \mid \text{GEN} \\
\mathcal{C} & ::= & \mathcal{C}_\perp \mid \mathcal{C}[\textbf{N} \mapsto E_s \times \iota] \\
\mathcal{F} & ::= & \mathcal{F}_\perp \mid \mathcal{F}[\textbf{N} \mapsto \tau] \\
\mathcal{S} & ::= & \mathcal{S}_\perp \mid \mathcal{S}[\textbf{N} \mapsto \tau]
\end{array}
$$

Figure 6: The Type Language

defines a collecting interpretation in the sense that a well-typed program has a type associated with every tuple-space that defines the structural properties of the tuples which can occupy that tuple-space. [3] gives a general discussion on type inference systems.

Operationally, the inference procedure can be thought of as a constraint system that imposes restrictions on a tuple-space's structure based on the context in which it occurs. Every tuple-space operation contributes to the type of a tuple-space: a tuple-space operation defines constraints on its argument tuple-space based on the constants, formals and actuals its argument tuple contains.

3.1 Preliminaries

Our inference system associates every TS expression with an expression in a type language defined by the grammar shown in Figure 6. Throughout the rest of the paper, we use the following naming conventions: we assume τ ranges over *types* and σ ranges over *type variables*. **N** ranges over integers, **S** ranges over strings, and **B** ranges over Booleans. ι ranges over all constants and E ranges over TS expressions. δ ranges over *tuple-types* and γ ranges over *tuple-space* types. We introduce the special ground type ϕ to denote the type of `out` and `eval` expressions. (Recall that these expressions have unspecified value and are executed for effect.)

There are three type constructors in our type language: $\times$ to build cross-products, $\rightarrow$ to build function types and **List** to construct list types.

A type can be either a ground type (*e.g.*, an integer, Boolean or string), a list type, a function type a tuple-type or tuple-space type. List types denote collections of homogeneous values (values of the same type); function types are used to type λ-abstractions.

A tuple-space type is defined as a set of tuple-types as described in figure 7.

3.2 Notation

We abbreviate a tuple-space type of the form:

$$TS_\perp[\delta_1][\delta_2]\ldots[\delta_n]$$

as:

$$TS(\delta_1, \delta_2, \ldots, \delta_n)$$

A similar notation applies over components of tuple-types. E.g.,

$$\mathcal{F}(i_1 \mapsto \tau_{i_1}, \ldots, i_k \mapsto \tau_{i_k})$$

defines a tuple whose i_j^{th} field contains a formal with type τ_{i_j}.

Finally, if δ is a tuple-type, then $\Pi(\delta)$ denotes a set of types, $\{\tau_1, \tau_2, \ldots, \tau_n\}$; we write $\Pi(\delta)[i]$ to denote τ_i. We define Π as follows: if

$$\delta = (\mathcal{K}, \mathcal{C}, \mathcal{F}, \mathcal{S}, n)$$

then

$\mathcal{C}(i) \downarrow 2 = \tau_i$, if $\Pi(\delta)[i] = \tau_i$.
$\mathcal{F}(j) = \tau_j$, if $\Pi(\delta)[j] = \tau_j$.
$\mathcal{S}(k) = \tau_k$, if $\Pi(\delta)[k] = \tau_k$.

(i, j, and k range over disjoint sets of natural numbers with the constraint that $i+j+k = n$.)

3.3 Subtyping

Tuple-space types are ordered under a subtype relation. Intuitively, we think of a type τ_1 as being a subtype of τ_2 if τ_2 is more constrained than τ_1. Stated another way, type τ_1 is a subtype of τ_2 if an expression of type τ_1 can be used in any context where an expression of type τ_2 is allowed.

The subtyping rule permits us to constrain the type of a tuple-space based on the expressions which operate over it. For example, if x is a tuple-space, the expression:

(out x *some tuple*)

- $\mathcal{K}$: the *kind* of tuple being described — READ if the tuple is associated with an **rd** or **in** expression; GEN if the tuple is associated with an **out** or **eval** operation. We write $\mathcal{K}(\delta)$ to denote the kind component of tuple-type δ.

- $\mathcal{C}$: the *constants* found within the tuple being described. $\mathcal{C}_\perp$ denotes tuples with no constants; a tuple-type with $\mathcal{C}$ component:

$$\mathcal{C}_\perp[i_1 \mapsto (E_{i_1} \times \iota_{i_1})][i_2 \mapsto (E_{i_2} \times \iota_{i_2})]\ldots[i_k \mapsto (E_{i_k} \times \iota_{i_k})]$$

denotes a tuple that has E_{i_j} with associated type τ_{i_j} in position i_j, $1 \leq j \leq k$.

$$\mathcal{C}(i_j) \downarrow 1$$

denotes E_{i_j} and

$$\mathcal{C}(i_j) \downarrow 2$$

denotes τ_{i_j}.

- $\mathcal{F}$: the *formals* found within the tuple being described. $\mathcal{F}_\perp$ denotes tuples with no formals; a tuple-type with $\mathcal{F}$ component:

$$\mathcal{F}_\perp[i_1 \mapsto \tau_{i_1}][i_2 \mapsto \tau_{i_2}]\ldots[i_k \mapsto \tau_{i_k}]$$

denotes a tuple that has formals in positions $i_1, i_2, \ldots, i_k$ with associated type $\tau_{i_1}, \tau_{i_2}, \ldots, \tau_{i_k}$.

- $\mathcal{S}$: the *actuals* found within the tuple being described. $\mathcal{S}$ has the same structure as $\mathcal{F}$.

- the last component of a tuple-type indicates the size of the tuple. If δ is a tuple-type, then $\mathcal{L}(\delta)$ gives the value of its size component.

Figure 7: The component elements of a tuple-type.

can be thought of as imposing a constraint on x (namely, that x must contain *some tuple*). This constraint can be couched in terms of a subtype relation which requires x's type to be a subtype of the type associated with a tuple-space (call it T) that contains *some tuple* as its sole element. Moreover, satisfaction of this constraint requires that x's type contain information regarding the structure of *some tuple*; if x can be used wherever T can, then x must contain at least as much information as found in the type of T.

If γ_1 and γ_2 are two tuple-space types, then we say that $\gamma_1 \leq \gamma_2$ if $\gamma_2 \subseteq \gamma_1$. In other words, if the set of tuple-types denoted by γ_1 is a superset of the set of tuple-types denoted by γ_2, then γ_1 is a subtype of γ_2 – it can be used in any type context where γ_2 can.

3.4 Type Environments

In presenting our inference rules, we use the symbol A to represent the current type environment. We use the notation

$$A \vdash e : \tau$$

to indicate that expression e has type τ given the type bindings defined in A.

If A is a type environment, then the type expression $A[x \mapsto \tau]$ defines a new type environment:

$$A[x \mapsto \tau](y) = \begin{cases} A(y) & \text{if } y \neq x \\ \tau & \text{otherwise} \end{cases}$$

3.5 Inference Rules

The axioms and inference rules for the type system are presented in a form similar to Gentzen's calculus of sequents[9]. Each inference rule consists of a set of statements called the *antecedents* and a statement called the *consequent*. In writing an inference rule, we separate antecedents and consequents by a horizontal line; axioms have no antecedents and no horizontal line is drawn.

(Type Variable Instantiation)

$$\frac{A \vdash e : \tau}{A \vdash e : \tau[\sigma/\tau_1]}$$

If τ and τ_1 are types and σ is a type variable, then the expression, $\tau[\sigma/\tau_1]$ replaces all free occurrences of σ in τ by τ_1.

(Subtype)

$$\frac{A \vdash e : \gamma}{A \vdash e : \gamma'} \qquad \gamma \leq \gamma'$$

(Identifiers)

$$A \vdash x : A(x)$$

(Abstraction)

$$\frac{A[x_i \mapsto \tau_i] \vdash e_b : \tau_b}{A \vdash (\lambda \ (x_1 \ x_2 \ \ldots \ x_n) \ e_b) : (\tau_1 \times \tau_2 \times \ldots \times \tau_n) \to \tau_b} \qquad 1 \leq i \leq n$$

(Application)

$$\frac{A \vdash e_\lambda : (\tau_1 \times \tau_2 \times \ldots \times \tau_n) \to \tau_f \qquad A \vdash e_i : \tau_i}{A \vdash (e_\lambda \ e_1 \ \ldots \ e_n) : \tau_f} \qquad 1 \leq i \leq n$$

(Conditional)

$$\frac{A \vdash e_b : \mathbf{B} \qquad A \vdash e_t : \tau \qquad A \vdash e_f : \tau}{A \vdash e_b \to e_t \ ; \ e_f : \tau}$$

(List)

$$\frac{A \vdash e_1 : \tau \qquad A \vdash e_2 : \tau}{A \vdash [e_1 : e_2] : \mathbf{List}[\tau]}$$

(Tuple-Space)

$$\frac{\sigma \text{ a fresh type variable}}{A \vdash \mathbf{make-ts} : \sigma}$$

(Generate)

Three auxiliary definitions are used in the type rules for tuple-space operations:

Definition 1 Let A be a type environment and let $t = (e_1, e_2, \ldots, e_n)$ be tuple expression. Then,

1. $Constants(A, (e_1, e_2, \ldots, e_n)) = \mathcal{C}(i_1 \mapsto (e_{i_1} \times \tau_{i_1}), i_2 \mapsto (e_{i_2} \times \tau_{i_2}), \ldots, i_k \mapsto (e_{i_k} \times \tau_{i_k}))$
   if $e_{i_1}, e_{i_2}, \ldots, e_{i_k}$ are constants found in t and $A \vdash e_{i_j} : \tau_{i_j}$ for $1 \leq j \leq k$.

2. $Formals(A, (e_1, e_2, \ldots, e_n)) = \mathcal{F}(i_1 \mapsto \tau_{i_1}, i_2 \mapsto \tau_{i_2}, \ldots, i_k \mapsto \tau_{i_k})$
   if $e_{i_1}, e_{i_2}, \ldots, e_{i_k}$ are the formals found in t and $A \vdash e_{i_j} : \tau_{i_j}$ for $1 \leq j \leq k$.

3. $Actuals(A, (e_1, e_2, \ldots, e_n)) = \mathcal{S}(i_1 \mapsto \tau_{i_1}, i_2 \mapsto \tau_{i_2}, \ldots, i_k \mapsto \tau_{i_k})$
   if $e_{i_1}, e_{i_2}, \ldots, e_{i_k}$ are the actuals found in t and $A \vdash e_{i_j} : \tau_{i_j}$ for $1 \leq j \leq k$.

Given these definitions, our type rule for **out** and **rd** operations are given as follows (the rules for **eval** and **in** are defined similarly):

$$\frac{A \vdash e_T : \gamma \quad t = (e_1, e_2, \ldots, e_n) \quad TS(\text{GEN}, Constants(A, t), Formals(A, t), Actuals(A, t), n) = \gamma}{A \vdash (\text{out } e_T \, (e_1, e_2, \ldots, e_n)) : \phi}$$

(Read)

$$\frac{\begin{array}{c} A \vdash e_T : \gamma \\ t = (e_1, e_2, \ldots, e_n) \\ F = Formals(A, t) = \mathcal{F}(i_1 \mapsto \tau_{i_1}, \ldots, i_k \mapsto \tau_{i_k}) \\ TS(\text{READ}, Constants(A, t), F, Actuals(A, t), n) = \gamma \\ A[e_j \mapsto \tau_j] \vdash e_b : \tau \quad j = i_1, \ldots, i_k \end{array}}{A \vdash (\text{rd } e_T \, (e_1, e_2, \ldots, e_n) e_b) : \tau}$$

3.6 Discussion

The inference rules given above do not define a type-checking algorithm; there are, in fact, many possible types that can be deduced for the same expression given different typing algorithms. Provided that the inference system is sound (*i.e.*, it does not yield a type for an expression inconsistent with the type of the expression's denotation), these types are all refinements of some principal (or most general) type. In our type-system the principle type of a tuple-space T is a set of tuple-types that contain precisely the tuples deposited into or read from T; the principal type defines a "minimal" type for an expression[5] A type assignment algorithm based on the inference rules given above can be found in [13].

A `make-ts` operation has a type variable as its type. A type variable is a variable that can be instantiated to a more specific type based on the type contexts in which it occurs. In our type system, a type variable can acquire a type that satisfies the constraints imposed by the type contexts in which its associated tuple-space occurs.

Constraints on type variables take place in the type rules for tuple operations. In order for `out` or `eval` operation to be well-typed we require that the type of its argument tuple-space (call this type γ) be the same as the tuple-space containing the tuple found as the operator's second argument. In order for such a constraint to be satisfied, the type of the argument tuple-space must be coercible (via the subtype rule) to γ. In other words, the expression denoting the argument tuple-space must have a tuple-space type that contains at least as many elements as defined by γ. Such a condition would permit application of the subtype rule on that type that would equate it with γ. A similar analysis holds over `in` or `rd` operations.

Consider the tuple operations applied to variable `sieve` in the prime number finder shown earlier. `Sieve` is defined as a tuple-space and is applied at various points to all four stream operators: `make-stream`, `stream-car`, `stream-cdr!` and `attach`. The structural type analysis for `sieve` binds `sieve`'s type to a set of tuple-types shown in figure 8; we partition the set based on the functions in which the tuple operations occur.

We first give an informal description of how an optimizer might use the information generated by the type inference system to construct a representation for tuple-space and then present a more precise description of the process.

Based on the structure of the tuples deposited into `sieve` we can deduce the following useful properties about this tuple-space:

1. It contains only tuples of length 2.

2. There are two constants (`"head"` and `"tail"`) used only in the first field of a tuple.

3. All formals appear only in the second field of any `read` tuple.

Given these properties, we can implement `sieve` as a structure with three components: two queues named `head` and `tail` and a symbol table (implemented in terms

---

[5] By "minimal type" we mean a type that contains no extraneous type information. Thus, a tuple-space type is minimal if the removal of any component tuple-type would violate a type constraint relative to some context in which it occurs.

make-stream					
$\mathcal{K}$	$\mathcal{C}$	$\mathcal{F}$	$\mathcal{S}$		$\mathbf{N}$
GEN	$0 \mapsto$ "head" $\times$ **S** $0 \mapsto 1$	–	–		2
GEN	$0 \mapsto$ "tail" $\times$ **S** $0 \mapsto 1$	–	–		2

stream-car				
$\mathcal{K}$	$\mathcal{C}$	$\mathcal{F}$	$\mathcal{S}$	$\mathbf{N}$
READ	$0 \mapsto$ "head" $\times$ **S**	$1 \mapsto \tau_1$	–	2
READ	–	$1 \mapsto \mathbf{N}$	$0 \mapsto \tau_1$	2

stream-cdr!				
$\mathcal{K}$	$\mathcal{C}$	$\mathcal{F}$	$\mathcal{S}$	$\mathbf{N}$
READ	$0 \mapsto$ "head" $\times$ **S**	$0 \mapsto \mathbf{N}$	–	2
GEN	$0 \mapsto$ "head" $\times$ **S**	–	$1 \mapsto \mathbf{N}$	2

attach				
$\mathcal{K}$	$\mathcal{C}$	$\mathcal{F}$	$\mathcal{S}$	$\mathbf{N}$
READ	$0 \mapsto$ "tail" $\times$ **S**	–	$1 \mapsto \mathbf{N}$	2
GEN	–	–	$0 \mapsto \mathbf{N}$ $1 \mapsto \tau_2$	2
GEN	$0 \mapsto$ "tail" $\times$ **S**	–	$1 \mapsto \mathbf{N}$	2

Figure 8: The type structure of variable `sieve`.

of a hashing function, trie, or any other suitable structure) that maps stream indices to their values. Out operations on sieve whose first field is a constant are implemented by appending to the appropriate queue; in or rd operations on these queue types simply remove the first element and block if the queue is empty. Reading or writing a stream element involves manipulating the symbol table: to read an element, the element's index is used as a key to select the appropriate element.

3.6.1 Transforming Types to Representations

In this section, we make precise the intuition given above by sketching an algorithm to generate representations for tuple-spaces given their types. The effectiveness of the algorithm lies in how cleverly it constructs a *partition* for the tuples that occupy any given tuple-space. A partition separates tuples into disjoint sets. Each set contains READ and GEN kind tuples that can potentially match with one another. The partition is constructed such that a GEN found in partition set s_1 is guaranteed *not* to match with any READ tuple found in partition set $s_j, j \neq i$. For example, tuples which have different lengths or whose corresponding fields have distinct types can never yield a non-empty substitution. A partition that contains tuples which enjoy a similar structure can be transformed into a particular data representation that takes advantage of this similarity; we describe some optimizations in this regard below.

We formalize our intuition of partitions as follows:

Definition 2 Let γ be a tuple-space type and let $\delta_1, \delta_2, \ldots, \delta_n$ be tuple-types found in γ.

A *partition* P of γ is a relation on tuple-types defined such that $(\delta_i, \delta_j) \in P$ iff

- $\mathcal{L}(\delta_i) = \mathcal{L}(\delta_j)$.
- $\Pi(\delta_i) = \Pi(\delta_j)$.

We can now define the tuple-space construction algorithm as follows:

Tuple Representation Algorithm:

    Input: A tuple-space type γ containing tuple-types, $\delta_1, \delta_2, \ldots, \delta_n$.

    Output: A *representation* for γ.

    Method:

Step 1 Partition the tuple-types found in γ.

    Optimization: If the tuples to occupy a given partition are defined purely in terms of constants (*e.g.,* (out T ("a","b")) or (in T ("c","d","e") e)), then we can implement each constant tuple as a general semaphore. Out operations perform a V operation on the corresponding semaphore; `in` or `rd` expressions perform a P operation.

Step 2 Compute the set of *search keys* for each partition. A search key is an index i defined such that no tuple field in any tuple found within such a partition contains a formal at position i. The set of search keys for a given partition defines exactly those fields that are involved in the matching procedure.

Optimization: If the search keys for a given partition denote tuple indices whose contents are all constants, the partition can be implemented as an n dimensional matrix where n denotes the number of search keys for the partition. The structure of this matrix is given by allocating a dimension for each tuple index corresponding to a search key; the contents of the nth dimension contains a queue to hold the binding-values for the formals found in `rd` or `in` expressions that access this partition.

For example, the partitions generated for `sieve`'s type would place tuples whose first fields are "head" and "tail" into the same partition. Since this first field is the only search key in this partition, we can build a vector of length 2 indexed by either "head" or "tail". Each element in the vector contains a queue. `Out` operations augment the queue; `in` and `rd` operations remove an element from the front, blocking if no such element exists.

Step 3 In the general case, a partition contains a set of search keys whose corresponding tuple-field contents are not known statically. The contents of the tuple-fields represented by the search keys are used here as keys in a generalized hashing procedure. An `out` expression is implemented by hashing the contents of each search key in its tuple argument to a pair containing the tuple and the search key. An `in` or `rd` expression computes the intersection of the set of tuples returned by hashing on each of the search key arguments. If this intersection is empty, it means that no matching tuple has yet been generated; if the intersection set contains more than one element, it means that several matching tuples have been deposited. Any tuple can be chosen from this set non-deterministically.

For example, given the following expressions:

```
(out T (a, b, c))
(rd  T (?d, f, g) E)
```

and assuming that the corresponding tuple-types reside in the same partition, we can use the second and third fields in the tuples as the search keys. To implement the out expression, we augment the hash structure by hashing the value of b to the pair:

< 1, (value of a, value of b, value of c) >

and the value of c to the pair:

< 2, (value of a, value of b, value of c) >

We translate the rd by first requiring the value of f and g to be used as hash keys to retrieve two sets of tuples. We extract from the first set all tuples belonging to pairs whose first field is 1; we extract from the second set all tuples belonging to pairs whose first field is 2. The intersection of these two sets gives us the set of tuples that match the template specified by the rd expression.

4 Conclusions

Our structural analysis technique enables us to construct a representation for first-class tuple-spaces similar to what an optimizing C.Linda compiler can generate given a more restrictive global tuple-space structure.

There is however a broad class of optimizations that still merit investigation. Our analysis has been restricted to a study of a tuple-space's structural properties; these properties are concerned with static attributes of a tuple, e.g., a tuple's length, the types of its fields, etc.. Flow analysis of $\mathcal{TS}$ programs would enable us to collect information on the dynamic attributes of tuple-spaces. For example, a given rd expression may potentially match with n out expressions; however, as a result of flow analysis, we may be able to deduce that only a small number (say k) of these n out's can actually be involved in any match operation with this rd expression. Such a situation would occur if the rd logically precedes (in the flow graph) the remaining $n - k$ out operations. Flow dependency information can be used to build a more refined partition scheme for tuple-spaces.

Time analysis is another non-standard analysis that can be profitably applied to construct efficient representations for tuple-spaces. Time analysis deals with inferring the amount of time a given expression takes to execute. In the context of tuple-space languages, time analysis can be used to answer questions of the form: given tuple expressions t_1 and t_2 found in two concurrently executing processes, will t_1 have executed before t_2 begins evaluating relative to some execution metric or scheduling policy M?

Such analysis can shed light on scheduling algorithms for active tuples as well as giving us further information on representation structures for tuple-spaces.

We intend to develop these analysis in greater detail in the near future as we experiment with various implementations of the ideas detailed here.

References

[1] Arvind, Rishiyur Nikhil, and Keshav Pingali. I-Structures: Data Structures for Parallel Computing. *Transactions on Programming Languages and Systems*, 11(4):598–632, October 1989.

[2] R. Bjornson, N. Carriero, D. Gelernter, and J. Leichter. Linda, the Portable Parallel. Technical Report RR-520, Yale Univ. Dept. of Computer Science, January 1988.

[3] Luca Cardelli and Peter Wegner. On Understanding Types, Data Abstraction, and Polymorphism. *ACM Computing Surveys*, 17(4):471–522, 1985.

[4] Nicholas Carriero and David Gelernter. Linda in Context. *Communications of the ACM*, 32(4):444 – 458, April 1989.

[5] Nick Carriero and David Gelernter. Applications Experience with Linda. In *Proceedings of the ACM Symposium on Parallel Programming*, pages 173–187, July 1988.

[6] Nick Carriero and David Gelernter. Tuple Analysis and Partial Evaluation Strategies in the Linda Precompiler. In *Second Workshop on Languages and Compilers for Parallelism*. MIT Press, August 1989.

[7] P. Cousot and R. Cousot. Abstract Interpretation: A Unified Lattice Model for Static Analysis of Programs by Construction or Approximation of Fixed-Points. In 4th *ACM Symposium on Principles of Programming Languages*, 1977.

[8] David Gelernter. Multiple Tuple Spaces in Linda. In *Proceedings of PARLE '89*, volume 2, pages 20–27, 1989.

[9] G. Gentzen. Investigations into Logical Deduction. In M.E.Szabo, editor, *The Collected Papers of Gerhard Gentzen*. North-Holland Press, 1969.

[10] Robert Halstead. Multilisp: A Language for Concurrent Symbolic Computation. *Transactions on Programming Languages and Systems*, 7(4):501–538, October 1985.

[11] Waldemar Horwat, Andrew Chien, and William Dally. Experience with CST: Programming and Implementation. In *ACM SIGPLAN '89 Conference on Programming Language Design and Implementation*, pages 101–109, June 1989.

[12] Susanne Hupfer. Melinda: Linda with Multiple Tuple Spaces. Technical Report YALEU/DCS/RR-766, Dept. of Computer Science, Yale University, 1990.

[13] Suresh Jagannathan. Semantics and Analysis of First-Class Tuple-Spaces. Technical Report DCS/RR-783, Yale University, April 1990.

[14] Neil Jones and Alan Mycroft. Data Flow Analysis of Applicative Programs Using Minimal Function Graphs. In 13th *ACM Symposium on Principles of Programming Languages Conf.*, pages 296–306, 1986.

[15] Wm Leler. Linda Meets Unix. *Computer*, 23(2):43–55, February 1990.

[16] Rishiyur Nikhil. ID Reference Manual (Version 88.0). Technical report, MIT, 1988. Computation Structures Group Technical Report.

[17] Ehud Shapiro. Concurrent Prolog: A Progress Report. *IEEE Computer*, 19(8):44–60, August 1986.

4 The Linda Program Builder
S. Ahmed, N. Carriero, D. Gelernter

Abstract

We present the Linda Program Builder, an emacs-based editor that supports incremental development of explicitly parallel C-Linda programs. The LPB supports programming paradigms that underlie most parallel programs. The programmer is guided through the use of templates. The LPB also develops and maintains a program-describing database during program construction. This database and the associated knowledge of the program serve as a basis for integration with other tools in the Linda programming environment. The LPB captures a methodology of programming without forcing complexity and rigidity on the base language. This is particularly important in light of the fact that the last twenty years have seen no major breakthroughs in "higher-level" languages, despite a demand in the programming community. Tools like LPB are the most likely candidates to fill the gap.

1 Introduction

The Linda Program Builder (LPB) is an emacs-based editor that supports incremental development of explicitly parallel C-Linda programs. Accumulated programming experience using Linda has made it clear that a small number of well-defined programming paradigms underlie most parallel programs. Each paradigm has a family of C-Linda implementations. We can abstract the basic features of these implementations into templates, and have a structured editor create program text using the templates under programmer guidance. A preliminary version of such a system has been implemented, in the shape of the LPB.

The work has several goals. First, the LPB can reduce the time and effort that goes into parallel programming. This holds in an "administrative" sense (the programmer types fewer keystrokes, thus spends less time and makes fewer mistakes), and in a conceptual one as well: having grasped the general structure of an appropriate coordination framework, I can implement it without worrying about (many of) the details governing the framework's implementation in Linda. Second, the LPB develops a program-describing database as it goes along. The database can be used to check for consistency, to guide program development and to document the code.

Finally, and most significant—though least exploited in the current prototype—the LPB "understands" the program under construction in ways that a compiler never could. The Linda coordination framework it constructs is understood to be the implementation of a particular paradigm. Where a compiler would see a collection of process and tuple-manipulation operations, with certain patterns (of obscure intent) governing the manipulation of tuple space, the LPB sees a master-worker program, a single-source multi-sink task queue, a shared global table. It understands the intent behind the program structures.

This knowledge can be used in many ways. The C-Linda compiler can use it to produce better codes. The Tuplescope program visualizer [BC90] can use it to produce better organized, "higher-level" displays. A yet-to-be-developed benchmarking utility can use it to drive automatic benchmarking and performance analysis; and the LPB's superior knowledge lays the foundation for an evolving expert-database approach to intelligent program development.

The LPB and allied approaches have significant implications for language design as well: they make it possible for you to have your cake and it too. The LPB is a promising solution to the general problem of capturing the methods and idioms that skilled programmers rely on, but *without* junking up the language itself with a galaxy of high-level, special-purpose constructs. The LPB's output is Linda code—making it a transparent utility. The programmer can see exactly what the LPB has done, and change it, extend it or throw it out as he chooses. When the LPB lacks a suitable paradigm, he can ignore it altogether (or use it as a mere administrative tool, allowing it to gather data for consistency-checking and documentation purposes). The LPB can evolve or be customized—can be extended with new tools and paradigms, and problem- or site-specific approaches—without necessitating any change either to the specification or the implementation of Linda. The programmer can draw on a wide spectrum of high-level structures and strategies; Linda itself remains simple and general.

The sections following describe an important template, some basic support functions and the LPB tuple database. Linda itself having been discussed extensively, we omit further description. [6] is a representative paper from our group; [8], [10] and [1] are good examples of other Linda-related research; [9] and [5] are examples of commercial Linda development; [4] and [2] give objective overviews. The LPB's most important template-editor predecessor is the Cornell Program Synthesizer[12]. SIGMACS [11] is an extensible environment for parallel programming.

2   The Master Worker Template

The LPB rests on a systematic programming methodology. The project would make no sense without one. Our goal isn't merely to save keystrokes; we hope to capture basic organizing strategies for parallel programs (basic coordination frameworks, in other words). We don't know what the basic strategies are unless we have a comprehensive methodology in hand.

This methodology is presented in [6] and [7]. It centers on three paradigms, called "specialist," "result" and "agenda" parallelism. Agenda parallelism is usually embodied in master-worker programs, in which each of a collection of identical, simultaneously-active workers grabs a task assignment, does the task and repeats until all tasks are done. The master-worker approach is flexible, robust and widely applicable, so we began LPB development by providing support for this paradigm. Future version will support result and specialist parallelism as well.

A simple coordination framework for master-worker programs looks like

```
master() {
    for number of workers {
        eval (''worker'', worker ());
    }
    for all tasks {
        /* Generate data for task in this iteration */
        ...
        out (''task'', data, ...);
    }
    for all tasks {
        in (''result'', ?res);
        /* Process result */
    }
```

```
        /* generate a poison pill */
        out (''task'', POISON, ...);
}

worker() {
    while (1) {
        in (''task'', ?data, ...);
        if (data == POISON) {
            /* regurgitate...*/
            out (''task'', POISON, ...);
            /* ...and expire */
            break;
        }
        /* execute task */
        out (''result'', res);
    }
}
```

The details are left out at this point. Lots of variations of this basic skeleton are possible. We could, for example, **eval** a worker for every task; the live tuples thus generated turn into passive result tuples which the master gathers up. The master might generate all task tuples itself, or might generate just one; workers generating futher tasks themselves. All these variants and others are supported by the LPB **master-worker** function.

When the programmer invokes the **master-worker** template, he;s asked a series of questions about the particular version he wants. He is then asked to enter declarations (in a new window provided for this purpose) for variables that figure in the task tuples. Depending on the master-worker version he's using, he'll be asked further questions; the answers guide the LPB in elaborating the coordination framework.

The templates provided by the editor for master-worker programs are useful to the programmer insofar as they restrict his own program-building to parts of the program that don't deal explicitly with parallelism. Figure 1 shows a C-Linda master-worker program generated using the **master-worker** function. The blanks have not been filled in. All the visible code was generated by the LPB automatically, based on information provided by the user in response to prompts.

```
tst.cl         Tue May 29 21:49:39 1990           1

#define POISON_VAL -999         /* The value of the poison pill for workers */

/* *** Insert any constant definitions here *** */

real_main (argc, argv)
     int argc;
     char **argv;
{
  int i;
  int iNumWorkers;
  int worker();
  int iStart;    /* The starting integer for the task */
  int iEnd;      /* The ending integer for the task */
  char arr[100]; /* The data array */
  long lRes;

  /* *** Insert additional variable declarations for master here *** */

  if (argc < 2) {
    /* # processors to be used is an argument to the program */
    printf ("usage: %s <# processors>\n");
    exit (1);
  }
  iNumWorkers = atoi(argv[1]);
  for (i = 0; i < iNumWorkers; i++) {
    /* Start the worker processes */
    eval ("worker", worker());
  }
  for (i = 0; i < iNumWorkers; i++) {

    /* *** Build task tuple in this iteration *** */

    out ("task", iStart, iEnd, arr:);
  }
  for (i = 0; i < iNumWorkers; i++) {
    in ("result", ?lRes);

    /* *** Code for what to do with read-in result goes here *** */

  }
  out ("task", POISON_VAL, iEnd, arr:);
  for (i = 0; i < iNumWorkers; i++) {
    in ("worker", ?int);
  }
}


worker ()
{
  int iStart;    /* The starting integer for the task */
  int iEnd;      /* The ending integer for the task */
  char arr[100]; /* The data array */
  long lRes;
  int len_arr;

  while (1) {
    in ("task", ?iStart, ?iEnd, ?arr:len_arr);

    if (iStart == POISON_VAL) {
      /* Check for poison pill */
      out ("task", POISON_VAL, iEnd, arr:);
      break;
    }

    out ("result", lRes);
  }
  return 0;
}
```

Figure 1: Sample Code Generated by the master-worker function

3 Creating distributed data structures

Tuples usually occur in the role of some distributed data structure: the average tuple isn't a mere tuple, it's part of a distributed array or a task bag, or it's a shared variable, and so on. To some extent these roles can be anticipated by coordination-framework templates of the sort described above. But sometimes the programmer must specify a particular distributed data structure; the LPB supports him.

3.1 Shared variables

In parallel programming, variables are often shared between processes. When this happens, the usual problems of simultaneous access arise. Linda solves the problem by putting shared variables into tuple space. Modification is achieved by an **in** followed by an **out**. The LPB provides a set of functions which cover the typical operations on shared variables. The **init-shared-var** function, for example, asks for the declaration of the shared variable in a separate window. The appropriate tuple is automatically generated using the variable name prefixed with a string as the tuple label. The user is prompted for the initial value of the shared variable. The **modify-shared-variable** function opens a new emacs window and provides a template for modification in the form of the necessary **in** and **out** operations. Input on the user's part is limited only to the assignment itself. If, for example, the shared variable is to be incremented by 3, the user simply postfixes "+3" to the field entry in the **out** operation. The user can now program the viewpoint of a shared variable abstraction, without worrying about how the abstraction is implemented.

3.2 Counter Variables

Counter variables are a sub-case of shared variables; they're so common that they deserve to be supported explicitly. As with shared variables, there is an **init-counter** function which asks for the name of the counter and its initial value. The type of a counter is assumed to be **long** by default. The modification operations on a counter are limited to an increment and a decrement function, both of which automatically insert the appropriate **in** and **out** operations into the code. In addition, there are functions to read a counter and to remove a counter from tuple space.

Counting Semaphores are supported in similar fashion.

3.3 Queues

Queues are as important in parallel as in sequential programming. In the conventional, sequential sense, there is typically one source and one sink, with the source writing at the tail of the queue, and the sink removing from the head of the queue. When we move to a parallel model, however, we are faced with more possibilities. We can have multiple sources, sinks, or both. In such a case, it is necessary to maintain some kind of synchronization or handshaking among the multiple sources or sinks. In Linda, we can share a head or tail pointer through tuple space. Since the pointer is shared, we must unsure exclusive access to a process that needs to modify it. Putting head or tail pointer in tuple space guarantees exclusive access to it.

The LPB provides the **create-queue** function to insert a template for a queue model. It will first furnish a new window in which the various queue models are named (Figure 2). One of these is selected by the user. Depending on the model, any combination of the tail pointer and the head pointer need to be shared or local. The corresponding code for queue manipulation is inserted at the current point in the program (Figure 3). There are three inserted functions, one to initialize the queue, one to add to the tail, and one to remove from the head. At any subsequent point in the program, performing a queue operation is limited to calling one of the three inserted functions.

Distributed **bags** and **arrays** will be supported in similar fashion in future versions.

3.4 A "Globals" Tuple

Linda is often used to parallelize existing sequential programs. A common practice in such conversions is to gather global variables occuring in the program into a single structure and output this to tuple space for access by the parallel processes. The LPB provides a **create-global** function for this purpose. It picks out all global variables at the head of the current C-Linda file and puts them in a new window. The user then selects which of these should go into the "globals" tuple. An appropriate structure definition is inserted at the head of the file. At any subsequent point, the user can call on any tuple operations using the globals tuple.

4 Basic Tuple Support

The LPB must support the programmer not only when he uses pre-cooked data structures but when he chooses to deploy Linda operations directly by himself.

```
/* *** Pick the desired model for queues by selecting \M-s or
       the L6 copy key on the line of the selected model *** */

SOURCE    SINK

Single    Single
Single    Multiple
Multiple  Single
Multiple  Multiple
```

`--**-Emacs: *queues*          [[(Fundamental)]]----All--------------------`

`--**-Emacs: tst.cl            [[(C)]]----Bot-----------------------------`

Figure 2: The Selection of Queue Models

```
mm_init_queue (name)
     char *name;
{
  out ("mm queue head ptr", name:strlen(name), 0);
  out ("mm queue tail ptr", name:strlen(name), 0);
}


mm_add_to_tail (name, val)
     char *name;
     long val;
{
  long ptr;

  in  ("mm queue tail ptr", name:strlen(name), ?ptr);
  out ("mm queue tail ptr", name:strlen(name), ptr+1);
  out ("mm queue", name:strlen(name), ptr, val);
}


long mm_take_from_head (name)
     char *name;
{
  long val;
  long ptr;

  in  ("mm queue head ptr", name:strlen(name), ?ptr);
  out ("mm queue head ptr", name:strlen(name), ptr+1);
  in  ("mm queue", name:strlen(name), ptr, ?val);
  return val;
}
```

--**-Emacs: tst.cl   [(C)]----Bot----------------------------

Figure 3: The Code for a Multiple Source, Multiple Sink Queue Model

4.1 General Tuple Operations in the Editor

Tuples generally have label strings in their first fields. These serve as identification tags, like the names of variables. The LPB institutionalizes this idiom. It assumes that tuples will always begin with string-valued identifier fields, and it uses these fields in referring to tuple types.

When manipulating tuples, we need to declare the variables involved in the tuple within the function in which we would like to use the tuple. This tuple may then be operated on in another function, which would require variables of the same type to be declared locally. The LPB automates the process of declaring variables. Variables for a particular tuple need only be declared once. Thereafter, we just specify the operation and the tuple label, and the LPB takes care of the variable declarations as well as the actual call to **in**, **out** or whatever the Linda operation may be.

4.1.1 For example: The tuple-out function

Consider an **out** operation on a tuple with three fields. The first field is an identifier string, which in our example will be "status." Our second field will be of type integer, and the third of type char. In order to insert the **out** operation, we move the cursor to the point in the program at which the **out** operation should be inserted. We then call the LPB's **tuple-out** function. The editor responds by asking for the tuple's label; the user types "status." The editor searches in its database of tuples to see whether a tuple by that name has already been defined. If we are defining "status" for the first time, the editor will not be able to find it. A new window will appear in which the user is asked to declare the variables that will be involved in the tuple. The label of the particular tuple being manipulated always appears in the caption bar of the appropriate emacs window. As shown in Figure 4, the programmer then enters the declarations for the variables, in this case an integer called *iStart* and a character named *cType*. Comments associated with the variables can also be specified at this stage. When the declarations are completed, the **out** operation, as well as the corresponding variable declarations, are inserted into the appropriate places of the surrounding function (figure 5). Had the tuple with label "status" already been defined at the time of invocation of **tuple-out** within the editor, the process of having the user declare the variables would have been skipped. Instead, the editor would have recalled the tuple and its associated variables inserted the **out** operation along with the necessary variable declarations immediately. (Initialization of variables remains the user's responsibility.)

The tuple-in, -rd and -eval functions are similar. We omit many details (for example the

```
/* *** This is a skeleton for the worker program, generated by the YALE
        editor *** */
worker ()
{
  int iCtr;      /* A counter */
  char a[20];    /* Data array */
  int res;       /* The result variable */
  int len;       /* Length for arrays in tuples */

  while (1) {
    in ("task", ?iCtr, ?a:len);

    if (iCtr == POISON_VAL) {
      /* Check for poison pill */
      out ("task", POISON_VAL, a:);
      break;
    }

    out ("result", res);
  }
  return 0;
}
```

```
--**-Emacs: tst.cl                    [(C)]----Bot--------------------------------
/* *** Insert declarations for variables in tuple in the same
        order as they will appear in the tuples.  One declaration
        per line please *** */

int iStart;    /* The starting data for the task */
char cType;    /* The type of the task */
```

```
--**-Emacs: *tuple:status             [(C)]----All--------------------------------
```

Figure 4: Declaring variables for a tuple

```
/* *** This is a skeleton for the worker program, generated by the YALE
   editor *** */
worker ()
{
   int iStart;     /* The starting data for the task */
   char cType;     /* The type of the task */
   int iCtr;       /* A counter */
   char a[20];     /* Data array */
   int res;        /* The result variable */
   int len;        /* Length for arrays in tuples */

   while (1) {
     in ("task", ?iCtr, ?a:len);

     if (iCtr == POISON_VAL) {
       /* Check for poison pill */
       out ("task", POISON_VAL, a:);
       break;
     }

     out ("status", iStart, cType);
     out ("result", res);
   }
   return 0;
}
```

--**-Emacs: tst.cl   (C)----63%----------------------------

Figure 5: The inserted out operation and the corresponding declarations

handling of actuals and formals, constants and arrays) that are essential to the user-LPB interaction, but not to the LPB's basic structure.

5 The Tuple Archive

Every tuple that the LPB deals with is entered in a global archive. The tuple's label, the declarations for variables used in that tuple and information about the nature of the tuple appear in the corresponding entry. This "nature of the tuple" information emerges when the tuple and its associated operations have been created by the LPB in response to the user's request for a "higher level" structure of some kind.

The archive is global across a user's LPB sessions. Tuples defined in one file or during a given session can be used in others without redefinition.

The data stored in the archive is generated automatically by the LPB. A second database maintains tuple information supplied by the user in the form of explicit comments. By invoking the function **tuple-info**, and supplying the label of the desired tuple when prompted for it, the user can add any text he wishes to the default information.

6 Menu Driven Tuple and Command Selection

The LPB's menu-driven interface for tuple and command selection. It enables the user to insert Linda operations throughout a program quickly and efficiently, while being sure that these are syntactically correct. A call to the editor function **tuple-list** will cause all the tuples that are known to the database to be listed by their labels in a new emacs window (see Figure 6). A user can now use the mouse or the cursor keys to select a particular tuple. A single keystroke causes another window to appear which contains information on this tuple from the information database (Figure 6). A different keystroke will cause a window to appear which displays all the editor functions which can be called on for this tuple (Figure 7). The list of functions on a particular tuple is dependent on the type of the tuple. For generic tuples, for example, one can expect **tuple-in, tuple-out**, etc., whereas for a shared variable tuple, one would expect **init-shared-variable, modify-shared-variable**, etc. Once again, the cursor keys or the mouse serve to pick out a function and a single keystroke will cause that function to be executed with the selected tuple.

This adds up to a powerful combination. Suppose we have a C-Linda program, and all the necessary tuples are already in our database. We now proceed to a point in the program where we wish a particular tuple operation to be entered, and call on **tuple-list**. We then select the desired tuple and the desired function. The appropriate operation gets

```
This is a shared counter variable
Types of fields in tuple:
long

This global counter is accessed by all the process through tuple space.
```

```
--**-Emacs: *tupinfo:counter_prog_counter     [[[(C)]]]----All----------------
This is a list of all the tuple labels of tuples that are
currently in the tuple table in memory.  Hitting \M-s or the
L6 function key on a selected line will display the available
tuple information for that tuple from the tuple information
table.  Hitting \M-c or L9 will provide a list of commands
can be executed on this tuple, one of which can subsequently
be selected for execution.
C-xC-s or function key F1 will will exit this mode.

worker
task
result
counter_prog_counter
shared_program_type
status
```

```
--**-Emacs: *tuple-list          [[[(Fundamental)]]]----All----------------
```

Figure 6: Tuple-list and information display

```
This is a list of commands that can be executed on the selected
tuple status.  Select one by pressing L6 or \M-s on the
appropriate line

tuple-in
tuple-out
tuple-rd
tuple-eval
tuple-delete


















--**-Emacs: *commands for tuple: status      [[[(Fundamental)]]]----All---------
This is a list of all the tuple labels of tuples that are
currently in the tuple table in memory.  Hitting \M-s or the
L6 function key on a selected line will display the available
tuple information for that tuple from the tuple information
table.  Hitting \M-c or L9 will provide a list of commands
can be executed on this tuple, one of which can subsequently
be selected for execution.
C-xC-s or function key F1 will will exit this mode.

worker
task
result
counter_prog_counter
shared_program_type
status









--**-Emacs: *tuple-list            [[[(Fundamental)]]]----All------------------
```

Figure 7: Tuple-list and selecting an editor function

inserted into our code, and the function window disappears, leaving the program window and the tuple window. We now proceed to another point in the program, switch to the tuple window, pick another tuple, and repeat the process.

7 Conclusions

Given increasingly widespread agreement that programmers will need to write explicitly-parallel programs, how should we support their efforts? Tools like the LPB, and related projects aimed at "semi-automatic" development of parallel programs, seem promising.

The LPB project bears on a wider question as well. Researchers have been mumbling since the late sixties and howling since the late seventies that programming languages are mostly too "low level." But in 1990, the greater part of all programs are written in languages derived from Fortran, Algol 60, Lisp and Cobol, all of which were in place by 1962. Today's most significant "new" development in language models, object-oriented programming, is derived from Simula 67. The only computing-language model dating from the 70's or 80's to have achieved any following among working programmers is Prolog; and its following, while real, is small. The hottest-ticket "higher-level language" concept of the late 70's and 80's, functional programming, seems to have no distinterested following among working programmers anywhere, and appears to be losing its cachet even among academics. Clearly, the idea that the "level" of most current programming languages is radically wrong needs some rethinking.

Great progress has been made in understanding programming methodology. But programmers (curiously) seem to dislike languages that are bent on shoving a particular methodology down their throats. Such languages are too complicated and too inflexible. Merely compare the fates of fundamentally similar 70's-era language like C on the one hand and Euclid on the other. Scheme is a big success and functional programming a big failure in part because Scheme merely supports while functional programming imposes a particular style.

Tools like the LPB represent one possible response to the handwriting on the wall. They capture a methodology and support it strongly; but they don't force complexity and rigidity on the base language, and they suggest rather than impose a particular approach. For all the research community's insistence that *it* knows what's best for the poor slobs who write the code, programmers have rejected this line of thinking, and the research community ought to support them.

The LPB itself is merely a preliminary stab at an integrated model-based editor. Much further work remains. But we're convinced that the direction is worth pursuing.

References

[1] V. Ambriola, P. Ciancarini and M. Danelutto, "Design and distributed implementation of the parallel logic language Shared Prolog," in *Proc. Second ACM SIGPLAN Symp. Principles and Practice of Parallel Programming,* (Seattle, March 1990):40-49.

[2] M. Ben-Ari, *Principles of Concurrent and Distributed Programming.* Prentice-Hall (Hertfordshire, UK: 1990).

[3] P. Bercovitz and N. Carriero. "TupleScope: A Graphical Monitor and Debugger for Linda-Based Parallel Programs," Research Report, Yale University Department of Computer Science (March 1990).

[4] H.E. Bal, J.G. Steiner and A.S. Tanenbaum, "Programming languages for distributed computing systems," *ACM Computing Surveys* 21,3(September:1989):261-322.

[5] S.Bogoch, I.Bason, J. Williams and M. Russel, "Supercomputers get personal." *Byte* (May 1990):231-237.

[6] Nicholas Carriero and David Gelernter, "Linda in Context," *Communications of the ACM*, April 1989

[7] Nicholas Carriero and David Gelernter, "Tuple Analysis and Partial Evaluation Strategies in the Linda Precompiler," *Second Workshop on Languages and Compilers for Parallelism*, August 1989

[8] C.J. Fleckenstein and D. Hemmendinger, "Using a global namespace for parallel execution of Unix tools." *CACM* 32,9 (Sept 1989)

[9] W. Leler, "Linda meets Unix." *IEEE Computer* 23,2(Feb. 1990):43-55.

[10] S. Matsuoka and S. Kawai, "Using tuple space communication in distributed object-oriented languages," Proc. OOPSLA '88 (Nov. 1988):276-284

[11] Bruce Shei and Dennis Gannon, "SIGMACS A Programmable Programming Environment," Proc. 3rd Workshop on Programming Languages and Compilers for Parallel Computing, August 1-3, 1990, Irvine, California

[12] Tim Teitelbaum, Thomas Reps, and Susan Horwitz, "The Why and Wherefore of the Cornell Program Synthesizer," *Software Development Environments*, November 16-20, 1981, IEEE Computer Society Press

5 SIGMACS: a Programmable Programming Environment
B. Shei, D Gannon

Abstract
Users of large scale parallel systems and multiprocessor supercomputers are primarily involved with the design of scientific software. Even though hardware technology has made parallel systems easily accessible, software, on the other hand, lags far behind. While it is true that compilers are getting much better and great strides have been made in parallel algorithms for various application areas, the process of designing, debugging and tuning new parallel programs is still extremely primitive. A number of software tools exist to aid users in converting programs from sequential forms into vectorized or parallelized forms. Unfortunately they are usually targeted at specific hardware and programming language. Here we present a programmable system that allows users to create new tools to fit their own needs.

1 Introduction

There are several experimental restructuring systems currently available. Some of them are based on extensions of batch oriented system such as KAP from KAI, VAST from Pacific Sieara Research, ParaFrase I and II from University of Illinois, and PTRAN from IBM [1, 2]. Some systems have been built that are interactive in nature. The most sophisticated and oldest one is R^n from Rice[7, 6]. Start/Pat is a joint project between Georgia Institute of Technology and the University of California at Santa Cruz[3]. ParaScope is yet another new tool from Rice University[5]. SIGMA is our own system which is part of the Indiana/Illinois Faust project[12, 13]. The advantage of the interactive systems is that, in principle, a user can help guide the system when data dependence analysis alone is not sufficient to resolve all the potential hazards of parallelization.

Unfortunately, none of the existing interactive systems have been widely used and there are several reasons for this. First, these systems are all new and experimental in nature. More significantly, all of these systems have some shortcomings such as handling only a single programming language, giving users access to only a limited number of transformations, and making it difficult to incorporate new tools into the system. What is needed is a set of software tools that provides a uniform interface that hides the complexity of different hardware and software systems from ordinary users while leaving room for experimentation by the experts. It can help users to correctly and quickly convert their existing programs to new platforms, to develop new programs and new algorithms while easing the burden of switching between different hardware platforms or parallel dialects.

The project SIGMACS is intended to provide an extensible environment for parallel programming. We have three major goals:

- It should be an extensible restructuring system. To achieve this goal, we have extracted a set of transformation primitives and build them into a special programmable database server. With a suitable user front-end, such as Emacs or UPSL, which we will discuss more later, it becomes a very flexible system. Users can build their own functions when necessary. In the later sections of this paper, we will show some examples how users can define their own application in the Emacs front-end.

- It should be easy to integrate new tools into the environment. It's often the case that many tools for such tasks as performance analysis, debugging and visualization may be needed by the user. The system should be kept flexible enough so that users can easily incorporate new tools into the environment. For example, we might want to invoke a performance analysis tool to help tune the program. If the performance tool needs help from the program database, such as providing a way for the user to automatically instrument the source code, this should be easy to arrange. (We will return to this issue later.)

- The system should be very portable. Currently SIGMACS runs on most UNIX[1] platforms. Also when using the Emacs front-end, users can work from a dial-up terminal or an X window based workstation.

In the following section, first we define some concepts that will be used in this paper. Then we introduce the programming model used in the database and the database server. Section 3 formally defines a selection of the primitives that will be used in the following examples. Section 4 presents several examples that shows the way to add new functionalities

---

[1] UNIX is a trademark of AT&T Bell Laboratories.

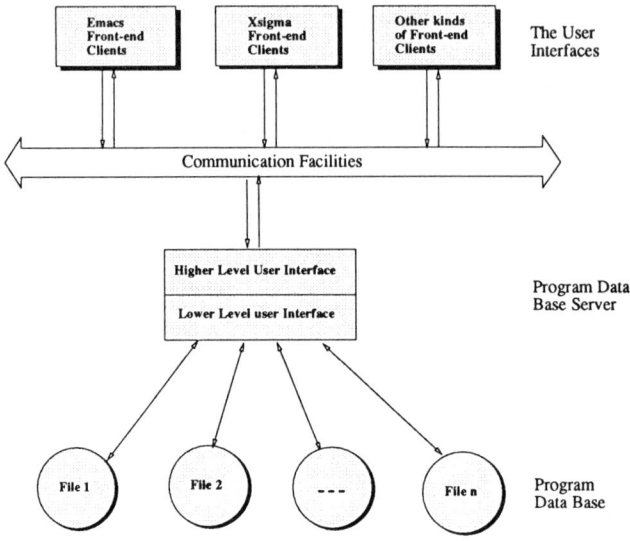

Figure 1: Structure of the SIGMACS System

to the system. First we will give two simple examples to show how to retrieve information from the database server. Then we show an example that performs the loop distribution, followed by an example of the loop vectorization which utilizes the loop distribution routine when necessary. The ways to incorporate new tools into our system is outlined in section 5. Finally, we end with a discussion of our future research.

2   System Organization

The SIGMACS system is composed of a set of parsers, program databases, a program database server and set of user interfaces. Currently we have a FORTRAN parser that understands some of the ANSI 90 extensions for parallel constructions such as vector expressions, vector assignment and several parallel DO loop forms. We also have a C++ parser, called VPC++, with various parallel and vector extensions. The parsers generate a special intermediate form, called a *dep* file, which contains all the information gathered in the compilation phase. The *dep* file contains a complete parse tree with dependence information embedded and it is used by different utilities in the system. A project is a collection of related *dep* files that correspond to the set of source files that make up the users application code. The database server plays the most important role in the system. It loads the project database upon request and then it can either retrieve the information stored in the database or perform restructuring operations as the user requests. Users talk to the database server via a set of client programs, as depicted in Figure 1.

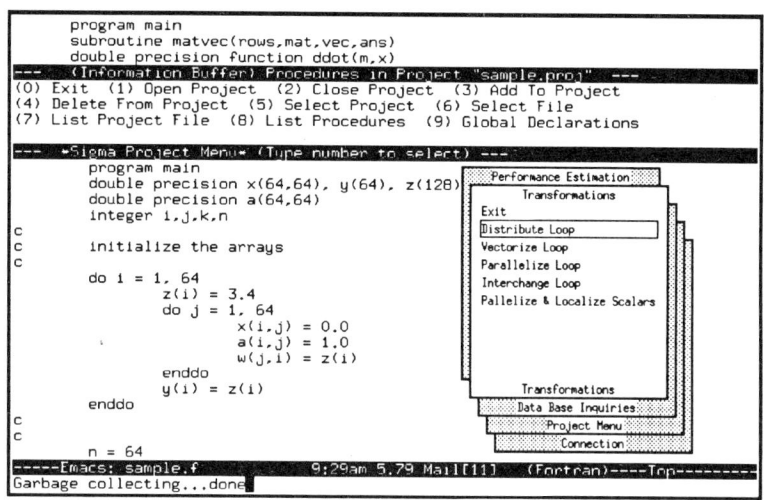

Figure 2: Emacs Front-end of SIGMACS

The client programs send requests to or receive responses from the database server through a communication media. Currently we are working on two user interfaces. One utilizes the popular GNU Emacs. Equipped with a set of GNU Emacs Elisp functions, users can perform many different operations. There are three user interfaces for users to choose from. The most basic level is the window menu interface. Upon invocation, the system pops up an Emacs window with a set of menu items that users can choose from. Another interface depends on the Emacs system being used. This version requires that Emacs be built with a special X window pop-up menu. With this interface, users can use a mouse to invoke a stack of menus (see Figure 2). The user can move the cursor to the statement he or she wants to manipulate and invoke the desired function from the pop-up menu item. The third way to use the system is, of course, the most familiar way to Emacs users — to use key bindings. Furthermore, we are developing yet another front-end that uses UPSL, an expert system derived from OPS5, to investigate the possibility of applying expert system techniques to the transformation system.

2.1 Definitions

In the following, we use the standard definitions for program dependence graph defined by Ferrante et al.[11, 8] and data dependences defined in Wolfe[17, 16].

Definition 2.1 A *control flow graph*, or CFG in short, is a directed graph $\mathcal{G}$ augmented with a unique *entry* note START and a unique *exit* node EXIT such that each node in the graph has at most two successors. The node with two successors is tagged with attributes

"T" (true) and "F" (false).

Definition 2.2 A node V is *post-dominated* by a node U in $\mathcal{G}$ if V belongs to every directed path from U to EXIT.

Definition 2.3 Let X and Y be nodes in a control flow graph $\mathcal{G}$. We say that Y is *control dependent* on X if there exists a nonempty path P from X to Y such that Y post-dominates every node after X on P and X is not post-dominated by Y.

Definition 2.4 If a statement S_1 modifies a variable v which is later referenced by the statement S_2, then we say there is a *flow dependence* from statement S_1 to statement S_2.

Definition 2.5 If a statement S_1 make reference to a variable v which is later modified by another statement S_2, then we say there is an *anti dependence* from statement S_1 to statement S_2.

Definition 2.6 If a statement S_1 modifies a variable v which is later modified again by another statement S_2, then we say there is an *output dependence* from statement S_1 to statement S_2.

Definition 2.7 Consider the directed graph formed by letting the statements be nodes and the dependencies be edges. We shall refer to the *strongly connected components* of a set of statements to be the strongly connected components of this associated graph.

Definition 2.8 The modification set, denoted as MOD, is the set of formal parameters and external variables that are modified by side effect in a function or subroutine. The use set, denoted as USE, is the set of those formal parameters and external variables that are referenced by a function or subroutine.

2.2 Project Database

As we mentioned before, a *project database* is a collection of related file objects and can be expressed nicely as a list $(file_1 \; file_2 \; \ldots \; file_n)$. These file objects correspond to the source code files of the application. This format has been used as the output of three very different kind of language parsers – Fortran, VPC++, and Blaze[15] and is general enough to be used for new platforms.

A *file object* is an extended control flow graph. It contains various kind of information gathered at the parsing phase. It has several categories of objects: statement nodes, expression nodes, symbol nodes, type nodes and dependence nodes which are denoted as $\mathcal{S}_t$, $\mathcal{E}$, $\mathcal{S}_y$, $\mathcal{T}$ and $\mathcal{D}$, respectively. Objets in each category are assigned a unique identification number and are referred to as *stmt-id*, *expr-id*, *symbol-id*, *type-id* and *dep-id*, respectively. Users access individual object in each category by its id number.

The *statement objects* correspond roughly to statements in the source program. Each node contains several important items of information: the node type, source file name, line number, lists of expression objects and dependence arcs. There are two ways to uniquely identify a source code statement in our scheme — by the *stmt-id* or the line number, *line-number* in the source file. We can view that a file object is a list of the form $(def_1 \; def_2 \ldots def_n)$ where def_i is the definition object which corresponds to a function or procedure definition, denoted as $func$, or global declarations, denoted as $decl$. The global declaration can be one of the following: typedef statements, struct statements or global variables in C language or class definitions in C++. The statements inside a function are stored as a control flow graph can be expressed naturally as list of lists. For example, the following function declaration with three statements (the numbers in parenthesis are *stmt-id* numbers)

(103)	**REAL FUNCTION** SUM(A, B)
(106)	SUM = A + B
(108)	**END**

can be thought as (103 (106 108) ()). Statements 106 and 108 are control dependent on the function statement 103, thus we call them *control-children* of 103 while 103 is the *control-parent* of these children. (The empty list after the list (106 108) is there because we view each statement as having two sets of control children so that conditionals are easily handled.) If we insert the following loop statement after the statement 103,

(107)	**DO** I = 1, 10
(109)	A = A + I
(200)	B = B + A
	END DO

then the function becomes (103 ((107 (109 200) ()) 106 108) ()). We will frequently refer to a statement as a *node* when no confusion arises.

The second category contains the "expression nodes" which representation all expressions in the program. They also can be represented as a list — $(term_1 \; term_2 \ldots term_n)$. For example, the statement "a = b + c" is represented as $(op_=$ (**ref** a) $(op_+$ (**ref** b) (**ref** c))) where (**ref** a) means a reference to the symbol a.

Of course there are implicit environments, such as variable declarations and type declarations, which must be considered. These are treated as property lists attached to the proper statement node, such as a function node, according to the scoping rules of the programming language used.

A *property list* is a list of paired elements where the first element is the property's name and the second element is the property. Thus a function node can have two property lists. One property list is the "variable declaration" (the property's name) and a list (the property) which contains a list of symbol table nodes for all variables declared in this function. The second property list is the "type declaration" which is a list which contains a list of type nodes. Each *symbol table node*, or *symbol node* in brief, is assigned a unique id number, referred to as *symb-id*. A symbol node contains a string for the variable name and a type node reference. A symbol node can have its property list which contains information specific to the node. For example, a function symbol node may have the USE or MOD information in its property list. Each *type node* also has a unique id number, denoted as *type-id*, and a tag to indicate the "type" it represents which could be of type integer, type real, or an array declaration. The first two are part of the fundamental building blocks, called the *base types*, that are used to construct more complex types such as arrays or structs. So the declaration "REAL X(1:100, -10:10)"[2] is represented as

```
Symbol Node      ( "X"   10   ((1 100) (-10 -10)) )
                      |
Type Node 10    ─▷( ARRAY   2 )
                           |
Type Node  2    ─▷( REAL )
```

The most important quantity in a restructuring system is, of course, the dependence information. They are also treated as a property list attached to a given statement node. It contains the information

$$(((from\text{-}stmt_1\ from\text{-}term_1)\ (to\text{-}stmt_1\ to\text{-}term_1)\ symb_1\ dep\text{-}type_1\ (v_{1,0}\ v_{1,1}\ \ldots))$$
$$((from\text{-}stmt_2\ from\text{-}term_2)\ (to\text{-}stmt_2\ to\text{-}term_2)\ symb_2\ dep\text{-}type_2\ (v_{2,0}\ v_{2,1}\ \ldots))$$
$$\ldots$$
$$((from\text{-}stmt_i\ from\text{-}term_i)\ (to\text{-}stmt_i\ to\text{-}term_i)\ symb_i\ dep\text{-}type_i\ (v_{i,0}\ v_{i,1}\ \ldots)))$$

where each component represents dependence information annotated at that statement node. The first pair represents the tail of the dependence arc while the second pair is the head of the arc. They are followed by the symbol table id, $symb_i$, of the variable involved, type (*flow-*, *anti-*, or *output-* dependence) of this dependence arc, $dep\text{-}type_i$, and the the distance vector, $(v_{i,0}\ v_{i,1}\ \ldots)$, calculated by the dependence analyzer. Putting together, this means "there is a dependence of type $dep\text{-}type_i$ about the variable $symb_i$ from the term $from\text{-}term_i$ in statement $from\text{-}stmt_i$ to the term $to\text{-}term_i$ in statement $to\text{-}stmt_i$".

---
[2]This is an extension of FORTRAN 77

2.3 Database Server

There are several important features in our system when compared with other systems:

- It handles multiple projects. The server can load multiple projects so that users can switch between different projects if they want.

- It handles multiple languages. The database has a built-in language type indicator so that the server understands which programming language the user is currently using. Thus it possible to mix different languages in the same project when the need arises.

- It is machine independent. The database was designed in such a way that it can be used across machine boundaries. A program database generated on one machine can be copied to another machine without being recompiled. This means that users can do the compilation phase on a faster, more powerful machine and then copy them to the machines they will be working on. This also means the program database can be accessed directly via NFS, the Network File System.

- It has restructuring primitives. The server has a set of specially designed primitives built in. When combined with suitable front end interface, it becomes a very powerful system which will be discussed further in the following sections.

3 Primitives

As we mentioned earlier, there is a set of built-in primitives in our server that can handle different kinds of requests that might arise in a programming environment. Basically they can be divided into several categories:

1. Project handling primitives which handle all project related requests such as opening or closing a project, adding files to a project, deleting files from a project or replacing files in the project.

2. Database inquiry primitives which retrieve information such as

    - list of all functions declared in the project.
    - type declaration of a given variable.
    - summary information of a function.
    - dependence information of statements

3. Restructuring primitives which are set of primitives that change the internal representation of the program loaded into the server. They consist of creating or deleting new nodes.

Generically, we can view the primitives as set of operations on the program database, i.e. given a control flow graph $\mathcal{G}$ in an file object, a primitive σ takes a list of (possibly empty) inputs, performs the operation and returns a list of (again possibly empty) outputs:

$$\sigma : \mathcal{G} \times \mathcal{I}^* \rightarrow \mathcal{G}' \times \mathcal{O}^*$$

where $\mathcal{I}$ designates the set of all possible inputs, such as line number, stmt-id, etc. and $\mathcal{O}$ is the set of all possible outputs, such as stmt-id or unparsed string for the given node. For example, given a line number the primitive statement-at-line returns the corresponding stmt-id from the database. If we denote the set of line numbers as $\mathcal{L}_{no}$ and the set of statement identification numbers as $\mathcal{I}_{stmt}$, then $statement\text{-}at\text{-}line = \sigma_1 \circ \pi$ where $\sigma_1 : \mathcal{G} \times \mathcal{L}_{no} \rightarrow \mathcal{G}' \times \mathcal{O}^*$ retrieves the information from the database and π is the projection from $\mathcal{O}^*$ to $\mathcal{I}_{stmt} \cup \{\bot\}$. It returns $\bot$ if there is no statement node corresponds to the given line number. In this case, G is not changed. Another example is the primitive copy-expr that takes an expr-id and creates a copy of the that expression tree. It returns the id of the new expression tree or $\bot$ if the operation failed. Most of the primitives are carefully designed so that they have inverse functions such as insert statement nodes and delete statement nodes.

In order to give a more concrete example, we will explain some of the primitives in more detail (using the Elisp function code).

- (statement-at-line *line-number*) — given a line number, it returns the statement's id *stmt-id*.

- (line-no *stmt-id*) — given a statement id, *stmt-id*, it returns its line number stored in the database. This is the inverse function of the *statement-at-line*.

- (statement-type *stmt-id*) — This function returns the type of the statement.

- (used-in-call *stmt-id*) — given the stmt-id of a function node, this function returns the id of the expression for the USE summary information. Users can either feed the output of this function to the unparse to see the information or use other primitives to investigate further.

- (control-children *stmt-id*) — returns a list in the form (((1 2 3) (4 5)) ((6 7) ())). It's a list of nested pairs of lists each representing the control children in one branch. Usually the second list is *nil* except for IF statements, in which case, the first list represents the children in true branch while the second list, the false branch.

- (tsort *stmt-id*) — It returns a list of strongly connected components of the set of control children in the form ((1 3 4) (2 5) (6 7 9 12)).

- (induct-vars *stmt-id*) — This function returns the symbol table id *symb-id* of the induction variable of a loop statement.

- (loop-bounds *stmt-id*) — returns a list of 2 or 3 expression ids in the form (start-expr end-expr inc-expr) where the *start-expr* is the id of the expression for the starting value, and the *end-expr*, id of the expression for the end value. If the increment is specified in the loop statement, then its expression id is returned as the third number in the list.

- (bad-cycles *stmt-id*) — It checks if there is any data dependence cycles that prohibit us from doing transformations like vectorizing a loop statement.

- (vector-expr *l-bound u-bound stride*) — Given the ids of expressions for lower bound, upper bound, and stride, it creates a new vector expression.

- (copy-expr *expr-id*) — This function makes a complete copy of the expression tree *expr-id* and returns the id of the new expression tree,

- (replace-var *expr-id$_1$ symb-id expr-id$_2$*) — It replaces all occurrence of symbol *symb-id* in expression *expr-id$_1$* by expression *expr-id$_2$*.

- (unparse-stmt *stmt-id*) — The server will unparse the statement with id, *stmt-id*, into the source code. It returns the unparsed string.

There are also help functions written in Elisp that assist in writing new functions:

- (get-line-number) — This function returns the line number where the cursor resides.

- (loop-p *stmt-id*) — This is a predicate that checks if the given node is a loop statement or not.

- (delete-statement *stmt-id start-line last-line*) — Given the statement id, its starting line number and its end line number, this function delete the given statement(s) from the database in the server as well as from the Emacs frontend.

- (insert-statement *line-no prev-id stmt-id*) — Given the line number, *line-no*, and the statement id of the node, *prev-id* after which the new statement node *stmt-id* will be inserted, it inserts the new nodes into the internal representation stored in the server's side. Also it requests the server to unparse this statement (in server's internal representation) back into the text string and then inserts this unparsed text into the Emacs window.

- (sigmacs-show-results *buffer-name message*) — This function will pop up to the Emacs buffer *buffer-name* and displays the string *message*.

```
;
; variable-type -- inquire the database for the type of the variable
;
(defun variable-type()
  (interactive)
  (let ((line-no (get-line-number))
        (var-name (get-variable-name)))
    (sigmacs-show-results "Variable Type Info"
                          (get-var-type line-no var-name))))
;
; get-summary-info -- the the summary information for a function/procedure
;
(defun get-summary-info ()
  (interactive)
  (let* ((stmt (get-line-number))
         (stmt-id (statement-at-line stmt))
         (id (used-in-call stmt-id)))
    (sigmacs-show-results "Summary of Use Info" (unparse-expr id))))
```

Figure 3: Simple Examples

4 Examples

In this section, we will present three examples in Elisp. The first one shows information retrieval from the database server. The second one shows how loop distribution is coded in the Emacs front-end. The third example shows how to utilize loop distribution in performing loop vectorization.

4.1 Simple Example

Figure 3 shows a simple example as how the Emacs front-end retrieves the information from the database server. The first part is the Elisp function `variable-type`. The user can move the cursor to the variable they want to examine, say z, and invoke this function. Then the system will pop up another window showing something like "double precision z(100)". In this simple function, we use `let` to allocate two local variables — *line-no* and *var-name*. The first one is assigned the value of the function call `get-line-number` which is a help function that returns the line number of the current line. The second one gets the returned value of the function call `get-variable-name` which is a small help function that extracts a variable or function name from where the cursor sits. Then we call the SIGMACS system primitive `get-var-type` which sends a request to the database server and return the response of server as a string. We pass this string to the system's help function `sigmacs-show-results` along with the buffer name ("Variable Type Info" here).

```
;
; distribute-loop -- distribute a loop statement
;
(defun distribute-loop (&optional stmt)
  (interactive)
  (save-excursion
    (let* ((stmt (or stmt (get-line-number)))
           (stmt-id (statement-at-line stmt))
           (children (car (control-children stmt-id)))
           (last-line (line-no (nth (1- (length children)) children)))
           prev)
      (if (loop-p (statement-type stmt-id)) ; if it's a loop statement
          (let* ((scc (tsort stmt-id))
                 (ind-var (induct-vars stmt-id))
                 (bounds (loop-bounds stmt-id))
                 (foo (function
                        (lambda (x) (new-loop FOR_NODE ind-var bounds x))))
                 new-loops)
            (setq new-loops (mapcar foo scc))
            (update-dep-info scc)
            (setq prev (delete-statement stmt-id stmt last-line))
            (insert-statement stmt prev new-loops)
            new-loops)
        (progn (message "Need to select a loop statement")
               nil)))))
```

Figure 4: Loop Distribution

The second part shows how to retrieve summary information from the server. Again, we use let* to allocate two local variables. The difference is that let* evaluates the first expression before going to the next. So *stmt-id* gets its value first and can be used in the second expression "(id (used-in-call stmt-id))". The function used-in-call is a SIGMACS primitive to retrieve from the server the USE information of a given function. Again we show the result by sigmacs-show-results.

4.2 Loop Distribution

The second example is a more complex one that distributes a loop statement (in Figure 4). The input *stmt* is the line number in the current active file. The first line in after the let* makes sure we get the line number. Then we fetch the statement id from the server. Also we request the server for a list of the loop's control children We also keep track of the line number of the last statement of the loop for later use. The call to the primitive function *tsort* gets a list of strongly connected components, the *scc*, of the control children of the loop statement which will be used to compose the new loops.

The local function *foo* requires a list of statement ids, passed in as x, which compose the body of the new loop. It creates new loop statement by passing this list to the SIGMACS primitive `new-loop` together with the induction variable, *ind-var* and loop bounds *bounds* we got earlier. The Elisp primitive `mapcar` takes a function and a list and applies the function to each element of the list, i.e. "(mapcar '1+ '(1 2 3 4))" will return (2 3 4 5). Thus by feeding each component of the *scc* to *foo*, we create as many new loop statements as required. We then update the dependency information, delete the old statement (from Emacs' window) and its node (from server), and then insert the new statements.

4.3 Loop Vectorization

This is an example function that vectorizes a given loop statement (see Figure 5). In the main program `vectorize`, we verify that the loop body contains only one statement. If not, then we call `distribute-loop` first which will returns a list of the *ids* of the new loop statements after loop distribution. The first part of `vectorize-w-id` gets the control-children of the loop statement. Then it makes sure that the following three conditions are satisfied before we perform the transformation. First it verifies that the given statement is a loop statement by the predicate function `loop-p`. Then it calls the help function `bad-cycles` to check if there is a flow-dependence cycles that prevents the loop from being vectorizable. If we pass the first two tests, then we check to see if the body of the loop is an assignment statement by `assign-p`.

If these three tests are passed, we get the symbol table id of the induction variable and assign it to *ind-var*, and get the line number of the end of the loop statement and assign it to *last-line*. Also we need the loop bound expression, *bounds* and the body of the loop statement, *body*. Then we request the server to create a vector expression from the loop bound by `vect-expr`. The SIGMACS primitive `get-both-sides` returns the left-hand side term and right hand-side term in a list. We use the SIGMACS `copy-expr` to make a copy for each of them. The SIGMACS primitive `replace-var` will replace all occurrences of the references to the induction variable *ind-var* by the newly created vector expression *new-expr*. `Replace-var` is called it twice — once for the left-hand side expression and once for the right-hand side to create vector forms for both sides. We then use these vector forms to form a new assignment statement by the SIGMACS primitives `make-assignment-stmt`. Then we update the dependence information for the new statement, delete the old loop statement and insert the new vector statement.

```
;
; vectorize-w-id -- vectorize a statement using the given id
;
(defun vectorize-w-id (stmt-id)
  (let ((ctrl-children (car (control-children stmt-id))))
    (if (and (loop-p (statement-type stmt-id)) ; a loop statement?
             (not (bad-cycles stmt-id)) ; Any dependence cycles?
             (assign-p (statement-type (car ctrl-children)))) ; an assignment?
        (let* ((ind-var (induct-vars stmt-id))
               (last-line (car (cdr (scope-line-numbers stmt-id))))
               (bounds (loop-bounds stmt-id))
               (body (car ctrl-children)) ; get the assignment statement
               (new-expr (vect-expr (list bounds)))
               (exprs (get-both-sides body))
               (lhs (copy-expr (car exprs)))
               (rhs (copy-expr (car (cdr exprs))))
               new-stmt prev)
          (setq new-stmt
                (make-assignment-stmt (replace-var lhs ind-var new-expr)
                                     (replace-var rhs ind-var new-expr)))
          (update-dep-info-1 stmt-id new-stmt)
          (setq prev (delete-statement stmt-id stmt last-line))
          (insert-statement stmt prev (list new-stmt))))))

;
; vectorize -- vectorize a loop statement under the cursor
;
(defun vectorize (&optional stmt)
  (let* ((stmt (or stmt (get-line-number)))
         (stmt-id (statement-at-line stmt))
         (ctrl-children (car (control-children stmt-id))))
    (if (= (length ctrl-children) 2)  ; only one statement?
        (vectorize-w-id stmt-id)
        (mapcar vectorize-w-id (distribute-loop stmt)))))
```

Figure 5: Loop Vectorization

5 Extensibility In The Large Sense

"One of the novel contributions of the UNIX system is the idea of a *pipe*.", said Brian Kernighan[14]. It's a simple, yet very powerful, way to combine several utilities to achieve your goal without the need to write a special purpose program for it. Of course, this requires that different programs understand a predefined protocol for them to be combined in a pipe. With the aid of special set of Elisp functions, it's easy to combine different tools into our environment. Here is a list of possible applications:

- Get a call graph from the database and send it to visualization programs to draw the call graph on a graphics workstation.
- A simple way to get a "history mechanism". Sometimes we wonder, at the middle of debugging, how a variable gets its current value and would like to see the whole modification history of that variable. Well, it's easy enough for the users in this system to implement it — just write an Elisp function that does the following:

  1. uses the SIGMACS primitives to get the *MOD* list of the variable, say x, from the database.

  2. transforms this list (with line number and filename) into *gdb*, the GNU debugger, commands and sends them to *gdb*:

     ```
     break filename:line_num
     commands
     silent
     step
     echo x is \040
     output x
     echo \n
     continue
     end
     ```

     This will set breaking points at all places where the variable x was modified and ask *gdb* to print its value and continue.

  3. grabs the values printed by *gdb* and shows them in a buffer.

- An intelligent "make" system. Make[10] is an indispensable tool in the Unix world. It checks the file dependence information stored in a special file and performs the necessary update. Its drawback is that it depends on a very coarse dependency information — the time stamp when files are created. If a file A depends on a file B and if user adds a comment to the file B after A was compiled, then next time he invokes *make*, it will recompile A again even though what he added was nothing but comments. It's possible to make *make* more intelligent by inquiring the program database server to see if a file was influenced by the modification. E.g. if you change variable declaration v in a header file H on which file A depends. If file A does not use v at all, then there is no need to recompile file A even H was modified.

- A performance analysis system. We have an interactive performance prediction tool[4] in our original SIGMA system that has been incorporated in the SIGMACS. This tool scans the assembly code generated for the program and collects performance related statistics and stores the information in the database as a property list of the corresponding statement node (by using the SIGMACS primitive `put-prop`). This information can be type of event, number of floating point operations, etc. Later, this information can be retrieved (by the `get-prop` primitive) from the database along with other information such as loop bounds so the system can calculate a performance prediction summary. The Elisp function can then extract the function and inquire users for the values of the free variables and sends the function to a plotting programs as shown in figure 6.

  In a related project, we are designing an interactive tool to allow users to use SIGMACS to indicate where they are interested in detailed performance statistics. SIGMACS will automatically make the source code modifications to generate the appropriate tracing facilities. The statistics from the actual execution can then be viewed by a separate client program.

- A data structure visualization system. The program database can also be used to provide an interface between a client program that animates application data structures during program execution. This work by using SIGMACS as the means for users to indicate which data structures in the source program he or she would like to see displayed while the application is executing. There are two roles played by the program database. The first is to provide symbol table information for the visualization client about the nature of the structure being animated. The second is to do the program transformations needed to insert the program breakpoints that synchronize with the animation kernel.

6 Work In Progress

6.1 Dependence Analysis Package

As the current state, the data dependence analysis is a built-in function of the parser and database server. It is a very sophisticated dependence analyzer that can do the interprocedural analysis. Still there are occasions that users can give compilers a hand. For

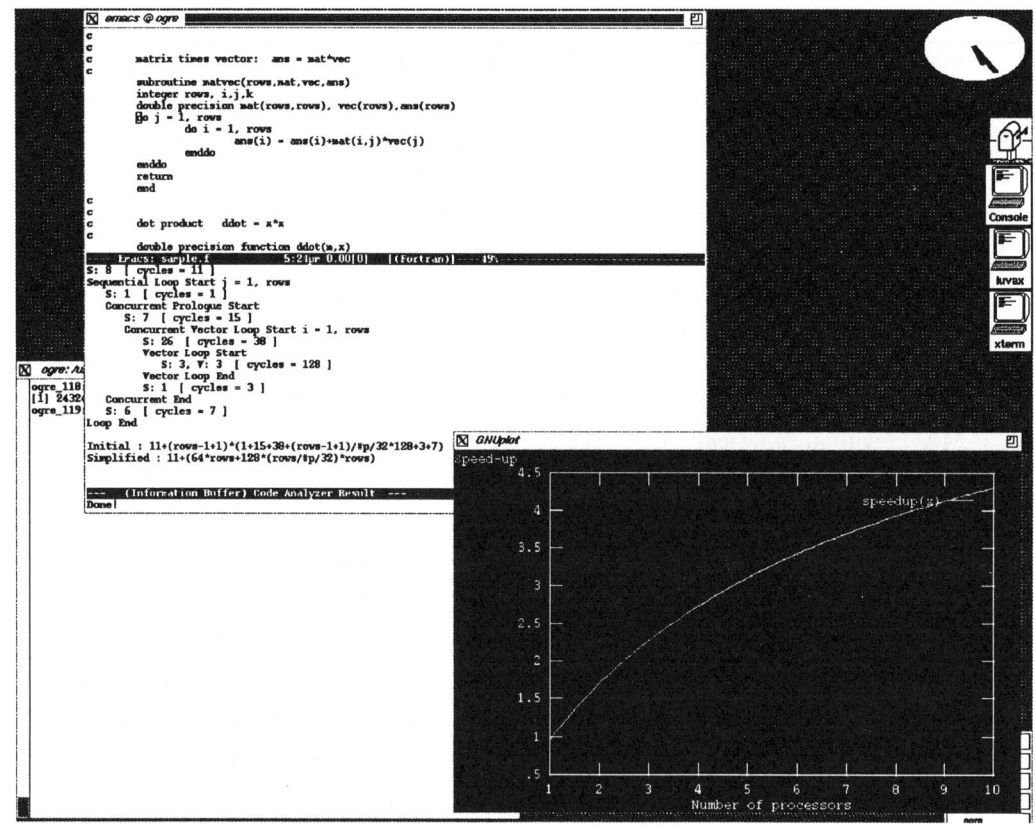

Figure 6: Performance Analysis System

example, in the following code

> **DO** I = 1, N
> A(ID(I)) = A(ID(I) + N)
> **END DO**

The dependence analyzer will conservatively say that there is a loop-carried dependence since it does not have the knowledge about the range of ID(I). If there is a compile directives that allows user to tell the compiler that the range of ID(I) is from 1 to N, such as "C $$Range(ID) = [1..n]", then the dependence analyzer can use this information to remove the dependence. Other possible annotations are aliases information such as "/* $$EQV(p->forward->back, p) */".

Another issue we are looking into is a way for the users to incorporate their own dependence analysis code into the system. Sometimes people want to test new dependence analysis methods. They are either interested in new algorithms for dependence analysis of array subscripts or pointer analysis and might want to be able to add their methods to the dependence analysis system. We are studying the way to implement it. The idea is to put the core of the dependence analysis into "user code" written in terms of the primitives so that users can add their own.

6.2 Reversibility

The returned values of the primitives are carefully designed in such a way that it's easy to perform the reverse functions, i.e. $\pi_1 \circ \sigma^{-1}(\sigma(\mathcal{G}, \mathcal{I}^*)) \sim \mathcal{G}$. Note that this is not really "equal" since there might be some intermediate nodes being created. For example, primitive delete-stmt takes a statement id *stmt-id* to be deleted and returns the id of the statement, *prev-id*, right before it. Thus if we want to revert back to the original state, all we have to do is to feed *prev-id* to the function insert-stmt along with the original *stmt-id* and the server will restore the deleted node back into the tree. The problem is that it is tedious to do all the bookkeeping since sometimes there might be hundreds of changes since the start of a transformation session. We are looking for a good way to automate the "undo" procedures. One way to implement this is for the server to take over all responsibility and store all information required to "undo" each change. In this example, the server will have to store something like (command *input output*) in its history list. Upon the "undo" request, it takes the *input* and *output* and restore the representation to the previous state. The crux of the problem is how to keep the information and minimize space requirements to achieve this goal.

6.3 Automatic Updating of Dependence Information

When doing program restructuring, it's unavoidable that we may need to delete some statements and insert new statements. This, of course, changes the dependence information we did at the compilation stage. Currently we rely on the informal rule that after each transformation, the Elisp code calls `update-deps` to update the dependence information explicitly. For example, in doing loop interchange, the Elisp function has to keep track of the nested loop level, say n, and calls the dependence updating primitive that interchanges the n-th and $(n+1)$-th elements of the direction vectors for each control child in the loop. A second option is for the Elisp to call the SIGMACS primitive `do-dep-analysis` to redo the dependence analysis for the entire function where the change has occurred. The server will then recalculate new *USE* and *MOD* information which are compared with the old *USE* and *MOD* information. If there is a change, the change must be propagated to other functions. (This can be a very expansive operation, but it cannot be avoided.)

Our goal is to provide more systematic ways to update the dependence information. The idea is that each transformation should not change the dependence graph very much. In fact, transformations should preserve the basic flow dependence structure and only change other dependences. Thus what we need is a set of primitives, such as delete-statement, insert-statement or replace-statement, that can update the dependence information automatically. For example, in the case of vectorizing a loop (see Figure 5), we construct a new vector statement, say with statement id $stmt\text{-}id_2$, from the original DO loop with statement id $stmt\text{-}id_1$. Then we can call (`replace-statement` $stmt\text{-}id_1$ $stmt\text{-}id_2$) which will delete the old DO statement, inserts the new vector statement, and "copy" the dependence arcs from the body of the DO loop to the new vector statement. As you can see, we can preserve most of the dependence arcs from the body of the DO loop except those that involve the induction variable of the original DO loop.

7 Conclusions

We have introduced a new programming environment for parallel systems and have demonstrated that this is a very open system in that new functionality can be added to the system easily. One example is that François Bodin has used SIGMACS to implement the idea of estimating the reference windows and their costs in their paper[9] in this volume. We have designed the SIGMACS to overcome the shortcomings of our original SIGMA system. Currently the prototype has been used in a high level compiler course here at Indiana University to identify the functionality users want most. Our initial experience with this system has been good.

References

1. Allen, F., Burke, M., Charles, P., Cytron, R., and Ferrante, J. An overview of the PTRAN analysis system for multiprocessing. In *Proceedings of the 1987 International Conference on Supercomputing* (Athens, Greece, 1987).

2. Allen, J. R., and Porterfield, A. Ptool: A preliminary design. Tech. Rep. TR85-17, Rice University, Mar. 1985.

3. Appelbe, B., Smith, K., and McDowell, C. Start/Pat: A parallel-programming toolkit. *IEEE Software 6*, 4 (July 1989), 29–38.

4. Atapattu, D., and Gannon, D. Building analytical models into an interactive performance prediction tool. In *Proceedings of Supercomputing '89* (Reno, Neveda, Nov. 1989), IEEE Computer Sciety and ACM SIGARCH, pp. 521–530.

5. Balasundaram, V., Kennedy, K., Kremer, U., McKinley, K., and Subhlok, J. The ParaScope editor: An interactive parallel programming tool. In *Proceedings of Supercomputing '89* (Reno, Neveda, Nov. 1989), IEEE Computer Sciety and ACM SIGARCH, pp. 540–550.

6. Carle, A., Cooper, K. D., Hood, R. T., Torczon, L., Kennedy, K., and Warren, S. A practical environment for scientific programming. *Computer* (Nov. 1987).

7. Copper, K. D., Kennedy, K., and Torczon, L. The impact of interprocedural analysis and optimization in the $I\!R^n$ programming environment. *ACM Transactions on Programming Languages and Systems 8*, 4 (Oct. 1986), 491–523.

8. Cytron, R., Ferrante, J., Rosen, B. K., Wegman, M. N., and Zadeck, F. K. An efficient method of computing static single assignment form. In *Conference Record of the Sixteenth Annual ACM Symposium on Principles of Programming Languages* (Austin, TX, Jan. 1989), ACM, pp. 25–35.

9. Eisenbeis, C., Jalby, W., Windheiser, D., and Bodin, F. A strategy for array management in local memory. In *Proceedings of the Third Workshop On Programming Languages and Compilers for Parallel Computing* (Irvine, CA, Aug. 1990).

10. Feldman, S. I. Make — a program for maintaining computer programs. *Software - Practice and Experience 9* (1977), 255–265.

11. Ferrante, J., Ottenstein, K. J., and Warren, J. D. The program dependence graph and its use in optimization. *ACM Transactions on Programming Languages and Systems 9*, 3 (July 1987), 319–349.

12. Gannon, D., Atapattu, D., Lee, M. H., and Shei, B. A software tool for building supercomputer applications. In *Parallel Processing For Scientific Computing* (Los Angeles, CA, Dec. 1987), G. Rodrigue, Ed., SIAM, pp. 301–305.

13. Guarna, Jr., V. A., Gannon, D., Jablonowski, D., Malony, A. D., and Gaur, Y. Faust: An integrated environment for parallel programming. *IEEE Software 6*, 4 (July 1989), 20–27.

14. Kernighan, B. W. *UNIX For Beginners – Second Edition.* Bell Laboratories, Sept. 1978.

15. Mehrotra, P., and Van Rosendale, J. R. The BLAZE language: A parallel language for scientific programs. *Parallel Computing 5*, 3 (Nov. 1987), 339–361.

16. Padua, D. A., and Wolfe, M. J. Advanced compiler optimizations for supercomputers. *Communications of the ACM 29*, 12 (Dec. 1986), 1184–1201.

17. Wolfe, M. J. *Optimizing Compilers for Supercomputers.* PhD thesis, University of Illinois at Urbana-Champaign, Urbana, Ill, Oct. 1982.

6 Detecting Data Races in Parallel Program Executions
R. Netzer, B. Miller

Abstract

Several methods currently exist for detecting data races in an execution of a shared-memory parallel program. Although these methods address an important aspect of parallel program debugging, they do not precisely define the notion of a data race. As a result, is it not possible to precisely state which data races are detected, nor is the meaning of the reported data races always clear. Furthermore, these methods can sometimes generate false data race reports. They can determine whether a data race was exhibited during an execution, but when more than one data race is reported, only limited indication is given as to which ones are real. This paper addresses these two issues. We first present a model for reasoning about data races, and then present a two-phase approach to data race detection that attempts to validate the accuracy of each detected data race.

Our model of data races distinguishes among those data races that actually occurred during an execution (*actual* data races), those that could have occurred because of timing variations (*feasible* data races), and those that appeared to have occurred (*apparent* data races). The first phase of our two-phase approach to data race detection is similar to previous methods and detects a set of data race candidates (the apparent data races). We prove that this set always contains all actual data races, although it may contain other data races, both feasible and infeasible. Unlike previous methods, we then employ a second phase which validates the apparent data races by attempting to determine which ones are feasible. This second phase requires no more information than previous methods collect, and involves making a conservative estimate of the data dependences among the shared data to determine how these dependences may have constrained alternate orderings potentially exhibited by the execution. Each apparent data race can then be characterized as either being feasible, or as belonging to a set of apparent data races where at least one is feasible.

Research supported in part by National Science Foundation grant CCR-8815928, Office of Naval Research grant N00014-89-J-1222, and a Digital Equipment Corporation External Research Grant.

1. Introduction

In shared-memory parallel programs, if accesses to shared data are not properly coordinated, a *data race* can result, causing the program to behave in a way not intended by the programmer. Detecting data races in a particular execution of a parallel program is an important part of debugging. Several methods for data race detection have been developed[1, 3, 4, 9, 15, 17]. Although these methods provide valuable tools for debugging, they do not precisely define the notion of a data race. As a result, we cannot precisely state which data races are detected by these methods. In addition, false data race reports can sometimes be generated. These methods can determine whether or not a data race occurred, but when more than one data race is reported, no indication is given as to which ones are real. Failure to characterize the detected data races, and the generation of false data race reports, can make it difficult to use these methods for debugging the program and locating the cause of the data races. This paper addresses these two issues. We first present a formal model in which to reason about data races, and then outline a two-phase approach to data race detection that is discussed entirely in terms of the model. The first phase performs essentially the same type of analysis as previous methods, and detects a set of candidate data races (which we call *apparent* data races). Unlike previous methods, we then employ a second phase that validates each of the apparent data races to determine which ones are real. By providing a model for reasoning about data races, the correctness of our techniques can be convincingly argued, and the meaning of the data race reports (generated by our methods or others) is made explicit. By validating the apparent data races, the programmer can be provided with information crucial to debugging.

One purpose of adding explicit synchronization to shared-memory parallel programs is to coordinate accesses to shared data. Some programs are intended to behave deterministically, and for these programs synchronization is usually designed to force all shared-data accesses to the same location to occur in a specific order (for some given program input). When the order of two shared-memory accesses made by different processes (to the same location) is not enforced, a *race condition* is said to exist[5, 6], possibly resulting in a nondeterministic execution. In contrast, other programs are not intended to be deterministic, and for these programs synchronization is usually added to ensure that some sections of code execute as if they were atomic (i.e., to implement critical sections). For example, consider a section of code that adds up a list of shared data representing the deposits to a bank account during a certain month. If this section of code does not execute as if it were atomic (because, for example, another section of concurrently executing code is debiting the account), the computed deposit total might not be correct. A section of code is guaranteed to execute atomically if the shared variables it reads and modifies are not modified by any other concurrently executing section of code[2]. If these conditions are not met, a *data race* is said to exist. Since nondeterministic behavior can result, a data race is a special case of the more general race condition. In this paper we focus on data race detection.

To provide a mechanism for reasoning about data race detection, we present a model for representing executions of shared-memory parallel programs, on sequentially consistent processors, that use fork/join and counting semaphores. Our model distinguishes between the ordering of events that *actually* occurred during execution and the ordering that *could have* occurred. Given an actual execution of the program, we characterize alternate event orderings that the execution could have exhibited. Possible orderings include those that could still allow the original data dependences among the shared data to occur and that do not violate the semantics of the explicit synchronization primitives used by the program. An execution exhibiting such an alternate ordering is called a *feasible program execution*. The characterization of feasible program executions in general requires knowledge of which shared-data dependences (if any) were exhibited between any two events performed by the execution. Since recording this information is not practical in general, we characterize approximate information in terms of our model. We show how the information recorded by previous methods can be used to define an *approximate program execution*. We then distinguish between three types of data races. *Actual* data races are those actually exhibited during an execution, *feasible* data races are those that could have occurred because of nondeterministic timing variations, and *apparent* data races are those that appeared to have occurred from analyzing the approximate information. Previous methods detect apparent data races. We show that apparent data races are not always actual or feasible, and show how a two-phase approach can be used to detect and then validate the apparent data races. The first phase is essentially identical to previous methods and simply detects the apparent data races. We prove that each actual data race is also apparent. The approach employed by previous methods is therefore safe in the sense that no actual data races are left undetected. We also employ a second phase that classifies each apparent data race as either feasible or as belonging to a set of data races that contains at least one feasible data race. Performing such a validation provides the programmer with some information as to which of the apparent data races should be investigated for debugging.

2. Previous Data Race Detection Methods

All previous methods for dynamic data race detection operate by first instrumenting the program so that information about its execution is recorded, and then executing the program and analyzing the collected information. These methods all analyze essentially the same information about the execution, but differ mainly in how and when that information is collected and analyzed. Two approaches to this information collection and analysis have been proposed: *on-the-fly* and *post-mortem*. On-the-fly techniques[4, 9, 17] detect data races by an on-going analysis during execution that encodes information about the execution so it can be accessed quickly and discarded as it becomes obsolete. Post-mortem techniques[1, 3, 15] detect data races after execution ends by analyzing trace files that are produced during execution. Although all previous methods never fail to detect any data races actually exhibited during execution (we prove this claim in Section 7), they do not precisely locate where these data races occurred. We briefly describe the common characteristics of these methods below.

Previous methods instrument the program to collect the same information: which sections of code executed, the set of shared variables read and written by each section of code, and the relative execution order between some synchronization operations. To represent this relative ordering, a DAG is constructed (either explicitly or in an encoded form), which we call the *ordering graph*, in which each node represents an execution instance of either a synchronization operation (a *synchronization event*) or the code executed between two synchronization operations (a *computation event*)†. Edges are added from each event to the next event belonging to the same process, and between some pairs of synchronization events (belonging to different processes) to indicate the order in which the synchronization events executed. The various methods differ in the types of synchronization handled, but they all handle **fork/join** (in one form or another). An edge is added from each **fork** event to the first event in each child created by the **fork**, and from the last event in each child to the corresponding **join** event.

The crux of data race detection is the location of events that accessed a common shared variable (that at least one wrote) and that either did or could have executed concurrently. Finding events that accessed a common shared variable is straightforward, since the sets of shared variables read and written by each event is recorded. To determine if two events could have executed concurrently, all previous methods analyze the ordering graph. Two computation events are assumed to have potentially executed concurrently if no path in the graph connects the two events. Data races are therefore reported between pairs of events that accessed a common shared variable and that have no connecting path. However, this assumption is not always true, and causes previous methods to generate potentially many false data race reports.

To illustrate these false reports, consider the program fragment in Figure 1. This program creates two identical children that remove from a shared queue the lower and upper bounds of a region of a shared array to operation upon, perform some computation on that region of the array, and loop until the queue is empty. The queue initially contains records representing disjoint regions of the array. A correct execution of this program should therefore exhibit no data races, since only disjoint regions of the shared array should be accessed concurrently. However, assume that the ''remove'' operations do not properly synchronize their accesses to the shared queue. An ordering graph for one possible execution of this program is also shown (the dotted lines only illustrate the data races and are not part of the graph). In this execution, the first ''remove'' operation performed by the left child completed before the first ''remove'' performed by the right child began (the nodes are staggered horizontally to indicate this order). The first two records were therefore correctly removed, and both children operated (correctly) on disjoint regions of the array. However, during the next iteration, the ''remove'' operations actually overlapped, and the right child correctly removed the fourth record, but the left child removed the upper bound (100) from the third record and the lower bound (300) from the fourth record. The left child therefore operated (erroneously) on region [100,299] of the array.

In this graph, no paths connect any nodes of the left child with any nodes of the right child. Since both children accessed the same queue, previous methods would report four data races between the ''remove'' operations (shown by the finely dotted lines). Similarly, since both children accessed a common region of the array, a data race would also be reported between these array accesses (shown by the coarsely dotted line). The latter data race report can be misleading, however, since the accesses by the left child to region [100,299] did not, and could never, execute concurrently with the accesses to region [200,299] made by the right child. For these accesses to execute concurrently, the second ''remove'' operation performed

---

† Some methods do not actually construct a node to represent a computation event but rather represent the event by an edge connecting the two surrounding synchronization events[4, 15].

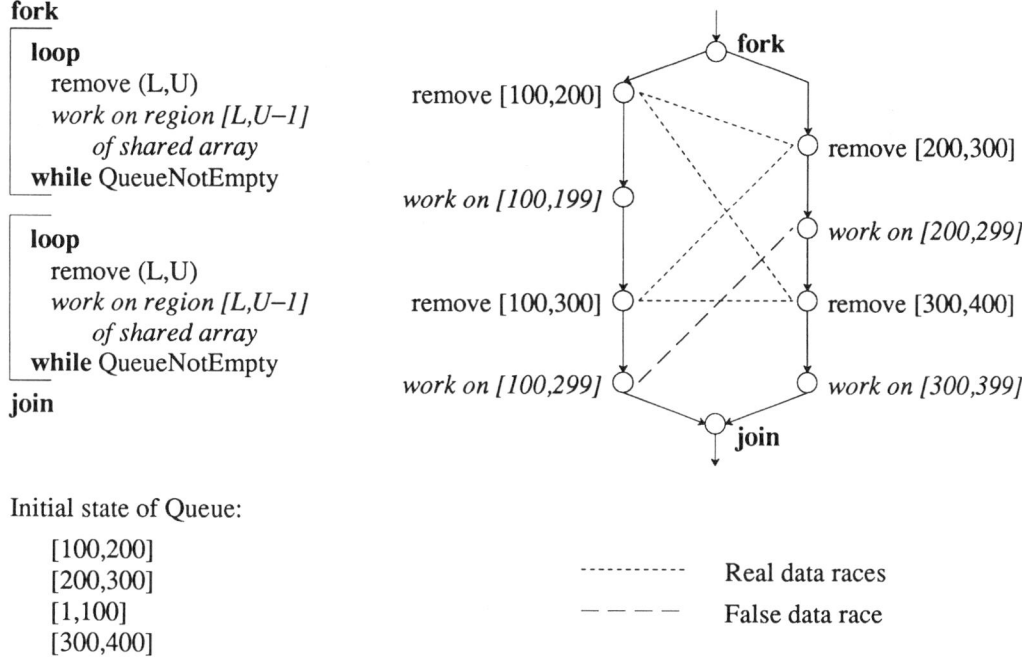

Figure 1. Example program fragment and ordering graph
(the dotted lines only illustrate the reported data races)

by the left child would have to execute before the second "remove" operation performed by the right child (with which it originally overlapped). If this would happen, the erroneous record [100,300] would not be removed by the left child, since it would no longer overlap with the other "remove" operation, and a different region of the array would be accessed.

If the array accesses were more complex, perhaps creating other children, there may have been many nodes in the graph representing these accesses. In such a case, many false data race reports would be generated, instead of only one. In this example, the data races are caused by lack of synchronization in the "remove" operations. The fact that non-disjoint regions of the array were accessed is an artifact of this missing synchronization, and does not represent a bug in the program. Reporting many false data races to the programmer, only one of which involves events that did (or could) execute concurrently, complicates the job of debugging.

False data race reports can result whenever shared variables are used (either directly or transitively) in conditional expressions or in expressions determining which shared locations are accessed (e.g., shared array subscripts). Accurate data race detection involves examining how shared data flowed through the execution and whether the execution might have changed had a different ordering occurred. This paper presents results showing how to validate the accuracy of each data race without recording additional information about the execution.

3. Program Execution Model

Before discussing data race detection, we first present a formal model to provide a mechanism for reasoning about shared-memory parallel program executions. The model contains the objects that represent a program execution (such as which statements were executed and in what order), and axioms that characterize properties those objects must possess. This model is useful as a notational device for describing behavior the execution *actually* exhibited. We later show how it can also be used to speculate on behavior that the execution *could have* exhibited (such as alternate event orderings) due to nondeterministic timing variations. Our model describes programs that use counting semaphores and the fork/join construct.

3.1. General Model

Our model is based on Lamport's theory of concurrent systems[13], which provides a formalism for reasoning about concurrent systems that does not assume the existence of atomic operations. In Lamport's formalism, a concurrent system execution is modeled as a collection of *operation executions*. Two relations on operation executions, *precedes* ($\rightarrow$) and *can causally affect* ($\dashrightarrow$), describe a system execution; $a \rightarrow b$ means that a completes before b begins (in the sense that the last action of a can affect the first action of b), and $a \dashrightarrow b$ means that some action of a precedes some action of b. We use Lamport's theory, but restrict it to the class of shared-memory parallel programs that execute on sequentially consistent processors[11].

When the underlying hardware guarantees sequential consistency, any two events that execute concurrently can affect one another (i.e., $a \leftrightarrow b \Leftrightarrow a \dashrightarrow b \wedge b \dashrightarrow a$).[†] Given sequential consistency, a single relation is sufficient to describe the temporal aspects of a system execution. For this purpose we introduce $\xrightarrow{T}$, the *temporal ordering* relation among events; $a \xrightarrow{T} b$ means that a completes before b begins, and $a \xleftrightarrow{T} b$ means that a and b execute concurrently (i.e, neither completes before the other begins). We should emphasize that we are defining the temporal ordering relation so it describes the order in which events *actually* executed during a particular execution; e.g., $a \xleftrightarrow{T} b$ means that a and b actually executed concurrently, and does not mean that a and b could have executed in any order. In Section 5 we show how to speculate on alternate temporal orderings that could have been exhibited.

In addition, we replace the $\dashrightarrow$ relation with the *transitive shared-data dependence* relation (or just *shared-data dependence* relation for brevity), $\xrightarrow{D}$. This relation shows when one event can causally affect another either because of a *direct* data dependence involving a single shared variable, or because of a chain of direct dependences involving several different variables. A direct shared-data dependence from a to b (denoted $a \xrightarrow{DD} b$) exists if a accesses a shared variable that b later accesses (where at least one access modifies the variable); we also say that a direct dependence exists if a precedes b in the same process, since data can in gen-

---

[†] In Lamport's terminology, we are considering the class of system executions that have global-time models. Throughout this paper, we use superscripted arrows to denote relations, and write $a \not\rightarrow b$ as a shorthand for $\neg(a \rightarrow b)$, and $a \leftrightarrow b$ as a shorthand for $\neg(a \rightarrow b) \wedge \neg(b \rightarrow a)$.

eral flow through non-shared variables which are local to the process. A transitive shared-data dependence ($a \xrightarrow{D} b$) exists if there is a chain of direct dependences from a to b (possibly involving events that access different shared variables); $\xrightarrow{D} = (\xrightarrow{DD})^+$, the irreflexive transitive closure of the direct shared-data dependence relation[‡]. This definition of data dependence is different from the standard ones[10] since we consider transitive dependences involving flow-, anti-, and output-dependences, and do not explicitly state the variables involved.

We define a *program execution*, P, to be a triple, $\langle E, \xrightarrow{T}, \xrightarrow{D} \rangle$, where E is a finite set of *events*, and $\xrightarrow{T}$ and $\xrightarrow{D}$ are the relations over E described above. We refer to a given program execution, P, as an *actual program execution* when P represents an execution that the program at hand actually performed. Each event $e \in E$ represents the execution of a set of program statements, and possesses two attributes, $READ(e)$ and $WRITE(e)$, the set of shared variables read and written by those statements. A *data conflict* is said to exist between two events if one events writes a shared variable that the other reads or writes. The temporal ordering and shared-data dependence relations must satisfy the following axioms:

A1. $\xrightarrow{T}$ is an irreflexive partial order.

A2.   If $a \xrightarrow{T} b \xleftrightarrow{T} c \xrightarrow{T} d$ then $a \xrightarrow{T} d$.

A3.   If $a \xrightarrow{D} b$ then $b \not\xrightarrow{T} a$.

No generality is lost by modeling each event, e, as having a unique *start time* (e_s) and *finish time* (e_f)[12]. A total ordering on the start and finish times is called a *global-time model*. Given a global-time model, the $\xrightarrow{T}$ relation is defined as follows: $a \xrightarrow{T} b$ iff $a_f < b_s$, and $a \xleftrightarrow{T} b$ iff $a_s < b_f \wedge b_s < a_f$. Axioms A1-A3 can also be written in terms of the start and finish times. We will occasionally employ such a view in proofs of our results.

3.2. Model Applied to Semaphores and Fork/Join

So far, the model does not describe any of the synchronization aspects of a program execution. By imposing some structure on the set of events, E, and by adding axioms that describe the semantics of synchronization operations, we extend the general model to describe programs that use counting semaphores and the fork/join construct. Other types of synchronization can be similarly accommodated.

We assume that a program execution consists of a number of processes, each of which either exists when the program execution begins or is created during execution by a *fork* operation. Similarly, a process either continues to exist until the program execution ends or until the process (and all others created by the same fork operation) is terminated by a *join* operation. The set of events belonging to process p is denoted by E_p, and therefore $E = \cup_p E_p$, for all

---

[‡] The transitive shared-data dependence relation is conservative in the sense that when data flows from a to b it always shows a dependence from a to b, but also sometimes shows a dependence when in fact no data flow occurs. A more precise characterization of causality would require examining the semantics of the individual actions performed by each event.

processes p that exist during the program execution. Each process is viewed as containing a totally ordered sequence of events, and the term $e_{p,i}$ will denote the ith event in the execution of process p. The following axiom describes the total ordering imposed on events belonging to the same process:

A4. $e_{p,i} \xrightarrow{T} e_{p,i+1}$ for all processes p and $1 \leq i < |E_p|$

To describe the presence of synchronization operations, we distinguish between different types of events. A *synchronization event* is an instance of a semaphore operation (a *P event* or a *V event*), a fork operation (a *fork event*), or a join operation (a *join event*). The set of all P and V operations on semaphore i is denoted by $E_{P(i)}$ and $E_{V(i)}$, respectively. A *computation event* is an instance of a group of statements, belonging to the same process, that executed consecutively, none of which are synchronization operations. Any arbitrary grouping of (consecutively executed) statement instances that does not include a synchronization operation defines a computation event.

To describe the semantics of synchronization operations, we add additional axioms to our model. A fork event, $Fork_{p,i}$, is assumed to precede all events in the child processes which it creates, and all events in these child processes are assumed to precede the subsequent join event in process p, $Join_{p,i+k}$:

A5. For all child processes, c, created by each $Fork_{p,i}$ and terminated at $Join_{p,i+k}$,

$$Fork_{p,i} \xrightarrow{T} e_{c,j} \xrightarrow{T} Join_{p,i+k} \quad 1 \leq j \leq |E_c|$$

We assume that in any program execution the semaphore invariant[7] is always maintained. For counting semaphores, the semaphore invariant is maintained iff at each point in the execution, the number of V operations that have either completed or have begun executing is greater than or equal to the number of P operations that have completed. For each semaphore, S, this invariant can be expressed by the following axiom:

A6. For every subset of P events, $P \subseteq E_{P(S)}$,

$$|\{ v \mid v \in E_{V(s)} \land \exists p \in P \ (v \xrightarrow{T} p \lor v \xleftarrow{T} p) \}| \geq |P|.$$

The above version of axiom A6 assumes that the initial value of each semaphore is zero. An arbitrary initial value, m, for some semaphore could be described by creating an artificial process that contains m V-events that precede all other events.

3.3. Higher-Level Views

It is useful to be able to view a program execution at different levels of abstraction, since information about the execution may be collected at that level, and because sometimes it is useful to abstract irrelevant details of part of an execution into a higher-level event. We can reason about a program execution at any level of abstraction by following Lamport and defining a *higher-level view*. A higher-level view of a program execution $P = \langle E, \xrightarrow{T}, \xrightarrow{D} \rangle$ is $\mathcal{P} = \langle \mathcal{E}, \xrightarrow{T}, \xrightarrow{D} \rangle$ where

(H1) $\mathcal{E}$ partitions E, and $\forall e' \in \mathcal{E}$,
$$READ(e') = \bigcup_{e \in e'} READ(e), \text{ and } WRITE(e') = \bigcup_{e \in e'} WRITE(e).$$

(H2) $A \xrightarrow{T} B \Leftrightarrow \forall a \in A, b \in B \ (a \xrightarrow{T} b)$, and

(H3) $A \xrightarrow{D} B \Leftrightarrow \exists a \in A, b \in B \ (a \xrightarrow{D} b)$.

A higher-level view always obeys axioms A1-A3. Since axioms A4-A6 are defined in terms of synchronization and computation events, they are also obeyed if each higher-level event consists of either a single synchronization event from E, or only a set of computation events from E. In such a case, each event $e' \in \mathcal{E}$ inherits its type from the type of the events comprising e'. When the higher-level events are defined to partition E in this way, $\mathcal{P}$ obeys axioms A1-A6 and is then itself a program execution.

4. Representing Actual Program Executions

The model we have presented so far captures complete information about a program execution in the sense that $\xrightarrow{T}$ shows the relative ordering in which any two events actually executed, and $\xrightarrow{D}$ shows the actual shared-data dependences between any two events. In practice, recording such complete information is not practical, and we now discuss how to represent partial information about a program execution in our model. Our intent is not to discuss details of program instrumentation, but rather to outline one type of information that is sufficient for data race detection, and show how this information is represented in our model. We will define *approximate* counterparts to the $\xrightarrow{T}$ and $\xrightarrow{D}$ relations capturing partial information about a program execution that is based on the type of information previous methods record. This information can be recorded without tracing every shared-memory access and without introducing a central bottleneck into the program. The resulting approximate relations, $\xrightarrow{\hat{T}}$ and $\xrightarrow{\hat{D}}$, define an *approximate program execution*, $\hat{P} = \langle E, \xrightarrow{\hat{T}}, \xrightarrow{\hat{D}} \rangle$. In Section 7 we show how $\hat{P}$ can be used for data race validation.

4.1. Approximate Temporal Ordering

As described in Section 2, previous data race detection methods record the temporal ordering among only some synchronization events. For example, the order among **fork** and **join** operations and their child processes is recorded, but the relative order of operations belonging to the different child processes is not. Recording incomplete ordering information is desirable because the required instrumentation can be embedded into the implementation of the synchronization operations without introducing additional synchronization. Not introducing additional synchronization ensures that the instrumentation will not create a central bottleneck which could reduce the amount of parallelism achievable by the program. We assume that the program is instrumented to record such incomplete ordering information, and that the ordering is represented by constructing a graph, called the *temporal ordering graph*, similar to the ordering graphs used by previous methods. For every event, e, this graph contains two nodes[†], e_s and e_f (corresponding to the start and finish of e), and an edge from e_s and e_f. The graph defines an

---

[†] In practice, it is not always necessary to actually construct two nodes per event, but we use such a representation here since it conceptually follows our model.

approximate temporal ordering relation, $\hat{\rightarrow}$, as follows: $a \hat{\rightarrow} b$ iff there is a path from a_f to b_s, $b \hat{\rightarrow} a$ iff there is a path from b_f to a_s, and $a \hat{\leftrightarrow} b$ otherwise. We assume the program instrumentation constructs a temporal ordering graph that gives $\hat{\rightarrow}$ the following properties:

(1) If $a \hat{\rightarrow} b$ then $a \xrightarrow{T} b$, and

(2) If $a \hat{\leftrightarrow} b$ then the explicit synchronization performed by the execution did not prevent a and b from executing concurrently.

The first property states that the ordering of events given by $\hat{\rightarrow}$ must be consistent with the order in which they actually executed (i.e., $\hat{\rightarrow} \subseteq \xrightarrow{T}$). The second property means that any linear ordering of the graph is a global-time model defining a temporal ordering that obeys the synchronization axioms (i.e., axioms A4-A6). Recall that $\xrightarrow{T}$ was defined to represent the actual order in which events executed; $a \xleftrightarrow{T} b$ means that a and b actually overlapped during execution. Since $\hat{\rightarrow}$ is an approximation of $\xrightarrow{T}$ (it is a subset), $a \hat{\leftrightarrow} b$ does not (necessarily) mean that a and b actually overlapped. Instead, it means that a and b were not forced to occur in a certain order by *explicit* synchronization (the graph does not contain enough information to determine their actual execution order). As illustrated in Figure 1, such events may nonetheless be ordered. The goal of data race validation (discussed in Section 7) is determining which events that are not ordered by $\hat{\rightarrow}$ could have indeed executed concurrently.

For programs using **fork/join**, the ordering graphs constructed by previous methods satisfy the above two properties. To accommodate semaphore synchronization, edges can be added to the temporal ordering graph by recording the order of all operations on a given semaphore. Such an ordering can be recorded without introducing additional synchronization into the program (as mentioned above for **fork/join** operations). To reflect this ordering in the graph, an edge can be drawn from each semaphore operation (on a given semaphore) to the next operation on the same semaphore. Since $\hat{\rightarrow}$ only needs to obey the synchronization axioms, other approaches for adding edges (that result in more events being unordered by $\hat{\rightarrow}$, allowing more data races to be detected) are possible. For example, previous methods that handle semaphores[3, 4, 15] construct edges only from a **V** operation to the **P** operation it allowed to proceed. More sophisticated approaches have also been investigated[8].

4.2. Approximate Shared-Data Dependences

Determining the actual shared-data dependences exhibited by an execution would in general require the relative order of all shared memory accesses to be recorded. However, in Section 2 we mentioned that previous methods record the *READ* and *WRITE* sets for each computation event. By using only these sets and the approximate temporal ordering, the actual shared-data dependences can be conservatively estimated. The *approximate shared-data dependence* relation, $\hat{\xrightarrow{D}}$, is defined by speculating on what the actual shared-data dependences might have been. Consider two events, a and b, that both access a common shared variable (where at least one access is a modification). If $a \hat{\rightarrow} b$, then there is a direct shared-data dependence from a

to b. When $a \overset{\hat{T}}{\leftrightarrow} b$, the direction of any direct dependence cannot be determined (since the actual temporal ordering between a and b is not known), and we make the conservative assumption that a direct dependence exists from a to b and from b to a. This assumption is conservative since it will always include the actual direct dependences, although it may introduce a dependence from b to a when in fact the only dependence was from a to b. The $\overset{\hat{D}}{\rightarrow}$ relation is then defined as the irreflexive transitive closure (see Section 3.1) of this approximation of the direct dependences. As we will see, for data race validation $\overset{\hat{D}}{\rightarrow}$ only needs to be computed between events a and b when $a \overset{\hat{T}}{\leftrightarrow} b$.

5. Characterizing Alternate Temporal Orderings

An actual program execution describes aspects of how the program *actually* performed, and does not contain any information regarding what the program might have done. For example, $\overset{T}{\rightarrow}$ is defined to represent the *actual* temporal ordering in which any two events were performed. In a given program execution, the temporal ordering between some events is not always enforced by (explicit or implicit) synchronization, but sometimes occurs by chance. It is possible that another execution of the program could perform exactly the same events, but exhibit a different temporal ordering among these events. In this section we characterize such alternate temporal orderings that an actual program execution, P, *could have* exhibited because of nondeterministic timing variations. To determine how much the temporal ordering of P can be disturbed without affecting the events performed, we consider the shared-data dependences exhibited by P. Any execution exhibiting these same dependences is capable of performing the same events. We later use this characterization of alternate orderings to distinguish between data races actually exhibited by an execution and data races that could have been exhibited.

For a given execution of a program, consider a particular view of the execution (called a *single-access* view) in which each computation event is defined to comprise at most one shared-memory access. The program execution describing this view, P_S, shows the data dependences among the individual shared-memory accesses made by the execution. These *single-access* shared-data dependences uniquely characterize the events performed. Since the execution outcome of each statement instance depends only upon the values of the variables it reads[14], the single-access dependences uniquely determine the program state at each step in each process.[†] Any temporal ordering that could still allow these data dependences to occur (and that would not violate the semantics of the synchronization operations) is an ordering the execution could have exhibited. Therefore, any other single-access program execution, P_S', possessing the same events and (single-access) shared-data dependences as P_S, represents an execution the program could actually exhibit, regardless of how its temporal ordering differs from that of P_S.

---

† For this statement to hold, interactions with the external environment must be modeled as shared-data dependences.

Similarly, this result also holds for higher-level views of the program execution. In higher-level views, computation events can consist of many shared-memory accesses. In the following theorem we show that any higher-level program execution possessing the same events and (higher-level) shared-data dependences as P describes an execution the program could actually exhibit, regardless of how its temporal ordering differs from that of P. We call a program execution that could actually be exhibited a *feasible program execution*. The following theorem gives sufficient conditions for a program execution to be feasible.

Theorem 5.1.

Let $P = \langle E, \xrightarrow{T}, \xrightarrow{D} \rangle$ be an actual program execution. $P' = \langle E, \xrightarrow{T'}, \xrightarrow{D'} \rangle$ is a feasible program execution if

(F1) P' is a valid program execution (axioms A1-A6 are satisfied), and

(F2) $\xrightarrow{D'} = \xrightarrow{D}$.

Proof.

We will use the result mentioned above that any single-access program execution possessing the same (single-access) shared-data dependences as those that actually occurred represents an execution the program could exhibit[14]. This theorem extends the result to higher-level program executions. Since computation events in higher-level program executions can consist of more than one shared-memory access, there may be more than one single-access program execution for which P, the actual program execution, is a higher-level view. Therefore, given a higher-level view, we do not always know which shared-data dependences actually occurred at the single-access level. To show that P' is a feasible program execution, we must show that it is a higher-level view of a single-access program execution possessing the actual single-access dependences. However, since these dependences are not known, we will show that the shared-data dependences exhibited by *each* single-access program execution described by P are also exhibited by *some* single-access execution described by P'. We will then be guaranteed that, no matter which single-access shared-data dependences were exhibited during P, an execution capable of exhibiting those same dependences is described by P'.

The single-access program executions that are described by P is given by the set $\{ P_S = \langle E_S, \xrightarrow{Ts}, \xrightarrow{Ds} \rangle \mid P$ is a higher-level view of $P_S \}$, and the single-access executions described by P' is given by $\{ P_S' = \langle E_S, \xrightarrow{Ts'}, \xrightarrow{Ds'} \rangle \mid P'$ is a higher-level view of $P_S'\}$. We must prove that each $\xrightarrow{Ds}$ is equal to some $\xrightarrow{Ds'}$. We first show that for any pair of higher-level events, we can always find some $\xrightarrow{Ds'}$ exhibiting the same shared-data dependences as any $\xrightarrow{Ds}$ among the lower-level events comprising these events, and then show that this guarantees some $\xrightarrow{Ds'}$ exists exhibiting the same dependences as any $\xrightarrow{Ds}$ among *all* the lower-level events comprising the actual program execution (which shows $\xrightarrow{Ds} = \xrightarrow{Ds'}$).

First, consider any P_S, and its (single-access) shared-data dependences among the lower-level events $a_S \in a$ and $b_S \in b$ comprising any two higher-level events a and b. We now show a P_S' exists exhibiting these same dependences. Since each lower-level event comprises at most one shared-memory access, it suffices to show that some P_S' exists such that $b_S \xrightarrow{Ts'} a_S$ whenever $a_S \xrightarrow{Ds} b_S$, and $a_S \xrightarrow{Ts'} b_S$ whenever $b_S \xrightarrow{Ds} a_S$, for any $a_S \in a$ and $b_S \in b$.

Case (1): $a \xrightarrow{T} b$ and $a \xrightarrow{T'} b$. In this case, $\xrightarrow{Ds}$ can only contain shared-data dependences from some a_S to some b_S, and all P_S' have $a_S \xrightarrow{T'} b_S$ for all $a_S \in a$ and $b_S \in b$.

Case (2): $a \xrightarrow{T} b$ and $a \xcancel{\xrightarrow{T'}} b$. As with case (1), $\xrightarrow{Ds}$ can only contain shared-data dependences from some a_S to some b_S. Some P_S' must exist in which $b_S \xrightarrow{Ts'} a_S$ for all $a_S \in a$ and $b_S \in b$, since otherwise $b_S \xrightarrow{Ts'} a_S$ for all $a_S \in a$ and $b_S \in b$ would imply $b \xrightarrow{T'} a$, contradicting the assumption $a \xcancel{\xrightarrow{T'}} b$.

Case (3): $a \xrightarrow{T} b$ and $b \xrightarrow{T'} a$. In this case, $\xrightarrow{Ds}$ can contain no shared-data dependences between any a_S and b_S (or else P' would violate A3).

Case (4): $a \xcancel{\xrightarrow{T}} b$ and $a \xrightarrow{T'} b$. Since $\xrightarrow{Ds}$ can contain shared-data dependences only from some a_S to some b_S (or else P' would violate A3), this case is analogous to case (1).

Case (5): $a \xcancel{\xrightarrow{T}} b$ and $a \xcancel{\xrightarrow{T'}} b$. In this case, $\xrightarrow{Ds}$ can contain shared-data dependences in both directions between the a_S and b_S, and since the set of single-access program executions described by P' contains all possible temporal orderings among the a_S and b_S that cause $a \xcancel{\xrightarrow{T'}} b$, some P_S' clearly exists with the desired properties.

Finally, we show that each $\xrightarrow{Ds}$ equals some $\xrightarrow{Ds'}$. Notice that when there are events a and b that overlap, P' describes more than one single-access program execution. These single-access program executions contain all possible (legal) temporal orderings among the lower-level events $a_S \in a$ and $b_S \in b$ that cause a and b to overlap. The set of all single-access program executions described by P' can be constructed by choosing, for each pair of higher-level events a and b, one such temporal ordering among the lower-level events comprising a and b. We showed above that for any $\xrightarrow{Ds}$, some $\xrightarrow{Ds'}$ exists exhibiting the same shared-data dependences among the lower-level events comprising any pair of higher-level events. Using this result, we can always find a $\xrightarrow{Ds'}$ exhibiting the same shared-data dependences as any $\xrightarrow{Ds}$ among *all* the lower-level events by independently considering each pair of higher-level events. Therefore, each $\xrightarrow{Ds}$ is equal to some $\xrightarrow{Ds'}$, which proves the theorem. ∎

Given an actual program execution, P, we are not attempting to predict the behavior of the program had different shared-data dependences occurred. Instead, the above theorem characterizes different program executions (performing the same events as P) that we can *guarantee* the program is capable of exhibiting. Indeed, there may be program executions that violate the above conditions but nevertheless perform the same events. However, characterizing such program executions requires analyzing the semantics of the program itself, to determine what effects different shared-data dependences would have on P.

6. Definition of Data Race

We can now characterize different types of data races in terms of our model. We distinguish between an *actual data race*, which is a data race exhibited during an actual program execution, and a *feasible data race*, which is a data race that could have been exhibited because of timing variations. We also characterize the *apparent data races*, those data races detected by searching the ordering graph for data-conflicting events that are not ordered by the graph (which are the data races reported by previous methods). As discussed in the next section, the problem of data race validation is determining which apparent data races are feasible.

Definition 6.1

A *data race under* $\xrightarrow{T}$ exists between a and b iff

(DR1) a data conflict exists between a and b, and

(DR2) $a \not\leftrightarrow^{T} b$.

Definition 6.2
An *actual data race* exists between a and b iff

(AR1) $P = \langle E, \xrightarrow{T}, \xrightarrow{D} \rangle$ is an actual program execution, and

(AR2) a data race under $\xrightarrow{T}$ exists between a and b.

Definition 6.3
A *feasible data race* exists between a and b iff

(FR1) there exists some feasible program execution, $P' = \langle E, \xrightarrow{T'}, \xrightarrow{D'} \rangle$, and

(FR2) a data race under $\xrightarrow{T'}$ exists between a and b.

Definition 6.4
An *apparent data race* exists between a and b iff

(AP1) $\hat{P} = \langle E, \xrightarrow{\hat{T}}, \xrightarrow{\hat{D}} \rangle$ is an approximate program execution, and

(AP2) a data race under $\xrightarrow{\hat{T}}$ exists between a and b.

7. Detecting Data Races

We now present our two-phase approach to data race detection. In the first phase, the apparent data races are located by using the approximate information collected about the execution to construct and then analyze the temporal ordering graph. This first phase performs the same type of analysis as previous data race detection methods. Unlike previous methods, we then employ a second phase to validate each apparent data race by attempting to determine whether or not the race is feasible. This determination is made by first augmenting the temporal ordering graph with additional edges representing a conservative estimate of the shared-data dependences, and then analyzing the resulting graph for cycles. Such a two-phase approach has the advantage that approximate information (such as that recorded by previous methods) can be used, but the programmer can still be provided with information regarding the feasibility of the reported data races. Throughout the remainder of this section, $\hat{P} = \langle E, \xrightarrow{\hat{T}}, \xrightarrow{\hat{D}} \rangle$ will denote an approximate program execution, and $P = \langle E, \xrightarrow{T}, \xrightarrow{D} \rangle$ will denote the actual program execution (which is unknown).

7.1. Phase I: Detecting Apparent Data Races

The first phase of our data race detection method identifies the apparent data races. The apparent data races are located by first constructing the temporal ordering graph and then searching the graph for pairs of data-conflicting events, a and b, whose nodes have no connecting path (implying that $a \xleftrightarrow{\hat{T}}\!\!\!\!\!/\, b$). In general, these data races include all actual data races, plus additional races, both feasible and infeasible. This phase cannot distinguish among these types of races since doing so would require knowledge of the complete temporal ordering.

Because the apparent data races are detected using an approximate temporal ordering, not all apparent data races are always actual or feasible. Figure 1 showed an example of an apparent data race that was not feasible. However, we now prove that each actual data race is also an apparent data race. The naive method of simply reporting all apparent data races to the user (which is the approach of previous methods) is therefore safe in the sense that no actual data races are left undetected.

Theorem 7.1.
Every actual data race is also an apparent data race.

Proof.
If there is an actual data race between a and b, then $a \xleftrightarrow{T}\!\!\!\!\!/\, b$. To show that there is an apparent data race between a and b, we must show that $a \xleftrightarrow{\hat{T}}\!\!\!\!\!/\, b$. By definition, the temporal ordering graph is constructed so that $a \xrightarrow{\hat{T}} b \Rightarrow a \xrightarrow{T} b$ (see Section 3). We must show that this implies $a \xleftrightarrow{T}\!\!\!\!\!/\, b \Rightarrow a \xleftrightarrow{\hat{T}}\!\!\!\!\!/\, b$. Consider that the contrapositive of the assumption is $a \xrightarrow{T}\!\!\!\!\!/\, b \Rightarrow a \xrightarrow{\hat{T}}\!\!\!\!\!/\, b$, which is equivalent to $a \xrightarrow{T} b \vee a \xrightarrow{\hat{T}}\!\!\!\!\!/\, b$, or $a \xrightarrow{T} b \vee b \xrightarrow{\hat{T}} a \vee a \xleftrightarrow{\hat{T}}\!\!\!\!\!/\, b$. But if $a \xrightarrow{\hat{T}} b \Rightarrow a \xrightarrow{T} b$, then this becomes $a \xrightarrow{T} b \vee b \xrightarrow{T} a \vee a \xleftrightarrow{\hat{T}}\!\!\!\!\!/\, b$, or $\neg (a \xleftrightarrow{T}\!\!\!\!\!/\, b) \vee a \xleftrightarrow{\hat{T}}\!\!\!\!\!/\, b$, which is equivalent to $a \xleftrightarrow{T}\!\!\!\!\!/\, b \Rightarrow a \xleftrightarrow{\hat{T}}\!\!\!\!\!/\, b$. ∎

Note that the proof of Theorem 7.1 does not make use of the specifics of how the temporal ordering graph is constructed. Indeed, any approximate temporal ordering, $\xrightarrow{\hat{T}}$, with the property $a \xrightarrow{\hat{T}} b \Rightarrow a \xrightarrow{T} b$ is sufficient to allow all actual data races to be detected as apparent data races. However, the more exhaustively the program is traced, the more accurately the apparent data races can be validated, as is shown below. As we will also show below, apparent data races have the property that the presence of an apparent data race implies that there is a feasible data race somewhere in the program execution, implying that when no actual data races occur, no apparent data races will be reported.

7.2. Phase II: Validating Apparent Data Races

The first phase of our data race detection method locates a set of apparent data races. We now outline the second phase, which validates each apparent data race by attempting to determine whether or not the race is feasible. This determination is made by first augmenting the temporal ordering graph with edges representing a conservative estimate of the actual shared-data dependences, and then searching the augmented graph for certain types of cycles. Each apparent data race can be characterized either as being feasible, or as belonging to a set of apparent data races where at least one is feasible.

To show that an apparent data race between a and b is feasible, we must guarantee that some feasible program execution, $P' = \langle E, \xrightarrow{T'}, \xrightarrow{D} \rangle$, exists such that $a \xleftrightarrow{T'} b$. To determine the feasibility of a program execution requires knowledge of $\xrightarrow{D}$, the shared-data dependences exhibited by the observed execution. When only an approximate program execution is available, however, the exact shared-data dependences are not known. By using the conservative estimate of these dependences, $\xrightarrow{\hat{D}}$, we can guarantee that some feasible program executions must exist. We augment the temporal ordering graph with edges, called *shared-data dependence edges*, representing this conservative estimate. Let G be the temporal ordering graph. We construct the *augmented temporal ordering graph*, G_{AUG}, by augmenting G with edges that ensure there is a path from $\mathbf{a_s}$ to $\mathbf{b_f}$ whenever $a \xrightarrow{\hat{D}} b$. These edges ensure that any possible shared-data dependence from a to b would be allowed to occur in certain program executions defined by G_{AUG} (shown below in the proof of Theorem 7.2). If $a \xrightarrow{\hat{T}} b$, then a path from $\mathbf{a_s}$ to $\mathbf{b_f}$ already exists. Edges are therefore added only when $a \xleftrightarrow{\hat{T}} b$. In this case, edges are added from $\mathbf{a_s}$ to $\mathbf{b_f}$ and from $\mathbf{b_s}$ to $\mathbf{a_f}$ if there is a data conflict between a and b, or if a has a data conflict with some other event c that also has a data conflict with b and $a \xleftrightarrow{\hat{T}} c \xleftrightarrow{\hat{T}} b$.

In general, G_{AUG} may contain cycles, due to the conservative approximation made about the actual shared-data dependences. By classifying the apparent data races into those that participate in cycles and those that do not, some apparent data races can be guaranteed to be feasible. We say that two events, a and b, are *tangled* if either $\mathbf{a_s}$ and $\mathbf{b_f}$, or $\mathbf{b_s}$ and $\mathbf{a_f}$, belong to the same strongly connected component[†] of G_{AUG}. A *tangled data race* is an apparent data race between two tangled events. Each strongly connected component defines a set of tangled data races, called a *tangle*. We now show (in Theorem 7.2) that any apparent data race between two events that are not tangled is guaranteed to be feasible. We then show (in Theorem 7.3) that in each tangle, at least one of the apparent data races is guaranteed to be feasible.

Lemma 7.1.

For a given execution, assume $P = \langle E, \xrightarrow{T}, \xrightarrow{D} \rangle$ and $\hat{P} = \langle E, \xrightarrow{\hat{T}}, \xrightarrow{\hat{D}} \rangle$ are the associated complete and approximate program executions. Let G be the temporal ordering graph defining $\xrightarrow{\hat{T}}$, and let G_{AUG-D} be G augmented with edges representing the actual shared-data dependences, $\xrightarrow{D}$. Any linear ordering of the nodes of G_{AUG-D} is a global-time model that defines a temporal ordering relation, $\xrightarrow{T'}$, such that $P' = \langle E, \xrightarrow{T'}, \xrightarrow{D} \rangle$ is a feasible program execution.

Proof.

We introduce G_{AUG-D} as a device for showing that certain feasible program executions must exist. G_{AUG-D} is identical to G_{AUG}, except that edges representing shared-data depen-

---

† A strongly connected component has the property that there is path from every node in the component to every other node, but no path from a node in one component to a node in another component and back.

dences that did not actually occur do not appear (they were conservatively added to G_{AUG} so that no actual shared-data dependences were missed). Even though we do not have enough information to construct G_{AUG-D}, it nonetheless exists, and in Theorems 7.2 and 7.3 we prove that it must possess certain properties. In this Lemma, we prove that any linear ordering of the nodes of this graph can be used to define a feasible program execution. Any such linear ordering defines a temporal ordering that satisfies the conditions for feasibility. The shared-data dependence constraint (axiom A3) is satisfied since G_{AUG-D} contains shared-data dependence edges representing the actual shared-data dependences. The synchronization constraints (axioms A4-A6) are satisfied since G_{AUG-D} contains at least as many edges as G, and by definition, any linear ordering of G obeys axioms A4-A6.

Let L be any linear ordering of the nodes of G_{AUG-D}, and let $\xrightarrow{T'}$ be the temporal ordering defined by L. We first show that $\xrightarrow{T'}$ satisfies axioms A1-A6:

A1. The $\xrightarrow{T'}$ relation is irreflexive, since if $a \xrightarrow{T'} a$ for some event a, then $\mathbf{a_f}$ would have to appear before $\mathbf{a_s}$ in L, which is not possible, since by definition G contains an edge from $\mathbf{b_s}$ to $\mathbf{b_f}$ for every event b. By the same argument, the $\xrightarrow{T'}$ relation is asymmetric. The $\xrightarrow{T'}$ relation is transitive, since if $a \xrightarrow{T'} b \wedge b \xrightarrow{T'} c$, then $\mathbf{a_f}$ appears before $\mathbf{b_s}$ in L, and $\mathbf{b_f}$ appears before $\mathbf{c_s}$. Since an edge exists from $\mathbf{b_s}$ to $\mathbf{b_f}$ for every event b, it follows that $\mathbf{a_f}$ appears before $\mathbf{c_s}$ in L, implying that $a \xrightarrow{T'} c$.

A2. Assume a, b, c, d exist such that $a \xrightarrow{T'} b \xleftrightarrow{T'} c \xrightarrow{T'} d$. By the definition of $\xrightarrow{T'}$, L must contain the nodes $\mathbf{a_f}\ \mathbf{b_s}\ \mathbf{c_f}\ \mathbf{d_s}$, in this order, implying that $a \xrightarrow{T'} d$.

A3. Since G_{AUG-D} contains an edge from $\mathbf{a_s}$ to $\mathbf{b_f}$ whenever $a \xrightarrow{D} b$, $\mathbf{a_s}$ will precede $\mathbf{b_f}$ in L, implying that $b \not\xrightarrow{T'} a$.

A4-A6. Because G_{AUG-D} contains no fewer edges than G, axioms A4 through A6 are satisfied since, by definition, any linear ordering of G obeys these axioms.

Since $\xrightarrow{T'}$ satisfies axioms A1-A6, $P' = \langle E, \xrightarrow{T'}, \xrightarrow{D} \rangle$ is a feasible program execution. ∎

Theorem 7.2.
  If there is an apparent data race between a and b, and a and b are not tangled, then the data race is feasible.

Proof.
We first show that G_{AUG} contains no path from $\mathbf{a_f}$ to $\mathbf{b_s}$, and no path from $\mathbf{b_f}$ to $\mathbf{a_s}$, and then show that this implies the apparent data race between a and b is feasible.

To show that G_{AUG} contains no path from $\mathbf{a_f}$ to $\mathbf{b_s}$, and no path from $\mathbf{b_f}$ to $\mathbf{a_s}$, we will establish a contradiction by assuming there is a path from $\mathbf{a_f}$ to $\mathbf{b_s}$, or a path from $\mathbf{b_f}$ to $\mathbf{a_s}$. Since a and b are not tangled, only one such path can exist. Assume the path from $\mathbf{a_f}$ to $\mathbf{b_s}$ exists. Since an apparent data race exists between a and b, G_{AUG} contains shared-data dependence edges from $\mathbf{a_s}$ to $\mathbf{b_f}$, and from $\mathbf{b_s}$ to $\mathbf{a_f}$. But these edges create the path $\mathbf{a_f}\ \mathbf{b_s}\ \mathbf{a_f}$ in G_{AUG}, implying that $\mathbf{a_f}$ and $\mathbf{b_s}$ belong to the strongly connected component, which cannot be true since a and b are not tangled. Therefore, there can be no path from $\mathbf{a_f}$ to $\mathbf{b_s}$, and no path from $\mathbf{b_f}$ to $\mathbf{a_s}$.

We finally show that the apparent data race between a and b is feasible. Consider the graph G_{AUG-D}, constructed by augmenting the temporal ordering graph, G, with edges representing the shared-data dependences that were actually exhibited by the program execution (see the proof of Lemma 7.1). This graph contains no more edges than G_{AUG}, since the edges in G_{AUG} represent the conservative estimate of the actual shared-data dependences. Since G_{AUG} cannot contain a path from a_f to b_s, or a path from b_f to a_s, G_{AUG-D} cannot contain such paths either. There is thus a linear ordering of the nodes of G_{AUG-D} in which a_s appears before b_f, and b_s appears before a_f. This linear ordering is a global-time model that defines a temporal ordering, $\xrightarrow{T'}$, such that $a \xleftarrow{T'} b$. By Lemma 7.1, $P' = \langle E, \xrightarrow{T'}, \xrightarrow{D} \rangle$ is a feasible program execution. Therefore, the apparent data race between a and b is feasible. ∎

The above theorem shows that the apparent data races between events that are not tangled are guaranteed to be feasible. Not all of the remaining apparent data races are infeasible, however. We now show that, in each tangle, at least one tangled data race is guaranteed to be feasible. Without more precise knowledge of the actual shared-data dependences (or without examining the semantics of the program execution), we cannot determine exactly which tangled data races are feasible.

Lemma 7.2.

Let G be a temporal ordering graph, let G_{AUG} be G augmented with edges representing the conservative estimate of the actual shared-data dependences, and let G_{AUG-D} be G augmented with edges representing the actual shared-data dependences (see the proof of Lemma 7.1). Assume T is a set of tangled events defined by a strongly connected component of G_{AUG}. Then there exists two events $a, b \in T$ such that an apparent data race exists between a and b, and no path from a_f to b_s, or from b_f to a_s, exists in G_{AUG-D}.

Proof.

Let **T** be the set of nodes in G_{AUG-D} representing the events in T. To establish a contradiction, assume that for all events $a, b \in T$ such that there is an apparent data race between a and b, there is either a path from a_f to b_s, or a path from b_f to a_s, in G_{AUG-D}. Since a path from a_f to b_s and a path from b_f to a_s cannot both exist (G_{AUG-D} is acyclic), assume that the path from a_f to b_s exists. Since there is an apparent data race between a and b, no such path exists in G. The path in G_{AUG-D} must therefore contain at least one shared-data dependence edge, which cannot emanate from a_f. This path must contain nodes for two events, c and d, such that there is a path from a_f to c_s, a shared-data dependence edge from c_s to d_f, and a path from d_f to b_s. Such a path implies that $a \xrightarrow{T} c$ and $d \xrightarrow{T} b$. Furthermore, c and d must belong to T, since **T** contains a strongly connected component.

The shared-data dependence edge from c_s to d_f exists either because there is a data conflict between c and d (and therefore also an apparent data race), or because c data conflicts with some other event that data conflicts with d (a *transitive* data conflict). Assume that the edge exists because of an apparent data race between c and d. Since c and d belong to T, our contradiction assumption implies that there must be a path from c_f to d_s. By applying the above argument to c and d, we conclude that the path from c_f to d_s must contain nodes for two events, $e, f \in T$, such that there is a path from c_f to e_s, a shared-data dependence edge from e_s to

$\mathbf{f_f}$, and a path from $\mathbf{f_f}$ to $\mathbf{d_s}$. Such a path implies that $c \xrightarrow{T} e$ and $f \xrightarrow{T} d$. Since $a \xrightarrow{T} c$ and $d \xrightarrow{T} b$, the events e and f must be different than c and d. By inductively applying the above argument, we find that we always need two more events, x and y, belonging to T, that are different than all other events in T. Since T is finite, we eventually arrive at a contradiction.

If the shared-data dependence edge exists from $\mathbf{c_s}$ to $\mathbf{d_f}$ because of a transitive data conflict between c and d, event c must participate in an apparent data race with some event e that has a (possibly transitive) data conflict with d. By applying an argument similar to the one above to c and e, we also arrive at a contradiction. Therefore, two events, $a,b \in T$, must exist such that there is an apparent data race between a and b, and there is no path from $\mathbf{a_f}$ to $\mathbf{b_s}$, and no path from $\mathbf{b_f}$ to $\mathbf{a_s}$, in G_{AUG-D}. ∎

Theorem 7.3.

Let G_{AUG} be an augmented temporal ordering graph, and let T be the set of tangled events defined by some strongly connected component of G_{AUG}. At least one of the apparent data races in T is feasible.

Proof.

Let G_{AUG-D} be the temporal ordering graph augmented with edges representing the actual shared-data dependences (see the proof of Lemma 7.1). By Lemma 7.2, there exists two events $a,b \in T$ such that there is an apparent data race between a and b, and there is no path from $\mathbf{a_f}$ to $\mathbf{b_s}$, and no path from $\mathbf{b_f}$ to $\mathbf{a_s}$, in G_{AUG-D}. By the argument at the end of the proof of Theorem 7.2, there is a feasible program execution, $P' = \langle E, \xrightarrow{T'}, \xrightarrow{D} \rangle$, such that $a \xleftrightarrow{T'} b$, showing that the apparent data race between a and b is feasible. Therefore, at least one of the tangled data races is feasible. ∎

For each tangle, the above theorem guarantees that at least one tangled data race in the tangle is always feasible. As illustrated in Section 2, however, not all of the tangled data races are always feasible. An infeasible tangled data race exists only when the outcome of one tangled data race *affects* another tangled data race. A data race between a and b can affect a data race between c and d if (1) a or b modifies a shared variable, V, and (2) either the shared locations accessed by c or d, or the presence of c or d, depend upon V. The presence of c or d can depend upon V if the outcome of some conditional statement depends upon V, and the outcome might either delay the execution of c or d, or cause c or d to not execute at all. This notion is similar to the *hides* relation of Allen and Padua[1]. A future paper will describe how to employ these ideas to locate tangled data races that can be guaranteed feasible.

8. Conclusion

This paper has addressed two issues regarding data race detection. We first presented a formal model for reasoning about data races, and then presented a two-phase approach to data race detection that validates the accuracy of each detected data race. Our model distinguished among the data races that actually occurred (actual data races), that could have occurred (feasible data races), and that appeared to have occurred (apparent data races). Such a model allowed us to characterize the type of data races detected by previous methods, and to develop and argue the correctness of our two-phase approach. The first phase of this approach is essentially identical to previous methods and detects the apparent data races. We proved that all actual data races are detected by this phase. Unlike previous methods, we then employed a second phase that validates the apparent data races. This phase augments the temporal ordering graph with edges representing a conservative estimate of the shared-data dependences. An apparent data race is validated by determining whether the events involved in the race belong to the same strongly connected component. We proved that each apparent data race involving two events belonging to different strongly connected components (or none at all) is feasible, and in each set of races belonging to a strongly connected component, at least one is feasible.

We are currently investigating several issues related to this work. First, we are developing more precise analyses for locating those apparent data races that are feasible. As mentioned in Section 7, tangled data races are infeasible only when one tangled data race affects the outcome (or the existence) of another. By examining when one event can affect another, the notion of a feasible program execution can be extended to characterize what an execution could have done had different shared-data dependences occurred. Using this extended notion of feasibility, certain tangled data races can be shown to be feasible. Second, we are examining different classes of feasible data races. We have proven that the problem of detecting all feasible data races is NP-hard[16] (even when the complete program execution is known). However, certain classes of feasible data races can be efficiently detected. Third, we are developing techniques for providing efficient data race detection in practice. These techniques include efficient program instrumentation, and algorithms for actually constructing, augmenting and analyzing the temporal ordering graph. For example, it is not necessary to model each event with two nodes in the temporal ordering graph. By appropriately modeling the end of one event as the start of the next event (in the same process), only one node per event is required. We are also investigating techniques for efficiently recording the *READ* and *WRITE* sets for each computation event. In addition, even though we presented a two-phase scheme, data race validation does not necessarily require a post-mortem approach. It may be possible to perform the validation phase on-the-fly. Finally, the ideas presented in this paper can be applied to shared-memory parallel programs that use synchronization primitives other than semaphores, such as event variables, barriers, or rendezvous. To gain practical experience with these ideas, we are currently incorporating them into a parallel program debugger[3, 15] under development at the University of Wisconsin–Madison.

Acknowledgements

This research was supported in part by National Science Foundation grant CCR-8815928, Office of Naval Research grant N00014-89-J-1222, and a Digital Equipment Corporation External Research Grant.

References

1. Allen, T. R. and D. A. Padua, "Debugging Fortran on a Shared Memory Machine," *Proc. of Intl. Conf. on Parallel Processing*, pp. 721-727 St. Charles, IL, (Aug. 1987).

2. Bernstein, A. J., "Analysis of Programs for Parallel Processing," *IEEE Trans. on Electronic Computers* **EC-15**(5) pp. 757-763 (Oct. 1966).

3. Choi, J.-D., B. P. Miller, and R. H. B. Netzer, "Techniques for Debugging Parallel Programs with Flowback Analysis," *Comp. Sci. Dept. Tech. Rep. #786*, Univ. of Wisconsin-Madison, (Aug. 1988).

4. Dinning, A. and E. Schonberg, "An Empirical Comparison of Monitoring Algorithms for Access Anomaly Detection," *Proc. of ACM SIGPLAN Symp. on Principles and Practice of Parallel Programming*, pp. 1-10 Seattle, WA, (Mar. 1990).

5. Emrath, P. A. and D. A. Padua, "Automatic Detection Of Nondeterminacy in Parallel Programs," *Proc. of the Workshop on Parallel and Distributed Debugging*, pp. 89-99 Madison, WI, (May 1988). Also *SIGPLAN Notices* **24**(1) (Jan. 1989).

6. Emrath, P. A., S. Ghosh, and D. A. Padua, "Event Synchronization Analysis for Debugging Parallel Programs," *Supercomputing '89*, pp. 580-588 Reno,NV, (Nov. 1989).

7. Habermann, A. N., "Synchronization of Communicating Processes," *Communications of the ACM* **12**(3) pp. 171-176 (Mar. 1972).

8. Helmbold, D. P., C. E. McDowell, and J.-Z. Wang, "Analyzing Traces with Anonymous Synchronization," *Proc. of Intl. Conf. on Parallel Processing*, St. Charles, IL, (Aug. 1990).

9. Hood, R., K. Kennedy, and J. Mellor-Crummey, "Parallel Program Debugging with On-the-fly Anomaly Detection," *Supercomputing '90*, New York, NY, (Nov. 1990).

10. Kuck, D. J., R. H. Kuhn, B. Leasure, D. A. Padua, and M. Wolfe, "Dependence Graphs and Compiler Optimizations," *Conf. Record of the 8th ACM Symp. on Principles of Programming Languages*, pp. 207-218 Williamsburg, VA, (Jan. 1981).

11. Lamport, L., "How to Make a Multiprocessor Computer That Correctly Executes Multiprocess Programs," *IEEE Trans. on Computers* **C-28**(9) pp. 690-691 (Sep. 1979).

12. Lamport, L., "Interprocess Communication," *SRI Technical Report*, (Mar. 1985).

13. Lamport, L., "The Mutual Exclusion Problem: Part I — A Theory of Interprocess Communication," *Journal of the ACM* **33**(2) pp. 313-326 (Apr. 1986).

14. Mellor-Crummey, J. M., "Debugging and Analysis of Large-Scale Parallel Programs," *Ph.D. Thesis, also Comp. Sci. Dept. Tech. Rep. 312*, Univ. of Rochester, (Sep. 1989).

15. Miller, B. P. and J.-D. Choi, "A Mechanism for Efficient Debugging of Parallel Programs," *Proc. of the Conf. on Programming Language Design and Implementation*, pp. 135-144 Atlanta, GA, (June 1988). Also *SIGPLAN Notices* **23**(7) (July 1988).

16. Netzer, R. H. B. and B. P. Miller, "On the Complexity of Event Ordering for Shared-Memory Parallel Program Executions," *Proc. of Intl. Conf. on Parallel Processing*, St. Charles, IL, (Aug. 1990).

17. Nudler, I. and L. Rudolph, "Tools for the Efficient Development of Efficient Parallel Programs," *Proc. of 1st Israeli Conf. on Computer System Engineering*, (1988).

7 A Strategy for Array Management in Local Memory
C. Eisenbeis, W. Jalby, D. Windheiser, F. Bodin

Abstract One major point in loop restructuring for data locality optimization is the choice and the evaluation of data locality criteria. In this paper we show how to compute approximations of window sets defined by Gannon et al. [3]. The window associated with an iteration i describes the "active" portion of an array: elements that have already been referenced before iteration i and that will be referenced after iteration i. Such a notion is extremely useful for data localization because it identifies the portions of arrays that are worth keeping in local memory because they are going to be referenced later. The computation of these window approximations can be performed symbolically at compile time and generates a simple geometrical shape that simplifies the management of the data transfers. This strategy allows derivation of a global strategy of data management for local memories which may be combined efficiently with various parallelization and/or vectorization optimizations. Indeed, the effects of loop transformations fit naturally into the geometrical framework we use for the calculations. The determination of window approximations is studied both from a theoretical and a computational point of view, and examples of applications are given.

1 INTRODUCTION

The impressive progress in raw arithmetic performance achieved by the recent generation of RISC and superscalar monoprocessors has stressed the problem of designing a memory system able to keep up with the memory request rate of the processor. This issue, already critical in the monoprocessor case, is exacerbated for shared-memory multiprocessors where memory contention (due to conflicts either at the level of the communication medium between the memory and the processors or at the level of the memory itself) can severely degrade main memory performance (cf. hot spot contention [12]). To overcome this problem, one of the most frequently used techniques consists of designing hierarchically-organized memory systems with several levels: typically, a low level of very limited size but that provides very fast access time (scalar/vector registers), an intermediate level of larger size but slightly slower (cache or local memory) and a high level (the main memory itself). These levels differ not only in their physical characteristics, but also in the policy used for moving data between these levels: some are entirely managed by the compiler (registers, local memory), some are entirely managed by the hardware (standard caches) and some are combining hardware and software management (caches that can be flushed by special instructions).

The underlying assumption for using such a hierarchical organization is that most of the data accesses can be made from the low or intermediate levels with a fast access time. In fact, the performance of such memory organizations is far from being uniform over the programs and is highly dependent upon the characteristics of the address stream of a program: its temporal locality (a same memory address referenced several times) and its spatial locality (references to consecutive memory addresses). Consequently, the analysis and improvement of data locality for a given program is of major importance. Three subproblems must be distinguished:

1. Detection and estimation of data locality. This problem concerns the quantification of the locality properties of a code.

2. Exploitation of data locality. This issue is specific to levels where transfers have to be explicitly managed by the software (registers, local memory). In such cases, specific problems of coherence (due to the existence of multiple copies of the same data item) have to be solved [1].

3. Improvement of data locality. This point covers possible program transformations to be applied to increase data locality.

In general, the problem as stated above is extremely difficult to solve. Furthermore, for vector or multiprocessors, data locality is not the only issue to be addressed; vectorization and parallelization have to be taken into account too. For such architectures, the real problem is optimizing simultaneously data locality and parallelization (and/or vectorization): the difficulty of such combining these two kinds of optimization is that they may seriously conflict; for example increasing vector length (for improving the usage of vector units) may turn out to decrease the amount of data locality. Tradeoffs between the two objectives have to be adjusted, which requires a precise quantification of the two problems.

However, for simple loop structures containing only linear references to arrays (which constitute a large fraction of the CPU time spent in numerical applications), several interesting solutions have been proposed. Before reviewing them briefly, let us mention that most of the previous studies have focused on points 1 and 3 (in fact, the target systems were cache-based) and that parallelization and vectorization were not taken into account. In [3], Gannon et al. have proposed a methodology for detecting and evaluating data locality and deriving guidelines for driving simple program transformations. In particular, they introduced the concept of the window to characterize "active" portions of arrays which should be kept in the cache. In [13], Porterfield used a different approach based on simulation of simple cache organizations, trying to evaluate miss ratios. He was also able to estimate the impact of loop blocking on the miss ratio and to apply automatically such transformations when necessary. In [4], Gannon et al. specialized on a specific subproblem of point 2), namely analyzing and quantifying the portions of arrays touched by linear references inside multiple-nested loops. They also developed code generation techniques for transferring such portions of arrays efficiently between different memory levels. In [16], Lam et al. focused more specifically on the problem of developing a strategy for applying loop transformations to simultaneously optimize data locality and parallelism. The scope of transformations was extensive (including loop reversal, non rectangular tiling) and both temporal and spatial locality were taken into account.

However all the previous studies except [4] were targeted at cache-based systems, greatly simplifying the problem in the sense that the transfers between levels are entirely managed by hardware. At the opposite for registers or local memory, exploiting the locality associated with a memory location referenced several times requires explicitly transferring the content of that memory location either into a register or into a local memory location. Furthermore, coherence has to be maintained; even in the uniprocessor case, great care has to be taken to avoid having simultaneously in the local memory, arrays portions overlapping. In the multiprocessor case, the situation is even more complex due to the presence of local memories associated with each processor. In this paper we will focus our attention on local memory-based systems and will try to define a coherent strategy for exploiting data locality for such systems. The key advantage of our approach is that our strategy of local memory optimization is systematically quantified (especially its benefits in terms of main memory access saved), which allows us to combine it with the optimization of parallelization and vectorization.

In section 2, the general framework and the concept of windows (originally introduced in [3]) is described. A simple management algorithm for the local memory is presented using windows combined with some simple metrics (size and degree of locality). This algorithm relies on a formulation of the management problem as a knapsack problem for which good approximate solutions exist (cf. [14]). The main difficulty for applying such a management strategy consists in determining the windows and their associated characteristics (size and degree of locality). Section 3 gives results for determining window approximations in the most common cases of linear addressing. In particular, window approximations are given in an analytical form which is of major interest for analyzing the impact of loop transformations. Section 4 indicates how these results can be used for driving loop restructuring, taking into account vectorization and/or parallelization criteria.

2 MOTIVATIONS AND FRAMEWORK

2.1 Some notations

For sake of clarity, we will restrict our analysis to data accessed by atomic references in structured variables within a set of perfectly nested (normalized) loops:

```
         DO 1 i₁ = 1, N₁
            DO 1 i₂ = 1, N₂
               ...
               DO 1 iₖ = 1, Nₖ
     S₁              ··· A[h(i₁, i₂, ···, iₖ)]
      ⋮                    ⋮
     S₂              ··· A[g(i₁, i₂, ···, iₖ)]
   1     CONTINUE
```

where the identifier A denotes an array of dimension d, and h and g are affine mappings from Z^k to Z^d. Furthermore we will assume that the loop body does not contain any procedure call or conditional statements.

We use the standard definitions for data dependencies (cf. [7], [8], [9], [10], and [11]). The reason for using the framework of data dependence analysis, originally introduced for vectorization, is that both vectorization problems and locality optimization have some strong common relations. In the first problem, the issue is to detect whether a specific memory location is referenced twice in order to enforce an execution order to preserve program semantics. For optimizing data locality, the first step is locality detection, which amounts to detecting if a same memory location is referenced several times. The major difference between the two problems is that, for data locality optimization, a quantitative measure is required (how many times the same memory location is referenced). Another difference is that in addition to the three classical dependencies (flow dependence, anti-dependence, and output dependence), we need to consider systematically input dependence, which arises whenever two successive reads are performed from the same memory location.

The *iteration space* $C \subset Z^k$ is defined by $C = \prod_{j=1}^{k}[1, N_j]$. The size of the iteration space is equal to $N = \prod_{j=1}^{k} N_j$. Each occurrence of an instruction is identified by an iteration vector $\vec{i} = (i_1, i_2, \cdots, i_k) \in C$ which specifies the current values of the loop indexes.

In the sequel, we will refer to a special of type of dependence which is very common:

Definition 2.1 (Uniformly Generated Dependencies)

A Uniformly Generated Dependence is a dependence existing between two statements S_1 and S_2 referencing respectively $X(h(\vec{i}) + d_1)$ and $X(h(\vec{i}) + d_2)$, where h is a mapping from Z^k to Z^d.

According to the semantics of a sequential nest of loops, the different occurrences of an instruction in the loop body are executed in lexicographic order. The order in which the different occurrences of instruction S are executed can be alternatively characterized by the *timing function*, which is a one-to-one mapping between C and $\{1, \ldots, N\}$. The *timing function* T is formally defined by: $T(\vec{i}) = T(i_1, i_2, \ldots, i_k) = \sum_{j=1}^{k}[(i_j - 1)P_j] + 1$ where $P_j = \prod_{q=j+1}^{k} N_q$ and $P_k = 1$. In cases where no ambiguity is possible, the iteration vector $\vec{i}$ and the corresponding time step $t = T(\vec{i})$ will be identified.

2.2 Definition of the window

For the moment, let us assume that the local memory is infinitely large and no coherence problem arises. With such assumptions, the optimal strategy for maximizing data reuse is rather straightforward: load the data in the local memory the first time it is referenced, then keep it in local memory. In practice, the limited size of local memories requires a more elaborate strategy; at least, we need to know how long the data is used so that after its last use, the data can be discarded and the freed local memory space can be reused. The basic idea of the window concept is to quantify precisely at each time t the portions of data arrays which are "alive" (i.e., which are worth keeping in local memory).

Definition 2.2 (Reference Window) *The reference window, $W_t(\delta_X)$, for a dependence $\delta_X : S_1 \rightarrow S_2$ on a variable X at time t is defined to be the set of all elements of X that are referenced by S_1 at or before t that are also referenced (according to the dependence) after t by S_2.*

For the sake of simplicity, when no ambiguity is possible, we will identify the reference window with the underlying set of indices.

Let us give an example of window:

```
       DO 1 i₁ = 1, N₁
       S₁           A(i₁) = X(i₁)
       S₂           D(i₁) = X(i₁ − 3)
   1   CONTINUE
```

The loop above has an input dependence δ_X^i from $S_1 < i_1 >$ to $S_2 < i_1 + 3 >$. If we set a breakpoint at the top of iteration $i_1 > 3$, we see:

$$W_{t=i_1}(\delta_X^i) = \{X(i_1 - 3), X(i_1 - 2), X(i_1 - 1)\} \tag{1}$$

If at any time t the corresponding window can be kept in the local memory (or registers), half of the memory references can be saved; in fact all the data accesses performed by S_2 on X can be done from the local memory.

In a more general way, we can prove the following property concerning reference windows:

Property 2.1 *Let us define the following loading strategy for the local memory:*

At any time t all the elements which are contained in $W_t(\delta_X)$ and were not already in $W_{t-1}(\delta_X)$ are loaded in the local memory, whereas all the elements in $W_{t-1}(\delta_X)$ which are no longer in $W_t(\delta_X)$ are discarded. In the following we make the assumption that the local memory is large enough to hold all these elements.

Then all the accesses made by S_2 on data already referenced by S_1 can be performed from local memory, and the cost in terms of local memory space is minimized.

This property stems directly from the definition of a reference window.

If the dependency graph contained only one arc (therefore only one reference window will be present), the previous property would give an intuitive guideline for loading the local memory. However, in practice, data dependency graphs contains many edges; therefore several window references are present and will compete for local memory space. This requires a more quantitative evaluation of the locality properties of a reference window:

Definition 2.3 (Cost and Benefit of a Reference Window)

*The **cost** of a reference window associated to a dependence δ_X is defined as:*
$Cost(W(\delta_X)) = \max_t |W_t(\delta_X)|$ *where $|W_t(\delta_X)|$ denotes the number of distinct elements of $W_t(\delta_X)$.*

*The **benefit** $Ben(W(\delta_X))$ of a reference window associated to the dependence δ_X is defined as the maximal number of data references performed by S_2 which can be executed from the local memory instead of the main memory (assuming the ideal loading strategy described in 2.1 is used).*

The cost and benefit metrics try to summarize the pros and cons of trying to keep a given window in local memory, over the whole loop execution. The cost estimates how much local memory space is required, while the benefit captures how many main memory references are saved. In our example, the costs and benefits associated with the window W are: $Cost(W(\delta_X)) = 3$ and $Ben(W(\delta_X)) = N_1 - 3$.

Although reference windows are very attractive from a theoretical point of view, their practical determination is in general extremely complex. A first problem is that their size and shape vary over time; in the previous example, at time 2 (beginning of second iteration), the window contains only one element $\{X(1)\}$. Then, at time 3, it contains two elements $\{X(1), X(2)\}$. It is only after the third iteration that the window has the generic shape as described by equation (1). For that reason, instead of dealing with exact reference windows, one solution consists in enclosing the reference window in a window slightly larger but with a much more regular behavior:

Definition 2.4 (Approximate Windows)

An **approximate window** *associated with a reference window* $W_t(\delta_X)$ *is a couple constituted of a mapping* m *from* Z^k *on* Z^d *and* W *a subset of* Z^d *such that for all* t, $\forall t, \; W_{t=\vec{i}}(\delta_X) \subset \{X(\vec{j}) / \vec{j} \in m(\vec{i}) + W\}$. *The number of elements of* W *is called the* **cost** *of the approximated window (denoted* $Cost(W)$).

For our example given above, an approximate window is: $m(i_1) = i_1 - 3$, $W = \{0, 1, 2\}$, $Cost(W) = 3$.

The key idea of the formulation of approximate windows is that the windows are enclosed in a moving frame of constant shape and size. First, using approximate windows instead of the exact reference windows simplifies greatly the evaluation of the local memory space required to hold the window and therefore will allow us to design a tractable management strategy. Second, the simple formula governing the motion of the window will reduce the complexity of loading the local memory: determining the set of elements which are contained in the approximate window at time t and were not in the window at time $t-1$ amounts to computing the difference between two sets which differ by a translation.

Finally, the impact of program transformation can easily be analyzed, and the task of selecting the more appropriate program transformation is made much easier. On the other hand, the approximation has to be accurate enough in order to avoid loading a large number of unnecessary elements.

Let us end this subsection with a slightly more complex example.

```
            DO 1 i₁ = 1, N₁
               DO 1 i₂ = 1, N₂
      S              B(i₁,i₂) = A(i₁ + i₂)
   1        CONTINUE
```

The loop above contains a self input-dependence on S due to A. At the beginning of iteration (i_1, i_2), the corresponding window is given by:

$$W_{t=(i_1,i_2)}(\delta_A^i) = \{A(j_1, j_2) / \ i_1 + 1 < j_1 + j_2 < i_1 + N_2\}$$

An approximate window is obtained by taking: $m(i_1, i_2) = i_1$ and $W = [1, N_2]$.

The cost is: $Cost(W) = N_2$. The computation of the benefit requires some more thought; the total number of accesses performed by S on A is $N_1 N_2$ and the number of **distinct** elements of A which are referenced is $N_1 + N_2 - 1$. In fact, it is easy to check that the set of elements referenced by S is $\{A(j) \ / \ 2 \leq j \leq N_1 + N_2\}$. Keeping the window inside the local memory allows us to save $N_1 N_2 - (N_1 + N_2 - 1)$ main memory references.

2.3 A global strategy for managing local memory

In a first approach, we will assume that there is no attempt to restructure the code for increasing data locality.

For determining a local memory management, three basic strategies have to be defined:

- LOADING STRATEGY: when to load an element or a portion of an array and in this latter case what portion of the array needs to be loaded

- UNLOADING STRATEGY: when to discard data or a portion of an array that was stored in local memory; furthermore if the data were modified, this requires writing it back to main memory

- MAINTAINING COHERENCE: inside the same processor and between processors.

2.3.1 Coherence constraints

Let us first state the problem in the uniprocessor case, on the following example:

```
            DO 1 i₁ = 1, N₁
               DO i₂ = 1, N₂
      S₁             X(h(i₁,i₂)) = ···
      S₂             ··· = ···X(g(i₁,i₂))···
   1        CONTINUE
```

where X is a one-dimensional array and h and g are two mappings from Z^2 onto Z.

In general there will be 4 dependencies and 4 windows associated:

$$\delta_{11}^o : S_1 \to S_1 \quad W_t(\delta_{11}^o) \qquad \delta_{12}^f : S_1 \to S_2 \quad W_t(\delta_{12}^f)$$
$$\delta_{21}^a : S_2 \to S_1 \quad W_t(\delta_{21}^a) \qquad \delta_{22}^i : S_2 \to S_2 \quad W_t(\delta_{22}^i)$$

If we apply the simple strategy described in the previous section, we will end up having 4 different windows (covering parts of the same array) coexisting in the local memory. A priori these four windows will be stored in disjoint subsets of memory locations: more precisely, if 2 windows overlap (which will be very likely when dealing with approximate windows), a same array element will have 2 different copies simultaneously alive in the local memory. The problem arises when one of these copies is modified, the other one needs to be either modified or invalidated accordingly. Such a phenomenon does appear in cache systems but is entirely managed by hardware [1]. In order to solve this problem, the idea is to avoid having multiple copies of the array element. For achieving that, we will use the notion of **Dominant Window** (DW_t), which has the main property to be such that for all t: $W_t(\delta_{11}^o) \cup W_t(\delta_{12}^f) \cup W_t(\delta_{21}^a) \cup W_t(\delta_{22}^i) \subset DW_t$

Let us define more formally the notion of **Dominant Window** :

Definition 2.5 (Dominant Window) *Let G be a connected component of the atomic data dependence graph related to the array X, a Dominant Window associated with G (noted $W_t(G)$) is a set of elements such that:*

$$\forall t \text{ and } \forall \delta \in G \quad W_t(\delta) \subset W_t(G)$$
$$\forall t, \quad DW_{t=\vec{i}}(G) = \{X(\vec{j}) / \vec{j} \in m(\vec{i}) + W\}$$

where m is a mapping from Z^k on Z^d and W a subset of Z^d.

The first condition imposed on the Dominant Window is going to enforce that every array element referenced will have a single copy present in the local memory. The second condition which is very similar to the condition imposed on the Approximate Windows simplifies the management of the Dominant Windows. In fact, in practice, we will first determine Approximate Windows, and then compute the Dominant Window using these approximate windows. In the case where all the dependencies involved are uniformly generated, the determination of a Dominant Window will be easy, because as we will see in subsequent sections, each of the reference windows $W_t(\delta)$ can be enclosed in an approximate window with the same mapping m: $\forall t, \forall \delta, W_{t=veci}(\delta) \subset m(\vec{i}) + W(\delta)$ where $W(\delta)$ is a subset of X depending only upon δ and no more upon time. Therefore, the determination of the Dominant Window amounts to compute a set containing all the $W(\delta)$.

In the case where not all the dependencies are uniformly generated, the computation of the Dominant Window might be extremely complex; for such a case, we chose the extreme solution of computing a Dominant Window for the whole loop entirely independent of time, which in fact amounts to compute "regions" as defined in [4]. The price of such a solution is that a large space in local memory may be wasted because the data stored in it will be referenced only at the beginning of the loop and not after that.

The problem of maintaining the coherence in the multiprocessor case with different local memories is much tougher because we need to propagate data from one local memory to another [15]. The approach which can be used is similar to the one proposed for a shared memory system. Independently of the presence of local memories, the existence of a data dependency across processors will require the generation of synchronization instructions to make sure that each processor gets the right value. In this case, the array element is in fact stored in local memory; the only thing needed is to generate code to explicitly move the data from one local memory to another, and this code will have to be inserted just before the synchronization instruction.

2.3.2 The complete algorithm

For the sake of clarity, let us consider the uniprocessor case. The algorithm proceeds in 5 steps:

1. Build the atomic dependence graph G.

2. For every dependence δ in the dependence graph, compute an approximate window $W(\delta)$

3. For every connected component G' in the data dependence graph, generate the Dominant Window $DW(G')$ as well its cost $Cost(DW(G'))$ and its benefit $Ben(DW(G'))$.

4. Solve the following knapsack problem:

   Find Γ a subset of the connected components such that:

   $$\begin{cases} \sum_{G' \in \Gamma} Cost(DW(G')) \leq LMS \\ \sum_{G' \in \Gamma} Ben(DW(G')) \text{ is maximal} \end{cases}$$

   where LMS stands for the local memory size. This knapsack problem is approximated via standard polynomial algorithms [14].

5. Then for every dependence in the set Δ, the corresponding windows are loaded into the local memory according to the strategy defined in 2.1.

It should be noted that two successive approximations of the reference window will be performed: first for computing the approximate windows then for computing the Dominant Window. In some very particular case (all the dependencies involved are input dependencies), the second approximation can be avoided.

Our final algorithm for the management of local memory will be the one described previously except that the determination of windows will be limited to uniformly generated dependencies.

3 Window Computation

This section presents the key points that allow us to compute symbolically approximated windows. For sake of simplicity, we show the case of data reuse due to a self reference $X(h(\vec{i}))$, where h is a linear mapping from the iteration space $C \subset Z^k$ into Z^d but the results extend directly to more general uniformly generated dependencies. Details and extensions of following results can be found in [2], just as code generation issues.

3.1 General Results

The first result is based on the use of the timing function (section 2.1) for rewriting the definition of the window: $T(\vec{i}) = T(i_1, i_2, \ldots, i_k) = \sum_{j=1}^{k}[(i_j - 1).P_j] + 1$ where $P_j = \prod_{q=j+1}^{k} N_q$ and $P_k = 1$.

Theorem 3.1 (Window Characterization)

The hyperplane $\mathcal{T}_t = \{\vec{i} \in Q^k, T(\vec{i}) = t\}$ splits the iteration space C into two regions C_t^- and C_t^+ such that $C_t^- = \{\vec{i} \in C \mid T(\vec{i}) \leq t\}$ and $C_t^+ = \{\vec{i} \in C \mid T(\vec{i}) > t\}$.

The reference window W_t at time t is equal to $W_t = h(C_t^-) \cap h(C_t^+)$.

From this characterization we deduce a first window approximation: instead of computing the intersection of the images of the two parts C_t^- and C_t^+, we compute the image of the frontier between the both: $\mathcal{F}_t = \mathcal{T}_t \cap \mathcal{E}$ where $\mathcal{E}$ contains all rational points of iteration space: $\mathcal{E} = \{(q_1, \cdots, q_k)/\forall i\ q_i \in Q \text{ and } 1 \leq q_i \leq N_i\}$.

Theorem 3.2 (First Window Approximation)

Let $\hat{W}_t$ be defined as: $\hat{W}_t = h(\mathcal{F}_t) \cap h(Z^k)$, then $W_t \subset \hat{W}_t$.

The shape of $\mathcal{F}_t$ varies over time, due to iterations bounds, making the window quite complex to deal with. To overcome this difficulty, we introduce the sets $\mathcal{F}_t^p = \mathcal{T}_t \cap \mathcal{E}^p, p \in \{1, \cdots, k\}$, where $\mathcal{E}^p = \{(q_1, \cdots, q_k)/ \forall i, q_i \in Q \text{ and } \forall i \in [1, p-1] \cup [p+1, k], 1 \leq q_i \leq N_i\}$. These sets present the advantage of having a much simpler geometric form and facilitate computations: for example, in 2D-space, the computation of $\mathcal{F}_t^p$ amounts to computing the intersection of a line with a stripe, while the computation of $\mathcal{F}_t$ amounts to compute the intersection of a line with a parallelogram. Moreover, the shape of $\mathcal{F}_t^p$ does not depend upon time.

Lemma 3.1 (Geometric Properties of $\mathcal{F}_t^p$)

$\forall\, t,\, t' \in \{1, \cdots, N\}$ and $\forall p \in \{1, \cdots, k\}$, $\mathcal{F}_t$ satisfies the following properties:

(i) $\mathcal{F}_t = \bigcap_{p=1}^{k} \mathcal{F}_t^p$

(ii) $\mathcal{F}_t^p$ is a parallelepiped

(iii) $\mathcal{F}_{t'}^p = \Theta_{\vec{u}}(\mathcal{F}_t^p)$ where $\Theta_{\vec{u}}$ is the translation of vector $\vec{u} = \frac{t'-t}{P_p}\vec{e}_p$.

This permits to define now **approximate windows**, in the sense of definition 2.4:

Theorem 3.3 (Second Window Approximation)

Let $\hat{W}_t^p = h(\mathcal{F}_t^p) \cap h(Z^k)$

- $\forall p \in \{1, \ldots, k\}$, $\hat{W}_t \subset \hat{W}_t^p$

- $\forall\, t,\, t' \in \{1, \ldots, N\}$, $\hat{W}_t^p = \Theta_{\vec{v}}(h(\mathcal{F}_1^p)) \cap h(Z^k)$, where $\Theta_{\vec{v}}$ is the translation of vector $\vec{v} = \frac{t-1}{P_p}h(\vec{e}_p)$.

From Theorems 3.2 and 3.3, we deduce the approximation chain for W_t:

$$\boxed{W_t \subset \hat{W}_t \subset \hat{W}_t^p, \forall p \in \{1, \cdots, k\}}$$

The next step in estimating the locality of a code is to evaluate the **cost** of the reference window (i.e, the maximum number of distinct elements in the window over time). Let us notice that the determination of this number may be complex: it represents the number of points with integer coordinates in the window, which may depend of the location of the window in the whole space and may therefore vary over time. The cost is often approximated and we will see in section 4.5 a example of approximation error (second order in the loop bounds) this may cause.

By using the previous chain, two approximations of the cost of the window W_t can be derived; the first one corresponds to the selection of an arbitrary integer p and the use of the number of elements of $\hat{W}_t^p$ for computing the approximation to the cost of W. The second requires the evaluation of all the costs associated with all the $\hat{W}_t^p$, then taking the minimum over p.

3.2 Examples of Window Computation

In this section, we apply the general results of the previous section to some special cases of mapping h of practical interest (in other words, which occur frequently in numerical computations). Previous results and a powerful approach detailed in [2] allow us to use a geometric approach for approximate windows computation and to consider the windows as projections of simple $(k-1)$-dimensional parallelepipeds on s-dimensional space, where s is the rank of the function h.

For each case, the window size can be determined analytically in function of the loop bounds and the mapping h. We give here some examples of results this approach permits to obtain. First, the case of an arbitrary linear mapping from Z^2 onto Z, then the generalization to the case where h is a $Z^k \to Z$ mapping are analyzed. This covers the cases when the rank of h is 1, by changing the basis as explained in [2]. Moreover, from a theoretical point of view, this even allows us to deal with the general case of the mapping Z^k onto Z^d by using linearization of d-dimensional arrays: the linearization procedure amounts to defining a linear function l from Z^d onto Z. Therefore the whole problem can be reformulated using the composition of the two mappings $h \circ l$, which is a Z^k onto Z mapping. However, one drawback of linearization is that the bounds of the array must be taken into account, introducing new variables in the computation; moreover the linearization procedure destroys the structure of the array that may help in code generation.

Last, we study the case of simple projections composed with permutations. This case is an important one (it appears in the matrix-matrix product, for example) and is very easy to handle in our geometrical framework.

For a $Z^2 \to Z$ mapping $h(i_1, i_2) = \lambda_1 i_1 + \lambda_2 i_2$, we obtain the following result:

Theorem 3.4

Let $\delta = \gcd(\lambda_1, \lambda_2)$. The approximate windows $\hat{W}_t^1$ and $\hat{W}_t^2$ are

$$\hat{W}_t^1 = (\frac{\lambda_1}{N_2}t + W^1) \cap \delta Z$$

where $W^1 = [min_{i_2 \in [1, N_2]} \lfloor \lambda_1 + \frac{1}{N_2}(\lambda_2 N_2 - \lambda_1) i_2 \rfloor, max_{i_2 \in [1, N_2]} \lceil \lambda_1 + \frac{1}{N_2}(\lambda_2 N_2 - \lambda_1) i_2 \rceil]$ and:

$$\hat{W}_t^2 = (\lambda_2 t + W^2) \cap \delta Z$$

where $W^2 = [min_{i_1 \in [1, N_1]} \lfloor (\lambda_1 - \lambda_2 N_2) i_1 + \lambda_2 N_2 \rfloor, max_{i_1 \in [1, N_1]} \lceil (\lambda_1 - \lambda_2 N_2) i_1 + \lambda_2 N_2 \rceil]$

This approximation gives a bound for the **cost** of the approximate window (definition 2.4):

Theorem 3.5

$$Cost(W) \leq \lfloor \tfrac{1}{\delta} \cdot \lvert \tfrac{N_2-1}{N_2}(\lambda_1 - \lambda_2 N_2) \rvert \rfloor + 1$$

This generalizes in the next theorem to the case when h is a $Z^k \to Z$ mapping:
$h(i_1, i_2, \cdots, i_k) = \lambda_1 i_1 + \lambda_2 i_2 + \cdots + \lambda_k i_k$

Theorem 3.6 *Let* $\delta = \gcd(\lambda_1, \lambda_2, \cdots, \lambda_k)$.

$$Cost(W) \leq \min_{p=1}^{k} \lfloor \tfrac{1}{\delta} \lvert \sum_{j=1, j \neq p}^{k} \tfrac{N_j - 1}{P_p} \lvert \lambda_j P_p - \lambda_p P_j \rvert \rvert \rfloor + 1$$

Now we give the results for the case where h is a simple projection composed with a permutation: h is from Z^k to Z^d and is defined by $h(i_1, i_2, \cdots, i_k) = (i_{\pi(1)}, i_{\pi(2)}, i_{\pi(d)})$, where π is a one-to-one mapping from $\{1, \cdots, d\}$ onto a d-elements subset Π of $\{1, 2, \cdots, k\}$.

The following approximation can be proved [2]:

Theorem 3.7

$$Cost(W) \leq \min(\min_{r=1}^{d}([\prod_{q=1, q \neq r}^{d} N_{\pi(q)}] \tfrac{1}{P_{\pi(r)}} [\sum_{j=1, j \neq \pi(r)}^{k} P_j N_j)], \prod_{q=1}^{d} N_{\pi(q)})$$

This formula will be used in the next section for the case of a matrix-matrix multiply.

4 LOOP TRANSFORMATIONS

In this section, the impact of loop transformations such as loop interchange, blocking or reversal on data locality is analyzed. Using the analytical characterizations for windows approximations detailed in the previous section, such an impact can be studied very easily, therefore simplifying the process of determining the most appropriate loop transformation for optimizing data locality, taking into account parallelization constraints.

4.1 Expressing the benefits of loop transformations

Up to now, all the computations were performed for a given loop structure and the goal was to exploit at best the data locality exhibited by the original loop structures. A much more powerful approach consists in transforming loops in such a way that data locality is increased. The problem is complex because all the legal transformations have to be considered: this number might be fairly large, for example, in a k-nested DO-loop, assuming any loop interchange is legal, there are $k!$ possible forms. Moreover, among all the possible transformations, one has to select the transformation yielding the "largest" data locality but which also preserves a sufficient amount of parallelism: in fact a subtle trade-off has to be reached in optimizing simultaneously these two criteria. For cache-based systems, Lam et al. describe a systematic methodology for reducing the complexity of searching the best solution ([16]).

In our case, the situation is different since via windows we have an entire control of the way locality is going to be exploited. Moreover the structure of the windows as well as its costs and benefits can be expressed in an analytical manner in function of h, the timing formula, and the loop bounds. Therefore any change of these parameters will not require any extra computation but just substitution. Let us examine the three cases:

- Changing the mapping h. This transformation corresponds either to the case where the array is restructured before loop execution or the case of loop reversal.

- Changing the timing function T. This corresponds to loop interchange, which might be viewed as a different sweep of the iteration space.

- Changing the loop bounds. This might be used for investigating loop blocking strategies; the amount of locality exhibited by the inner blocks can be easily obtained by substituting the values of the block sizes in place of the original loop bounds. Moreover, because of the simple analytical expressions of the window size, the values of the block sizes maximizing locality usage can be determined.

As a consequence, the computations of the window for a given loop may guide for the choice of a good transformation, and eliminate a priori a large set of transformations that would otherwise have had to be tried explicitly.

In the next section, we show how to express the usual transformations in our framework.

4.2 Example of loop interchange

As mentioned above, loop interchange can be viewed as a change in the timing function. For instance, instead of having $T(i_1, i_2) = (i_1 - 1)N_2 + i_2$, we get $T'(i_1, i_2) = (i_2 - 1)N_1 + i_1$. As an example, let us consider the loop

$$\text{DO } 1 \; i_1 = 1, 20$$
$$\text{DO } 1 \; i_2 = 1, 30$$
$$\cdots A(4 * i_1 - 6 * i_2) \cdots$$
$$1 \qquad \text{CONTINUE}$$

For this configuration, by applying the formula of section 3, ($N_1 = 20, N_2 = 30, \lambda_1 = 4, \lambda_2 = -6, \delta = 2$), we obtain a window of size:
$Cost(W) = \lfloor \frac{1}{\delta} | \frac{N_2 - 1}{N_2}(\lambda_1 - \lambda_2 N_2) | \rfloor + 1 = \mathbf{89}$. Now, assuming loop interchange is legal, such

a transformation would result in a new window of size: $Cost(W') = \lfloor \frac{1}{\delta} | \frac{N_1 - 1}{N_1}(\lambda_2 - \lambda_1 N_1)|\rfloor + 1$
$= 41$. It should be noted that in both cases, the benefit associated with each window will be the same (in fact loop interchanging does not affect that characteristic); therefore it is preferable to choose the second loop order, since it will provide the same benefit at a lower cost in terms of local memory space.

4.3 Loop Reversal

Loop reversal amounts to a change in the mapping h; reversing the innermost loop on i_2 in the previous loop results in:

$$\text{DO 1 } i_1 = 1, 20$$
$$\text{DO 1 } i_2 = 1, 30$$
$$\cdots A(4 * i_1 - 6 * (30 - i_2 + 1)) \cdots$$
$$1 \qquad \text{CONTINUE}$$

The coefficient $\lambda_2 = -6$ of i_2 in h is changed into $\lambda'_2 = 6$. So the size of new window is: $Cost(W'') = \lfloor \frac{1}{\delta} | \frac{N_2 - 1}{N_2}(\lambda_1 - \lambda'_2 N_2)|\rfloor + 1 = 86$.

Now if we first perform interchanging followed by a loop reversal of the innermost loop, it is easy to check that we obtain a final window of size **36**. Since the benefit is affected neither by loop interchanging nor loop reversal, this latter form results in the best solution.

4.4 Loop Blocking

Loop blocking consists in dividing the iteration space into smaller blocks and modifying the way the iteration space is swept. The innermost loops consists in sweeping the iterations inside a block while the outermost loops define the order in which the blocks themselves are executed. The window relative to the iterations associated within a block can be easily computed by substituting the values of the block size. For instance, the latter loop could be blocked (if semantically legal) in the following way:

$$\text{DO 1 } j_1 = 1,20,b_1$$
$$\text{DO 1 } j_2 = 1,30,b_2$$
$$\text{DO 1 } i_1 = j_1, \min(20, j_1 + b_1 - 1)$$
$$\text{DO 1 } i_2 = j_2, \min(30, j_2 + b_2 - 1)$$
$$\cdots A(4 * i_1 - 6 * i_2) \cdots$$
$$1 \qquad \text{CONTINUE}$$

where b_1 and b_2 give the block sizes. The size of the resulting window (when considering the two innermost loops) is: $Cost(W_b) = \lfloor \frac{1}{\delta} | \frac{b_2 - 1}{b_2}(\lambda_1 - \lambda_2 b_2)|\rfloor + 1$. By choosing $b_2 = 15$, the resulting window size is **44**. If before blocking, loop interchange was performed, the resulting size of the window would have been: $Cost(W_{ib}) = \lfloor \frac{1}{6} | \frac{b_1-1}{b_1}(\lambda_2 - \lambda_1 b_1) | \rfloor + 1 = \mathbf{21}$, for $b_1 = 10$, for example. For each case, the benefit depends on b_1 and b_2: $Ben(W_b) = Ben(W_{ib}) = b_1 b_2 - 2b_1 - 3b_2 + 4$. This formula is obtained as the difference between the total number of references to the array A ($b_1 b_2$) and the number of *distinct* elements referenced ($2b_1 + 3b_2 - 4$).

Now, let us try to solve the inverse problem: assuming that blocking is semantically legal, let us compute the maximal size of the block such that the corresponding window requires less than S memory locations. This consists in finding b_1 and b_2 such that:
$\lfloor \frac{1}{6} | \frac{b_2-1}{b_2}(\lambda_1 - \lambda_2 b_2) | \rfloor + 1 \leq S$ (for the first case when innermost loop is on i_2) or
$\lfloor \frac{1}{6} | \frac{b_1-1}{b_1}(\lambda_2 - \lambda_1 b_1) | \rfloor + 1 \leq S$ (for the second case when innermost loop is on i_1).

Let us notice that it is useless to block the i_1-loop in the first case because b_1 does not appear in the formula, and to block the i_2-loop in the interchanged loop for the same reason. Suppose $S = 16$, we can choose $b_2 = 5$ (first case) and $b_1 = 7$ (second case), so that the whole window fits into the memory.

When a true 2-dimensional blocking is not possible because of the presence of data dependencies, it is always possible to block the innermost loop. Then, we can still apply the window theory to that innermost loop and determine the best blocking.

This section has shown how to handle the loop transformations in our framework. We have seen that they result in very minor changes in the window computation, and also that they provide interesting guidelines for the choice of a transformation to improve data locality.

4.5 Matrix-matrix Product

Let us consider the computation of the product of a matrix B of size $N_1 \times N_2$ by a matrix C of size $N_2 \times N_3$, the result being stored in a matrix A of size $N_1 \times N_3$. After a phase of initialization, the computation looks like :

```
        DO 1 i₁ = 1, N₁
           DO 1 i₂ = 1, N₂
              DO 1 i₃ = 1, N₃
                 A(i₁,i₃) = A(i₁,i₃) + B(i₁,i₂) * C(i₂,i₃)
    1      CONTINUE
```

The size of the window has to be evaluated for the the six possible orders of nesting (i_1, i_2, i_3), (i_1, i_3, i_2), (i_2, i_1, i_3), (i_2, i_3, i_1), (i_3, i_1, i_2), (i_3, i_2, i_1). The timing function is $T(i_1, i_2, i_3) = P_1(i_1 - 1) + P_2(i_2 - 1) + P_3(i_3 - 1) + 1$. We intentionally do not explicit the coefficients (P_j) and use them as parameters for using directly the formula computed in theorem 3.7. Arrays A, B, and C are accessed via respectively h_A, h_B, h_C, defined by $h_A(i_1, i_2, i_3) = (i_1, i_3)$, $h_B(i_1, i_2, i_3) = (i_1, i_2)$, $h_C(i_1, i_2, i_3) = (i_2, i_3)$. Let w_A, w_B, w_C denote the size of the windows generated respectively by the three access functions. By applying the formula of theorem 3.7, we get

$$w_A = \min(\frac{N_3}{P_1}(P_3N_3 + P_2N_2), \frac{N_1}{P_3}(P_1N_1 + P_2N_2), N_1N_3)$$

$$w_B = \min(\frac{N_2}{P_1}(P_2N_2 + P_3N_3), \frac{N_1}{P_2}(P_1N_1 + P_3N_3), N_1N_2)$$

$$w_C = \min(\frac{N_3}{P_2}(P_3N_3 + P_1N_1), \frac{N_2}{P_3}(P_2N_2 + P_1N_1), N_2N_3)$$

Now expliciting the values of the (P_j) coefficients results in:

	Nesting order					
	(i_1, i_2, i_3)	(i_1, i_3, i_2)	(i_2, i_1, i_3)	(i_2, i_3, i_1)	(i_3, i_1, i_2)	(i_3, i_2, i_1)
w_A	N_3	$1 + N_3$	N_1N_3	N_1N_3	$1 + N_1$	N_1
w_B	$1 + N_2$	N_2	$1 + N_1$	N_1	N_1N_2	N_1N_2
w_C	N_2N_3	N_2N_3	N_3	$1 + N_3$	N_2	$1 + N_2$
w	$1 + N_2 + N_3$ $+ N_3N_2$	$1 + N_3 + N_2$ $+ N_2N_3$	$1 + N_1 + N_3$ $+ N_1N_3$	$1 + N_1 + N_3$ $+ N_1N_3$	$1 + N_1 + N_2$ $+ N_1N_2$	$1 + N_1 + N_2$ $+ N_1N_2$

The last line gives the sum $w = w_A + w_B + w_C$ of the three window sizes and represents the amount of memory space required for loading the variables only once from main memory and then working on them from the local memory.

For evaluating the accuracy of our approximation for computing windows, the exact window sizes are given in the table below:

	Nesting order					
	(i_1, i_2, i_3)	(i_1, i_3, i_2)	(i_2, i_1, i_3)	(i_2, i_3, i_1)	(i_3, i_1, i_2)	(i_3, i_2, i_1)
w'	$1 + N_3$ $+ N_3N_2$	$1 + N_2$ $+ N_2N_3$	$1 + N_3$ $+ N_1N_3$	$1 + N_1$ $+ N_1N_3$	$1 + N_2$ $+ N_1N_2$	$1 + N_1$ $+ N_1N_2$

It can be noted that the approximated results are close to the exact ones. The difference comes from the computation of the size of the window corresponding to the input dependence induced by the innermost loop invariant ($B(i_1, i_2)$ for the nesting order (i_1, i_2, i_3) for instance). This is an example of phenomena described at the end of section 3.1. It can be found easily that in that simple case the window size is 1 instead of $1 + N_2$. It is clear that such cases could be detected by a special preprocessing phase before the computation of windows using the general formulas.

In the following, the approximate sizes of windows as obtained by the general formula will be used. Due to the symmetric nature of the window sizes for the different ordering, the minimal window size is $\min_{ij}(1 + N_i + N_j + N_i N_j)$. This value is obtained for the ordering which assigns the largest number of iterations ($\max_i N_i$) to the outermost loop. For example if $N_1 = 10, N_2 = 50, N_3 = 100$, then the best order of nesting is (i_3, i_2, i_1), which result in a size of $w' = 1 + N_1 + N_2 + N_1 N_2 = \mathbf{561}$ of local memory required for loading every data only once.

Blocking the loop requires to determine the size of the block (b_1, b_2, b_3) and the order in which the iterations inside a block are swept. The order of the three outermost loops does not matter because locality is only used inside a block. The determination of the best block size is reduced to the following standard optimization problem: maximizing the quantity $4b_1b_2b_3 - b_1b_2 - b_2b_3 - b_1b_3$ (i.e. the benefit) under the constraints that $\min_{ij} 1 + b_i + b_j + b_i b_j \leq LMS$ (i.e. the windows corresponding to the block fit in the local memory) and $1 \leq b_i \leq N_i$ ($i = 1, 2, 3$). The complexity of this optimization procedure can be simplified further by imposing the possible blocks to be square; instead of functions of multiple variables, only simple polynomials have to be manipulated.

4.5.1 Combining parallelization / vectorization with data locality optimization

The problem here is to find the best parallel or vector form of a program, taking into account data locality. For that purpose, we have to answer such questions as: is it better to have vectors of length 30, and 600 hundred main memory accesses, rather than vectors of length 20, and only 400 hundred main memory accesses? To be answered correctly, such questions require detailed knowledge of specific characteristics of the machine such as timings of the vector operations and memory accesses. More generally, this requires a more or less accurate analytical model of the machine performance, for a given program. Such models can be derived using static code analysis combined with empirical data obtained through experimentation. An example of such a model is the *Load-Store* model which was used in [5] and [6].

The key advantage of our approach is that all the computations involved in our local memory management strategy are entirely parameterized and most of the standard loop transformations can be easily taken into account. In particular, as a by product of our scheme, we get analytical expressions of the benefits, which allows us to compute precisely how many memory references are saved. Similarly, the extra operations which might be involved in moving to and/or from the local memory can be precisely evaluated (cf. Section 6). Such information can be used as input to an analytical model of the performance for determining what is the best parallel/vector structure of a program.

Let us give a small example which is a variant of the example given in section 4.2. Let us assume that we have to optimize the following piece of code on a vector machine:

$$\text{DO } 1 \ i_1 = 1, 20$$
$$\text{DO } 1 \ i_2 = 1, 30$$
$$B(i_1, i_2) = A(4 * i_1 - 6 * i_2)$$
$$1 \qquad \text{CONTINUE}$$

In such a form, the cost associated with the window relative to the self dependence on A is 89 words (cf section 4.2). The innermost loop is clearly vectorizable with vector of length 30. It is clear that interchanging is legal. If interchanging is performed, the cost of the window will be reduced down to 41 words (cf section 4.2) but the vector length will be also reduced down to 20. However, in both versions, the benefits (number of memory references saved) are the same. Now if we assume that the local memory has a size bigger than 89, it is clear that the original version of the code will perform better due to the longer vector length.

If the local memory size lies between 41 and 89, the right form of the loop is tougher to determine. However, the interchanged version might end up to perform better because it will not only save memory references but memory references with stride 2 which in general perform badly in interleaved memory systems.

The case of the matrix multiply is also typical of a situation where a trade off between parallelism and data locality has to be precisely quantified. The results of the previous section provides us analytical formula (in function of the block sizes) for the benefit in terms of locality. Assuming that the unit of computation allocated to a processor is the computation over a whole block (i.e. parallelism is used between blocks), these formula quantify the performance of a single processor. Now the amount of parallelism as well its costs can be quantified (using simple performance models) in function of N_i/b_i. By combining together the two aspects, a correct tradeoff can be found.

5 CONCLUSION

In this paper we have developed a global strategy for managing a local memory. First, "active" portions of arrays (windows) are detected and characterized; these windows can be enclosed in simple constant geometric shape moving regularly across the array. Associated with each window, two metrics (size and degree of locality) are evaluated. We have shown that for the most important cases (self-reference windows), all these quantities can be computed symbolically in function of the loop bounds, the index function and the way the iteration space is swept. This allows us to reduce the management of the local memory to a classical knapsack problem. Furthermore the symbolic form of the windows and their characteristics enable to perform a simple analysis of the impact on locality of the most common loop transformations. Finally, several examples showing the power of the approach have been detailed. The strategy described is currently being integrated into an interactive parallelization environment developed by D. Gannon at University of Indiana.

Several problems deserve further refinement:

- The choice of the best strategy to perform the transfers needs to be explored; there is a trade-off between the speed at which the window moves inside the array and the size of the window. Choosing large windows simplifies the transfer policy at the potential price of keeping too many elements in local memory

- The tradeoffs between data locality and parallelism require further investigation; in particular, a systematic strategy has to be determined to select an appropriate trade-off (criteria). This should be achieved by integrating the techniques described here into a performance evaluation system.

- The management strategy described in this paper was mainly focused on local memory; however similar techniques can be applied to registers. This is becoming increasingly attractive as the number of registers available in recent RISC processors has increased; such a large number of registers can be used systematically for retaining data across iterations (exploiting "long-term" locality) in addition to the classical use of registers for exploiting locality inside a given iteration.

References

[1] Chi, C.H., and Dietz, H., *Unified Management of Registers and Cache Using Liveness and Cache Bypass*, SIGPLAN 89, Conf. on Prog. Lang. Des. and Impl.

[2] Eisenbeis, C., Jalby, W., Windheiser, D., Bodin, F., *A Strategy for Array Management in Local Memory*, Rapport de Recherche INRIA, to appear, 1990.

[3] Gannon, D., Jalby, W. and Gallivan, K., *Strategies for Cache and Local Memory Management by Global Program Transformation*, Proceedings of the International Conference on Supercomputing, Springer Verlag, New York, 1987 and Journal of Parallel and Distributed Computing, Oct 1988.

[4] Gallivan, K., Gannon, D. and Jalby, W., *On the Problem of Optimizing Data Transfers for Complex Memory Systems*, Proceedings of ACM International Conference on Supercomputing, ACM Press, 1988, pp.238-253

[5] Gallivan, K., Jalby, W., Malony, A., and Wijshoff, H. *Performance prediction of loop constructs on multiprocessor hierarchical memory systems.* Proceedings of ACM International Conference on Supercomputing, ACM Press, 1989, pp.433-442.

[6] Gallivan, K., Gannon D., Jalby, W., Malony, A., and Wijshoff, H. *Experimentally Characterizing the Behavior of Multiprocessor Memory Systems: A Case Study* IEEE Transaction on Software Engineering, Feb 1990, Vol16, no 2

[7] Burke, M. and Cytron, R. *Interprocedural analysis and parallelization* Proc. SIGPLAN 86 Symposium on Compiler Construction, July 1986, pp. 162-175.

[8] Kennedy, K., *Automatic translation of Fortran programs to vector form* Technical Report, Rice University, Houston, Texas, 1980.

[9] Kuck, D., Kuhn, R., Leasure, B., and Wolfe, M., *Dependence graphs and compiler optimizations* Proc. ACM Symp. POPL, January 1981.

[10] Padua, D., and Kuck, D., *High-speed multiprocessors and compilation techniques*, IEEE Trans. Comput., C-29, 9, pp. 763-776.

[11] Padua, D., and Wolfe, M., *Advanced compiler optimizations for supercomputers*, CACM, 29, 12, pp. 1184-1201.

[12] Pfister, G., and Norton, A, *Hot spot contention and combining in multistage interconnection networks*, Proc. 1985 Int. Conf. on Parallel Processing, pp. 790-797.

[13] Porterfield, A., *Compiler management of program locality* Technical Report, Rice University, Houston, Texas, January 1988.

[14] Sahni, S., *Approximate algorithms for the [0,1] knapsack problem*, JACM. 22, January 1975, pp. 115-124.

[15] Veidenbaum, A., Cheong, H., *Cache Coherence Scheme with Fast Selective Invalidation*, Proceedings of the International Symposium on Computer Architecture, June 1988.

[16] Wolf, M., and Lam, M., *An algorithm to generate sequential and parallel code with improved data locality* Technical Report, Stanford University 1990.

8 On the Performance of Parallel Strips-Based Lists
J. Solworth

Abstract

This paper presents some results of implementing strips-based lists on a parallel processor. Strips-based lists enable highly parallel operations on lists including iteration, deletion, and converting a list to an array. In addition, most sequential operations on strips-based lists have the same asymptotic performance as on traditional linked lists.

1 Introduction

Perhaps the most important of all pointer-based structures is the linked list. Linked lists can directly represent sequences, queues, stacks, and bags. In addition, lists of lists can be used to represent trees and arrays of adjacency lists can be used to represent graphs. Hence, in sequential algorithms, lists play an important role both directly and in the construction of complex data structures.

Unfortunately, traditional linked lists require $O(n)$ time to access the nth element of a list. Techniques such as CDR-coding decrease the access time by at most a constant factor [11]. Harrison and Padua have proposed a list structure for their parallel Lisp PARCEL which is composed of subsequences which can be accessed as arrays, enabling non-sequential access [4]. Although this structure is well suited for Lisp, it has a limitation:

elements may be neither added nor deleted from the array segments.

In this paper, we describe strips-based lists, based on our original work in [9]. The original description of strips-based lists assumed a CREW PRAM model; in the paper, a suitable implementation is given for a more realistic architecture (with a grid interconnect) and performance figures based on that architecture are presented.

The paper is organized as follows. In section 2, strips-based lists are described. In section 3, we describe some features of *PARSEQ*, a parallel programming language that we are developing. Although strips-based lists can be used with other programming languages, *PARSEQ* forms the conceptual framework in which strips-based lists were designed and indicates some ways strips-based lists might be used. In section 4 we describe the implementation used in strips-based lists for a parallel processor with a grid interconnect as opposed to the PRAM model presented in section 2. We present the performance results in section 5.

In what follows, N is the size of the linked list and P is the number of processors.

2 Strips-based lists

In this section, we review our results for strips-based lists using the popular theoretical model, the CREW PRAM. The PRAM is completely synchronous, and has a global shared memory which can be accessed simultaneously by all processors in unit time. Concurrent reads are allowed (there is no penalty for multiple processors accessing the same location), but if any processor writes a location, no other may access it during that cycle.

Strips-based lists have the following features not found in traditional linked lists:

1. An *arbitrary* element of the linked list can be accessed in unit time.

2. A strip-based list of size $P \log(P)$ can be converted into an array in time $O(\log(P))$. This operation is called *reordering*.

3. If the strip is reordered, an element can be random accessed in unit time.

4. Parallel insertion, deletion, and iteration over both reordered and unreordered strips

can take place with high performance.

5. Serial insertion, deletion, and iteration over strips-based lists requires the same asymptotic time as with traditional algorithms.

An *arbitrary* element refers to some element belonging to the list; in general it is indeterminate which element is returned or even the position of the element within the linked list. Arbitrary selection semantics play an important role both in sequential and parallel programming languages: examples of arbitrary selection semantics include Linda's *in* selector (when there are multiple matches) [1] and SETL's set element selectors [7]. If the strips-based list is *reordered*, then a specific element can be accessed in unit time by specifying the ith element of the list, for any i. Reordering is a highly parallel operation based upon parallel prefix.

High-performance parallel operations are not enough: when the number of lists to be operated on in parallel exceeds the processor resources, a single processor can be assigned to each list and the operations performed sequentially. Hence, sequential operations should be as efficient as possible. Strips-based linked lists enable efficient sequential operations of iterations, element insert and delete, and appending two lists.

These advantages are not without cost: implicit tail sharing is prohibited and there is an overhead in both storage costs and running time. However, since strips-based lists can be declared, and since strips-based lists can be mixed with traditional linked lists, this overhead need be incurred only if there is sufficiently parallelism to justify it.

To enable unit-time arbitrary element access to lists, it is necessary to be able to compute quickly the locations of elements of the linked list. The easiest way to do this is to store the elements in contiguous storage. Unfortunately, this prohibits an element from being a member of multiple lists simultaneously. For example, in languages like C or Pascal, a structure can be declared with arbitrary number of pointer fields; each pointer field can link the element into a different linked list. In addition, copying costs for maintaining contiguous allocation during an insertion or deletion requires time proportional to the size of the element, instead of constant time. But the greatest practical problem is tracking pointers: if an element is moved, then either the runtime system or the programmer must track and update any live pointers to that element.

To circumvent these problems of contiguous list storage, strips-based list storage is separated into two halves: the elements which can be located anywhere in storage and *strips* which are units of contiguous storage. A strip is an array of *cells*, each cell holding a pointer. Elements' strips-based pointers point only to strips cells; strip cells point only to elements. Any cell not pointing to an element contains a null value. These constraints ensure that the elements of the list are exactly the elements pointed to by the non-null strips cells — enabling all elements to be accessed in parallel directly through the contiguous strip storage, without accessing any successor fields. In addition, elements are reachable through predecessor elements in the list, first by dereferencing the pointer to reach a strips cell and then dereferencing the strips cell to reach the successor.

The order of pointers in the strip is unspecified, with the exception of first cell (indexed by zero) which points to the first element of the list.

An example of a 5 element strips-based linked list is shown in figure 1, and consists of the elements e_0, e_1, e_2, e_3, e_4, and the strip s. The list can be sequenced through starting either at $s[0]$ or at a pointer to e_0. The successor to e_0 is found by dereferencing e_0's successor field, obtaining $s[1]$ and then dereferencing $s[1]$ obtaining e_1. Note that it is not a requirement that $s[i]$ point to e_i except when $i = 0$ — for example, e_2 is pointed to by $s[5]$ — and that null values are scattered throughout the list.

The allocation of processors to strips is static and uniform (there are N/P elements per processor). Hence, a set of processors are associated with each strips-based list. The static allocation enables finer grain sizes and increases the algorithm's ability to take advantage of locality. This style of algorithm is reminiscent of the data parallel algorithms [5] of the Connection Machine and other SIMD architectures in which each object logically has its own processor. In addition to increased locality and static binding, data parallel algorithms are synchronous and thus neither incur the overhead of synchronization nor the *skew* or waiting time of a processor waiting to rendezvous with another processor.

Although the algorithms presented here are MIMD they are in the spirit of data parallel algorithms. For example, the algorithm achieves the same locality and static binding properties as data parallel. The skew is reduced (and approximates the data parallel algo-

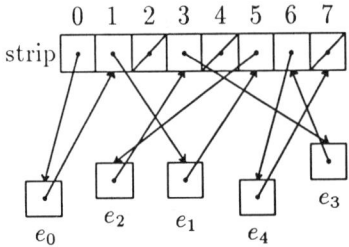

Figure 1: An 8-processor strips-based list with one element per processor

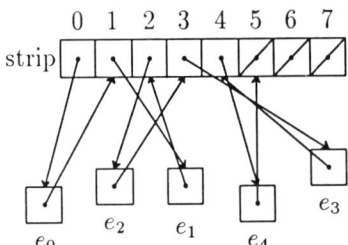

Figure 2: An 8-processor strips-based list which has been reordered

rithm) since the work each processor is performing is highly predictable. High-performance synchronization hardware reduces synchronization overhead while allowing caching techniques to be used. In addition, the MIMD nature allows the number of processors to be allocated to the data structure to be a function of the size of the data structure rather than being the entire parallel computer.

Although the strip in figure 1 enables an arbitrary element to be accessed in unit time, it does not enable the ith element to be accessed directly. While it is possible, when $N = P$ to access the ith element directly in time $O(\log(P))$, a better way is to number each element with its index. This too requires $O(\log(P))$ time using either deterministic coin tossing techniques [2] or randomized techniques. Furthermore, this same bound holds when $P = N/\log(N)$, resulting in work of $O(1)$ per element. Once the index is obtained with parallel prefix, the strips pointers can be permuted (with corresponding changes in the successor pointers of the elements) in unit time per element. The result is that the strip is reordered, that is $s[i]$ points to e_i. For example, the resulting structure after reordering of the strip in figure 1 is shown in figure 2.

Reordering, by using parallel prefix, is the key to the more sophisticated uses of strips. By reordering, the linked structure is converted into an array. The array structure then

```
1    struct T {
2        int val;
3        struct T *<strips>   stripsSuccessor;
4        struct T *<strips>   anotherStripsSuccessor;
5        struct T *           ordinaryPointer;
6    }
```

Figure 3: Declaration of strips based and non-strips based list in the same structure

enables the full range of array-based optimization and parallelization techniques to be applied to linked list operations.

We shall assume that strips-based lists are declared and that the only programmer visible pointers to a strips-based list are to its constituent elements. For example, using an extended C syntax, a structure T is declared in figure 3. The structure contains an integer value *val* and three pointer fields, each of which point to the same type of object. Two of those pointers are strips-based *stripsSuccessor* and *anotherStripsSuccessor*. Since an element can only belong once to a linked-list, each strips declaration unambiguously declares that it is a member of a separate strips-based list.[1]

Finally, an ordinary pointer is a traditional linked list pointer structure — there is no strip for this one.

Syntactically, if *e* is a pointer to an element, then its successor is specified identically, independent of whether the pointer field is strips based or not. Hence, the successor on *stripsSuccessor* is specified

    e→stripsSuccessor

while that on *ordinaryPointer* it is specified similarly.

    e→ordinaryPointer

The compiler will generate different code depending on the declaration. For the *ordinaryPointer* field the code generated is the same as would be generated by a C compiler. For the *stripsSuccessor*, the code generated is

---

[1] It is possible to emulate tail sharing by having a bit which specifies either a successor within the same strip, or a successor in another strip, but this reduces parallel access.

*(e→stripsSuccessor)

to compensate for the double layer of indirection.

3 PARSEQ

Strips-based lists were designed for the programming language we are developing called *PARSEQ* [10]. The acronym *PARSEQ* stands for a *PA*Rallel programming language with *SEQ*uential semantics. Sequential semantics means that program execution can be understood in terms of a single program counter execution of the program; the language is parallel because the user can predict and control how the compiler parallelizes a program, hence parallelization is transparent.

Our approach is closest to Refined Languages [3], which extend existing sequential languages with independence information, enabling parallelization. Like refined languages, errors cannot arise from undetected race conditions since all parallelism is implicit. Because *PARSEQ* is a new language, we are able to change language semantics in ways not possible with Refined Languages, for example to control storage allocation and management.

A primary looping structure in *PARSEQ* is the *forall* loop. The *forall* loop specifies an iteration over a (possibly strips-based) list. The iteration semantics are sequential, as are all *PARSEQ* semantics, but the iteration *order* is unspecified — the runtime system is free to choose as an iteration order any permutation of the list elements. The goal of the *PARSEQ* compiler (and the runtime system) is to choose a sequential order which results in the fastest execution time given the processor resources. Consider the case of a large number of processors and the the program shown in figure 4. Since there are no dependencies between iterations, any execution order will result in a parallel schedule with maximal parallelism. This is a trivial program, but these techniques also apply to loops with intra-iteration dependencies.

More complex loops must be parallelized by taking advantage of the list structure. For example, the program fragment in figure 5 is the inner loop of a sorting algorithm. If the *forall* loop is iterated in list order, then the resulting sort is bubble sort – and

```
1   forall x ∈ l do
2       x.val := 0;
```

Figure 4: Forall iteration over a list

```
1   forall x ∈ l do
2       if x.val > x.next.val then
3           t := x.val;
4           x.val := x.next.val;
5           x.next.val := t;
```

Figure 5: Inner loop of a sorting algorithm

bubble sort's inner loop is complete sequential (although the outer loop is pipelinable). On the other hand, if the iteration order is chosen so that all of the odd elements are selected, followed by all of the even elements, then the whole loop can be executed in two steps. Note that these orders are not equivalent, at least without examining the outer loop. So without programmatic specification, the compiler would require a much higher level of sophistication to transform the iteration order of a non-arbitrary order loop into a different iteration order.

The index of each element can be determined by parallel prefix. The index can then be used to test odd versus even elements and hence schedule the parallelism. The computed parallel prefix numbering remains valid as long as the structure of the list is not modified. Note that the advantage of strips-based lists derives not from refining what can be done in parallel, but from removing the sequential bottleneck of accessing elements. Strips-based lists and arbitrary-order semantics are therefore complementary mechanisms.

An alternative to arbitrary-order would be to write the loop as two separate loops — one for odd elements and one for even. When the loop can be scheduled at compile time it is always possible to rewrite the loop into separate, completely parallelizable loops. However, manually splitting loops increases the programmer burden and requires dependency information to be computed by the programmer; small changes in the code can require reformulation of the loops to ensure that the parallelism is exploited. When the loop cannot

```
1    while task ≠ [] do
2        x := arb_less task;
3        task := task concat p(x);
```

Figure 6: Self service paradigm

be scheduled statically, manual loop splitting would be ineffective to achieve parallelism. Hence, non-determinism reduces the programmer load and may increase opportunities for parallelization. Moreover non-deterministism is the natural way to specify many pointer-based algorithms — although correctness often depends on non-trivial convergence proofs. Hence, determining what changes in iteration order are possible would be difficult to do automatically.

The arbitrary order semantics of the *forall* loop are a fundamental technique for achieving parallelism. For example, consider the *PARSEQ* arbitrary-order selector *arb_less* which removes an unspecified member from the list and returns that former member as its value. The program in Figure 6 removes elements from a task queue and computes new tasks using the procedure *p(x)*. If different invocations of *p* can be run in parallel, then the semantics of this program enable greedy scheduling, that is, the self-service paradigm which is often used for load balancing. A specified order would decrease the parallelism in the event that the first computation took a very long time relative to other computations; in this case, tasks not on the initial task list could not execute until the first task completed computation.

4   Towards more realistic architectures

There are several problems when the PRAM algorithms are applied to real machines:

1. Real machines do not have unit time memory access. Locality and possibly bandwidth limitations must be compensated for.

2. Linked lists have varying sizes.

3. Constants frequently overwhelm the asymptotic analysis for realistic problem sizes and machines.

Randomization techniques are often used to achieve good average case access patterns. Unfortunately, while such techniques eliminate (with high probability) worst case access patterns they also eliminate locality. Locality is a precious commodity since it enables a larger amount of parallelism to be applied to smaller problem sizes without the loss of efficiency, and hence reduces the degree of virtualization necessary to hide latency. It is even more important in computers which do not have sufficient interconnect bandwidth to hide latency.

It is not easy to characterize the amount of locality in strips-based list structures since locality depends on complex interactions between the run-time environment (for example, garbage collection) and the algorithms which use strips-based lists. The implementation presented takes advantage of locality, and results are presented both for which there is and is not locality.

The algorithms presented here are very simple and only need infrequent synchronizations. This reduces the constant overheads, making these techniques effective for a larger range of processor sizes.

The numbers obtained are for a two dimensional grid with limited bandwidth. Two dimensional grids were chosen for our simulation since we could achieve large-scale effects with smaller number of processors than in a three dimensional grid. Moreover, grids have higher latency than many networks proposed for parallel processing such as hypercube and omega. Hence, the performance figures presented are lower bounds for computers with similar CPU, switch, and memory parameters.

4.1 Strip headers

We have not implemented the theoretical algorithms for PRAMs alluded in section 2 because of their requirement for massive amount of synchronizations (which has no cost in the PRAM model) and because they do not take advantage of locality. The randomization techniques we use do not destroy locality, but attempt to provide approximately equal sized

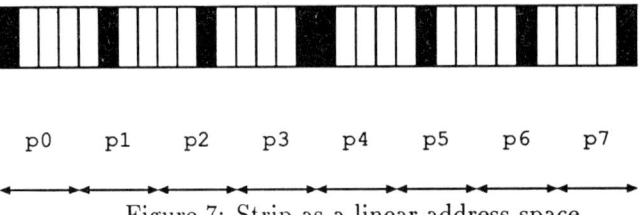

Figure 7: Strip as a linear address space

sublists to each processor.

In all of the algorithms we implemented, each processor operates on a sublist and then the results of each processor are merged in a tree phase. To access a sublist, a parallel algorithm must use the strips since the elements are spread throughout memory. In an unordered strip, there is no restriction on the relationship between the index of an element in the linked list and the index of the cell pointing to the element.

The problem is then to ensure that the sublists assigned to each processor are disjoint, and the union of all the sublists is the entire list. The method we have implemented is to choose a subset of the strip cells as *headers*. The sublist associated with that header consists of all of the list elements, from the element pointed to by the header until the first element that points to a strip cell which is a header. Since each header is assigned to one processor, and since no sublist spans headers, each sublist is disjoint. To see that the union of sublists is the entire list, it is sufficient to see that the first element of the list is pointed to by a header cell. Since $s[0]$ points to e_0, this requirement is met by making $s[0]$ a strip header.

There are several desirable properties for a practical algorithm:

1. There should be at least as many strip headers as there are processors so that each processor has a sublist. In fact, when the strips are unordered, it is desirable to have several strip headers per processor since this will reduce the variance in the number of elements per processor — an important factor since the running time is the time of the last processor to complete.

2. Each sublist header (and ideally each element in the sublist) should be near the processor associated with that header to increase locality. This decreases the latency to access an element and also decreases bandwidth requirements for the interconnection

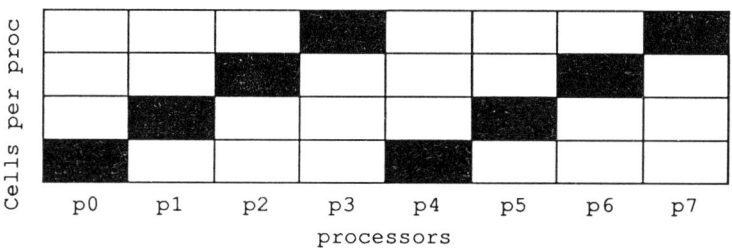

Figure 8: Strip for an 8 processor strip of height 4

network.

3. To reduce the overhead of synchronization, there should be multiple elements per processors.

4. To increase the robustness of the algorithm, the likelihood of access patterns on which the algorithm perform poorly should be minimized.

When viewed as a linear address space, the strip cells are configured as shown in Figure 7. There are a constant number of headers per processor, but the headers are skewed. This mirrors a common practice in vector machines, where strides of a power of two result in dramatically reduced memory bandwidth.

Since there are multiple elements per processor, the strip can be viewed as a two dimensional matrix with the horizontal dimension being processors and the vertical dimension is word in the local memory of a processor as shown in figure 8. The single list is allocated over eight processors labeled p_0 through p_7, each processor has its own locally accessibly (but globally addressable) memory. The number of cells per processor is called the *height* — in this example the height is 4. The entire 32 cell strip is contain in contiguous region of the grid containing 8 nodes. In a three dimensional grid the contiguous region would be a $2 \times 2 \times 2$ subgrid. An important feature of this algorithm is that on ordered lists all elements in a sublist are contained in two adjacent processors, and so excellent locality is obtained.

The algorithms for operating on strips-based lists have the form of a tree. Level 0 of the tree contains sublists whose union is the entire list, successive levels i are defined recursively as containing lists of the lists at level $i-1$. The hierarchy of lists is represented

```
1   for i:= 0 to MaxLevels do
2       foreach h ∈ Header_p^i do
3           e := h;
4           repeat
5               < process e >;
6               last := e;
7               e := e→ next^i;
8           until isHeader^i(e);
9           h→ next^{i+1} := last;
10      endif;
11  endfor;
```

Figure 9: Parallel iteration over all elements of a strips-based list

by a hierarchy of strip headers with the top of the hierarchy containing a single strip header. A strips cell c is a header at level i if $isHeader^i(c)$ is true.

The algorithm shown in figure 9 shows how all elements of a list are iterated over. This code is executed by each processor p assigned to the strips-based list. The algorithm proceeds in levels from 0 to $MaxLevels$. At each level, a subset of the strips cells are designated as strip headers ($Header_p^i$). In the initial iteration, $e \rightarrow next^0$ is the successor of e in the list.

For simple iterations which don't have dependencies between iterations a single level suffices. However, for more complex algorithms such as deletion, a hierarchy of levels are needed, each level involving fewer elements and processors. On each successive level, the number of strip headers decreases with

$$Header_p^i \subset Header_p^{i+1}, \qquad (1)$$

until the number of strip headers is equal to 1. The values of $e \rightarrow next^i$ consists only of the strip headers of at $i-1$. In the case of parallel prefix, the algorithm is a little more complicated than shown in figure 9, since the hierarchy must first be ascended and then descended.

As a concrete example, consider the deletion of elements which match a given key. At the first level, any element satisfying the condition is deleted from each of the sublists. Successive levels concatenate the resulting sublists together, forming ever larger sublists, until the final list is constructed. Note that this concatenation cannot be efficiently performed in a single level since an arbitrary number of sublists may be empty — resulting in a worse case serial algorithm in which the first sublist would have to examine all successive (and empty) sublists to find its successor.

4.2 Hierarchy of sizes

Linked lists come in a variety of sizes which grow and shrink during program execution. To prevent wasting processor resources, the number of processors allocated to a strip should be approximately equal to the number of elements in the strip. Moreover, to enhance locality and reduce bandwidth requirements, the strip should be allocated on a collection of adjacent processors.

Strip space is organized into a hierarchy of levels. Small strips are contained at the bottom most level, and as strips grow they are promoted to the next higher level, thereby at least doubling the number of cells and processors assigned to the strip. The promotion is performed by copying; hence the time is proportional to the size of the list. However, if the cost is amortized over the number of elements added, then promotion has only constant cost per added element. And, of course, promotion is a completely parallel operation.

The strip is interleaved over a set of contiguous nodes, with small strips interleaved over small sets of nodes and the very largest strips interleaved over the entire parallel processor. For example, in figure 10 the processors are arranged in levels. At level i, up to $f(2^i)$ elements can be represented.[2] If the list grows larger than this size, it is promoted up to the next larger level.

Strips are aligned. A strip which uses k processors will begin at a processor number which is divisible by k. The alignment serves two purposes. First, in grid networks, successively numbered elements are not necessarily physically adjacent — but, if aligned, they are guaranteed to be close. Second, the alignment enables the start and size of a

---

[2]In two dimensional grids, the levels might grow by 2^{2i} and in three by 2^{3i}.

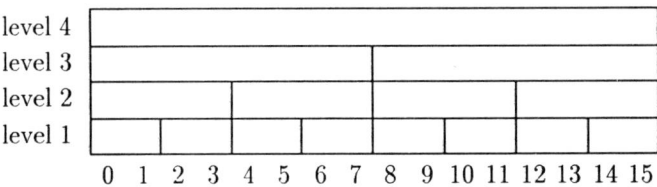

Figure 10: Strips-based lists come in an hierarchy of sizes, from some lower bound l to P processors per strip

strip to be determined from any pointer to the strip. This enables the set of processors participating in a strips-based algorithm to be completely determined from any pointer either to an element or a cell of the strip.

The hierarchy of lists ensures that there is at most twice the number of list cells as there are elements in the list, thus ensuring that parallel resources are not scheduled for operating on null cells.

4.3 Architecture

Although Microflow [8] has no architectural features specific to strips-based lists, it is worth describing Microflow architecture on which our numbers are based.

The two most interesting aspects of Microflow in respect to strips based lists are the network topology and the ratio of switches to processors. The Microflow topology is a three dimensional grid with a routing switch, processor, and memory at every node. This topology does not have sufficient bandwidth to inject a new memory request every processor cycle — that is, the bandwidth across the bisection is only $O(p^{2/3})$ instead of the $O(p)$ bandwidth necessary to support random communications patterns. For grid architectures for which this restriction does not hold, such as the Horizon [6], our numbers form lower bounds on the performance of such machines.

Hence, as the number of processors grows large, problem performance is increasingly likely to be limited by bandwidth restrictions. To fully take this effect into account, we have simulated a two dimensional grid of 256 processors (16 × 16), which has the same proportional bandwidth as a three dimensional grid with 4096 processors (16 × 16 × 16). Smaller sized grids will be less bandwidth constrained.

Parameter	Performance
Switch routing time	25ns
Packets per switch	2
CPU cycle time	25ns
Cycles to complete instruction	3
Memory Access (and Cycle) time	100ns
Memory Module per node	2

Table 1: Microflow simulation parameters

The simulation parameters shown in table 1 were used in a detailed simulator for the Microflow architecture. For each node there is a switch, memory, and processor. Each memory has a 100ns access and cycle time, and there are two memory modules per node. Multiple memory modules were used primarily to compensate for the fact that the architecture does not yet have a cache (and hence the memory system must provide greater bandwidth).[3] A switch contains fully duplexed connections in 4 directions, and requires 2 packets to contain a message, each packet requires 25ns to transit the switch. The switch ports contain queues in order to enhance bandwidth.

Finally, the processor has a 25ns cycle time, a RISC-style instruction set, and requires 3 cycles (pipeline stages) to complete an instruction. There is no delay slot for branches — the pipeline simply stalls.

5 Results

We simulated 4 algorithms on a linked list of size 2^{16} which was spread out evenly over the 256 processor grid. Although this list is very large, it places a much heavier burden on the interconnect than smaller lists. These algorithms were compared to a serial version over the equivalent traditional linked list, with the processor located at the center of the grid.

The parallel algorithm was run on 3 different list patterns. The first was a random element location and strip pointer location. In the second case, the strips were ordered

---

[3]Since in a bandwidth constrained computer, non-local request arrival time is restricted by network bandwidth and not memory speed, multiple memory modules per node are unlikely to be needed.

Prefix		
operation	time (μsec)	speedup
serial (traditional linked lists)	60,400	1:1
parallel, no locality	1,200	50.3:1
parallel, ordered strips	633	95.4:1
parallel, local elements	534	113.1:1

Table 2: Performance of prefix computation

Reorder (Prefix + Permute)		
operation	time (μsec)	speedup
serial (traditional linked lists)	60,400	1:1
parallel, no locality	1,608	37.6:1
parallel, ordered strips	949	63.6:1
parallel, local elements	770	78.4:1

Table 3: Performance of reorder computation

but the elements were randomly scattered. In the third case both the elements and the strips were local to the processor. Only one set of numbers is given for the serial case since the pattern only affects the order in which locations are accessed and hence has no effect on the total running time of the algorithm.

Table 2 shows the performance of prefix. Prefix is an expensive operation because it involves a traversal both up and down the hierarchy of headers. The sequential time, is dominated by memory/network access time. The parallel speedup from randomly distributed elements and strips pointers is 50 fold, or about 20% efficiency. When just the strip is reordered (with the elements unmoved), the speedup and efficiency almost doubles. A small incremental savings is obtained by localizing the elements.

The performance of reordering is shown in table 3. Reordering is more expensive than just prefix because it involves modifying all of the pointers of the elements and all of the cells of the strip. It is interesting to note that reordering substantially reduces the cost of other operations, and so on an amortized basis is usually worthwhile if multiple parallel operations are to be performed on the list.

Simple iteration, such as initializing a field in each element of a linked list is the simplest execution requiring only a single level of headers. Efficiency ranges from 35% to 75%, as shown in table 4.

Simple Iteration		
operation	time (μsec)	speedup
serial (traditional linked lists)	57,306	1:1
parallel, no locality	639	89.7:1
parallel, ordered strips	375	152.8:1
parallel, local elements	296	193.6:1

Table 4: Performance of simple iterations

Deletion		
operation	time (μsec)	speedup
serial (traditional linked list)	63,053	1:1
parallel, no locality	1,210	52.1:1
parallel, ordered strip	728	86.6:1
parallel, local elements	649	97.2:1

Table 5: Performance of deletions

Finally, consider the task of deleting every other element in a linked list. While this involves only a traversal up the tree it is almost computationally as expensive as prefix since there is a large number of writes. The performance is shown in table 5.

6 Conclusions

We have described an algorithm and implementation for parallel lists on grid computers with limited bandwidth. These algorithms exhibit speedups of between 50 and 193 on a 256 processor computer with limited bandwidth.

The strips-based lists yield efficient parallel and sequential executions. On the one hand, a single element can be inserted (or deleted) from a strips-based list using a single processor and execution time not much different than that for a traditional linked lists. On the other hand, highly parallel operations can also be performed on these lists. This mix of serial and parallel operations can be arbitrarily mixed. Whether the operation is parallelized or not, the programming notation is the same for ordinary linked lists. In fact, strips-based lists and ordinary lists can be freely intermixed in the same program.

Strips-based lists support a duality for parallel processing between lists and arrays. When viewed as an array, classical array parallelization techniques can be used. When viewed as a lists, the flexibility of linked lists is provided in a parallel setting.

The results presented here are preliminary. We expect improvements to come from two different sources. First, better compilation techniques would reduce the overhead of parallel prefix which is a complex program relative to serial prefix. On the other hand, not much improvement can be expected from the sequential programs since they are almost entirely bound by memory/network latency. The second improvement is the use of a processor cache, which is not yet in Microflow. Once again, the sequential algorithms benefit little since currently, either a location is register based or accessed only once. Parallel prefix, on the other hand, must access each element of the list twice; once as it traverses up the tree and once as it traverses down.

Acknowledgments

Thanks to Jerry Stamatopoulos and Paul Wilson for proof reading earlier versions of this paper. Support for this work was provided in part by ONR-N00014-88-K-0423.

References

[1] S. Ahuja, N. Carriero, and David Gelertner. Linda and friends. *Computer*, 19(8):26–34, August, 1986.

[2] Richard Cole and Uzi Vishkin. Deterministic coin tossing and accelerating cascades: micro and macro techniques for designing parallel algorithms. *PROC 18th STOC*, pages 206–219, 1986.

[3] Henry Dietz and David Klappholz. Refined C: A sequential language for parallel processing. *ICCP*, pages 442–449, August, 1985.

[4] W. Ludwell Harrison, III and David A. Padua. Representing S-expressions for the efficient evaluation of lisp on parallel processors. *Proceedings of the 1986 International Conference on Parallel Processing*, pages 703–710, August, 1986.

[5] W. Daniel Hillis and Guy L. Steele, Jr. Data parallel algorithms. *CACM*, 29(12):1170–1183, DEC 1986.

[6] J. T. Kuehn and B. J. Smith. The horizon supercomputer system: Architecture and software. *Supercomputing 88*, November 1988.

[7] Jacob T. Schwartz, R. B. K. Dewar, E. Dubinsky, and E. Schonberg. *Programming with sets: an introduction to SETL*. Springer-Verlag, New York, New York, 1986. setl book.

[8] Jon A. Solworth. The Microflow architecture. In *International Conference on Parallel Processing*, volume 1, pages 113–117, St. Charles, Ill., August 15-20 1988. IEEE.

[9] Jon A. Solworth. Programming language constructs for highly parallel operations on lists. *The Journal of Supercomputing*, 2:331–347, 1988.

[10] Jon A. Solworth. The PARSEQ project: An interim report. In *Languages and Compilers for Parallel Computing*, pages 490—510. Pittman/MIT, 1990.

[11] Guy L. Steele. Destructive reordering of cdr-coded lists. *Artificial Intelligence Memo No. 587*, August, 1980.

Authors address:

Dept. of EECS (m/c 154), 1120 SEO, University of Illinois, P.O. Box 4348, Chicago, IL, 60680. E-mail: solworth@bert.eecs.uic.edu.

9 An Efficient Monolithic Array Constructor
G Gao, R Yates, J. Dennis, L Mullin

Abstract

Despite their importance in scientific computation, arrays have posed a serious persistent challenge to the efficient implementation of functional languages. In this paper, we propose a new monolithic array constructor which provides a solution to two major problems arising in the implementation of monolithic arrays: (1) the overhead of scheduling and synchronization for recursively defined arrays; (2) the copying of the many intermediate arrays during array construction. Our array constructor allows an index domain to be constructed from a set of rectangular *index regions* and combinations of these. An ordered sequence of regions may be specified in a fashion which can be checked by a compiler using simple subscript analysis techniques. An array is also allowed to be monotonically defined in an iterative fashion without using incremental array update operations. Program examples arising in scientific computation are used to illustrate the principles and advantages of the new constructor.

1 Introduction: Arrays in Functional Languages

Issues concerning the efficient implementation of arrays have received little attention from the designers of functional programming languages. From the beginnings of interest in functional programming to the present, most published work has developed within the framework of symbolic applications and interactive computing [9]. This is surprising in view of the intense current interest in expoiting the power of parallel computers for high performance scientific and engineering computation, since the absence of side effects in functional languages facilitates the identification of program parts that may be executed concurrently. Notable exceptions have been APL [23] (although not truly a functional language), and the work on array theory [28,29]. Two functional programming languages, Val and Sisal [2,27], have been designed specifically for scientific computation and include expression forms for the construction of multidimensional arrays. Id-Nouveau has also paid considerable attention to supporting arrays for scientific computation [31].

Two cases of array construction are important. In the first case, each element of the array has a value obtained using only values available before construction of the array begins, and elements may be computed concurrently without conflict or hazard. This case is supported by many languages, e.g., the **forall** of Val and the parallel **for** expression in Sisal. These constructs are *monolithic* in the sense that their elements are defined "all at once" at the moment the array value is created [3].

The second case occurs if the expression for the value of an array element contains references to other elements of the array being constructed. This case often arises in scientific computation when the array elements are determined by a mathematical recurrence – each array element may depend on several elements of the same array. In Val and Sisal this requires use of the array update operation and leads to the copying of array values in unoptimized machine code.

An array update operation (also sometimes called "append") A[i:v] generates a new array which agrees everywhere with the old array A except at the ith position, where it has the value v. The creation of the new array leaves the old array intact, thereby preserving referential transparency. However, such *incremental* array update operations, when implemented literally, incur large costs in time and space due to copying.

There have been many attempts to eliminate or reduce incremental array copying in functional languages. In early proposals it was suggested that arrays might be implemented as trees and copying avoided by proper sharing of subarrays [1,13]. But implementing arrays as trees sacrifices the efficient accessing of elements supported by familiar memory system architectures. Another approach combines static analysis with runtime reference counting to eliminate some copying and memory management operations [7,12,16,19,34]. It is not clear how far these methods can be extended. An alternative is to refine the programming language so that the function of the append operation is replaced by constructs more amenable to analysis by a compiler.

In recent years, monolithic arrays have been included in several functional languages, including FEL [24], Alfl [15], Id-Nouveau [32] and Haskell [20]. Related proposals can also be found in [36] and [37]. Hudak [17] has summarized the two major difficulties confronting the implementors of languages that include these array constructors: (1) the overhead of scheduling and synchronization for recursively defined arrays; and (2) the copying of the many intermediate arrays during array construction.

More powerful array operations are being considered in extending conventional programming languages We lack the space to give even a short survey, and we refer the readers to Fortran 8X as a representative example of a general trend in this direction [21]. In the language FIDIL [14], domains and maps play a central role and constitute an extension of the array types found in other programming languages. A FIDIL domain corresponds to an index set similar to our index region and maps are functions which can monolithically construct an array based its index domain. A rich set of operations on domains and maps is included in the language. FIDIL's objective is to reduce the semantic distance between abstract descriptions of finite difference and particle methods and programs that implement them, making abstract mathematical descriptions into programs. To this effect, FIDIL encourages programmers to build arbitrary complex array object in single expressions, using its powerful array operations.

The objective of this paper is to study issues in funtional language design that influence our ability to achieve efficient implementation of monolithic arrays intended for scientific and engineering computation. Careful attention to language design can make the construction of efficient code much more straightforward. Toward this end, we propose a new monolithic array constructor which allows an index domain to be constructed from a set of rectangular *index regions* and combinations of these. An ordered sequence of regions may be specified in a fashion which can be checked by a compiler using simple subscript analysis techniques. An array is also allowed to be monotonically defined in an iterative fashion without using incremental array update operations. Program examples arising in scientific computation are used to illustrate the principles and advantages of the new constructor.

In section 2 we review monolithic array constructors as they have been defined in existing functional programming languages, and illustrate some deficiencies of current languages for scientific computation. Section 3 introduces our basic monolithic array constructor for non-recursive array definitions. In section 4 the new array constructor is extended to recursive array definitions and illustrated for the wavefront computation. Sections 6 and 7 treat subscript analysis. The problem of minimizing copying, using LU decomposition as an example, is illustrated in section 8; a new approach to copy elimination is presented in section 9. The paper concludes with comments on future work.

2 Monolithic Array Constructors

It is the recursive array definitions that provide the greatest challenge for the design of a monolithic array constructor. One would like to ensure that: (1) arbitrary dependences can be expressed; (2) "in place" construction may be used to minimize storage allocation needs; (3) possible concurrency in the evaluation of array elements can be exploited. Two interesting proposals for meeting these objectives exist in the facilities provided in Id and in the newly proposed language Haskell.

The intention in Id is that array definitions having arbitrary recursive dependences be written using the *I-structure* mechanism of Id. This mechanism alows for explicit allocation of storage for an array with all elements undefined, and supports write and read operations on the array elements. It is invalid to write the same element twice (an error that can only be detected during program execution). Any reads of an array element are delayed until the element becomes defined. The general implementation of I-structures requires a special memory organization and a resource scheduling mechanism that may be invoked for each element of the constructed array. To avoid the penalties of using I-structures, the Id program could be analyzed by a compiler to recognize the important simple forms for which more efficient code can be constructed. The problems of doing this are similar to those for the monolithic array constructor in Haskell, which we introduce next.

The functional programming language Haskell [20] has been proposed as a standard functional language for a broad range of applications. Haskell provides an expression form in which an array is specified by a list of pairs of the form (*index, value*), where *index* is a tuple of integers, one for each dimension of the array being constructed, and *value* is an object of element type. The list is written as a concatenation of one or more *list comprehensions* [33]. Such an expression defines an array monolithically and is known as an *array comprehension*. As an example, the wavefront computation may be written as follows [17]:

```
A = array ((1,m),(1,n)) [ ((1,1),1) ]
                     ++ [ ((i,1),1) | i <- [2..m] ]
                     ++ [ ((1,j),1) | j <- [2..n] ]
                     ++ [ ((i,j), A!(i-1,j) + A!(i,j-1) + A!(i-1,j-1) )
                              | i <- [2..m], j <- [2..n]]
```

The right hand side of this definition consists of the keyword `array`, a bounds expression `((1,m),(1,n))` that specifies the rank and index ranges of the constructed array, and a group of four list comprehensions combined with the concatenate operator "++". The first list contains a single element that defines the corner element to be one. The next two lists define the remaining elements of the first column and the first row of the array. The last list is specified using the Zermelo-Frankel set abstraction notation to express the dependence of the interior array elements on their neighbors to the north, west and northwest. The exclamation point "!" is the subscripting operator.

In this way the Haskell program uses list comprehensions to specify four different regions which cover the index domain of A. In the wavefront example, the list comprehension for the interior region is created by two generators, one for i and one for j, producing index pairs for all points (i,j) not part of the north and west boundaries. To appreciate the semantics of an array comprehension, it is important to know that the order in which array elements are specified in the list *does not* specify the order in which element values are to be computed; the list is only a device for specifying the *values* of array elements. It is the responsibility of the implementation (the compiler and runtime system) to use an order of evaluation that honors the dependences expressed in the array comprehension. For a parallel computer it is also the job of the implementation to determine which elements may be safely evaluated concurrently. In the wavefront example, it is the sets of elements that make up the secondary diagonals of the array.

In many scientific computations an array may be recursively defined, but the pattern of self reference is regular, as in a linear recurrence or the wavefront computation. In these cases it is important that the inefficiencies of the general implementation of the Id and Haskell array constructors be avoided. Compile-time analysis can help if the regularities in the dependence relation can be identified and used to partition array elements into groups that can be safely evaluated in parallel. As will be shown in section 6, array constructors can be designed to make this process straightforward.

3 A New Monolithic Array Constructor

In this section we introduce the basic form of our monolithic array constructor. This form applies to arrays defined without self-dependence. The extension to recursive array definition is made in section 4.

We consider an array to be a function whose domain is a set of tuples of integers. Such a domain may be thought of as a rectangular subset of n-dimensional space. We call this rectangular region the *index domain* of the array. Our array constructor lets the

```
mono-array-constructor  ::= for index-list in domain-spec construct [id]
                              mono-body
                            endfor
domain-spec             ::= [ shape , lowbd ]
mono-body               ::= region-constructor [ ; mono-body ]
                          | region-constructor [ ! mono-body ]
region-constructor      ::= region-spec-list : expression
region-spec-list        ::= region-spec [ , region-spec-list ]
                          | otherwise
region-spec             ::= [ shape , lowbd ]
                          | point-list
shape                   ::= ( param-expr-list )
lowbd                   ::= point
point-list              ::= point [ , point-list ]
point                   ::= ( param-expr-list )
param-expr-list         ::= param-expr [ , param-expr-list ]
param-expr              := integer expressions evaluated prior to array constructor
expression              := arbitrary expression of array element type
```

Figure 1: Syntax for the basic monolithic array constructor

programmer specify an array by giving separate rules for several *index regions* within the index domain. Each index region may be specified as a union of rectangular regions and points. Although this could be expressed using nested conditional expressions that test index values, the use of expressions guarded by region specifications yields a more natural and compact format. This is done by allowing the body of the array constructor to consist of a set of pairs, each consisting of a list of *region specifications* and an array element expression.

The syntax of the basic array constructor is given in Figure 1. An n-dimensional rectangular index region R can be denoted by a pair [*shape, lowbd*], where both *shape* and *lowbd* are ordered n-tuples of integers. This format is adapted from [29]. Each element of the *shape* tuple is the length of the corresponding dimension of the specified region; the *lowbd* tuple specifies the origin of the region. For example, a 10-by-10 two-dimensional index region with lower bound at (0,0) is represented by [(10,10),(0,0)].

The *domain-spec* defines the index region as a shape/lower bound pair. The *region-constructor-list* specifies a list of region constructors separated by the parallel or sequential composition operators ";" and "!". A region constructor may be a *region-spec* followed by an expression for computing array elements in that region. Each region-spec defines a subspace within the index domain by specifying a rectangular subspace, or by giving a list of points.

The semantics of the array constructor is strict: the construct fails to returns an array value if the computation of any element fails to complete. This decision is based on the observation that strict semantics is satisfactory for most arrays constructed in scientific computation. The difference between strict and nonstrict semantics is important. Some expressions that terminate with valid results under nonstrict semantics will fail to terminate under strict semantics. There is a debatable question as to whether programs for which this distinction exists are "good" programs. Another difference is that greater parallelism may be exploitable under a nonstrict semantics because, for example, the consumer of an array value may begin processing elements before the producer has given values to all elements. However, implementations honoring strict semantics can also use elements before all have been computed.

The convenience of the array constructor for real scientific computation may be illustrated by an example from the SIMPLE benchmark – the NodeReflect routine[8]. In this routine, the boundary elements of a data array are defined by different formulas for each part of the boundary.

As shown in Figure 2, there are 13 pieces that must be separately defined. The complexity of assembling the result array is illustrated by the Sisal code for NodeReflect given in Figure 3. In this form of the code the 13 components are constructed as separate arrays and concatenated, horizontally and then vertically, to form the result. Though current Sisal compilers are actually able to determine that this code may be optimized to the construction of a single array without any copying, this style of programming is very awkward. Alternatively, it could be written in Sisal as a single parallel **for** expression in which the body is an elaborate nested conditional that tests which of the 13 regions apply to the current index values and selects the proper formula. Although the tests on the indices may be optimized away, the new code would still be awkward.

Conventional languages with their side effects can use assignment statements to write the values into memory slots at will, thus avoiding the problem of having to combine various bits and pieces explicitly into a coherent whole. But by using the new monolithic array constructor with a partitioned index domain as shown in Figure 2, we can keep the important advantage of referential transparency found in purely functional languages, yet avoid the problems of incremental construction. The new code uses no concatenations, no copying, and no conditionals.

The level of performance that is achievable for programs using the monolithic array constructor will depend on characteristics of the target machine and on the information available at compile time. If the parameter values that determine the position and shape of the index domain and the region specifications are not known to the compiler, then many decisions about storage allocation and process partitioning and scheduling must be deferred to execution time. If parameter values are known at compile time, the compiler can check that the specified regions do not overlap and that they collectively fill up the index domain.

Index regions of other shapes such as diagonals or hyperplanes are also useful in scientific computation. We will illustrate their specification later in the paper. The next section extends the constructor to recursively defined arrays.

```
                K_min-1              K_max K_max+1
              ┌─────┬─────────────────┬─────┬─────┐
   L_min-1    │ C_1 │     Top Mid     │ D_1 │ C_2 │
              ├─────┼─────────────────┼─────┼─────┤
              │     │                 │     │     │
              │ Lft │        X        │ Rgt │     │
              │     │                 │     │     │
   L_max      │ D_2 │                 │ D_3 │     │
              ├─────┼─────────────────┼─────┼─────┤
   L_max+1    │ C_3 │     Bot Mid     │ D_4 │ C_4 │
              └─────┴─────────────────┴─────┴─────┘
```

```
for (i,j) in [(Lmax-Lmin+1,Kmax-Kmin+1),(Lmin-1,Kmin-1)] construct
  [(1,1),(Lmin-1,Kmin-1)] : 0.0                                  % C1
  [(1,1),(Lmin-1,Kmax+1)] : 0.0                                  % C2
  [(1,1),(Lmax+1,Kmin-1)] : 0.0                                  % C3
  [(1,1),(Lmax+1,Kmax+1)] : 0.0                                  % C4
  [(1,1),(Lmin-1,Kmax)]
       : Projct( X[Lmin,Kmax], X[Lmin,Kmax-1], X[Lmin+1,Kmax]); % D1
  [(1,1),(Lmax,Kmin-1)]
       : Projct( X[Lmax,Kmin], X[Lmax-1,Kmin], X[Lmax,Kmin+1]); % D2
  [(1,1),(Lmax+1,Kmax)]
       : Projct( X[Lmax,Kmax], X[Lmax,Kmax-1], X[Lmax-1,Kmax]); % D3
  [(1,1),(Lmax+1,Kmax)]
       : Projct( X[Lmax,Kmax], X[Lmax,Kmax-1], X[Lmax-1,Kmax]); % D4
  [(1,Kmax-Kmin),(Lmin-1,Kmin)]
       : Projct( X[Lmin,j], X[Lmin,j+1], X[Lmin+1,j] );         % TopMid
  [(1,Kmax-Kmin),(Lmax+1,Kmin)]
       : Projct( X[Lmax,j], X[Lmax,j+1], X[Lmax-1,j] );         % BotMid
  [(Lmax-Lmin,1),(Lmin,Kmin-1)]
       : Projct( X[L,Kmin], X[L+1,Kmin], X[L,Kmin+1] );         % Lft
  [(Lmax-Lmin,1),(Lmin,Kmax+1)]
       : Projct( X[L,Kmax], X[L+1,Kmax], X[L,Kmax-1] );         % Rgt
  otherwise              : X[i,j]                                % interior
end for
```

Figure 2: NodeReflect written with new monolithic constructor.

```
function NodeReflect(X:TwoDim; Kmin,Kmax,Lmin,Lmax:integer returns TwoDim)
let
  C1,C2,C3,C4 := 0.0, 0.0, 0.0, 0.0;
  D1      := Projct( X[Kmin,Lmax], X[Kmin,Lmax-1], X[Kmin+1,Lmax] );
  D2      := Projct( X[Kmax,Lmax], X[Kmax-1,Lmax], X[Kmax,Lmax-1] );
  D3      := Projct( X[Kmax,Lmin], X[Kmax-1,Lmin], X[Kmax,Lmin-1] );
  D4      := Projct( X[Kmax,Lmax], X[Kmax,Lmax-1], X[Kmax-1,Lmax] );
  TopMid := for L in Lmin,Lmax-1
            returns array of Projct( X[Kmin,L], X[Kmin,L+1], X[Kmin+1,L] )
            end for;
  BotMid := for L in Lmin,Lmax-1
            returns array of Projct( X[Kmax,L], X[Kmax,L+1], X[Kmax-1,L] )
            end for;
  MidRows:= for K in Kmin,Kmax-1
              Lft := Projct( X[K,Lmin], X[K+1,Lmin], X[K,Lmin+1] );
              Rgt := Projct( X[K,Lmax], X[K+1,Lmax], X[K,Lmax-1] );
              Row := array [Lmin-1:Lft] || X[K] || array [1:Rgt]
            returns array of Row
            end for;
  TopRow := array [Lmin-1:C1] || TopMid || array [1:D1,C2]
  LowRow := array [Lmin-1:D2] || X[Kmax] || array [1:D3];
  BotRow := array [Lmin-1:C3] || BotMid || array [1:D4,C4]
in    array [Kmin-1:TopRow]
  || MidRows
  || array [1:LowRow]
  || array [1:BotRow]
end let
end function
```

Figure 3: NodeReflect written in Sisal.

4 Recursive Array Construction

An array is *recursively defined* if some elements of the array depend on other elements. For example, the array A in the wavefront example introduced earlier is recursively defined: each element of A depends on its north, west and northwest neighbours (except the elements of the top and left boundaries).

The data dependences between elements of a recursively defined array may put constraints on the order of their evaluation. In the Haskell array comprehension, the order of evaluation of array elements is not explicitly specified by the programmer. If a compiler does not identify the dependences, a general (and inefficient) implementation scheme must be used.

Two strategies that may be used to avoid such overhead in implementations of monolithic array constructors are:

Strategy 1: Have the compiler attempt to identify dependences without assistance from the programmer. Use optimized code for common regularities that can be recognized. Use a general implementation scheme as the default.

Strategy 2: Provide means in the language to explicitly indicate evaluation order where this information may help a compiler to construct a more efficient implementation.

Researchers have been working on both compile-time and runtime methods based on strategy 1 [3,4]. Subscript analysis, originally developed for vectorizing/parallelizing compilers of imperative languages, can be adapted to find some efficient and safe evaluation order.

To pursue strategy 2 for recursive array definition, we extend our basic monolithic array constructor with features which allow programmers to express explicitly sequential evaluation orderings wherever they are needed both within and between regions. We add a *sequence-region-constructor* which specifies a region of the array to be recursively defined:

region-constructor	::=	*basic-region-constructor*
		sequence-region-constructor
basic-region-constructor	::=	*region-spec : expression*
sequence-region-constructor	::=	**ordered by** *id* **from** *range*
		region-constructor

Let us illustrate the construct by an example. The following program constructs an array where each column is computed by a first-order linear recurrence.

```
for (i,j) in [(n,n),(1,1)] construct AT
    [(1,n),(1,1)] : 1 !                         % Init top row first,
ordered by i from [2..n]                        % then iterate over
    [(1,n),(i,1)] : B[i,j] + AT[i-1,j] + C[i,j] % the lower n-1 rows.
end for
```

First, we note that an internal name, AT, for the recursively defined array is introduced after the keyword **construct**. The semantics allows AT to be referenced inside the scope of the monolithic constructor, making it possible to reference the elements of the array before it is completely constructed.

The above program partitions the index region into rows. Following initialization of the first row, the ordered clause specifies that the remaining rows be evaluated in ascending sequence, row 2, row 3, etc., up to row n. Because no other ordering is specified, evaluation of array elements within each row can, by default, be performed in parallel.

The order specified between the regions will be checked by a compiler to confirm that the array elements are in fact defined before they are used in the array construction. If such checks fail, appropriate measures must be taken to warn the user. In may cases, our array constructor makes such checks straightforward. We discuss the issue further in the next section.

5   A Solution to the Wavefront Problem

So far, we have considered simple partitions of the index domain such as rows or columns. Other partitions may be more beneficial depending on the computation to be performed. The wavefront program discussed earlier is a good example where maximum parallelism would be achieved by evaluating the upper and left border elements all in parallel, then processing each of the secondary diagonals in sequence starting from the upper left corner (elements within each diagonal can be evaluated in parallel). There has been interesting work done on automatic detection and parallelization of wavefronts [6,22,25]. Our monolithic array constructor can express such an evaluation scheme:

```
for (i,j) in [(n,n),(1,1)] construct AT
    [(1,n),(1,1)]                : 1;  % initialize top row
    [(n-1,1),(2,1)]               : 1!  % initialize left column
    ordered by k from [4..2*n-1]        % fill the interior by diagonals
        [i+j=k] & [(n-1,n-1),(2,2)] : AT[i-1,j] + AT[i,j-1] + AT[i-1,j-1]
endfor
```

In this code the entire index domain is partitioned such that the first row and first column are initialized simultaneously. The rest of the index domain is partitioned into $2n - 3$ secondary diagonals. Note that the diagonals are specified by a new kind of *region-spec*, i.e. the equation $i + j = k$ of a line in the index space. More precisely, the region is implicitly defined as the intersection ("&") of the straight lines $i + j = k$ and the enclosing rectangular region [(n-1,n-1),(2,2)], for $k = 4..2n - 1$.

The construction of the diagonals is ordered explicitly by the ascending range given for k, and proceeds from top-left to bottom-right. The elements in any one diagonal may, by default, be evaluated in parallel. It is easy to check that the specified evaluation order is consistent with the data dependences. We only need to check the following condition for consistency: all references to the result array must lie in a region already defined, i.e., on the boundary or on one side of the diagonal line $i + j = k$. In this particular example, the subscripts of AT[i-1,j], AT[i,j-1], and AT[i-1,j-1] all do in fact meet this straightforward test.

The role of array subscript analysis is the subject of the next section.

6 Compile-time Checking

First, we would like to contrast our subscript analysis to the traditional approach taken by parallelizing compilers for von Neumann languages such as Fortran and to the approach an optimizing compiler of a functional language such as Haskell may take.

Programs written in imperative languages *overspecify* the evaluation order of array elements: the sequential execution of statements yields a sequence of assignments to array elements. A parallelizing/vectorizing compiler performs array subscript analysis to detect the true dependences so the program may be transformed to exploit parallelism. The transformation must be *safe*, i.e., one that preserves all true dependences. In order to assure safety, a compiler must decide whether or not a given set of linear Diophantine equations in N variables has an integer solution in a certain index region [5]. No efficient algorithm has been found to derive a necessary and sufficient condition for such a test in general. To ensure safeness, a compiler must be conservative if the tests fail to exclude the possibility of dependence.

At the other extreme, a monolithic array constructor such as the Haskell array comprehension *underspecifies* the evaluation order. In fact no evaluation ordering is given at all. An optimizing compiler needs to perform subscript analysis to determine a correct evaluation order, if one exists.

The monolithic array constructor described in this paper allows the programmer to introduce explicit sequential ordering between regions of the array. The default "ordering" is parallel. In contrast to the two types of compilers mentioned above, the role of our compiler is to check that the programmer-specified order is consistent with the data dependences of the array definition. In other word, the compiler must check that the specified order of regions ensures that array elements are defined before they are used. Unlike a parallelizing compiler for Fortran, our compiler has no "first-order" obligation to parallelize the sequential order explicitly introduced by the programmer. Unlike an optimizing compiler for Haskell, our compiler does not need to discover a safe sequential order.

In the next section we discuss a simple subscript analysis that answers the consistency question for our array constructor.

7 Subscript Analysis

In a recursive array definition, an array element may be computed from other elements of the same array. In using the proposed array constructor, it is the programmer's responsibility to specify a correct evaluation order. The compiler should detect data dependences that are inconsistent with the specified order and report these as errors. In our case, the test to be made is that recursive references must fall only in regions that are earlier in the specified evaluation order. This amounts to making sure that a read of an array element is performed only after it has been defined (or "written", in the parlance of imperative languages).

Let us consider the general case:

```
for (x₁, ..., xₙ) in region-spec
construct A
    ... (initialization here) ...
    ordered by k from range
    [k = c₁x₁ + c₂x₂ + ... + cₙxₙ]                              % a hyperplane
        : ... A[f₁(x₁,..., xₙ), f₂(x₁, ..., xₙ), ..., fₙ(x₁, ..., xₙ)] ...   % recursive ref
end for
```

where the user specifies a sequence of hyperplanes H_k ($\forall k \in$ range) in an n-dimensional index region and the k-th hyperplane H_k is defined using a linear function with n indices $x_1, x_2...x_n$:

$$c_1 x_1 + c_2 x_2 + ... + c_n x_n = k \qquad (1)$$

We assume that $c_1, c_2...c_n$ are integer constants known at compile time. Using the monolithic array constructor, the elements of an array A lying on the hyperplane H are computed, with possible references to other elements of array A in the form

$$A[f_1(x_1, ..., x_n), f_2(x_1, ..., x_n), ..., f_n(x_1, ..., x_n)]$$

where the f_i are linear, i.e.

$$f_i(x_1, ..., x_n) = a_{i,0} + a_{i,1}x_1 + a_{i,2}x_2 + ... + a_{i,n}x_n \qquad (2)$$

and $a_{i,0}, a_{i,1}...a_{i,n}$ are constants. The problem is to check that for all k, the following holds:

$$c_1 f_1(x_1, ..., x_n) + c_2 f_2(x_1, ..., x_n) + ... + c_n f_n(x_1, ..., x_n) < k \qquad (3)$$

under the conditions

$$l_i \leq x_i \leq h_i \qquad \forall i \in 1..n \qquad (4)$$

where l_i, h_i are the bounds on the i-th dimensions of the index region.

For example, in the wavefront program, the hyperplanes are just the secondary diagonals of the 2-dimensional index region

$$c_i = 1, \quad \forall i \in 1..2$$

Consider, for instance, the array reference A[i-1,j-1]. We have

$$a_{1,1} = a_{2,2} = 1$$
$$a_{1,0} = a_{2,0} = -1$$
$$a_{i,j} = 0 \quad \text{otherwise}$$

The consistency check is trivial in this case.

For the general case, the test expressed by inequality (3) can be rewritten in the form:

$$\sum_{i=1}^{n} b_i x_i - k < -b_0 \qquad (5)$$

where

$$b_i = \sum_{j=1}^{n} c_j a_{j,i} \qquad \forall i \in 0..n \qquad (6)$$

Substituting the left hand side of (1) for k in (5):

$$\sum_{i=1}^{n} b_i x_i - \sum_{i=1}^{n} c_i x_i < -b_0 \qquad (7)$$

then collecting terms we end up with

$$\sum_{i=1}^{n} d_i x_i < -b_0 \qquad (8)$$

where

$$d_i = b_i - c_i \qquad (9)$$

Note that the a_i, b_i, c_i and d_i are all compile-time constants. Therefore, our problem of testing whether inequality (8) holds under condition (4) reduces to the standard problem of computing the bounds of a linear function in a trapezoidal region [5](Chapter 4). Both closed form solutions and reasonable algorithms exist, and the test can be performed without having to solve a system of linear Diophantine equations (what a relief!). In fact, for the most common cases the test is really trivial, as we have seen in the wavefront example. If the test succeeds, we are assured that the specified order is consistent with the data dependences. If the test fails, the program is erroneous and the compiler should report back to the programmer for debugging purposes.

The analysis described above can be put to even better use. Often an iterative relaxation algorithm will read old values from in front of the wavefront as well as new values from behind the wavefront, e.g.:

$$A^{t+1}[i,j] = (A^{t+1}[i-1,j] + A^{t+1}[i,j-1] + A^t[i,j+1] + A^t[i+1,j])/4$$

Under such conditions the the preceding analysis will verify that an implementation may safely overwrite A^t with A^{t+1}.

The analysis method we have presented assumes that array references in the body expression have only linear subscript expressions. From previous parallelization work for conventional languages such as Fortran [26], a substantial percentage of scientific programs appear to satisfy this requirement. Finally, if the body expression contains function calls, the compiler may need to perform analysis of the function invocation. We believe such analysis will be much simpler than a general interprocedural analysis for conventional languages due to the absence of side effects.

8 The LU-decomposition Problem

One problem that has attracted a lot of attention as a test case for array facilities in functional languages is LU-decomposition of matrices.[1] In this section we present our solution to the problem and illustrate its advantges.

LU decomposition is used to solve systems of linear equations of the form:

$$\begin{bmatrix} a_{1,1} & \cdots & a_{1,n} \\ & \cdots & \\ a_{n,1} & \cdots & a_{n,n} \end{bmatrix} \begin{bmatrix} x_1 \\ \vdots \\ x_n \end{bmatrix} = \begin{bmatrix} b_1 \\ \vdots \\ b_n \end{bmatrix}$$

This can be expressed by the equation $Ax = b$, where A is a square matrix. In LU-decomposition A is decomposed into two submatrices:

- L: A lower triangular matrix which excludes the diagonal
  (more precisely, all diagonals of LU are equal to 1 and are omitted);

- U: An upper triangular matrix which includes the diagonal.

$$\begin{bmatrix} & U \\ L & \end{bmatrix}$$

One solution method for LU-decomposition is to use Gaussian elimination [35]. To simplify the discussion, we assume that no pivoting is performed. The structure of the algorithm is illustrated in Figure 4.

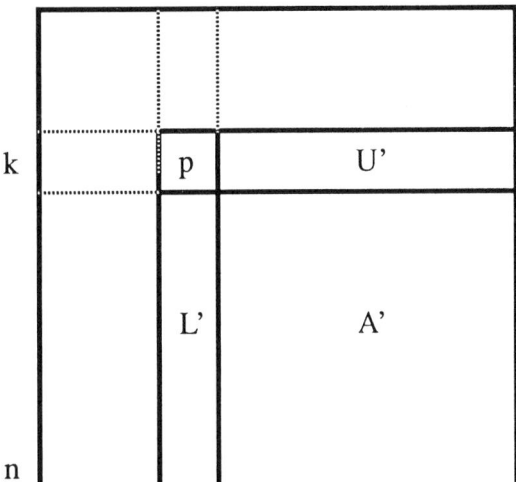

p = (A[k, k]) = pivot element at step k

L' : the new column of multipliers generated at step k, i.e.
   A[i, k] = A[i, k]/A[k, k]
      for i=k+1...n

A' : the k-1 by k-1 submatrix generated by elimination at step k:
   A[i, j] = A[i, j] - A[i, k] * A[k, j]
      for i, j = k+1...n

Figure 4: LU-Decomposition using Gaussian elimination

---

[1]LU-decomposition was suggested as a revealing exercise by Arvind during the IFIP WG 2.8 meeting in Mystic, Connecticut in May, 1989.

The algorithm proceeds in n steps. At each step k, it uses the pivot element p at $A[k,k]$ to generate a new partial column L', then using elements from the current partial row U' it performs elimination on the $k-1$ by $k-1$ submatrix.

In programs written in a conventional language such as Fortran, the new data for L and U overwrite corresponding locations of A and are unchanged for the remainder of the computation. Using previous proposals of monolithic array constructors, coding Gaussian elimination may involve the creation of a sequence of $n-1$ intermediate arrays, which may lead to excess overhead due to computation-less copying and waste memory space. The problem was pointed out by Nikhil [30] in a discussion of his draft solution (see Figure 5). To avoid such problems, both Hudak and Nikhil have given solutions to the LU-decomposition using a different algorithm (the Crout method) [18,31].

```
def LUD A_initial N =
            -- As[1] is the original matrix to be decomposed.
            -- As[k] (k in 2..N) is an (N-k+1) by (N-k+1) matrix
            -- obtained by elimination from A[k-1] and L[k-1].
    { As = {vector (1,N)
          | [1]   = A_initial
          | [k+1] = elim As[k] L[k] k      || k <- 1 to N-1};

            -- L[k] (k in 1..N-1) is the column of multipliers from step k.
      L = {vector (1,N-1)
          | [k]   = multipliers As[k] k    || k <- 1 to N-1};

            -- U[i] (i in 1..N) is just a copy of the top row of As[i].
      U = {vector (1,N)
          | [i]   = {vector (i,N)
                    | [j] = As[i][i,j]     || j <- i to N}
                                           || i <- 1 to N}
      def multipliers Ak k
         = {vector (k+1,N)
           | [i]   = Ak[i,k]/Ak[k,k]       || i <- k+1 to N};

      def elim Ak Lk k
         = {matrix (k+1,N),(k+1,N)
           | [i,j] = Ak[i,j]-Ak[k,j]*Lk[i] || i <- k+1 to N
                                           &  j <- k+1 to N};
    in L,U }
```

Figure 5: LU-Decomposition written in Id-Nouveau

9 Monotonic Definition of an Iteration Variable

It is quite natural (to us at least) to specify the highly recursive computation of LU decomposition using explicit evaluation steps, as required by the Gaussian elimination method. We observe that the use of unnecessary intermediate arrays is due to the single assignment style of functional programming – at each step a new (temporary) array is defined. However, one of the main reasons for only allowing single assignment in applicative languages is to eliminate side-effects in programs (and keep referential transparency). Now let us ask what side-effects may appear if we eliminate those intermediate arrays.

First, let us begin with a simple example of an iterative definition of a scalar in Val:

```
x := for   i := 1;
           t := t1
      do if i = N then t
         else iter
             i := i+1;
             t := f(t)        % assume that f is some unary function
         enditer endif
      endfor
```

In this loop expression the internal name t will be bound to a sequence of intermediate values during the tail-recursive computation. However, t is not visible outside the loop. A compiler should not allocate an array to hold these intermediate values of t because only the final value may be used outside the loop. In a dataflow interpreter [10], t is carried by successive tokens during each iteration through the loop. The sequence of "overwrites" to t may be viewed as a sequence of operations which *monotonically* defines the final result.

Now let us apply these observations to provide for the monotonic definition of arrays using the new array constructor. This may be done by adding an iteration facility. Using this facility, the LU-decomposition can then be written as:

```
AA := for i,j in [1,n]
      construct AT iterby k from [1..n]
      initial AT := A repeat

          [(n-k,1),(k+1,k)]:            % First process current column
            AT[i,k]/AT[k,k]             % by computing the multipliers.
          !
          [(n-k,n-k),(k,k+1)]:          % Then process the current row:
            AT[i,j]-(NEW AT)[i,k]*AT[k,j] % eliminate in n-k by n-k region

      end for
```

The line construct AT iter by k from [1..n] means that the body of the code is to be executed once for each value of k using a single copy of the array AT. Right-hand-side references to AT refer to values as defined by the previous iteration (or the initial value) A reference to NEW AT refers to values defined in the current iteration. References to elements that are not yet defined and overwrites of already defined elements are programming errors.

During each step of **k**, the two regions are evaluated in sequence (as specified by the sequential composition operator "!"): the computation of the column multipliers is performed first, follwed by elimination of the remaining (n−k)-by-(n−k) region.

Evaluation of array elements within either of the two regions can be done in parallel by default. Values of elements of AT outside these two regions will not change, thus avoiding useless copying. In each iteration, the specified binding regions and the default regions form a partition of the indexdomain of the array constructor.

Something like the above code could be written in Sisal using the iterative **for initial** loop with incremental update of the array. The advantage of our proposal is that it avoids the use of incremental array update operations, making it easy for a compiler to determine that only a single array need be allocated for the result.

10 Future Work

One problem which has not been fully addressed in this paper is the detection that the subregions making up a partition are mutually exclusive and collectively exhaustive. Neither have we proven that all array references can be shown conclusively at compile time to lie within or outside a defined region. Although both are clearly programming errors, we are seeking a solution which will ensure that such errors should be manifested by the implementation in a deterministic fashion for debugging purpose. We are currently evaluating existing solutions proposed for Haskell or Id Nouveau through runtime detection and resolution mechanism, as well as investigating our own schemes. We plan to report our solution in another publication.

We plan to continue experimenting with the new array constructor on a number of representative benchmark programs. Based on these experiments, we hope to improve the design and study its implementation on the McGill dataflow architecture model [11].

References

1 W.B. Ackerman. A structure processing facility for data flow computers. In *Proceedings of the 1978 International Conference on Parallel Processing*, Aug. 1978.

2 W.B. Ackerman and J.B. Dennis. *VAL — A Value-Oriented Algorithmic Language*. Technical Report 218, Laboratory for Computer Science, MIT, 1979.

3 S. Anderson and P. Hudak. Compilation of Haskell array comprehensions for scientific computing. In *Proc. of the ACM SIGPLAN Conference on Programming Language Design and Implementation (SIGPLAN Notices, vol. 25, no. 6)*, pages 137–149, June 1990.

4 Arvind, R.S. Nikhil, and K.K. Pingali. I-Structures: Data structures for parallel computing. *ACM TOPLAS*, 11(4):598–632, Oct 1989.

5 U. Banerjee. *Dependence Analysis for Supercomputing*. Kluwer Academic Publishers, Boston, Ma., 1988.

6 U. Banerjee. Unimodular transformations of double loops. In *Proc. of the Third Workshop on Programming Languages and Compilers for Parallel Computing*, Irvine, Ca., Aug 1990. To be published by Pitman in their series Monographs in Parallel and Distributed Computing.

7 D.C. Cann. *Compilation Techniques for High Performance Applicative Computation*. PhD thesis, Colorado State University, 1989.

8 W.P. Crowley, C.P. Henderson, and T.E. Rudy. *The SIMPLE code*. Technical Report UCID-17715, Lawrence Livermore National Laboratory, Feb 1978.

9 J. Darlington, P. Henderson, and D.A. Turner. *Functional Programming and its Applications — An Advance Course*. Cambridge University Press, 1982.

10 J.B. Dennis. First version of a data-flow procedure language. In *Proceedings of the Colloque sur la Programmation*, pages 362–376, Springler-Verlag, 1974.

11 G.R. Gao. A flexible architecture model for hybrid dataflow and control-flow evaluation. In *Proc. of the International Workshop: Dataflow — A Status Report*, in conjunction with the ACM Annual Symposium on Computer Architecture, Israel, May 1989. To be published by Prentice-Hall.

12 K. Gopinath and J.L. Hennessy. *Copy Elimination with Abstract Interpretation*. CLaSSiC Project Manuscript CLaSSiC-87-17, Stanford University, 1987.

13 K.P. Gostelow and R.E. Thomas. A view of dataflow. In *AFIPS Conf. Proc., vol. 48*, pages 629–636, 1979.

14 P.N. Hilfinger and P. Colella. *FIDIL: A Language for Scientific Processing*. Technical Report UCRL 98057, Lawrence Livermore National Laboratory, Jan 1988.

15 P. Hudak. *ALFL Reference Manual and Programmer's Guide*. Technical Report YALEU/DCS/TR-322, Yale University, July 1984.

16 P. Hudak. Arrays, non-determinism, and parallelism: A functional perspective. In *Graph Reduction*, pages 312–327, Springer-Verlag, LNCS-279, 1987.

17 P. Hudak. Conception, evolution, and application of functional programming languages. *Computing Surveys*, 21(3), Sept. 1989.

18 P. Hudak and S. Anderson. *Haskell Solutions to the Language Session Problems at the 1988 Salishan High-Speed Computing Conference*. Technical Report YALEU/DCS/RR-627, Yale University, Jan 1988.

19 P. Hudak and A. Bloss. The aggregate update problem in functional systems. In *Proc. of the 12th ACM Symp. on Principles of Prog. Lang.*, pages 300–314, 1985.

20 P. Hudak and P. Wadler (editors). *Report on the Programming Language Haskell, A Non-strict Purely Functional Language (Version 1.0)*. Technical Report YALEU/DCS/RR777, Yale University, Department of Computer Science, April 1990.

21 American National Standards Institute. Fortran 8X draft. *Fortran Forum*, 8(4), Dec 1989.

22 F. Irigoin and R. Triolet. Supernode partitioning. In *Proc. of the 15th ACM Symp. on Principles of Prog. Lang.*, pages 319–329, 1988.

23 Kenneth E. Iverson. *A Programming Language*. John Wiley and Sons, New York, 1962.

24 R.M. Keller. *FEL (Function Equaation Language) Programmer's Guide*. Technical Report AMPS Technical Report 7, University of Utah, April 1983.

25 M. Lam and M. Wolf. Maximizing parallelism via linear loop transformations. In *Proc. of the Third Workshop on Programming Languages and Compilers for Parallel Computing*, Irvine, Ca., Aug 1990. To be published by Pitman in their series Monographs in Parallel and Distributed Computing.

26 Z. Li, P.-C. Yew, and C.-Q. Zhu. An efficient data dependence analysis for parallelizing compilers. *IEEE Trans. on Parallel and Distributed Systems*, 1(1):26–34, Jan 1990.

27 J.R. McGraw, S. Skedzielewski, et al. *SISAL: Streams and Iteration in a Single Assignment Language — Language Reference Manual Version 1.2*. Technical Report M-146, Lawrence Livermore National Laboratory, 1985.

28 T. More. Notes on the diagrams, logic and operations of array theory. In Bjorke and Franksen, editors, *Structures and Operations in Engineering and Management Systems*, Tapir Pub., Trondheim, Norway, 1981.

29 L.M.R. Mullin. *A Mathematics of Arrays*. PhD thesis, Syracuse University, 1988.

30 R.S. Nikhil. Solution to the LU decomposition problem posed at IFIPS WG 2.8 meeting. May 1989. Unpublished communication.

31 R.S. Nikhil and Arvind. *Id: A Language with Implicit Parallelism*. Computation Structures Group Memo 305, Laboratory for Computer Science, MIT, 1990.

32 R.S. Nikhil, K. Pingali, and Arvind. *Id Nouveau*. Computation Structures Group Memo 265, Laboratory for Computer Science, MIT, 1986.

33 S.L. Peyton Jones. *The Implementation of Functional Programming Languages*. Prentice-Hall International Series in Computer Science, 1987.

34 J.E Ranelletti. *Graph Transformation Algorithms for Array Memory Optimization in Applicative Languages*. PhD thesis, University of California, Davis, 1988.

35 G.W. Stewart. *Introduction to Matrix Computation*. Academic Press, Inc., 1973.

36 P.L. Wadler. A new array operations. In *Graph Reduction*, pages 328–335, Springer-Verlag, LNCS-279, 1987.

37 D. Wise. Matrix algebra and applicative programming. In G. Kahn, editor, *Funct. Prog. Lang. and Comp. Arch.*, pages 301–324, Springer-Verlag, LNCS-274, 1987.

10 Unimodular Transformations of Double Loops

U. Banerjee

Abstract

The aim of this paper is to present a unified matrix-based theory for transforming a nest of loops, in order to determine those instances of the loop-body that can execute in parallel. The transformation we are dealing with is the general wavefront method that includes loop interchange, loop reversal, and loop skewing as special cases. A nest of two loops with constant loop limits is taken as the program model for this paper; however, the transformation is not restricted to this model. We study the transformation of the nest into a new nest, caused by an arbitrary unimodular matrix acting on the index variables. Theorems and algorithms are presented dealing with the questions that arise naturally: validity of such a transformation, computation of loop limits of the new nest, feasibility of parallel execution of the outer or the inner loop of the transformed nest, existence of matrices that allow such parallel execution, identification of matrices that produce the well-known loop transformations mentioned above, etc. This uniform treatment includes and generalizes known results in the area and produces several new ones.

1. Introduction

In the area of automatic restructuring of double loops for parallel processing, the transformations called the Wavefront or Hyperplane Method (Lamport [8]), and Loop Interchange (Wolfe [11, 12], Allen & Kennedy [1]) are well-known. The transformations of Skewing (Wolfe [10]) and

Loop Reversal are also used sometimes. The last three transformations are actually special cases of the Wavefront Method, although they are not normally viewed as such. In this paper, we treat the Wavefront Method in terms of matrix transformations of the index vector of the original double loop. This enables us to create a rigorous theory of loop transformations that contains all the known results in this area and produces new results and algorithms, all in a natural unified way. Instead of having to apply the transformations mentioned above in an *ad hoc* manner, we just apply one matrix transformation, where the choice of the matrix is determined by the nature of the problem. This transformation may be an interchange, a reversal, a skewing, a general wavefront, or a certain combination of these. There is no longer any need to consider the order, validity, or usefulness of applying the elemental transformations to a particular case.

To give an idea of the subject matter, we consider a simple example:

L_1:   do I_1 = 0, 3, 1
L_2:   do I_2 = 0, 2, 1
   S: $A(I_1, I_2) = A(I_1 - 1, I_2) + A(I_1, I_2 - 1)$
              end do
           end do

The index vector of the double loop is (I_1, I_2); it takes the 12 values indicated in Fig. 1, which constitute the iteration space of the program. There are two dependence distance vectors: $(1, 0)$ and $(0, 1)$. The outer loop L_1 cannot be executed in parallel, since the four instances of the inner loop L_2, corresponding to the four values 0, 1, 2, 3 of I_1, are not mutually independent. For any given value of I_1, the inner loop cannot be executed in parallel, since the three instances of S, corresponding to the three values 0, 1, 2 of I_2, are not independent. Loop interchange, although valid here, would not solve the problem. The standard practice in this case is to sweep the iteration space by a packet of straight lines of the form

$I_1 + I_2$ = constant.

This constitutes a 'wave' in the direction of the vector $(1, 1)$. There are exactly six lines of this form that contain at least one point of the iteration space (Fig. 2).

We first execute the single point on line 0, then the two points on line 1 simultaneously, then the three points on line 2 simultaneously, and so on. This mode of execution is valid, since it preserves the dependence of the program statement on itself. To rewrite the original program in a form that gives this order of execution, we need to define two new variables. The first variable,

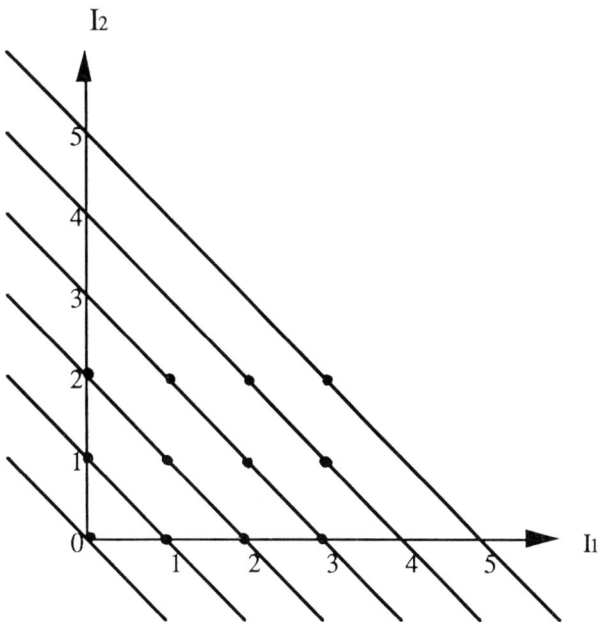

Fig. 1. Iteration Space of Example and a Wave

Line	Points
$I_1 + I_2 = 0$	(0, 0)
$I_1 + I_2 = 1$	(1, 0), (0, 1)
$I_1 + I_2 = 2$	(2, 0), (1, 1), (0, 2)
$I_1 + I_2 = 3$	(3, 0), (2, 1), (1, 2)
$I_1 + I_2 = 4$	(3, 1), (2, 2)
$I_1 + I_2 = 5$	(3, 2)

Fig. 2. Lines Covering the Iteration Space of (L_1, L_2)

call it K_1, should step through the six lines from line 0 to line 5. Obviously,

$$K_1 = I_1 + I_2 \quad \text{and} \quad 0 \leq K_1 \leq 5.$$

The choice for the second variable, call it K_2, is not that clear cut. We can take $K_2 = I_2$ and transform the given program into the following double loop:

```
        do K₁ = 0, 5, 1
            do K₂ = max{0, K₁ − 3}, min{2, K₁}, 1
S:              A(K₁ − K₂, K₂) = A(K₁ − K₂ − 1, K₂) + A(K₁ − K₂, K₂ − 1)
            end do
        end do
```

We had to replace I_1 by $K_1 - K_2$, and I_2 by K_2 to express the statement in terms of the new variables.

Let us now examine what has been done. We have moved from the given variables I_1, I_2, to a pair of new variables K_1, K_2 by the matrix transformation

$$(K_1, K_2) = (I_1, I_2) \cdot U \quad \text{where } U \text{ is the } 2 \times 2 \text{ matrix } \begin{bmatrix} 1 & 0 \\ 1 & 1 \end{bmatrix}.$$

Note that U is an integer matrix and unimodular ($\det(U) = 1$). The distance vectors $(1, 0)$ and $(0, 1)$ in the original loop have turned into the distance vectors $(1, 0)$ and $(1, 1)$, respectively, in the new loop. Since there is no longer a dependence at level 2 (i.e. for a fixed instance of the outer loop), the inner loop in the new program can be executed in parallel. The first column of U is the vector that defines the direction of the wavefront. The second column is chosen so that U is unimodular. The unimodularity is needed to guarantee that U^{-1} is an integer matrix, which ensures that an integer vector (K_1, K_2) will always map back into an integer vector (I_1, I_2). (It is not sufficient for U to be nonsingular.) There are infinitely many choices for the second column, e.g. $(1, 2)^T$, where the superscript denotes transpose. The limits of the K_2-loop are different in this case, although we still cover the same set of iteration points in each instance of the inner loop (in the new program).

There are also infinitely many choices for the first column of U. This is to be expected, since the iteration space of the original program can obviously be swept by many wavefronts. The current first column of U is optimal in the sense that the iteration count of the K_1-loop is minimized.

Some of these concepts were already in [8], although Lamport used a language slightly different from the one we use today in discussions on parallelization of serial programs. For related work, see [6] and [9] and the references in those two papers.

In the rest of the paper, we will make precise the concepts outlined informally above. Some background is described in Section 2, and Section 3 is devoted exclusively to unimodular matrices. In Section 4, we study the transformation of a double loop under an arbitrary unimodular matrix: we derive the limits of the new loop, give conditions for the validity of the transformation, and also point out when the outer or the inner loop in the new program can be executed in parallel. Section 5 looks at the special transformations of loop reversal, loop interchange, and loop skewing. In Section 6, we consider the existence of a unimodular matrix so that a given double loop could be transformed into a nest in which the outer or the inner loop can be executed in parallel. Finally, Section 7 reports some conclusions.

2. Basic Concepts

Let $\mathbf{Z}$ denote the integers. The sign of an integer x is indicated by sig(x), where sig(x) is 1, 0, or -1, if x is positive, zero, or negative, respectively. We will deal with points in $\mathbf{Z}^2$, the integer vectors of length 2. Let $\mathbf{0}$ denote the zero vector $(0, 0)$. For two vectors (i_1, i_2) and (j_1, j_2), we define

$(i_1, i_2) <_1 (j_1, j_2)$ if $i_1 < j_1$;
$(i_1, i_2) <_2 (j_1, j_2)$ if $i_1 = j_1$ and $i_2 < j_2$;
$(i_1, i_2) < (j_1, j_2)$ if   either $(i_1, i_2) <_1 (j_1, j_2)$, or $(i_1, i_2) <_2 (j_1, j_2)$.

The inverse relations of $<_1$, $<_2$ and $<$ are denoted by $>_1$, $>_2$ and $>$, respectively, and the notations like $\leq$ and $\geq$ have the usual meanings. A vector (i_1, i_2) is *positive*, if $(i_1, i_2) > \mathbf{0}$. Note that in our terminology, the vector $(1, -1)$ is positive.

The program model for this paper is the double loop

    L_1:   **do** $I_1 = n_1, N_1, 1$
    L_2:   **do** $I_2 = n_2, N_2, 1$
                  $H(I_1, I_2)$
           end do
      end do

where n_1, N_1, n_2 and N_2 are integer constants. We often refer to this construct as a loopnest, or simply a nest. Loops with strides different from 1 can be reduced to this model, if we consider iteration numbers as the primary variables. Variable loop limits can also be allowed at the cost of additional complexity in the algebraic expressions. The *index vector* of the nest is the ordered pair (I_1, I_2). The *iteration space* of the nest is the set of all possible values of (I_1, I_2), i.e. the set of points

$$\{(i_1, i_2) \in \mathbf{Z}^2 : n_1 \leq i_1 \leq N_1,\ n_2 \leq i_2 \leq N_2\}.$$

There are $(N_1 - n_1 + 1) \cdot (N_2 - n_2 + 1)$ points in the iteration space, each of which represents an iteration of the nest. In the serial execution of the nest, an iteration (i_1, i_2) is executed before an iteration (j_1, j_2) iff $(i_1, i_2) < (j_1, j_2)$. The *body* of the nest, H, may contain any program statements, including other loops. We write $H(I_1, I_2)$ in place of H to emphasize the fact that in general, H contains the loop indexes I_1 and I_2. The notation $H(i_1, i_2)$ then refers to the *instance* of H that corresponds to a particular iteration $(I_1, I_2) = (i_1, i_2)$ of the nest.

We say that there is a *dependence* in the nest, if there are iterations (i_1, i_2) and (j_1, j_2), and a memory location M, such that in the serial execution of the nest

1. The iteration (i_1, i_2) precedes the iteration (j_1, j_2), i.e., $(i_1, i_2) < (j_1, j_2)$;

2. Both instances $H(i_1, i_2)$ and $H(j_1, j_2)$ of the body reference M, and at least one of the references is a write;

3. There is no iteration (k_1, k_2) such that $(i_1, i_2) < (k_1, k_2) < (j_1, j_2)$, and M is written by the instance $H(k_1, k_2)$.

If these conditions hold, we also say that the instance $H(j_1, j_2)$ *depends* on the instance $H(i_1, i_2)$. There is a *dependence* in the nest *with a (dependence) distance vector* (D_1, D_2), if two iterations (i_1, i_2) and (j_1, j_2) exist satisfying the above conditions and $(j_1 - i_1, j_2 - i_2) = (D_1, D_2)$. There is a *dependence* in the nest *with a (dependence) direction vector* (s_1, s_2), if there is dependence with any distance vector (D_1, D_2), such that $\text{sig}(D_1) = s_1$ and $\text{sig}(D_2) = s_2$. Usually, it is convenient just to say that the nest *has* a certain distance or direction vector. Dependence at a level is dependence with a direction vector of a particular form. There is a *dependence* in the nest *at level* 1, if the nest has a direction vector of the form $(1, s_2)$. *Dependence at level* 2 means having the direction vector $(0, 1)$.

Thus, a distance vector is always positive. Level-1 dependence is indicated by a distance vector (D_1, D_2) such that $(D_1, D_2) >_1 0$, and level-2 dependence is indicated by a distance vector (D_1, D_2) such that $(D_1, D_2) >_2 0$. Similar statements can be made about direction vectors. In the literature, dependence is usually defined in terms of input and output variables of individual program statements. Dependence between statements within a fixed iteration of the nest is then possible, and there arise the concepts of level-3 dependence, zero distance vectors, and zero direction vectors. We choose to define dependence in terms of the body of the nest, since it is the entire body as a unit that we will be dealing with in the loop transformations to be considered.

The set of all distance vectors in the nest obviously carries more information than the set of all direction vectors, and specifying the direction vectors may tell us more than making a simple statement that there is dependence at level 1 and/or level 2. However, as expected, of any two of these sets, the set with the greater information content is costlier to compute and maintain. In the paper, we will first try to state a condition in terms of dependence levels, and then in terms of direction vectors or distance vectors.

The transformations we are dealing with do not affect the internal structure of the body of the nest, H. We are given a fixed set of instances of H, and are told that they should be executed serially in a certain order. The goal, of course, is to find groups of these instances that could be executed in parallel. The outer loop can be run in parallel iff there is no dependence at level 1. The inner loop can be run in parallel iff there is no dependence at level 2. If none of these works, then we try to reorder the instances of H by changing the index variables. In this endeavor, one must not violate the dependence structure of the given program. Suppose an instance $H(j_1, j_2)$ of H depends on an instance $H(i_1, i_2)$. If instances are reordered, $H(j_1, j_2)$ must follow $H(i_1, i_2)$; how closely $H(j_1, j_2)$ follows $H(i_1, i_2)$ is immaterial. The distance vector $(j_1 - i_1, j_2 - i_2)$ is allowed to change as long as it remains positive; and the direction vector $(sig(j_1 - i_1), sig(j_2 - i_2))$ may change, provided it remains positive. This leads us to the following formal statement:

Principle of Program Transformations: A reordering of the instances of the body of the given nest is valid iff each distance vector remains positive, or equivalently, iff each direction vector remains positive.

We will need Lemma 2.1 to compute the extreme values of a linear function of a single variable; see Banerjee [2, 3] for details. The positive part a^+ and the negative part a^- of a real number a are defined by $a^+ = \max\{a, 0\}$ and $a^- = \max\{-a, 0\}$. The extended Euclidean Algorithm [7] will also be useful; it is stated here for convenience.

Lemma 2.1. The minimum and maximum values of a function $f(x) = ax$ in a range $p \leq x \leq q$ are $(a^+p - a^-q)$ and $(a^+q - a^-p)$, respectively.

Algorithm 2.1. (Extended Euclidean Algorithm). Given two integers a and b, this algorithm finds $g = \gcd(a, b)$, and two integers x_0 and y_0 such that $ax_0 + by_0 = g$.

```
    (x₁, x₂) ← (1, 0)
    (c₁, c₂) ← (|a|, |b|).          /* Initialize */
    while c₂ > 0, do begin
        q ← ⌊c₁/c₂⌋
        x₁ ← x₁ - q*x₂
        c₁ ← c₁ - q*c₂
        Interchange x₁ and x₂, c₁ and c₂
    end
    g ← c₁
    x₀ ← sig(a)*x₁
    if b = 0
      then y₀ ← 0
      else y₀ ← (g - a*x₀)/b.                              ∎
```

3. Unimodular Matrices

Some familiarity with matrix theory is assumed on the reader's part. An *integer* matrix is a matrix with integer elements. Unless otherwise stated or implied, a matrix in this paper is always an integer matrix.

When dealing with integer matrices, the operations of addition, subtraction, matrix multiplication, scalar multiplication by an integer, augmentation, and taking the transpose always result in integer matrices. But, the inverse of a nonsingular integer matrix is not always an integer matrix. This is where the concept of a unimodular matrix comes in. A square integer matrix $\mathbf{A}$ is *unimodular* if $|\det(\mathbf{A})| = 1$. The important properties of unimodular matrices we will need are listed below:

Lemma 3.1. (i) The product of two unimodular matrices is a unimodular matrix.

(ii) A unimodular matrix is nonsingular. The inverse of a unimodular matrix is a unimodular matrix.

Proof. Let $\mathbf{A}$ and $\mathbf{B}$ denote two $n \times n$ unimodular matrices. For the first part, simply note that the product $\mathbf{AB}$ is an integer matrix and that $|\det(\mathbf{AB})| = |\det(\mathbf{A}) \cdot \det(\mathbf{B})| = |\det(\mathbf{A})| \cdot |\det(\mathbf{B})| = 1$.

Since $\det(\mathbf{A}) \neq 0$, matrix $\mathbf{A}$ is nonsingular. All elements of $\mathbf{A}$ being integers, the cofactor of each element is also an integer. Since $\det(\mathbf{A}) = \pm 1$, it follows from the definition that $\mathbf{A}^{-1}$ is an integer matrix. Also, we have $\det(\mathbf{A}^{-1}) = 1/\det(\mathbf{A}) = \pm 1$, so that $\mathbf{A}^{-1}$ is unimodular. ∎

We now define some particular unimodular matrices. For any n, the $n \times n$ unit matrix, denoted by $\mathbf{I}_n$, is clearly unimodular. Consider three other classes of matrices that can be easily derived from $\mathbf{I}_n$:

reversal matrices: obtained by negating a diagonal element of $\mathbf{I}_n$;

interchange matrices: obtained by interchanging two columns (or rows) of $\mathbf{I}_n$;

skewing matrices: obtained by replacing a zero element in $\mathbf{I}_n$ by a nonzero integer. If a zero above the main diagonal is replaced, we get an *upper skewing matrix*. If a zero below the main diagonal is replaced, we get an *lower skewing matrix*.

Direct computation shows that each such matrix is unimodular.

Among 2×2 matrices, there are two reversal matrices

$$\begin{bmatrix} -1 & 0 \\ 0 & 1 \end{bmatrix} \text{ and } \begin{bmatrix} 1 & 0 \\ 0 & -1 \end{bmatrix},$$

one interchange matrix $\begin{bmatrix} 0 & 1 \\ 1 & 0 \end{bmatrix}$, one set of upper skewing matrices and one set of lower skewing matrices

$$\begin{bmatrix} 1 & p \\ 0 & 1 \end{bmatrix} \text{ and } \begin{bmatrix} 1 & 0 \\ p & 1 \end{bmatrix},$$

where p denotes any integer.

These matrices are called *elementary matrices* as they can be used to perform the elementary matrix operations. The *elementary row operations* for any integer matrix are:

row (sign) reversal: multiply a row by -1,

row interchange: interchange two rows,

skewing a row by another row: replace a given row r, by row r plus an integral multiple of another row s. The *elementary column operations* are defined in an exactly similar manner.

The proofs of the following lemmas are tedious and are omitted:

Lemma 3.2. For any integer matrix **A**, an elementary row operation can be accomplished by forming the product **E·A** (i.e. premultiplying **A** by **E**), and an elementary column operation can be accomplished by forming the product **A·F** (i.e. postmultiplying **A** by **F**), where **E** and **F** are suitable elementary matrices. Either elementary matrix is a reversal, an interchange or a skewing matrix, if the operation is a reversal, an interchange or a skewing, respectively.

Lemma 3.3. The product of a finite number of elementary matrices is a unimodular matrix. Conversely, each unimodular matrix can be expressed as a product of a finite number of elementary matrices.

Corollary. A lower (upper) skewing matrix S_L can be expressed as $S_L = T_1 S_U T_2$ where S_U is an upper (lower) skewing matrix and T_1, T_2 are interchange matrices. Consequently, any unimodular matrix can be expressed as the product of reversal, interchange and upper skewing matrices, and also as a product of reversal, interchange and lower skewing matrices.

Lemma 3.4. If a matrix **A** is unimodular, then it remains unimodular after any sequence of elementary row and/or column operations. Conversely, if the result of a number of elementary operations to **A** is a unimodular matrix, then **A** itself is unimodular.

4. Validity of Unimodular Transformations

We start with the double loop

    L_1:   **do** $I_1 = n_1, N_1, 1$
    L_2:   **do** $I_2 = n_2, N_2, 1$
                      $H(I_1, I_2)$
              end do
        end do

where n_1, N_1, n_2, and N_2 are integer constants. Consider an arbitrary 2×2 unimodular integer matrix

$$U = \begin{bmatrix} u_{11} & u_{12} \\ u_{21} & u_{22} \end{bmatrix}$$

and let Δ denote $\det(U)$. Then, $\Delta = \pm 1$ and the inverse matrix

$$U^{-1} = \begin{bmatrix} u_{22}/\Delta & -u_{12}/\Delta \\ -u_{21}/\Delta & u_{11}/\Delta \end{bmatrix} = \frac{1}{\Delta}\begin{bmatrix} u_{22} & -u_{12} \\ -u_{21} & u_{11} \end{bmatrix} = \Delta\begin{bmatrix} u_{22} & -u_{12} \\ -u_{21} & u_{11} \end{bmatrix}$$

is also a unimodular integer matrix. (Note that Δ and $1/\Delta$ have the same value, so that they could be used interchangeably.) The transformation

$$(K_1, K_2) = (I_1, I_2) \cdot U = (u_{11}I_1 + u_{21}I_2, u_{12}I_1 + u_{22}I_2) \tag{1}$$

carries each given (I_1, I_2) into a unique (K_1, K_2). The inverse transformation

$$(I_1, I_2) = (K_1, K_2) \cdot U^{-1} = (\Delta u_{22}K_1 - \Delta u_{21}K_2, -\Delta u_{12}K_1 + \Delta u_{11}K_2) \tag{2}$$

carries each given (K_1, K_2) back into a unique (I_1, I_2). The important point is that (K_1, K_2) is an integer vector whenever (I_1, I_2) is an integer vector, and conversely.

The serial program (L_1, L_2) consists of a number of instances of the loop-body H, that are executed in the direction of increasing (I_1, I_2). (An instance $H(i_1, i_2)$ is executed before an instance $H(j_1, j_2)$ iff $(i_1, i_2) < (j_1, j_2)$.) Each such instance is also described by a unique value of the variables (K_1, K_2). The transformation $(L_1, L_2)^U$ of the double loop (L_1, L_2) under the matrix U is the serial program that consists of the same instances of H as in (L_1, L_2), but where the instances are executed in the order of increasing (K_1, K_2). The following theorem shows that $(L_1, L_2)^U$ can be expressed in the form of a double loop.

Theorem 4.1. Two integers m_1, M_1 and two integer-valued functions m_2, M_2 can be determined such that $(L_1, L_2)^U$, the transformation of the nest (L_1, L_2) under a unimodular matrix U, is represented as the double loop (L_1^U, L_2^U):

$L_1^U:$ do $K_1 = m_1, M_1, 1$

$L_2^U(K_1):$ do $K_2 = m_2(K_1), M_2(K_1), 1$

             $H^U(K_1, K_2)$

        end do

    end do

where $H^U(K_1, K_2)$ denotes the loop-body $H(I_1, I_2)$ after we replace (I_1, I_2) by $(K_1, K_2) \cdot U^{-1}$.

Proof. Replace (I_1, I_2) by $(K_1, K_2) \cdot U^{-1}$ in the loop-body $H(I_1, I_2)$ to get

$$H((K_1, K_2) \cdot U^{-1}) = H(\Delta u_{22} K_1 - \Delta u_{21} K_2, -\Delta u_{12} K_1 + \Delta u_{11} K_2)$$

which is denoted by $H^U(K_1, K_2)$. Each point in the iteration space can be represented by a value of (I_1, I_2) and also by a value of (K_1, K_2). It is sufficient to show that the iteration space, which is represented by the set $\{I_1 = n_1, n_1 + 1, ..., N_1;\ I_2 = n_2, n_2 + 1, ..., N_2\}$, can also be represented by a set of the form

$$\{K_1 = m_1, m_1 + 1, ..., M_1;\ K_2 = m_2(K_1), m_2(K_1) + 1, ..., M_2(K_1)\}.$$

Note that $K_1 = u_{11} I_1 + u_{21} I_2$ from (1). The minimum value m_1 and the maximum value M_1 of K_1, as I_1 varies from n_1 to N_1 and I_2 varies from n_2 to N_2, can be computed by applying Lemma 2.1 to each term:

$$m_1 = \min(u_{11} I_1) + \min(u_{21} I_2)$$
$$= (u_{11}^+ n_1 - u_{11}^- N_1) + (u_{21}^+ n_2 - u_{21}^- N_2) \quad (3)$$

$$M_1 = \max(u_{11} I_1) + \max(u_{21} I_2)$$
$$= (u_{11}^+ N_1 - u_{11}^- n_1) + (u_{21}^+ N_2 - u_{21}^- n_2). \quad (4)$$

Next, using the bounds on I_1 and I_2, we get from (2) that

$$n_1 \leq \Delta u_{22} K_1 - \Delta u_{21} K_2 \leq N_1 \quad (5)$$

and $n_2 \leq -\Delta u_{12} K_1 + \Delta u_{11} K_2 \leq N_2.$ (6)

If $u_{21} = 0$, then (5) is trivially satisfied: In this case, $\Delta = u_{11}u_{22}$ so that $u_{11} = \pm 1$ and $u_{22} = \pm 1$. Thus, $\Delta u_{22} = u_{11}(u_{22})^2 = u_{11}$. The expressions for m_1 and M_1 are simplified and we have

$$u_{11}^+ n_1 - u_{11}^- N_1 \leq K_1 \leq u_{11}^+ N_1 - u_{11}^- n_1.$$

If $u_{11} = \Delta u_{22} = 1$, then $n_1 \leq K_1 \leq N_1$ and therefore $n_1 \leq \Delta u_{22} K_1 \leq N_1$, which is (5) for the case $u_{21} = 0$. If $u_{11} = \Delta u_{22} = -1$, then $-N_1 \leq K_1 \leq -n_1$ and therefore we again have $n_1 \leq \Delta u_{22} K_1 \leq N_1$. Similarly, if $u_{11} = 0$, then (6) is trivially satisfied. The inequalities (5) and (6) imply

$$n_1 - \Delta u_{22}K_1 \leq (-\Delta u_{21})K_2 \leq N_1 - \Delta u_{22}K_1$$
and
$$n_2 + \Delta u_{12}K_1 \leq (\Delta u_{11})K_2 \leq N_2 + \Delta u_{12}K_1.$$

A set of bounds for K_2 is obtained from these inequalities (see Step 4 of Algorithm 4.1). Note that both u_{21} and u_{11} cannot be zero at the same time, since $\det(U) \neq 0$. Thus, K_2 has always at least one lower and one upper bound. Define $m_2(K_1)$ to be the ceiling of the maximum of the lower bound functions, and $M_2(K_1)$ the floor of the minimum of the upper bound functions.

For any given (I_1, I_2) in the range $\{n_1 \leq I_1 \leq N_1, n_2 \leq I_2 \leq N_2\}$, the corresponding value of (K_1, K_2) will be in the range $\{m_1 \leq K_1 \leq M_1, m_2(K_1) \leq K_2 \leq M_2(K_1)\}$. Conversely, suppose for a given K_1 in $m_1 \leq K_1 \leq M_1$, we have $m_2(K_1) \leq M_2(K_1)$. Then, working the above steps backwards, we see that for that K_1 and each integer K_2 in $m_2(K_1) \leq K_2 \leq M_2(K_1)$, the corresponding (I_1, I_2) will be an integer in the range $\{n_1 \leq I_1 \leq N_1, n_2 \leq I_2 \leq N_2\}$. Thus, both nests (L_1, L_2) and (L_1^U, L_2^U) have the same set of instances of the loop-body H. However, in the transformed nest, the instances are executed in the order of increasing (K_1, K_2). ∎

The iteration count of the outer loop in the transformed program can be found easily; the iteration counts of the different instances of the inner loop satisfy certain upper bounds:

Corollary 1. The number of iterations of the outer loop L_1^U is

$$|u_{11}| \cdot (N_1 - n_1) + |u_{21}| \cdot (N_2 - n_2) + 1.$$

Proof. Using (3) and (4), we get

$$M_1 - m_1 = (u_{11}^+ + u_{11}^-)(N_1 - n_1) + (u_{21}^+ + u_{21}^-)(N_2 - n_2)$$

$$= |u_{11}| \cdot (N_1 - n_1) + |u_{21}| \cdot (N_2 - n_2)$$

since $a^+ + a^- = |a|$ for any integer a. The number of iterations of the outer loop is $(M_1 - m_1 + 1)$, and the result follows. ∎

Corollary 2. The number of iterations of any instance of the inner loop $L_2^U(K_1)$ cannot exceed

$$\frac{(N_1 - n_1)}{|u_{21}|} + 1 \quad \text{if} \quad u_{21} \neq 0,$$

$$\frac{(N_2 - n_2)}{|u_{11}|} + 1 \quad \text{if} \quad u_{11} \neq 0.$$

Proof. If $u_{21} \neq 0$, then $(n_1 - \Delta u_{22}K_1)/(-\Delta u_{21})$ and $(N_1 - \Delta u_{22}K_1)/(-\Delta u_{21})$ are a pair of lower and upper, or upper and lower bounds for K_2. The absolute difference between the two bounds being $(N_1 - n_1)/|u_{21}|$, it follows that the number of points in the range of K_2 (i.e. the number of instances of $L_2^U(K_1)$) cannot exceed $[(N_1 - n_1)/|u_{21}| + 1]$. The second part follows if we consider the other pair of bounds for K_2: $(n_2 + \Delta u_{12}K_1)/(\Delta u_{11})$ and $(N_2 + \Delta u_{12}K_1)/(\Delta u_{11})$. ∎

The essential steps of the above theorem are stated in the form of an algorithm:

Algorithm 4.1. Given a double loop (L_1, L_2):

L_1:   do $I_1 = n_1, N_1, 1$
L_2:   do $I_2 = n_2, N_2, 1$
             $H(I_1, I_2)$
           end do
         end do

where n_1, N_1, n_2, and N_2 are integer constants, and a 2×2 unimodular integer matrix

$$U = \begin{bmatrix} u_{11} & u_{12} \\ u_{21} & u_{22} \end{bmatrix},$$

this algorithm finds the program $(L_1, L_2)^U$, the transformation of (L_1, L_2) under U, in the form of a double loop (L_1^U, L_2^U):

L_1^U: do $K_1 = m_1, M_1, 1$
$L_2^U(K_1)$:   do $K_2 = m_2(K_1), M_2(K_1), 1$
                    $H^U(K_1, K_2)$
                  end do
                end do

Here m_1, M_1 are two integers, and m_2, M_2 are two integer-valued functions that are computed from the integers n_1, N_1, n_2, and N_2. Also, $H^U(K_1, K_2)$ denotes the loop-body $H(I_1, I_2)$ after (I_1, I_2) has been replaced by $(K_1, K_2) \cdot U^{-1}$.

1. Set $\Delta \leftarrow \det(U)$.
   If $|\Delta| \neq 1$, then terminate (U is not a unimodular matrix).

2. [Find the expressions for I_1 and I_2 in terms of K_1 and K_2.]
   Set
   $$\iota_1(K_1, K_2) \leftarrow (\Delta u_{22})K_1 + (-\Delta u_{21})K_2$$
   $$\iota_2(K_1, K_2) \leftarrow (-\Delta u_{12})K_1 + (\Delta u_{11})K_2.$$

   Replace I_1 by $\iota_1(K_1, K_2)$ and I_2 by $\iota_2(K_1, K_2)$ in the loop-body $H(I_1, I_2)$ to get $H^U(K_1, K_2)$.

3. Set
   $$m_1 \leftarrow (u_{11}^+ n_1 - u_{11}^- N_1) + (u_{21}^+ n_2 - u_{21}^- N_2)$$
   $$M_1 \leftarrow (u_{11}^+ N_1 - u_{11}^- n_1) + (u_{21}^+ N_2 - u_{21}^- n_2).$$

4. Label $(n_1 - \Delta u_{22} K_1)/(-\Delta u_{21})$ a lower bound for K_2 if $(-\Delta u_{21}) > 0$, an upper bound if $(-\Delta u_{21}) < 0$.

   Label $(N_1 - \Delta u_{22} K_1)/(-\Delta u_{21})$ an upper bound for K_2 if $(-\Delta u_{21}) > 0$, a lower bound if $(-\Delta u_{21}) < 0$.

   Label $(n_2 + \Delta u_{12} K_1)/(\Delta u_{11})$ a lower bound for K_2 if $(\Delta u_{11}) > 0$, an upper bound if $(\Delta u_{11}) < 0$.

   Label $(N_2 + \Delta u_{12} K_1)/(\Delta u_{11})$ an upper bound for K_2 if $\Delta u_{11} > 0$, a lower bound if $\Delta u_{11} < 0$.

   Define $m_2(K_1)$ to be the ceiling of the maximum of the lower bound functions, and $M_2(K_1)$ the floor of the minimum of the upper bound functions. ∎

The next problem is to determine when the new nest is equivalent to the old nest. This is the subject of the following theorem.

Theorem 4.2. The transformation (L_1^U, L_2^U) of the double loop (L_1, L_2) by a unimodular matrix U, is equivalent to the original program iff for each distance vector $(D_1, D_2) > \mathbf{0}$ in (L_1, L_2), we have $(D_1, D_2) \cdot U > \mathbf{0}$.

Proof. Let (D_1, D_2) denote a dependence distance vector in the original nest (L_1, L_2). Then there are iterations (i_1, i_2) and (j_1, j_2), such that $(D_1, D_2) = (j_1, j_2) - (i_1, i_2)$. In the transformed loop (L_1^U, L_2^U), these iterations are given by $(K_1, K_2) = (j_1, j_2) \cdot U$ and $(K_1, K_2) = (i_1, i_2) \cdot U$, respectively, so that (D_1, D_2) is transformed into the vector $(D_1, D_2) \cdot U$. By the principle of program transformations, the transformed nest is equivalent to the original nest iff $(D_1, D_2) \cdot U \geq 0$ for each distance vector (D_1, D_2) in (L_1, L_2). ∎

Corollary. Suppose the transformed nest (L_1^U, L_2^U) is equivalent to the original nest (L_1, L_2). Then, the outer loop L_1^U can be executed in parallel, iff there is no distance vector (D_1, D_2) in (L_1, L_2), such that $(D_1, D_2) \cdot U >_1 0$. The inner loop L_2^U can execute in parallel, iff there is no distance vector (D_1, D_2) in (L_1, L_2), such that $(D_1, D_2) \cdot U >_2 0$.

Proof. Each distance vector in (L_1^U, L_2^U) is of the form $(D_1, D_2) \cdot U$ where (D_1, D_2) is a distance vector in (L_1, L_2). The outer loop L_1^U in the new nest can execute in parallel iff there is no dependence in (L_1^U, L_2^U) at level 1, i.e. iff there is no distance vector $(D_1, D_2) > 0$ in (L_1, L_2) with $(D_1, D_2) \cdot U >_1 0$. The inner loop L_2^U in the new nest can be executed in parallel iff there is no dependence in (L_1^U, L_2^U) at level 2, i.e. iff there is no distance vector $(D_1, D_2) > 0$ in (L_1, L_2) with $(D_1, D_2) \cdot U >_2 0$. ∎

Example 4.1. The nest

L_1:   do $I_1 = 0, 10, 1$
L_2:   do $I_2 = 0, 10, 1$
       S: $A(I_1, I_2) = A(I_1 - 1, I_2) + A(I_1, I_2 - 1) + A(I_1 - 2, I_2 + 1)$
                end do
                end do

has the distance vectors $(1, 0)$, $(0, 1)$ and $(2, -1)$. Consider the matrix $U = \begin{bmatrix} 1 & 0 \\ 1 & 1 \end{bmatrix}$. Since

$$(1, 0) \cdot U = (1, 0) > \mathbf{0},$$
$$(0, 1) \cdot U = (1, 1) > \mathbf{0},$$
and $(2, -1) \cdot U = (1, -1) > \mathbf{0},$

it follows from Theorem 4.2 that the transformation of the nest caused by the matrix U will be valid. Thus, the given double loop is equivalent to the transformed double loop

L_1^U: do $K_1 = 0, 20, 1$
$L_2^U(K_1)$:   do $K_2 = \max\{0, K_1 - 10\}, \min\{10, K_1\}, 1$
        $A(K_1 - K_2, K_2) = A(K_1 - K_2 - 1, K_2) + A(K_1 - K_2, K_2 - 1)$
                        $+ A(K_1 - K_2 - 2, K_2 + 1)$
    end do
end do

which we found by an application of Algorithm 4.1. The original nest has a dependence at level 1, and hence the outer loop L_1 cannot be run in parallel. For the same reason, the outer loop in the transformed nest cannot be run in parallel. Since the original nest has a dependence at level 2, the inner loop L_2 cannot be executed in parallel. However, there is no dependence at level 2 in the transformed nest, so that the inner loop $L_2^U(K_1)$ can be executed in parallel for each fixed K_1.

5. Special Cases

If we take one of the elementary matrices for U, we get a special unimodular transformation. The transformation $(L_1, L_2) \to (L_1^U, L_2^U)$ is called

a *loop reversal* if U is a reversal matrix;
a *loop interchange* if U is the interchange matrix;
a *loop skewing* if U is a skewing matrix.

A skewing of the inner loop by the outer loop results if U is an upper skewing matrix; a lower skewing matrix U causes a skewing of the outer loop by the inner loop. Unless otherwise stated, by a 'loop skewing' we will mean a skewing of the inner loop by the outer loop, which is caused by an upper skewing matrix. This is the commonly accepted meaning of 'skewing' [10]. Skewing the outer loop by the inner loop (caused by a lower skewing matrix) will be treated as part of the general transformation.

The forms of the transformed loops in the special cases given below can be easily derived from Algorithm 4.1.

Outer Loop Reversal:

The matrix $U = \begin{bmatrix} -1 & 0 \\ 0 & 1 \end{bmatrix}$ with inverse $U^{-1} = \begin{bmatrix} -1 & 0 \\ 0 & 1 \end{bmatrix}$

transforms (L_1, L_2) into the loop

    do $K_1 = -N_1, -n_1, 1$
        do $K_2 = n_2, N_2, 1$
            $H(-K_1, K_2)$
        end do
    end do

Inner Loop Reversal:

The matrix $U = \begin{bmatrix} 1 & 0 \\ 0 & -1 \end{bmatrix}$ with inverse $U^{-1} = \begin{bmatrix} 1 & 0 \\ 0 & -1 \end{bmatrix}$

transforms (L_1, L_2) into the loop

    do $K_1 = n_1, N_1, 1$
        do $K_2 = -N_2, -n_2, 1$
            $H(K_1, -K_2)$
        end do
    end do

Loop Interchange:

The matrix $U = \begin{bmatrix} 0 & 1 \\ 1 & 0 \end{bmatrix}$ with inverse $U^{-1} = \begin{bmatrix} 0 & 1 \\ 1 & 0 \end{bmatrix}$

transforms (L_1, L_2) into the loop

    do $K_1 = n_2, N_2, 1$
        do $K_2 = n_1, N_1, 1$
            $H(K_2, K_1)$
        end do
    end do

Skewing of the Inner Loop by the Outer Loop:

The matrix $\mathbf{U} = \begin{bmatrix} 1 & q \\ 0 & 1 \end{bmatrix}$ with inverse $\mathbf{U}^{-1} = \begin{bmatrix} 1 & -q \\ 0 & 1 \end{bmatrix}$

transforms (L_1, L_2) into the loop

        do $K_1 = n_1, N_1, 1$
           do $K_2 = n_2 + q*K_1, N_2 + q*K_1, 1$
              $H(K_1, K_2 - q*K_1)$
           end do
        end do

The integer q is called the *skewing factor*.

Since each unimodular matrix is the product of a finite number of reversal, interchange and upper skewing matrices (Corollary to Lemma 3.3), the following theorem is clear.

Theorem 5.1. Any unimodular transformation of the loop nest (L_1, L_2) can be accomplished by a finite sequence of loop reversals, interchanges, and skewings of the inner loop by the outer loop.

We now derive some known results: the special versions of Theorem 4.2 and its Corollary for the four special transformations described above. The theorems on loop reversals follow trivially. Loop reversals are generally known, although seldom discussed in print; they were formally considered by Hoeflinger [5]. Loop interchange was introduced by Wolfe and studied in detail by Wolfe [11, 12], and Allen and Kennedy [1]; loop permutations in arbitrary nests were investigated in Banerjee [4]. Loop skewing was introduced by Wolfe [10] who implemented the wavefront method by skewing and interchanging.

Theorem. 5.2. (i) Outer loop reversal of (L_1, L_2) is valid iff there is no dependence in (L_1, L_2) at level 1.

(ii) Suppose outer loop reversal is valid. The outer loop in the transformed nest can always be executed in parallel. The inner loop in the transformed nest can be executed in parallel iff there is no dependence in (L_1, L_2) at levels 1 and 2.

Theorem. 5.3. (i) Inner loop reversal of (L_1, L_2) is valid iff there is no dependence in (L_1, L_2) at level 2.

(ii) Suppose inner loop reversal is valid. The inner loop in the transformed nest can always be executed in parallel. The outer loop in the transformed nest can be executed in parallel iff there is no dependence in (L_1, L_2) at levels 1 and 2.

Theorem. 5.4. (i) Loop interchange of (L_1, L_2) is valid iff the nest (L_1, L_2) does not have the direction vector $(1, -1)$.

(ii) Suppose loop interchange is valid. The outer loop in the transformed nest can be executed in parallel iff (L_1, L_2) does not have the direction vectors $(1, 1)$ and $(0, 1)$. The inner loop in the transformed nest can be executed in parallel iff (L_1, L_2) does not have the direction vector $(1, 0)$.

Proof. Let U denote the interchange matrix. The distances in the transformed nest are of the form $(D_1, D_2) \cdot U = (D_2, D_1)$, where (D_1, D_2) is a distance in the original nest (L_1, L_2). Loop interchange is valid iff $(D_2, D_1) > \mathbf{0}$ whenever $(D_1, D_2) > \mathbf{0}$. This condition fails to hold for a distance (D_1, D_2) iff $D_1 > 0$ and $D_2 < 0$, i.e. iff the direction vector of the distance is $(1, -1)$. This proves part (i).

Suppose that loop interchange is valid. The outer loop after interchange can be made parallel iff there is no dependence in (L_1, L_2) with a distance (D_1, D_2) such that $(D_2, D_1) = (D_1, D_2) \cdot U >_1 \mathbf{0}$, i.e. $D_2 > 0$. In other words, the nest (L_1, L_2) cannot have direction vectors $(1, 1)$ and $(0, 1)$. Similarly, the inner loop after interchange can be made parallel iff there is no dependence distance (D_1, D_2) in (L_1, L_2), such that $(D_2, D_1) >_2 \mathbf{0}$, i.e. $D_2 = 0$ and $D_1 > 0$. This rules out the direction vector $(1, 0)$. ∎

Remark. Loop interchange interchanges the components of a distance vector, and hence the components of a direction vector. A level-1 dependence in (L_1, L_2) with direction vector $(1, 1)$ remains a level-1 dependence after interchange. A level-1 dependence in (L_1, L_2) with direction vector $(1, 0)$ becomes a level-2 dependence after interchange. However, a level-2 dependence in (L_1, L_2) must have the direction vector $(0, 1)$, and it always becomes a level-1 dependence after interchange.

Theorem. 5.5. A skewing of the inner loop by the outer loop in (L_1, L_2) is always valid. The outer loop in the transformed nest can execute in parallel iff there is no dependence in (L_1, L_2) at level 1. The inner loop in the transformed nest can be executed in parallel iff there is no dependence in (L_1, L_2) at level 2.

Proof. Let U denote the skewing matrix $\begin{bmatrix} 1 & q \\ 0 & 1 \end{bmatrix}$. The dependence distances in the transformed nest are of the form

$$(D_1, D_2) \cdot U = (D_1, qD_1 + D_2),$$

where (D_1, D_2) is a distance in (L_1, L_2). Note that $(D_1, D_2) \cdot U >_1 \mathbf{0}$ iff $D_1 > 0$, i.e. iff $(D_1, D_2) >_1 \mathbf{0}$. Also, $(D_1, D_2) \cdot U >_2 \mathbf{0}$ iff $D_1 = 0$ and $D_2 > 0$, i.e. iff $(D_1, D_2) >_2 \mathbf{0}$. Since $(D_1, D_2) \cdot U > \mathbf{0}$ whenever $(D_1, D_2) > \mathbf{0}$, a skewing of the inner loop by the outer loop (by any factor) is always valid. The other two parts of this theorem follow from Theorem 4.2. ∎

Remark. A skewing does not change the level of a dependence, but it may change a distance or a direction vector. A skewing does not change the iteration count of the outer or the inner loop.

6. Existence of Suitable Unimodular Transformations

Given a double loop (L_1, L_2) and a unimodular matrix U, we can find the double loop which is the transformation of (L_1, L_2) caused by U, and decide if the transformed program is equivalent to the original program. If the two double loops are equivalent, we can also decide if the inner or the outer loop in the transformed nest could be executed in parallel. Consider now the problem of finding a matrix to fit a particular situation. Given a double loop, the big question is: What transformation will make the loop execute the fastest on a given machine?. For the purposes of this paper, we limit ourselves to the question: Given a double loop (L_1, L_2), does there exist a unimodular matrix U such that the outer or the inner loop in the transformed nest can be executed in parallel?

Theorem 6.1. There exists a 2×2 unimodular integer matrix U such that the transformation (L_1^U, L_2^U) of the double loop (L_1, L_2) is equivalent to the original nest and the outer loop L_1^U can be executed in parallel, iff there is a fixed integer vector $(a_1, a_2) > \mathbf{0}$, such that each dependence distance in (L_1, L_2) is of the form $\alpha(a_1, a_2)$, where α is a positive integer.

Proof. The 'if' Part. Suppose that there exists an integer vector $(a_1, a_2) > \mathbf{0}$ such that each dependence distance in (L_1, L_2) is of the form $\alpha(a_1, a_2)$, where α is a positive integer. Let $g = \gcd(a_1, a_2)$. Then, $g > 0$ since a_1 and a_2 cannot both be zero. Define a 2×2 integer matrix

$$U = \begin{bmatrix} u_{11} & u_{12} \\ u_{21} & u_{22} \end{bmatrix},$$

by $u_{11} = a_2/g$, $u_{21} = -a_1/g$, and (u_{12}, u_{22}) = any pair of integers for which $a_1 u_{12} + a_2 u_{22} = g$. (See Algorithm 2.1.) This matrix is unimodular, since

$$\det(U) = (u_{11} u_{22} - u_{21} u_{12}) = (a_2 u_{22} + a_1 u_{12})/g = 1.$$

For each distance vector $(D_1, D_2) = \alpha(a_1, a_2)$ in (L_1, L_2), we have

$$(D_1, D_2) \cdot U = \alpha(a_1, a_2) \cdot U = \alpha(a_1 u_{11} + a_2 u_{21}, a_1 u_{12} + a_2 u_{22}) = (0, \alpha g) >_2 0.$$

By Theorem 4.2 and its Corollary, the transformed nest (L_1^U, L_2^U) is equivalent to the original nest and the outer loop L_1^U can be executed in parallel.

The 'only if' Part. Assume that there exists a unimodular matrix U such that the transformed nest is equivalent to the original nest and the outer loop in the transformed nest can be executed in parallel. Then, by Theorem 4.2 and its Corollary, any dependence distance (D_1, D_2) in (L_1, L_2) must satisfy $(D_1, D_2) \cdot U >_2 0$, i.e.

$$D_1 u_{11} + D_2 u_{21} = 0$$
and $$D_1 u_{12} + D_2 u_{22} > 0.$$

The general solution to the equation is $(D_1, D_2) = (-u_{21} t, u_{11} t) = t(-u_{21}, u_{11})$, where t is any integer. Substituting for D_1 and D_2 in the inequality, we get $t\Delta > 0$, where $\Delta = \det(U)$. Then, recalling that $\Delta^2 = 1$, one can write $(D_1, D_2) = (t\Delta) \cdot \Delta(-u_{21}, u_{11}) = \alpha(a_1, a_2)$, where $\alpha > 0$, and $(a_1, a_2) > 0$ since $(D_1, D_2) > 0$. ∎

Example 6.1. Consider the nest

L_1:   do $I_1 = 5, 100, 1$
L_2:   do $I_2 = 16, 80, 1$
   S: $A(I_1, I_2) = A(I_1 - 2, I_2 - 4) + A(I_1 - 3, I_2 - 6)$
         end do
      end do

There are two distance vectors in the nest: $(2, 4)$ and $(3, 6)$. Note that $(2, 4) = 2(1, 2)$ and $(3, 6) = 3(1, 2)$. Since the distance vectors are of the form $\alpha(a_1, a_2)$, where $\alpha > 0$ and $(a_1, a_2) > 0$, there exists a unimodular matrix U such that after the given nest is transformed by U, the outer loop in the new nest could be run in parallel (Theorem 6.1). By Algorithm 2.1, find $\gcd(a_1, a_2)$

$= \gcd(1, 2) = 1$, and two integers $u_{12} = 1$ and $u_{22} = 0$, such that $1 \cdot u_{12} + 2 \cdot u_{22} = 1$. The integers $u_{11} = a_2/\gcd(a_1, a_2) = 2$, and $u_{21} = -a_1/\gcd(a_1, a_2) = -1$ are then computed, and we have

$$U = \begin{bmatrix} 2 & 1 \\ -1 & 0 \end{bmatrix}.$$

Now, we use Algorithm 4.1 to get the transformation of (L_1, L_2) caused by U:

S:
```
do K₁ = −70, 184, 1
    do K₂ = ⌈max{5, 8 + K₁/2}⌉, ⌊min{100, 40 + K₁/2}⌋, 1
        A(K₂, −K₁ + 2*K₂) = A(K₂ − 2, −K₁ + 2*K₂ − 4) + A(K₂ − 3, −K₁ + 2*K₂ − 6)
    end do
end do
```

The outer K_1-loop in this new nest can be executed in parallel. The distance vectors $(2, 4)$ and $(3, 6)$ should have been transformed into the distance vectors $(0, 2)$ and $(0, 3)$. Examining the new nest, we see directly that indeed is the case. ∎

The steps of Theorem 6.1 are stated in the form of an algorithm. If there are two choices for the matrix U, we pick the one that maximizes the iteration count of the outer loop.

Algorithm 6.1. Given a nest (L_1, L_2), this algorithm finds a unimodular matrix U such that
(i) The transformed nest (L_1^U, L_2^U) is equivalent to the original nest;

(ii) The outer loop L_1^U can be executed in parallel;

(iii) The iteration count of L_1^U is maximized.

1. Find all the dependence distance and direction vectors in (L_1, L_2).

2. If there are no (positive) distance vectors, then set

$$U \leftarrow \begin{bmatrix} 1 & 0 \\ 0 & 1 \end{bmatrix} \text{ if } N_1 - n_1 \geq N_2 - n_2,$$

$$U \leftarrow \begin{bmatrix} 0 & 1 \\ 1 & 0 \end{bmatrix} \text{ otherwise,}$$

and go to step 5.

3. If all dependence distance vectors in (L_1, L_2) are of the form $\alpha(a_1, a_2)$, where α is a positive integer and $(a_1, a_2) > 0$, then go on to the next step. Otherwise, terminate the algorithm with the

message : "There is no unimodular transformation U such that the outer loop can be executed in parallel in the transformed nest (L_1^U, L_2^U)."

4. By Algorithm 2.1, find $g = \gcd(a_1, a_2)$ and a pair of integers (u_{12}, u_{22}) such that
$$a_1 u_{12} + a_2 u_{22} = g.$$
Set
$$(u_{11}, u_{21}) \leftarrow (a_2/g, -a_1/g),$$
and
$$U \leftarrow \begin{bmatrix} u_{11} & u_{12} \\ u_{21} & u_{22} \end{bmatrix}.$$

5. If U is the identity matrix, then simply label the outer loop as parallel. Otherwise, find by Algorithm 4.1, the transformed loop (L_1^U, L_2^U) and mark the outer loop L_1^U parallel. ∎

Thus, a transformation exists after which the outer loop could run in parallel, iff all distance vectors in the given nest are 'parallel' to each other. This is a relatively uncommon situation. On the other hand, no matter what distance vectors are present, one can always transform the given loopnest so that the new inner loop could run in parallel. This does not mean, however, that we have found a magical cure for that double loop in which each iteration (except the first) depends on the previous iteration. In an extreme case like that, the parallel inner loop would contain only one iteration. In general, as far as the transformations considered in this paper are concerned, if there is parallelism to be found in a nest, either Algorithm 6.1 or Algorithm 6.2 will find it.

Theorem 6.2. There always exists a 2×2 unimodular matrix U such that the transformation (L_1^U, L_2^U) of (L_1, L_2) is equivalent to the original nest and the inner loop L_2^U can execute in parallel.

Proof. If there is a dependence distance (D_1, D_2) in (L_1, L_2) such that $D_1 > 0$ and $D_2 < 0$, then let μ denote $\lfloor \max\{-D_2/D_1\} + 1 \rfloor$, where the maximum is taken over all distances (D_1, D_2) in the original nest such that $D_1 > 0$ and $D_2 < 0$. Otherwise, let $\mu = 1$. Take the unimodular matrix
$$U = \begin{bmatrix} \mu & 1 \\ 1 & 0 \end{bmatrix}.$$

Consider the sign of the expression $(\mu D_1 + D_2)$ for a positive distance (D_1, D_2) in (L_1, L_2). Since $\mu > 0$, the sign is clearly positive if $D_1 > 0$ and $D_2 > 0$, or if $D_1 = 0$ and $D_2 > 0$. The sign is also positive if $D_1 > 0$ and $D_2 < 0$, since we have $\mu > (-D_2/D_1)$. The result then follows from Theorem 4.2 and its Corollary, since $(D_1, D_2) \cdot U = (\mu D_1 + D_2, D_1) >_1 0$. ∎

Remark. It is clear from the above proof that any integer greater than μ will also work, so that there are again infinitely many matrices that can be used to get a parallel inner loop. Since the total number of instances of the nest is fixed, to get as many parallel instances in a group as possible, we minimize the number of iterations of the (usually serial) outer loop L_1^U. The matrix U of the last theorem is the best choice in many cases, but sometimes simpler matrices are better. The essence of Theorem 6.2 is summarized in the following algorithm:

Algorithm 6.2. Given a nest (L_1, L_2), this algorithm finds a unimodular matrix U such that
(i) The transformed nest (L_1^U, L_2^U) is equivalent to the original nest;

(ii) The inner loop L_2^U can be executed in parallel;

(iii) The iteration count $[|u_{11}| \cdot (N_1 - n_1) + |u_{21}| \cdot (N_2 - n_2) + 1]$ of the outer loop L_1^U is

minimized.

We are trying to find a matrix U such that $(D_1, D_2) \cdot U >_l \mathbf{0}$ for each distance vector in the given nest. We start with a list LIST of 'good' choices for the first column $(u_{11}, u_{21})^T$ of the matrix U. A choice $(u_{11}, u_{21})^T$ is deleted if there is a distance vector (D_1, D_2) present in the loop, such that $D_1 u_{11} + D_2 u_{21} \leq 0$. In most cases, this can be done by examining only the direction vectors. ('Deleting' an item x from the list means deleting it only if x is on the list.) On one occasion, a choice is also added to the list. Then, the 'best' choice is picked from the final list. The second column $(u_{12}, u_{22})^T$ is chosen to make U a unimodular matrix.

1. Find all the dependence distance and direction vectors in (L_1, L_2).

2. Set
$$\text{LIST} \leftarrow \{(1, 0)^T, (0, 1)^T, (0, -1)^T, (1, 1)^T\}. \quad \text{/* Initialize LIST */}$$

3. /* Get the final list */

   if the nest has the direction vector $(1, 0)$
   then delete $(0, 1)^T$ and $(0, -1)^T$ from LIST;
   if the nest has the direction vector $(0, 1)$
   then delete $(1, 0)^T$ and $(0, -1)^T$ from LIST;
   if the nest has the direction vector $(1, 1)$
   then delete $(0, -1)^T$ from LIST;
   if the nest has the direction vector $(1, -1)$

then begin
   delete $(0, 1)^T, (1, 1)^T$ from LIST,

   set $\mu \leftarrow \lfloor \max\{-D_2/D_1\} + 1 \rfloor$, where the maximum is taken over all distance vectors (D_1, D_2) such that $D_1 > 0$ and $D_2 < 0$;

   add $(\mu, 1)^T$ to LIST,
end;

4. /* Get the best choice for $(u_{11}, u_{21})^T$ */

   Case 4.1. $(N_1 - n_1) \leq (N_2 - n_2)$.
   Take the first vector from the sequence that is present in LIST:

   $(1, 0)^T, (0, 1)^T, (0, -1)^T, (1, 1)^T, (\mu, 1)^T$.

   Case 4.2. $(N_1 - n_1) > (N_2 - n_2)$.
   Take the first vector from the sequence that is present in LIST:

   $(0, 1)^T, (0, -1)^T, (1, 0)^T, (1, 1)^T, (\mu, 1)^T$.

5. If the best choice for $(u_{11}, u_{21})^T$ is $(1, 0)^T$, then simply mark the inner loop L_2 of the given nest as parallel; no other transformation is needed. (This is same as taking the 2×2 identity matrix for **U**.) Otherwise, form **U** by taking for the first column its best choice, and for the second column the vector $(1, 0)^T$. Transform the nest (L_1, L_2) by the unimodular matrix **U** (Algorithm 4.1), and mark the inner loop of the final nest as parallel.

Proof. After the transformation **U**, a distance vector (D_1, D_2) in the original nest becomes the vector $(D_1, D_2) \cdot \mathbf{U}$. The transformed program will be equivalent to the original program and the inner loop in the new program can be executed in parallel, iff we have $(D_1, D_2) \cdot \mathbf{U} >_1 0$, i.e.

$$D_1 u_{11} + D_2 u_{21} > 0, \tag{1}$$

for each distance vector (D_1, D_2).

The iteration count of the outer loop L_1^U will be $[|u_{11}| \cdot (N_1 - n_1) + |u_{21}| \cdot (N_2 - n_2) + 1]$. Of all the available choices for the first column $(u_{11}, u_{21})^T$ of **U**, we want to pick the one that minimizes this iteration count. This means minimizing the absolute values of u_{11} and u_{21}. The first eight vectors with minimum values of its components are

$\{(1, 0)^T, (-1, 0)^T, (0, 1)^T, (0, -1)^T, (1, 1)^T, (-1, 1)^T, (1, -1)^T, (-1, -1)^T\}.$

Any of the first four vectors is better than any of the last four, from the point of view of minimizing the iteration count of the outer loop. One of the vectors $(1, 0)^T$ and $(-1, 0)^T$ is better than one of $(0, 1)^T$ and $(0, -1)^T$, iff L_1 has fewer iterations than L_2. We can discard half of this list right away, since the vectors $(-1, 0)^T, (1, -1)^T, (-1, 1)^T$, and $(-1, -1)^T$ can always be replaced by a better choice. For example, if the vector $(1, -1)^T$ is acceptable, then the direction vector $(0, 1)$ must be absent, so that we can use the choice $(1, 0)^T$. Thus, we can start with the initial list of Step 2.

If the nest has the direction vector $(1, 0)$, i.e. a distance vector $(D_1, 0)$ with $D_1 > 0$, then u_{11} must be positive. Hence, $(0, 1)^T$ is not an acceptable choice for $(u_{11}, u_{21})^T$. Similarly, if the nest has the direction vector $(0, 1)$, then u_{21} has to be positive, so that $(1, 0)^T$ must be ruled out. Also, the direction vector $(1, 1)$ rules out the choice $(0, -1)^T$.

Now, suppose there is a distance vector (D_1, D_2) with $D_1 > 0$ and $D_2 < 0$. Then, $(u_{11}, u_{21})^T = (0, 1)^T$ will not satisfy (1). We also need to rule out $(u_{11}, u_{21})^T = (1, 1)^T$, unless $D_1 + D_2$ is always positive. More generally, we write (1) as

$$u_{11} > (-D_2/D_1)u_{21}. \tag{2}$$

Let μ be defined as in the algorithm. After the possible choices of $(1, 0)^T, (0, 1)^T$, and $(0, -1)^T$, we have $(\mu, 1)^T$ as the best choice for the first column of $\mathbf{U}$, that will satisfy (1).

Step 4 should now be clear in view of the comments made earlier about the choices $(1, 0)^T$, $(0, 1)^T, (0, -1)^T$ and the relative sizes of the loops L_1 and L_2. The list LIST is never empty. After the first column of $\mathbf{U}$ has been chosen, we choose the second column in such a way that $\mathbf{U}$ is a unimodular matrix. ∎

Remark. The part about choosing a value of μ in the presence of the direction vector $(1, -1)$ is similar to choosing a suitable skewing factor in [10].

Example 6.2. Consider the program

```
L₁:        do I₁ = 5, 100, 1
L₂:           do I₂ = 5, 100, 1
    S:           A(I₁, I₂) = A(I₁, I₂ – 1) + A(I₁ – 2, I₂ + 3) + A(I₁ – 3, I₂ + 7)
              end do
           end do
```

The nest has the distance vectors (0, 1), (2, −3) and (3, −7). We want to transform this into a nest where the inner loop can be executed in parallel and the iteration count of the outer loop is minimized. Algorithm 6.2 is applied towards this goal. Since the nest has the direction vector (0, 1), the vectors $(1, 0)^T$ and $(0, -1)^T$ are dropped as possible choices for the first column of $\mathbf{U}$. Since the direction vector $(1, -1)$ is present, the vectors $(0, 1)^T$ and $(1, 1)^T$ are dropped as well. Next, we compute μ:

$$\mu = \lfloor \max\{-(-3)/2, \ -(-7)/3\} + 1 \rfloor = \lfloor 7/3 + 1 \rfloor = 3.$$

The desired matrix is then $\mathbf{U} = \begin{bmatrix} 3 & 1 \\ 1 & 0 \end{bmatrix}$. After an application of Algorithm 4.1, the transformed nest is found to be

```
      do K₁ = 20, 400, 1
         do K₂ = ⌈max{5, (K₁ − 100)/3}⌉, ⌊min{100, (K₁ − 5)/3}⌋, 1
S:          A(K₂, K₁ − 3*K₂) = A(K₂, K₁ − 3*K₂ − 1) + A(K₂ − 2, K₁ − 3*K₂ + 3)
                             + A(K₂ − 3, K₁ − 3*K₂ + 7)
         end do
      end do
```

The inner loop in this nest can be run in parallel. ∎

7. Conclusions

We have tried to present a unified theory of a certain class of loop transformations for a loopnest of length 2, called unimodular transformations. We have shown that the wavefront method, loop reversal, loop interchange and loop skewing are all members of this class and that they need not be considered separately. Based on the dependence structure of a given loopnest, we can always find directly an equivalent nest (if one exists) where the outer or the inner loop will run in parallel. Subscript forms are immaterial as long as dependence analysis can produce the needed distance and direction vectors. This theory subsumes the existing results in this area. Extensions to more general loopnests will be presented in future papers.

Acknowledgment. The author would like to thank Kevin Smith, David Sehr, Michael Lake, Celso Mendes and Jin-Ho Tan for pointing out several errors in an earlier version of the paper and for suggesting improvements.

References

1. Allen, J. R., and Kennedy, K. Automatic Loop Interchange. *Proceedings of the SIGPLAN '84 Symposium on Compiler Construction.* Montreal, Canada (June 17–22, 1984), 233–246.
2. Banerjee, U. Data Dependence in Ordinary Programs. *M.S. Thesis,* Dept. of Computer Science, University of Illinois at Urbana-Champaign, Urbana, Illinois, Report 76-837 (November 1976).
3. Banerjee, U. *Dependence Analysis for Supercomputing.* Kluwer Academic Publishers, Norwell, Mass., 1988.
4. Banerjee, U. A Theory of Loop Permutations. In *Languages and Compilers for Parallel Computing,* D. Gelernter, A. Nicolau & D. Padua, Eds. The MIT Press, Cambridge, Mass., 1990, pp. 54-74.
5. Hoeflinger, J. Unpublished paper.
6. Irigoin, F. and Triolet, R. Dependence Approximation and Global Parallel Code Generation for Nested Loops. In *Parallel and Distributed Algorithms,* M. Cosnard et al, Eds. Elsevier (North-Holland), New York, NY, 1989, pp. 297-308.
7. Knuth, D. E. *The Art of Computer Programming,* Vol. 1, *Fundamental Algorithms,* Second Edition, Addison-Wesley, Reading, Mass., 1973.
8. Lamport, L. The Parallel Execution of DO Loops. *Comm. of the ACM,* 17, 2 (February 1974), 83-93.
9. Wolf, M. E. & Lam, M. S. Maximizing Parallelism via Loop Transformations. This Proceedings.
10. Wolfe, M. J. Loop Skewing: The Wavefront Method Revisited. *Int'l. J. of Parallel Programming,* 15, 4 (August 1986), 279-293.
11. Wolfe, M. J. Advanced Loop Interchanging. *Proceedings of the 1986 Int'l Conf. on Parallel Processing.* St. Charles, Ill. (Aug. 19-22, 1986), 536-543.
12. Wolfe, M. J. *Optimizing Supercompilers for Supercomputers.* Pitman Publishing, London, 1989.

11 Parallelism Evaluation and Partitioning of Nested Loops for Shared Memory Multiprocessors

E. Ayguadé, J. Labarta, J. Torres, J. M. Llaberia, M. Valero

Abstract

In this paper we describe how the parallelism of a loop can be evaluated from its data dependence graph. We also describe **Graph Traverse Scheduling (GTS)** as a loop partitioning method targeted to shared-memory multiprocessors. Both aspects are considered in this paper for multiple-nested loops including one or several recurrences.

The parallelism evaluated from the data dependence graph allows the compiler to make decisions when parallelizing its associated loop. The loop partitioning method tries to include in the sequential execution of the computation assigned to each processor as many dependences as possible minimizing the number of them that require explicit synchronization. The method achieves minimum execution time of the parallel code assuming that a sufficient number of processors is available and synchronization cost is negligible.

1 INTRODUCTION

Parallelizing compilers exist today for high performance parallel computers in order to efficiently execute sequential programs written in conventional languages such as Fortran and C. These compilers mainly examine DO loops trying to obtain parallel code semantically equivalent to the original sequential one. DO loops offer a great amount of potential parallelism in numerical programs.

Several parallelizing compilers such as Parafrase I and II [12, 18] from Illinois, PFC from Rice University [3], IBM PTRAN [1], KAP from Kuck and Associates, VAST from Pacific Sierra, to name a few, have been developed over the years.

Such parallelizing compilers rely on data dependence analysis. In loop partitioning it is important to analyze data dependences between statements involving array references within the scope of each loop. Dependences reflect an execution order of operations of the loop that must be preserved in the transformed code in order to keep the semantics of the original sequential program.

Many methods have been presented in the literature for partitioning DO loops into computations that can be executed in parallel. It is possible to obtain fully parallel code when there are no cyclic dependence chains, running all the iterations of the loop independently in a DOALL-like loop. *Loop distribution* [7] splits a loop into a sequence of loops including either a single statement or statements involved in a cyclic dependence relationship.

Problems arise when dependences form recurrences or cycles in the dependence graph. In this case, parallelizing methods can be classified in (a) methods that try to obtain fully independent partitions, i.e., there are no dependences between computations that belong to different blocks of the partition, and (b) methods that try to obtain more parallelism by synchronizing dependent computations assigned to different processors.

Alignment techniques [2, 14, 15] can be used in conjunction with partitioning techniques in order to increase the parallelism obtained or to reduce the synchronization required.

Partial Partitioning [14] obtains an independent partition of the iteration space whose cardinality is given by the product of the greater common divisors of the dependence distances in each dimension of the loop. In [20] two approaches, called the *Partitioning Vector* and the *Smith Normal Form approaches*, for identifying independent partitions of algorithms with uniform dependences are given. The *Minimum Distance Method* [16] and *Hollander's partitioning method* [10] transform the original dependence matrix into upper-triangular and diagonal matrices respectively which are used to identify an independent partition. The number of independent partitions is given by the product of the elements in the diagonal.

Other methods such as *DOACROSS* [10] and *Cycle Shrinking* [17] obtain more parallelism by synchronizing the computations assigned to the processors. The first one partially overlaps the execution of successive iterations of the loop in order to satisfy all the dependences of the graph. The second one executes in parallel as many successive iterations in each dimension as possible. It uses barrier synchronization in order to guarantee the correctness of its execution.

It is worth knowing a priori the degree of parallelism that can be obtained out of the loop, allowing the compiler to decide the validity of the restructuring process. However, parallelism on its own does not determine the performance of the execution on a multiprocessor system. The overhead due to synchronization and scheduling must be also taken into consideration.

The cardinality of the independent partitions obtained by [10, 16, 20] and the average parallelism of the loop whose evaluation is presented in this paper can be used to establish a trade-off between actual parallelism of the transformed loop and communication and synchronization costs. Although nowadays multiprocessor systems are more efficient when processors execute independent computations, it is interesting to know which could be the maximum parallelism that we could obtain out of the loop if the overhead associated to parallel computation were low in near future systems.

In this paper we first describe how the parallelism of a loop can be evaluated from its data dependence graph. Parallelism is a characteristic of the loop that allows the compiler to decide a priori whether the restructuring process will obtain good results or not. It can also be used as an absolute reference to compare different parallelization techniques.

We also describe **Graph Traverse Scheduling (GTS)** as a method for partitioning recurrences included in multiple nested loops and the generation of code well-suited for shared memory multiprocessor systems. This method was proposed in [4] and presented in [5] as a method for parallelizing or vectorizing recurrences in single-nested loops. GTS performs the partitioning of the loop from the dependence graph and obtains a fully independent partition when a single hamiltonian recurrence appears in the graph. In other case, GTS needs the use of some intertask synchronization mechanism to achieve the maximum parallelism available. The parallel code generated by GTS always attains this parallelism although more than the strictly necessary processors can be used. In [6] the method is extended in order to minimize the number of processors used and balance the load assigned to them.

The outline of the remaining sections in this paper is as follows. In section 2 we review some concepts and definitions used along this paper. The evaluation of the parallelism from the data dependence graph is presented in section 3. Section 4 presents GTS as a parallelizing method for nested loops, describing how to obtain the computations that will be assigned to each processor, the synchronization between dependent computations and code generation. The main concluding remarks and future work are given in section 5.

2 DEFINITIONS AND NOTATION

2.1 Dependences

Restructuring compilers are based on the analysis of dependences among a collection of statements (S_1, S_2, ..., S_s) within the scope of normalized nested loops (L_1, L_2, ..., L_n). Dependence relations reflect a given execution order that cannot be altered.

As a result of dependence analysis, a directed dependence graph G (N, E) is obtained, in which N is a set of nodes

$$N = \{S_1, \ldots, S_s\}$$

representing statements in the loop body, and E is a set of arcs

$$E = \{d_{ij} \mid S_i, S_j \in N\}$$

representing dependence relations between statements of the loop.

There are two basic kinds of dependence relations: data and control dependences. Data dependences are due to the use of a given variable by the two statements. Control dependences appear when the execution of a given statement depends on the result obtained in the execution of a previous one.

A statement S_j is said to be data dependent on S_i (denoted $S_i \; \delta \; S_j$), if S_i is executed in the sequential execution before S_j, both statements access the same scalar variable or element of a structured variable, and at least one statement writes the variable. Some data dependences are defined [13]: flow-dependence appears when S_j reads a variable that S_i can write; anti-dependence appears when S_i reads a variable that can be written by S_j; output dependence appears when both statements write the same variable. The statement S_i is called the statement source and S_j the statement sink of the dependence relation.

Each node S_i of the set N has an associated label S_i that represents its execution time. On the other hand, each arc d_{ij} of the set E has an associated dependence distance vector

$$\tilde{d}_{ij} = <d_{ij}^1, d_{ij}^2, \ldots, d_{ij}^n>$$

where d_{ij}^k represents the number of iterations the dependence extends across in the kth dimension of the loop.

Arcs associated to control dependences always have a zero-distance vector associated to them while arcs associated to data dependences always have a positive distance in the smallest non-zero element due to the temporal ordering of dependent operations.

There is an arc between two nodes if a dependence test results affirmative. Dependence analysis is easy when only scalar variables are involved. Various tests have been developped [8, 21] for the case of subscripted variables with linear subscript expressions. In this paper we will consider data dependences with constant associated distance known at compile time.

2.2 Chains and Recurrences

A *chain* C_{ij} is an ordered set of arcs

$$C_{ij} = \{d_{ik}, d_{kl}, \ldots, d_{mj}\}$$

between two statements S_i and S_j such that each node in the chain is visited only once.

Let C_{ij}^* be the set of nodes traversed by the chain C_{ij}. Several chains can exist between any pair of nodes.

Given a chain C_{ij}, we define its *weight vector* $\bar{w}(C_{ij})$ as the number of iterations the dependence chain extends across in all the dimensions of the loop. It is a vector whose k^{th} component is

$$w^k(C_{ij}) = \sum_{d_{lm} \in C_{ij}} d_{lm}^k$$

representing the number of iterations in the associated dimension between the two statements S_i and S_j linked by the chain C_{ij}. We can also define the *execution time* of a chain $t(C_{ij})$ as

$$t(C_{ij}) = \sum_{S_k \in C_{ij}^*} S_k$$

When all statements of the loop take one time unit, the execution time of a chain C_{ij} is given by the cardinality of C_{ij}^*

$$t(C_{ij}) = |C_{ij}^*|$$

A *recurrence* R is a cycle or closed chain in the dependence graph. The weight of the recurrence will be represented by

$$\bar{w}_R = <w_R^1, w_R^2, ..., w_R^n>$$

Recurrences imply sequential execution of the statements participating in them, and for this reason, they have been one of the points of interest of researchers working on parallelizing compilers. A *Hamiltonian Recurrence* is a recurrence R that involves all the nodes of the dependence graph, so $|R^*|$ = s.

Let B be the set of recurrences in a given dependence graph G. This graph G is an *acyclic dependence graph* when B=Ø and it is a *cyclic dependence graph* when $|B| \geq 1$. When at least one recurrence of B is hamiltonian, the graph is called *hamiltonian graph*.

2.3 Iteration Spaces and threads

Next we review and define some spaces on which we will represent the statements and iterations of the loop. The *Iteration Space* (IS) is a set of points defined by a vector index

$$\bar{i} = <i_1, ..., i_n>$$

in a space with dimensionality equal to the depth of the nested structure of the loop. We will refer to the *Unbounded Iteration Space* as

$$UIS = \{ \bar{i} \mid i_k \in Z, 1 \leq k \leq n \}$$

leading to an infinite iteration space. The *Bounded Iteration Space* is the finite subset of UIS

$$BIS = \{ \bar{i} \mid 1 \leq i_k \leq N_k, 1 \leq k \leq n \}$$

being N_k the upper limit of the loop control variable in the kth dimension of the loop. Each point in this space represents an iteration of the loop body.

We now define the *Statement per Iteration Spaces* in order to take into account the statements of the loop. The *Unbounded Statement per Iteration Space* (USIS) is defined as the cartesian product UIS∗N. It is a set of points in an infinite space representing all the possible iterations of each statement of the loop. The *Bounded Statement per Iteration Space* (BSIS) is the cartesian product BIS∗N. It is a finite space representing the actual set of statements and iterations that must be executed. It can be described as

$$BSIS = \{ S_r^{\bar{i}} \mid 1 \leq r \leq s, \bar{i} \in BIS \}$$

where $S_r^{\bar{i}}$ represents iteration $\bar{i}$ of statement S_r of the loop. BSIS is a subset of USIS.

Given a dependence graph G (N, E), each dependence d_{ij} in E imposes an execution order between any pair of vertices

$$S_i^{\bar{i}} \quad \text{and} \quad S_j^{\bar{i}+\bar{d}_{ij}}$$

in the USIS. If the source vertex of the dependence does not belong to the BSIS, the correspondent sink vertex is named *free-point*.

Given a dependence chain in G, we define a *thread* as the set of points in the USIS among which an execution order is implied by the dependence chain. One thread is characterized by a free-point from which it is possible to obtain the intersection of the thread with the BSIS following the dependence chain. For a given thread only its intersection with BSIS has to be executed.

3   PARALLELISM EVALUATION

In this section we define the parallelism of a loop and describe how it can be evaluated from its data dependence graph. Parallelism is a characteristic of the loop that allows the compiler to decide a priori whether the restructuring process will obtain good results or not. It can also be used as an absolute reference to compare different parallelization techniques.

Some measures of the parallelism in applications have been presented in the literature [11, 19] such as the average parallelism, the maximum and minimum parallelism and the parallelism profile.

The average parallelism of a loop is the average number of active processors executing computations of the loop when an unlimited number of processors are available, assuming neither synchronization nor run-time scheduling overhead.

In a data-flow execution scheme of the loop, the instantaneous parallelism is defined as the number of active processors at a given instant. The parallelism profile is defined as the instantaneous parallelism over the execution time of the loop.

There are applications in which if the number of processors allocated is less than the height of a peak in the parallelism profile the execution time of the application increases. In other situations, the use of less processors than the indicated in the peak does not increase the execution time, because the work assigned to them can be delayed in order to fill valleys in the parallelism profile.

In this paper we will refer in general to parallelism as the average parallelism of a loop. This parallelism can be evaluated as the quotient between the time to execute the sequential version and the time to execute the longest critical dependence chain through the whole BSIS. The parallelism of a loop will, in general, depend of the dependence graph as well as the shape and size of BSIS.

The sequential execution of n perfect-nested normalized loops $(L_1, ..., L_n)$ including s statements in the body of the innermost loop takes

$$T * \prod_{i=1}^{n} N_i$$

being T the execution time of one iteration of the body in the innermost loop and N_i the upper limit of each loop L_i. In order to compute the execution time of the longest dependence thread in BSIS we consider acyclic anc cyclic graphs separately.

3.1 Acyclic Dependence Graphs

The execution time for an acyclic dependence graph is determined by the execution of the longest thread in BSIS. This thread is generated by the longest chain C of the dependence graph. So the quotien The parallelism in this case is given by

$$\| = \frac{T * \prod_{i=1}^{n} N_i}{t(C)}$$

gives us the average parallelism of the loop. Observe that parallelism does not depend on the distances associated to the arcs of E.

Figure 1.a shows an acyclic dependence graph associated to a single-nested loop and a portion of its BSIS. Observe that the longest dependence chain that determines the execution time of the loop is $S_1 \delta S_2 \delta S_4$. The parallelism will be $(N \cdot 4 / 3)$ if we assume that all statements take one time unit to be executed.

3.2 Cyclic Dependence Graphs

In the case of cyclic dependence graphs, each recurrence $R \in B$ limits the parallelism of the loop because it forms a thread that extends across the whole BSIS of the loop.

We first consider the effect of a single recurrence R. For example, figure 1.b shows a cyclic dependence graph associated to a single-nested loop with a single hamiltonian recurrence R that involves all statements of the loop. Observe that R generates a thread that traverses the whole BSIS from an initial dependence free-point.

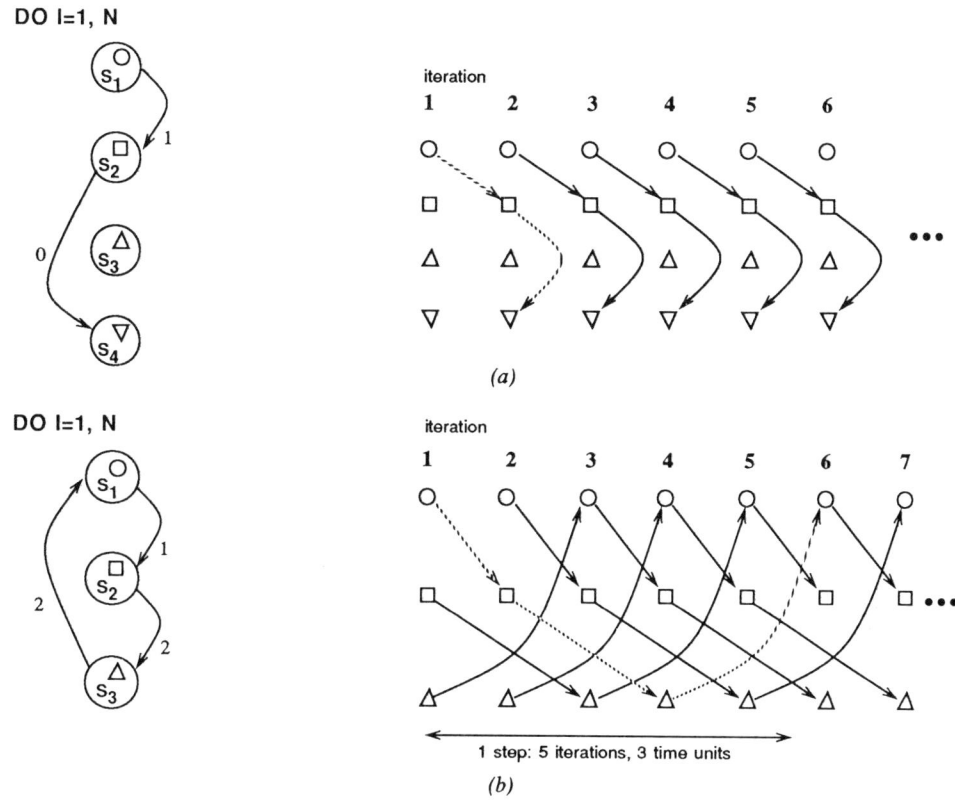

Figure 1: Parallelism evaluation for (a) an acyclic and (b) a cyclic graph with a single recurrence.

In general, all threads that appear formed by a recurrence R are characterized by a cyclic pattern defined by:

- in each step, the thread goes forward w_R^k iterations in the kth dimension;
- the number of time units required to execute a step is given by $t(R)$;
- the cyclic pattern is repeated

$$\frac{N_k}{|w_R^k|}$$

times through the BSIS in the kth dimension of the loop. If this quotient is not an integer value, the last repetition of the pattern will not be completed.

In the general case, the dimension k^{th} in which the cyclic pattern is repeated less times determines the execution time of the thread and therefore the parallelism of the loop.

The parallelism for a cyclic dependence graph associated to a multiple-nested loop can be expressed as

$$\| \| = \frac{T * \prod_{i=1}^{n} N_i}{t(R) * \min_{1 \le i \le n} (N_i / |w_R^i|)} \qquad (1)$$

Observe that parallelism depends on the size of the problem as well as on the dimension k^{th} that determines the parallelism of the loop. Observe also that in this expression we approximate the time to execute an incomplete repetition of the thread with the proportional part of the time to execute the whole pattern. The error is small if loop limits are large enough in comparison with w_R.

For example, by applying this expression to the dependence graph of figure 3.a associated to a double-nested loop, a parallelism of 14 is obtained limited by the outer dimension of the loop. Remember that this is the average parallelism of the loop. We can observe that the parallelism profile of this loop starts with a maximum parallelism of 26 and decreases until an minimum instantaneous parallelism of 8 at the end of its execution.

The expression of the parallelism obtained for a single recurrence can be rewritten as

$$\| \| = T * \|_s (R)$$

being $\|_s$ the *parallelism per statement* of a recurrence

$$\|_s (R) = \frac{|w_R^k|}{t(R)} * \prod_{\substack{1 \le i \le n \\ i \ne k}} N_i$$

and k the loop dimension that determines the parallelism

$$\frac{N_k}{|w_R^k|} \le \frac{N_i}{|w_R^i|} \quad \forall i$$

In the single-nested loop case, when several recurrences appear in G, the the parallelism of the loop is determined by the parallelism per statement of the most restrictive recurrence of G, so

$$T * \min_{R \in B} (\|_s (R))$$

In the multiple-nested loop case, the parallelism is not always determined by the recurrence with less parallelism per statement as in the single-nested case. In this case, the longest path through the BSIS may not be covered by traversing a single recurrence. Observe in the example of figure 2.a that the longest dependence chain can traverse first recurrence <0, 1> until the end of dimension J is reached and then recurrence <1, 0> until the end of dimension I is reached.

The existence of recurrences with components of different sign or even zero in their weight vectors implies the possibility of traversing the BSIS back and forward in a given dimension of the loop several times without leaving it. Observe this fact in the example of figure 2.b. In this case, dimension J is traversed several times following the recurrences of the dependence graph.

In general, the problem of finding the longest dependence chain can be formulated as an integer linear programming problem. Meanwhile, the parallelism of the most restrictive recurrence gives an upper-bound of the loop parallelism and processors required to achive the theoretical parallelism evaluated.

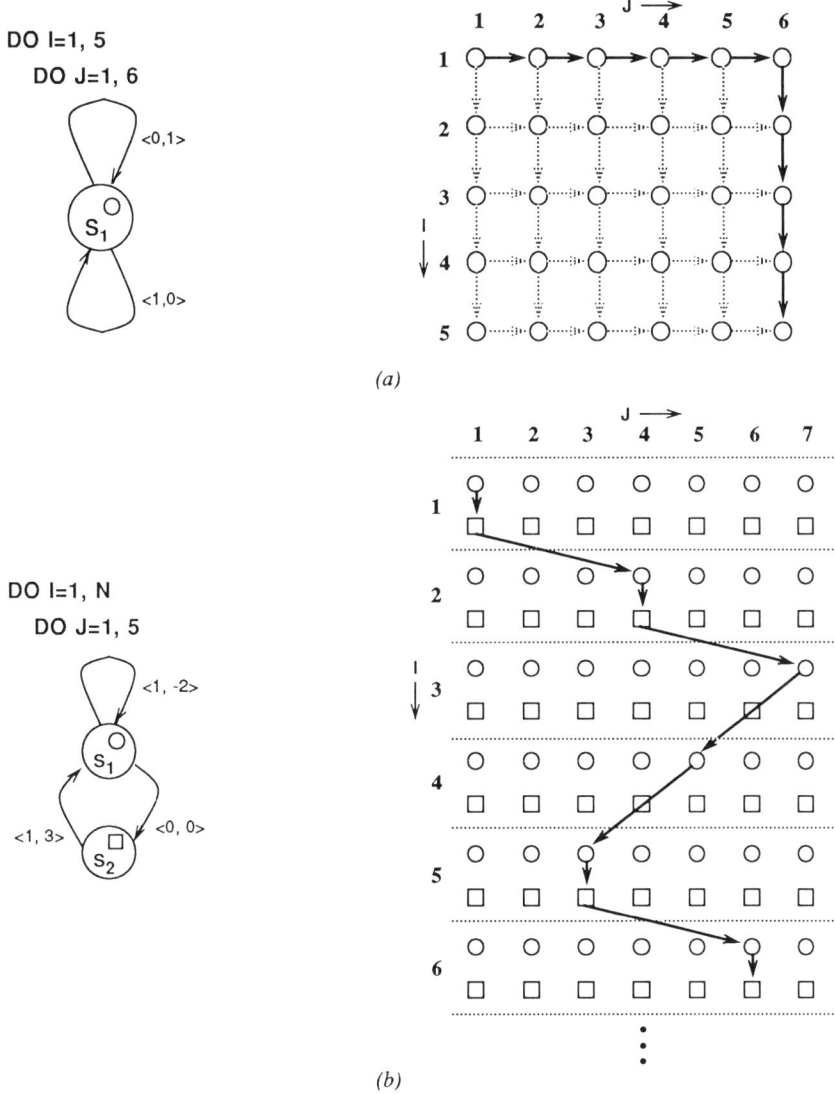

Figure 2: (a) Longest dependence chain traversing first recurrence <0,1> until the end of jth dimension and recurrence <1,0> until end of ith dimension.(b) Longest dependence chain traversing BSIS back and forward through both recurrences of the dependence graph.

4 GRAPH TRAVERSE SCHEDULING

In this section we present GTS as a method for obtaining a maximal partition of BSIS in threads while minimizing synchronization between them. The partitioning algorithm is based on the existence of a hamiltonian recurrence that goes through all the statements of the loop and on which the partitioning algorithm is applied. If there is no such recurrence, one must be obtained by adding dummy dependences that do no limit the parallelism of the loop.

Each thread consists of a set of points of BSIS among which an execution order is forced by a hamiltonian recurrence. The maximal partition is obtained by finding the minimum set of threads that cover the whole BSIS. The alignment implicitely done by GTS covers the maximum number of possible dependences within the sequential execution of each thread. Other dependences need explicit synchronization in order to enforce the execution order imposed by them.

First we describe the method for single-recurrence hamiltonian graphs focussing on the partitioning algorithm. After that we consider the multiple-recurrence case, taking into consideration how dependences not included in the hamiltonian recurrence are explicitely synchronized. We also describe the structure of the parallel code generated by GTS.

4.1 Single-recurrence Hamiltonian Graphs

In the case of single-recurrence hamiltonian graph, fully independent threads are obtained. Each thread can be characterized by the first point of the thread that intersects BSIS and from which it is possible to obtain the whole thread by traversing the hamiltonian recurrence.

4.1.1 Free-point and Thread Sets

We define the *Free-Point set* (FP) as the subset of points of BSIS which do not depend on any previous execution. In the example of the figure 3, points of FP are shown with filled shapes. Observe that several points of FP can belong to the same thread in USIS, as for example $S_1^{<1,1>}$ and $S_1^{<3,2>}$.

The set of points that define FP can be expressed as follows. Each distance vector $<d_{ij}^1, d_{ij}^2, \ldots d_{ij}^n>$ associated to dependence arc d_{ij} of G defines the subset of points fp (S_j) associated to the statement sink S_j that can be initially executed

$$fp(S_j) = \bigcup_{1 \leq k \leq n} fp^k(S_j) \qquad (2)$$

being $fp^k(S_j)$ those free points associated to statement S_j determined by the kth component of the dependence vector. These points can be expressed as:

$$fp^k(S_j) = \{S_j^{i_1, i_2, \ldots i_n} \mid 1 \leq i_k \leq d_{ij}^k, 1 \leq i_m \leq N_m, \forall m \neq k\} \quad \text{if } d_{ij}^k \geq 0$$

$$fp^k(S_j) = \{S_j^{i_1, i_2, \ldots i_n} \mid N_k - d_{ij}^k + 1 \leq i_k \leq N_k, 1 \leq i_m \leq N_m, \forall m \neq k\} \quad \text{if } d_{ij}^k < 0$$

depending on the sign of the component. Subset **FP** is defined by

$$FP = \bigcup_{1 \le j \le s} fp\,(S_j)$$

Let *thread set* **TS** be the subset of points in **FP** that belong to different threads in **USIS**. In the example of figure 3.b, the characterization of **TS** is shown with points filled in black.

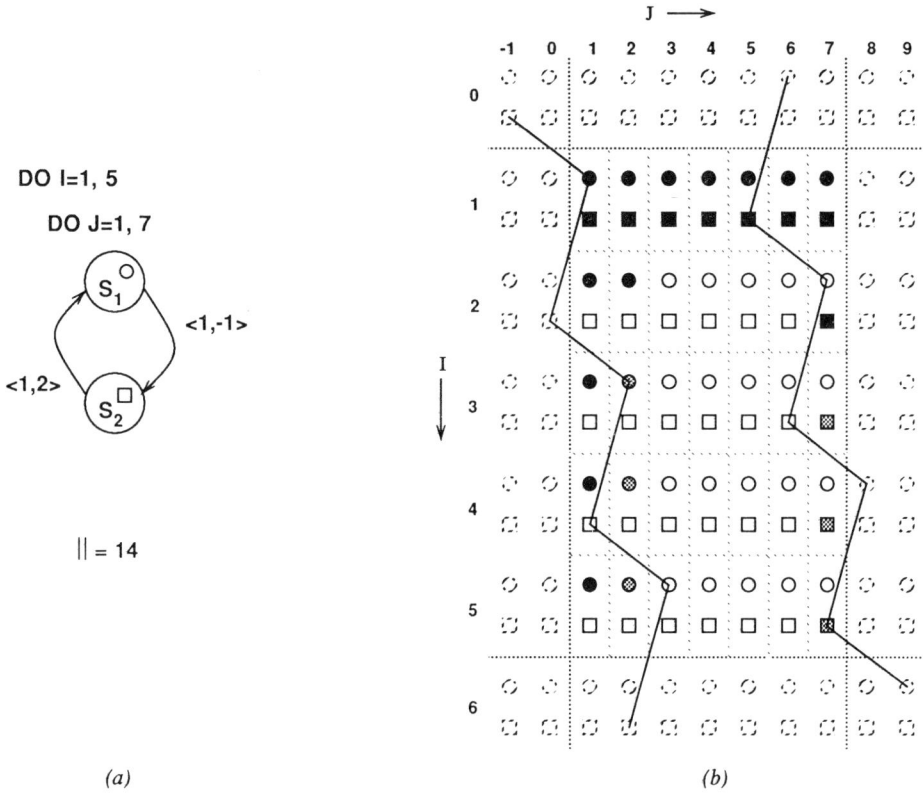

*Figure 3: (a) Dependence Graph and (b) Statement per Iteration Spaces, **FP** set (filled points) and **TS** (black points).*

GTS assigns each thread generated by the hamiltonian recurrence R to a different task or processor of the system. In this case each thread generated from hamiltonian recurrence R includes all dependences of the graph and there are no interthread dependences.

Next we give a graphical description of how **FP** and **TS** can be obtained for two-dimensional loops. The mechanism is valid for the n-dimensional case.

4.1.2 Aligned and Collapsed Space

If we consider the **BSIS** as a set of planes corresponding to each of the s statements, dependences among statements connect points in the **BSIS** from two such planes. The alignment of the hamiltonian recurrence R can be obtained by fixing the plane associated to a given statement (i.e. S_1), traversing R backwards and shifting each plane s_j of BSIS by a vector equal to $\bar{w}_{j1}$ relative to the fixed plane S_1. We will refer to $\bar{w}_{ij}$ as the weight of chain a C_{ij} included in R.

Once the shifting has been done all dependences in the recurrence except one are aligned with the statement dimension in BSIS. We can now project along the statement dimension and obtain a new shape in the BIS we will call the *aligned and collapsed space* (ACS). Each point in this ACS represents one iteration of the aligned loop and may not contain all the statements of the loop.

In figure 4.a we show the shifting of the planes after alignment process for the example of figure 3. The light grey plane represents statement S_1 and the dark one statement S_2. Each cell in a plane represents an iteration of the statement associated to the plane. Points of FP are shown with a circle or square inside the cell, depending on the statement they represent.

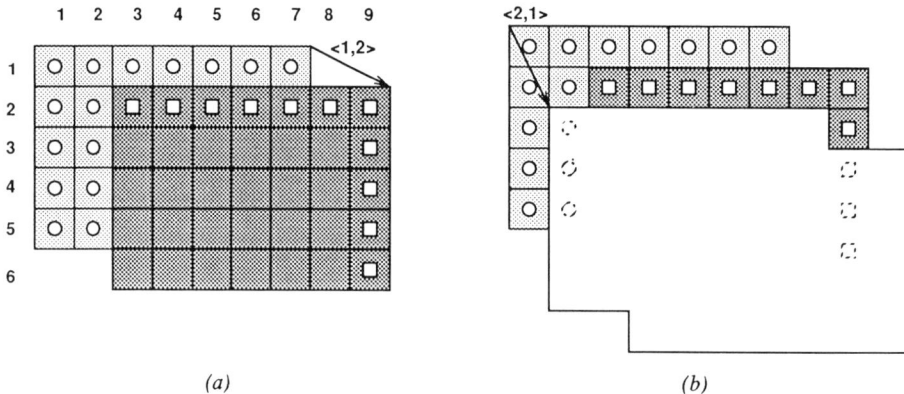

(a)   (b)

Figure 4: (a) shifting of the statement planes of BSIS traversing the hamiltonian recurrence backwards in order to obtain the ACS. (b) TS characterization obtained by overlapping ACS shifted the weight of the hamiltonian recurrence..

The TS can be characterized by those points in ACS that would not be covered by ACS shifted with $\bar{w}_R$. Each of the resulting points defines a thread that can be identified by the coordinates of the point. Observe that $\bar{w}_R$ corresponds to the distance of the dependence with non zero distance after the alignment process.

Figure 4.b shows the obtaining of TS characterization for the example of figure 3. TS is obtained by overlapping both ACS and ACS shifted the weight of recurrence R. All visible points belong to TS. As one can see, those initial points of FP hidden by the shifted space do not belong to TS.

In this characterization of TS, each thread is defined by the first point of the thread that intersects BSIS. Observe that the shape can be quite irregular in the general case. A thread could also be characterized by a point that do not belong to the BSIS but from which the same intersection with the BSIS can be reached by traversing the recurrence in the USIS. Later in this section we describe a transformation that produces a simpler characterization of the TS.

4.1.3 Thread Numeration

It is interesting to obtain other more compact and regular characterizations of TS in order to ease code and synchronization generation. These characterizations need not necessarily consist of points included in BSIS of the loop.

The new shape for TS we propose is a volume limited to a width w_R^k in the kth dimension that determines the parallelism of the loop. Remember that this dimension fulfils

$$\frac{N_k}{|w_R^k|} \leq \frac{N_i}{|w_R^i|} \quad \forall i$$

In order to obtain the new shape of TS, points out of this proposed volume are projected following recurrence R into the proposed volume.

Each thread will be identified in this new characterization with a *thread tuple*

$$\bar{t} = (t_1, t_2, ..., t_n)$$

For any point s_j^i in BSIS, the thread $\bar{t}$ on which it will be mapped can be obtained by applying the following transformation:

$$t_k = \Delta \bmod w_R^k \quad , \quad \Delta = i_k + w_{j1}^k - 1$$
$$t_m = (i_m + w_{j1}^m - \lfloor \Delta/w_R^k \rfloor \cdot w_R^m - 1) \quad (3)$$

being k dimension that determines the parallelism and m the rest of loop dimensions. This transformation reflects the projection process described above. Upper (TU$_i$) and lower (TL$_i$) limits of this TS in each dimension can be obtained by applying (3) to the corners of ACS. These limits will be used to define semaphore arrays and generate an easier parallel code.

Figure 5.a shows the obtaining of the new TS characterization and thread numeration for the example of figure 3. This characterization can be obtained by applying (3) only to the points in FP. Figure 5.b shows the composition of each thread in terms of points of BSIS.

Observe that the length of the threads is not constant so the load of the processors will not be balanced if as many processors as threads are allocated. If a number of processors equal to the parallelism of the loop are allocated we could try to schedule long threads first and leave short threads to balance the load at the end. From this point of view, the method can lead to a good load balance.

Another characteristic of the numeration proposed is that contiguous threads in a given loop dimension execute consecutive iterations of a statement in this dimension. This feature is unimportant at this point but it will ease synchronization generation when needed.

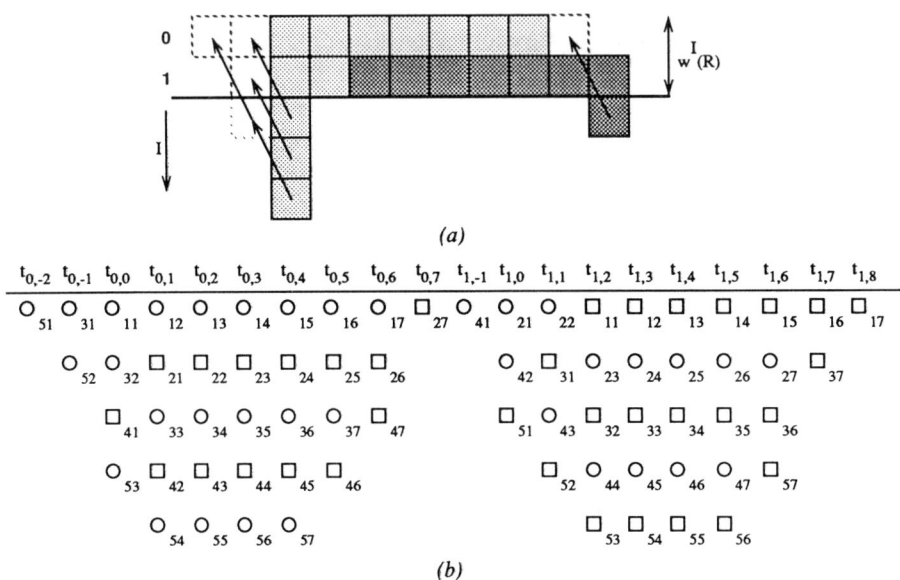

Figure 5: (a) Thread projection in order to obtain a more regular and simpler characterization of TS and numeration proposed. (b) Composition of threads generated.

4.2 Multiple-recurrence Hamiltonian Graphs

In the case of a loop with more than one recurrence, the scheduling is performed by applying to a hamiltonian recurrence of the loop the same procedure described in the preceding section. We will call scheduling recurrence a recurrence R_{sch} that includes all the statements of the loop.

Once R_{sch} has been obtained, dependences not included in the scheduling recurrence represent dependences that must be explicitly synchronized by using some intertask synchronization mechanism. On the other hand, dependences included in the scheduling recurrence will be embedded in the sequential execution of each task.

4.2.1 Thread Synchronization

Explicit synchronization must be introduced for any arc $d_{ij} \notin R_{sch}$ in the graph going from node S_i to node S_j. Many mechanisms can be used to perform this synchronization. We shall use counting semaphores as synchronization objects. As coupling between tasks will be very tight, we need a fast implementation of primitives on semaphores.

The statement S_i source of the dependence will signal the end of its execution to the statement S_j sink of the same dependence, in order to allow its execution. Observe that different pairs of threads use different pairs of synchronizing objects avoiding hot spots and distributing load on synchronizing objects. For each arc $d_{ij} \notin R_{sch}$:

- We will use a d-dimensional array of semaphores $sem_{ij}(\bar{t})$ defined by the rectangular characterization of **TS** ($TL_i \leq t_i \leq TU_i$).

- We decide to insert a *signal* operation on semaphore $sem_{ij}(\bar{t})$ in thread $\bar{t}$ after the execution of the source statement S_i. A *wait* operation on the same semaphore must be executed in thread $\bar{t}'$ before the execution of the sink statement S_j of the same dependence.

Due to the thread numbering proposed above, the relationship between both threads is:

$$t'_k = \Theta \bmod w_R^k \quad , \quad \Theta = t_k + d_{ij}^k - w_{ij}^k$$

$$t'_m = (t_m + d_{ij}^m - w_{ij}^m - \lfloor \Theta / w_R^k \rfloor * w_R^m) \quad (4)$$

Figure 6.a shows a dependence graph with a hamiltonian recurrence on which it is possible to apply the partitioning algorithm and a dependence that must be explicitly synchronized. Figure 6.b shows the characterization of **TS** and its projection taking into consideration that the parallelism is limited by dimension J of the loop. Figure 6.c shows the regular pattern required by the explicit synchronization of dependence d_{32} after the alignment in **ACS**. Figure 6.d shows the same pattern as a relationship between synchronized threads of **TS**.

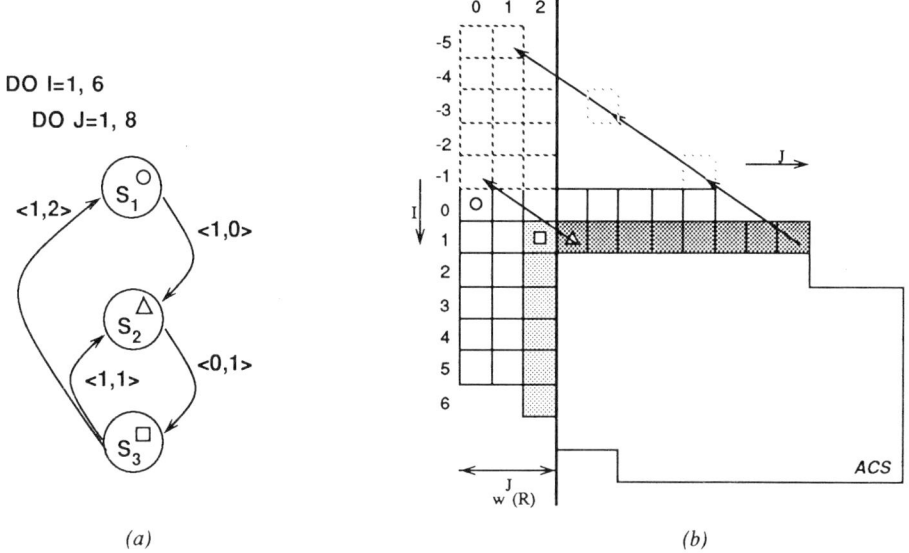

Figure 6: (a) Multiple-recurrence dependence grap and (b) **TS** characterization and projection.

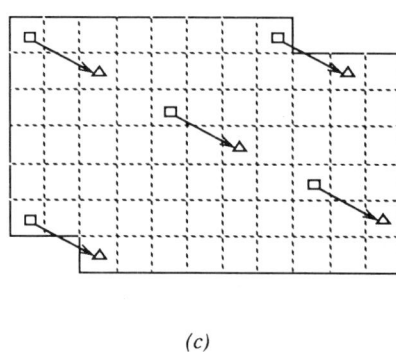
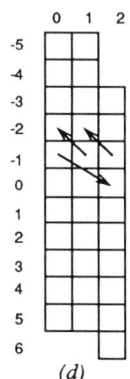

(c) (d)

Figure 6 (cont.): (c) Synchronization pattern in ACS and (d) Synchronization pattern between threads of TS.

4.2.2 Semaphore Initialization

All semaphores must be initialized to zero except those on which threads perform a wait operation before the execution of a sink statement for which the source statement is outside the BSIS space. In this case no signal operation is executed so the semaphore must be initialized in order to allow the execution of these sink statements.

For a given dependence d_{ij}, expression (2) determines the set of points fp (S_j) in BSIS associated to the sink statement S_j for which the points associated to the source statement S_i are outside BSIS. Each point of fp (S_j) is executed in a thread $\bar{t}'$ given by expression (3). The semaphore $sem_{ij}(\bar{t})$ that must be initialized is the one on which this thread performs the wait operation, obtained from (4):

$$t_k = \Phi \bmod w_R^k \quad , \quad \Phi = t'_k - d_{ij}^k + w_{ij}^k$$

$$t_m = (t'_m - d_{ij}^m + w_{ij}^m - \lfloor \Phi / w_R^k \rfloor * w_R^m). \qquad (5)$$

Combining expressions (2) and (5) we can obtain that, for each free-point, the semaphore that must be incremented from its zero initial value is:

$$t_k = \Omega \bmod w_R^k \quad , \quad \Omega = i_k + d_{ij}^k - w_{i1}^k$$

$$t_m = (i_m + d_{ij}^m - w_{i1}^m - \lfloor \Omega / w_R^k \rfloor * w_R^m).$$

Figure 7 graphically shows the semaphore initialization process for dependence d_{32} in figure 6.a. Figure 7.a identifies the set of free-points associated to statement S_2 and the set of points associated to statement S_3 source of the same dependence relation. Observe that points associated to S_3 are out of the plane associated to the plane in BSIS. Figure 7.b shows the elements of semaphore array sem_{32} initialized to one (striped cells). These semaphore elements are associated to threads that executes the dummy-points of S_3.

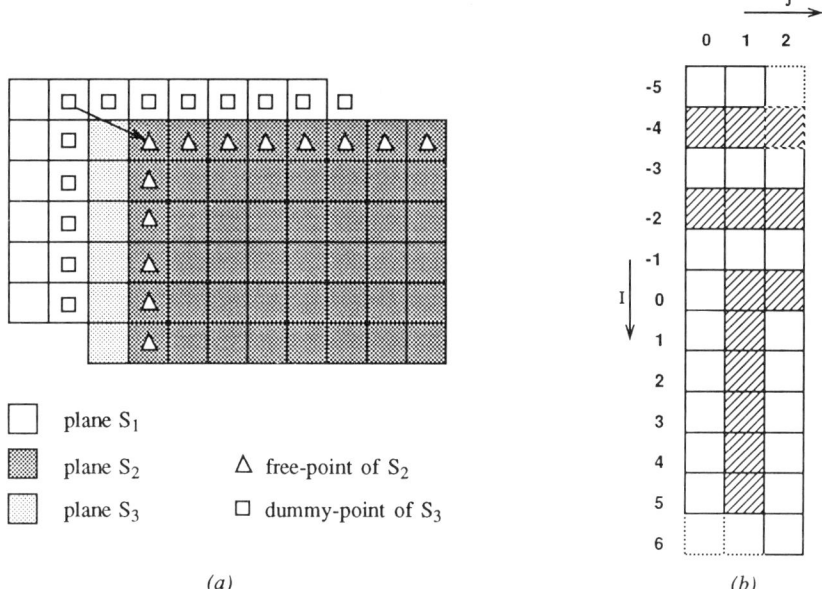

Figure 7: (a) Free-points of S_2 and dummy-points of S_3 for dependence d_{32}. (b) Semaphore array sem_{32} and initialization (striped cells).

Observe that if we consider a new dependence relation d_{11} in the graph of figure 6.a with an associated distance vector d_{11} = <2,3>, it will not need explicit synchronization because it is already enforced by the hamiltonian recurrence used for scheduling purposes. From the above expressions we can determine if a given dependence must or must not be explicitly synchronized. A dependence $d_{ij} \notin R_{sch}$ does not require explicit synchronization if there is an alternative path in the dependence graph through R_{sch} or even traversing other dependences explicitly synchronized.

4.3 Parallel Code Generation

In this section we describe the structure of the parallel code generated by GTS. Parallel code must be generated so that each processor of the system executes a given thread within the original BSIS and perform the appropriate synchronization operations.

The general structure of the code proposed is shown in figure 8. In the code of a thread we can distinguish three parts: *prolog, core and epilog*. Without loss of generality, we have assumed that $S_i \delta S_{i+1}$ ($1 \le i \le s-1$) and $S_s \delta S_1$. If this is not the case, the compiler will reorder the statements to let the previous condition be satisfied.

The prolog part initially executes a useless WHILE loop that locates the beginning of the thread in the BSIS. It also executes some points of each thread extracted from the core part in order to use the same code for all processors.

```
                         DOALL t̄ ∈ TS
...........................................................................
                         v̄ = t̄
                         WHILE (v̄ ∉ ACS) DO v̄ = v̄ + w̄_R ENDWHILE
                         v̄ = v̄ + 1̄
                         IF ((v̄ - w̄_{21}) ∈ BIS) S_2(v̄ - w̄_{21}) ENDIF      prolog part
                         ...
                         IF ((v̄ - w̄_{s1}) ∈ BIS) S_s(v̄ - w̄_{s1}) ENDIF
...........................................................................
DO ī = 1̄ , N̄             WHILE (v_k.LE.(N_k - w_{1s}^k)) DO
   S_1(ī)                   IF (v̄ ∈ BIS) S_1(v̄) ENDIF
   S_2(ī)
   ...                      IF ((v̄ + w̄_{12}) ∈ BIS) S_2(v̄ + w̄_{12}) ENDIF
   S_s(ī)                   ...                                              core part
ENDDO                       IF ((v̄ + w̄_{1s}) ∈ BIS) S_s(v̄ + w̄_{1s}) ENDIF
                         v̄ = v̄ + w̄_R
                         ENDWHILE
...........................................................................
                         IF (v̄ ∈ BIS) S_1(v̄) ENDIF
                         ...                                                  epilog part
                         IF ((v̄ + w̄_{1 s-1}) ∈ BIS) S_{s-1}(v̄ + w̄_{1 s-1})
...........................................................................
                         ENDDOALL
      (a)                            (b)
```

Figure 8: (a) Sequential DO loop and (b) General structure of the parallel code generated by GTS.

The core part consists of a sequential WHILE loop controlled by a vector index $\bar{v}$ that traverses the BSIS through recurrence R In the general case, the cardinality of the FP set can be greater than the cardinality of the TS because the recurrence can connect two points in the BSIS through some points that are not in the BSIS. This is why the conditionals in the main WHILE loop must be introduced. The compiler should rewrite each statement in order to include the offset indicated by the alignment process. The WHILE loop ends when the last point associated to S_s in the thread is executed.

The epilog part includes those statements and iterations not executed in the core part that must be executed to complete the computation assigned to each thread.

Figure 9.a shows the code obtained for the example of figure 3. Observe the possible overhead introduced due to the computation at run time of the limits in the inner DOALL loop.

The proposed code can be simplified if we characterize TS the set of points $\bar{t}$ such that $TL_i \leq t_i \leq TU_i$. Figure 6.b shows the resulting code when this approximation is done. Observe that simpler limits for the DOALL loops are obtained. The additional cost is that some threads are generated with no computation assigned. The conditionals in the thread body guarantee that no computation is performed by these tasks.

```
DOALL TI=0, 1
    IF TI=0 THEN TJL=-2;
                TJU=7;
    ELSE TJL=-1
         TJU=8;
    FI
    DOALL TJ=TJL, TJU
        I=TI+1;
        J=TJ+1;
        WHILE (I.LT.1).OR.(J.LT.1) DO
            I=I+2;
            J=J+1;                                          prolog
        ENDWHILE
        IF (I.GT.1).AND.(J.GT.2) THEN S₂(I-1,J-2);
        WHILE (I.LE.4).AND.(J.LE.8) DO
            IF (J.GE.1).AND.(J.LE.7) THEN S₁(I,J);
            IF (J-1.GE.1) THEN S₂(I+1,J-1);
                                                            core
            I=I+2;
            J=J+1;
        ENDWHILE
        IF (I.LE.5).AND.(J.LE.7) THEN S₁(I,J);              epilog
    ENDOALL
ENDOALL
                        (a)
DOALL TI=0, 1
    DOALL TJ=-2, 8
        I=TI+1;
        J=TJ+1;
        :
          same code of figure 9.a
        :
    ENDOALL
ENDOALL
                        (b)
```

*Figure 9: Parallel code generated by **GTS** for the example of figure 3.*

Figure 10 shows the parallel code generated by **GTS** including synchronization primitives for the example of the figure 5 (we have omitted the initialization of the semaphores used). Observe that conditionals in the inner WHILE loop are not necessary because all points in each thread must be executed (there are no negative components in distance vectors).

```
;semaphore initialization
DOALL TJ=0,2
    IF TJ .LE.1 THEN    TIL=-5
                        TIU= 5;
    ELSE    TIL= -3;
            TIU=  6;
    FI
    DOALL TI= TIL, TIU
        I=TI+1;
        J=TJ+1;
        WHILE (I.LT.1).OR.(J.LT.1) DO                                   prolog
            J=J+3;
            I=I+2;
        ENDWHILE
        IF (I.GT.1).AND.(J.GT.3)    THEN
            wait (sem31[(TI+1)-((TJ+1)/3)*2,(TJ+1) mod 3]);
            S2(I-1,J-3);
        FI
        IF (I.GT.1).AND.(J.GT.2)    THEN
            S3(I-1,J-2);
            signal (sem31[TI, TJ]);
        FI
        WHILE ( I.LE.5) .AND. (J.LE.7) DO                               core
            S1(I,J);
            wait (sem31[(TI+1)-((TJ+1)/3)*2,(TJ+1) mod 3]);
            S2(I+1,J);
            S3(I+1,J+1);
            signal (sem31[TI, TJ]);
            I=I+2;
            J=J+3;
        ENDWHILE
        IF (I.LE.6).AND.(J.LE.8) THEN S1(I,J); FI                       epilog
        IF (I+1.LE.6).AND.(J.LE.8) THEN
            wait (sem31[(TI+1)-((TJ+1)/3)*2,(TJ+1) mod 3]);
            S2(I+1,J);
        FI
    ENDOALL
ENDOALL
```

Figure 10: Parallel code and synchronization primitives for the example of figure 6.

5 CONCLUSIONS AND FUTURE WORK

In this paper we have presented a method for evaluating the parallelism from the data dependence graph and a partitioning algorithm that obtains the parallelism evaluated.

The compiler can use the parallelism as a good characterization of the loop to make decisions when parallelizing it. This characteristic alone does not determine the performance of the parallel code obtained because overhead associated to synchronization and run time scheduling are not taken into consideration. It would be worth that the compiler could know the trade-off between parallelism and synchronization cost of a given dependence graph in order to take more accurate decisions when parallelizing the loop.

The evaluation of the parallelism in presence of control dependences due to conditional statements has not been considered in this paper. In this case the parallelism of the loop depends of the sequence of branches executed. The compiler can obtain bounds of this parallelism and select an appropriate scheduling recurrence if the branch sequence can be predicted at compile time [4].

The partitioning method presented assumes the existence of a hamiltonian recurrence in the dependence graph. This is not the common case, so the problem must be taken into consideration. A hamiltonian recurrence can be obtained by adding a set of dummy dependences E' such that the parallelism of the loop is not limited by the new set of recurrences that appear in the dependence graph. Set E' should be obtained so that the number of threads generated is minimized and the number of dummy arcs is minimum in order to minimize synchronization between processors. Fast heuristics for obtaining good E' arcs should be looked into.

The method proposed does not balance the load assigned to the processors if as many processors as threads are allocated. The number of threads generated is greater than the parallelism evaluated and threads take different time to complete their execution. In the case of a single recurrence, the program can be executed by a number of processors equal to the parallelism of the loop. In this case a good load balancing can be obtained if long threads are scheduled first. Observe that the length of a thread can be evaluated by the compiler so that information for the run-time scheduler could be included in the parallel code.

In the case of multiple recurrences with multiple nested loops, the minimum number of processors needed to achieve the minimum execution time could also be evaluated at compile time. This number will in general be larger than the mean parallelism of the loop.

A new step that can be added [6] to the partitioning algorithm is the reduction of number of threads generated without increasing the execution time of the parallel loop. Several threads can be grouped in tasks in order to reduce the number of processors needed without overcoming the execution time of the longest thread before grouping. It is important to guarantee that the grouping of threads in tasks is deadlock-free when dependences of the graph require explicit synchronization.

REFERENCES

1. Allen F., Burke M., Charles P., Cytron R. and Ferrante J. (1988) "An Overview of the PTRAN Analysis System for Multiprocessing", Journal of Parallel and Distributed Computing, 5, pp. 617-640.
2. Allen J.R., Callahan D. and Kennedy K. (1987) "Automatic Decomposition of Scientific Programs for Parallel Execution", Proceedings of the 14th ACM Symposium Principles of Programming Languages, pp. 63-76.
3. Allen J.R. and Kennedy K. (1987) "Automatic Translation of FORTRAN Programs to Vector Form", ACM Trans. on Programming Languages and Systems, vol. 9, n. 4, pp. 491-542.

4. Ayguadé E. (1989) "Automatic Parallelization of Recurrences in Numerical Sequential Programs", Ph.D. Thesis, Departament d'Arquitectura de Computadors, Universitat Politècnica de Catalunya (in spanish).
5. Ayguadé E., Labarta J., Torres J. and Borensztejn P. (1989) "GTS: Parallelization and Vectorization of Tight Recurrences", Proc. of the Supercomputing'89, Reno-Nevada, pp. 531-539.
6. Ayguadé E., Torres J., Labarta J., Llaberia J.M. and Valero M. (1990) "Grouping Threads in GTS", Departament d'Arquitectura de Computadors, Universitat Politècnica de Catalunya, UPC/DAC Research Report RR-90/10.
7. Banerjee U., Chen S., Kuck D.J. and Towle R.A. (1979) "Time and Parallel Processor Bounds for Fortran-like Loops", IEEE Transactions on Computers, vol. C-28, n. 9, pp. 660-670.
8. Banerjee U. (1988) "Dependence Analysis for Supercomputing", Kluwer Academic Publishers, Boston.
9. Cytron R.G. (1986) "Doacross: Beyond Vectorization for Multiprocessors", Proc. of the International Conference on Parallel Processing, pp. 836-844.
10. D'Hollander E.H. (1989) "Partitioning and Labeling of Index Sets in Do Loops with Constant Dependence Vectors", Proc. of the International Conference on Parallel Processing, vol. II, pp. 139-144.
11. Eager D.L., Zahorjan J. and Lazowska E.D. (1989) "Speedup versus efficiency in parallel systems", IEEE Transactions on Computers, vol. 38, n. 3, pp. 408-423.
12. Kuck D.J., Kuhn R.H., Leasure B. and Wolfe M. (1984) "The Structure of an Advanced Vectorizer for Pipelined Processors", Tutorial on Supercomputers: Design and Applications, (Ed: K. Hwang), IEEE Press, New York, pp. 967-974.
13. Kuck D.J., Kuhn R.H., Padua D.A., Leasure B. and Wolfe M. (1981) "Dependence Graphs and Compiler Optimizations", Proc. of the 8th ACM Symposium on Principles of Programming Languages, Williamsburg, pp. 207-218.
14. Padua D.A. (1979) "Multiprocessors: Discussions of Some Theoretical and Practical Problems", Ph.D. Thesis, Univ. of Illinois at Urbana-Champaign, DCS Report No. UIUCDCS-R-79-990.
15. Peir J. (1986) "Program Partitioning and Synchronization on Multiprocessor Systems", Ph.D. Thesis, University of Illinois at Urbana-Champaign.
16. Peir J. and Cytron R. (1989) "Minimum Distance: A Method for Partitioning Recurrences for Multiprocessors", IEEE Transactions on Computers, vol. 38, n.8, pp. 1203-1211.
17. Polychronopoulos C.D. (1988) "Parallel Programming and Compilers", Kluwer Academic Publishers, London.
18. Polychronopoulos C.D., Girkar M., Haghighat M.R., Lee C.L., Leung B. and Schouten D. (1989) "Parafrase-2: An Environment for Parallelizing, Partitioning, Synchronizing and Scheduling Programs on Multiprocessors", Proc. of the International Conference on Parallel Processing, vol. II, pp. 39-48.
19. Sevcik K.C. (1989) "Characterizations of Parallelism in Applications and Their Use in Scheduling", ACM Performance Evaluation Review, 17, pp. 171-180.
20. Shang W. and Fortes J.A.B. (1988) "Independent Partitioning of Algorithms with Uniform Dependencies", School of Electrical Engineering, Purdue University.
21. Wolfe M. (1989) "Optimizing Supercompilers for Supercomputers", Reasearch Monographs in Parallel and Distributed Computing, PITMAN Publishing, London.

Author's address[*]: *Departament d'Arquitectura de Computadors. Universitat Politècnica de Catalunya. Facultat d'Informàtica de Barcelona, Pau Gargallo, 5. 08028-Barcelona. SPAIN.*
E-mail: *eduard@ac.upc.es*

[*] This work has been supported by the Ministry of Education of Spain (CICYT) in programs TIC 299/89 and 392/89

12 An Algorithmic Approach to Compound Loop Transformations
M. Wolf, M. Lam

Abstract

This paper presents a theory that unifies many existing loop transformations, including loop interchange or permutation, skewing, reversal, tiling, and combinations of these elementary transformations. This theory provides the foundation for solving an open question in compilation for parallel machines: Which loop transformations and, in what order, should be applied to achieve a particular goal, such as maximizing parallelism or data locality. This paper presents an efficient loop transformation algorithm based on this theory to maximize the degree of parallelism in a loop nest.

1 Introduction

Loop transformations, such as loop interchange, reversal, skewing and tiling (or subblocking)[2, 4, 18] have been shown to be useful for two important goals: parallelism and efficient use of the memory hierarchy. Previous work on loop transformations focused on the application of *individual* transformations: when it is legal to apply a transformation, and if the transformation directly contributes to a particular goal. It remains an open question as to how to combine these transformations to optimize general loop nests for a particular goal. This paper introduces a theory of loop transformations that answers this question.

A technique commonly used in today's parallelizing compilers is to decide *a priori* the order in which the compiler should attempt to apply transformations. This technique is inadequate because the effectiveness of a given transformation often depends on the future transformations that can be applied. Another proposed technique is to "generate and test", that is, to apply all different possible combinations of transformations. This "generate and test" approach is

---

This research was supported in part by DARPA contract N00014-87-K-0828.

expensive. Differently transformed versions of the same program may trivially have the same behavior and so need not be explored. For example, when vectorizing, the order of the outer loops is not significant. More importantly, generate and test approaches cannot search the entire space of transformations that have potentially infinite instantiations. Loop skewing is such a transformation, since a wavefront can travel in an infinite number of different directions.

For loops whose data dependences are distance vectors, a more rigorous mathematical approach has been proposed. In this approach, loop interchange, reversal, and skewing transformations are unified as linear transformations in the iteration space. This mathematical formulation of a loop has been used in the study of generating systolic arrays and tiling[6, 7, 10, 11, 14, 15]. The restriction that data dependences must be distance vectors excludes loops that contain any "serializing" loops. That is, in this notation, an n-dimensional iteration space trivially can be transformed to produce $n - 1$ parallel loops. We are interested in representing general loop nests and transforming the loops to maximize the number of parallel loops.

Our approach combines the rigor of the iteration space approach with the general program domain of the vectorizing and concurrentizing compilers. Our dependence vectors can incorporate both distance and direction information. The various transformations, interchange, reversal and skewing are unified as linear transformations. Compound transformations are just another linear transformation. This unification provides a general condition to determine if the code obtained via a compound transformation is legal, as opposed to a specific test for each individual elementary transformation. This makes it possible to search through the transformation space efficiently to achieve a given goal. Moreover, the relationships and interactions between different transformations can be analyzed in this unified model. Similarly, this model supports the derivation of the new loop bounds directly after a compound transformation. If loop bounds were derived for every transformation, the final expressions derived may be more complex than necessary.

Using this notation, we have developed algorithms for improving the parallelism and locality of a loop nest via loop transformations. Our parallelizing algorithm maximizes the degree of parallelism, that is, the number of parallel loops, within a loop nest. By finding the maximum number of parallel loops, multiple consecutive loops can be coalesced to form a single loop with all the iterations; this facilitates load balancing and reduces synchronization overhead. The different degrees of parallelism can be exploited directly by processors with different levels of parallelism, such as a multiprocessor with superscalar nodes. Moreover, some of the loops may contain a small number of loop iterations. Parallelizing only one loop may not fully exploit all the parallelism in the machine. The algorithm can generate coarse-grain and/or fine-grain parallelism; the former is useful in multiprocessor organizations and the latter is useful for vector machines and superscalar machines, machines that can execute multiple instructions per cycle. It can generate code for machines that can use multiple levels of parallelism, such as a multiprocessor with vector nodes.

We have also applied our representation of transformations successfully to the problem of data locality. All modern machine organizations, including uniprocessors, employ a memory hierarchy to speed up data accesses; the memory hierarchy typically consists of registers, caches, primary memory and secondary memory. To use this memory hierarchy efficiently, our locality optimization seeks to maximize the reuse of data that has been recently accessed. As the processor speed improves and the gap between processor and memory speeds widens, data locality becomes more important. Even with very simple machine models (for example, uniprocessors with data caches), complex compound loop transformations may be necessary [8, 9, 13]. The consideration of data locality makes it more important to be able to combine primitive loop transformations in a systematic manner.

The loop transformation algorithm has been implemented in our Stanford University parallelizing compiler. The implementation has taken only about two man-months, demonstrating that the implementation is made simple by the theory.

This paper introduces our model of loop dependences and transformations. We describe how the model facilitates the application of compound transformation, using parallelism as our target. The model is important in that it enables the choice of an optimal transformation without an exhaustive search. Here we will only present the parallelization algorithm; the proof that it finds the optimal transformation[16] is outside the scope of this paper. The derivation of the optimal compound transformation consists of two steps. The first step puts the loops into a canonical form, and the second step tailors it to specific architectures. While the first step can be expensive in the worst case, we have developed an algorithm that is feasible in practice. We apply a cheaper technique to handle as many loops as possible, and use the more general and expensive technique only on the remaining loops. We expect to find the optimal transformation in $O(n^3 d)$ time for most programs, where n is the depth of the loop nests and d is the number of dependence vectors. The second step of specializing the code for different granularities of parallelism is straightforward and cheap. After deciding on the compound transformation to apply, the code including the loop bounds is then modified.

The organization of the paper is to first present the representation of the loop nests and the modeling of loop transformations. After establishing the notation, we illustrate the algorithm of parallelization by stepping through a simple example and showing the output code for different machine organizations. Finally, we describe a method for deriving the bounds of a loop after a compound transformation.

2 Representation

2.1 Program Representation

Our approach is applicable to perfectly nested loop nests; we assume that all optimizations have been applied to create perfectly loop nests whenever possible [1]. The upper and lower loop bounds must be linear expressions of the loop indices and the loops are normalized to have unit step sizes. In our model, a loop nest of depth n corresponds to a finite convex polyhedron of iteration space Z^n, bounded by the loop bounds. Each iteration in the loop corresponds to a *node* in the polyhedron, and is identified by its index vector $\vec{p} = (p_1, p_2, \ldots, p_n)$; p_i is the loop index of the i loop in the nest, counting from the outermost to innermost loop. In the sequential program, the iterations are therefore executed in lexicographic order of their index vectors.

The scheduling constraints of the loop are represented as dependence vectors. The only dependences of interest are loop carried dependences, and not loop independent dependences. It is not necessary to classify the different dependence types such as control, anti- or output dependence, nor is the identity of the related memory accesses of any significance.

A dependence vector in an n-nested loop is denoted by a vector $\vec{d} = (d_1, d_2, \ldots, d_n)$. Each component d_i is a range of integers, represented by

$$[d_i^\mu, d_i^\nu], \text{ where } d^\mu \in \mathcal{Z} \cup \{-\infty\}, d^\nu \in \mathcal{Z} \cup \{\infty\} \text{ and } d^\mu \leq d^\nu.$$

A single dependence vector represents a set of distance vectors, known as the *distance vector set*:

$$\mathcal{E}(\vec{d}) = \{(e_1, \ldots, e_n) | e_i \in \mathcal{Z} \wedge d_i^\mu \leq e_i \leq d_i^\nu\}.$$

Each distance vector defines a set of edges on pairs of nodes in the iteration space. We say that an edge $(\vec{p_1}, \vec{p_2})$ exists if and only if $\exists \vec{e} \in \mathcal{E}(\vec{d})$ for some dependence vector $\vec{d}$, such that $\vec{p_2} = \vec{p_1} + \vec{e}$. The dependence vectors thus define a partial order on the nodes in the iteration space, and any topological ordering on the graph is a legal execution order, as all dependences in the loop are satisfied.

This notation allows us to represent both direction [3, 17] and distance information in a uniform notation. For example, the Wolfe direction vector '<' would be represented in our notation as $d^\mu = 1$ and $d^\nu = \infty$, or $[1, \infty]$ for short. If a dependence has a constant distance δ, then the dependence is represented as $[\delta, \delta]$, and we use the shorthand δ to represent that distance when the context is clear. Finite ranges of distance components are represented by separate dependence vectors; that is, if $d^\mu \neq d^\nu$, then $d^\mu = -\infty$ or $d^\nu = \infty$ or both.

The arithmetic and comparison operators over the domain of components are defined in a straightforward way to give useful meanings. For example, arithmetic operators are defined so that $2 + [-3, \infty] = [-1, \infty]$. We also utilize the multiplication of a distance by a scalar when taking dot products. We use the straightforward definition that

$$s[a, b] = \begin{cases} [sa, sb], & \text{if } s \geq 0 \\ [sb, sa], & \text{otherwise} \end{cases}$$

and $s \cdot \infty$ is ∞ for positive s, 0 if s is 0, and $-\infty$ for negative s, and likewise for a factor times $-\infty$. These definitions of addition and multiplication are conservative in that

$$\vec{e_1} \in \mathcal{E}(\vec{d_1}) \text{ and } \vec{e_2} \in \mathcal{E}(\vec{d_2}) \Rightarrow f(\vec{e_1}, \vec{e_2}) \in \mathcal{E}(f(\vec{d_1}, \vec{d_2}))$$

where f is a function that performs a combination of multiplications and additions on its operands. The converse, that

$$\vec{e} \in \mathcal{E}(f(\vec{d_1}, \vec{d_2})) \Rightarrow \exists \vec{e_1} \in \mathcal{E}(\vec{d_1}) \wedge \vec{e_2} \in \mathcal{E}(\vec{d_2}) : f(\vec{e_1}, \vec{e_2}) = \vec{e},$$

is not necessarily true unless $\vec{d_1}$ and $\vec{d_2}$ are themselves distance vectors.

A component d is *positive*, written $d > 0$, if its minimum d^μ is a positive integer. It is *non-negative*, written $d \geq 0$, if its minimum is non-negative. Likewise, d is *negative* or *non-positive* if its maximum d^ν is negative or non-positive respectively. We use the notation '+' as shorthand for $[1, \infty]$, '−' as shorthand for $[-\infty, -1]$, and '*' as shorthand for $[-\infty, \infty]$.

Since the nodes are initially executed in lexicographic order, the scheduling constraints can be captured by a set of *lexicographically positive* dependence vectors. A dependence vector $\vec{d}$ is lexicographically positive, written $\vec{d} \succ \vec{0}$, if $\exists i : (d_i > 0 \text{ and } \forall j < i : d_j \geq 0)$. A dependence vector $\vec{d}$ is lexicographically non-negative, written $\vec{d} \succeq \vec{0}$, if it is lexicographically positive or its components are all non-negative. A zero vector is one with all components equal to 0, written $\vec{0}$.

The procedure for extracting data dependence for this representation is similar to those used in previous vectorizing and parallelizing compilers. The only difference is that we require the data dependences of the original programs be represented as lexicographically positive data dependence vectors. For example:

   for $i := 0$ to n do
     for $j := 0$ to n do
        $b := g(b)$;

The dependence vectors are $\{(0, `+`), (`+`, `*`)\}$. The lexicographical positive property of the dependences is crucial in simplifying the modeling of loop transformations.

2.2 Transformation Representation

The scope of loop transformations addressed in this paper is restricted to transformations that manipulate entire iterations and reorganize them within a loop nest. A loop transformation is defined by two mapping functions. The first is a one-to-one and onto mapping between a node in the convex polyhedron representing the original loop nest and a node in another convex polyhedron in an iteration space of possibly different dimensions. The second function maps the original set of dependence vectors, such that if a distance vector exists between a pair of nodes in the original loop, one also exists between the corresponding nodes in the transformed loop. We note that there may not be a one-to-one correspondence between the dependence vectors of the two loops because infinite sets of distance vectors can be represented only along the basis of the iteration space. This notation is chosen because it is efficient and it captures most of the dependences found in real programs. We say that a transformation is *valid* if the transformed dependence edges are acyclic. Traditionally, we say that it is *legal* to apply a transformation to a loop nest if the transformed code can be executed sequentially, or in lexicographic order of the iteration space. We observe that if nodes in the transformed code are executed in lexicographic order, all data dependences are satisfied if the transformed dependence vectors are lexicographically positive. This observation leads to a general definition of a legal transformation.

Definition 2.1 *A loop transformation is* legal *if the transformed dependence vectors are all lexicographically positive.*

Many of the loop transformations used in vectorizing and parallelizing compilers can be generalized as *linear transformations*; these include permutation, reversal and skewing. An important non-linear loop transformation is tiling.

2.2.1 Linear Transformations

A linear transformation T, where T is a non-singular, unimodular matrix, maps iteration $\vec{p}$ to iteration $T\vec{p}$ and dependence vector $\vec{d}$ to iteration $T\vec{d}$. T is unimodular so that T^{-1} maps the transformed iteration $\vec{p'}$ back to integral points in the original iteration space $\vec{p} = T^{-1}\vec{p'}$. We consider only $n \times n$ matrices, where n is the nest depth. Three of the common loop transformations, permutation, reversal and skewing, are elementary transformations.

- *Permutation:* A permutation σ on a loop nest transforms iteration $(p_1,\ldots,p_n)$ to $(p_{\sigma_1},\ldots,p_{\sigma_n})$. This transformation can be expressed in matrix form as I_σ, the $n \times n$ identity matrix I with rows permuted by σ.

- *Reversal:* Reversal of loop i is represented by the identity matrix, but with the ith diagonal element equal to -1 rather than 1.

- *Skewing:* Skewing loop l_j by an integer factor f with respect to loop l_i [18] maps iteration
$$(p_1,\ldots,p_{i-1},p_i,p_{i+1},\ldots,p_{j-1},p_j,p_{j+1},\ldots,p_n)$$
to
$$(p_1,\ldots,p_{i-1},p_i,p_{i+1},\ldots,p_{j-1},p_j+fp_i,p_{j+1},\ldots,p_n).$$
The transformation matrix that produces skewing is the identity matrix, but with the element $t_{i,j}$ equal to f rather than zero. Since $i < j$, T must be lower triangular.

A compound transformation can be synthesized from a sequence of primitives, and the effect of the transformation is represented by the products of the various transformation matrices for each primitive transformation. Such a transformation is always unimodular. If the computation is to be executed sequentially in lexicographic order, then it must be the case that $T\vec{d} \succ \vec{0}$. This observation allows us to devise a simple legality test for general linear transformations.

Theorem 2.1 (Linear Transformation Test). *Let D be the set of dependence vectors of a computation. A linear transformation T is legal if T is non-singular and unimodular, and if $\forall \vec{d} \in D : T\vec{d} \succ \vec{0}$.*

The proof is a simple consequence of the definition of legal and that if $\vec{d} \in D$ then $\vec{e} \in \mathcal{E}(\vec{d}) \rightarrow T\vec{e} \succ \vec{0}$. Since our arithmetic operators are only conservative for general dependence vectors, it is the case that $\vec{d} \in D$ then $T^{-1}(T\vec{d}) = \vec{d}$ only under the two common cases stated in Theorem 2.2.

Theorem 2.2 *Let D be the set of dependence vectors of a computation. Suppose either of the following is true:*

1. *all $\vec{d} \in D$ are distance vectors, or*

2. *the linear transformation T can be synthesized exclusively from a combination of permutation and loop reversals.*

Then the linear transformation T is legal if and only if $\forall \vec{d} \in D : T\vec{d} \succ \vec{0}$.

As an example, let us consider the following code:

```
for i := 1 to n do
  for j := 1 to n do
    a[i, j] := f(a[i, j],a[i + 1, j − 1]);
  end for
end for
```

This code has the dependence $(1, -1)$. Loop interchange is represented by $T = \begin{bmatrix} 0 & 1 \\ 1 & 0 \end{bmatrix}$ mapping iteration (i, j) to (j, i). However, $T(1, -1)$ is $(-1, 1)$ which is lexicographically negative, rendering loop interchange illegal on this loop. On the other hand, the transformation represented by $T' = \begin{bmatrix} 0 & -1 \\ 1 & 0 \end{bmatrix}$ is legal. Note that $\begin{bmatrix} 0 & -1 \\ 1 & 0 \end{bmatrix} = \begin{bmatrix} -1 & 0 \\ 0 & 1 \end{bmatrix} \begin{bmatrix} 0 & 1 \\ 1 & 0 \end{bmatrix}$ so the legal transformation can be considered an interchange followed by a reversal of the outermost loop.

We say that a set of adjacent loops i through j is *fully permutable* if it is legal to reorder the loops in all possible permutations. Full permutability is an important property that is exploited by transformations for both parallelism and data locality.

Theorem 2.3 (Full Permutability Test.) *Loops i through j of a legal computation with dependence vectors D are fully permutable if*

$$\forall d \in D : ((d_1, \ldots, d_{i-1}) \succ \vec{0} \vee (\forall i \leq k \leq j : d_k \geq 0))$$

2.2.2 Tiling

Tiling [17] is not a linear transformation. When we tile loops $i, \ldots, j$ by sizes $b_i, \ldots, b_j$, the iteration space gains $j - i + 1$ new dimensions, and the iteration

$$(p_1, \ldots, p_{i-1}, p_i, \ldots, p_j, p_{j+1}, \ldots, p_n)$$

is mapped to

$$(p_1, \ldots, p_{i-1}, p'_i, \ldots, p'_j, p''_i, \ldots, p''_j, p_{j+1} \ldots, p_n)$$

where $p'_k = \lfloor p_k/b_k \rfloor$, and $p''_k = p_k \bmod b_k$, for each $i \leq k \leq j$.

Define the function

$$s(d) = \begin{cases} 0 & \text{if } d = 0 \\ \text{`}+\text{'} & \text{if } d \neq 0 \text{ and } d \text{ non-negative} \\ \text{`}-\text{'} & \text{if } d \neq 0 \text{ and } d \text{ non-positive} \\ \text{`}*\text{'} & \text{otherwise.} \end{cases}$$

A dependence vector $(d_1, \ldots, d_n)$ is transformed into up to 2^{j-i+1} new vectors of the form

$$(d_1, \ldots, d_{i-1}, d'_i, \ldots, d'_j, d''_i, \ldots, d''_j, d_{j+1}, \ldots, d_n),$$

where for each $i \leq k \leq j$, either $d'_k = s(d_k)$ and $d''_k = \text{`}*\text{'}$ or $d'_k = 0$ and $d''_k = d_k$, except that if $d_k = 0$ then $d'_k = 0$ and $d''_k = 0$.

From examination of the above, it is clear that if loops i through j of a legal computation are fully permutable, then they are also tilable. Since the resulting dependence vectors are independent of the size of the tile, it is not necessary to determine that size at loop transformation time.

3 The Parallelizing Algorithm

Iterations of a loop can execute in parallel if and only if there are no dependences carried by that loop. Suppose the loop nest $(p_1, \ldots, p_n)$ can be executed correctly in lexicographic order. The loop p_i of a legal sequential loop nest is parallelizable if and only if for all dependence vectors $(d_1, \ldots, d_{i-1}) \succ \vec{0}$ or $d_i = 0$. Such a loop is called a DOALL loop. To maximize the degree of parallelism is to transform the loop nest to maximize the number of loops that satisfy this property.

We divide the problem of parallelization into two parts. We first transform the original loop nest into nests of largest fully permutable loop nests. This is the canonical form from which maximum degrees of coarse and fine grain parallelism can be obtained. Then different techniques are applied to obtain the granularities of parallelism appropriate for the target machine. We illustrate this algorithm using the following example:

```
for i := 1 to n do
  for j := 1 to n do
    for k := 1 to n do
      (a[i,k],b[i,j,k]) := f(a[i,k], a[i+1,k-1], b[i,j,k], b[i,j,k-1]);
```

The loop body above is represented by a cube in a three-dimensional iteration space with sides of length n. Discarding $(0,0,0)$, the dependence vectors are,

$$D = \{(0, `+`, 0), (1, `*`, -1), (0, 0, 1)\}.$$

None of the three loops in the source program can be parallelized as it stands; however, there is one degree of parallelism that can be exploited at either a coarse or fine grain level.

In the description below, we will show the code resulted from each step of the transformation process. In reality, code is generated once only at the end of the entire algorithm.

3.1 Canonical Form

A loop is in canonical form for parallelization if it contains the maximally outermost fully permutable loops under linear transformations. Once in canonical form, the loops can be translated mechanically to suit a particular parallel architecture.

For the example above, the algorithm *permutes* the j and k loops, and *skews* the k loop with respect to loop i by a factor of 1, resulting in the code below:

```
for i := 1 to n do
  for k := i+1 to i+n do
    for j := 1 to n do
      (a[i,k-i],b[i,j,k-i]) := f(a[i,k-i], a[i+1,k-i-1], b[i,j,k-i], b[i,j,k-i-1]);
```

The transformation matrix T and the transformed dependences D are

$$T = \begin{bmatrix} 1 & 0 & 0 \\ 1 & 1 & 0 \\ 0 & 0 & 1 \end{bmatrix} \begin{bmatrix} 1 & 0 & 0 \\ 0 & 0 & 1 \\ 0 & 1 & 0 \end{bmatrix} = \begin{bmatrix} 1 & 0 & 0 \\ 1 & 0 & 1 \\ 0 & 1 & 0 \end{bmatrix}$$

and
$$D = \{(0, 0, \text{'+'}), (1, 0, \text{'*'}), (0, 1, 0)\}.$$

The transformation is legal since the dependences remain lexicographically positive. The first two loops form one set of fully permutable loop nest, since interchanging loops i and j leaves the dependences lexicographically positive. The loop k is in a (degenerate) set of permutable loops by itself.

We will briefly outline the algorithm that is used in transforming the code into canonical form[16]. The algorithm constructs the final set of loops incrementally starting with the outermost subnest and working inwards. The same procedure of finding the currently outermost, largest fully permutable loop nest is applied recursively. For each subnest, the algorithm adds loops to it one at a time. A loop may first be reversed and/or skewed with respect to outer loops before it can be permuted to be included into the current subnest. This permute-reverse-skew does not always deliver the optimal result. However, it is optimal in common cases such as when the nest contains less than four loops, or when all the dependences in the original program are distance vectors. In those cases where this algorithm cannot order all the loop, we apply general 2-D transformations[14, 15] on pairs of loops to improve parallelism. With this transformation, our algorithm is optimal for loops nests of depth four or less in $O(n^3 d)$ where n is the loop nest depth and d is the number of dependences[16].

3.2 Targeting for Specific Architectures

In the following, we first show that the loops in the canonical format can be trivially transformed to give coarsest granularity of parallelism. We then show these loops can be transformed to give the same degree of fine-grain parallelism, suitable for superscalar and VLIW architectures. We then return to the multiprocessor architecture, and show how the same degree of parallelism can be obtained via lower synchronization cost, and how both fine- and coarse-grain parallelism can be produced.

3.2.1 Coarse Grain Parallelism

A nest of n fully permutable loops can be transformed to code containing at least $n - 1$ degrees of parallelism [11]. In the degenerate case when no dependences are carried by these n loops, the degree of parallelism is n. Otherwise, $n - 1$ loops can be obtained by skewing the innermost loop in the fully permutable nest by each of the other loops and moving the innermost loop to the outermost position. For example, the two-loop fully permutable set in the example above can be transformed to provide one level of parallelism:

for k := 3 to 3*n do
  doall i := max(1,⌈(k-n)/2⌉) to min(n,⌊(k-1)/2⌋) do
    for j := 1 to n do
      (a[i,k-2*i],b[i,j,k-2*i]) := f(a[i,k-2*i], a[i+1,k-2*i-1], b[i,j,k-2*i], b[i,j,k-2*i-1]);

1	2	3	4	5
2	3	4	5	6
3	4	5	6	7
4	5	6	7	8

Figure 1: Order of DOALLs in tiled 2-dimensional iteration space

The transformation matrix T for this phase of transformation, and the transformed dependences D are

$$T = \begin{bmatrix} 0 & 1 & 0 \\ 1 & 0 & 0 \\ 0 & 0 & 1 \end{bmatrix} \begin{bmatrix} 1 & 0 & 0 \\ 1 & 1 & 0 \\ 0 & 0 & 1 \end{bmatrix} = \begin{bmatrix} 1 & 1 & 0 \\ 1 & 0 & 0 \\ 0 & 0 & 1 \end{bmatrix}$$

and

$$D = \{(0, 0, \text{`+'}), (1, 1, \text{`*'}), (1, 0, 0)\}.$$

Applying this skew and interchange transformation to all the fully permutable loop nests will produce a loop nest with the maximum degree of parallelism. Moreover, the parallelism is contained in the outermost possible loops, and thus of the coarsest granularity possible[16].

3.2.2 Fine Grain Parallelism

If the target is a superscalar or VLIW machine, it is desirable that the parallel loop be innermost. If loop m is a parallel loop and $m < n$, then loop i can be permuted into the innermost loop via the transformation I_σ, where $\sigma = 1, \ldots, m-1, m+1, \ldots, n, m$. It is obvious that originally lexicographically positive dependences remain so if loop m is a parallel loop. Thus if there is a DOALL anywhere in the loop nest, we can create fine-grain parallelism for a machine that can use it. In fact, any number of DOALL loops can be permuted to be inner loops. This may be useful if code scheduling techniques such as software pipelining[12] are used. The overhead of starting and finishing a parallel loop is further reduced by coalescing the multiple DOALL loops. Since the transformation in Section 3.2.1 creates the largest possible number of DOALL loops, the maximum degree of fine-grain parallelism can be obtained by simply moving these DOALL loops innermost.

3.2.3 Reducing Global Barriers

Whenever a DOALL loop is nested within a non-DOALL loop, all processors must be synchronized at the end of each DOALL loop with a barrier. We can reduce the synchronization cost by tiling [17]. In the following, we show two variations.

After transforming the code to obtain the outermost fully-permutable loop nests, we do not skew and permute as suggested in Section 3.2.1. Instead, starting with the canonical form of the nest from Section 3.1, we tile the outermost fully-permutable nest. Using our simple example again, the tiled code becomes:

```
for ii := 1 to n by B do
  for kk := ii+1 to ii+n by B do
    for i := ii to min(ii+B, n) do
      for k := max(kk,i+1) to min(kk+B, n) do
        for j := 1 to n do
          (a[i,k-i],b[i,j,k-i]) := f(a[i,k-i], a[i+1,k-i-1], b[i,j,k-i], b[i,j,k-i-1]);
```

The outer loop nests obtained by tiling (*ii* and *kk* in the example) can be skewed and permuted to run in parallel just as the original loops. The advantage is that the synchronization cost is reduced by the block size. The i and k dimensions are plotted in Figure 1. Tiles are numbered by the index of their outer loops so that tiles with the same number are executed in parallel. Tiles numbered n cannot execute until all those numbered $n-1$ have executed.

Tiling has two other advantages. First, within each tile, fine-grain parallelism can easily be obtained by skewing the loops *within* the tile and moving the DOALL loop innermost. Second, tiling can improve data locality if there is data reuse across several loops [8].

To further reduce the synchronization cost, we can apply the concept of a DOACROSS loop to the tile level [5] [17]. After tiling, instead of skewing the loops statically to form DOALL loops, the computation is allowed to skew dynamically by explicit synchronization between data dependent tiles. In the DOALL loop approach, tiles of each level must be completed before the processors may go on to the next, requiring a global barrier synchronization. In the DOACROSS model, each tile can potentially execute as soon as it is legal to do so. That is, referring to Figure 1, those numbered n can execute as soon as their neighbors that are numbered $n-1$ have executed. This ordering can be enforced by local synchronization. Furthermore, different parts of the wavefront may proceed at different rates as determined dynamically by the execution times of the different tiles. In contrast, the machine must wait for the slowest processor at every level with the DOALL method.

3.3 Summary

We have outlined our two-step algorithm in finding parallelism for the different machines. The first is to transform the code into nests of maximal fully permutable loop nests. The second is to tailor the code to specific architectures. The step of transforming the loop nests into nests of fully permutable loops can be quite expensive, whereas the transformation of targeting to different machine architectures is straightforward.

4 Determining Loop Bounds

In this section we present a method to determine the loop bounds after a series of skews, permutations, reversals, general two dimensional transformations and tilings.

4.1 Scope

The class of loops that the loop bound calculation can handle is of the form

$$\text{for } I_i := \max(L_i^1, L_i^2, \ldots) \text{ to } \min(U_i^1, U_i^2, \ldots) \text{ do}$$

where

$$L_i^\alpha = \left\lceil \left(l_{i,0}^\alpha + \sum_{k=1}^{i-1} l_{i,k}^\alpha I_k \right) / l_{i,i}^\alpha \right\rceil$$

$$U_i^\alpha = \left\lfloor \left(u_{i,i}^\alpha + \sum_{k=1}^{i-1} u_{i,k}^\alpha I_k \right) / l_{i,i}^\alpha \right\rfloor$$

and all $l_{i,k}^\alpha$ and $u_{i,k}^\alpha$ are known constants, except possibly for $l_{i,0}^\alpha$ and $u_{i,0}^\alpha$, which must still be invariant in the loop nest. (If a ceiling occurs where we need a floor it is a simple matter to adjust $l_{i,0}^\alpha$ and $u_{i,0}^\alpha$ and replace the ceiling with the floor, and likewise if a floor occurs where we need a ceiling.) If any loop increments are not one, then they must first be made so, for example via loop normalization. If the bounds are not of the proper form, then the given loop cannot be involved in any transformations, and the loop nest is effectively divided into two: those outside the loop and those nested in the loop.

Loop skewing followed by permutation can easily produce bounds of this complexity, with minima, maxima, floors and ceilings. Since we wish to be able to take permuted and skewed loops and perform further transformations, we need full generality.

4.2 Determining the Bounds after Skewing or Reversal

Loop reversal can be implemented by negating the step and exchanging the upper and lower bounds, and applying loop normalization to make the step again unity. It is also easy to determine the bounds after loop skewing [18]. Moreover, if the bounds were previously in the class of bounds we can transform, then they remain so after the loop bound transformations for skewing and reversal.

4.3 Determining the Bounds after Permutation

We outline our method for determining the bounds of a loop nest after permutation by σ. We explain the general method and demonstrate it by permuting the following loop nest to make k the outermost loop and i the innermost loop.

for $i := 1$ **to** n_i **do**
  for $j := 2i$ **to** n_j **do**
    for $k := 2i + j - 1$ **to** $\min(j, n_k)$ **do**
      $S;$

The inequalities extracted from the above loop nests are:

$$\begin{array}{ll} i \geq 1 & i \leq n_i \\ j \geq 2i & j \leq n_j \\ k \geq 2i + j - 1 & k \leq j \quad k \leq n_k \end{array}$$

From these inequalities, we can find the maximum and minimum possible values of each loop index. This can be easily done by substituting the values obtained from the outermost loop to innermost. The minimum and maximum values are:

$$i \geq 1 \qquad\qquad i \leq n_i$$
$$j \geq 2 \times 1 = 2 \qquad\qquad j \leq n_j$$
$$k \geq 2 \times 1 + 2 - 1 = 3 \qquad k \leq \min(n_j, n_k).$$

We define for loop i

$$\min(I_i) = \max_\alpha (L_i^{*\alpha})$$

where

$$L_i^{*\alpha} = \left\lceil \left(l_{i,0}^\alpha + \sum_{k=1}^{i-1} l_{i,k}^\alpha I_{i,k}^{*\alpha} \right) / l_{i,i}^\alpha \right\rceil$$

and

$$I_{i,k}^{*\alpha} = \begin{cases} \min(I_k), & \mathrm{sgn}(l_{i,k}^\alpha) = \mathrm{sgn}(l_{i,k}^\alpha) \\ \max(I_k), & \text{otherwise.} \end{cases}$$

Similar formulas hold for $\max(I_i)$.

The inequalities can be expressed in a more uniform notation. We first note that $I_i \geq \lceil f(\ldots) \rceil$ if and only if $I_i \geq f(\ldots)$ since I_i is an integer. Thus in the inequality $I_i \geq L_i^\alpha$ we can remove the ceiling in the L_i^α. We can then move the I_i term to the same side as the summation and multiply the inequality through by $l_{i,i}^\alpha$ to get

$$l_{i,0}^\alpha - l_{i,i}^\alpha I_i + \sum_{k=1}^{i-1} l_{i,k}^\alpha I_k \leq 0, \text{if } l_{i,i}^\alpha > 0.$$

The sense of the inequality is reversed if $l_{i,i}^\alpha < 0$. We can perform the same manipulations of the upper bound expressions. We can also multiply through by -1 when the test is $\geq$. Again we can perform the same manipulations for the upper bound inequalities. This results in a series of inequalities of the form

$$e_{i,0}^\alpha + \sum_{k=1}^{i} e_{i,k}^\alpha I_k \leq 0$$

where the $e_{i,k}^\alpha$ are compile time constants and $e_{i,0}^\alpha$ is a loop nest invariant.

To determine the loop bounds for loop index i after permutation by σ, we first rewrite each inequality containing i, producing a series of inequalities $i \leq f(\ldots)$ and $i \geq f(\ldots)$. Each inequality of the form $i \leq f(\ldots)$ contributes to the upper bound. If there is more than one such expression, then the minimum of the expressions is the upper bound. Likewise, each inequality of the form $i \geq f(\ldots)$ contributes to the lower bound, and the maximum of the right hand sides is taken if there is more than one. Each inequality of the form $i \geq f(j)$ is considered twice. Suppose loop j is placed outside of i, the expression does not need to be changed since the loop bound of i can be a function of the outer index j. As for loop index j, we must substitute i by its minimum or maximum, whichever minimizes f. A similar procedure is applied to the upper loop bounds.

We demonstrate this method for the above example. Substituting the minimum and maximum of i and j into bounds of loop k, and those of i into bounds of loop j, we obtain:

$$k \geq 2i + j - 1 \qquad k \leq j \qquad k \leq n_k$$
$$k \geq 3 \qquad\qquad k \leq n_j \qquad k \leq n_k$$

$$j \geq 2i \qquad k \leq j \quad j \leq n_j \quad k \geq 2i + j - 1$$
$$j \geq 2i \qquad j \geq k \quad j \leq n_j \quad j \leq k - 2i - 1$$
$$j \geq 2 \qquad j \geq k \quad j \leq n_j \quad j \leq k - 2 - 1 = k - 3$$

$$i \geq 1 \qquad\qquad i \leq n_i \quad j \leq k - 2i - 1$$
$$i \geq 1 \qquad\qquad i \leq n_i \quad i \leq (k - j - 1)/2 = i \leq \lfloor (k - j - 1)/2 \rfloor$$

The transformed bounds are the following:

for $k := 3$ **to** $\min(n_k, n_j)$ **do**
  for $j := k$ **to** $\min(n_j, k - 3)$ **do**
    for $i := 1$ **to** $\min(n_i, \lfloor (k - j - 1)/2 \rfloor)$ **do**
      S;

The loop bounds produced as a result of permutation again belong to the class discussed in Section 4.1, so that our methods can calculate the loop bounds after further transformation of these loops.

4.4 Determining the Bounds for General 2-D Loop Transformations

The process for determining the bounds after a general 2-D transformation T is similar to that for permutation. First, we produce the set of inequalities relating the original loop indices i and j, and calculate the maxima and minima for the indices. Transformation T maps i and j to a linear combination of i' and j'. We replace all references to i and j by the equivalent linear combinations of i' and j' in the inequalities. The inequalities remain linear. We then apply the same transformation T to the maxima and minima of i and j to produce those for i' and j'. Once these are known, the loops are placed in the desired order and the bounds are calculated, just as in the permutation case.

4.5 Determining the Bounds after Tiling

It has been suggested that strip-mining and interchanging be applied to determine the bounds of a tiled loop. However, it is not straightforward when the loop bounds are not rectangular [18]. A more direct method is as follows. When tiling, we partition the iteration space, whatever the shape of the bounds, as in Figure 2. Each rectangle represents a computation performed by a tile; some tiles may contain little or even no work.

We replace the loop nest to be tiled, $(p_i, \ldots, p_j)$, with $(p'_i, \ldots, p'_j, p_i, \ldots, p_j)$. The lower bound on the p_k loops, $i \leq k \leq j$, is the maximum of the original lower bound and p'_k; similarly, the upper bound is the minimum of the original upper bound and $p'_k + S_k - 1$, where S_k is the size of the tile in the k loop. For loops p'_k, the lower and upper bounds are simply

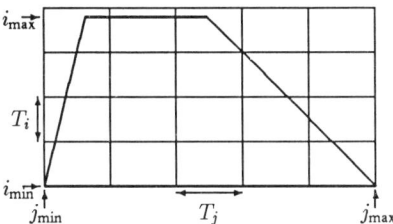

Figure 2: Tiling a trapezoidal loop (2-D)

the minimum and maximum values of loop index k. As shown in Figure 2, some of these tiles are empty. The time wasted in determining that the tile is empty should be negligible when compared to the execution of the large number of non-empty tiles in the loop. The p'_k loops step by S_k.

Applying these methods to the permuted example loop nest, we can tile to get the following: (Note that k', j' and i' can be permuted at will.)

```
for k' := 3 to min(n_j, n_k) by T_k do
for j' := 2 to n_j by T_j do
for i' := 1 to n_i by T_i do
  for k := max(3, k') to min(n_k, n_j, k' + T_k - 1) do
  for j := max(k, j') to min(n_j, k - 3, j' + T_j - 1) do
  for i := max(1, i') to min(n_i, ⌊(k - j - 1)/2⌋, i' + T_i - 1) do
    S;
```

After tiling, the loops *within* the tiles are again in the form we need to perform further permutation, skewing and so on. This property is very useful for tiling for coarse-grain parallelism and then skewing and permuting to create fine-grain DOALL parallelism. The loops *controlling* the tile have a step chosen by the compiler and therefore known at compile time. However, it may not be possible to normalize the loop in such a way that those bounds will still be in the class we need to perform further permutation with loops controlling these tile loops.

5 Conclusions

We have developed a theory that unifies various previously proposed loop transformations, and enables the application of compound transformations. This theory is general enough to encompass both parallelizable and non-parallelizable loops. Previous approaches focus on either specific elementary transformations on general loop nest representation, or general linear transformations on a subclass of loops, namely, the set of loops whose dependences can be represented as a set of distance vectors. This uniform notation is necessary to allow reasoning about the space of all transformations to reduce the search for the optimal transformation.

We have applied this theory to the problem of maximizing the degree of parallelism in loop nests. This paper proposes a practical approach to maximize the degree of parallelism for various different machine architectures via general linear transformations. There are many different possible sequences of linear transformations that can be applied and the algorithm to find the optimal can potentially be expensive. We reduce the problem of maximizing parallelism for different architectures to finding a series of coarsest fully permutable loop nests. By showing that it is easy to transform the loops in this canonical form to suit different architectures, we unify all these different parallelization problems into one. This problem formulation reduces the general parallelization problem into the problem of finding the outermost, largest, fully permutable nest, thus significantly reducing the search space.

We have also applied this theory to the problem of finding loop bounds after transformation. By considering the loop nest as a whole, the general algorithm for determining loop bounds is simplified. For example, in the case of tiling there is no need to have different versions of the transformation for constant loop bounds and for "triangular loops" — the bounds can be determined in a uniform manner.

References

[1] R. Allen, D. Callahan, and K. Kennedy. Automatic decomposition of scientific programs for parallel execution. Technical Report Rice COMP TR86-42, Rice University, Nov 1986.

[2] R. Allen and K. Kennedy. Automatic translation of fortran programs to vector form. Technical Report Rice COMP TR84-9, Rice University, Jul 1984.

[3] U. Banerjee. Data dependence in ordinary programs. Technical Report 76-837, University of Illinios at Urbana-Champaign, Nov 1976.

[4] U. Banerjee. A theory of loop permutations. In *2nd Workshop on Languages and Compilers for Parallel Computing*, Aug 1989.

[5] R. Cytron. *Compile-time Scheduling and Optimization for Asynchronous Machines*. PhD thesis, University of Illinois at Urbana-Champaign, 1984.

[6] J.-M. Delosme and I. C. F. Ipsen. Efficient systolic arrays for the solution of toeplitz systems: an illustration of a methodology for the construction of systolic architectures in vlsi. Technical Report 370, Yale University, 1985.

[7] J. A. B. Fortes and D. I. Moldovan. Parallelism detection and transformation techniques useful for vlsi algorithms. *Journal of Parallel and Distributed Computing*, 2:277–301, 1985.

[8] Dennis G., William J., and Kyle G. Strategies for cache and local memory management by global program transformation. *Journal of Parallel and Distributed Computing*, 5:587–616, 1988.

[9] K Gallivan, W. Jalby, U. Meier, and A. Sameh. The impact of hierarchical memory systems on linear algebra algorithm design. Technical report, University of Illinios, 1987.

[10] F. Irigoin and R. Triolet. Computing dependence direction vectors and dependence cones. Technical Report E94, Centre D'Automatique et Informatique, 1988.

[11] F. Irigoin and R. Triolet. Supernode partitioning. In *Proc. 15th Annual ACM SIGACT-SIGPLAN Symposium on Principles of Programming Languages*, January 1988.

[12] M. Lam. Software pipelining: An effective scheduling technique for vliw machines. In *Proc. ACM SIGPLAN 88 Conference on Programming Language Design and Implementation*, pages 318–328, June 1988.

[13] A. Porterfield. *Software Methods for Improvement of Cache Performance on Supercomputer Applications*. PhD thesis, Rice University, May 1989.

[14] P. Quinton. Automatic synthesis of systolic arrays from uniform recurrent equations. In *Proc. 11th Annual International Symposium on Computer Architecture*, June 1984.

[15] R. Schreiber and J. Dongarra. Automatic blocking of nested loops. 1990.

[16] M. E. Wolf and M. S. Lam. Maximizing parallelism via loop transformations. Technical report, Stanford University, 1990.

[17] M. J. Wolfe. More iteration space tiling. In *Supercomputing '89*, Nov 1989.

[18] M. J. Wolfe. *Optimizing Supercompilers for Supercomputers*. MIT Press, 1989.

13 The Suppression of Compensation Code

T. Gross, M. Ward

Abstract

Trace scheduling is a code generation technique that selects a sequence of operations (called a "trace") from different basic blocks and schedules these operations together as if they were in a single basic block. When scheduling the trace, an operation that appeared in the code above a branch may move below the branch. Whenever this happens, a simple code scheduler has to insert a copy of the moved operation into the off-trace code. Such a copy is called *compensation code* since it compensates for the scheduling of the trace. However such a copy may not be necessary. In this paper, we present the precise conditions that allow a code generator to *suppress* compensation copies and then discuss how this optimization can be included in a compiler that employs trace scheduling. The key is to provide the code generator with a more global view of scheduling so that is can determine if a compensation copy is unnecessary. A simple algorithm can deal with most practical cases, and we report briefly on the implementation for the TRACE 300, a VLIW machine developed by Multiflow Inc.

1. Introduction

Trace scheduling is an effective code generation technique that has been used for VLIW processors as well as pipelined processors. The key idea of trace scheduling is that the code generator selects a group of basic blocks, either based on heuristics or actual frequency information, and produces code for these block as if they were a single basic block [6]. Since the trace scheduler does not see any of the original basic blocks, it can move operations around

---

Michael Ward was employed by Multiflow Inc., Branford, CT, while the implementation described in this paper was done.

freely, for example to fill slots in a wide instruction word or to utilize a load delay.

Determining the order of operations is one of the key tasks for a code generator. By considering different basic blocks together, trace scheduling provides the code generator with more operations to deal with. This improves the chances that a good schedule can be found since the code generator has more choices available to fill a "hole" in a schedule. However, if operations are moved across basic block boundaries, such optimizations require that the overall program be fixed up to account for the code movements.

Trace scheduling is just one code generation technique that requires adjustment of the unscheduled parts of the code to counterbalance the decisions of the code generator. Perlocation scheduling is another code generation technique that moves operations during scheduling and that also requires adjustments [8].

1.1. Trace scheduling

The machine model that we use in this discussion is a simple load/store architecture with a load delay of one where all instructions take the same amount of time to execute. (A load delay of one means that the result of a load instruction is not available to the instruction immediately following the load instruction.) In this machine, each machine instruction performs a single (machine) operation. These simplifications keep the description of the problem simple and concise; our actual implementation is for a VLIW machine (i.e. each instruction includes multiple machine operations) and that includes instructions with different execution times [2]. For example, load, floating point, and integer operations take a different number of clocks.

Consider this code fragment that we want to compile for such a machine.

```
if (c != 0)
    { b = a / c; }
else
    { b = 0; };
f = g + h;
```

Figure 1-1: Program segment

After the usual local optimizations, the compiler obtains a sequence of machine operations as shown in Figure 1-2. For our simplified machine model, each machine operation maps into exactly a single instruction, and the task of the trace scheduler is to find a good execution sequence.

Figure 1-3 shows the flow graph for this code segment. Each node represents a single machine operation, and boxes represent basic blocks. Notice that "goto" instructions do not show up explicitly in the flow graph; control transfers are indicated by arcs between basic blocks.

Let us assume that (c != 0) most of the time, so the most likely execution path includes the then-clause of the if-statement as shown in Figure 1-3. All the operations in the darkly shaded region are processed by the trace scheduler together, and the resulting schedule of instructions for operations 1 to 9 is shown in Figure 1-4. For example, instruction A consists of the first operation, **load a**, instruction B consists of operation 3, etc. Notice how operations 6

```
START:
        load c
        branch if c = 0 goto ELSE
THEN:
        load a
        t1 = a / c
        store b
        goto NEXT
ELSE:
        store b
        goto NEXT
NEXT:
        load g
        load h
        t2 = g + h
        store f
```

Figure 1-2: Machine code

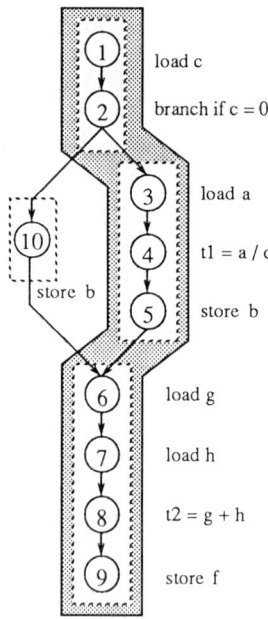

Figure 1-3: Flow graph for Figure 1-1

and 7 have moved relative to the other operations in the flow graph.

Since operation 6 has moved, the instruction that contains this operation cannot be any longer the target of the branch (operation 2) after scheduling. Instead, a new target must be found. Furthermore, the code shown in Figure 1-4 causes a problem if the branch of operation 2 *is taken* (that is, (c == 0)), and the else-clause is executed. With the current schedule, operation 7 (load h) cannot executed without performing the division of the then-clause.

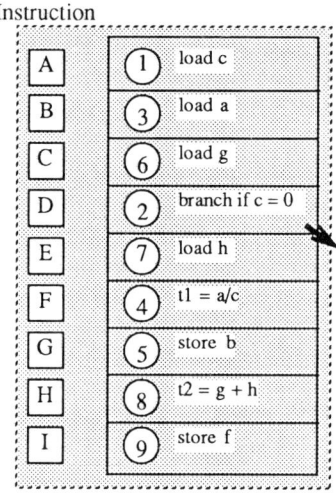

Figure 1-4: Partial schedule for Figure 1-3

The solution to these problems is part of the core of trace scheduling [6, 5, 3], but before we describe how trace scheduling deals with these two problems, we introduce some terminology.

1.2. Terminology

The trace scheduler takes a sequence of operations, called the *trace*, and generates a sequence of target machine instructions, called the *schedule*. Operations that are not part of the trace are called *off-trace*. Each instruction can consist of multiple operations, although our figures and examples here depict only a single operation per (machine) instruction. Since we use graphs to illustrate some of the concepts, we sometimes use the term *node* to refer to specific operations. In the figures for this paper, operations are represented by circles and instructions by rectangles.

A trace is an ordered sequence of operations, and each operation in the trace has a unique position, called the *trace position*. Instructions are also ordered, and each instruction is associated with a unique *schedule cycle*, which indicates the place of the instruction in the schedule. There exists a map *TS* that maps each trace position into a schedule cycle. This map is a one-to-one mapping for our demonstration target machine and a many-to-one map for a machine with multiple operations per instruction word. However, this map does not preserve the ordering: for two operations O_i and O_j, *traceposition*(O_i)<*traceposition*(O_j) does not imply that *schedulecycle*(*TS*(O_i))<*schedulecycle*(*TS*(O_j)). For example, operation 2 appears before operation 3 in the trace of Figure 1-3 but is actually scheduled after operation 3 in the schedule shown in Figure 1-4.

A *split operation*, or *split* for short, is a conditional branch operation (an operation with more than one successor operation) on the trace. One of the two successors is on the trace and is called the fall-through successor. The other successor is the target of the branch that is not on the trace. In our example operation 2 is a split. Node 3 is the on-trace successor, and Node 10 is the off-trace target.

A *join operation*, or *join* for short, is an operation on the trace that is the target of a branch operation. After a trace is scheduled, branches to join operations must be adjusted to reflect the scheduling decisions for the trace. The code generator must find an appropriate instruction that can serve as the branch target; just choosing the instruction that contains the join operation is not correct. For example, join operations may have moved relative to other operations, as seen by operation 6 in Figure 1-3. Therefore, the trace scheduler must translate each *join position JP* into a *rejoin cycle RC* so that if a branch operation targeted the join J at position JP, the corresponding branch instruction targets instruction R in cycle RC. The rejoin cycle RC of join J must satisfy the constraint that all operations O that appeared prior to J in the trace (that is, *traceposition(O)<traceposition(J)*) must be scheduled before instruction R. If this constraint is satisfied, then the trace scheduled code behaves exactly as if the code was scheduled conventionally, that is one block at a time. For example, in Figure 1-4, the rejoin cycle for join position 6 is 8. Operation 5, the last operation on the trace before the join, is scheduled in instruction G, therefore the rejoin cycle is 8, and the off-trace branch (represented by the arc from the block that contains operation 10 to an operation on the trace) must be adjusted: it rejoined the trace at trace position 6 and now must be targeted at operation 8 in instruction H.

Whenever the trace scheduler moves an operation above a join, it must insert a copy of this operation on the off-trace joining edge, as shown in Figure 1-5. Otherwise, the moved operation will not be executed if the path through Node X on the off-trace code is taken.

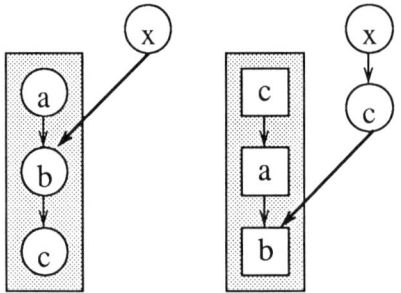

Figure 1-5: Join compensation code

Similarly, whenever the trace scheduler moves an operation below a split, it must insert a copy of this operation on the off-trace splitting edge, as shown in Figure 1-6. However, since we are trying to fill load delays, load operations tend to move up towards the beginning of the schedule, and this situation is less frequent in practice.

If we add the compensation copies required by the code schedule of Figure 1-4, we obtain the complete schedule for the graph of Figure 1-3 as shown in Figure 1-7.

2. Problem statement

Clearly, the introduction of compensation code is undesirable. Adding copies of moved operations to the program increases the program size, with its well-known negative impact on cache performance and compilation time. Furthermore, insertion of a compensation copy penalizes the off-trace code. Depending on the operations in the off-trace code, it may not be possible to schedule the compensation copy together with other off-trace operations.

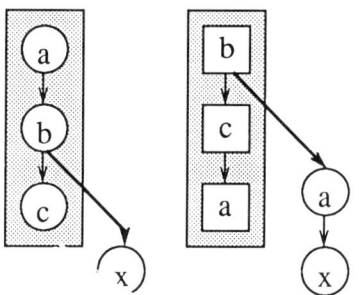

Figure 1-6: Split compensation code

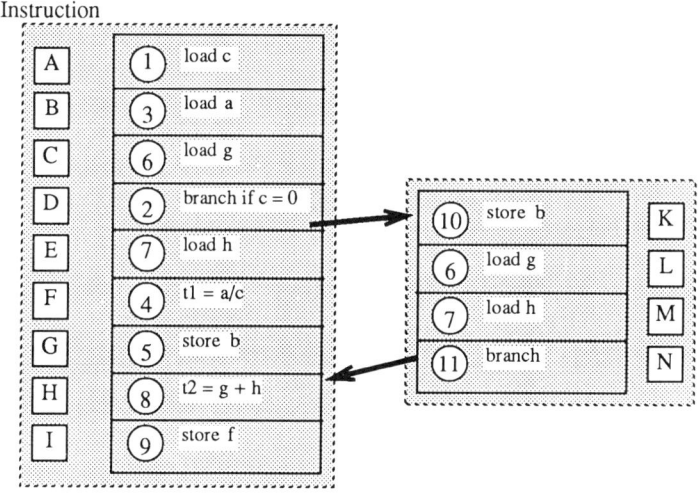

Figure 1-7: Complete schedule for Figure 1-3

Furthermore, not all compensation copies are necessary, as has been noticed earlier [3]. The simple-minded trace scheduler notices that an operation was moved above a join and inserts a copy. However, upon inspection of Figure 1-7, we notice that instruction L (**load g**), the copy of operation 6, is redundant. Operation 6 moved up so high in the schedule (instruction C) that it will be executed regardless which path through the program graph is taken. Even if the off-trace path with operations 10 and 11 is selected, operation 6 is executed.

The effect of inserting compensation code is that the off-trace code contains extra operations. In the case above, these copied operations are executed *twice* whenever the path through the off-trace branch is taken: first, the moved operation is executed, and second, the copied operation is executed. This is a real problem if the off-trace code is executed frequently as well (e.g. in the case of a 60/40 branch that is taken 60% of the time, the off-trace code is nevertheless executed 40% of the time).

This observation forms the basis for the optimization of compensation code. First we define when a copy is redundant.

Definition 1: A compensation copy C of an operation O for a split or join SJ is *redundant* if O has been moved to an instruction I that is executed whenever SJ is executed, and the sources and destinations of O are live at SJ.

By demanding that the sources of O are still live at SJ, we guarantee that the copy C computes the same results as O. If the sources are no longer live, then we have to insert a copy for correctness. And we require that the destination is live as well, otherwise we have to recompute the result of O to ensure correctness.

In the rest of this section, we will discuss further under what conditions an instruction I satisfies the condition that it is executed whenever RC is executed. The *join compensation code optimization problem* can then be stated as follows:

Join compensation code optimization problem:
    Given a trace T, a join operation J, an operation O such that $traceposition(O) > traceposition(J)$, and a schedule S for the trace T with rejoin instruction R at rejoin cycle RC for J such that $schedulecycle(TS(O)) < RC$.
    Determine if C is redundant and remove the copy if this is the case.

The reason to include the liveness requirement in the definition of redundancy is obvious. If the operation O modifies any storage elements (registers, memory, etc.), then we have to make sure that no other instruction I' executing after I and before RC modifies any of these storage resources. Otherwise, the compensation copy does useful work and is not redundant.

There exists the dual *split compensation code optimization problem*, which can then be stated as follows:

Split compensation code optimization problem:
    Given a trace T, a split operation B, an operation O such that $traceposition(O) < traceposition(B)$, and a schedule S for the trace T such that $schedulecycle(TS(B)) < schedulecycle(TS(O))$.
    Determine if C is redundant and remove the copy if this is the case.

However, as we stated earlier, since our goal is to fill load delays (or other pipeline delays), operations with a high latency tend to move up towards the top of the schedule, not downwards. For this reason, we decided to delay the investigation and implementation of split compensation code until there was a compelling performance reason to include it in the compiler. The rest of the paper then describes our algorithm and results for join compensation code.

3. Approaches to suppress compensation code

Our goal was to incorporate this optimization into an existing compiler, the trace scheduling compiler of Multiflow Inc. This decision had three consequences: First, the overall structure of the compiler could not be changed. The structure of the code generator of this compiler is similar to the original description of a trace scheduler [6]; a complete block is compacted and then the book-keeper inserts join and split compensation copies. The important point is that all operations of the trace are scheduled *before* the compensation copies are inserted. Second, including this optimization should not increase the compilation time noticeably. Third, this compiler performed a number of optimizations on the intermediate code before trace scheduling. For example, the flow graphs contained no dead nodes, loops had been identified, and loop invariants had been recognized and moved.

Although the optimization had been introduced before [3], we do not know of any implementation. And although it has some similarity with other, more conventional optimizations, upon close inspection this similarity does not lead to a strategy to incorporate this optimization into a compiler.

3.1. Dead code elimination

At first sight, the optimization of compensation code looks similar to the elimination of dead code; since this optimization also removes (or suppresses) operations, would it not be possible to detect such operations at the time dead code elimination is performed? Unfortunately, this view is incorrect, for two reasons.

Dead code elimination is usually performed prior to code generation [1]. At this time however, the traces (therefore of course also the schedules for these traces) are completely unknown. Compensation copies are inserted *during* code generation, not before.

More important is a fundamental difference. Consider the flow graph segment shown in Figure 3-1, with a compensation copy of node 4 (labeled "x" in the off-trace code). Resource R, which is defined by operation 4, cannot be dead after node 4; otherwise, earlier phases of the compiler would eliminate this node. Therefore, resource R must be live at instruction N, and this implies that the destination of operation x is not dead but live. Therefore, dead code elimination would never be able to remove this operation.

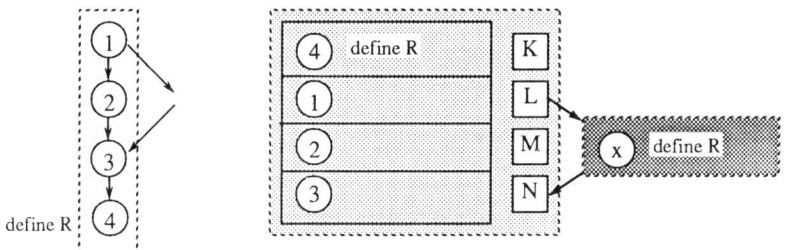

Figure 3-1: Resource R is not dead

3.2. Code hoisting

Another way to approach the problem of eliminating unnecessary copies is to consider code hoisting, another well-known optimization. In Figure 3-1, the compensation copy "x" can be eliminated because the original node moved above the branch operation (node 1). However, this is different from code hoisting, where copies of the same operation appear in both successor blocks of a branch.

3.3. Domination

In Figure 1-7, the compensation copy can be eliminated because the original operation is executed in any case, whether the branch is taken or not. That is, the new position of operation 6 dominates the off-trace branch, and this was the approach suggested earlier [3]. Unfortunately, this approach is overly restrictive and may not work in practice when loops are unrolled.

Consider the flow graph on the left hand side of Figure 3-2. The trace consists of the nodes 1 to 8, and the schedule for this trace is shown on the right hand side. For example, instruction B contain contains operation 7. The first rejoin instruction is instruction D, for the rejoin that was targetted to operation 3. Instruction G is the rejoin instruction for the rejoin that was targetted to operation 6.

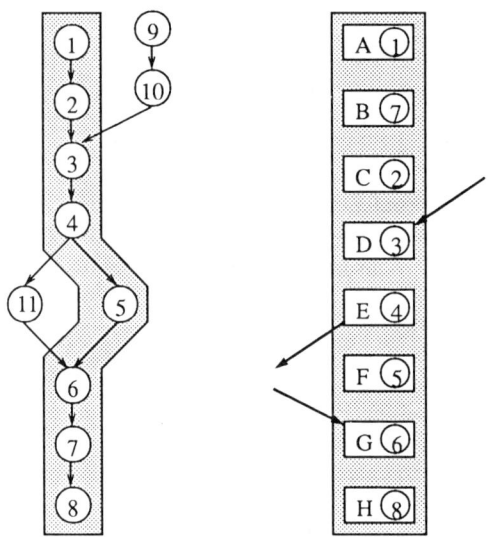

Figure 3-2: Sample trace with schedule

Operation 7 moved from below the join at position 6 up into the second instruction. The rejoin cycle for this join is instruction G (the second to last instruction). Now let us consider if we need to insert a compensation copy of operation 7 into the off-trace code for this join. This off-trace code contains so far operation 11. Instruction B does not dominate instruction G since a there is path through nodes 9 and 10 that joins at instruction D and that does not include instruction 2. However, there is no need to introduce a copy of operation 7 for join position 6! It is necessary to insert a copy for join position 3 (with rejoin instruction D), since operation 7 moved also above this join. After this is done (see Figure 3-3), operation 7 is executed on any path through the program that includes the rejoin instruction, instruction G. Either the (moved) operation 7 in instruction B *or* the compensation copy in instruction M in the off-trace branch joining at instruction D is executed.

Often loops are unrolled by the compiler to increase the number of operations in the loop body that are available for scheduling. Figure 3-4 shows a sample flow graph before and after unrolling twice. If we required that a moved operation dominates the off-trace code, then whenever operation 2' or 3' (resulting from unrolling) is scheduled between the branch operations 1 and 4, a compensation copy must be generated.

From this we conclude that domination is a sufficient but not a necessary condition to eliminate a compensation copy.

Theorem 2: Given a trace T, a join operation J, an operation O such that $traceposition(O) > traceposition(J)$, and a schedule S for the trace T with rejoin instruction R at rejoin cycle RC for J such that $schedulecycle(TS(O)) < RC$. Further-

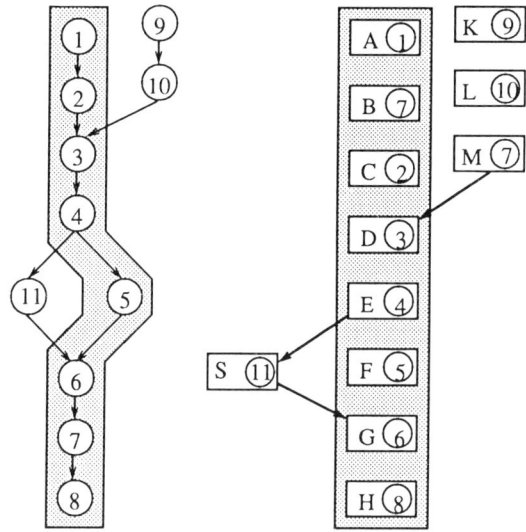

Figure 3-3: Schedule with compensation copy in instruction L

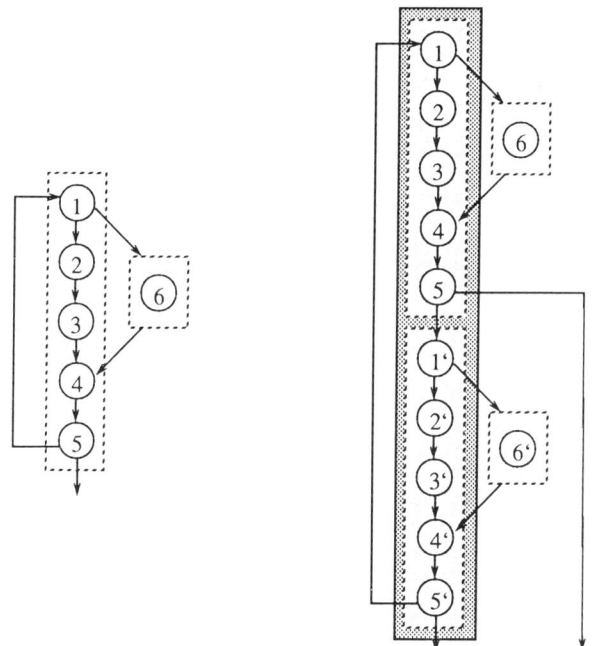

Figure 3-4: Unrolled loop

more, the destinations of $TS(O)$ are live at cycle RC in the schedule S.

If $TS(O)$ dominates R, then this is a sufficient condition for the redundancy of the compensation copy C for O, but it is not a necessary condition.

Proof: From the example of Figure 3-3 it is clear that domination is not a necessary condition. The rest of the proof follows immediately from the next lemma.

Lemma 3: Given a trace T, a join operation J, an operation O such that $traceposition(O) > traceposition(J)$, and a schedule S for the trace T with rejoin instruction R at rejoin cycle RC for J such that $schedulecycle(TS(O)) < RC$. The compensation copy C for O is redundant if

1. $TS(O)$ dominates R.

2. The destinations of $TS(O)$ are live at cycle RC in the schedule S.

Proof: Call I the instruction that holds operation O, i.e. $TS(O)=I$. The first clause of the above theorem guarantees that instruction I is executed on every path from the START instruction of the program to instruction R, the rejoin instruction[1]. Furthermore, the second clause states that the result of O is still available at cycle RC. This means that no instruction on the trace or off the trace that is executed after I and before R modifies any of the destinations of O. Therefore, the compensation copy C is redundant for rejoin instruction R; there is no need to insert a copy of O into the off-trace rejoining edge.

3.4. Our solution

Since domination is only sufficient but not necessary, we have to find a more precise criterion to determine if a compensation copy is redundant.

Theorem 4: Given a trace T, a join operation J, an operation O such that $traceposition(O) > traceposition(J)$, and a schedule S for the trace T with rejoin instruction R at rejoin cycle RC for J such that $schedulecycle(TS(O)) < RC$. The compensation copy C for O is redundant if

1. Instruction $TS(O)$ or a successor instruction of $TS(O)$, instruction D, such that D is different from R, dominates R.

2. The destinations of $TS(O)$ are live at cycle RC in the schedule S.

Proof: There are two cases to consider. If instruction $TS(O)$ dominates the rejoin instruction R, then the conditions of Lemma 3 hold and the compensation copy C for O is redundant.

If $TS(O)$ does not dominate but a successor instruction D dominates, then there must be join onto the trace between instructions $TS(O)$ and D. (If there is no join onto the trace, D cannot dominate R.) Let us call D' the rejoin instruction on the trace that dominates D. If there are multiple rejoin instructions that dominate D, we pick the instruction D' that is scheduled in the earliest instruction (i.e. has the lowest schedule position). Then $TS(O)$ cannot dominate D'; otherwise it would dominate R as well. That means that for rejoin instruction D', compensation code is required. However, once a compensation copy is inserted for the rejoin at instruction D', there is no need to insert a copy at rejoin instruction R, since either the moved instruction or an earlier compensation copy is executed on any path to R.

---

[1]Given a directed graph G with a special START node such that (1) START has no predecessors in G, and (2) every node of G can be reached by at least one path from START. For two nodes D and N, we say D *dominates* N if and only if every path from START to N contains D [1].

Since every instruction dominates itself, we have to ensure that the rejoin instruction D' above is different from R. R is always a successor of $TS(O)$, so it meets the first condition, but since we currently analyze the compensation code for this rejoin, the above argument cannot apply to R's compensation code.

4. Algorithm

Our algorithm exploits Theorem 4 to suppress compensation copies. The main difficulties are finding a suitable instruction D that is a successor to $TS(O)$ and dominates R without incurring a high compile-time cost, and testing that the resources of an operation to be copied are still live.

Given a trace T and a schedule S for this trace. For each join operation J with join position JP

- Determine the corresponding join instruction R at rejoin cycle RC.
- Determine the sequence of operations $O_1, O_2, ...$ that satisfy $traceposition(O_i) > JP$ and $schedulecycle(TS(O_i)) < RC$.
- Order the sequence O_j so that $traceposition(O_i) < traceposition(O_{i+1})$.
- For each operation O_k in $O_1, O_2, ...$, in trace position order,

  1. Find a rejoin instruction $D'_k \neq R$ in the schedule that has a higher schedule position and that dominates the rejoin instruction R.

  2. If no D'_k cannot be found (i.e. $D'_k = R$, insert a compensation copy for O_k and proceed to the next operation O_{k+1}.

  3. Check that the destinations of O_k are still live at instruction R, i.e. the last instruction to modify these destinations is $TS(O_k)$. You must consider the off-trace code to determine liveness.

  4. Check that the sources of O_k have not been modified since they were read by $TS(O_k)$. The off-trace code must be checked for instructions that destroy the sources of O_k.

  5. If the destinations or sources are *not live*, a compensation copy for O is needed. Otherwise, no compensation copy is required.

The reason to process the operations in trace position order is that after a compensation copy for one operation O was made, all other operations that use one of the destinations of O as a source operand will have to be copied as well, since the destinations will not be live any more.

5. Results

The above algorithm was implemented in the framework of the trace scheduling FORTRAN compiler for a VLIW machine, the Multiflow TRACE/300. Table 5-1 gives the percentage of compensation copies that are optimized away for those of the Lawrence Livermore Kernels that contain conditional branches [7, 4].

For two of the programs, Kernel 2 and Kernel 24, no compensation code is required, and therefore this optimization cannot apply. The other kernels are good representatives of the two

Program	Compensation copies removed
Kernel 2	n/a
Kernel 15	10 %
Kernel 16	36 %
Kernel 17	0%
Kernel 20	95 %
Kernel 24	n/a

Table 5-1: Effect of compensation code optimization for Livermore Loops

groups of programs that we have seen so far. The first group includes programs for which our implementation removes around 30 % of the compensation copies, and Kernels 15, 16, and 17 fall into this group. Kernel 15 contains many control transfer instructions resulting in a large number of rejoins, and most of the moved operations (82 %) do not dominate the respective rejoin instruction. Kernel 17 poses the same problem (and there are only a few compensation copies anyhow). The results for Kernel 16 are better, but 59 % of the moved operations do not dominate. The second group includes programs for which the algorithm is highly effective and removes in excess of 90 % of the compensation copies. Kernel 24 is an example of such a program.

The results that we report on for the Livermore Loops match what we observe for other applications programs[2]. If no compensation code is required, then this optimization does not apply. But since there are no compensation copies in such a program, the size of the program has not been changed by the the trace scheduler. Programs with compensation code fall into two classes: programs in which the moved operations do *not* dominate the rejoins, and programs in which the rejoins are dominated by the moved operations. For the first group, even a more expensive algorithm that is based on Theorem 4 does not help. For the second class of programs the optimization is highly effective, removing most of the compensation copies.

The described optimization was incorporated into the released compiler. Although we can only report on the effect of this optimization for a small number of programs, the compiler that includes this optimization has been used extensively to compile large programs. We are therefore fairly confident that our implementation is complete and that we did not overlook any special cases. Performing this optimization had no noticeable effect on the compilation speed.

6. Conclusions

Trace scheduling aims to devise a good schedule for operations from multiple basic blocks, possibly at the cost of making the rest of the code less efficient. Compensation copies are one of the noticeable side effects of this effort to schedule the trace as well as possible; they add operations to the off-trace code and thereby increase the cache miss frequency as well as the compilation time. However, a number of compensation copies can be optimized away, and a

---

[2]Multiflow Inc. closed its doors at the end of March 1990, so it is very unlikely that we will be able to report the data for other programs that we used to evaluate the effectiveness of this optimization.

simple test based on dominator information produces good results in practice.

Using dominator information to optimize compensation code is just one example how a code generator with more global view can produce a superior schedule. Trace scheduling, by expanding the code generator's viewpoint beyond a single basic block, provides a good framework for such global code generation techniques.

Acknowledgements

The authors appreciate the comments and contributions of other members of the Multiflow compiler group: Cindy Collins, Stefan Freudenberger, Woody Lichtenstein, Geoffrey Lowney, and John Ruttenberg.

References

1. Aho, A. V., Sethi, R., and Ullman J. D.. *Compilers*. Addison-Wesley, 1986.

2. Colwell, R. P., Nix, R. P., O'Donnell, J. J., Papworth, D. B., and Rodman, P. K. . "A VLIW Architecture for a Trace Scheduling Compiler". *IEEE Trans. on Computers 37*, 8 (August 1988), 967-979.

3. Ellis, J. R. Bulldog: A Compiler for VLIW Architectures. Tech. Rept. DCS/RR-364, Yale Univ., Feb., 1985.

4. Feo, J. T. "An Analysis of the Computational and Parallel Complexity of the Livermore Loops". *Parallel Computing 7*, 2 (June 1988), 163-186.

5. Fisher,J.A., Ellis, J.R., Ruttenberg, J.C., and Nicolau, A. Parallel Processing: A Smart Compiler & a Dumb Machine. Proc. ACM SIGPLAN '84 Symposium on Compiler Construction, Montreal, June, 1984, pp. 37-47.

6. Fisher, J.A. "Trace Scheduling: A Technique for Global Microcode Compaction". *IEEE Trans. on Computers C-30*, 7 (July 1981), 478-490.

7. McMahon, F. H. The Livermore Fortran Kernels: A Computer Test of the Numerical Performance Range. Tech. Rept. UCRL-53745, University of California, Lawrence Livermore National Laboratory, December, 1986.

8. Nicolau, A. Percolation Scheduling: A Parallel Compilation Technique. Tech. Rept. 85-678, Cornell, May, 1985.

Authors' addresses

Thomas Gross, School of Computer Science, Carnegie Mellon University, Pittsburgh, PA 15213. Michael Ward, IBM Corporation T.J. Watson Research Center P.O. Box 704 Yorktown Heights, NY 10598

14 A Realistic Resource-Constrained Software Pipelining Algorithm

A. Aiken, A. Nicolau

Abstract

This paper presents a new approach to resource-constrained compiler extraction of fine-grain parallelism in loops. We present an algorithm which integrates resource limitations into software pipelining. Our approach does not sacrifice generality in the software pipelining algorithm in order to handle resource constraints; furthermore, the scheduling choices are made with truly global information. This is in contrast with previous approaches which either applied only to conditional-free code, or limited the parallelization process by imposing local heuristic resource constraints early in the scheduling process.

1 Introduction

Software pipelining is a compiler loop parallelization technique. Software pipelining algorithms compute a static parallel schedule overlapping the instructions of a loop body in much the same way that a hardware pipeline overlaps instructions in a dynamic instruction stream. The schedule computed by a software pipelining algorithm is suitable for execution on a synchronous, tightly-coupled parallel machine, such as a super-scalar or VLIW (Very Long Instruction Word) machine.

Software pipelining algorithms are interesting for three reasons. The first reason is that super-scalar and VLIW machines are being built. IBM's System 6000 can execute four instructions in parallel; Intel's i860 chip can execute two instructions in parallel. The largest tightly-coupled synchronous machine built to date is Multiflow's TRACE-14, which has 14 functional units. The second reason is that these tightly-coupled machines must be programmed at a very low level. Someone writing a program for a tightly-coupled machine must develop a parallel schedule, which means that person must know about and account for details of the hardware design such as instruction timings and resource conflicts between functional units. This is extremely time-consuming and error-prone; compilation techniques are needed to translate programs written at a reasonably high level into good parallel schedules.

The final reason is that software pipelining techniques hold the promise of producing better code with faster compilation time than other scheduling techniques. Briefly, other scheduling techniques, notably Trace Scheduling, schedule instructions only within a loop body. Because parallelism is often present across loop iterations and not within a loop body, the loop is usually unrolled before scheduling. While this allows parallelism to be exploited between some iterations of the original loop, there is still sequentiality imposed between iterations of the unrolled loop body. Software pipelining provides a direct way of exploiting parallelism across all iterations of a loop without the expense of explicit unrolling.

This paper describes an algorithm for *resource-constrained* software pipelining. To our knowledge, no general resource-constrained software pipelining algorithms have been proposed. Some software pipelining algorithms have dealt with only weak forms of resource constraints [5] (i.e., the number of instructions that can be executed in parallel); others have assumed that machine-dependent constraints could be handled entirely in a fix-up phase after software pipelining [3,2]. One software pipelining algorithm has been designed with resource constraints in mind, but it is tuned to a particular machine and it is not clear how to generalize it to other architectures [9,12].

The algorithm we present smoothly integrates software pipelining with the treatment of resource constraints. Intuitively, a machine-dependent *scheduler* is used to incrementally build a parallelized loop from a sequential loop. At each step, the scheduler makes strictly local decisions about which instructions to schedule based on global data dependence information. As the parallelized loop is constructed, our software pipelining algorithm checks for repeating states that can be "pipelined". The software pipelining algorithm itself is very simple; the difficulty lies in establishing restrictions on the scheduler and data dependence information that guarantee the correctness and termination of the software pipelining algorithm.

The rest of this paper is divided into six sections. Section 2 defines the model of parallel computation used to develop the algorithm. Section 3 works through a small example to give an intuitive idea of how the software pipelining algorithm works. Section 4 describes the algorithm and sketches a proof of correctness. Section 5 outlines an incremental analysis technique, developed by Ebcioğlu and Nicolau [6], that lies at the heart of our algorithm. Section 6 presents a result which suggests that our algorithm achieves the best feasible results in the presence of resource constraints. The final section discusses some extensions and future work.

2 Basic Terminology

This section develops a simple model of a tightly-coupled, synchronous parallel machine. The formalism is used to explain the algorithm and to provide a basis for a proof of correctness.

A *program* is an automaton $\langle X, \delta, n_0, S \rangle$. X is a set of n instructions $\{x_0, \ldots, x_{n-1}\}$. Instructions are divided into *assignments* which read and write a global store, *tests* (boolean-valued functions) which affect the flow of control, and a distinguished instruction *stop*.

The body of the program is a set of *states* S which are subsets of X. The state n_0 is the *start state* of the program. The states represent parallel instructions; intuitively, when control reaches a state n, all instructions in n are executed simultaneously. For simplicity, we assume that all instructions execute in unit time. Extensions to multi-cycle instructions and pipelined functional units are straightforward [1].

A *configuration* is a pair $\langle n, s \rangle$ where n is a state and s is a store (the contents of memory locations and registers). The *transition function* δ maps configurations into configurations. An *execution* is a sequence of configurations $\langle \ldots, \langle n_i, s_i \rangle, \ldots \rangle$ such that $\delta(\langle n_i, s_i \rangle) = \langle n_{i+1}, s_{i+1} \rangle$.

The *successors* $succ(n)$ of a state n are the states in the set $\{n' | \exists s \text{ s.t. } \delta(\langle n, s \rangle) = \langle n', s' \rangle\}$. When n is executed, control is transferred to some $n' \in succ(n)$. A state that contains the instruction *stop* cannot contain other instructions and cannot have any successors.

The transition function describes how a tightly-coupled, synchronous machine actually executes a parallel instruction. We deliberately avoid defining a transition function in any detail. The transition functions of super-scalar and VLIW machines are complex and vary considerably from machine to machine. The greatest source of complexity is defining what it means to execute more than one test in parallel (multi-way jumps). As an example, in one possible model tests within a state n are always organized into a binary decision tree with a unique root. One branch of each test in the decision tree is labeled *true*, the other is labeled *false*. Each leaf of the decision tree is a pointer to an element of $succ(n)$. When the state is executed, all of the tests are evaluated in parallel in the store. The next state to be executed is the leaf that terminates the (unique) path from the root where every branch is labeled by the value of that test in the store. This is only one possible implementation of multi-way jumps; many other mechanisms have been implemented and proposed [7,10,4,5].

We next define a meaning function μ for programs.

Definition 2.1 Let P be a program $\langle X, \delta, n_0, S \rangle$. If there is an execution

$$\langle \langle n_0, s \rangle, \ldots, \langle \{stop\}, s' \rangle \rangle$$

then $\mu(P, s) = s'$. If no such execution exists, then $\mu(P, s)$ is undefined.

Software pipelining is a loop parallelization technique, so we must describe the loops we are interested in parallelizing. A *sequential loop* is a program with i instructions $x_0, \ldots, x_{i-1}$ and i states $n_i = \{x_i\}$. There is a single backedge from n_{i-1} to n_0; that is, $succ(n_{i-1}) = \{n_0\}$. Every other state has only forward branches; that is, for all n_j such that $0 \leq j < i-1$, if $n_k \in succ(n_j)$ then $k > j$.

3 An Example

Given a sequential loop L, the software pipelining algorithm incrementally builds a parallelized program from L. An important data structure used by the algorithm is an incrementally maintained set A of *available instructions*. At each point in time during execution of the algorithm, A contains a set of instructions available for scheduling in the current state. How this set is maintained is discussed in Section 5.

Initially, the new program graph is empty and A contains all instructions available for scheduling in the first state. Consider the program in Figure 1. We display programs as control-flow graphs with the convention that true branches of tests are to the left and false branches are to the right. Not all instructions can be scheduled in the first state; for example, c must be scheduled after b, since c references a value that b writes. In standard compiler terminology, there is a *data dependence* from b to c [11].

For this example, we assume a machine model in which all reads take place before any writes during a parallel instruction, and write conflicts are not permitted. In this model, the instructions a, b, and f are all available for scheduling in the first state. Because the algorithm may overlap instructions from different iterations, we superscript instructions with the scheduled iteration from which they came. In addition, we subscript the available instruction set to keep track of its different values over time. Thus, initially $A_0 = \{a^0, b^0, f^0\}$.

Another component of the pipelining algorithm is the *scheduler*. The scheduler selects from A a set of instructions to schedule in the current state. Together, the procedure to maintain the set of available instructions and the scheduler encapsulate all machine-dependent information.

A pipelined version of the loop in Figure 1 is given in Figure 2. The rest of this section describes how the software pipelining algorithm computes this parallel schedule from the sequential loop. For the first state n_0, assuming that the machine has sufficient resources, the scheduler could choose to schedule all available instructions. A_0 is then updated to contain a new set of available instructions, given that a^0, b^0 and f^0 have been scheduled. Because f is a test, there will be two successors of the first state—one for the case where f evaluates to true, and one for the case where f evaluates to false. The sets of available instructions are different for the two continuations.

Consider the successor n_1 of n_0 for the case where f^0 evaluates to false. This is an easy case, as the program terminates on this branch. The new set A_1 of available instructions is $\{c^0, d^0, e^0\}$. Because write conflicts are not permitted, d^0 and e^0 cannot be scheduled in the same state, but both are "available"— at this point, all dependences on the two statements have been satisfied. Assume that the scheduler selects instructions c^0 and d^0 for state n_1. Instruction c^0 is a test, so there are two successors of this state. For the successor n_2 where c^0 evaluates to false, the set A_2 is $\{e^0\}$. Assume that the scheduler place e^0 in n_2. For the single successor n_3 of n_2 the set of available instructions A_2 is just $\{g^0\}$, the stop instruction. Thus n_3 contains only g^0. Backing up to n_1, the set of available instructions for the branch where c^0 evaluates to true is also $\{g^0\}$, so the successor of n_1 on this path is also n_3.

This completes the terminating path from n_0. On the other path, where f^0 evaluates to true, the new set of available instructions A_4 is $\{c^0, d^0, e^0, a^1\}$. As before, d^0 and e^0 cannot be scheduled in the same state, but both are available for scheduling. Note that the instruction a^1 from the next iteration is available for scheduling in parallel with statements from the first iteration.

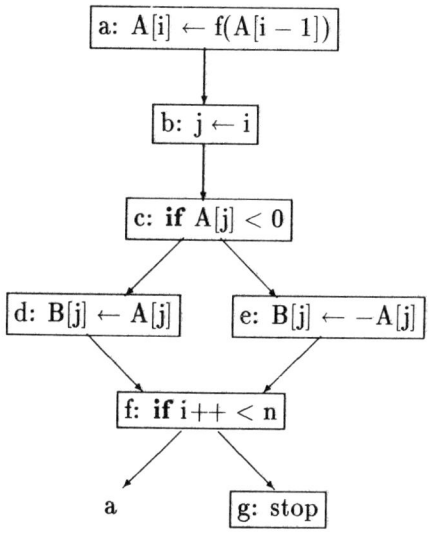

Figure 1: An example loop.

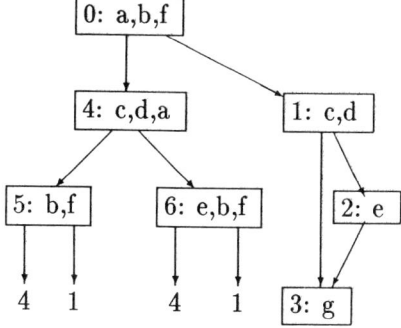

Figure 2: The loop after software pipelining.

Assume that the scheduler selects instructions c^0, d^0, and a^1 for state n_4. Instruction c^0 is a test, so there are two successors of this state. For the successor n_5 where c^0 evaluates to true, the set A_5 is $\{b^1, f^1\}$. Assuming that the scheduler places both instructions in n_2, the set of available instructions for the successor of n_5 on the path where f^1 is true is $\{c^1, d^1, e^1, a^2\}$. Note that, except for the superscripts, this set is exactly the same as A_4. The superscripts are just a way of keeping track of the iteration of each instruction; the sets have the same instructions. Rather than continue scheduling at this point, the pipelining algorithm simply makes n_4 a successor of n_5. Similarly, the set of available instructions for the successor of n_5 where f^1 evaluates to false is $\{c^1, d^1, e^1\}$. Except for superscripts, this is exactly the same as A_1. As before, the pipelining algorithm makes n_1 a successor of n_5.

Backing up, the pipelining algorithm next considers the successor n_6 of n_4 where c^0 evaluates to false. The set of available instructions A_6 is $\{e^0, b^1, f^1\}$. Assuming that the scheduler places all three instructions in n_6, the sets of available instructions for the two successors of n_6 are the same as for n_5 and scheduling proceeds just as it did for n_5. The algorithm terminates with the schedule in Figure 2.

There are two technically difficult aspects of the software pipelining algorithm. The first is computing the sets of available instructions. An algorithm for maintaining these sets incrementally was first presented in [6]; a brief overview of the method and some simple extensions needed for this algorithm are included in Section 5. The second problem, and the main technical contribution of this paper, is justifying the step where previously scheduled states are "reused", such as when the pipelining algorithm decided to make n_4 the successor of n_5. We have simply implied that this step is correct, and in the example it happens to be correct, but in general this is *not* a safe transformation. Intuitively, the problem is that just because two sets of available instructions happen to be the same for two different states, that does not by itself guarantee that all subsequent sets of available instructions would be the same in all continuations from those states.

We illustrate the difficulties that can arise with the loop in Figure 3a. To make the example as simple as possible, there are no conditional statements or exits from the loop. Assuming that the variable i is always zero upon entering the loop, note that statements b and c are independent for the first 50 iterations and data dependent for the next 50 iterations. If dependence analysis recognizes that the b and c are independent for the first 50 iterations, then as the parallelized loop is built the scheduler could place b and c together in the first 50 iterations. Following the pipelining strategy for the previous example, repeating states would be detected in the second iteration, leading to the

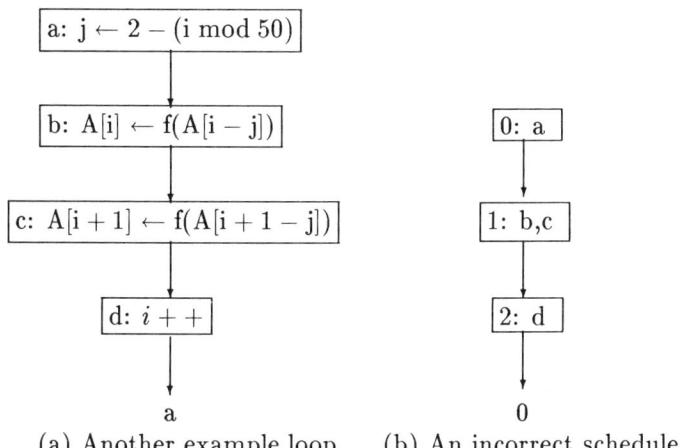

(a) Another example loop. (b) An incorrect schedule.

Figure 3: Another example loop.

parallelized program in Figure 3b, which is clearly incorrect. In this example, irregular dependencies make it difficult to detect repeating behavior. Section 4 formalizes the software pipelining algorithm and provides constraints on the scheduler and instruction availability information that guarantee the correctness and termination of the software pipelining algorithm.

4 The Algorithm

We first present constraints on the components used by algorithm. These constraints are needed to present the algorithm and prove its correctness. The following definition is used in the discussion of the constraints.

Definition 4.1 Let $X = \{\ldots, x_i^{j_i}, \ldots\}$ be a set of instructions. The set X^c is the set $\{\ldots, x_i^{j_i+c}, \ldots\}$.

As discussed in Section 3, one component of the software pipelining algorithm is a *scheduler* for a specific machine. We place the following constraint on schedulers.

Constraint 4.2 The scheduler S must be a function from sets of instructions to sets of instructions. Furthermore, we require that

$$S(A) = B \Rightarrow \forall i \; S(A^i) = B^i$$

The need for this constraint is discussed below, after presentation of the software pipelining algorithm. At this point, however, it is natural to ask whether this constraint is reasonable, since it forces the scheduler to rely only on very local information; conceivably, a scheduler with a more global view of the optimization process could make better decisions. The potential advantage of a global scheduler is, unfortunately, illusory, because scheduling problems with finite resources are intractable. Very simple forms of the instruction scheduling problem are NP-hard [8]. Thus, heuristics are required at some level in any practical algorithm. This constraint still permits a wide range of heuristics tuned to a particular machine. In addition, this particular constraint has a significant design benefit: it cleanly separates the scheduler from the rest of the algorithm, thus isolating the most machine-dependent portion of the code. Any scheduler satisfying this constraint will work with the software pipelining algorithm.

A second constraint is placed on the instruction availability information. Recall that at any moment there is a set of instructions A which are available for scheduling. Also, there is an update function $Next(A, S, C) = A'$ that takes a set of available instructions A, a set of scheduled instructions S where $S \subseteq A$, and a continuation from the scheduled instructions C, and returns a new set of available instructions A'.

Constraint 4.3 For all sets A, S, A' and all continuations C from S,

$$Next(A, S, C) = A' \Rightarrow \forall i \; Next(A^i, B^i, C) = A'^i$$

Once again, we must defer justification of the need for Constraint 4.3 until after presentation of the software pipelining algorithm. Intuitively, Constraint 4.3 says that the instructions available may depend on which instructions have already been scheduled and the relative distance (in iterations) between instructions already scheduled, but it cannot depend on the actual values of the iterations of instructions already scheduled. Whether Constraint 4.3 is satisfied or not depends on the form of the data dependence analysis used to maintain instruction availability information. Standard data dependence graphs satisfy Constraint 4.3, as do extensions to dependence graphs, such as labeling edges with distance vectors. In fact, as far as we know, every proposed representation of dependence information satisfies this constraint.

```
function pipeline(A)
    if ∃c s.t. DoneBefore[A^c] ≠ ∅ then
        return (DoneBefore[A^c])
    else
        let State ← schedule(A) in
            begin
                DoneBefore[A] ← {State}
                for each continuation c from State do
                    succ(Node) ← succ(Node) ∪ pipeline(Next(A, State, c))
                return ({State})
            end

∀x DoneBefore[x] ← ∅
pipeline(InitialAvail)
```

Figure 4: The software pipelining algorithm.

The software pipelining algorithm is given in Figure 4. Given some initial set of available instructions, the function *pipeline* invokes the scheduler, and then applies *pipeline* recursively to the sets of available instructions in all possible continuations from the scheduled state. If at any point the algorithm encounters the same set of available instructions (modulo iteration numbers) a second time, it returns the previously scheduled state.

The two constraints given above are needed to show the correctness of the pipelining algorithm. We present an informal proof of correctness; a more rigorous version can be developed using the techniques in [1].

Figure 5 gives the key construction for the proof of correctness. The algorithm in Figure 5 is identical to the one in Figure 4 in all but two respects:

- The algorithm in Figure 5 constructs a schedule to some fixed depth k on all paths.

- The algorithm in Figure 5 does not reuse previously scheduled states.

The first step in the proof is to relate the schedules produced by the algorithm in Figure 5 to the original loop.

```
function pipeline2(A, k)
    if k = 0 then
        return (∅)
    else
        let State ← schedule(A) in
            begin
                for each continuation c from State do
                    succ(Node) ← succ(Node) ∪ pipeline2(Next(A, State, c), k −
                return ({State})
            end

pipeline(InitialAvail)
```

Figure 5: An approximate software pipelining algorithm.

Lemma 4.4 Let $L_k = pipeline2(InitialAvail, k)$. For every store s, there exists a k such that $\mu(L, s) = \mu(L_k, s)$ or $\mu(L, s)$ is undefined.

Proof: Immediate by the correctness of the scheduler and the incremental availability information, and by the fact that some L_k contains every terminating computation of L. □

The second step in the proof is to relate the partial schedules L_k to the fully pipelined loop.

Lemma 4.5 Let $L' = pipeline(InitialAvail)$. Every execution of L_k of length k or less is also an execution of L'.

Proof: [sketch] The proof is by induction on k, using Constraints 4.2 and 4.3 to show that states reused by the pipelining algorithm are the same as corresponding states in L_k. □

Constraints 4.2 and 4.3 are needed to prove Lemma 4.5. These constraints ensure that having the same instructions available for two states implies that all possible continuations from those states would also be the same. Combining Lemmas 4.4 and 4.5 gives a proof of correctness.

Theorem 4.6 If the pipelining algorithm produces a loop L' from an initial loop L, then for all s, $\mu(L',s) = \mu(L,s)$ or $\mu(L,s)$ is undefined.

Proof: If $\mu(L,s)$ is defined, then by Lemma 4.4 there is a k such that $\mu(L,s) = \mu(L_k,s)$. By Lemma 4.5 it follows that $\mu(L,s) = \mu(L',s)$. □

Theorem 4.6 states that the software pipelining algorithm can only produce correct results; however, it does not show that the software pipelining algorithm always terminates. To show termination, we must show that the recursive function *pipeline* terminates. The function terminates when it finds a set of instructions A such that A^c has been scheduled previously. Let $\equiv$ be the equivalence relation $A \equiv B \Leftrightarrow \exists c$ s.t. $A = B^c$. To prove termination it is sufficient to show that there are only finitely many equivalence classes under $\equiv$.

Unfortunately, there may be infinitely many equivalence classes and in fact the function *pipeline* is not necessarily terminating under the constraints given so far. Consider, for example, what happens if the A sets simply increase in size on each recursive call. A necessary condition for $A \equiv B$ is that $|A| = |B|$; if there are sets of unbounded cardinality, then there are infinitely many equivalence classes. An additional constraint is placed on the availability information to limit the size of the set of instructions available for scheduling.

Constraint 4.7 There is a constant k such that for all possible availability sets A, if $x_i^c \in A$ then no $x_j^{c+k} \in A$.

This constraint states that instructions can be available from at most k consecutive iterations at one time. This provides the scheduler with a "sliding window" of instructions, and until instructions in the earliest iteration are scheduled, a new iteration cannot be added to the end.

Lemma 4.8 Constraint 4.7 ensures that there are only finitely many equivalence classes of sets of instructions under $\equiv$.

Proof: If there are n instructions in a loop body and k consecutive iterations can appear in *Avail*, then every available instruction set is a subset of $\{\ldots, x_i^{c+j_i}, \ldots\}$ for some c, $0 \leq i < n$, and $0 \leq j_i < k$. □

The value k of Constraint 4.7 is a parameter of the software pipelining algorithm. It need not be the same for every loop scheduled (i.e., it can be computed dynamically), but it must have a maximum value for any particular loop.

While Constraint 4.7 is motivated by the need to guarantee termination, it also leads to a good implementation of the function *pipeline*. The most expensive part of executing *pipeline* is checking whether the current set of available instructions A has ever been scheduled before for some A^c. Instruction availability information for iterations c through $c + k - 1$ can be represented as a bit vector of length kn, where n is the number of instructions in the sequential loop. The bit $jn + i$ is 1 if instruction x_i^{c+j} is available for scheduling; otherwise it is 0. When iteration c has been completely scheduled (this occurs when the first n bits are all 0) the bit vector is shifted left n bits, discarding information for iteration c, and the last n bits are set to reflect the availability of instructions in iteration $c + k$. With this representation, checking whether the same availability information has been seen before only requires checking whether the same bit vector has been seen before, which can be implemented very efficiently through hashing.

5 Available Instructions

Sets of available instructions were, for historical reasons, originally termed "unifiable ops" in [6]. This component plays a role in our algorithm similar to the role global dataflow analysis plays in traditional optimizing compilers. At each step of the parallelization process, the set of available instructions contains all instructions which could potentially be scheduled in the current state.

While intuitively simple, the details of computing accurate available operations sets and the efficient maintenance of these sets during scheduling can be quite complex. A thorough description of efficient, incremental algorithms for computing and maintaining these sets is given in [6]. For the purposes of this paper, we only need to understand the concept of available operations and their computation.

Briefly, the algorithm in [6] works with acyclic (loopless) programs. The first step is a backward pass over the entire program, propagating information about how early instructions can be scheduled. Once this is completed, the information associated with the start state is exactly the set of instructions available for scheduling in the first state of a parallelized program. As scheduling proceeds, the instruction availability information is updated by removing scheduled instructions and repeating as much of the backward analysis as necessary. An important fact is that the portion of the analysis that has to be recomputed is small [6].

Because of the restriction to loopless programs, a simple extension of the technique in [6] is needed for our purposes. The key observation is that Constraint 4.7 forces the available instruction information to span no more than k iterations at one time. Thus, we can make use of the incremental available instructions algorithm by using k "straight line" iterations of the program. When the first iteration is completely consumed by the scheduler, the next iteration is added to the available instruction sets using the incremental techniques in [6].

6 On Optimal Software Pipelining

In this section we briefly review research on the limitations of software pipelining, especially a recent result showing that optimal software pipelining is unachievable [13]. Given this result, we show that our algorithm is "as good as possible" in the sense that it can produce schedules arbitrarily close to optimal.

Research in software pipelining has naturally focused on discovering algorithms for computing pipelined schedules, both in general and for specific machines. Concurrently, researchers have investigated the theoretical limitations of software pipelining. One of the central theoretical questions is whether or not there is a software pipelining algorithm that produces optimal pipelined schedules for an arbitrary loop. Because scheduling algorithms are based on preserving data dependences, the natural meaning of "optimality" is with respect to the length of dependence chains.

Definition 6.1 A program L is *time optimal* if for every execution $\langle\langle x_0, s_0\rangle, \ldots, \langle\langle \{stop\}, s_n\rangle$ of L, n is the length of the longest dependence chain in the execution.

The obvious form of the optimality question is stated as follows: is there an algorithm which takes as input a machine description (i.e., resource constraints, instruction timings, etc.) and a loop, and produces a time optimal schedule for that machine? This problem statement is not very useful, however, because scheduling problems with finite resources are computationally intractable even without software pipelining. To gain some insight into software pipelining itself, researchers have usually abstracted the problem as: given unbounded resources and a loop L, is there an algorithm which computes a time optimal schedule for L?

The answer to this question is trivially "no" for some programs, such as the one in Figure 1. Recall that instructions d and e cannot be scheduled in the same instruction because they write the same store location. One branch of the test must always be optimized at the expense of the other branch, and thus there does not exist a parallel version L that is time optimal. The conflict between d and e in Figure 1 is usually classified as another type of dependence—an *output* dependence [11]. To avoid this problem, we can rephrase the question again: given unbounded resources and a loop L without output dependences, is there an algorithm which computes a time optimal schedule for L?

This question was recently resolved negatively [13]. Again the problem is that for some loops an optimal parallel version does not exist. We briefly sketch an alternative proof to the one in [13] that sheds some light on the behavior of our resource-constrained algorithm.

Definition 6.2 A scheduling algorithm is *bounded* if for any loop L there is a constant c such that for every scheduled state n, if x^i is in n then no y^{i+c} is in n.[1]

An unbounded scheduling algorithm cannot be pipelined; it produces an infinite number of different states [1]. In [13], a loop is presented for which a time optimal schedule can be produced only by an unbounded scheduler. Therefore, there are loops for which no software pipelining algorithm produces a time optimal schedule.

Boundedness is very closely related to Constraint 4.7; in fact, Constraint 4.7 guarantees that our algorithm is bounded and therefore succeeds in pipelining any loop. By adjusting the parameter k of Constraint 4.7 our algorithm can be arbitrarily close to optimal.

Theorem 6.3 (Asymptotic Optimality) Let L be a loop without output dependences, and let $t(L, s)$ be the length of the execution of L in store s. We apply the pipelining algorithm to L for a target machine with unbounded resources and using the *greedy scheduler*, which schedules every instruction as soon as it is available. Define L_k to be the result of applying *pipeline* where k iterations are available for scheduling at each step. Then

$$\lim_{k \to \infty} t(L_k, s) = t(L, s)$$

Theorem 6.3 is a very theoretical result, since it completely ignores resource constraints and realistic schedulers. However, it does show that within the framework of our algorithm it is possible to get as close to optimal as practical, subject to the ability of the scheduler to make good scheduling decisions for finite resources.

---

[1]This definition of boundedness is slightly weaker than the definition used in [1].

7 Extensions and Future Work

We have presented our resource-constrained software pipelining algorithm using a very simple model. In practice, a few extensions are necessary. For example, for a machine with multi-cycle instructions, the set of resources available for scheduling may vary from state to state depending on the instructions scheduled in earlier states. For such a machine, it is desirable to base scheduling decisions not only on the set of instructions available (Constraint 4.2), but also on the resources available in a given step. In fact, Constraint 4.2 can be relaxed. The only important aspects of the scheduler are that it is deterministic (a function) and that the domain of possible inputs is finite. Thus, any finite amount of information can be used by the scheduler and the results of Section 4 will hold. Of course, the test for termination in function *pipeline* must be extended to check not just whether the same set of available instructions has been seen before, but whether the same "scheduler input" (i.e., everything on which the scheduler depends) has been seen before.

Another desirable extension is to integrate other compiler optimizations into the software pipelining algorithm. For example, variable renaming frequently eliminates dependences between statements, allowing shorter schedules. It is trivial to add these optimizations either before or after the pipelining algorithm; it is more interesting to consider performing optimizations "on the fly" as an integral component of scheduling. A solution to this problem, combined with our resource constrained algorithm, would yield a completely general, practical software pipelining algorithm.

References

1. A. Aiken. *Compaction-Based Parallelization*. PhD thesis, Cornell, 1988. Department of Computer Science Technical Report No. 88-922.

2. A. Aiken and A. Nicolau. Optimal loop parallelization. In *Proceedings of the 1988 ACM SIGPLAN Conference on Programming Language Design and Implementation*, June 1988.

3. A. Aiken and A. Nicolau. Perfect Pipelining: a new loop parallelization technique. In *Proceedings of the 1988 European Symposium on Programming*, pages 221–235, Springer Verlag Lecture Notes in Computer Science no. 300, March 1988. Also available as Cornell Technical Report TR 87-873.

4. M. Annaratone, E. Arnould, T. Gross, H. T. Kung, M. Lam, O. Menzilcioglu, K. Sarocky, and J. A. Webb. Warp architecture and implementation. In *Proceedings of*

the 13th Annual Symposium on Computer Architecture, pages 346–356, June 1986.

5. K. Ebcioğlu. A compilation technique for software pipelining of loops with conditional jumps. In *Proceedings of the 20th Annual Workshop on Microprogramming*, pages 69–79, December 1987.

6. K. Ebcioğlu and A. Nicolau. A global resource-constrained parallelization technique. In *Proceedings of the ACM SIGARCH International Conference on Supercomputing*, June 1989.

7. J. Fisher. 2^n-way jump microinstruction hardware and an effective instruction binding method. In *Proceedings of the 13th Annual Workshop on Microprogramming*, pages 64–75, December 1980.

8. M. R. Garey and D. S. Johnson. *Computers and Intractability: A Guide to the Theory of NP-Completeness*. W. H. Freeman and Company, 1979.

9. T. Gross and M. Lam. Compilation for a high-performance systolic array. In *Proceedings of the 1986 SIGPLAN Symposium on Compiler Construction*, July 1986.

10. K. Karplus and A. Nicolau. Efficient hardware for multi-way jumps and pre-fetches. In *Proceedings of the 18th Annual Workshop on Microprogramming*, pages 11–18, December 1985.

11. D. J. Kuck, R. Kuhn, D. Padua, B. Leasure, and M. Wolfe. Dependence graphs and compiler optimizations. In *Proceedings of the 1981 SIGACT-SIGPLAN Symposium on Principles of Programming Languages*, pages 207–218, January 1981.

12. M. Lam. *A Systolic Array Optimizing Compiler*. PhD thesis, Carnegie Mellon University, 1987.

13. U. Schwiegelshohn, F. Gasperoni, and K. Ebcioğlu. *On Optimal Loop Parallelization*. Technical Report RC-14595, IBM T. J. Watson Research Center, 1989.

Authors' Addresses: Alexander Aiken
IBM Almaden Research Center
650 Harry Rd.
San Jose, CA 95120
email: aiken@ibm.com

Alexandru Nicolau
Dept. of Information and Computer Science
UC Irvine
Irvine, CA 92717
email: nicolau@ics.uci.edu

15 Handling Unresolvable Array-Access Aliases in Refined C

A. Kallis, D. Klappholz

Abstract
Refined C is a language in which it is possible to express parallelism, but impossible to inadvertently create races or deadlocks. In the version of Refined C discussed here, not only are races and deadlocks impossible, but code is guaranteed to be strictly deterministic, i.e., all executions of a program with the same input data are guaranteed to either terminate normally, producing exactly the same results, or to terminate abnormally with exactly the same error messages. Later papers will discuss the more general dialect of Refined C in which deterministic behavior is not necessarily enforced -- or desired -- but freedom from races and deadlocks is still guaranteed. The fundamental ideas behind the Refined Language approach were originally proposed in 1984 ([28]: basics), 1985([27]: Refined C), and 1986 ([26]: Refined Fortran), and are developed further in [23]-[25]. The present paper supersedes all earlier work on those aspects of the subject which it addresses.

1. Introduction

The Refined Language approach eliminates the problem of potential races and deadlocks in parallel code by extending conventional imperative languages with data-oriented constructs which enable the programmer to specify not only *what* code segments may be executed in parallel with one another, but *why* their parallel execution would be race-free and deadlock-free. Refined Language compilers utilize analysis techniques originally developed for use in *automatic parallelism detection* [1]-[22] to verify the safety of parallel execution. (In the context of Refined Languages, these techniques are more appropriately thought of as *parallelism-recognition* techniques.)

The Refined Language compiler generates parallel code only if the programmer's explanation of *what* and *why*, possibly in concert with run-time checks, is sufficient to guarantee freedom from races and deadlocks. Statically-detectable errors in the programmer's explanation result in loss of parallelism rather than irrepeatable behavior. Errors in the programmer's explanation which cannot be detected until run-time result in repeatable fatal error messsages rather than races or deadlocks.

We have added the Refined Language constructs to conventional imperative programming languages such as Fortran and C, rather than creating entirely new languages, because of the large number of users of languages such as Fortran and C, and because of the large investment in code already written in such languages.

The Refined Language approach embodies two independent theses. The first thesis is that it is possible to extend sequential imperative programming languages with data-oriented constructs in such way as to endow them with the expressive power of control-parallelism-extended languages. That is, we are attempting to endow Refined C, for example, with the power to express any strictly deterministic parallel computation expressible in C extended with **spawn**, **wait**, and **signal** constructs, or any other set of equivalent control-oriented parallel constructs. We make no claim that the version of Refined C presented here has the full desired expressive power. Examples presented here and in [23]-[24], however, suggest that it may not be far from this goal.

The second thesis of the Refined Language approach, independent of the first, is that a compiler can do an acceptable job of *packaging* parallel code, i.e., of deciding when specified parallelism can be cost-effectively exploited on the target architecture and when not. With this thesis in mind, we note that in a Refined Language a programmer's indication *that* (and explanation of *why*) code segments *may* be executed in parallel with one another is not an indication that they *must* be executed in that way, at least not in the strictly deterministic version of Refined C discussed here, and not unless the programmer specifies so through the use of *override* directives which will be detailed in a later paper. Rather, the compiler makes the determination of which potentially-parallel-executable code segments will actually be executed in parallel on the basis of its evaluation of cost effectiveness. I.e., it chooses the granularity of parallelism appropriate to the target architecture. The present paper addresses only issues related to the first thesis, that of the expression of potential parallel execution.

In Refined C the programmer specifies potential parallel execution of a fixed number of code segments $\Sigma_1, \Sigma_2, \ldots, \Sigma_n$ by writing them in such way as to make it clear that there are no read/write, write/read, or write/write dependences between any two of $\Sigma_1, \Sigma_2, \ldots, \Sigma_n$, i.e., that there is no memory location which is accessed by more than one of $\Sigma_1, \Sigma_2, \ldots, \Sigma_n$ and written by at least one of $\Sigma_1, \Sigma_2, \ldots, \Sigma_n$. The specification of a *doall* or *forall* loop, i.e., a loop all of whose iterations may be executed in parallel with one another, is a straightforward extension of this method; the specification of a *doacross* loop, i.e., a loop whose iterations' parallel execution requires the introduction of synchronization is also a straightforward extension.

Given the Refined Language method for expressing parallelism, it might well be asked why any language extensions are required. The programmer simply uses different names for different memory locations, and satisfies the conditions for parallel execution when parallel execution is desired. The reason, of course, is the same as the reason that automatic parallelism detection sometimes runs into trouble, i.e., the aliasing caused by array references and pointer references. In [23] we have provided a rudimentary exposition of how Refined C deals with the problems caused by array-reference aliases and pointer-reference aliases. [23] is not, however, very detailed in its exposition of Refined C constructs. Since the publication of [23] the details of array-reference alias handling have been developed somewhat further. The details of pointer-reference alias handling have been radically changed. The latter will be dealt with in specific detail in a later paper. The present paper presents the current status of array-reference alias handling techniques in Refined C. Its details supersede those of all previous expositions of the subject of handling array-reference aliases.

2. Problems Caused by Array References

Consider the Gaussian elimination code of Figure 1. *gauss(a, m, n, k)* reduces the rows of the m × n array *a* using the k-th row as pivot.

Suppose that the programmer wishes to indicate that both *for* loops may be executed as *forall* loops. It would be difficult for a compiler to detect the fact that doing so is safe since its safety depends upon the fact that there is never a k-th iteration of the outer loop.

2.1 An Inefficient Solution

A simple, but inefficient, way to handle this problem would be to rewrite the code as in Figure 2 in which the contents of the pivot row are moved into a one-dimensional array named *pivrow* and the contents of array *a*, except for the pivot row, are moved into a two-dimensional array named *rest*.

```
gauss(a,m,n,k)
float a[][];
int  m,n,k;
    {
      int i,j;

      for (i=0; i < m; i++)
          {
            if ( i != k )
               {
                 for (j=0; j<n; j++)
                    {
                      a[i][j] = a[i][j] - a[i][j] * (a[k][j]/a[k][k]);
                    }
               }
          }
    }
```

ANSI C Code for Gaussian Elimination
Figure 1

The compiler has no problem recognizing the desired parallelism:

- the i-th iteration of the i-loop both reads and writes the i-th row (only) of array *rest*

- the i-th iteration of the i-loop (only) reads *pivrow*

- the j-th iteration of the j-loop both reads and writes the j-th column (only) of array *rest*

- the j-th iteration of the j-loop (only) reads *pivrow*

- *rest* and *pivrow* have been allocated via two distinct calls to *malloc*, so they are non-overlapping

```
gauss(a,m,n,k)
float a[][];
int m,n,k;
    {
      int i,j;
        float *pivrow, **rest;

        pivrow = (float *) malloc(n * sizeof(float));
        rest = (float **) malloc( n * sizeof(float *));

      for (i=0; i < m; i++)
          {
              rest[i] = (float *) malloc(n*sizeof(float));
          for (j=0; j < n; j++)
              {
               if (i == k)
                  {
                      pivrow[j] = a[k][j];
                  }
               else
                  {
                      rest[i][j] = a[i][j];
                  }
              }
          }

      for (i=0; i < m; i++)
          {
          if ( i != k )
              {
              for (j=0; j<n; j++)
                  {
                   rest[i][j] = rest[i][j]
                              -rest[i][j] * (pivrow[j]/pivrow[k]);
                  }
              }
          }
    }
```

Code of Figure 1 Re-written to Enable
Parallel Execution
Figure 2

The problem of expressing the parallelism has been solved by changing name spaces. In the old name space there are unresolvable potential aliases; in the new name space there are none. The name space transformation is effected by physically moving the relevant data from one name space to another.

2.2 The Refined C Approach

A more efficient solution, one which requires no data movement, would be to rewrite the code into Refined C as in Figure 3. In Refined C no data is moved; rather the program's name space is directly transformed, by the programmer, into a new name space in which the desired parallelism is easily recognized.

The generic problem created by array references is that it is often impossible for the compiler to determine that expressions which, in fact, reference *disjoint* parts of an array actually do so rather than referencing overlapping parts. The construct introduced by Refined C to enable the programmer to solve this problem is the *disjoint construct*[1]. The disjoint construct utilizes two types of statement, the *decname* statement and the *disjoint* statement.

In Figure 3 the *disjoint* statement

```
disjoint a
{
    rest[i:(i != k )][];
    pivrow[][];
}
```

effects the name space transformation τ_1

$$\tau_1(a[i][j]) = \begin{cases} rest[i][j] & \text{if } i \neq k \\ pivrow[i][j] & \text{otherwise} \end{cases}$$

The result of executing the *disjoint* statement is to make the new names, *pivrow* and *rest*, aliases for non-overlapping access-restricted parts of array *a*. Since *a* is an array of arrays, i.e., a two-dimensional array, *pivrow* and *rest* are also two dimensional arrays, i.e., references to elements of *pivrow* and *rest* must include two subscripts, e.g., *pivrow[k][j]* and *rest[i][j]* (see Figure 3).

---

[1] In earlier publications, e.g., [23], the *disjoint* statement was referred to as the *partition* statement. The introduction of the new terminology is motivated by our feeling that it is more appropriate

```
gauss(a,m,n,k)
float a[][];
int m,n,k;
    {
    int i,j;
        decname float pivrow[][],rest[][];

    disjoint a
        {
        rest[i:(i != k )][];
        pivrow[][];
        }

    for (i=0; i < m; i++)
        {
        if ( i != k )
            {
            for (j=0; j<n; j++)
                {
                rest[i][j] = rest[i][j]
                            -rest[i][j] * (pivrow[k][j]/pivrow[k][k]);
                }
            }
        }
    }
```

Code for Gaussian Elimination in Refined C

Figure 3

If, for specific values of i and j, $\tau(a[i][j]) \neq rest[i][j]$, then a reference to rest[i][j] is illegal, and causes a fatal error; if, for specific values of i and j, $\tau(a[i][j]) \neq pivrow[i][j]$, then a reference to pivrow[i][j] is illegal, and causes a fatal error.

A (parallelism-recognizing) Refined C compiler has no problem determining that the iterations of both *for* loops of Figure 3 may all be executed in parallel with one another:

•the i-th iteration of the i-loop both reads and writes the i-th row
 (only) of that part of array *a* named *rest*

•the j-th iteration of the j-loop both reads and writes the j-th
 column (only) of that part of array *a* named *rest*

- the i-th iteration of the i-loop (only) reads that part of array *a* named *pivrow*

- the j-th iteration of the j-loop (only) reads that part of array *a* named *pivrow*

- *pivrow* and *rest* are declared disjoint parts of array *a*

There are, therefore, no inter-iteration (loop-carried [2]) dependences.

The *decname* statement is used to declare that the names *pivrow* and *rest* will appear together in a *disjoint* statement, and to declare their type.

In order to ensure freedom from races the compiler appends to every reference of the form *pivrow[a][b]* a test for a = k, and to every reference of the form rest[a][b] a test for a ≠ k. A failed test results in a fatal error.

The Gaussian elimination example leads to a first, tentative, version of the rule for indicating in Refined C that a *for* loop may be executed as a *forall* loop. The *for* loop is written as:

```
for(i = init; i <= limit; i++)
{
        loop_body
}
```

with the following constraints:

- init and limit are arbitrary integer-valued expressions

- *loop_body* contains no definition (write) of the iteration variable *i*

- every pair of potentially data-dependence-creating array references in *loop_body* is a pair of array references of the form:

    - $A[exp_1][exp_2] ... [exp_t]$

and

$$\bullet A[exp'_1][exp'_2] \ldots [exp'_t]$$

and for at least one k, $1 \le k \le t$, $exp_k = i = exp'_k$

- there are no potentially data-dependence-creating scalar references in *loop_body*.

A *forall* loop may also be written using a Refined C *while* loop or *do while* loop with appropriate constraints. Finally, various more restricted forms of parallel loop, e.g., *doacross* loops, may be written in Refined C. The full-length version of the present paper will contain details of all of these.

3. Formal Detail

The programmer may use the *disjoint* statement to transform into verifiably disjoint sub-spaces the name space associated with any C expression whose type is an array type. The syntax of the *disjoint* statement is detailed in Figure 4.

array_exp is the expression whose name space is to be transformed. The *name*'s which appear in the *name_def*'s of the *name_def_list* are the names of the disjoint sub-spaces.

If *array_exp* denotes an m-dimensional array, then the general *disjoint* statement of Figure 5 effects the name space transformation τ

$$\tau(array\_exp[i_1][i_2] \ldots [i_m]) = \begin{cases} name_1[i_1][i_2] \ldots [i_m] & \text{if } pred\_exp\_list_1 \text{ is true} \\ name_2[i_1][i_2] \ldots [i_m] & \text{if } pred\_exp\_list_2 \text{ is true} \\ & \text{and } pred\_exp\_list_1 \text{ is false} \\ name_3[i_1][i_2] \ldots [i_m] & \text{if } pred\_exp\_list_3 \text{ is true} \\ & \text{and } pred\_exp\_list_2 \text{ is false} \\ & \text{and } pred\_exp\_list_1 \text{ is false} \\ \vdots \end{cases}$$

```
disjoint_stmt  :      'disjoint' array_exp '{' name_def_list '}'

name_def_list  :      name_def
                    | name_def name_def_list

name_def  :           name pred_exp_list ';'

name  :               identifier
                    | identifier index_list

index_list  :         index
                    | index index_list

index  :              '<' index_dummy '>'

pred_exp_list  :      pred_exp
                    | pred_exp pred_exp_list

pred_exp  :           '[' pred_dummy ':' '(' predicate ')' ']'

pred_dummy  :         identifier

index_dummy  :        identifier
```

BNF of the *disjoint* Statement

Figure 4

The result of executing the *disjoint* statement is to make the new names, $name_1$, $name_2$, ... , $name_k$ aliases for non-overlapping access-restricted parts of the array denoted by *array_exp*. Before the names $name_1$, $name_2$, ... , $name_k$ are used together in a *disjoint* statement, they must be declared in a *decname* statement in which their type is also declared. That type must be the same as that of *array_exp*. A reference to any of $name_1$, $name_2$, ... , $name_k$ therefore requires exactly as many subscripts as does a reference to *array_exp*.

If, for specific values of a, $i_1, i_2, \ldots, i_m$,

$$\tau(array\_exp[i_1][i_2] \ldots [i_m]) \neq name_a[i_1][i_2] \ldots [i_m]$$

then a reference to $name_a[i_1][i_2] \ldots [i_m]$ is invalid, and causes a fatal error. Checks for validity of references are inserted by the Refined C compiler. The question of limiting the amount of run-time checking required to test for validity of references will be addressed in a later section.

```
disjoint  array_exp
        {
                name₁(pred_exp_list₁)
                name₂(pred_exp_list₂)
                       ·
                       ·
                       ·
                nameₖ(pred_exp_listₖ)
        }
```

General *disjoint* Statement
Figure 5

3.1. Scalar Names

In the general *disjoint* statement each $name_i$, $1 \leq i \leq k$, is either a scalar name or an indexed name. The names *pivrow* and *rest* in the Refined C code of Figure 3 are examples of *scalar names*.

Note that we have termed the names *pivrow* and *rest* "scalar names" even though neither refers to a single memory location. It is the *names* which are scalar, not the region of memory which each denotes. When the number of required names (sub-spaces) can be determined statically, by the programmer, scalar names are used. When the number required varies dynamically, indexed names are used.

3.2. Indexed Names

The term *scalar* is applied to names like *pivrow* and *rest* to distinguish them from *indexed names* such as the name *segment<j>* in the Refined C code of Figure 6.

```
decname int segment<>[];

s = 1;
for (i = 0; i < lg(n); i++)
        {
        s = 2*s;

        disjoint x
                {
                segment<m; n/s>[k:((m*s) <= k && k <= (m*s)+(s/2))];
                }

        for(j=0; j < n/s; j++)
                {
                segment<j>[j*s] = segment<j>[j*s] + segment<j>[j*s+(s/2)];
                }
        }
```

Refined C Code for Log-Sum
Figure 6

Before considering the code of Figure 6, we consider that of Figure 7, from which it arose.

```
s = 1;
for (i=0; i < lg(n); i++)
        {
        s = 2*s;
        for (j=0; j < n/s; j++)
                {
                x[j*s] = x[j*s] + x[j*s+(s/2)];
                }
        }
```

ANSI C Code for Log-Sum
Figure 7

The code of Figure 7 sums the elements of an n-element one-dimensional array x, leaving the sum in $x[n-1]$. This code utilizes the standard log-time parallel algorithm for solving first-order linear recurrences, successively dividing the array into halves, quarters, eighths, etc.

After each division, the individual segments may be processed in parallel with one another, i.e., the iterations of the inner *for* loop may be executed in parallel with one another.

Figure 6 shows Refined C code for the parallel array summation algorithm. On each iteration of the outer *for* loop, array *x*'s name space is partitioned into the number of segments appropriate to that iteration. Since the *j*-th iteration of the inner *for* loop references only *segment<j>* the Refined C compiler recognizes that all iterations may be executed in parallel with one another.

In Figure 6 the *disjoint* statement

$$\text{disjoint } x$$
$$\{$$
$$\text{segment<m;n/s>}[k:((m*s) <= k \ \&\&\ k <= (m*s)+(s/2))];$$
$$\}$$

invokes the set of names *segment<0>*, *segment<1>*, ... , *segment<n/s - 1>*, and effects the name space transformation τ_2 shown below. The variable *m* is used as a dummy in defining the various new indexed names; index values go from 0 to n/s - 1.

$$\tau_2(x[k]) = \begin{cases} \text{segment } <0> [k] & \text{if } (0*s) \le k \le (0*s) + (s/2) \\ \\ \text{segment } <1> [k] & \text{if } (1*s) \le k \le (1*s) + (s/2) \\ & \text{and } \neg\ ((0*s) \le k \le (0*s) + (s/2)) \\ & \vdots \\ \text{segment } <i> [k] & \text{if } (i*s) \le k \le (i*s) + (s/2) \\ & \text{and } \neg\ (((i-1)*s) \le k \le ((i-1)(*s) + (s/2)) \\ & \vdots \\ & \text{and } \neg\ ((0*s) \le k \le (0*s) + (s/2)) \\ \vdots \end{cases}$$

If, for specific values of i and k, $\tau_2(x[k]) \ne$ segment<i>[k], then a reference to segment<i>[k] is illegal, and causes a fatal error.

The term *indexed* is applied to names like *segment* for obvious reasons. *segment* is an "array" of names, with "subscripts" in angle brackets rather than square brackets, to distinguish between "arrays of names" and "arrays of memory locations." An indexed name may have one or more *index dimensions*; *segment*, for example, has a single index dimension.

This last example leads to the general rule for specifying the equivalent of a *forall* loop in Refined C. The *for* loop is written as:

    for(i = init; i <= limit; i++)
    {
        loop_body
    }

with the following constraints:

- init and limit are arbitrary integer-valued expressions

- *loop_body* contains no definition (write) of the iteration variable i

- every pair of potentially data-dependence-creating references in *loop_body* is either a pair of array references or a pair of indexed-name references, i.e., they are of the form:

  - $A<exp_{11}><exp_{12}> \ldots <exp_{1r}>[exp_{21}][exp_{22}] \ldots [exp_{2t}]$ [1]

  and

  - $A<exp'_{11}><exp'_{12}> \ldots <exp'_{1r}>[exp'_{21}][exp'_{22}] \ldots [exp'_{2t}]$

  and for at least one k, $1 \leq k \leq r$, $exp_{1k} = i = exp'_{1k}$

  or for at least one k, $1 \leq k \leq t$, $exp_{2k} = i = exp'_{2k}$

- there are no potentially data-dependence-creating scalar references in *loop_body*.

3.3. Predicates Which Define Names

The general *name_def* in a *disjoint* statement is of the form

  name pred_exp_list

---

[1] r may equal zero or t may equal zero, but not both.

The *name* has zero (if it is scalar) or more (if it is indexed) *index*'s in angle brackets. I.e., it is of the form

$$\text{identifier}<m_1; \text{ext}_1><m_2; \text{ext}_2> \ldots <m_r; \text{ext}_r>$$

where $r \geq 0$. The *pred_exp_list* consists of one or more *pred_exp*'s, i.e. it is of the form

$$[k_1: (\pi_1(m_1, m_2, \ldots, m_r, k_1))] [k_2: (\pi_2(m_1, m_2, \ldots, m_r, k_1, k_2))]$$
$$\ldots [k_t: (\pi_t(m_1, m_2, \ldots, m_r, k_1, k_2, \ldots, k_t))]$$

where

- each k_i, $1 \leq i \leq t$, is a *pred_dummy*

- each π_i, $1 \leq i \leq t$, is a *predicate*

Each *predicate* is a Boolean expression involving the indicated *index_dummy*'s and *pred_dummy*'s. Any Boolean expression π which satisfies the following restrictions may be used as a predicate:

- π may not contain any pointer variables

- a function called in the evaluation of π, if any, may reference only its calling parameters and its local variables, and may write only its local variables

- other than writes to local variables of called functions, the evaluation of π may cause no side effects

The *pred_exp_list*

$$[k_1: (\pi_1(m_1, m_2, \ldots, m_r, k_1))] [k_2: (\pi_2(m_1, m_2, \ldots, m_r, k_1, k_2))]$$
$$\ldots [k_t: (\pi_t(m_1, m_2, \ldots, m_r, k_1, k_2, \ldots, k_t))]$$

represents the Boolean expression

$$\pi_1(m_1, m_2, \ldots, m_r, k_1) \wedge (\pi_2(m_1, m_2, \ldots, m_r, k_1, k_2) \wedge$$
$$\ldots \wedge (\pi_t(m_1, m_2, \ldots, m_r, k_1, k_2, \ldots, k_t)$$

4. The *cdisjoint* Statement

When a large number of instances of an indexed name is invoked, run-time checking can become excessive; the required check for a reference to *name<i>* is that the defining predicate is true for i and false for $0, 1, \ldots, i-1$.

As an example, consider the Refined C log-sum code of Figure 6. The reference to *segment<j>[j*s]* in the body of the *for* loop requires a check that

$$(j*s) \leq j*s \leq (j*s)+(s/2)$$

$$\wedge \neg (((j-1)*s) \leq j*s \leq ((j-1)*s)+(s/2))$$

$$\bullet$$
$$\bullet$$
$$\bullet$$

$$\wedge \neg (((0)*s) \leq j*s \leq ((0)*s)+(s/2))$$

While arbitrarily complex indexed names, requiring arbitrarily complex, non-optimizable, run-time checking can be written in Refined C, many, if not most, algorithms of interest utilize indexed names which "partition" *array_exp* in highly stylized ways. In the Refined C log-sum code of Figure 6, for example, this "partitioning" is into contiguous sections of the original array (see Figure 8).

segment<0>	segment<1>	...	segment<n/s - 1>

Indexed Names in Refined C Log-Sum Code of Figure 6

Figure 8

In other cases, "partitioning" is into a *shuffle-exchange, butterfly (FFT)* or other similar patterns.

Refined C provides specialized versions of the *disjoint* statement, versions which allow often-used indexed-name patterns to be invoked with minimal checking overhead. The particular version which we consider in the present section is the *cdisjoint* (contiguous disjoint) statement, whose syntax is shown in Figure 9.

cdisjoint_stmt :	'cdisjoint' array_exp '{' cdisjoint_name_list '}'
cdisjoint_name_list :	cdisjoint_name
	| cdisjoint_name cdisjoint_name_list
cdisjoint_name :	identifier index_def_list ';'
index_def_list :	index_def
	| index_def index_def_list
index_def :	'<' initial ';' increment ';' number '>'
initial :	expression
increment :	expression
number:	expression

BNF of the *cdisjoint* Statement
Figure 9

The general cdisjoint statement invokes indexed names as shown in Figure 10.

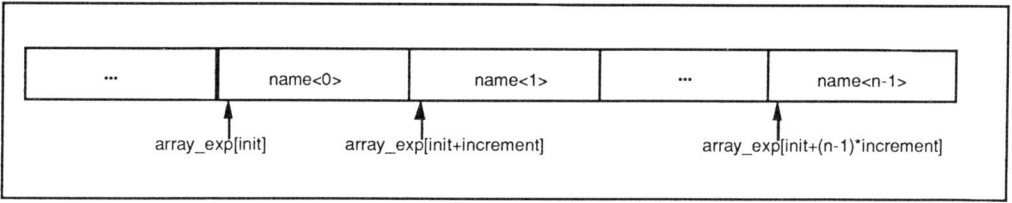

Names Created by the *cdisjoint* Statement
Figure 10

The Refined C code for log-sum, re-written using *cdisjoint*, is shown in Figure 11. The check on each reference to *segment* amounts to no more than a single lower and upper bounds check.

```
s = 1;
for(i=0; i < lg(n); i++)
    {
    s = 2*s;

    cdisjoint x
        {
        segment< 0; s/2 ; n>;
        }

    for(j = 0; j < n/s; j++)
        {
        segment<j>[j*s] = segment<j>[j*s] + segment<j>[j*s+(s/2)];
        }
    }
```

Refined C Code for Log-Sum Using *cdisjoint*
Figure 11

Additional versions of the disjoint statement will be discussed in the full-length version of the present paper.

References

[1] Allen, Fran, Michael Burke, Philippe Charles, Ron Cytron, and Jeanne Ferrante, "An Overview of the PTRAN Analysis System for Multiprocessing" Proc of the 1987 Int'l Conference on Supercomputing, Athens, Greece (1987)

[2] Allen, J.R., "Dependence Analysis for Subscripted Variables and its Application to Program Transformations", Ph.D. Thesis, Rice University, April, 1983

[3] Allen, J.R., and K. Kennedy, "Automatic Translation of Fortran Programs to Vector Form," *ACM Transactions on Programming Languages and Systems*, Vol. 9, No. 4, October, 1987.

[4] Banerjee, U., "Data Dependence in Ordinary Programs," M.S. thesis, Univ. of Ill at Urbana-Champaign, Nov., 1976.

[5] Banerjee, U., "Speedup of Ordinary Programs," Ph.D. thesis, Univ. of Ill at Urbana-Champaign, 1979.

[6] Banerjee, U., *Dependence Analysis for Supercomputing*, Kluwer Academic Publishers, Norwell, Mass., 1988.

[7] Burke, M., and R. Cytron, "Interprocedural Dependence Analysis and Parallelization," Proceedings of SIGPLAN '86 Symposium on Compiler Construction, Palo Alto, CA, June, 1986.

[8] Lamport, L. "The Parallel Execution of DO Loops," *Communications of the ACM*, Vol. 17, No. 2, February, 1974.

[9] Towle, R.A., "Control and Data Dependence for Program Transformations," Ph.D. thesis, University of Illinois at Urbana-Champaign, 1976.

[10] Wolfe, Michael, "Optimizing Supercompilers for Supercomputers," Ph.D. Thesis, Univ. of Ill. at Urbana-Champaign, Oct., 1982.
[11] Wolfe, Michael, *Optimizing Supercompilers for Supercomputers*, Pitman Publishing Co., London, and MIT Press, Cambridge, Mass, 1989.
[12] Wolfe, M.J., and U. Banerjee "Data Dependence and its Application to Parallel Processing," *International Journal of Parallel Programming*, Vol. 16, No. 2, April, 1987.
[13] Kong, Xiangyun, David Klappholz, and Kleanthis Psarris, "The I Test: A New Test for Subscript Data Dependence," to appear in Proceedings of 1990 International Conference on Parallel Processing, August, 1990.
[14] Horwitz, S., P. Pfeiffer, and Thomas Reps, "Dependence Analysis for Pointer Variables," Proceedings of SIGPLAN '89 Conference on Programming Language Design and Implementation, June, 1989.
[15] Larus, J.A., and Paul N. Hilfinger, "Detecting Conflicts between Structure Accesses," Proc. of the SIGPLAN '88 Conference on Programming Language Design and Implementation, 1988.
[16] Hendren, L.J., and A. Nicolau, "Parallelizing Programs with Recursive Data Structures," in IEEE Transactions on Parallel and Distributed Computing, Vol. 1, No. 1, January, 1990.
[17] Hendren, L.J., "Interference Analysis Tools and Parallelization Techniques for C Programs with Recursive Data," in Proceedings of the 1989 ACM International Conference on Supercomputing, June, 1989.
[18] Hendren, L.J., and A. Nicolau, "Parallelizing Programs with Recursive Data Structures," Proceedings of 1989 International Conference on Parallel Processing, August, 1989.
[19] Banning, John P., "An Efficient Way to Find the Side Effects of Procedure Calls and the Aliases of Variables," Proceedings of ACM Conference on Principles of Programming Languages, 1979.
[20] Cooper, Keith D., "Analyzing Aliases of Reference Formal Parameters," Proceedings of ACM Conference on Principles of Programming Languages, 1985.
[21] Myers, Eugene W., "A Precise Inter-Procedural Data Flow Algorithm," Proceedings of ACM Conference on Principles of Programming Languages, 1981.
[22] Weihl, William E., "Interprocedural Data Flow Analysis in the Presence of Pointers, Procedure Variables, and Label Variables," Proceedings of ACM Conference on Principles of Programming Languages, 1980.
[23] Klappholz, D., Kallis, A., and Kong, X., "Refined C - An Update" Proceedings of the Second Workshop on Languages and Compilers for Parallel Computing, in *Research Monographs in Parallel and Distributed Processing*, MIT Press and Pitman Publishing Co., Cambridge, Mass., and London, 1989.
[24] Klappholz, D., Kong, X., and Kallis, A., "Refined Fortran - An Update" Proceedings of Supercomputing '89, Reno, NV, November, 1989.
[25] Klappholz, D., H. G. Dietz, K. Stein, H. C. Park, and X. Kong, "Refined Languages: An Evolutionary Approach to the Use of Sequential Languages for Programming Parallel(MIMD) Machines," in Parallel Processing: State of The Art Report, Pergamon-Infotech, Maidenhead, Berkshire, U.K., 1987.
[26] Dietz, Henry, and David Klappholz, "Refined FORTRAN: Another Sequential Language for Parallel Programming," Proc. Int'l Conference on Parallel Processing, August, 1986.
[27] Dietz, Henry, and David Klappholz,"Refined C: A Sequential Language For Parallel Programming." in Proceedings of the International Conference on Parallel Processing, Saint Charles, Illinois, August, 1985.
[28] Dietz, Henry, and David Klappholz,"Refining a Conventional Language for Race-Free Specification of Parallel Algorithms," in Proceedings of the International Conference on Parallel Processing, Bellaire, Michigan, August, 1984.

16 Symbolic Dependence Analysis for High-Performance Parallelizing Compilers
M. Haghighat, C. Polychronopoulos

Abstract

The effectiveness and efficiency of parallelizing compilers and other parallel programming tools, depend solely on the accuracy and effectiveness of data dependence analysis techniques. Although powerful dependence analysis techniques exist and have been employed in commercial and experimental systems, all these schemes fail in the presence of symbolic terms and pointers. In this paper we introduce a framework for solving the dependence problem in the presence of unknown symbolic terms. Our scheme, built on abstract interpretation based on lattice theoretic models, and classical dependence analysis, can be used to accurately compute dependences in the presence of symbolic terms, and can be extended to handle pointers. Several examples of array references with symbolic terms were extracted from common numerical packages, and are discussed in this paper. We also gathered statistics about the frequency of symbolic terms in index expressions and loop upper bounds, which provide an indication about the importance and usefulness of symbolic dependence analysis schemes. The details of implementation of *symbolic dependence analysis* in Parafrase-2[1] [25] is also presented.

1 Introduction

As sequential computer technology reaches its limitations imposed by the laws of physics, parallelism seems to be the most promising alternative for satisfying the demand for computational speed [24]. *Parallel processing* is an efficient form of information processing

---

[1] Parafrase-2 is a multilingual vectorizing/parallelizing code restructurer developed at the Center for Supercomputing Research and Development at the University of Illinois at Urbana-Champaign.

which emphasizes the exploitation of concurrent events in the computing process. Parallelism can be exploited in one or more levels (i.e. at job, program, subroutine, loop, statement, or instruction level) [18]. Parallel languages to support parallel processing have been proposed in recent years, but none has been widely accepted [9]. Therefore, it is essential to have compilers that can detect and exploit parallelism in sequential programs. For this reason, *restructuring compilers* have been developed [2], [7], [8],[9],[18], [23][24], [27].

Program restructuring consists of rewriting a program to make a better use of machine architecture. Restructuring compilers use a number of program transformations to achieve this goal. Several transformations are known today, and probably new ones will come in future to match the evolution of supercomputer architectures [9].

The effectiveness of program transformations and optimizations directly depends on compiler's ability to perform accurate data and control dependence analysis and to expose the partial order imposed on the program statements by the semantics of the languages as precisely as possible. Symbolic dependence analysis serves this purpose and complements existing dependence analysis tests by extending the compilers ability of dependence analysis in the presence of unknown symbolic terms.

1.1 An Intuitive Approach to Dependence Analysis

The sequential nature of early uniprocessors is reflected in the semantics of the programming languages developed to run on these machines. The total ordering imposed by sequential languages is more restrictive than is necessary to guarantee a correct program output [5]. In other words, the correct output of a program can often be obtained by other statement orderings. However, portions of the original ordering are essential to maintain the program correctness. These constraints arise because of the way program variables are defined and used. These required orderings are abstracted by the concept of *dependence*. In general, the more precise information a compiler has about dependence constraints, the better transformed code it can generate. The basic dependence problem is to decide if two indexed elements of an array (in a loop nest) can represent the same memory location under certain constraints imposed by the loop iteration space. This leads to the question of existence of an integer solution to a diophantine equation satisfying a set of constraints. This equation which is called the *dependence equation*, is a diophantine equation in terms of loops index variables. The constraints are imposed by the boundaries of the loop iteration space. The subject of dependence has been studied over the years, and there are methods to analyze the problem in cases where no symbolic terms are involved in the dependence equation or in its constraints. By symbolic terms, we mean those variables other than loop indices, whose values are not known at compile time. The theory of dependence analysis is studied in detail in [9].

Section 2 presents the basic definitions and a brief review of theory of dependence analysis. Section 3 introduces a framework to solve the dependence problem in the presence of unknown symbolic terms. It also contains the details of implementation of symbolic constant propagation and symbolic dependence analysis in Parafrase-2 [25], and some preliminary measurements.

2 Dependence Analysis of Programs

Dependence analysis theory has evolved over the years with contributions by a number of authors. Some of the references are : [20], [7], [18], [8], [10], [19], [5], [4], [12], [6], [28], [26]. Banerjee gives a rigorous theory of dependence analysis, presenting much of the published research in a coherent form [9].

The basic problem of dependence is to decide if two indexed elements of an array would represent the same memory location under certain given conditions [9]. In a more general approach, we are looking for the intersection of two regions in the iteration space generated by a nest of loops. Since loop indexes are integers, these problems reduce to finding integer solutions to a set of diophantine equations under a set of constraints imposed by loops upper and lower bounds. In cases that nonlinear functions are involved, even if complete information about the system of equations and inequalities is available, the compiler may not be able to do much. But, empirical statistics from common mathematical packages indicate that the subscripts of array elements and limits of loop indexes are usually linear functions [26].

The existence of dependence in the linear case can be investigated by integer programming methods. However, all such methods are prohibitively expensive and inefficient in a compiler. Approximate tests that find bounds of linear functions and solutions to linear diophantine equations have proved to be quite adequate for real programs.

2.1 Dependence Tests

The basic dependence problem reduces to the existence of solution to a system of linear diophantine equations subject to a set of linear constraints. There are two major categories of dependence tests: exact and approximate. In the case of exact tests, we find all the solutions to the system of linear diophantine equations and then check to see if any of the solutions satisfy all the constraints. In such a case, the two statements S_v and S_w are dependent. If no such a solution exists, then statements S_v and S_w are independent. For an extensive treatment of dependence tests see [9].

GCD Test: The *gcd test* is a simple test which can detect independence [7], [17], [6], [28], [9], [27]. This test can be stated as follows:

Given a linear diophantine equation $a_1 x_1 + a_2 x_2 + \cdots + a_n x_n = c$, and a region $\Re \subset \mathbf{Z}^n$, if $\gcd(a_1, a_2, \ldots, a_n)$ does not divide c, the equation has no solution in $\Re$.

Banerjee's Inequality: One of the most popular data dependence tests is *Banerjee's Inequality* [7], [10]. It has been studied extensively in the literature and modified for several different purposes [5], [3], [6] [27]. It can be stated as follows:

Given a linear diophantine equation

$$\sum_{k=1}^{n} a_k x_k = c, \tag{1}$$

and a region $\Re \subset \mathbf{Z}^n$, defined by $\Re = \{\langle x_1, x_2, \ldots, x_n \rangle \in \mathbf{Z}^n \mid p_1 \leq x_1 \leq q_1,\ p_2 \leq x_2 \leq q_2,\ \ldots,\ p_n \leq x_n \leq q_n\}$, if the inequality

$$\sum_{k=1}^{n}(a_k^+ p_k - a_k^- q_k) \leq c \leq \sum_{k=1}^{n}(a_k^+ q_k - a_k^- p_k) \tag{2}$$

is not satisfied, then there is no solution to the equation in $\Re$. However, if the inequality is satisfied, there may or may not be a solution to the equation in $\Re$.

In Banerjee's inequality, the *positive part* a^+ and the *negative part* a^- of a real number a are defined by $a^+ = \max\{a, 0\}$ and $a^- = \max\{-a, 0\}$. Note that for any real number a, $a^+ \geq 0$ and $a^- \geq 0$.

Banerjee's Inequality can be generalized to the case where $\Re$ is a trapezoid. This has been done by giving an algorithm that computes the lower and upper bounds of a linear function f of n variables in a trapezoidal region $\Re \subset \mathbf{R}^n$ [9].

3 Symbolic Dependence Analysis of Programs

Banerjee's gcd and inequality tests need all the values involved (loop bounds and variables in array subscript expressions) to be known at compile time. This restriction makes these dependence tests to be of no use in most cases where array subscript expressions contain unknown symbolic terms. We have found that in certain numerical packages over 50% of array references inside loops contain at least one unknown symbolic term, other than loop index variables (Table 2). Traditionally, parallelizing compilers have resolved some of these cases by applying classical optimization techniques such as constant propagation, loop induction variable substitution, and statement forward substitution. User assertions and interprocedural analysis can also be used to reduce unknown symbolic terms [26]. Nevertheless, standard dependence tests can not be applied on many of the unresolved cases, due to lack of information about the values of certain variables at compile time. Flow analysis and approximate semantic analysis are quite helpful in handling these cases. In the following sections, we look at some program segments, extracted from common numerical packages, that require symbolic dependence analysis. Then, we discuss the importance of symbolic constant propagation in dependence analysis, and also the details of its implementation in Parafrase-2. We also describe how approximate semantic analysis and partial symbolic execution of programs can create a flow analysis framework, under which dependence analysis can be quite powerful.

3.1 Motivation

Consider the loop of Figure 1. Since n is not modified inside the loop, the gcd test will lead to verifying the existence of integer solutions to the equation $2i_1 + \text{n} = 2i_2 + \text{n} + 1$. This equation which can be simplified to $2i_1 - 2i_2 = 1$ does not have an integer solution because 2 divides the left hand side of the equation but not the right hand side. So, there is no output dependence, and this loop can be either vectorized or parallelized.

To see an example where symbolic inequality test is useful, consider the loop of Figure 2, which has been extracted from a block tridiagonal solver [11]. A simple symbolic manipulation of subscripts of array F shows that the inner loop forms a recurrence and the outer loop can be executed in parallel. That is because in different iterations of the outer loop, say j_1 and j_2, there can be no dependence due to the index expressions (p-1)*q+j_1 and (p-1)*q-m+k. Because the latter is always less than or equal to (p-1)*q, (this is a consequence of the fact that k $\leq$ m), while the former is greater than (p-1)*q

```
do i := low, high
    A[2*i+n]   := B[i]
    A[2*i+n+1] := C[i]
enddo
```

Figure 1: Use of symbolic expression simplification in dependence test.

```
do j := 1, m
    do k := 1, m
        F[(p-1)*q+j]:=F[(p-1)*q+j]-V[k,j,p-1]*F[(p-1)*q-m+k]
    enddo
enddo
```

Figure 2: Example of use of symbolic inequality dependence test.

(because $j_1 \geq 1$).

Some cases with subscripted subscript expressions have the same property as the above example. The code in Figure 3 has also been extracted from the same block tridiagonal solver.

```
l := m+1
do j := 1, Q[i]
    do k := 1, m
        F[S[i]+j] := F[S[i]+j]-V[k,j,i-1]*F[S[i]-m+k]
    enddo
enddo
```

Figure 3: Example of a subscripted subscript case.

Note that i and thus S[i] are constants during the execution of the loop. Hence, a similar analysis shows that the outer loop can be executed in parallel, and the inner loop forms a recurrence.

Semantic analysis also eliminates some of the dependences which may be assumed otherwise [23]. For instance, consider the loop in Figure 4. The loop cannot be executed unless m > 0; therefore, it can be vectorized. The compiler can discover this by examining the condition in the if statement.

3.2 Types of Symbolism

Recall from Section 2 that the gcd test involves verifying the divisibility of c by the gcd of a_is in Equation 1. On the other hand, the inequality test in Equation 2 involves computing the minimum and maximum of function f in $\Re$, and then verifying whether c lies within those bounds. The inequality test can be applied only if c, a_is and the loop bounds p_is

```
        if (m > 0) then
            do i := low, high
                A[i] := B[i]+A[i+m]
            enddo
        endif
```

Figure 4: Example of use of semantic analysis in dependence detection.

and q_is are constant. The types of symbolism that arise within loops can be classified into three categories:

- *Loops with Symbolic Bounds*, as in the loop of Figure 5. The symbolic case that arises most often is the case of symbolic loop upper bounds. This has no effect on the gcd test. The reason is that the gcd test determines the existence of solutions to the dependence equation over the set of integers; it is independent of region boundaries. However, the inequality test relies on the region imposed by the loop bounds. For example, the symbolic evaluation of Banerjee's inequality for the loop of Figure 5 leads to the verification of the inequality $n \leq 100$; the loop can be vectorized if and only if n is less than or equal to 100. The compiler can evaluate this inequality within a flow analysis framework.

```
do i := 1, n
    A[i+100] := A[i]+···
enddo
```

Figure 5: Example of a loop with a symbolic upper bound.

- *Symbolic Additive Terms*, as in the case of the loop of Figure 6. Symbolic evaluation of Banerjee's inequality for this loop indicates that there exists a dependence relation between statements s_1 and s_2 if and only if the following condition holds:

$$((m < 0) \wedge (-99 \leq m \leq -1)) \vee (m = 0) \vee ((m > 0) \wedge (1 \leq m \leq 99))$$

This condition can be simplified to the inequality $-99 \leq m \leq 99$. The compiler can come up with the decision about dependence relation between statements s_1 and s_2 by evaluating the above inequality within a flow analysis framework discussed in the following. The compiler can also use the above constraints for multiversion code generation for the loop [21].

- *Symbolic Multipliers*, as in the case of the loop of Figure 7. If m is evaluated to a constant on all flow paths to the loop, symbolic constant propagation can be quite useful. However, if m is not a constant, general symbolic dependence analysis may resolve the case. Symbolic evaluation of Banerjee's inequality for this loop indicates a dependence between different instances of statement s_1, if and only if $-99 \leq m \leq 0$. Thus, the compiler can assume no dependence, if it has the information that either

```
do i := 1, 100
   s₁: A[i+m] := ...
   s₂: ... := A[i]+...
enddo
```

Figure 6: Example of a loop with a symbolic additive term.

$m > 0$ or $m < -99$ when the control reaches statement s_1 (such an information can be the result of approximate semantic analysis of the program).

```
do i := 1, 100
   s₁: A[m*i+100] := A[i]
enddo
```

Figure 7: Example of a loop with a symbolic multiplier.

3.3 Symbolic Constant Propagation

The constant propagation problem can be solved in a monotone framework $\langle\langle L, \cap \rangle, F\rangle$, where F is a monotone operation space, each element of which models the effect of a flow graph node [16], [1]. The way that F is implemented has an important role in the effectiveness of the constant propagation algorithm.

Traditionally, F has been implemented as follows. Let $G = \langle N, E, n_0 \rangle$ be a flow graph, $n \in N$ be a flow graph node, and in_n be the information available at the beginning of node n. Then, n is a sequence of program statements, i.e. $n = \langle s_{b_n}, \ldots, s_{e_n} \rangle$, where s_{b_n} and s_{e_n} are the first and last statements of the flow graph node n. Corresponding to each statement s of the program, there is a function f_s that models that statement. Function f_n, that models the flow graph node n, is the composition of the functions corresponding to the statements in that node, i.e. $f_n(in_n) = f_{e_n}(\cdots(f_{b_n}(in_n))\cdots)$.

Let statement s be an assignment statement, i.e. $s = \langle v, e(\vec{x}) \rangle$, where v is a program variable, $\vec{x}$ represents the program variables, and e is a function on the set of program variables. The effect of function f_s on the information that reaches statement s is as follows. If evaluation of e, in the environment defined by the information that reaches statement s, results in a constant, then the information is updated by deleting any binding of variable v, if such a binding exists, and adding a new binding $\langle v, e(\vec{x}) \rangle$ to the information of that environment. Note that an environment is a set of bindings of variables to their corresponding constant values.

A more precise scheme is implemented in Parafrase-2. Instead of loosing information about the assignment statements whose right hand sides do not result in constant values, their result values are kept symbolically in the environment. Hence, in this model, an environment is a set of bindings of variables to their corresponding symbolic values. In this model, some constants are captured that may not be caught otherwise. We call these *hidden constants*. A constant is hidden if it is the result of cancellation of nonconstant variables in an expression. As an example, consider the program segment shown in Figure 8. Assume that c has been evaluated to the same constant value along all control flow paths that reach the given code segment. Also assume that v could have taken different values on different paths that reach the given code segment. By using the traditional constant propagation models, variable x would not be evaluated as a constant. Consequently, variable y would not be a constant either. But, in our model, the symbolic value of x is used in evaluation of y. Thus, the variable v will be canceled out, and y results in a constant value c+1. Hence, y is a hidden constant.

```
    ⋮
x := v+c
y := x-v+1
    ⋮
```

Figure 8: Example of a hidden constant.

3.4 Symbolic Dependence Analysis

Symbolic constant propagation can be considered as a special case of *constraint propagation*, in which, certain constraints among program variables remain constant. A substantial set of linear constraints among program variables can be discovered by the scheme proposed in [14]. An extension of this scheme, which is based on the abstract interpretation of programs, is a part of the frame we use for symbolic dependence analysis [15]. Following is a description of a framework in which the constraint propagation problem is solved.

3.4.1 Constraint Propagation

Let $\langle\langle \mathbf{C}, \cap\rangle, F\rangle$ represent the constraint propagation problem, where $\mathbf{C}$ is the set of all convex polyhedra, as defined in [14]. The zero element of $\mathbf{C}$ is the set $\mathbf{R}^n$, where n is the number of program variables. The meet operation is the convex-hull operation. Intuitively, $P \in \mathbf{C}$ represents the information that we may assume at certain points of the program flow graph. $\vec{x} \in P$ means that all the linear constraints that characterize the polyhedron P, hold among the program variables.

Each basic block of the flow graph can be modeled as an operation on $\mathbf{C}$, as follows (for simplicity, let us ignore the aliasing problem). First, symbolically execute the code in the basic block in an environment, created by assigning all variables their symbolic names. This will transform each basic block to a form in which each variable is the target of at most a single assignment statement. This transformation is performed only once for each basic block. This method has the advantage that the intermediate subexpressions, that are canceled out, do not have any effect on the computation. Hence, they do not cause any approximation. As an example, consider the code segment shown in Figure 9. Assuming that a and b are nonconstant program variables, the expression on the right hand side of statement s_2 is nonlinear in terms of program variables. Therefore some information is lost by using the method of abstract interpretation (because of the above nonlinearity). Hence, there is some approximation in evaluation of the right hand side of statement s_3 that uses the value of x. But, in our model, because of the cancellation of the nonlinear term a*b, statement s_3 is simplified to a linear statement, although s_2 remains nonlinear.

```
       ⋮                              ⋮
s₁: y := 4*a*b+2*c            s'₁: y := 4*a*b+2*c
s₂: x := (2*a+3)*(2*b+1)      s'₂: x := 3+2*a+4*a*b+6*b
s₃: z := x-y                  s'₃: z := 3+2*a+6*b-2*c
       ⋮                              ⋮
       (a)                            (b)
```

Figure 9: (a) A code segment and (b) its symbolic execution.

After the above partial symbolic execution of the code is performed, we find the corresponding transformation of each of the statements of each basic block, using the methods described in [15]. The function representing each basic block consists of the composition of functions that represent each statement within the basic block.

Having F defined as above, the framework is monotone. Hence, the general iterative algorithm for monotone frameworks [16], [1] can be used to solve the constraint propagation problem. After the application of this algorithm, for each point of the program we have a set of valid linear constraints.

3.4.2 Symbolic Inequality Test

The basic problem of dependence, as introduced in Section 2, is to decide if two indexed elements of an array would represent the same memory location under certain given conditions imposed by the iteration space of a loop nest.

If the subscript expressions contain the same symbolic term, we must assure that both of them use the same instance of the corresponding variable. In other words, the corresponding variables of the symbolic terms common in both expressions must not be updated along all control flow paths between the two statements. As we shall see later, in some cases *induction variable substitution* can transform the code so that the above condition is satisfied and hence, symbolic dependence test can be applied.

Let s_1 and s_2 be the two statements for which we want to answer the dependence question. Also, let P_{s_1} and P_{s_2} be the convex polyhedra of s_1 and s_2 respectively. Now, Banerjee's inequality can be simplified symbolically. Then, we test the simplified inequality in the convex-hull of P_{s_1} and P_{s_2} using the method described in [15]. That answers the dependence question.

Example: We illustrate the symbolic dependence analysis of programs on the code segment of Figure 10. In the first step, linear constraints among the program variables are

```
      m := 2
      n := 0
      while ... do
          m := m + 2
          if ... then
              m := m + 2
          else
              n := n + 1
          endif
      endwhile
      do i := 1, 100
          do j := 1, 50
              s₁: A[3*i+2*j+m+k+100] := ...
              s₂: A[-i+5*j+n+k-143] := ...
          enddo
      enddo
```

Figure 10: Example of application of symbolic dependence analysis.

detected. For simplicity, we just consider the program variables m and n. Figure 11(a) shows the convex polyhedron corresponding to the point of program right before the while loop. This polyhedron is transformed to the one in Figure 11(b) by the statements inside the loop and by the merge of transformed information, with that of the point before the while loop, shown in Figure 11(a). Note that a convex-hull operation is used to find the convex polyhedron associated with the merge of the then and else paths of the if statement. The merge, associated with the loop junction node, is also done with a convex-hull operation. The polyhedron associated with the first two iterations of the while loop is shown in Figure 11(c). When the while loop body is analyzed, a *widening* operation takes place at the loop junction node [14], [15]. A widening operation is an approximation of the transformation for ordinary junction nodes and ensures stabilization. This results in the convex polyhedron of Figure 11(e), which approximates the effect of the while loop. The polyhedron associated with only the third iteration of the while loop, shown in Figure 11(d), is included in the polyhedron associated with the loop. The program analysis converges and the polyhedron of Figure 11(e) represents the linear constraints among program variables m and n after the while loop.

Now, suppose we want to decide about the output dependence relation between statements s_1 and s_2. Variables k, m, and n are invariant along all control flow paths between s_1 and s_2. Hence, Banerjee's inequality test for dependence at level 1 (after substitution and simplification in Equation 2) reduces to the verification of the inequality $0 \leq n - m \leq 735$. Note that k is cancelled out in the symbolic evaluation of the inequality. The region for dependence at level 1 is shown in Figure 12(a). There is no intersection between this region and the convex polyhedron of Figure 11(e) that shows the linear constraints among program variables m and n. This fact can be concluded from verification of the above inequality in the convex polyhedron of Figure 11(e), using the algorithm described

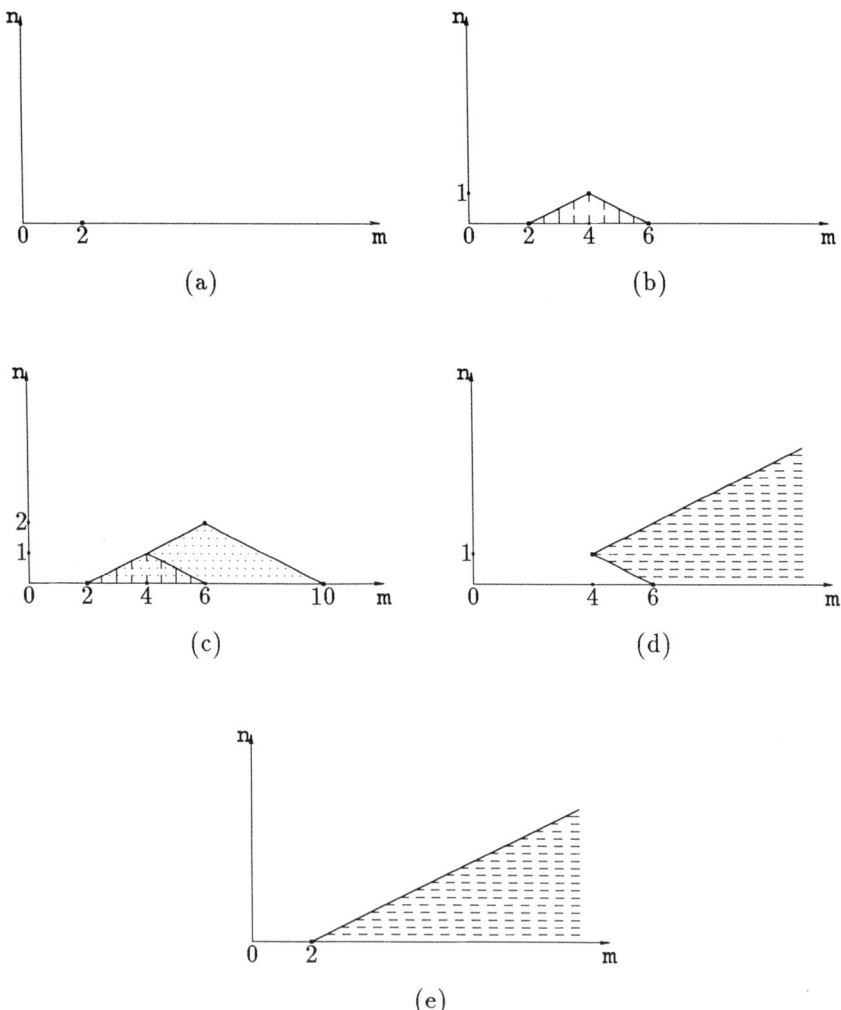

Figure 11: Detection of linear constraints among program variables.

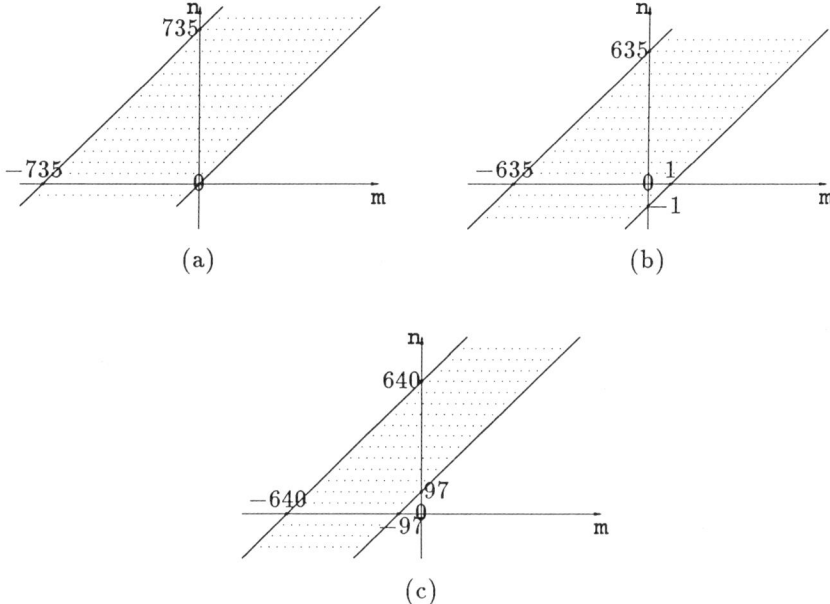

Figure 12: Regions for dependence at (a) level 1, (b) level 2, and (c) level 3.

in [14], [15]. Therefore there is no output dependence between statements s_1 and s_2 at level 1. Similarly, the question of dependence at levels 2 and 3 reduces to the verification of inequalities $-1 \leq n - m \leq 635$ and $97 \leq n - m \leq 640$ respectively. The associated regions for dependence at levels 2 and 3 are shown in Figure 12(b), and 12(c). Neither of these regions have intersection with the convex polyhedron of Figure 11(e). Hence, there is no output dependence between statements s_1 and s_2. Therefore, both of the do loops can be parallelized.

3.4.3 Induction variable substitution

Variables in loops whose successive values form an arithmetic progression are called *induction* variables; the most obvious example of an induction variable is the index variable of a loop [23]. In traditional optimizing compilers, induction variable elimination is used to optimize the array address calculation [1]. In parallelizing compilers, detection of induction variables is very important. Occurrences of induction variables on the right hand side of statements inside a loop are replaced with expressions in terms of loop index variables. This eliminates the corresponding symbolic terms in array subscript expressions, and hence makes the dependence tests more accurate [5]. As an example consider the loop in Figure 13(a). We would like to know if there is any dependence between different instances of the statement s_1. Note that **k** is a symbolic term in the corresponding subscript expressions. Also, note that **k** is updated on a path from s_1 to s_1, i.e. on the path corresponding to a single iteration of the loop. Therefore, we can not use symbolic dependence test unless the assignment to **k** is legitimately eliminated.

```
k := 0
do i := 1, n                          do i := 1, n
  s₁: X[n-k] := Y[i]+Z[n-i+1]           s'₁: X[n-i+1] := Y[i]+Z[n-i+1]
  s₂: k := k+1                        enddo
enddo                                 k := n
     (a)                                   (b)
```

Figure 13: Example of a loop with an induction variable.

However, **k** is an induction variable which can be replaced with the expression **i-1**. This results in the code segment shown in Figure 13(b). Now, the symbolic dependence test can be applied to the transformed code. In the symbolic inequality test, the symbolic term **n** will be canceled out and the test indicates that there is no dependence relation between different instances of the statement s_1. Thus, this loop can be vectorized.

3.5 Data Structures for Implementation of Symbolic Dependence Analysis

Among the various Parafrase-2 data structures, those that represent symbolic expressions have an important role in the implementation of symbolic dependence analysis. Following is a description of these structures.

3.5.1 Symbolic Expressions

Symbolic expressions are represented as summation of symbolic terms. Each symbolic term is the product of a real number and a subset of program variables. The internal representation of the symbolic expression $2yx - 7wxt - z + 3ts + 5$ is shown in Figure 14.

For efficient manipulation of symbolic terms, such as addition, subtraction, multiplication, and comparison, the list of program variables in each symbolic term is lexicographically sorted. For the similar reason, the list of symbolic terms in each symbolic expression is lexicographically sorted.

3.6 Preliminary Measurements

We used Parafrase-2 to study array referencing behavior on a number of numerical packages (Table 1). Besides frequently used scientific packages, such as Linpack and Eispack, ordinary programs were also studied. This sample reflects the array referencing behavior in both the library routines and user written programs (Table 4, 5). These data are summarized in Table 2 and Table 3.

Our results (Table 2) indicate that over 50% of array references inside loops contain symbolic terms other than loop index variables. The majority of these cases were symbolic additive terms. We also discovered that close to 95% of loops have symbolic bounds (Table 3). Parallelizing compilers handle many of these cases by applying classical optimization techniques such as constant propagation, loop induction variable substitution,

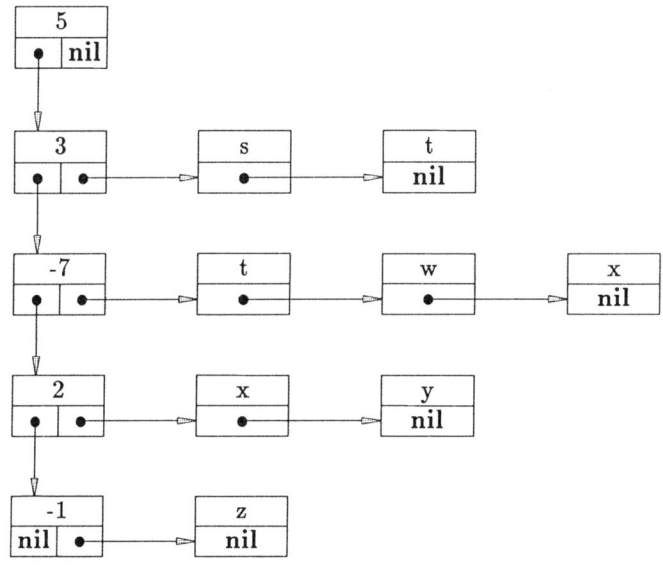

Figure 14: Representation of the expression $2yx - 7wxt - z + 3ts + 5$.

forward substitution, and interprocedural analysis. User assertions can also be used to reduce unknown symbolic terms. Nevertheless, standard dependence tests can not be applied on many of the unresolved cases, due to lack of information about the values of certain variables at compile time. Hence, a more sophisticated and yet efficient symbolic dependence testing is required to analyze these cases [22], [26]. In the following section, we give examples of common loop structures in standard numerical packages where traditional dependence tests can not be applied. However, symbolic dependence analysis handles them quite successfully.

Package	Description	Lines
ACM	Sample algorithms from ACM	2712
EISPACK	Eigensystem package	11700
FISHPAK	Separable elliptic partial differential equations package	22647
ITPACK	Iterative algorithms for sparse matrices	5591
LINPACK	Linear system package	10175
NAS	Perfect Club benchmark	5003
SMPL	Flow analysis program	2072
Total		59900

Table 1: Analyzed packages

	Array reference subscript expressions in loops			
Array dim.	References with no symb. terms	References with 1 symb. term	References with ≥ 2 symb. terms	References with symb. terms
1	52.33%	47.20%	0.47%	47.67%
2	40.60%	39.00%	20.40%	59.40%
≥ 3	65.24%	28.61%	6.15%	34.76%
Total	49.64%	43.45%	6.91%	50.36%

Table 2: Array references

Loops with no symbolic bounds	Loops with symbolic lower bound	Loops with symbolic upper bound	Loops with symbolic stride	Loops with symbolic bounds
5.16%	23.62%	94.69%	0.92%	94.84%

Table 3: Loop types

	Array reference subscript expressions in loops			
Package	References with no symb. terms	References with 1 symb. term	References with ≥ 2 symb. terms	References with symb. terms
ACM	279	200	18	218
EISPACK	1353	1098	469	1567
FISHPAK	3429	2963	284	3247
ITPACK	693	282	0	282
LINPACK	1008	1392	282	1674
NAS	1454	1312	45	1357
SMPL	365	263	97	360

Table 4: Array references in analyzed packages

Package	Total number of loops	Loops with symbolic bounds
ACM	157	152
EISPACK	627	610
FISHPAK	1242	1212
ITPACK	96	90
LINPACK	274	274
NAS	242	166
SMPL	76	70

Table 5: Loop types in analyzed packages

3.7 Common Examples from Standard Numerical Packages

In this section we give some common loop structures in standard numerical packages, where traditional optimization techniques can not eliminate unknown symbolic terms, consequently, classical data dependence tests can not be applied. However, symbolic dependence analysis in the framework we described, detects parallelism in all of those cases.

```
                         m1 := ...
                         m2 := ...
m := ...                 do i1 := 1, n1
do i := 1, n                do i2 := 1, n2
   s1: A[i+m]:=A[i+m]+...       A[i1+m1,i2+m2]:=A[i1+m1,i2+m2]+...
enddo                       enddo
                         enddo

    (a)                           (b)
```

Figure 15: Cancellation of unknown symbolic terms.

Consider the loop of Figure 15(a). If m is not evaluated to a constant, constant propagation and even statement forward substitution can not help to handle the case. However, since m is not modified along all control flow paths from statement s_1 to itself, m will be canceled out in a symbolic evaluation of Banerjee's inequality test. Hence, no self-dependence is imposed by statement s_1, and the loop can be parallelized. A similar analysis for the loop of Figure 15(b) shows that both loops of that figure can be parallelized. Both of these loops are frequently found in FISHPAK.

Now, look at the loop of Figure 16 whose structure has frequently been observed in FISHPAK. If m has not been evaluated to a constant when control reaches the given code segment, neither constant propagation nor statement forward substitution can help in analysis of dependence relation between statements s_1 and s_2. However, as far as the given loop is concerned, the relation mp1 = m+1 holds in the loop iteration space.

```
    mp1 := m+1
    do i := 1, n
      s₁: A[i,m]   := ...
      s₂: ...      := A[i,mp1]
    enddo
```

Figure 16: Example of use of constraint propagation in dependence analysis.

```
    nm1 := n-1
    do i := 1, nm1
      s₁: k   := n-i
      s₂: A[k] := A[k]+...
    enddo
```

Figure 17: Dependence testing in the existence of loop induction variables.

Hence, statements s_1 and s_2 always access different columns of array A. Therefore there is no dependence between statements s_1 and s_2. There is no self-dependence imposed by statement s_1 either, because different instances of statement s_1 access different rows of array A. Hence, the loop can be parallelized.

In the loop of Figure 17, k is an induction variable. Even if statement forward substitution is used to substitute n-i for all occurrences of k in statement s_2, the classical dependence tests can not be applied dut to the unknown symbolic term n in the subscript expressions. However, symbolic dependence analysis indicates that no self-dependence is imposed by statement s_2. Therefore the loop can be parallelized.

In the loop of Figure 18, suppose that m1 and n are not constants. Even if statement forward substitution is used to substitute m1-n for all occurrences of m2 in statement s_1, classical dependence tests can not be applied because of existence of unknown symbolic term m1 in the subscript expressions, and because the loop upper bounds are unknown. However, as far as the given loop nest is concerned, all the references to variables m1 and m2 refer to the same instances of those variables, a condition easily recognizable by symbolic testing. Hence, the relation m2 = m1-n holds in the loop iteration space. Note that i1 $\geq$ 1 in the loop iteration space, therefore m1+i1 > m1. We also have m2+i2 = m1-n+i2 $\leq$

```
    m2 := m1-n
    do i1 := 1, n
        do i2 := 1, n
          s₁: A[i1+m1] := A[i1+m1]+B[i2,i1]*A[i2+m2]
        enddo
    enddo
```

Figure 18: Example from a block tridiagonal solver.

m1, because i2 $\leq$ n. Hence, there is no dependence due to subscript expressions m1+i1 and m2+i2. Therefore, the outer loop can run in parallel, while the inner loop forms a recurrence.

```
mp1 := m+1
do i1 := mp1, n
    do i2 := 1, m
        s₁: A[C[k]+i2] := A[C[k]+i2]+B[i2,i1]*A[c[k]-m+i2]
    enddo
enddo
```

Figure 19: A subscripted subscript case from a block tridiagonal solver.

A similar analysis can be used for some of the cases with subscripted subscript expressions. For example consider the loop of Figure 19. Classical optimization techniques can not eliminate the unknown symbolic expression C[k], and the unknown symbolic term m from subscript expressions. Also, the unknown symbolic terms m and n can not be eliminated from loop bounds by those techniques. However, as far as that loop nest is concerned, the relation mp1 = m+1 holds in the loop iteration space, and C[k] is also loop invariant. Note that i2 $\geq$ 1 in the loop iteration space, therefore C[k]+i2 > C[k]. Also, we have C[k]-m+i2 $\leq$ C[k], because i2 $\leq$ m. Hence, there is no dependence due to subscript expressions C[k]+i2 and C[k]-m+i2. Therefore, the outer loop can run in parallel, while the inner loop forms a recurrence.

Loop of Figure 20 often results from blocking a loop, then unrolling the inner loop [13]. Note that n2 and n3 are computed outside of the loop to avoid redundant computations. This can also be the result of *code motion*. Code motion is an optimization technique that takes an expression that yields the same result independent of the number of times a loop is executed (a *loop-invariant computation*) and places the expression before the loop [1]. If n is not a constant, even if statement forward substitution is used, classical dependence tests can not come up with any decision about dependence relations of statements s_1, s_2, and s_3. However, symbolic dependence analysis indicates that it is not possible that two of these three statements access the same memory location unless n=0. In such a case, the loop will not be executed at all, because n is the loop upper bound, and the loop lower bound is 1. Therefore there is no dependence relation between s_1, s_2, and s_3. Hence, the loop can run in parallel.

The framework we described in this thesis, resolves all the cases we discussed in this section. Implementation of this framework in Parafrase-2 is underway.

4 Conclusion

Dependence analysis is the key for effective vectorizing and parallelizing compilers for supercomputers. Our measurements show that a significant number of array references inside program loops contain unknown symbolic terms. We also noticed that the majority of loops have symbolic bounds. Classical data dependence tests require that index variable

```
n2 := n*2
n3 := n*3
do i := 1, n
  s₁: A[i+n]  := ...
  s₂: A[i+n2] := ...
  s₃: A[i+n3] := ...
enddo
```

Figure 20: Example of loop blocking and urolling with code motion.

coefficients in subscript expressions be known at compile time. Hence, more sophisticated, and yet efficient symbolic dependence analysis is necessary to handle cases where unknown symbolic terms are involved. We introduced a framework to solve the dependence problem in the presence of unknown symbolic terms. This framework creates an environment in which a significant number of constraints between program variables, at each point of the program, is known at compile time. Classical data dependence tests can then be applied in this environment. If these tests can not come up with dependence decision due to lack of information, or because of imprecise approximation (introduced by approximate semantic analysis), they can generate conditions that can be used for multiversion code generation. Procedures, by their very nature, tend to hide information. This information may be necessary for dependence analysis. Our framework can be extended to incorporate interprocedural information. The same idea can also be used to do dependence analysis in the presence of pointers.

Acknowledgements

This work was supported in part by the National Science Foundation under Grant No. NSF-CCR-89-57310, the U. S. Department of Energy under Grant No. DOE-DE-FG02-85ER25001, AT&T-AFFL-71-POLYCH, and Digital Equipment Corporation.

References

[1] A. V. Aho, R. Sethi, and J. D. Ullman. *Compilers : Principles, Techniques and Tools*. Addison Wesley, March 1986.

[2] F. E. Allen and J. Cocke. A catalogue of optimizing transformations. In R. Rustin, editor, *Design and Optimization of Compilers*, pages 1–30. Prentice-Hall, Englewood Cliffs, New Jersey, 1972.

[3] J. R. Allen and K. Kennedy. Automatic loop interchange. In *Conference Proceedings - The SIGPLAN '84 Symposium on Compiler Construction*, volume 19(6), pages 233–246, Montreal, Canada, June 17-22 1984.

[4] J. R. Allen, K. Kennedy, C. Proterfield, and J. Warren. Conversion of control dependence to data dependence. In *Proceedings of the 10th Annual ACM Symposium on Principles of Programming Languages*, pages 177–189, Austin, Texas, January 24-26 1983.

[5] R. Allen. *Dependence analysis for subscripted variables and its application to program transformations*. PhD thesis, Rice University, Houston, Texas, April 1983.

[6] R. Allen and K. Kennedy. Automatic translation of FORTRAN programs to vector form. *ACM Transactions on Programming Languages and Systems*, 9(4), October 1987.

[7] U. Banerjee. Data dependence in ordinary programs. Master's thesis, Department of Computer Science, University of Illinois at Urbana-Champaign, Urbana, Illinois, November 1976.

[8] U. Banerjee. *Speedup of Ordinary Programs*. PhD thesis, Department of Computer Science, University of Illinois at Urbana-Champaign, Urbana, Illinois, October 1979.

[9] U. Banerjee. *Dependence Analysis for Supercomputing*. Kluwer Academic Publishers, 1988.

[10] U. Banerjee, S. C. Chen, D. J. Kuck, and R. A. Towle. Time and parallel processor bounds for fortran-like loops. *IEEE Trans. on Computers*, C-28(9):660–670, September 1979.

[11] C. S. Beckman-Davies. Improving parallelism in linpack. Technical Report UIUCDCS-R-83-1138, Dept. of Computer Science, UIUC, Urbana, Illinois 61801, May 1983.

[12] M. Burke and R. Cytron. Interprocedural dependence analysis and parallelization. In *Conference Proceedings - The SIGPLAN '86 Symposium on Compiler Construction*, volume 21(7), pages 162–175, Palo Alto, California, June 25-27 1986.

[13] D. Callahan, J. Cocke, and K. Kennedy. Estimating interlock and improving balance for pipelined architectures. In *Proceedings of the 1987 International Conference on Parallel Processing*, pages 295–304, St. Charles, IL, August 1987.

[14] P. Cousot and N. Halbwachs. Automatic discovery of linear restraints among variables of a program. In *Proceedings of the 5th Annual ACM Symposium on Principles of Programming Languages*, pages 84–97, Tucson, AZ, January 1978.

[15] M. R. Haghighat. Symbolic dependence analysis for high performance parallelizing compilers. Master's thesis, Department of Computer Science, University of Illinois at Urbana-Champaign, Urbana, Illinois, 1990.

[16] M. S. Hecht. *Flow Analysis of Computer Programs*. Elsevier North-Holland, 1977.

[17] K. Kennedy. Automatic vectorization of fortran programs to vector form. Technical report, Rice University, Houston, TX, October 1980.

[18] D. J. Kuck. *The Structure of Computers and Computations, Volume I*. John Wiley and Sons, New York, 1978.

[19] R. H. Kuhn. *Optimization and Interconnection Complexity for: Parallel Processors, Single-Stage Networks, and Decision Trees*. PhD thesis, Department of Computer Science, University of Illinois at Urbana-Champaign, Urbana, Illinois, February 1980.

[20] L. Lamport. The parallel execution of DO loops. *Communications of the Association for Computing Machinery*, 17(2):83–93, February 1974.

[21] B. P. Leung. Issues on the design of parallelizing compilers. Master's thesis, Department of Computer Science, University of Illinois at Urbana-Champaign, Urbana, Illinois, 1990.

[22] A. Lichnewsky and F. Thomasset. Introducing symbolic problem solving techniques in the dependence testing phases of a vectorizer. In *Supercomputing 88*. IEEE Computer Society Press, July 1988.

[23] D. A. Padua and M. Wolfe. Advanced compiler optimizations for supercomputers. *Communications of the ACM*, 29(12):1184–1201, December 1986.

[24] C. D. Polychronopoulos. *On Program Restructuring, Scheduling and Communication for Parallel Processor Systems*. PhD thesis, University of Illinois, August 1986.

[25] C. D. Polychronopoulos, M. B. Girkar, M. R. Haghighat, C. L. Lee, B. Leung, and D. A. Schouten. Parafrase-2: An environment for parallelizing, partitioning, synchronizing and scheduling programs on multiprocessors. In *Proceedings of the 1989 International Conference on Parallel Processing*, St. Charles, IL, August 1989. Penn State.

[26] Z. Shen, Z. Li, and P. C. Yew. An empirical study on array subscripts and data dependences. In *Proceedings of the 1989 International Conference on Parallel Processing*, volume II, pages 145–152, St. Charles, IL, August 1989.

[27] M. J Wolfe. *Optimizing Supercompilers for Supercomputers*. The MIT Press, Cambridge, MA, 1989.

[28] M. J. Wolfe and U. Banerjee. Data dependence and its application to parallel processing. *International Journal of Parallel Programming*, 16(2):137–178, April 1987.

17 Parallelism in Numeric and Symbolic Programs
J. R. Larus

Abstract

This paper explains a new technique for estimating and understanding the speed improvement from executing programs on a parallel computer. This approach traces a sequential program to record a small set of significant events. From this compact trace, a parallelism analyzer (`llpp`) regenerates a full address trace that also identifies events such as loop initiation and termination. The analyzer uses this information to simulate parallel execution of the program's loops.

In addition to predicting parallel performance, `llpp` measures many aspects of a program's dynamic behavior. This paper presents measurements of six substantial C programs. These results indicate that the three symbolic (non-numeric) programs differ substantially from the numeric programs and, as a consequence, cannot be parallelized automatically with the same compilation techniques.

1 Introduction

Programmers often want to know whether a program would benefit from parallel execution. One way to answer this question is to write a parallel version of the program and run it on a parallel computer. This approach has several disadvantages. First, it requires a parallel program. Writing such a program, or even modifying a sequential program to run concurrently, may require considerable effort. Similarly, compiler writers need to know whether a large class of programs (e.g., Fortran or C programs) could benefit from parallel execution—before they write a restructuring compiler. Again, this information is difficult to collect without actually writing the compiler.

Another disadvantage of the traditional approach is that the speed of a program on a parallel computer says little about the program's inherent parallelism. Implementation details may hobble the program's performance. Errors of this kind are difficult to detect and correct because the program functions correctly. A programmer needs detailed information about loop speedups and data dependences to identify portions of the program that fail to take proper advantage of parallelism. Few tools provide this information.

This paper presents a simple, mechanizable technique for estimating a program's speed improvement on a parallel computer and for understanding limits on its performance. The technique requires no additional programming and minimal effort by a programmer. A modified compiler adds tracing code to the sequential program to record a small set of significant events. When the program runs, it produces a compact trace file that serves as input to an analyzer (`llpp`), which determines the potential speedup of the program. The process uses an innovative technique to reduce the cost of tracing and the size of the trace file, which permits long executions to be economically measured. `llpp` also measures and reports many characteristics of the program—for example, the dynamic size of loop bodies, number of loop iterations, and number and type of loop-carried data dependences—that form a basis for improving parallel execution.

This paper contains measurements of six substantial C programs. Three are non-numeric symbolic applications and two are array-manipulating (numeric) programs. The sixth is an optimization program that performs many floating point operations, but manipulates a graph data structure. Its behavior falls between the two groups and it can be classified as a numeric symbolic application. The measurements clearly demonstrate that the array-manipulating programs are very different from the other programs in two ways: the number and size of loop iterations and the quantity and quality of loop-carried data dependences. The differences prevent Fortran-style compilation techniques from producing parallel symbolic programs.

Needless to say, the technique has limitations. Since the analysis is driven by a program trace, it reflects a particular execution of a program and does not necessarily predict the program's performance with other input data. Of course, empirical speedup measurements share this problem. Also, the analysis currently looks for parallelism between loop iterations and assumes an idealized parallel computer with a unbounded number of processors and no-cost synchronization. If desirable, the analyzer easily could be modified to make the execution model more realistic. However, the current assumptions ensure that the estimated parallelism is a upper bound on the program's performance on a real computer. Finally, and perhaps most significantly, the analysis currently does not account for the potential benefits of optimizations that a compiler or a programmer could use to increase the program's parallelism. However, `llpp` could estimate these benefits by ignoring some of the data dependences in the program under the assumption that an optimization eliminated them.

This paper contains four sections. The next section briefly discusses related work. Section 3 describes the model of parallel execution. Section 4 shows how `llpp` analyzes a program's parallelism. Finally, Section 5 presents some measurements of C programs. The appendix explains the technique for tracing a program.

2 Related Work

Several lines of research are related to this work. Sarkar directly measured the execution frequency of basic blocks and used the results to estimate the execution cost of portions of a program. The PTRAN parallel compiler uses this information to partition the program for parallel execution [9]. Unlike PTRAN, llpp does not estimate a program's execution cost or produce a parallel program. Instead, it measures the program's actual cost—and other features such as its memory reference pattern—and uses this data to estimate how the program would execute on a parallel computer.

Several groups have built tools for tracing parallel programs. TRAPEDS is a system that traces the memory reference pattern of programs running on a parallel computer [12]. MPTrace produces address traces of programs running on shared-memory multiprocessors [3]. Both systems capture the memory reference behavior of an existing parallel program. Unlike llpp, they do not record program structures (such as loops) that would permit them to simulate a program's behavior on other computers. Also, llpp's tracing mechanism is more efficient than either system's, which permits tracing of longer program executions.

The Rice Parallel Processing Testbed (RPPT) has goals similar to llpp's [1]. This system measures a parallel program and uses the resulting trace to drive a simulator of a parallel computer. The major differences are that RPPT requires the original program to be written for a parallel machine and permits a programmer to investigate changes to the architecture of the computer and the assignment of processes and data to processors. llpp has a more static model of the target computer but captures more information about the program. This detail permits llpp to simulate the program's execution under a variety of models.

Nicolau and Fischer used a technique similar to llpp's to estimate the instruction-level parallelism available to a VLIW computer [8]. They ran their programs on a detailed simulator of a hypothetical computer, which limited the size and duration of the programs. They also sought a much finer grain of parallelism and did not attempt to characterize the behavior or dependences in the programs.

Kumar studied the parallel execution of Fortran programs with aims similar to this research, but a different technique [5]. His COMET system modifies Fortran programs so they dynamically calculate the earliest time at which a statement can execute while satisfying its control and flow dependences. The modified program produces a histogram of the number of concurrently-executing statements. COMET, unlike llpp, assumes all statements execute in unit time and ignores anti- and output dependences. COMET presumes a fine-grain, almost dataflow, granularity of parallelism, rather than the loop-level parallelism sought by llpp. COMET also does not collect information about the program's structure and behavior.

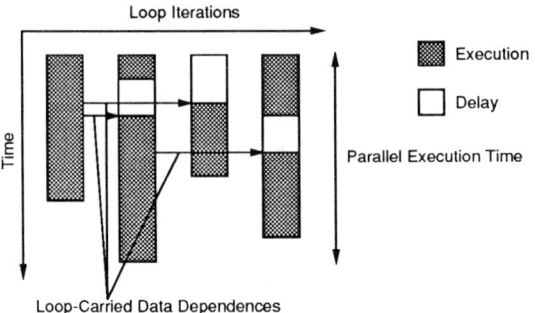

Figure 1: *Doacross* scheduling of parallel loop execution. All iterations of a loop begin execution simultaneously. Loop-carried data dependences are synchronized by delaying a conflicting statement in a later iteration until an earlier statement accesses a common memory location. The loop finishes when the iteration with the longest combined delay and execution time completes.

3 Parallel Execution Model

This paper concentrates exclusively on parallel loop execution and ignores other opportunities for parallelism.[1] The idealized execution model used by llpp assumes a unbounded number of parallel processors that communicate and synchronize at no cost through a shared memory. Each loop iteration runs on a separate processor. A loop's iterations begin simultaneously when the loop starts executing. Synchronization introduces delays to serialize loop-carried data dependences. If statement S_1 conflicts with statement S_2 in a later iteration, then synchronization delays the memory reference in S_2 until S_1 reads or writes the common memory location. A loop terminates when all iterations complete, so its parallel speedup is the ratio of time to execute the loop sequentially to the time spent in the iteration with the longest combined delay and execution time. Figure 1 illustrates this model, which is Cytron's *doacross* scheduling [2].

4 Analyzing Parallelism

AE is a system that economically collects detailed traces of a program's execution (see Appendix A). We can use the traces collected by AE to simulate a program's execution on a parallel machine. The parallelism analyzer (llpp) receives a stream of events from the trace regeneration program. These events indicate: an instruction execution (with its address); a read or write of a memory location (with its address); the initiation, iteration, and termination of a loop (with a unique loop identifier); or entry and exit of a function (with its address).

llpp simulates the parallel execution of a program's loops with the aid of two data structures: the loop nest and conflict table. The *loop nest* is a stack of *loop descriptors* (top half of Figure 2). This stack contains a descriptor for every uncompleted loop. When

---

[1]However, the framework described below can accommodate other parallel execution strategies—for example, fine-grained data flow—by modifying the analyzer described in Section 4.

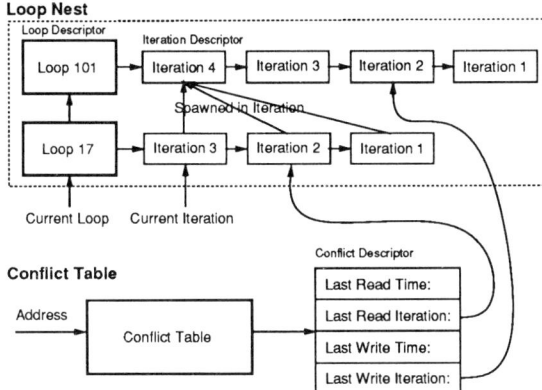

Figure 2: llpp's loop nest and conflict table data structures. The loop nest keeps track of loop nesting and iterations. The table maps a memory address to a conflict descriptor, which records when the address was last read and written.

a loop begins, a new descriptor is pushed onto the nest. When a loop terminates, its descriptor is popped. Each loop descriptor points to a stack of *iteration descriptors*. When the top loop begins a new iteration, a new iteration descriptor is pushed on its stack. When the loop terminates, its iteration descriptors may not be deallocated since the conflict table can contain references to them. Iteration descriptors record the nesting of loops by maintaining a pointer to the iteration of the surrounding loop.

llpp's other data structure is the *conflict table*, which is a hash table that maps a memory address into a *conflict descriptor* (bottom half of Figure 2). These descriptors record when a memory location was last read and written. They contain both the time of the access and the iteration descriptor of the innermost loop surrounding the statement that referenced the location. On each access to a memory location, llpp compares the values stored in the location's descriptor against the current time and loop to detect loop-carried data dependences.[2]

For example, consider detecting loop-carried flow dependences. On a read of a memory location, llpp examines the loop iterations in which the location was last modified. If the location was written in a different iteration than the one currently executing, the loop containing both iterations has a loop-carried flow dependence. When a conflict occurs, llpp uses the access times to calculate the delay necessary to ensure that the location is not read until after it is written.

The algorithm for finding loop-carried data dependences is:

---

[2] The idea is analogous to the abstract interpretation used by Horwitz, Pfieffer, and Reps to detect data dependences in pointer-manipulating programs [4]. However, their technique is applied by a compiler to the static text of the program to determine potential—not actual—dependences.

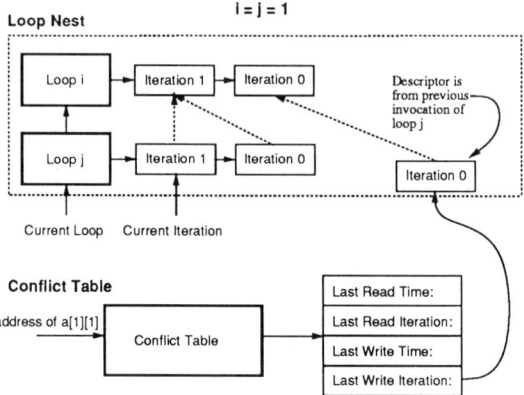

Figure 3: Example of detecting a loop-carried flow dependence.

On a read of memory location M:
1. Record read time and iteration.
2. Find the loop in the nest, L, that is the least-common ancestor of the current iteration and the last write iteration.
3. If the read and write occur in different iterations of L, then record a Flow Dependence.

On a write to memory location M:
1. Record write time and iteration.
2. Find the loop, L, that is the least-common ancestor of current iteration and last read iteration.
3. If the read and write occur in different iterations of L, then record an Anti-Dependence.
4. Find the loop, L, that is the least-common ancestor of current iteration and last write iteration.
5. If the writes occur in different iterations of L, then record an Output Dependence.
6. Remove record of read of location.

To make this discussion more concrete, consider the loops:

```
for (i = 0; i < 100; i = i + 1)
    for (j = 0; j < 100; j = j + 1)
        a[i+1][j+1] = a[i][j];
```

Both have loop-carried flow dependences. For example, when $i = j = 1$, the location read (a[1][1]) was written in the previous iteration of the outer loop. The iteration descriptor for this loop is still in the loop nest (see Figure 3). The iteration descriptor for the j

sgefa	Number of Dependences (% of Memory References)							
	Flow		Anti		Panti		Output	
regs	1,012,253	(28.7%)	23,893	(0.7%)	688,341	(19.5%)	957,253	(27.1%)
no regs	3,756,769	(31.0%)	1,079,983	(8.9%)	2,906,008	(23.8%)	3,283,637	(27.1%)

Table 1: Frequency of loop-carried data dependences with and without registers.

loop is not on the stack since the first invocation of that loop has finished. However, the descriptor persists since it is referenced by the conflict descriptor for the array location. Since the outer loop is the least-common ancestor of both accesses and the read and write occur in different iterations, the loop has a loop-carried flow dependence.

This technique detects all loop-carried flow and output data dependences, but only a subset of the anti-dependences. Conflict descriptors record only the last read of a location, not all reads since the last modification. Therefore, they cannot detect anti-dependences between the earlier reads and a write. However, by counting reads since the previous write to a location, we can compute a upper bound to the number of anti-dependences—called *panti-dependences* for potential anti-dependences. This bound can be conservative since some of the reads may occur outside of a loop and therefore not cause a loop-carried anti-dependence. In computing the delays, llpp uses anti- (not panti-) dependences.

Another problem is that llpp does not detect dependences carried by variables stored in registers since references to them do not appear in the address trace. This problem is less important for anti- and output dependences, which can be eliminated by renaming variables. As an experiment, the program *sgefa* (see Section 5) was compiled without registers, but with optimization still enabled. Table 1 shows the number of dependences and the proportion of memory references that cause a dependence. Allocating variables on the program stack greatly increased the number of memory references and dependences. The proportion of flow and output dependences did not change appreciably, although anti-dependences increased in frequency ten times. It is a hypothesis that most additional conflicts involved loop indices. In the measurements below, variables are register-allocated because the speedup is extremely limited by variable conflicts. A compiler for a parallel machine can precisely analyze scalar variable-carried dependences and eliminate most conflicts—in particular, those involving loop indices—without much effort.

llpp does not find spurious dependences caused by reuse of locations on the program stack. This problem arises when a loop repeatedly invokes a function. Stack locations referenced in the first invocation will likely be used by subsequent invocations. They will cause dependences that would not occur if the calls used separate stacks—as they would on a parallel computer. llpp avoids this problem by removing all stack locations referenced by a function from the conflict table when the function terminates. llpp avoids spurious dependences in dynamically-allocated storage by the same technique. When a block of storage is freed, llpp clears the conflict descriptors for all locations in the block.

llpp uses the cycle count of the executed instructions as a measure of time. Most instructions take 1 *tick*, except loads, which require 2 ticks, and some floating point operations, which require up to 20 ticks. The times are from the MIPS R2000 and are similar for most RISC computers. However, the numbers ignore the effect of cache misses on loads and stores.

Program	Purpose	Size (lines)	Time (ticks)	# Loops
gcc	C compiler	87,838	24,522,714	1139
xlisp	Lisp interpreter	7,741	20,220,999	126
espresso	PLA minimization	14,838	30,794,533	750
sgefa	Gaussian elimination	1,219	18,255,659	73
dcgc	Conjugate gradient	1,060	19,295,194	55
costScale	Feasible flows in networks	2,128	79,998,720	50

Table 2: Characteristics of the test programs.

When a loop terminates, llpp examines each iteration descriptor to find the iteration that finished last. In addition, llpp records a wealth of information about the loop, such as how many times it executed, the cost of each iteration, and the number and distance of the loop-carried dependences.

A loop's *speedup* is the ratio of its sequential to parallel execution time. This definition has a unusual aspect. If an inner loop has a large speedup, it will reduce the parallel execution time of every iteration of the surrounding loop, thereby permitting that loop's speedup to exceed the number of its iterations. A program's speedup can be estimated from its loop speedups. Since loops nest, llpp cannot simply add the parallel execution times to compute the program's cost. This cost is the sum of the cost of the top-level (non-nested) loops and the top-level non-looping code.

This analysis is not particularly expensive. On a DECstation 3100 (a 14 MIPS computer), llpp analyzes about 80,000 simulated ticks per second of DECstation time (175 times slower). A slightly more serious problem is the memory cost of llpp's data structures. Their size is proportional to the number of referenced locations and the number of iterations in loops. With virtual memory and large physical memories, this overhead is not exorbitant, although it clearly limits llpp's ability to analyze extremely large programs.

Several schemes could reduce both costs. First, many memory references are irrelevant to parallelism analysis since they correspond to memory accesses that cannot cause loop-carried dependences. These references can be eliminated from the schema file. Another possibility is to group together several locations (e.g., by truncating the low-order bits of the address). However, neither technique has yet proven necessary.

5 Measurements of C Programs

This section presents measurements of six C programs. Three are symbolic applications that perform few floating-point operations: *gcc*, *xlisp*, and *espresso*. *gcc* is the GNU C compiler optimizing and compiling a 775-line file. *xlisp* is a lisp interpreter running a program that solves the 5-queens problem. *espresso* is a PLA minimization program running on a 7-input, 10-output PLA. These programs form most of the integer portion of the SPEC benchmark suite [10]. The other three programs perform numeric computations: *sgefa*, *dcgc*, *costScale*. *sgefa* is a gaussian elimination program running a variety of test cases. *dcgc* is a preconditioned conjugate gradient package running a variety of test cases. *costScale* finds a feasible flow in a network that minimizes a linear cost function. Although

Program	Sequential/Parallel Time (Speedup)
gcc	2.5
xlisp	1.4
espresso	4.5
sgefa	106.3
dcgc	259.4
costScale	5.0

Table 3: Calculated speedup for the test programs.

it performs many floating-point operations, it uses data structures similar to those in symbolic programs. The programs range in size from a thousand to a hundred thousand lines. Table 2 characterizes the programs in more detail.

Table 3 contains the ratio of the programs' sequential to parallel execution times—the speedup—calculated by llpp. Although llpp's parallel execution model is optimistic, only the two numeric programs that manipulated arrays (*sgefa* and *dcgc*) significantly benefited from parallelism. The discussion below shows that this difference is the consequence of fundamental differences in program structure and data usage.

Figure 4 shows the distribution of loop speedups in the programs. Most loop invocations (58%–93%) in the two numeric programs have a speedup of 50 or more. Almost all symbolic loops (90–95%) have a speedup of 10 or less and almost no invocations ($< 0.25\%$) have a speedup of 100 or more. In addition, in numeric programs, large speed improvements occurred in fairly expensive loops and consequently caused a large reduction in total time. In symbolic programs, large speedups occurred in less expensive loops, which did not have much effect on the programs' total cost.

Two factors limit a loop's speedup in the *doacross* model: the number of iterations and the frequency and distance of loop-carried data dependences. Figure 5 shows the number of iterations per loop invocation. The figure again illustrates a difference between numeric and symbolic programs. Numeric loops iterate many times. Symbolic loops generally iterate 10 or fewer times, which limits their potential speedup. A possible objection to these measurements is that the number of iterations is proportional to the size of the problem and that with different input, symbolic programs would iterate more times. However, the inputs were chosen so all programs executed for roughly the same time. Increasing the problem size would also benefit numeric programs. In addition, simply increasing the length of the input to programs such as *gcc* and *xlisp* would not cause most loops to iterate more times, unless the input also changed qualitatively.

Another way to compare loops is to examine their sequential execution cost. Loops that execute few instructions—even if they iterate many times—have little potential for parallel execution, particularly on real computers in which initiating a parallel task has non-trivial overhead. In addition, large speedups on these loops have little effect on the overall program cost. Figure 6 shows the sequential time per loop invocation. Most loops in symbolic programs (70–90%) execute in fewer than 100 ticks. By contrast, only 1–3% of the loops in numeric programs (including *costScale*) executed in fewer than 100 ticks.

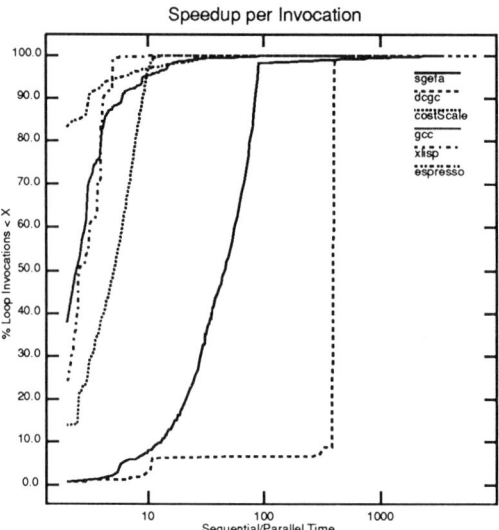

Figure 4: Distribution of loop speedups. This graph shows the percentage of loop invocations in each program that had a speedup less than the x-value.

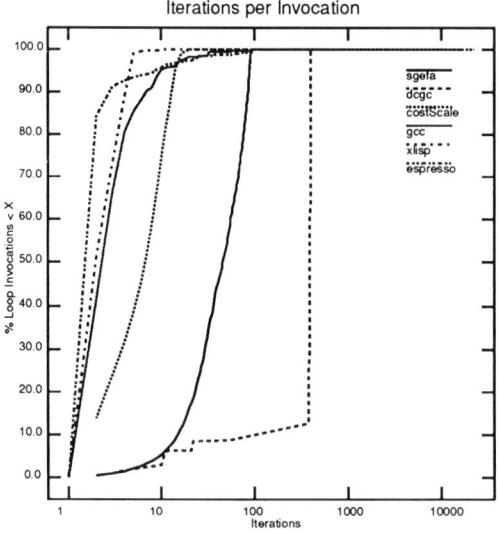

Figure 5: Distribution of iterations.

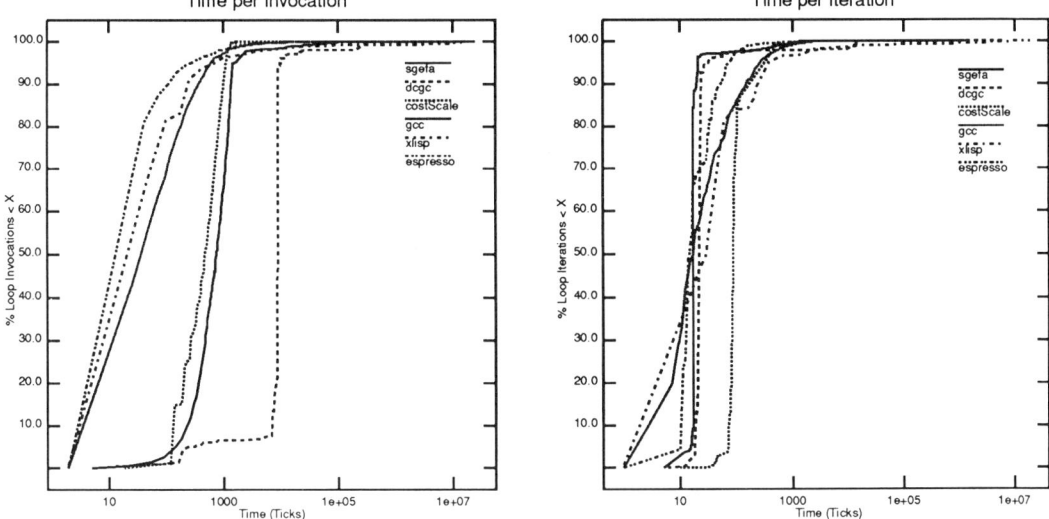

Figure 6: Sequential execution cost of loops.

Most loops in these programs execute in 500–10,000 ticks. However, the situation changes when we examine the cost per iteration (not invocation). Figure 6 shows that iterations in both symbolic and numeric programs typically execute in 10–100 ticks. *dgcg* and *sgefa* appear to have particularly short iterations. The difference in invocation costs is primarily due to the number of iterations per invocation. However, the symbolic programs also have a significant number of iterations (40%) that execute in fewer than 10 instructions. The long tails on the distributions are due to programs' top-level loops, which encompass most of their computation.

Another difference is the variance in both the cost and number of loop iterations. Table 4 shows the variance in the time and number of iterations per loop invocation. The first column is the sum of the coefficient of variation for each loop. The second column contains the sum weighted by each loop's contribution to the program's execution time. Unweighted variance is a better metric since the weighted numbers can be dominated by an outer loop, which may be invoked once and have no variance. The unweighted variances of symbolic programs (except *xlisp*) are much larger than those of the numeric programs. In addition, in the symbolic (but not numeric) programs, the time variance is larger than the variance in the number of iterations. These programs are performing different actions, which require different amounts of time, in each iteration.

The other constraint on a program's speedup is the data dependences that inhibit concurrent execution of loops. Figure 7 illustrates the number of loop-carried flow dependences per loop iteration. In numeric programs, 97% of loop iterations incur no loop-carried flow dependences and most other iterations have only one dependence. *costScale* is different since almost all iterations have exactly two flow dependences. In symbolic programs, more iterations have one flow dependence, although few have more than 5 such dependences. The distance of loop-carried dependences also limits a loop's speedup. Figure 7 also illustrates the distances of the loop-carried flow dependences. The difference between numeric

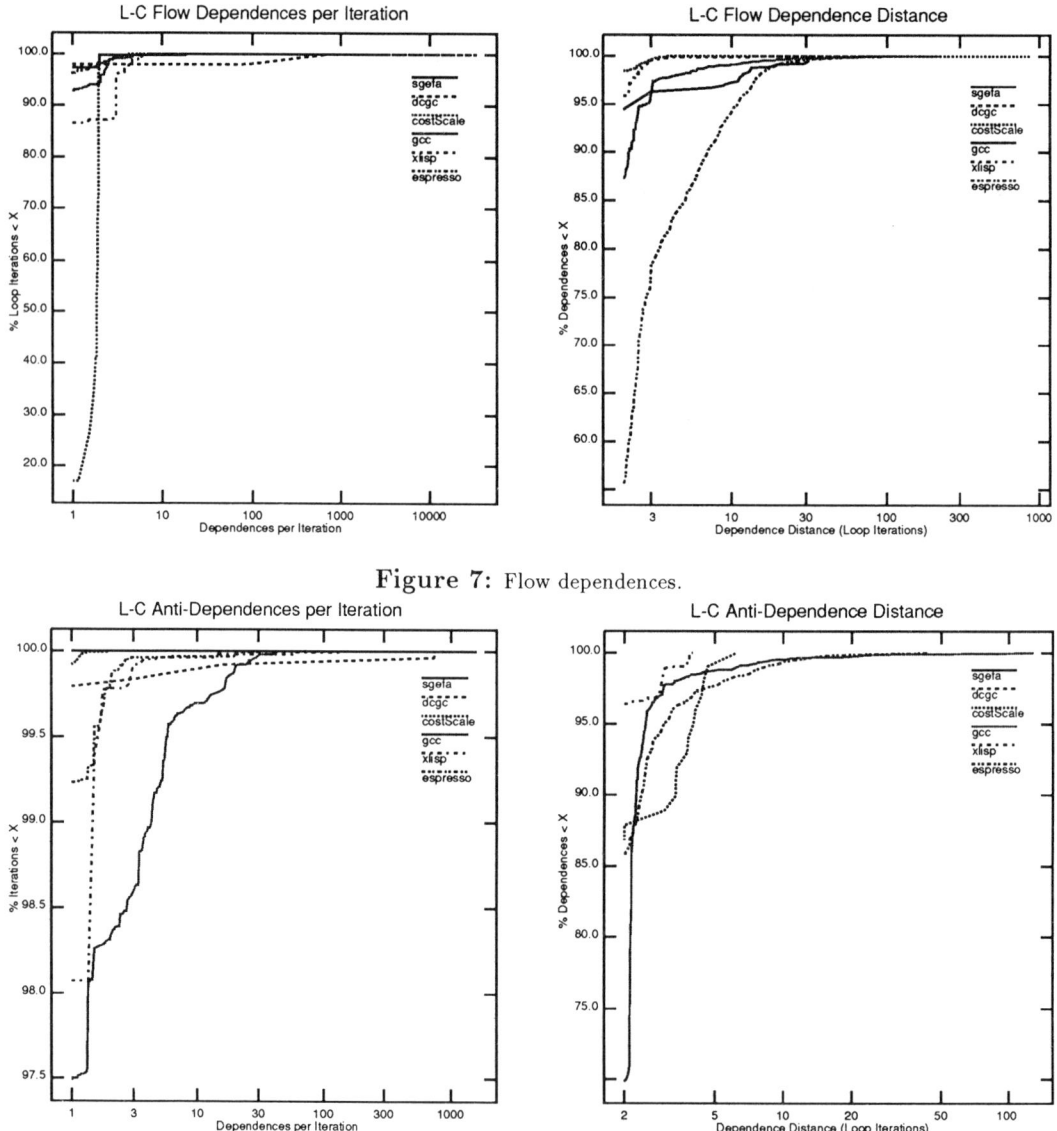

Figure 7: Flow dependences.

Figure 8: Anti-dependences.

		Sum of Per-Loop Coefficient of Variances	
Program		Unweighted	Weighted
gcc	Time	274.8	0.9
	Iterations	183.0	1.1
xlisp	Time	16.8	1.3
	Iterations	19.2	323.8
espresso	Time	111.7	0.9
	Iterations	101.7	1.8
sgefa	Time	13.4	0.5
	Iterations	18.9	1.6
dcgc	Time	14.1	0.2
	Iterations	17.0	1.2
costScale	Time	2.3	0.4
	Iterations	2.7	0.8

Table 4: Variance in execution time and the number of iterations per loop invocation.

Program	Number of Dependences (% of Memory References)							
	Flow		Anti		Panti		Output	
gcc	822,503	(11.4%)	124,202	(1.7%)	1,245,036	(17.3%)	460,732	(6.4%)
xlisp	461,156	(6.5%)	17,987	(0.3%)	181,166	(2.6%)	299,282	(4.2%)
espresso	544,205	(7.4%)	99,151	(1.4%)	515,655	(7.0%)	519,029	(7.1%)
sgefa	1,012,253	(28.7%)	23,893	(0.7%)	688,341	(19.5%)	957,253	(27.1%)
dcgc	1,148,072	(17.8%)	22,550	(0.3%)	45,102	(0.7%)	774,227	(12.0%)
costScale	5,658,096	(23.1%)	129,727	(0.5%)	204,531	(0.8%)	2,341,341	(9.6%)

Table 5: Frequency of loop-carried data dependences.

and symbolic programs is not as clear for this measure. Numeric programs have a higher percentage of flow dependences of distance one (for example, all of *dcgc*'s dependences). However, *sgefa* has more dependences of distance ten or more than any program except *espresso*.

The distances in *espresso* are very different from those in other programs. This program has more dependences of all types and these dependences extend over many loop iterations. Most of *espresso*'s time is spent sorting arrays with a quicksort algorithm. The conflicts arise as values move between array locations in a data-dependent pattern.

Figure 8 illustrates that anti-dependences are less common than flow dependences and are extremely uncommon in numeric programs. They also extend over a smaller number of iterations. Both differences may be artifacts of recording only the last read of a location. Figure 9 shows that output dependences are almost as frequent as flow dependences. However, unlike flow dependences, output dependences almost always have a distance of one (again excepting *espresso*).

Loop-carried data dependences, although they occur in few loop iterations, occur on a high percentage of memory references. Table 5 shows the frequency of loop-carried dependences and the percentage of memory references that result in a loop-carried dependence. Flow dependences are the most common, followed by output dependences, and by anti-

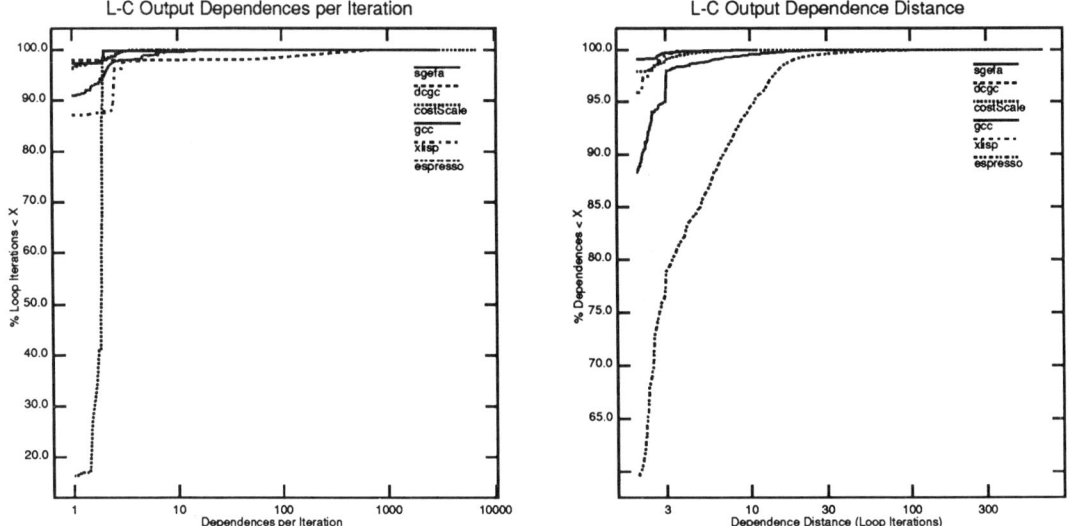

Figure 9: Output dependences.

	Percent of Conflicts					
	gcc	xlisp	espresso	sgefa	dcgc	costScale
Flow						
Heap Static	10.5	33.2	0.5	0.0	0.0	0.0
Heap Dynamic	78.0	50.8	98.1	100.0	100.0	100.0
Stack	11.5	16.0	1.4	0.0	0.0	0.0
Heap Array/Struct	77.6	50.8	60.4	5.7	0.0	99.8
Heap Variable/Pointer	11.0	33.2	38.3	94.3	100.0	0.0
Stack Array/Struct	9.0	10.5	0.3	0.0	0.0	0.0
Stack Variable/Pointer	2.6	5.5	1.1	0.0	0.0	0.2
Anti						
Heap Static	51.2	89.5	97.2	99.6	100.0	100.0
Heap Dynamic	0.00	0.0	0.0	0.0	0.0	0.0
Stack	48.8	10.5	2.8	0.4	0.0	0.0
Heap Array/Struct	38.1	89.1	76.3	0.0	0.0	100.0
Heap Variable/Pointer	13.2	0.4	20.9	99.6	99.7	0.0
Stack Array/Struct	18.1	0.9	0.0	0.3	0.0	0.0
Stack Variable/Pointer	30.6	9.6	2.9	0.1	0.3	0.0
Output						
Heap Static	50.1	74.3	98.4	100.0	100.0	100.0
Heap Dynamic	0.0	0.0	0.0	0.0	0.0	0.0
Stack	49.9	25.7	1.6	0.0	0.0	0.0%
Heap Array/Struct	35.8	28.3	73.3	5.0	0.0	99.8
Heap Variable/Pointer	14.4	46.0	25.0	95.0	100.0	0.0
Stack Array/Struct	28.7	17.3	0.3	0.0	0.0	0.0
Stack Variable/Pointer	21.2	8.4	1.3	0.0	0.0	0.2

Table 6: Breakdown of loop-carried data dependences.

dependences. However, the difference narrows when panti- dependences (see Section 4) are considered. Flow and output dependences are far more common in numeric than symbolic programs. Anti-dependences are relatively more common in symbolic programs. Since the proportion of conflicting memory references is higher than the proportion of loop iterations that contain a conflict, conflicts are not evenly distributed among loop iterations, but tend to cluster so a few iterations contain most of them.

Table 6 categorizes loop-carried dependences by the referenced object's type and the form of the reference. The first three entries for each dependence identify the referenced object. *Heap static* objects are global data whose size is known to the compiler. *Heap dynamic* objects are allocated by `malloc`. *Stack* objects are variables, structures, and arrays local to a procedure that are stack allocated. The next four entries classify the type of memory reference in the second-executed statement in a conflict. *Heap array/struct* are references to data structures or arrays that residing in the heap (both dynamically and statically allocated). *Heap variable/pointer* are references to scalar variables or references through a C pointer. The first category may not include all references to arrays since *gcc* does not determine that a pointer accesses an array. *Stack array/struct* and *stack variable/pointer* are similar, except that the objects reside on the stack.

Different programming styles cause conflicts to appear in different places in the programs. Typically, flow dependences are centered in dynamically-allocated objects, which, curiously, never cause anti- or output dependences. Unfortunately, data dependence analysis for dynamically-allocated objects (in particular, structures) is more complex and less precise than array analysis [6]. In symbolic programs (except *espresso*), the anti- and output dependences are divided between static and stack objects. In the numeric programs and *espresso*, almost all of these dependences are due to static objects.

The program statements causing conflicts also vary among the programs. In numeric programs (except *costScale*), most conflicting references are *heap pointer*, which implies that *gcc*'s analysis could not determine that the reference object was an array. In the symbolic programs, a wider variety of statements cause the conflicts. However, the high percentage of pointer references implies that precise analysis of these programs would be difficult.

6 Conclusion

This paper has shown how to study the parallelism of a program without creating and running a parallel version of the program. The system currently computes an optimistic upper bound to the speedup. However, it could produce accurate estimates by using a more realistic execution model. The current measurements not only provide a basis for predicting the performance of the program on a parallel computer—and hence a baseline against which the program's actual performance can be compared—but they also provide a wealth of detail about a program's dynamic behavior. This information is valuable the program's author, compiler writers, and people who construct languages and systems for parallel programming.

Because of the AE profiling system, these measurements require little effort on a programmer's part and do not consume much time during execution or require large amounts of disk space. By adapting techniques from AE to other compilers, it would be possible to analyze the parallelism in programs written in other languages, for example Fortran or Lisp.

The measurements of these C programs demonstrate a profound difference between the two array-manipulating numeric programs and the other programs. This difference has two components. First, symbolic programs have smaller loops that execute fewer iterations. Second, the symbolic programs have more loop-carried data dependences that constrain execution. Most compilation techniques (including the *doacross* model) were developed for array-manipulating programs and do not perform well for the symbolic programs. New compilation techniques, execution models, and even programming languages, are likely to prove necessary to compile symbolic programs for parallel machines.

Acknowledgments

Mark Hill generously provided disk space and a copy of the SPEC benchmarks, which facilitated this work. He and Diana Stone greatly improved this paper with their perceptive comments.

References

[1] R.C. Covington, S. Madala, V. Mehta, J.R. Jump, and J.B. Sinclair. The Rice Parallel Processing Testbed. In *Proceedings of the 1988 ACM SIGMETRICS Conference on Measuring and Modeling of Computer Systems*, pages 4–11, May 1988.

[2] Ronald G. Cytron. Compile-Time Scheduling and Optimization for Asynchronous Machines. Technical Report UIUCDCS-R-84-1177, Department of Computer Science, University of Illinois at Urbana-Champaign, October 1984. PhD thesis.

[3] Susan J. Eggers, David R. Keppel, Eric J. Koldinger, and Henry M. Levy. Techniques for Efficient Inline Tracing on a Shared-Memory Multiprocessor. In *Proceedings of the 1990 ACM SIGMETRICS Conference on Measuring and Modeling of Computer Systems*, pages 37–47, May 1990.

[4] Susan Horwitz, Phil Pfeiffer, and Thomas Reps. Dependence Analysis for Pointer Variables. In *Proceedings of the SIGPLAN '89 Conference on Programming Language Design and Implementation*, pages 28–40, June 1989.

[5] Manoj Kumar. Measuring Parallelism in Computation-Intensive Scientific/Engineering Applications. *IEEE Transactions on Computers*, 37(9):1088–1098, September 1988.

[6] James R. Larus. Restructuring Symbolic Programs for Concurrent Execution on Multiprocessors. Technical Report UCB/CSD 89/502, Computer Science Division (EECS), University of California at Berkeley, May 1989. PhD thesis.

[7] James R. Larus. Abstract Execution: A Technique for Efficiently Tracing Programs. Technical Report 912, Computer Sciences Department, University of Wisconsin–Madison, February 1990.

[8] Alexandru Nicolau and Joseph A. Fischer. Measuring the Parallelism Available for Very Long Instruction Word Architectures. *IEEE Transactions on Computers*, C-33(11):968–976, November 1984.

[9] Vivek Sarkar. Determining Average Program Execution Times and their Variance. In *Proceedings of the SIGPLAN '89 Conference on Programming Language Design and Implementation*, pages 298–309, June 1989.

[10] SPEC. SPEC Benchmark Suite Release 1.0, Winter 1990.

[11] Richard M. Stallman. *Using and Porting GNU CC*. Free Software Foundation, September 1989.

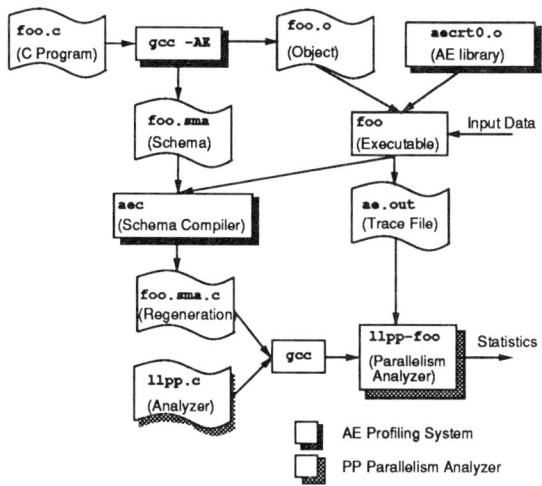

Figure 10: Overview of the AE program measurement system. The -AE flag to the GNU C compiler (gcc) causes it to add tracing code to the compiled program and to produce a schema file (foo.sma). The schema file describes how to interpret the trace file (ae.out) produced by running the program. The schema compiler (aec) translates a schema into a C program (foo.sma.c) that reads the trace file and generates a full program trace. This program is linked with the parallelism analyzer (llpp.c), which uses the trace to estimate the program's speedup.

[12] Craig B. Stunkel and W. Kent Fuchs. TRAPEDS: Producing Traces for Multicomputers Via Execution Driven Simulation. In *Proceedings of the 1989 ACM SIGMETRICS Conference on Measuring and Modeling of Computer Systems*, pages 70–78, May 1989.

Appendix

A Tracing Programs

The parallelism analyzer (llpp) depends on the program measurement system AE [7] to record the events during a program's execution that are necessary to predict parallel behavior. llpp needs two kinds of information. The first is details of a loop invocation— how many times the loop iterates and which instructions execute in each iteration. The other information is a complete record of the memory locations referenced by the program. This information is voluminous and could be expensive to collect and store. However, AE uses a new technique that greatly reduces the size of traces. Below is a brief description of AE.

AE is composed of two pieces. The first is a modified version of the GNU C compiler gcc [11]. This compiler performs two tasks beyond compiling a program. First, it adds a small amount of code to the compiled program to record *significant events* in a trace file. As illustrated by the example below, these events form a basis for reconstructing the program's control flow and its memory accesses. Not all branches and address calculations need to be recorded. Most can be recalculated later when producing the full trace. gcc also produces a condensed version of the program, called a *schema*, that describes how to interpret the trace file to regenerate a full program trace. Regeneration is carried out by a C program produced from the schema by the schema compiler aec. Figure 10 shows the pieces of the system.

An execution of the traced program produces a file (ae.out) containing the significant events that fully characterize the execution. These files can be interpreted only with the aid of the program's schema since they are highly compressed and omit information that can be recalculated. aec translates schema files into a C program that regenerates a full trace from the significant event trace. A simple example demonstrates this process. Consider the program:

```
main ()
{
  int i;
  int *a = (int *) malloc (sizeof (int) * 100);
  for (i = 0; i < 100; i = i + 1)   a[i] = i * i;
}
```

gcc will produce machine code for the loop similar to:

```
      move R4, 100
      call malloc
      move R5, R2         # R2 is result
      move R3, 0
      branch gt, R3, 100, end
loop: shift-left-logical R2, R3, 2
      add R2, R5, R2
      mult R6, R3, R3
      store R6, 0(R2)
      add R3, R3, 1
test: branch lt, R3, 100, loop
end:
```

In the program above, AE records only two types of significant events. First, to reproduce the program's control flow, AE adds tracing code at the beginning of basic blocks that are the target of a conditional branch. Each time such a block executes, this code records the block's number. These numbers permit the regeneration program to follow a conditional branch. Unconditional control flow is fully described by the schema and does not require significant events. AE also records the address of array a since its location cannot be determined by the regeneration program. The schema describes both the instructions produced by gcc and the significant events.

```
start_block 0
uneventful_inst 2 4
call_inst malloc
record_defn R2
compute_defn_0 R5 R2
compute_defn_0 R3 0
uneventful_inst 2 4
end_block_cjump 0 1 3

start_block_target 1
uneventful_inst 1 4
end_block_next_target 1 %loop_entry(2 0)

start_block_target 2
compute_defn_2 R2 R3 << 2
compute_defn_2 R2 R5 + R2
uneventful_inst 1 4
store_inst R2 + 0
compute_defn_2 R3 R3 + 1
end_block_cjump 2 3 2 %loop_exit(3 0) %loop_back(2 0)
```

The schema omits details of the portions of the program that produce values, as opposed to addresses. It describes instructions that compute memory addresses, reference memory, or affect control flow. The operation record_defn means that a value used in an address calculation (such as the result of malloc) cannot be regenerated. The value is recorded in the trace file. By contrast, the regeneration program can recalculate the expressions in compute_defn's, so they do not record anything during execution. uneventful_inst are placeholders for instructions that do not contribute to memory references or control flow—in general, instructions that produce and consume values. The schema also indicates which arcs between basic blocks enter and leave loops and which begin new iterations.

The trace file for this program contains 103 items:

Stack Pointer Upon Entry	4 bytes
Result from malloc	4 bytes
Block 1	1 byte
⋮	
Block 1	1 byte
Block 3	1 byte

This file contains 109 bytes. The full address trace contains 3610 bytes (618 instructions and 104 memory references at 5 bytes each), so AE reduces the size of the trace by a factor of 33.[3]

James R. Larus

---

[3]This ratio can be increased to 106 times by compressing ae.out to 34 bytes with the Unix utility compress.

18 An Efficient Implementation of Thread-Specific Data
M. Guzzi, R. Simpson, D. Parce

Abstract

Parallel languages are generally classified by the method they employ to express parallelism. However, the nature of memory and data defines the programming model as much as the multitasking method. While only a few basic methods of expressing parallelism have been used, a wide variety of memory models have been employed. From this varied field, system standards, such as Posix Pthreads, have been proposed that favor a fully shared address-space model. Unfortunately, parallel algorithms inevitably need some amount of data private to each thread. This paper will describe Encore's pseudo-private memory implementation which provides thread-specific data in a fully shared address space.

1. Introduction

Parallel languages are often classified by the method they employ to express parallelism. From the large number of parallel languages that have been implemented or proposed, only two basic parallel methodologies have emerged: *explicit tasking* and *block-parallel constructs*. Explicit tasking involves breaking the problem into chunks, called *tasks* or *threads,* that can execute more or less independently [5]. Block-parallel constructs are language statements that specify local parallel execution. They may create one or more new execution threads, but all such threads are slaves to the thread which invoked the block-parallel construct.

In a parallel system, the nature of memory and data defines the programming model as much as the multitasking method. A wide variety of memory models have been employed. The variety is great because many factors, such as the underlying architecture, the operating system, and the programming language, all affect the memory model presented to the programmer. For example, loosely-coupled multiprocessor architectures such as the Illiac IV[2], hypercube architectures[9], and the transputer[15] provide only local memory. Therefore, languages on such systems usually present a task-private memory model to the user. To share information, data must be explicitly transmitted from one node or task to another.

At the other end of the spectrum, shared-memory multiprocessor architectures such as the Encore Multimax[18] and Sequent Symmetry[11] can provide a fully shared address space for all threads in a program. Until recently, however, shared memory and parallel programming were often treated as extensions to the sequential programming model. Data that was to be shared would have to be declared explicitly, or linked in a special section. Parallel execution was typically created by making multiple Unix[*] fork() calls followed by some type of share() call that would specify the region of memory to be shared.

Recently, the overall perception of parallelism and shared memory has been changing. Parallel systems and parallel programming are moving into the mainstream of computer science. System standards have been proposed that favor a fully shared address-space model. Posix Pthreads[14], OSF/1[10], and the Unix International multiprocessor proposal[17] all specify a fully shared virtual address space among threads in a program.

The fully shared memory model has been adopted because of efficiency and simplicity. The shared memory model allows light-weight threads to be be created with far less overhead than traditional heavy-weight process creation. Unfortunately, it has also been recognized that parallel algorithms inevitably need some amount of data private to each thread. The amount of private data used in applications is usually small, but as with registers or cache it is intensively accessed.

---

[*]Unix is a trademark of AT&T.

In this model private data is provided by language based restrictions on access to a pool of data in the shared area. We call this thread-specific data because it is owned by a particular thread but is private only by agreement. For example the Posix Pthreads proposal provides the functions pthread_getspecific() and pthread_setspecific() to read and write thread-specific data.

This paper will describe current methods of providing thread-specific data in a fully shared address space. These methods will be compared to the virtual-memory based method which provides truly private data. Finally, these methods will be compared to Encore's pseudo-private memory implementation which is an efficient compiler and run-time based method providing thread-specific data in a fully shared address space.

2. Thread-Specific Memory

Several types of thread-specific memory are in common usage today. In fact, any multi-threaded program in a shared address space, such as cthreads[4] on Mach[3], must provide thread-specific stack areas for each thread. The stack of each thread is private only by convention. A thread does not usually access anothers stack area, but such access is possible. Such variables may be passed by reference to another thread, or in the case of Ada[13], a task may access variables on its parent's stack if the variable is visible in the child task's scope. Additionally, any data allocated from a heap in a shared address space is thread-specific memory.

Thread-specific stacks and heaps do not provide all the functionality needed in multi-threaded programs, however. There is a need to provide private data with a global reference. In order to provide this functionality, some parallel language implementations turn to the operating system for assistance. Private and shared data are placed into separate memory sections. Access to shared data sections is propagated to newly created threads or tasks, while private data sections are duplicated as needed using some copy-on-write virtual-memory technique. This is truly private data protected by the page tables in the operating system. This method is used by Cedar Fortran[8] on the Xylem[6] operating system, and by early versions of Encore Parallel Fortran (EPF)[12] on Unix.

Truly private data, however, has several disadvantages. First, it is incompatible with the pthreads, OSF, and UI environments. Second, it lacks the efficiency of the fully shared address-space model. The operating system is required to keep separate page tables for each thread, adding to thread-creation and context-switch times. Finally, this private data can never be passed by reference to another thread, since the whole region would be duplicated in the address space of each thread.

In Fortran and other languages which pass data by reference, VM-private memory places a limitation on data usage. For example, in Parallel Computing Forum[*] Fortran[12] the concept of partially-shared common maps precisely into pseudo-private. Partially-shared common arises in nested parallelism where the outer level of parallelism has some private common blocks, but within each thread there is nested parallelism where the private common blocks now need to be shared among the nested parallel threads. VM-private memory does not work; an indirect reference to a shared memory area is needed.

Posix Pthreads attempts to remedy the limitations of VM-private memory by defining a run-time interface for creating and referencing thread-specific data. Pthreads provides global references to thread-specific data via globally allocated *keys*. The key is simply a run-time system data structure that is shared by all threads in a program. A thread may associate a private value with a key using the pthread_setspecific() call. This value may later be retrieved using the pthread_getspecific() call. For such calls, the run-time system must perform a lookup operation based on the thread id. This interface to thread-specific data is somewhat cumbersome and has limited application because it is not efficient when compared with normal memory references. It would be prohibitively expensive to implement all accesses to a PCF partially-shared common using this run-time system lookup scheme.

In the ideal solution to this problem, thread-specific data is allocated in the shared VM space, references to thread specific data are accommodated in the global program scope, and references to thread-specific data are as efficient as references to normal global data.

---

[*]The Parallel Computing Forum is a group comprised of corporate and academic representatives coordinated by Kuck and Associates, Inc. developing parallel Fortran extensions that include both block-parallel constructs and explicit tasking.

The pseudo-private memory implementation presented here has all of these characteristics.

All pseudo-private memory is allocated out of shared memory at thread creation. The programmer's interface to pseudo-private memory is very simple. Pseudo-private data is declared in the same manner as all other data with the additional keyword of `private`. Pseudo-private declarations may be used in all cases where global, static, or common data declarations would be used in a sequential program. In the following C example, an array of pseudo-private integers is declared and then initialized.

```
private int pdata[10];

void pdata_init()
{
    register int i;
    for (i=0; i<10; i++) pdata[i] = i;
}
```

The same initialization could be done at compile time with the following declaration:

```
private int pdata[10] = { 0,1,2,3,4,5,6,7,8,9 };
```

In Fortran, the private declaration can be used with `Common` blocks and data declared `Save`. In the following Encore Parallel Fortran (EPF) example, the common block `Pdata` is declared to be pseudo-private:

```
Subroutine Example
Common /Pdata/ A(100), B(50)
Private /Pdata/
```

In EPF, pseudo-private common blocks can also be initialized using the Fortran `Data` statement. In PCF, the partially-shared `Scommon` blocks would be implemented with pseudo-private memory as well.

References to pseudo-private variables are as efficient as references to global variables because there is no run-time lookup of the private area. The references are generated directly by the compiler using a similar code sequence as is used for referencing global data. On the National Semiconductor 32532, our current processor, and on the Motorola 88100, our next processor, references to pseudo-private memory have exactly the same instruction count as any other external reference.

3. Implementation

The implementation of pseudo-private memory required extensions to the compilers, linkers, and run-time systems. Since pseudo-private memory is allocated at task-creation time, pseudo-private memory addresses cannot be fully resolved at compile time or even link time. Pseudo-private memory addresses are resolved as relative offsets to a base. Special code sequences and references had to be generated by the compilers. The linker had to resolve the offsets. Finally, the run-time system must allocate and initialize the pseudo-private data area for each thread, and then setup the current thread to properly reference its pseudo-private data area.

3.1. Object Format Extensions

In the standard Unix COFF[16] object format, data definitions are placed into memory sections. The program text is placed in the *.text* section, the initialized data is placed in the *.data* section, and the uninitialized data is placed in the *.bss* section. To support pseudo-private data, two new sections, *.prvdata* and *.prvbss*, have been added. Initialized pseudo-private data is placed in the .prvdata section, and uninitialized pseudo-private data is placed in the .prvbss section.

The relocation information has also been extended to accommodate pseudo-private data. In an object file, relocation information is attached to each symbol reference. The linker will later use this information to resolve references. A new relocation type, *PRIVREL*, has been added to COFF. This relocation type indicates that this symbol must be resolved as an offset from the pseudo-private base.

3.2. Compiler Extensions

Since pseudo-private memory references are relative offsets, each thread must have a unique base pointer. In the fully shared address-space model, only registers are truly private to a thread. A register is dedicated as the base pointer for the pseudo-private area. This register is never used for other purposes and it provides efficient access to the private data.

On the National Semiconductor 32532 chip, our current processor, a base register, called the static base (SB) register, is provided. The intented function of this register was to provide hardware support for module-based languages such as Modula and Ada. The SB register was to be used to point to the module level or package level data, and it would be reset each time the execution moved from one module to another. We do not believe that this register was ever used for this purpose, and often went entirely unused.

This SB register has been adopted as pseudo-private base register. All references to pseudo-private data are generated as offsets relative to the SB register. Since the SB is intended to be a base register, the ns32532 provides a full range of SB-based addressing modes.

Pseudo-private memory references are generated by the compilers in a manner similar to that used for other external references. Declarations of pseudo-private data are placed in the .prvdata or .prvbss sections. Instructions with a pseudo-private argument are output using an SB-based addressing mode. The symbol relocation information specifies that this is a PRIVREL reference.

3.3. Linker Extensions

The linker must now deal with the extended COFF objects to form a normal executable file (a.out in Unix). First, it must coalesce the like sections from all object files to form single .text, .data, .bss, .prvdata, and .prvbss sections. The .text, .data, and .bss sections will be present in the a.out. The .prvdata and .prvbss sections are not maintained as independent sections.

Once the .prvdata and .prvbss sections have been formed and relative offsets of all pseudo-private symbols have been calculated, the .prvdata and .prvbss sections will be embedded in the .data and .bss sections. For convenience, we call this the privdata area. The beginning of the privdata area, the end of the initialized pseudo-private data, and the end of the privdata area are marked with external symbols that will be accessible to the program when it executes. The run-time system will use this area in the a.out image as a master copy of the pseudo-private data area. Part of the initialization of each thread will be to make its own copy of the pseudo-private area.

As the linker resolves relocation references, any PRIVREL relocations encountered will not be turned into addresses but into offsets from the beginning of the pseudo-private area. In generated instructions, references to pseudo-private data will be an offset from the contents of the pseudo-private base register.

There is one type of reference that cannot be resolved with pseudo-private data. Since the reference to pseudo-private data exists only as an offset from a base register, the address of a particular instantiation of a pseudo-private variable cannot be resolved until run time. Therefore, in languages without run-time data initialization, it is impossible to initialize an external variable to the address of a pseudo-private variable. In the C language, for example, the following code sequence cannot be resolved:

```
private int pdata[10];
int *pdata_pntr = &pdata[0];
```

The compilers have been modified to flag such references as errors.

Pseudo-private data is also supported in a dynamic loader, dynload, which is based on the System V rel 3.1 linker, ld. Dynload must recognize the existing private data area in the address space and combine it with any new private data being loaded. Dynload must recognize the existing pseudo-private data symbols, their offsets, and the total size of the pseudo-private area. In creating this expanded pseudo-private data area, existing .prvdata initializations must be copied to the front of the new area. New private data initializations are placed at the end of the new area. Finally boundary variables in the user address space are updated with the addresses of the beginning and end of the new area so that the run-time can locate the new private area. This procedure may be repeated for multiple dynamic loads.

3.4. Run-time Support

The run-time system is entrusted with the task of insuring that all threads have a properly allocated and initialized pseudo-private area. A pseudo-private memory initialization routine is called as part of the program and thread startup routines. The initialization is quite simple. First, the size of the pseudo-private area is determined by subtracting the start address of pseudo-private master area from the end address. An area of memory of the proper size is then allocated, and a copy is done from the master area to the newly allocated space. Finally, the pseudo-private base register is set to point to this newly allocated space.

4. Performance

The reader may suspect that the initialization of the privdata area could be quite expensive. The expense actually depends on several factors. The experimental results below indicate that the virtual-memory manipulations provided by the operating system have the greatest impact on the expense of pseudo-private memory initialization. Cost also varies with the size of privdata area and how much of it is initialized.

Pseudo-private memory has been implemented under the Mach operating system using threads and under the nUnix[1] operating system, an Encore extension to System V Unix that provides light-weight processes. The Mach implementation uses the Mach vm_copy() routine to setup the pseudo-private area. The vm_copy() routine virtually copies one region of memory to another by manipulating the program's page tables. The page-table entries will share the same physical page of memory, marked copy-on-write. Only when an attempt is made to modify a page does the page-fault handler make a new copy of the page. System V does not provide powerful vm-manipulating primitives. Therefore, the System V implementation uses sbrk() for allocation and must physically copy all initialized data.

Experiments were performed to compare pseudo-private memory creation overhead vs. VM-private memory creation overhead on both Mach and nUnix. All experiments were conducted on Encore Multimax 520 systems which use the ns32532 processor. In this discussion, we will use "thread" to refer to Mach threads as well as nUnix lightweight processes.

In the first experiment, the cost of VM-private memory creation was measured with varying amounts of private memory. This was accomplished by timing Unix fork() operations with varying amounts of private data allocated. Timings were done for uninitialized and initialized data. No shared memory was used in this experiment.

In the second experiment, timings for thread creation were measured with varying amounts of shared memory. This was done to provide a baseline to measure against thread creation with pseudo-private memory. The results of experiments one and two are summarized in Figure 1. The data indicates that the thread-creation times in both Mach and nUnix were independent of the amount of shared memory. For more performance information on Mach and nUnix, the reader should consult [1].

When using pseudo-private data, thread-creation time has two components: the actual creation of the thread resource performed by the creating thread and the initialization of the pseudo-private data area performed by the created thread. This differs from the first

	Unix Fork (VM-Private Mem)	Mach Thread Create (Shared Mem)	nUnix Shared Fork (Shared Mem)
Uninitialized			
1 kb	16920 uSec	4149 uSec	2020 uSec
8 kb	18140 uSec	4422 uSec	1980 uSec
128 kb	16300 uSec	4379 uSec	1840 uSec
1 Mb	17040 uSec	4349 uSec	2180 uSec
4 Mb	26040 uSec	5266 uSec	2120 uSec
16 Mb	49720 uSec	4208 uSec	2100 uSec
Initialized			
1 kb	16820 uSec	4755 uSec	2140 uSec
8 kb	18660 uSec	3977 uSec	1980 uSec
128 kb	17220 uSec	4524 uSec	1960 uSec
1 Mb	23500 uSec	4653 uSec	1880 uSec
4 Mb	41020 uSec	4349 uSec	1980 uSec
16 Mb	113680 uSec	5032 uSec	2220 uSec

Times are averages of 1000 iterations in a timesharing environment on lightly-loaded machines.

Figure 1. Creation Times for Unix, Mach, and nUnix

experiment where thread-creation time and VM-private memory initialization time where all incurred by the creating process. In the following two experiments, the creation time of the operating system thread resource and the initialization time of pseudo-private memory will be measured. The results of experiments three and four have been summarized in Figure 2.

In the third experiment, timings for thread and light-weight-process creation were measured with varying amounts of pseudo-private data. This experiment measures only the operating-system creation of the thread resource as experienced by the creating thread and was done to verify that pseudo-private memory does not affect the creating thread. The overhead for pseudo-private memory is incurred by the created thread. This overhead is measured in the fourth experiment. The experiments were run with initialized and uninitialized pseudo-private data. Comparing the thread-creation times given in Figure 1 with the thread-creation times given in Figure 2 confirms that pseudo-private memory does not affect the thread-creation time experienced by the creating thread.

The fourth experiment measured the timings for allocation and setup of pseudo-private data in the newly created thread. Again, the experiments were run with uninitialized and initialized data. Both systems performed well with uninitialized data, but the Mach system performed much better for initialized data. This was due entirely to the vm_copy() memory primitive.

The results of these experiments have shown that pseudo-private memory can be used to efficiently provide thread-specific memory on both Mach and nUnix in most cases. On Mach the combined overhead of thread-creation and pseudo-private initialization was always substantially less than the Unix fork() time with the equivalent amount of VM-private memory (shown in Figure 1, column 1). It was only with large amounts of initialized pseudo-private data on nUnix that pseudo-private memory became prohibitively expensive.

	Mach		**nUnix**	
	Thread Create (creator)	Pseudo-Priv Init. (new thread)	Shared Fork (creator)	Pseudo-Priv Init. (new process)
Uninitialized				
1 kb	4149 uSec	1614 uSec	1980 uSec	240 uSec
8 kb	4722 uSec	1311 uSec	1980 uSec	280 uSec
128 kb	4894 uSec	1591 uSec	1880 uSec	240 uSec
1 Mb	5166 uSec	1877 uSec	2380 uSec	200 uSec
4 Mb	5489 uSec	1602 uSec	2440 uSec	280 uSec
16 Mb	5266 uSec	1533 uSec	2400 uSec	400 uSec
Initialized				
1 kb	4755 uSec	1433 uSec	2120 uSec	1000 uSec
8 kb	3977 uSec	1583 uSec	1920 uSec	7940 uSec
128 kb	4524 uSec	1916 uSec	2380 uSec	166000 uSec
1 Mb	4653 uSec	2497 uSec	2320 uSec	1437000 uSec
4 Mb	4349 uSec	5158 uSec	2380 uSec	5650000 uSec
16 Mb	5032 uSec	9816 uSec	2320 uSec	28320000 uSec

Times are averages of 1000 iterations in a timesharing environment on a lightly loaded system, except for the Pseudo-Private Init times on nUnix for 1 Mb, 4Mb and 16 Mb which are averages of 20 iterations.

Figure 2. Pseudo-Private Initialization Times for Mach and nUnix

5. Architectural Considerations

It may appear that this pseudo-private memory implementation may not be practical for some architectures. The cost of a dedicated processor register may seem prohibitively expensive on register-poor CISC architectures. This is a valid concern.

However, it should be noted that a dedicated register is only necessary in true multiprocessor systems. On uniprocessor systems, the private register can be simulated with a global memory location. Pseudo-private references would have to be generated as offsets from the contents of this global memory location. The only additional requirement would be that this global memory location be saved and restored with the processor state on a context switch.

Another point to be considered is that RISC architectures are becoming more prominent, especially in the multiprocessor arena. These register-rich architectures can much more easily afford a dedicated register for pseudo-private access.

Encore has selected the Motorola 88100 processor for its next generation of multiprocessor systems. Like other RISC architectures, the 88100 has a large number of general-purpose registers. The 88open consortium, a Motorola-sponsored industrial consortium developing object and binary standards for the 88100 processor, has recently agreed to dedicate register r27 as the pseudo-private base register.

When comparing pseudo-private memory references to global memory references, pseudo-private memory on the 88100 is actually more efficient than on the National 32532. On the 88100, two instructions are necessary to access a global memory location – one instruction loads the high half of the address into a register, the second instruction loads the low half of the address and accesses the location. Any register can serve as a base register with a 16 bit offset. Therefore, if the amount of pseudo-private memory is less than 64k, pseudo-private accesses can be accomplished with a single instruction. With more than 64k of pseudo-private memory, a three-instruction access sequence is required – two instructions to load the high and low halves of the address into a register followed by the load or store of that location. In practice, we expect the amount of private memory to usually be small, so pseudo-private references will often be cheaper than other external memory references.

6. Conclusion

In most situations, pseudo-private memory combines the advantages of light-weight threads with efficient access to thread-specific memory. Unlike other thread-specific memory methods, pseudo-private memory requires no run-time lookup, and it provides global references to thread-specific data. The Mach implementation demonstrates that powerful VM primitives can greatly extend the amount of initialized pseudo-private memory that can be efficiently allocated.

References

1. Aral, Z., Bloom, J., Doeppner, T., Gertner, I., Langerman. A. & Schaffer, G., Variable Weight Processes with Flexible Shared Resources. *Conference Proceedings, 1989 Winter USENIX Technical Conference*, USENIX Assocation, Berkeley, CA 1989.
2. Barnes, G., Brown, R., Kato, M., Kuck, D., Slotnick, D., & Stokes, R., The Illiac IV Computer. *IEEE Transactions on Computers*, Vol C-17 No. 8 (Aug. 1968), pp. 746-757.
3. Baron, R., Rashid, R., Siegel, E., Tevanian, A., & Young M., MACH-1: A Multiprocessor Oriented Operating System and Environment. In Arthur Wouk (editor), *New Computing Environments: Parallel, Vector, and Symbolic*. SIAM, 1986.
4. Cooper, E. and Draves, R., Cthreads. Department of Computer Science, Carnegie Mellon University, July 20,1987.
5. Dennis, J. & Van Horn, E., Programming Semantics for Multiprogrammed Computations. *Communications of the ACM*, Vol. 9 No. 3 (March 1966), pp. 143-155.
6. Emrath, P., Xylem: An Operating System for the Cedar Multiprocessor. *IEEE Software*, Vol. 3 No. 4 (July 1985), pp. 30-37.
7. *Encore Parallel Fortran User's Guide*, Encore Computer Corporation, Marlborough, Mass. 1988.
8. Guzzi, M., Cedar Fortran Programmer's Manual *CSRD doc. no. 601*, U of I Center for Supercomputing R and D, Jan. 1987.
9. Heath, M. ed., Hypercube Multiprocessors, *Proc. of the First Conference on Hypercube Multiprocessors*, SIAM 1966.
10. *OSF/1 Press Releases*, Open Software Foundatation, Cambridge, MA 1990.
11. Osterhaug, A., *Guide to Parallel Programming on Sequent Computer Systems*, Sequent Computer Systems, Inc., Beaverton, Oregon 1986.
12. *PCF Fortran: Language Definition*, Parallel Computing Forum, Kuck & Associates, Champaign, IL 1989.
13. *Reference Manual for the Ada Programming Language*, ANSI/MIL-STD-1815 A, U.S. Department of Defense 1983.
14. P1003.4a, *Thread Extenstion for Portable Operating Systems -- P1003.4a/D2*, Technical Committee on Operating Systems of the IEEE Computer Society, January 1990.
15. *Transputer Reference Manual*, Inmos 1986.
16. *Umax V Programmer's Guide, Part 2* Encore Computer Corporation 1989.
17. *UNIX System V Multiprocessing: A Standard Path to the Future*, UNIX International, Parsippany, NJ 07054, January 1990.
18. Woodbury, P., Wilson, A., Shein, B., Gertner, I., Chen, P.Y., Bartlett, J., & Aral, Z., Shared Memory Multiprocessors: The Right Approach to Parallel Processing, *COMPCON Spring 1989 Conference*.

19 Programming Distributed Memory Architectures Using Kali

P. Mehrotra, J. Van Rosendale

Abstract

Programming nonshared memory systems is more difficult than programming shared memory systems, in part because of the relatively low level of current programming environments for such machines. This paper presents a new programming environment, Kali, which provides a global name space and allows direct access to remote data values. In order to retain efficiency, Kali provides a system of annotations, allowing the user to control those aspects of the program critical to performance, such as data distribution and load balancing. This paper describes the primitives and constructs provided by our language, and also discusses some of the issues raised in translating a Kali program for execution on distributed memory systems.

1 Introduction

Current programming environments for distributed memory machines provide very little support for the distribution of data and code across the processors. This makes programming such machines very difficult since the user has to encode all the low-level details required to implement the algorithm. Thus, the resulting program is extraordinarily complex and also inflexible.

We have been working for several years on a programming environment, called Kali, designed to alleviate this problem in the context of scientific computation. The goal

---

[0] Research supported by the National Aeronautics and Space Administration under NASA contract NAS1-18605 while the authors were in residence at ICASE, Mail Stop 132C, NASA Langley Research Center, Hampton, VA 23665.

of our approach is to allow programmers to focus on high-level algorithm design and
performance issues, while relegating the minor but complex details of interprocessor
communication to the compiler and run-time environment.

This paper describes the Kali environment in relative detail, focusing on a Fortran-
style syntax for our language primitives. This kind of language extension can be done
with almost any sequential, procedural language supporting arrays. The version of these
primitives here, known as KF1 (Kali Fortran 1), is natural in scientific programming,
since most scientific programming is done in Fortran. Syntax is, however, not the issue;
in earlier papers [9, 10] we have discussed this kind of language extension in the context
of BLAZE [14], a Pascal-like data-flow language. We focus here on Fortran, primarily
because of its greater acceptance in scientific computing.

The remainder of this paper is organized as follows. Section 2 describes the programming model employed by Kali. Section 3 describes the primitives provided by the
language, while section 4 addresses the issues of portability and scalability. Section 5
presents an overview of the analysis and transformations needed to map a Kali program
to a nonshared memory architecture. Finally, section 6 compares our work with other
approaches, and section 7 gives a brief set of conclusions.

2 Kali Programming Model

The Kali programming environment is targeted to scientific applications. Such applications frequently consists of parallel operations on large "structures" such as grids,
matrices, and so forth. These operations can generally be expressed as parallel loops
manipulating arrays representing these structures.

The fundamental goal of Kali is to allow programmers to treat distributed data structures as single objects. Kali thus provides a software layer supporting a global name
space on distributed memory architectures. The computation is then specified via a set
of parallel loops, using this global name space exactly as one does on a shared memory architecture. The danger here is that since true shared memory does not exist, one
might easily sacrifice performance. However, Kali requires the user to explicitly control
data distribution and load balancing, thus forcing awareness of those issues critical to
performance on nonshared memory architectures. In effect, the user retains the ease of
programmability of the shared memory model, while exploiting the performance characteristics of nonshared memory architectures.

In Kali, one specifies parallel algorithms in a high-level, distribution independent manner. The compiler then analyzes this high-level specification and translates it into a

system of processes which communicate via messages. The generated code runs in what has been termed the SPMD mode (Single Program Multiple Data). That is, identical process code is down loaded onto each processors of the architecture. These processes then execute asynchronously, interacting via message-passing. These exchanges of data through messages are generally enough to maintain the semantics of the source code. However there are a few situations where barrier synchronizations are required in order to produce the correct results (see for example doall loops in section 3.3).

There are two major issues in restructuring Kali source code for parallel execution. First, the parallel loops must be partitioned across the processors. This is generally easy, since the compiler distributes the parallel loop iterations based on annotations provided by the user, as described in the next section. Second, all remote accesses have to be "compiled" into message passing communication. That is, the compiler must analyze all references to identify potentially nonlocal accesses. It then generates communication phases, causing the data to be moved to the processes requiring it.

There are two ways to translate sequential code for execution on a distributed memory architecture. One can either specify a "king processor," which executes all sequential code, communicating the results to all others, or one can replicate the sequential operations on all processors. We followed the latter approach, since it generally yields better performance.

The other issues to be addressed as part of our programming model are the issues of scaling and portability. These issues will be addressed in section 4, where we can discuss them in the context of specific Kali constructs.

3 Kali Language Primitives

In this section we describe the primitives provided by Kali. A Kali programmer must specify three things, in addition to the original (sequential) algorithm: a) the processor array on which the program is to be executed, b) the distribution of the data structures across these processors, and c) the parallel loops and where they are to be executed. The following subsections describe each of these specifications in more detail.

3.1 Processor Arrays

The first thing that needs to be specified is a "processor array." This is an array of physical processors across which the data structures will be distributed, and on which the algorithm will execute. A processor array is declared in the main program in KF1 using a syntax similar to that of Fortran array declarations:

> **parameter**(maxprocs = 128)
> **parameter**(p ∼ maxprocs)
>
> **processors** procs(p)

Here *procs* has been declared as a one-dimensional array of processors. The size of this processor array, *p*, is an integer constant whose value is between 1 and *maxprocs*, as set by the **parameter** statement. **Parameter** statements are standard Fortran, but the tilda notation here is new. It's meaning is that the value of *p* is dynamically chosen in this range by the run-time system, and will remain constant throughout the program's execution.

Allowing the size of the processor array to be dynamically chosen is important, since it allows programs to be parametrized by the number of processors. Our approach provides portability, scalability, and avoids dead-lock in case fewer processors are available than expected. There are, however, other approaches one could take to achieving this same end, an issue we will return to in the next section.

KF1 also allows multi-dimensional processor arrays to be declared:

> **parameter**(px ∼ 128)
> **parameter**(py = 2*px)
>
> **processors** procs(px, py)

Here *procs* is a two-dimensional array which has twice as many processors in the second dimension as in the first. Processors can be referenced in the code like any other array element, e.g., *procs(i, j)* is the *(i,j)*th processor.

3.2 Data Distribution Primitives

Given a processor array, the programmer must specify the distribution of data structures across the array. Currently the only distributed data type supported is distributed arrays, though "lists" may be supported in future versions of the language. Scalar variables and arrays that are not distributed are simply replicated, with one copy assigned to each of the processors in the processor array.

A **dist** statement can be used to specify the distribution functions for arrays. Kali provides notations for the most common distribution patterns: **block**, **cyclic**, and **block_cyclic**:

> **processors** procs(p)
>
> **real** A(N), B(N), C(N)
>
> **dist** A(**block**), B(**cyclic**), C(**block_cyclic**(b))

Here, arrays A, B, and C are distributed across the p processors of the one-dimensional processor array *procs*. Array A is distributed by blocks such that each processor receives a contiguous block of elements of the array. Conversely, array B has its rows cyclically distributed. Here, if p were 10, processor 1 would store elements in rows 1, 11, 21, and so on, while processor 10 would store rows which were multiples of 10. Array C is distributed in a block-cyclic fashion with size b. That is, the elements of C are first divided into blocks of size b, and then these blocks are cyclically distributed across the set of processors.

The number of dimensions of an array that are distributed must match the number of dimensions of the underlying processor array. Asterisks are used to indicate dimensions of data arrays which are not distributed, as in the case of *D1*, *D2* and *E* shown here:

> **processors** procs(p)
>
> **real** D1(N, N), D2(N, N), E(N, M, L)
>
> **dist** D1(block, *), D2(*, block), E(*, block, *)

Since the processor array *procs* is one-dimensional, only one dimension of the arrays *D1*, *D2* and *E* is distributed. In the case of array *D1*, the first dimension is distributed across the p processors, i.e., the rows are blocked with a block of rows assigned to each processor. Array *D2*, on the otehr hand, has its second dimension distributed. Similarly, for array *E*, the second dimension is distributed with each processor getting a slice of the array.

User defined distributions

In addition to system defined distributions, KF1 supports general user defined distributions. The **map** statement uses syntax similar to the Fortran statement function, and allows the user to provide a mapping from array indices to processor indices. For example, in the code fragment below, the distribution function *ublock* is equivalent to the system defined **block** distribution.

> **processors** procs(p)
>
> **real** F(N), G(N,M)
>
> **map** ublock(i) = p*(i-1)/N + 1
> **dist** F(ublock), G(ublock, *)

Here *ublock* takes one argument, an array index, and produces a corresponding processor index. The identifier i is a dummy argument, local to the **map** function. Such user defined distributions can then be used in the **dist** statement in place of the system defined distribution patterns.

The **map** statement is special in that it can return multiple values, as required for processor indices in the case of multi-dimensional processor arrays. This is illustrated in the following code fragment by the distribution function *cyc2d*, which takes as argument two integers and returns two integer values to be used as processor indices.

> **processors** procs(p, p)
>
> **real** H(N, N), P(N, M, L), Q(N, N, N)
> **map** cyc1d(i) = mod(i-1, p)+1
> **map** cyc2d(i,j) = mod(i-1, p)+1, mod(j-1, p) + 1
> **dist** H(cyc2d), P(cyc2d, *), Q(block, cyc1d, *)

As shown here, array distributions can be specified using a combination of system defined distributions, user defined distributions, and asterisks which denote undistributed dimensions. This system is completely general, yet convenient for the commonly occurring cases.

Dynamic Distributions

Along with the static mechanisms for data distributions described above, KF1 allows the distribution of array elements to be changed dynamically. This can be done by using the **distribute** statement:

> **processors** procs(p)
>
> **real** U(N), V(M), W(N)
> **map** static(i) = mod(i-1, p) + 1
> **map** dyn(i) = p * (i-1) / k + 1
> **dist** U(block), V(static), W(dyn)
>
> ...
> k = ...
> ...
> **distribute** U, V, W
> ...

The effect of the **distribute** statement depends on the distributions associated with the respective arrays. If the mapping function is based on constants, then the distribution statement is a null operation. For example, the array U is mapped using system defined distribution **block** while the array V is distributed using the map *static* which involves only constants. Hence the distribution of the arrays U and V will remain unchanged when the **distribute** statement is executed.

On the other hand, the mapping function *dyn* is dependent on the variable k. Thus when the **distribute** statement is executed, the system will redistribute W if and only if the value of the variable k has changed since the last redistribution. When the mapping function involves an array (possibly distributed) or a function call, the compiler may use the conservative approach and redistribute without checking. Note that arrays that have dynamic distribution functions, that is, the distribution function depends on variables rather than constants, have to be *distributed* before they can be accessed or modified. That is, such arrays must occur in a **distribute** statement before being referenced in the code.

In general, the redistribution of an array implies that the data elements comprising the array are moved to new processors. As a compiler optimization, in some cases it can be determined that the array elements are not being accessed before being redefined, so that the values themselves do not need to be transported. Note that this is slightly different from live-variable analysis, since all the elements of the array have to be "dead" for this optimization to be applicable.

3.3 Doall Loops

Operations on distributed data structures are specified by **doall** loops:

> **processors** procs(p)
>
> **real** A(N)
> **dist** A(block)
>
> **doall** 10 i = 1, N **on owner**(A(i))
>   A(i) = ...
>   ...
>   10   **continue**

The iterations of a **doall** loop cannot have inter-iteration dependencies. That is, any memory location assigned to in one iteration cannot be accessed or modified in any other iteration. This allows the iterations to be logically executed in parallel. There is an implied synchronization at the beginning and the end of the parallel loop, i.e., all the parallel threads start concurrently and all threads have to finish execution of their iterations before any other statement is executed.

In addition to the range specification in the header of the **doall**, there is also an **on** clause. The expression associated with the clause specifies the processor on which each loop invocation is to be executed. In the above program fragment, the **on** clause causes the ith loop invocation to be executed on the processor owning the ith element of the array A. The system defined function **owner** returns the home processor of its argument. Although this is the most common use of the **on** clause, it is also possible to name the processor directly by indexing into the processor array, as shown below, where the ith iteration is executed on processor $P(i)$.

> **processors** procs(p)
>
> **real** A(N)
> **dist** A(block)
>
> **doall** 10 i = 1, p **on** (procs(i))
> ...
> 10 **continue**

In KF1, the loop headers of perfectly nested **doall** loops can be combined into a single header as shown:

> **processors** procs(p,p)
>
> **real** A(N, M)
> **dist** A(block, block)
>
> **doall** 10 (i, j) = [1, N]*[1, M] **on owner**(A(i, j))
> ...
> A(i, j) = ...
> ...
> 10 **continue**

Here, a product of ranges is used to specify that for each value of the outer loop index, i, in the range $[1, N]$, the inner loop index, j, assumes each of the values in the range $[1, M]$.

3.4 Parallel Subroutines

In addition to ordinary Fortran subroutines and functions, KF1 supports parallel subroutines, which manipulate distributed data structures in parallel. For example, the header of a parallel subroutine looks like:

> **parsub** jacobi(u, f, n; procs)
>
> **processors** procs(p, p)
>
> ...

The keyword, **parsub** declares *jacobi* to be a parallel subroutines. For a parallel subroutine, the processor array on which the subroutine will execute has to be passed in as a special parameter, in the case here, *procs*. In this case, *procs* is a two-dimensional processor array of size p by p. The size of the processor array argument is "open", and is determined by the actual size of the processor array passed at the point of call. It does not need to be explicitly passed into the subroutine. The identifier p reflects this value, and can be used as a constant in the body of the subroutine.

The calling sequence for parallel subroutines is the same as that of ordinary subroutines, except for the special parameter representing the set of processors on which it will execute. For example, in the code fragment below, the subroutine *jacobi* is passed in the whole set of processors, *procs*.

> **processors** procs(p, p)
> ...
> **call** jacobi(u, f, n; procs)

Subsets of processors can also be passed:

> **processors** procs(p, p)
>
> **real** A(N, N)
> **dist** A(block, block)
> ...
> **doall** 10 i = 1, N **on** owner(A(i,*))
>   **call** Q(A(i, *), N; owner(A(i, *)))
> 10 **continue**
> ...
> **stop**
> **end**
>
>
> **parsub** Q(B, N; pr)
>
> **processors** pr(p)
>
> **real** B(N)
> **dist** B(block)
> ...
> **return**
> **end**

Here, subroutine Q accepts as argument a real vector B, distributed by blocks across a one-dimensional processor array *pr*, of size p. In the calling routine, we have a two-dimensional array A distributed by blocks on a two-dimensional processor array *procs*. The ith iteration of the **doall** loop conceptually executes on the "owner" of the ith row of the array A (represented by $A(i, *)$). That is a whole row of processors execute the i th iteration. In this example, the subroutine Q is called by each processor in the row in a distributed manner, each with its own piece of the i th row of the array A. The set of processors passed to subroutine Q is again supplied by the system function **owner**. In this example, the **doall** loop is supplying one level of parallelism, while the second level is provided by the parallel subroutine Q

Note that the set of processors passed in to a parallel subroutine must cover all the distributed data structures being passed as arguments. That is, the set of processors owning the individual pieces of distributed arguments need to be passed to the parallel subroutine.

3.5 An Example: ADI Iteration

As an example of how these constructs fit together, we show here how to program a simple example, an ADI algorithm. More detailed versions of this example are given in [15]. This example is appropriate here, since while straight forward in KF1, the analogous message-passing code is quite awkward. It is also typical of the kind of algorithms one must support in any scientific programming language.

ADI is a well known method for solving partial differential equations in multiple dimensions, in which one solves tridiagonal linear systems along the x- and y-lines of a grid at every step. The KF1 code for this algorithm is straight forward, as shown in Figure 1. In this version of the algorithm, we employ a sequential tridiagonal solver, *seqtri*, transposing the data arrays vx and vy so that either x-lines or y-lines do not cross processor boundaries. Then the sequential tridiagonal solver will run without interprocessor communication. The transpose here is implicit. Assigning array vx distributed (**block**, *) to vy distributed (*, **block**) induces the required interprocessor communication.

The notation **dynamic** here is new. Arrays declared dynamic are dynamically (stack) allocated. Sun Microsystems Fortran supports a similar construct, but standard Fortran does not. Thus one typically emulates dynamic allocation by hand using space in common blocks. KF1 does not currently support common blocks, and even when it does, this use of common arrays would be rather messy. This **dynamic** construct is natural here, and much simpler than dealing with distributed common blocks.

The version of ADI here is only one of a number of ways of distributing the computation; alternatives are given in [6, 12, 15]. The point is that all versions of this algorithm are equally easy to express in KF1. Moreover, changing distributions, or changing from calls to the sequential tridiagonal solver used here to calls to a parallel tridiagonal solver, is completely trivial. That is the power of this kind of language, in marked contrast to

```
      parsub adi (u,f,nx,ny; procs)
c
c ...... procedure which performs one step of ADI iteration
c
      processors procs(nprocs)

      real        u(nx,ny), f(nx,ny)
      dynamic real vx(nx,ny), vy(nx,ny)

      dist u(*, block), f(*, block), vx(*, block)
      dist vy(block, *)
c
c ...... compute residual
c
      call resid(vx,u,f,nx,ny; procs)
c
c ...... perform tridiagonal solves in x direction
c
      doall 100 j = 1,ny on owner(vx(*, j))
         call seqtri(vx(*, j), nx)
100   continue
c
c ...... perform transpose across processors
c
      vy = vx
c
c ...... perform tridiagonal solves in y direction
c
      doall 200 i = 1,nx on owner(vy(i, *))
         call seqtri(vy(i, *), ny)
200   continue
c
c ...... perform transpose
c
      u = vy

      return
      end
```

Figure 1: ADI Algorithm in KF1

the situation with message-passing languages, where such minor changes typically induce weeks of programming.

4 Portability and Scalability

Portability and scalability are central concerns in parallel programming. The necessity of portability is clear; it is a real waste of human effort to repeatedly program the same algorithms for machines from different manufactures, or machines having slightly different topologies. Scalability is of equal importance; it is, after all, the raison d'êetre for distributed memory architectures. Thus a programming environment should allow programs to run essentially unchanged on architectures having varying numbers of processors, and should make as few assumptions as possible about the underlying architecture and its topology. At the same time, there needs to be enough specificity in the programming environment to adequately exploit machine performance, and to allow programmers to "tune" programs for efficient execution on specific machines. Balancing these conflicting requirements is quite difficult.

On the issue of portability, Kali assumes a distributed memory architecture on which one can allocate processor arrays of at least two dimensions. With this assumption, both hypercube and mesh connected architectures suffice. Programs that use only one or two dimensional arrays will run well on either architecture. Programs using processor arrays of higher dimensions may suffer performance degradation on mesh architectures, depending on compiler implementation details, and the way in which the processor array is used in the program. This level of performance penalty is unavoidable since portability entails some compromise in performance. Given the great importance of portability, this level of compromise seems acceptable.

On the issue of scalability, the simplest approach is to provide arrays of virtual processors, which can be of any size desired. This is the approach taken, for example, in the Connection Machine language, C*. This approach is natural, and is easy to use, but one soon runs into subtle semantics and performance issues when one has multiple data arrays of various sizes and shapes [8]. Either the compiler must guess at the appropriate size for the virtual processor array, at the mapping from virtual processors to physical processors, and at the distributions of the data arrays, or one must provide annotations allowing the user to specify things more precisely. That is, in order to achieve performance, one must break the abstraction of virtual processors, and show the user at least part of the mechanism by which they are implemented.

The alternative followed here is to provide arrays of physical processors rather than virtual processors at the language level. This approach is simpler, and allows full control of the mapping. On the other hand it is occasionally awkward, since programs must be written to accommodate the varying sizes of processor arrays selected by the runtime system. With virtual processors, the programmer is sheltered from this issue, at the cost of serious potential performance penalties. In effect, we are avoiding potentially serious performance penalties, through the sacrifice of a small amount of language elegance.

To see why we have followed this path, consider the code fragment for a tree summation as shown in Figure 2. Here the first N/p steps of the summation are done sequentially on each processor, while the final $log_2(p)$ steps require interprocessor communication. The point is that one needs to know p in order to produce this code. Without knowing p, it is impossible to know how far the sequential operations on each processor should be carried before one resorts to interprocessor operations. Thus one could only program this as though p and N were equal, incurring a substantial overhead.

This particular example is "made up" in the sense that there is a built in primitive **sum=** which accomplishes this tree summation without all of this code. However the same issue arises in a variety of contexts, including fast tridiagonal solvers, Fast Fourier transforms, and adaptive quadrature algorithms [15]. Given only virtual processor arrays, one cannot write programs which are nearly as efficient, in most of these cases.

5 Program Transformation

In this section we describe some of the transformations performed by the compiler to restructure high-level Kali code for execution on distributed memory machines. As indicated before, the compiler produces SPMD-style code. The distributed data structures are partitioned such that each process gets the appropriate portion of the data structure. The scalar and non-distributed variables are replicated, and a current copy is maintained by each process. This is done by replicating the sequential parts of the source code in each process and inserting send-receive pairs whenever distributed variables are accessed.

The major focus of the KF1 compiler is to distribute the parallel loops using message-passing to transfer data between processes executing the different iterations of the loop. A parallel loop is "strip mined" across the processors based on the associated on clause, that is, each processor gets a set of iterations to execute sequentially. Based on the references made to distributed data structures made in this set of iterations, we can define $in(p, q)$ as the set of data elements that are referenced by processor p but stored in processor q. This set can be inverted into the set $out(p, q)$ which is the set of elements owned by processor p and required by processor q. Given the latter set, each processor

```
      processors procs(p)

      integer U(N), Rep(p)
      dist U(block), Rep(block)

c
c ...... perform summation locally on each processor
c

      doall 10  i = 1, p on procs(i)
         Rep(i) = 0
         do 100  j = N*i−1+1, N*i
            Rep(i) = Rep(i) + U(j)
100      continue

10    continue

c
c ...... perform logarithmic tree summation across processors
c

      do 20  k = 1, log(p)
         istep = 2 ** k
         doall 200  i = 1, p on procs(i)
            if (mod(i, istep) .eq. 0) then
               Rep(i) = Rep(i) + Rep(i−istep)
            endif
200      continue
20    continue
```

Figure 2: Code for Tree Summation

can then send the appropriate data to the appropriate processors before the computation is performed.

In some cases we can analyze the program at compile-time and precompute the sets symbolically. Such an analysis requires the distribution of the referenced data structures, the **on** clause of the associated loops, and the subscripts in the array references to be of a form such that closed form expressions can be obtained for the communications sets. If such an analysis is possible, the compiler generates the message-passing statements necessary to communicate the data between the processes. In this paper we will not pursue this optimization; interested readers are referred to [9], which gives some flavor of the analysis.

However, such compile time analysis is not possible for programs in which the array references in a **doall** loop depend on the run-time values of the variables involved. This situation arises, for example, in PDE solvers using an irregular grid. The grid is generally represented using adjacency lists which denotes the neighbors of a particular node of the grid. Figure 3 presents a KF1 subroutine to perform a "relaxation" operation on such an irregular grid.

Here the n node grid is represented by the vector u. Each node has a maximum of *maxnbrs* neighbors with indices of these neighbors being stored in the two-dimensional array *nbrs*. We assume that the grid is generated on the fly by some algorithm and hence the values in the array *nbrs* are set at run-time before the routine *relax* is called. In the code, the arrays are shown distributed by block; proper distribution of the arrays in this case raises load balancing issues outside the scope of this paper. The **doall** loop ranges over the grid points updating the value with a weighted sum of the values at the grid point's immediate neighbors.

The important point here is that to access the values at neighboring nodes, the elements of the vector *utmp* are indexed by the array *nbrs*. Thus the compiler cannot determine at compile-time which elements will be accessed. In such cases, the communication sets must be computed at run-time. We do this by running a modified version of the **doall** called the *inspector* before running the actual **doall**. The inspector only checks whether references to distributed arrays are local. If a reference is local, nothing more is done. If the reference is not local, a record of it and its "home" processor is added to a list of elements to be received. This approach generates the $in(p, q)$ sets. To construct the $out(p, q)$ sets, we note that $out(p, q) = in(q, p)$. Thus, we need only route the sets to the correct processors using a global communication phase. To avoid excessive communications overhead we use Fox's Crystal router [4] which handles such communications without creating bottlenecks. Once this is accomplished, we have all the sets needed to execute the communications

```
          parsub relax(u, nbrs, coef, n; procs)

          processors procs(p)

          parameter(niters = 100)
          parameter(maxnbrs = 12)

          real u(n)
          dynamic real utmp(n)

          real coef(n, maxnbr)
          integer nbrs(n, maxnbr)

          dist u(block), utmp(block), coef(block, *), nbrs(block, *)

          do 400 iter = 1, niters
c
c.........copy u into utmp
c
          utmp = u

c
c.........update u
c
          doall 300 i = 1,n on owner(u(i))

             u(i) = 0.0
             do 200 j = 1, maxnbrs
               if (nbrs(i,j) .eq. 0) goto 300
               u(i) = u(i) + coef(i,j) * utmp( nbrs(i,j) )
200          continue

300       continue

400       continue

          return
          end
```

Figure 3: Sweep over an unstructured mesh

and computation of the original **doall**, which are performed by the part of the program which we call the *executor*.

Such run-time analysis obviously adds overhead. It is not clear a priori whether this overhead will be low enough to justify the use of run-time analysis. However, the variables controlling the communications sets often do not change for many executions of the **doall** loop. We take advantage of this by computing the *in* and *out* sets only the first time they are needed and saving them for later loop executions. This amortizes the cost of the run-time analysis over many repetitions of the **doall**, lowering the overall cost of the computation. This method is generally applicable and relatively efficient. A detailed description of this approach and its performance is given in [10].

6 Related Work

Since the issue of effectively programming distributed memory architectures is so pressing, a number of other projects have sprung up in an attempt to provide cleaner environments for these machines. These projects fall into two major groups: those which attempt automatic distribution of data values and code and those which require the user to explicitly specify data distribution. Our approach is, in a sense, intermediate: we currently require the user to explicitly specify distributions, but are studying ways to automate array distribution. To show how our work relates to that of other researchers in this field, we briefly describe the principal alternative approaches being explored.

Among those following the first approach of automatic distribution of data and code, Quinn and Hatcher [18], and Reeves et al. [3, 19] compile languages based on SIMD semantics. These groups perform automatic distribution, while attempting to minimize the interprocessor synchronizations inherent in SIMD execution. The compiler for SPOT [23], an SIMD language designed specifically for point-iterative methods, performs compile-time analysis similar to ours to aggregate mesh point operations into larger processes. The AL compiler [24], targeted to one-dimensional systolic arrays, distributes only one dimension of the arrays. Based on the one dimensional distribution, this compiler allocates the iterations to the cells of the systolic array in a way that minimizes inter-cell communications.

Another approach is that of Linda [1], which is an explicit tasking language requiring the programmer to write code for each process. However, it does provide a shared name space called a *tuple space*, which can be implemented on distributed memory architectures. The language provides special primitives to access and modify this tuple space.

There are also a variety of projects following the second approach of leaving the distribution of data to the user. Pingali and Rogers [20] extend the dataflow language Id Nouveau with array distributions. Their compiler analysis appears similar to ours, and they also suggest run-time resolution of communications. However, they have not attempted to save run-time information over repeated execution of the parallel loops, and hence conclude that run-time resolution is "fairly inefficient". The Onyx environment [13], on the other hand, uses run-time analysis similar to that described here to handle communication patterns based on run-time data.

Griswold et al. [5] introduce the concept of *ensembles* to partition data, code and communication ports. The data is partitioned into sections, each section being mapped to a processor. This allows the data to scale with the number of processors as is the case with our system. The communication graph and the actual movement of data has to be explicitly specified by the programmer along with code for each processor. This allows them not only to distinguish between global and local computation but also to support the pure MIMD semantics.

Kennedy and coworkers [2, 7] and the SUPERB project [25] extend Fortran with array distributions. The approach there is to decompose the array into partitions and then specify a one-to-one mapping of partitions to processors. They utilize optimizing compiler transformations similar to our compile-time analysis to generate the processes and the necessary communications. The programmer can specify blocks of local data which have images on other processors. These blocks can then be explicitly "moved" by the programmer allowing the efficient copying of data across processors.

The language DINO [21] proposed by Rosing and Schnabel takes a similar approach by extending a C-like language with data distribution primitives. The user can then invoke parallel functions on these distributed data structure, however, the user needs to annotate off-processor data accesses. The language allows users to specify portions of data which are mapped to several processors. The copies are kept consistent automatically by the system thus allowing overlapping distributions to be programmed fairly easily. The compile-time analysis required for their approach is again similar to ours, however, as in most other approaches they do not provide any support for run-time analysis of communication patterns.

Run-time analysis of communications patterns has also been proposed in [16, 22], while [11, 17] study the efficiency of data structures required to support such run-time extraction of communication patterns.

7 Conclusions

Current programming environments for distributed memory architectures provide inadequate support for mapping applications to the machine. In particular, the lack of a global name space forces algorithms to be specified at a relatively low level. This greatly increases the complexity of programs, and also locks in algorithm design choices, inhibiting experimentation with alternate algorithm choices or problem decompositions. Thus, the relatively low-level of the programming environment leads, perhaps paradoxically, to poor performance, as well as burdening the programmer unnecessarily.

In this paper, we have described an environment which allows the user to specify data parallel algorithms at a high level, while still retaining control over those details critical to performance. It is important to note that there are no message-passing statements in KF1. Instead, the programmer views the program as operating within a global name space. The compiler analyses the program and produces the low level details of the message-passing code required to support the sharing of data on the distributed memory machines.

The support of a shared memory model provides a distinct advantage over message-passing languages; in those languages, communications statements often substantially increase the program size and complexity [4]. The global name space model used here allows the bodies of the **doall** loops to be independent of the distribution of the data and processor arrays used. If only local name spaces were supported, this would not be the case, since the communications necessary to implement two distribution patterns would be quite different. In a message-passing language, changing distribution patterns would involve extensive rewriting of the communications statements, and perhaps of the whole program. With our primitives, a variety of distribution patterns can easily be tried by trivial modification of this program. In this sense, Kali allows programming at a higher level of abstraction. Kali allows one to focus on the global algorithm, and worry less about machine-dependent details of the implementation.

The paper also outlined the transformations performed by the Kali compiler in order to efficiently map the KF1 programs to distributed memory machines. Our system relies on both compile-time and run-time analysis of the program. Compile-time analysis results in faster programs, but is only applicable when the compiler has adequate information. Run-time analysis is much more general, but also entails performance penalties. However, in many cases, the costs of run-time analysis can be effectively masked by the number of loop iterations performed, resulting in negligible overhead.

References

[1] S. Ahuja, N. Carriero, and D. Gelernter. Linda and friends. *IEEE Computer*, 19:26–34, August 1986.

[2] D. Callahan and K. Kennedy. Compiling programs for distributed-memory multiprocessors. *Journal of Supercomputing*, 2:151–169, 1988.

[3] A. L. Cheung and A. P. Reeves. The paragon multicomputer environement: A first implementation. Technical Report EE-CEG-89-9, Cornell University, July 1989.

[4] G. Fox, M. Johnson, G. Lyzenga, S. Otto, J. Salmon, and D. Walker. *Solving Problems on Concurrent Processors, Volume 1*. Prentice-Hall, Englewood Cliffs, NJ, 1986.

[5] W. Griswold, G. Harrison, D. Notkin, and L. Snyder. Scalable abstractions for parallel programming. In *Proceedings of the Fifth Distributed Memory Computing Conference*, April 1990.

[6] S. L. Johnsson, Y. Saad, and M. H. Schultz. Alternating direction methods on architectures. Technical Report YALEU/DCS/RR-382, Yale Research Report, October 1985.

[7] K. Kennedy and H. Zima. Virtual shared memory for distributed-memory machines. In *Proceedings of the Fourth Conference on Hypercube Concurrent Computers and Applications*, March 1989.

[8] K. Knobe, J. D. Lukas, and G. L. Steele. Data optimization: Allocation of arrays to reduce communication on SIMD machines. *Journal of Parallel and Distributed Computing*, 8(2):102–118, 1990.

[9] C. Koelbel and P. Mehrotra. Compiler transformations for non-shared memory machines. In *Proceedings of the 4th International Conference on Supercomputing*, volume 1, pages 390–397, May 1989.

[10] C. Koelbel, P. Mehrotra, and J. Van Rosendale. Supporting shared data structures on distributed memory architectures. In *2nd ACM SIGPLAN Symposium on Principles Practice of Parallel Programming*, pages 177–186, March 1990.

[11] C. Koelbel, P. Mehrotra, J. Saltz, and H. Berryman. Parallel loops on distributed machines. In *Proceedings of the Fifth Distributed Memory Computing Conference*, April 1990.

[12] D. S. Lim and R. V. Thanakij. A survey of ADI implementations on hypercubes. In *Proceedings of the Second Conference on Hypercube Multiporcessors*, 1987.

[13] R. Littlefield. Efficient iteration in data-parallel programs with irregular and dynamically distributed data structures. Technical Report 90-02-06, University of Washington, Seattle, February 1990.

[14] P. Mehrotra and J. Van Rosendale. The BLAZE language: A parallel language for scientific programming. *Parallel Computing*, 5:339–361, 1987.

[15] P. Mehrotra and J. Van Rosendale. Parallel language constructs for tensor product computations on loosely coupled architectures. In *Proceedings Supercomputing '89*, pages 616–626, November 1989.

[16] R. Mirchandaney, J. H. Saltz, R. M. Smith, D. M. Nicol, and Kay Crowley. Principles of runtime support for parallel processors. In *Proceedings of the 1988 ACM International Conference on Supercomputing , St. Malo France*, pages 140–152, July 1988.

[17] S. Mirchandaney, J. Saltz, H. Berryman, and P. Mehrotra. Parallel loops on distributed machines. In *Proceedings of the Fifth Distributed Memory Computing Conference*, April 1990.

[18] M. Quinn and P. Hatcher. Implementing a data parallel language on a tightly coupled multiprocessor. Technical Report 89-60-20, Oregon State University, Corvallis, OR, 1989.

[19] A. P. Reeves. Paragon: a programming paradigm for multicomputer systems. Technical Report EE-CEG-89-3, Cornell University, January 1989.

[20] A. Rogers and K. Pingali. Process decomposition through locality of reference. In *Conference on Programming Language Design and Implementation*, pages 69–80. ACM SIGPLAN, June 1989.

[21] M. Rosing and R. Schnabel. An overview of DINO - a new language for numerical computation on distributed memory multiprocessors. Technical Report CU-CS-385-88, University of Colorado, Boulder, 1988.

[22] J. Saltz, K. Crowley, R. Mirchandaney, and H. Berryman. Run-time scheduling and execution of loops on message passing machines. *Journal of Parallel and Distributed Computing*, 8(2):303–312, 1990.

[23] D. Socha. An approach to compiling single-point iterative programs for distributed memory computers. In *Proceedings of the Fifth Distributed Memory Computing Conference*, April 1990.

[24] P.-S. Tseng. An AL compiler for the Warp sytolic computer. In *Proceedings of the Fifth Distributed Memory Computing Conference*, April 1990.

[25] H. Zima, H. Bast, and M. Gerndt. Superb: A tool for semi-automatic MIMD/SIMD parallelization. *Parallel Computing*, 6:1–18, 1988.

20 Implementing a Data Parallel Language on a Tightly Coupled Multiprocessor

M. Quinn, P. Hatcher, B. Seevers

Abstract

Our thesis is that data parallel programs can be translated into programs that execute efficiently on a variety of architectures. Currently we are focusing on the data parallel programming language C*[TM], developed by Thinking Machines Corporation for the Connection Machine[TM] processor array. Previous papers have described the design of a cross-compiler for hypercube multicomputers. In this paper we propose the design of a cross-compiler that translates C* programs into C programs suitable for compilation and execution on a tightly coupled multiprocessor, the Sequent Balance 21000[TM]. The C* language is based upon a synchronous model of parallel computation, while the resulting C code executes asynchronously on the multiprocessor. We present a polynomial time algorithm that, given certain reasonable assumptions about dependences between expressions in parallel code, produces a minimal set of barrier synchronizations necessary to ensure the correctness of the translated program. We conclude by presenting evidence that compiled C* programs may be able to achieve reasonable speedup on tightly coupled multiprocessors.

C* and Connection Machine are trademarks of Thinking Machines Corporation. Balance is a trademark of Sequent Computer Systems.

1. Introduction

At a time when academics debate the merits of various processor organizations and vendors appear and disappear at an alarming rate, software portability is an important concern to parallel programmers. In the last few years a number of high level parallel programming languages and methodologies have been proposed, including Actus [14, 15], Blaze [9], Booster [13], C* [22], Coherent Parallel C [3], Dino [23], The Force [6], Kali [7], Linda [2], Orca [1], the paralation model [24], Parallel Pascal [20, 21], Poker [25], Seymour [10], and Vector C [8]. To the extent that these languages are based upon abstract models of parallel computation, they are more machine independent and, hence, more portable.

Our work has focused on the data parallel programming language C*, designed by Thinking Machines Corporation for its Connection Machine processor array. Previous papers have described preliminary [19] and refined [17, 18] designs for a compiler that translates C* programs into C programs suitable for execution on the NCUBE family of multicomputers. These compiler-generated C programs often rival and occasionally match the speed of hand-coded C programs written for the NCUBE. In this paper we present the design of a C* compiler for tightly coupled multiprocessors, and we give preliminary evidence that these programs can achieve reasonable speedup.

A *multiprocessor* is a multiple-CPU computer with a single address space [16]. Every processor can read from and write to every memory location. In a *tightly coupled multiprocessor* all processors work through a central switching mechanism to reach a shared global memory. The tightly coupled multiprocessor used for a testbed in this paper is the Sequent Balance 21000, which uses a high speed bus as its central switching mechanism.

2. The Data Parallel Programming Language C*

We believe a synchronous, massively parallel model in which all the processes change state in a simple, predictable fashion leads to understandable programs. In this kind of model parallelism comes from the simultaneous execution of a single operation across a large data set.

The first advantage of the data parallel approach is its simple control flow. It is easy to determine the state of the processes, since they are either active or inactive as a universal program counter works through the various control statements. A second advantage is that results of computations are deterministic and independent of the number of physical processors used. A third advantage is that it is straightforward to build a debugger. Breakpoints make sense on a single instruction stream model. Lastly, we mean to show that data parallel programs are portable.

We want to emphasize that data parallel languages are not **the** solution to programming multiprocessors; they are only a solution. While many problems, such as low-level vision, protein mechanics, and most linear algebra problems, are amenable to solution via data parallel programs, a data parallel language is not appropriate for implementing programs with multiple asynchronous processes, such as data base management systems and multiprogrammed operating systems. More insight into the data parallel approach can be gained by reading the article by Hillis and Steele [5].

The language C* is an extension of C that incorporates features of the data parallel programming model. We briefly describe a few important features of C*. For further details, see the paper by Rose and Steele [22].

All data in C* are divided into two kinds, scalar and parallel, referred to by the keywords mono and poly, respectively. C* allows the programmer to express algorithms as if there were an unbounded number of processors onto which the data can be mapped. Once every piece of parallel data has been mapped to its own processing element, several simple program constructs allow parallel operations to be expressed. The most important of these constructs is an extension of the class type in C++. A class is an implementation of an abstract data type. Instances of variables of a particular class type are manipulated with that class's member functions. In C* member functions operate on a number of instances of a class in parallel. This "parallel class type" is called a *domain*.

In C* variables of a domain type are mapped to separate processing elements, and all instances of a domain type may be acted upon in parallel by using that domain's member functions and the selection statement (which is illustrated below). Within parallel code each sequential program statement is performed in parallel for all instances of the specified domain.

The following code segment computes the element-wise maximum of two arrays.

```
domain vector { real a, b, max; } x[100];
< Intervening code >
[domain vector].{
   if (a > b) max = a;
   else max = b;
}
```

The domain type vector defines a domain containing two real values named a and b. By declaring x to be a 100-element array of vector, 100 instances of the variable pair are created, one pair per processing element. The selection statement [domain vector] activates every processing element whose instance has domain type vector; i.e., every element of x. Every active processing element executes the statements contained within the selection statement. In this case every processing element evaluates the expression a > b. The universal program counter enters the **then** clause, and those processing elements for which the expression is true perform the assignment statement **max** = a. Next the universal program counter enters the **else** clause, and those processing elements for which the expression is false perform the assignment statement **max** = b.

Within a C* program, any expression can contain a reference to any variable in any domain. For example, consider the following code segment, in which every active processing element sets its own value of **temp** to be the average of the **temp** values of its predecessor and successor processing elements:

```
#define N 100
domain rod { real temp; } x[N];
< Intervening code >
[domain rod].{
    int index = this-x;   /* Meaning of this is same as in C++ */
    < Intervening code >
    if ((index > 0) && (index < N-1))
        temp = (x[index-1].temp + x[index+1].temp)/2.0;
}
```

Each processing element's value of **index** gives its unique position in the domain, a value in the range 0...N−1. All active processing elements evaluate the right hand side of the assignment statement together, then they all perform the assignment of values together. Hence an old value cannot be overwritten before an adjacent processing element has had the opportunity to read it.

3. Evaluating the Cost of Synchronizations

Previous implementations of C* have been on architectures in which each processor has its own local memory. Processing elements are tightly bound to the physical processors emulating them, and when a processing element accesses a variable of a processing element mapped to a different physical processor, message passing is required. On a tightly coupled multiprocessor every processor has access to every memory location. The Balance C programming language allows variables to be declared as shared, meaning every CPU can read and write their values. Because the variables of all processing elements are accessible to all physical processors, this need for passing messages vanishes.

On the other hand, the values of variables in active domain instances must still be buffered at times. For example, consider the C* assignment statement

```
temp = (x[index-1].temp + x[index+1].temp)/2.0
```

taken from the second example in the previous section. Because the physical processors execute asynchronously on a multiprocessor, every processor must be guaranteed access to the old temp values before they are overwritten. If the only processor synchronization mechanism is the barrier synchronization, then either the old values of temp or the value of the expression must be buffered before the barrier. After the synchronization the assignment can take place, using the values stored in the buffers.

In this section we evaluate the effect that this copying and synchronization overhead can have on the performance of the parallel program.

The maximum efficiency possible per processor is a function of grain size; that is, a function of both the number of data elements per processor and the number of computations performed on these data elements between synchronizations. Assume each processor's share of the data is n elements. Suppose at the heart of the parallel algorithm is an iteration in which each processor performs $f(n)$ operations on n elements, buffers n results, and then synchronizes with the other processors.

If K is the time spent per arithmetic operation, then the time needed to perform the computation is $Kf(n)$. Let p be the number of processors, S be the synchronization time per processor, and C be the time needed to copy one data element into temporary storage. The overhead of the parallel program, then, is $Sp + 2Cn$, and the efficiency of the parallel program is

$$\text{Efficiency} = \frac{Kf(n)}{Kf(n) + Sp + 2Cn}$$

Reasonable estimates of the values of these constants on the Sequent Balance are $C = 23$ μsec, $K = 41$ μsec, and $S = 50$ μsec. Given these values, we have shown in Figure 1 the maximum efficiency possible, as a function of data set size, for $f(n) = n$, $f(n) = n \log n$, and $f(n) = n^2$ on a 30-processor system.

The graph shows that for small-grained computations, buffering and synchronization time can dramatically lower the peak efficiency achievable by the parallel program. Hence it is vital that the number of synchronizations be minimized, especially inside loops.

To illustrate this concept with an actual example, we have hand-translated a C* Gaussian elimination program into a Sequent Balance C program and compared its speedup against the speedup achieved by a program executing on the NCUBE/7 hypercube multicomputer [17]. Figure 2 illustrates the results. Figure 2-a shows the speedups achieved on a system of 64 equations. The speedups vary widely, because the grain size is small enough that the time spent communicating has a large impact on speedup. The NCUBE/7 has lower speedup, since its synchronization and copying times are much higher. In Figure 2-b the computers are solving a system of 256 equations. The grain size is larger, so the time spent copying values is relatively less important, and the speedup curves are quite similar.

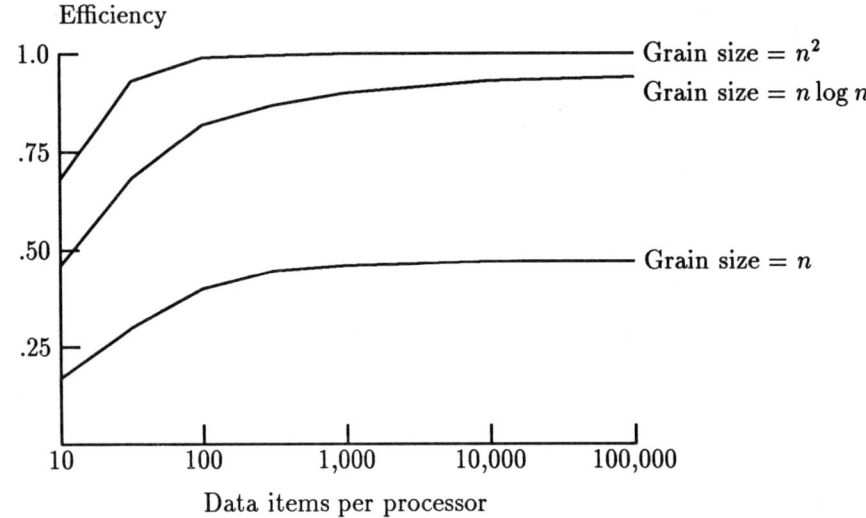

Figure 1. Maximum efficiency possible per processor as a function of number of data elements per processor and number of computations performed on these data elements (30-processor Sequent Balance 21000).

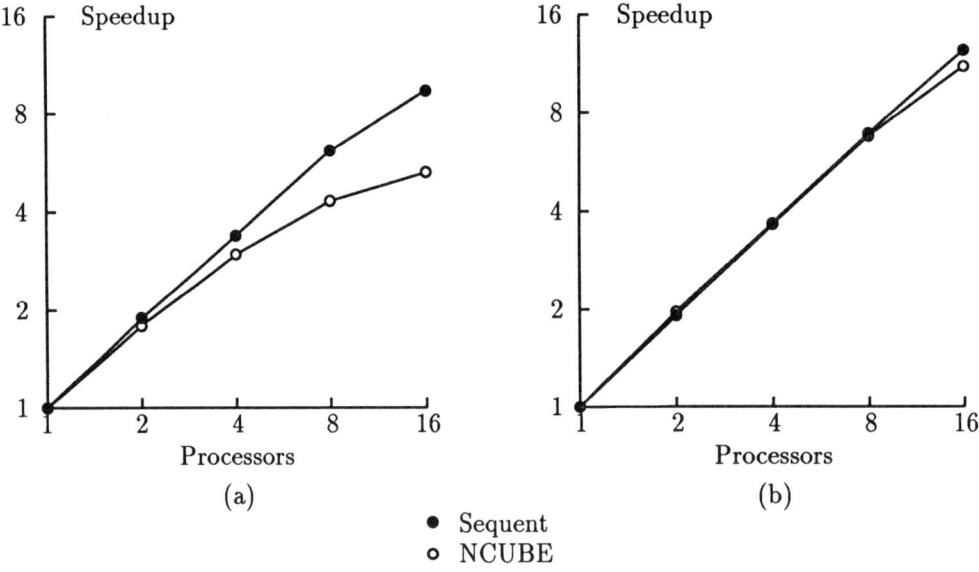

- Sequent
- ○ NCUBE

Figure 2. Performance of two parallel programs that decompose a dense system of linear equations into its LU factorization using Gaussian elimination. (a) Speedup achieved decomposing a system of size 64. (b) Speedup achieved decomposing a system of size 256.

4. The Translation of C* Programs

Our compiler design must address two fundamental issues. The first issue is the insertion of synchronization points into the C program produced by the compiler so that (1) every processor participates in every barrier synchronization; and (2) the semantics of the C program asynchronously executing on the multiprocessor is identical to the semantics of the original C* program. The second is the emulation of processing elements. Data parallel programs often assume a very large number of processing elements. If these programs are to run efficiently on a multiprocessor with far fewer physical processors, then there must be an efficient mechanism for emulating processing elements on physical processors.

4.1. Minimizing Number of Processor Synchronizations

We approach the synchronization issue by asking the following question: how much can we loosen the synchronization requirements of the language without affecting the behavior of programs? If a set of processing elements were executing the same block of code and were only accessing their own local variables, it would not matter if they synchronized after every statement, after every other statement, or only at the end of the block. However, if halfway through the block each processing element reads a value from its neighbor and that value may have been written after the last synchronization point, then the processors must be synchronized prior to accessing that value in shared memory, in order to guarantee that the value retrieved by each processor is the same as it would be under a fully synchronous implementation. Similarly, if a processing element writes a value into the memory of another processing element, and that memory location has been read from by another processing element after the last synchronization, then a synchronization is required in order to preserve the semantics. Hence synchronization is required between statements in which different processing elements access the same memory location. To determine the intervals that must include at least one synchronization, the compiler performs data flow analysis, building def-use and use-def chains at those places where different processing element interact.

A single block of code may have more than one data dependency requiring a synchronization. For example, consider the following code segment:

```
1.  mono float csum;
2.  domain foo { float a, b, c; } x[100];
3.  <Intervening code>
4.  [domain foo].{
5.     csum += c;
6.     a = b + c;
7.     (this-1)->b = b;
8.     c = c / csum;
```

Given: List L of n pairs (i, j) representing expression ranges. The existence of pair (i, j) implies there must be a synchronization barrier placed immediately before at least one of the expressions in the range $i \ldots j$.

Result: Minimal set B of expressions immediately before which barrier synchronizations should be placed.

1. $B = \emptyset$
2. Sort list L by first value. Call resulting list F.
3. Sort list L by second value. Call resulting list S.
4. While list S is not empty do
   4a. $B = B \cup \{j\}$, where (i, j) is the first pair in S
   4b. While $j \leq k$, where (k, l) is the first pair in list F do
       Remove pair (k, l) from list F and list S

Figure 3. Algorithm *SelectSyncs*, which finds a minimal set of synchronization points, given a list of synchronization requirements.

Because active processing elements access in line 8 the value of csum, which is defined in line 5, there must be a barrier synchronization between lines 5 and 8. Because every active processing element overwrites in line 7 another processing element's variable, b, that is read in the line 6, there must be a barrier synchronization between lines 6 and 7. A single barrier synchronization, placed between lines 6 and 7, is sufficient to achieve both purposes.

Adding Synchronization Points to Basic Blocks. Gavril [4] showed that, given a set of intervals, finding the minimum number of points such that every interval spans at least one point can be done in polynomial time. A simple greedy algorithm can extract a minimal set of synchronizations from a list of synchronization requirements. Our algorithm, called *SelectSyncs*, is shown in Figure 3, and an example of its operation appears in Figure 4.

Complexity analysis. Let n denote the number of data dependences and e the number of expressions in the basic block. Step 1 requires constant time. If we use a bucket sort, then Steps 2 and 3 have complexity $\Theta(e + n)$. The body of loop 4b is executed exactly n times during the course of the algorithm. Removing the first element from list F can be done in constant time. By doubly-linking list S and linking elements of F with the corresponding element in list S, the second deletion can be accomplished in constant time as well. Step 4a, too, is executed exactly n times during the course of the algorithm, and it requires constant time. Hence the total time complexity of step 4 of the algorithm is $\Theta(n)$. Algorithm *SelectSyncs* has time complexity $\Theta(e + n)$.

Adding Synchronization Points to Loops. Next we explain how to add synchroniza-

Input:
    L: (2,6), (3,4), (6,8), (2,5), (7,10), (4,6)

Sort list L into lists F and S:
    F: (2,6), (2,5), (3,4), (4,6), (6,8), (7,10)
    S: (3,4), (2,5), (4,6), (2,6), (6,8), (7,10)

Add {4} to B.
Remove (2,6),(2,5), (3,4), (4,6) from F and S.
    F: (6,8), (7,10)
    S: (6,8), (7,10)

Add {8} to B.
Remove (6,8), (7,10) from F and S.

Algorithm terminates. B = $\{4, 8\}$

Figure 4. Example of operation of algorithm *SelectSyncs*.

tion points to a loop. Midkiff [11] and Midkiff and Padua [12] have presented algorithms for inserting synchronization points into the bodies of FORTRAN DO loops marked for parallel execution. Midkiff [11] has shown that the problem of eliminating redundant dependences is NP-hard. The C* programmer does not have to rely upon concurrent execution of multiple loop iterations to achieve parallelism, since parallelism is explicit in the C* selection statement. Therefore, we make the reasonable simplifying assumption that all loop data dependences between points E_1 and E_2 imply that there must be at least one barrier synchronization between the time that the global flow of control leaves point E_1 and the time it reaches point E_2. Given this assumption, our algorithm finds the minimal number of barrier synchronizations to insert into a loop.

If the loop contains only forward data dependences, it is handled using the basic *SelectSyncs* algorithm. If the loop contains backward data dependences, then there may or may not be an expression not spanned by a data dependence. If there is an expression not spanned by a data dependence, then the loop may be cut at that point and the basic algorithm applied to the resulting segment with "forward-only" dependences (see Figure 5). Given a loop with d data dependences and e expressions, it may require time $\Theta(e)$ to find an appropriate expression at which to cut the loop. Hence the complexity of the algorithm is $\Theta(e + d)$.

If data dependences span every expression in the loop, then we must try cutting the loop at the end point of every data dependence. By putting a synchronization before

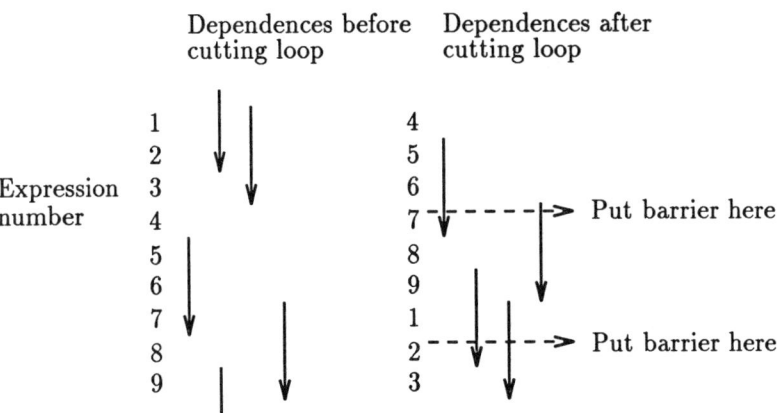

Figure 5. Determining synchronization points in a loop where data dependences do not span entire loop.

that expression and removing all data dependences ensured by that synchronization, all remaining data dependences are "forward" and the elementary algorithm can be applied. After attempting to cut the loop at all such data dependence end points, we choose the solution requiring the fewest synchronizations. The algorithm has complexity $\Theta(e + d^2)$, where d is the number of data dependences and e is the number of expressions in the loop.

Adding Synchronization Points to an Entire Program. Synchronization points are added to an entire program in the following manner. First the necessary synchronization points are added to the loops. In the case of nested loops, the algorithm works outward from the innermost loop. The remaining data dependences are all in the forward direction. Those which span a synchronization point can be removed. Of those that remain, the loop portions of those that enter or leave loops are removed (since we do not wish to add any more synchronization points inside loops). Once these modifications have been made, algorithm *SelectSyncs* can be applied to the remaining dependences to determine the remaining synchronization points.

Transforming Control Structures. Because a barrier synchronization requires the participation of all physical processors, we must guarantee that if any processing elements are still executing a loop with at least one synchronization, all physical processors must be executing at least the barrier synchronization. In other words, no processing element can execute the statement after the loop until all processing elements have exited the loop. This constraint forces all processing elements to compute a global logical *OR* of the Boolean loop control values. A processing element can exit the loop only when the global logical *OR* is *false*.

Of course, a processing element does not actually execute the body of the loop

The C* construct: is translated into the following C code:

```
while (condition) {                temp = TRUE;
    statement_list₁;               do {
    barrier_synchronization;           if (temp) temp = condition;
    statement_list₂;                   if (temp) {
}                                          statement_list₁;
                                       }
                                       barrier_synchronization;
                                       gtemp = global_or (temp);
                                       if (temp) {
                                           statement_list₂;
                                       }
                                   } while (gtemp);
```

Figure 6. Translation of C* while loop.

The C* construct: is translated into the following C code:

```
if (condition) {                   temp = condition;
    statement_list₁;               if (temp) {
    barrier_synchronization;           statement_list₁;
    statement_list₂;               }
}                                  barrier_synchronization;
                                   if (temp) {
                                       statement_list₂;
                                   }
```

Figure 7. Translation of simple if statement.

after its local loop control value has gone to *false*. Rather, the physical processor on which it resides participates in the barrier synchronization and the global *OR* operation. This means that our C* compiler must rewrite the control structures of input programs. Figure 6 illustrates how while loops are rewritten.

The requirement that all physical processors must actively participate in any barrier synchronization forces our compiler to rewrite all control statements that have inner statements requiring a synchronization. We must rewrite the statement in order to bring the synchronization to the surface of the control structure. Figure 7 illustrates how an if statement is handled.

Synchronizations buried inside nested control structures are pulled out of each en-

The C* construct: is translated into the following C code:

```
if (condition₁) {                        temp₁ = condition₁;
    statement_list_1;                    if (temp₁) {
    if (condition₂) {                        statement_list₁;
        statement_list₂;                     temp₂ = condition₂;
        barrier_synchronization;             if (temp₂) {
        statement_list₃;                         statement_list₂;
    }                                        }
    statement_list₄;                     }
}                                        barrier_synchronization;
                                         if (temp₁) {
                                             if (temp₂) {
                                                 statement_list₃;
                                             }
                                             statement_list₄;
                                         }
```

Figure 8. Translation of nested `if` statements.

closing structure until they reach the outermost level. Figure 8 shows a nested if statement.

The technique just described will not handle arbitrary control flow graphs. For this reason we have not implemented the `goto` statement. We can, however, handle the `break` and `continue` statements.

4.2. Efficiently Emulating Processing Elements

Once the barrier synchronizations have been brought to the surface of the control structures, emulation of processing elements is straightforward. We statically allocate work to processors; every physical processor emulates an equal share of processing elements. The compiler puts `for` loops around the blocks of code that have been delimited by the synchronization steps. During each iteration of a `for` loop a physical processor emulates the actions of a different processing element. Since within the delimited blocks there is no interaction between processing elements, it makes no difference in which order the physical processors perform the operations of the processing elements.

4.3. Summary

To summarize, the compiler must first locate the expression ranges that must include a barrier synchronization. Second, the compiler must generate a set of synchronizations that satisfy the synchronization requirements. Third, the compiler must transform the control structure of the input program to bring these synchronization steps to the outermost level. Finally, in order to allow a single physical processor to emulate a number of processing elements, the compiler must insert `for` loops around the blocks of code that

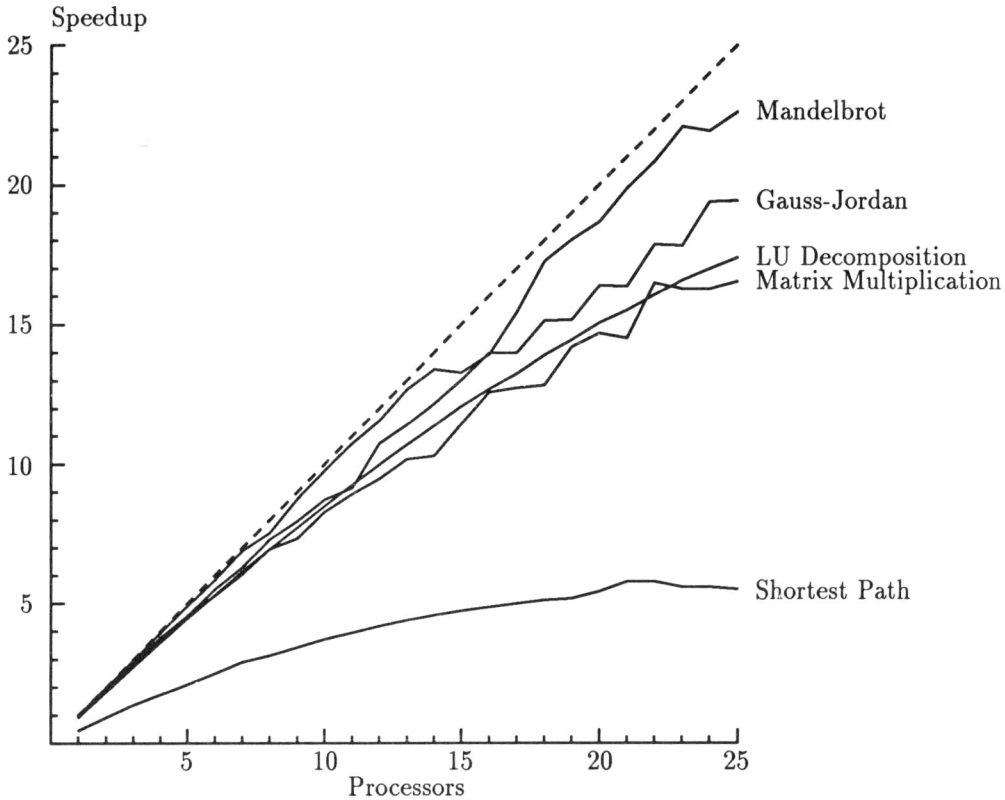

Figure 9. Speedup achieved by five hand-compiled C* programs on Sequent Balance 21000 multiprocessor.

are delimited by the barrier synchronizations.

5. Experimental Results

To evaluate the potential of the design outlined above to yield a compiler that produces executables with acceptable performance, we have hand-translated five benchmark programs from C* into Sequent C, then compiled the C programs using the GNU C compiler. The speedups achieved by these programs are illustrated in Figure 9. Speedup is computed by comparing the time of the parallel program on p processors with the time of the best known sequential implementation of the algorithm on 1 processor.

The first program explores how well the compiler can handle "embarrassingly parallel" programs in which there are no interactions between virtual processors. The program computes the Mandelbrot set for 16,384 points constituting a square on the complex plane bounded by the points (-2,-2) and (2,2). The program achieves nearly linear speedup; the performance degradation observed can be attributed to contention for the shared bus.

The second and third programs solve dense systems of linear equations. Because of the large grain size—$\Theta(n^2)$ operations per synchronization step—these algorithms, too, achieve nearly linear speedup until the system bus becomes a limiting resource. The speedup curves shown illustrate the performance of both programs reducing a 192 × 192 system. The Gauss-Jordan achieves slightly higher speedup than simple Gaussian elimination, because it reduces every row every iteration, whereas Gaussian elimination reduces only those rows which have not been used as pivots.

The fourth C* program is a parallelization of matrix multiplication, another $\Theta(n^3)$ sequential algorithm. The algorithm is "row parallel"; that is, every virtual processor in the C* program is responsible for a row of the first factor matrix, a column of the second factor matrix, and a row of the product matrix. The figure illustrates the speedup of the hand-translated program multiplying two 128 × 128 integer matrices. Because the processors perform $\Theta(n^2)$ operations per synchronization, this algorithm, too, achieves reasonable speedup.

The fifth C* program solves the single source, all paths problem using Dijkstra's algorithm, having sequential time complexity $\Theta(n^2)$. The program performs $n-1$ iterations, and each iteration requires that the virtual processors interact at several points. Hence the grain size per synchronization is $\Theta(n)$, and the resulting speedup is poor.

Most of the speedup curves in Figure 9 exhibit irregularities. These irregularities are due to an unequal distribution of work among the processors. Recall that our compiler performs a static allocation of work to processes; no attempt is made at run time to redistribute the workload.

The efficiency of Dijkstra's shortest path algorithm is particularly low: we measured a speedup of 0.45 on one processor. This 55% drop in efficiency relative to the best sequential algorithm can be traced to a several factors. Two factors are particularly important: the C* compiler's inability to recognize the "tournament idiom" (to be described later), and the large number of local variables introduced by the C* compiler.

The most significant factor leading to poor efficiency of Dijkstra's algorithm is the insertion of an extra barrier synchronization in the portion of the program where the unmarked vertex closest to the source is found. In C*, the code to find this vertex is found inside a domain select:

```
if (!marked) {
   if (dist == (<?= dist))
      choice = ID;
}
```

A virtual processing element is associated with every vertex of the graph. The first `if` condition screens out processing elements associated with marked vertices—those for which a shortest path has already been found. The unary reduction operator `<?=` returns the smallest value of `dist` among all unmarked processing elements. By comparing the local value of `dist` with the minimum value, the second `if` condition screens out those processing elements whose vertices are not closest to the source. After the (possibly parallel) assignment of `ID` to `choice`, `choice` contains the number of the processing element whose vertex is to be marked next. Immediately afterward, processing elements use the value of `choice` to examine and possibly update their values of `dist`.

This code segment is an example of what we call the "tournament idiom," a situation in which we are more concerned about which processing element "wins" than we are about the "winning" value. A C programmer, understanding the objectives, can perform this operation using only a single barrier synchronization. The C* compiler, relying solely upon its data flow analysis, inserts two barrier synchronizations: one after each assignment statement. The extra barrier synchronization reduces by 35% the single-processor efficiency of the compiled C* program relative to its hand-coded C counterpart.

The large number of local variables used by the compiled C* program is the second most significant cause of poor efficiency. The C program resulting from our translation of the C* code has more local variables than the hand-coded C program, and there are not enough registers in a National Semiconductor 32032 CPU to accommodate all of them. This shortage of registers reduces by another 14% the single-processor efficiency of the compiled C* program.

6. Conclusions

We have examined some key issues in the translation of C* programs into semantically equivalent C programs suitable for compilation and execution on a tightly compiled multiprocessor. The existence of a shared global memory eliminates the need for communicating values of domain instances from one physical processor to another. However, copying values into temporary locations in global storage and synchronizing the physical processors are needed at times. We have examined how synchronizations can affect the efficiency of the parallel program, and we have presented an algorithm that introduces barrier synchronizations into the C program. Finally, we have presented evidence that a C* compiler can generate programs that achieve reasonable speedup.

Acknowledgments

This work was supported by National Science Foundation grant CCR-8906622.

References

1. Bal, H. E., Kaaschoek, M. f., and Tanenbaum, A. S. Experience with distributed

processing in Orca. In *Proceedings of the IEEE Computer Society 1990 International Conference on Computer Languages*, New Orleans, LA (March 1990), pp. 79–89.

2. Carriero, N., and Gelernter, D. Linda in context. *Communications of the ACM* 32, 4 (April 1989), pp.444–458.

3. Felten, E. W., and Otto, S. W. Coherent Parallel C. In *Proceedings of the Third Conference on Hypercube Concurrent Computers and Applications*, ACM Press, 1988, pp. 440–450.

4. Gavril, F. Algorithms for minimum coloring, maximum clique, minimum covering by cliques, and maximum independent set of a chordal graph. *SIAM Journal on Computing* 1, 2 (1972), pp. 180–187.

5. Hillis, W. D., and Steele, G. L., Jr. Data parallel algorithms. *Communications of the ACM* 29, 12 (December 1986), pp. 1170–1183.

6. Jordan, H. The Force. In *The Characteristics of Parallel Algorithms*, L. H. Jamieson, D. B. Gannon, and R. J. Douglass, eds., The MIT Press, Cambridge, MA, 1987, pp. 395–436.

7. Koelbel, C., and Mehrotra, P. Supporting shared data structures on distributed memory architectures. Technical report, Department of Computer Sciences, Purdue University, 1989.

8. Li, K.-C., and Schwetman, H. Vector C: a vector processing language. *Journal of Parallel and Distributed Computing* 2 (1985), pp. 132–169.

9. Mehrotra, P., and Van Rosendale, J. The BLAZE language: A parallel language for scientific programming. *Parallel Computing* 5 (1987), pp. 339–361.

10. Miller, R., and Stout, Q. F. An introduction to the portable parallel programming language Seymour. In *Proceedings of the Thirteenth Annual International Computer Software and Applications Conference*, IEEE Computer Society, 1989.

11. Midkiff, S. P. Automatic generation of synchronization instructions for parallel processors. M.S. thesis, University of Illinois at Urbana-Champaign, CSRD Report 588 (May 1986).

12. Midkiff, S. P., and Padua, D. A. Compiler algorithms for synchronization. *IEEE Transactions on Computers* C-36, 12 (December 1987), pp. 1485–1495.

13. Paalvast, E. M. R. M. The Booster language. TNO-rapport 89-ITI-B-18, Instituut voor Toegepaste Informatica TNO, Delft, The Netherlands, 1989.

14. Perrott, R. H. *Parallel Programming*. Addison-Wesley, Wokingham, England, 1987.

15. Perrott, R. H., Crookes, D., Milligan, P., and Martin Purdy, W. R. A compiler for an array and vector processing language. *IEEE Transactions on Software Engineering* SE-11, 5 (May 1985), pp. 471–478.

16. Quinn, M. J. *Designing Efficient Algorithms for Parallel Computers*, McGraw-Hill, New York, NY, 1987.

17. Quinn, M. J., and Hatcher, P. J. Compiling SIMD programs for MIMD computers. In *Proceedings of the IEEE Computer Society 1990 International Conference on Computer Languages*, New Orleans, LA (March 1990), pp. 291–296.

18. Quinn, M. J., and Hatcher, P. J. Data parallel programming on multicomputers. *IEEE Software* (September 1990).

19. Quinn, M. J., Hatcher, P. J., and Jourdenais, K. C. Compiling C* programs for a hypercube multicomputer. In *Proceedings of the ACM/SIGPLAN PPEALS 1988, Parallel Programming: Experience with Applications, Languages, and Systems*, July 1988, *SIGPLAN Notices* 23, 9 (September 1988), pp. 57-65.
20. Reeves, A. P. Parallel Pascal: An extended Pascal for parallel computers. *Journal of Parallel and Distributed Computing* 1 (1984), pp. 64-80.
21. Reeves, A. P., and Bergmark, D. Parallel Pascal and the FPS hypercube supercomputer. In *Proceedings of the 1987 International Conference on Parallel Processing*, IEEE Press, 1987, pp. 385-388.
22. Rose, J. R., and Steele, G. L., Jr. C*: An extended C language for data parallel programming. Tech. report PL 87-5, Thinking Machines Corporation, Cambridge, MA, 1986.
23. Rosing, M., Schnabel, R. B., and Weaver, Dino: Summary and examples. In *Proceedings of the Third Conference on Hypercube Concurrent Computers and Applications*, ACM Press, 1988, pp. 472-481.
24. Sabot, G. W. *The Paralation Model.* MIT Press, Cambridge, MA, 1988.
25. Snyder, L. Parallel programming and the Poker programming environment. *Computer* 17, 7 (July 1984), pp. 27-36.

Michael J. Quinn is an associate professor of computer science at Oregon State University, Corvallis, OR 97331.

Philip J. Hatcher is an assistant professor of computer science at the University of New Hampshire, Durham, NH 03824.

Bradley K. Seevers is a graduate student in computer science at Oregon State University.

21 Automating the Coordination of Interprocessor Communication
J. Li, M. Chen

Abstract

This paper presents methods for ensuring correct synchronization and scheduling of message-passing in the context of compiling shared-memory programs onto distributed-memory machines. We show that from a given source loop nest, there corresponds a *maximum granularity* where the computation can go on without the need for any communication, and a *communication window* within which a communication command must occur and can occur anywhere legally. Better overall efficiency can then be achieved by playing with the granularity parameter using more frequent communication than that for the maximum granularity case.

1 Introduction

In compiling a shared-memory program to a distributed-memory target machine, explicit communication commands to achieve interprocessor data transfer must be generated from the references in the source program. The generation process has three parts to it: first, selecting appropriate communication primitives (the *synthesis* part), placing the calls to these primitives in appropriate location in the target program text to ensure correct statement sequencing and scope (*scheduling*), and setting up correct conditions for invoking these primitives (*synchronization*). This paper addresses the latter two issues, referred to together as the issues of *coordinating* interprocessor communication. We present a solution which ensures that the data dependency of the original shared-memory program is preserved in the target message-passing program. Two important notions are developed for coordination: the *maximum granularity* of a loop nest where the computation can go on without the need for any communication, and a *communication window* within which a communication command must occur and can occur anywhere legally.

First we provide some background for our work on coordination of interprocessor communication.

Crystal Approach The Crystal approach to programming parallel computers is to begin with a machine-independent, high-level problem specification. A sequence of transformations, either suggested by the programmer or generated by the compiler, are then applied to this specification. These transformations are tuned for each particular machine architecture so that efficient target code with explicit communication can be generated. Our approach to compilation consists of the following components:

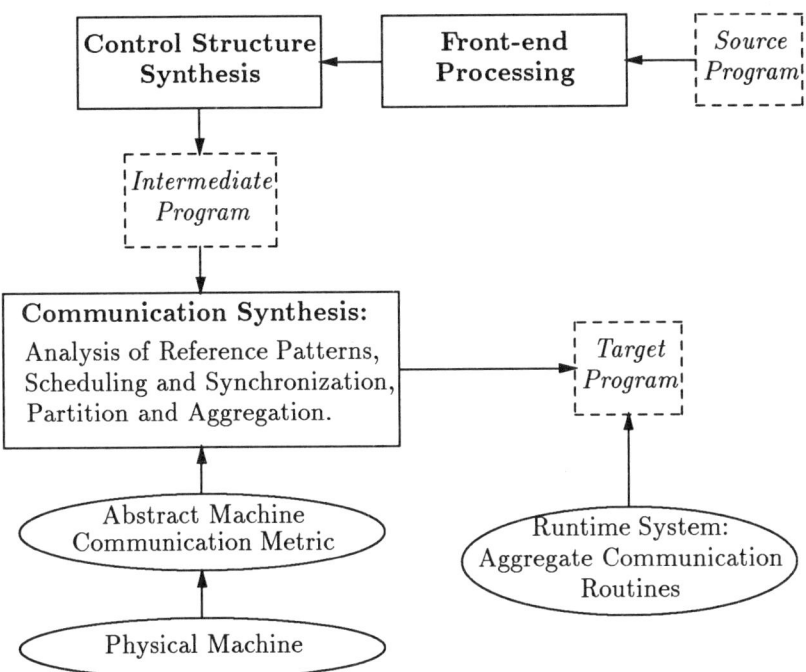

Figure 1: A High Level View of the Communication Synthesis Module

1. *Control structure synthesis:* deriving a parallel control structure from a functional specification or a sequential program. This component as shown in Figure 1 generates an intermediate program in which parallel schedule and flow of control are made explicit, but the references are still based on a global shared memory.

2. *Data distribution:* mapping the program data structure to a virtual network and then embedding the virtual network into the physical network. Specifically, we consider virtual networks which are multi-dimensional grids and use the standard Gray code embedding of a grid into a hypercube. The mapping from data structures to the virtual network consists of (1) *partitioning* the program data structures into appropriate grain sizes in such a way that communication overhead is reduced and workload is balanced, and (2) determining the relative locations of data structures so as to minimize interprocessor communication (we call this process *domain alignment*).

3. *Communication synthesis:* translating all references to data structures to either local memory accesses or interprocessor communication. The reference patterns of the intermediate program are matched with a library of aggregate communication routines and those which minimize network congestion and overhead are chosen. Once such calls to communication routines are determined, they need to appear in the program text under the correct conditions, statement sequence, and scope. This issue of coordinating interprocessor communication is the topic of this paper.

Issues in Coordinating Interprocessor Communication We use the following example to illustrate some issues arising in automating the coordination of interprocessor communication. The following loop nest contains a segment of a shared-memory program with explicit parallel control using forall loops:

for $(t : [0..n])$
  forall $((i,j) : [1..n] \times [1..n])$
    $a(i,j,t) =$ if $(t > 1)$ and $(i > j) \rightarrow a(i+1, j-2, t-1);$
                else $\rightarrow i + j;$

The program is written in a single-assignment, C-like notation which will be described in more detail in Section 2. The array a has been expanded with an extra dimension so as to allow the single assignment form of statement, however, its implementation will actually be a two-dimensional array using side-effecting assignment statements.

Suppose we distribute the forall loops over the two-dimensional domain to a two-dimensional network of processors. Let each processor be denoted by a pair (x,y), and let processor (x,y) be responsible for a range of iterations specified by the intervals $D_1 = [I_l(x,y)..I_u(x,y)]$ and $D_2 = [J_l(x,y)..J_u(x,y)]$. The following is the program for each processor (x,y) which is assigned a portion of array a:

Program for processor (x,y) :
for $(t : [0..n])$
  forall $((i,j) : D_1 \times D_2)$
    if $(t > 1)$ && $(i > j)$
      $a[i][j][t] = a[i+1][j-2][t-1];$
    else $a[i][j][t] = i + j;$

For any given iteration $t : [0..n]$, the reference pattern of the program indicates that for every element (i,j) in the domain $[1..n] \times [1..n]$, the value of a needs to be shifted to another element which is offset by $(1,-2)$ steps from itself.

Recognizing such a pattern symbolically, we can match these references with the following send and receive commands, and the target message passing program will look like

Program for processor (x,y) :
for $(t : [0..n])\{$
  forall $(\langle(i,j)$ on boundary of $D_1 \times D_2\rangle)$ {
    if $(t > 1)$ && $(i - 1) > (j + 2)$
      send$((-1, 2), a);$
    if $(t > 1)$ && $(i > j)$
      receive$((1, -2), a);$
  }
  forall $((i,j) : D_1 \times D_2)$

$$\text{if } (t > 1) \,\&\&\, (i > j)$$
$$a[i][j][t] = a[i+1][j-2][t-1];$$
$$\text{else } a[i][j][t] = i + j;$$
}

As we see above, the destination addresses of the **send** and **receive** commands are the inverses (to be defined later) of each other, and so are the predicates of the statements in which they appear. Since such information is not explicit in the shared-memory program, it needs to be derived symbolically. Also, there are many possible choices for when a communication can occur; for instance, it can occur immediately before the statement where the transferred data are to be used or it can occur much earlier. In addition, the actual target code generated will be more complex than what is shown above due to the need to aggregate many individual send commands into a single send command to avoid overhead involved in each invocation of a communication command. There are alternative ways to aggregate which can have significant performance impact.

Related Work The problem of automatically generating communication for distributed-memory machines from program references is addressed by several research projects [1, 9, 13, 14, 15, 16, 18] In terms of coordinating interprocessor communication, most of the proposed ideas use *run-time analysis* to solve the synchronization problem, which works as follows. A processor sends out a request whenever there is a need for a piece of data which is not available locally, and the request will interrupt the source processor. In this setting, scheduling is by default (communication occurs whenever there is a request). Rogers and Pingali [15] also describe a *compile-time resolution* in which processors are assigned to every computation node in the abstract-syntax tree of the source program at compile-time so that the source and destination of each message can be determined. The scheduling problem is not specifically discussed in that paper.

2   Context

To make this paper self-contained, we first describe the framework for generating communication commands from source program references. We introduce concepts and notations that are pertinent to the problems addressed in this paper. We first define the form of the input programs, called *shared-memory programs*. Then we introduce the notions and representations of *index domains* and *reference patterns*, which provide essential information regarding the latent parallelism and communication in a program. Next, we describe a set of run-time communication routines, which will be used by the compiler to implement interprocessor communication. We also describe *standard data partition strategies* since data layout affects the communication to be generated. Finally, we describe the method for selecting calls to run-time communication routines based on analyzing the reference patterns appearing in the shared-memory program.

```
for (t : [0..n]) {
    forall ((i, j) : [1..n] × [1..n])
        b(i, j, t) = if (j = t) →
                    \ + {a(i, x, t − 1) | 1 ≤ x ≤ n};
                    else → 1;
    forall ((i, j) : [1..n] × [1..n])
        a(i, j, t) = if (t = 0) → 0;
                    else if (i = b(0, t, t)) → a(i, j, t − 1);
                    else → b(i, t, t);
}
```

Figure 2: A Shared-Memory Program

2.1 Shared-Memory Programs

The input program to the communication synthesis module shown in Figure 1 is given in a C-like notation augmented with parallel control structures to be described below. Suitable pre-processing can be applied to programs written in exiting parallel shared-memory languages or sequential languages augmented with parallel control structures (see [17] for FORTRAN extensions) to obtain this form (with un-essential syntactic variations). An example shared-memory program is given in Figure 2.

We have the following assumptions on the form shared-memory programs:

Single assignment: Each array element can be assigned to only once. However, an array can appear on the left-hand side of many assignment statements (so long as different array elements are assigned to each time).

Left-hand side subscripts are index variables: Array subscript expressions on the left-hand side of an assignment statement must be index variables. For instance, the following statement
$$a(i, j - 1) = b(i + 2, j)$$
should be written as
$$a(i, j) = b(i + 2, j + 1).$$

Arrays are aligned: Within each loop nest, arrays are aligned to have a common *index domain* (see [12] for a detailed discussion on domain alignment). The boundaries of each individual array are appropriately adjusted according to the alignment. In the example shown in Figure 2, the index domain of the loop nest is the Cartesian product of intervals $[1..n] \times [1..n] \times [0..n]$.

We use the notation $(t : [0..n])$ to denote a **for** or **forall** loop indexed by t with lower bound 0 and upper bound n, and the notation of Cartesian product of intervals as in

$((i, j) : [0..n] \times [0..n])$ for doubly nested loops. A for loop is just a conventional sequential loop. A forall is a parallel loop whose iterations can be executed in parallel with the assumption that proper synchronization is enforced. For example, given the following loop

$$\text{forall } (i \in D_1)$$
$$\text{for } (j \in D_2)$$
$$a(i,j) = a(2, j-1),$$

the iterations of the forall loop can be executed in parallel, however, they have to be synchronized by the iterations of the for loop, i.e. no iteration of the forall loop should go on to the $j+1$th iteration of the for loop, unless all the iterations finish the jth iteration.

General data structures using pointers as in C are not allowed in the shared-memory program defined above. Notice also that arrays in a shared-memory program are expanded with extra dimensions so as to allow the single assignment form of statements. In the code generation stage, however, the extra dimensions of an array will be collapsed, and the array restored to its original shape.

Reference Patterns For each pair of array references appearing on the two sides of an assignment statement in a loop,

$$\text{for } (i_1 : D_1, \ldots, i_n : D_n)$$
$$a(i_1, \ldots, i_n) = \text{if } \gamma \rightarrow \cdots b(\tau_1, \ldots, \tau_n) \cdots;$$
$$\text{else } \rightarrow \cdots;$$

the symbolic form (as a quoted string of characters)

$$\ulcorner a(i_1, \ldots, i_n) \leftarrow b(\tau_1, \ldots, \tau_n) : \gamma \urcorner$$

is called a *reference pattern*, where the formals $(i_1, \ldots, i_n)$ are quantified over the index domain $D_1 \times \cdots \times D_n$, and γ is the guard of the conditional branch that $b(\tau_1, \ldots, \tau_n)$ is in.

The following reference patterns can be derived from the program in Figure 2,

$$P_1 : \ulcorner b(i,j,t) \leftarrow a(i,x,t-1) : j = t \text{ and } 1 \le x \le n \urcorner,$$
$$P_2 : \ulcorner a(i,j,t) \leftarrow b(0,t,t) : t \ne 0 \urcorner,$$
$$P_3 : \ulcorner a(i,j,t) \leftarrow a(i,j,t-1) : t \ne 0 \text{ and } i = b(0,t,t) \urcorner,$$
$$P_4 : \ulcorner a(i,j,t) \leftarrow b(i,t,t) : t \ne 0 \text{ and } i \ne b(0,t,t) \urcorner.$$

A reference pattern represents a collection of data dependencies. We emphasize this aggregate form rather than each instance of a reference because the key for generating efficient target message-passing programs is to extract correlated references and issue a single aggregate communication routine that is optimized both for the pattern and the target architecture.

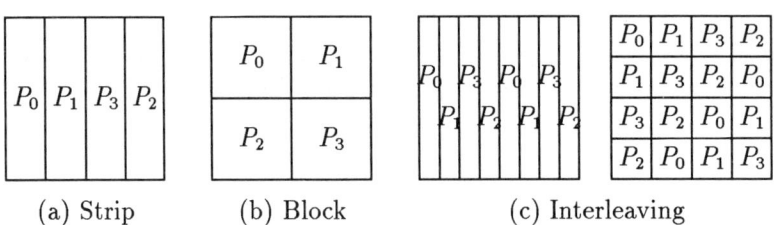

Figure 3: Standard Partition Strategies

2.2 Partition Strategies

Clearly, distribution of arrays affects what data need to be passed by messages between processors. Generally speaking, optimizing for data layout and minimizing communication overhead are two inter-dependent activities. We use a straightforward approach here by considering a few often-used, standard data layouts for programs with regular data structure, called *standard partition strategies*, which include *block partition*, *strip partition*, and *interleaving partition* (Figure 3). In each strategy, an index domain is partitioned into more or less equal-size sub-domains. Strategies differ in the resulting shape and size (the granularity) of the partitioned sub-domains. In the following, we call a dimension of an index domain *spatial* if the subdomain along that dimension is mapped to different processors; otherwise we call it *temporal*. In Figure 3, the horizontal dimension of the index domain is partitioned in all of the four cases, while the vertical dimension is partitioned only in the second and fourth cases.

Partitioned Shared-Memory Program Applying a partition strategy to a shared-memory program results in a *partitioned* shared-memory program. For example, suppose that the forall loops in the program in Figure 2 are partitioned over a two-dimensional network of processors such that processor (x, y) is responsible for a sub-domain $[I_l(x,y)..I_u(x,y)] \times [J_l(x,y)..J_u(x,y)]$ of (i,j). Figure 4 shows the partitioned version of the program.

Although the partitioned program is to be executed sequentially by each individual processor, we still use forall to represent sections of parallel loops derived from a forall loop. The reason here is that knowing the absence of data dependence of a forall loop helps in scheduling communication in such a way that better performance can be obtained.

Canonical Form of Loop Nests For reasons which will become clear later, we want to perform loop interchange (see [17] for a survey on this topic) on a partitioned shared-memory program to obtain a *canonical form* where all for loops appear outside of forall loops. Note that there is a top-level forall loop that ranges over the processors and is invisible from each processor's standpoint. The forall loops in a canonical form reveal the maximum granularity between synchronization points between iterations.

The validity of the interchange of two adjacent for and forall loops can be easily shown for the partitioned shared-memory program as defined (due to the single assignment form

```
for (t : [0..n]) {
    forall ((i, j) : [I_l(x, y)..I_u(x, y)] × [J_l(x, y)..J_u(x, y)])
        b(i, j, t) = if (j = t) →
                        \ + {a(i, x, t − 1) | 1 ≤ x ≤ n};
                     else → 1;
    forall ((i, j) : [I_l(x, y)..I_u(x, y)] × [J_l(x, y)..J_u(x, y)])
        a(i, j, t) = if (t = 0) → 0;
                     else if (i = b(0, t, t)) → a(i, j, t − 1);
                     else → b(i, t, t);
}
```

Figure 4: A Partitioned Shared-Memory Program

of the array assignment statements). Suppose that we are given a loop nest and its interchanged version, as shown below:

```
for (i : D_1)              forall (j : D_2)
    forall (j : D_2)           for (i : D_1)
        S(i, j);                   S(i, j);
```

Consider two arbitrary instances of the loop body, $S(i_1, j_1)$ and $S(i_2, j_2)$, where $i_1 < i_2$. In the first nest, $S(i_1, j_1)$ will be executed first, since i is the outer loop. In the second nest, the same is also true, since the **for** loop appears in every iteration of the **forall** loop, and it forces synchronization between the iterations. For two instances with the same i value, $S(i, j_1)$ and $S(i, j_2)$, the execution order does not matter, since there is no data dependence between them.

Spatial Reference Patterns As described above, a given partition of the index domain of a loop nest also separates the domain coordinates into two kinds: spatial and temporal. Clearly, for the purpose of determining the form of interprocessor communication, it is sufficient to consider only the spatial part of a reference pattern (called a *spatial reference pattern*). Using the program and partition strategy in Figure 4 as an example, we can derive the following spatial reference patterns:

$$\ulcorner a@(i, x) \Rightarrow (i, j) : j = t \text{ and } 1 \leq x \leq n \urcorner,$$
$$\ulcorner b@(0, t) \Rightarrow (i, j) : t \neq 0 \urcorner,$$
$$\ulcorner a@(i, j) \Rightarrow (i, j) : t \neq 0 \text{ and } i = b(0, t, t) \urcorner,$$
$$\ulcorner b@(i, t) \Rightarrow (i, j) : t \neq 0 \text{ and } i \neq b(0, t, t) \urcorner.$$

Compared with the reference patterns above, we see that different notations are used: in a reference pattern, we use $b(x) \leftarrow a(y)$ to denote that $a(y)$ is needed to compute $b(x)$.

Primitive	Pattern	Cost
One-All-Broadcast$(D, \mathbf{s}, a)$	⌜$a@\mathbf{s} \Rightarrow \mathbf{i}$⌝	$\mathcal{O}(B \log |N|)$
All-One-Reduce$(D, \mathbf{d}, a, \oplus)$	⌜$a@\mathbf{i} \Rightarrow \mathbf{d}$⌝	$\mathcal{O}(B \log |N|)$
All-All-Broadcast(D, a)	⌜$a@\mathbf{i} \Rightarrow \mathbf{j}$⌝	$\mathcal{O}(B|N|)$
Single-Send-Receive$(D, \mathbf{s}, \mathbf{d}, a)$	⌜$a@\mathbf{s} \Rightarrow \mathbf{d}$⌝	$\mathcal{O}(B)$
Uniform-Shift$(D, \mathbf{c}, a)$	⌜$a@\mathbf{i} \Rightarrow \mathbf{i} + \mathbf{c}$⌝	$\mathcal{O}(B \log |N|)$
Affine-Transform$(D, M, \mathbf{c}, a)$	⌜$a@\mathbf{i} \Rightarrow M\mathbf{i} + \mathbf{c}$⌝	$\mathcal{O}(B \log |N|)$

Table 1: General Communication Primitives over Domain D and Their Costs

By contrast, in a spatial reference pattern, we use $a@y' \Rightarrow x'$, where x' and y' contain only the spatial coordinates to denote that the element of array a in spatial location y' needs to be sent to spatial location x'.

For convenience and in situations where there is no confusion, we will simply call the spatial reference pattern a reference pattern in the rest of this paper.

2.3 Communication Primitives

We define an abstract distributed-memory machine to which shared-memory programs will be compiled. The abstract machine will then be embedded into the target machine. The abstract machine is configured as an n-dimensional grid of size $N_1 \times \cdots \times N_n$ and modeled as an index domain $D = [1..N_1] \times \cdots \times [1..N_n]$.

We select a set of aggregate communication routines[1] defined over D as primitives, as shown in Tables 1 and 2. Let B denote the message size, N the number of virtual processors modeled by the index domain D, and N_p the number of processors along the pth dimension of the domain. We also use bold-face letters $\mathbf{i}$, $\mathbf{s}$, $\mathbf{d}$ as shorthand for index tuples $(i_1, i_2, \ldots, i_n)$, $(s_1, s_2, \ldots, s_n)$, $(d_1, d_2, \ldots, d_n)$. In Table 2, l_1 and l_2 denote lists of indices $(i_1, \ldots, i_{p-1})$ and $(i_{p+1}, \ldots, i_n)$, respectively.

Primitives in Table 1 are called *general primitives*. Those in Table 2 are called *simple primitives*. Each simple primitive describes collective communication which is confined in a single dimension (denoted by index p) of the multi-dimensional grid of the abstract machine. Each simple primitive has a corresponding general primitive, but its data movement is constrained. Tables 1 and 2 can be extended to include more primitives, such as **gather**, **scatter**, and **shuffle-exchange**.

These communication primitives can be implemented as part of a run-time system on a specific target machine. Each primitive uses a routing algorithm that takes advantage of its particular pattern of communication, and is carefully tuned for performance for each

---

[1]called *collective communication routines* by Fox et al.[6], and Johnsson and Ho[7, 8]. They have developed a collection of efficient collective communication routines for hypercube machines, and have shown that programs using these routines are more efficient than those using asynchronous message passing (i.e. individual **send** and **receive** pairs) in many scientific and engineering applications.

Primitive	Pattern	Cost
Spread(D, p, s, a)	$\ulcorner a@(l_1, s, l_2) \Rightarrow (l_1, i, l_2) \urcorner$	$\mathcal{O}(B \log |N_p|)$
Reduce$(D, p, d, a, \oplus)$	$\ulcorner a@(l_1, i, l_2) \Rightarrow (l_1, d, l_2) \urcorner$	$\mathcal{O}(B \log |N_p|)$
Multi-Spread(D, p, a)	$\ulcorner a@(l_1, i, l_2) \Rightarrow (l_1, j, l_2) \urcorner$	$\mathcal{O}(B|N_p|)$
Copy(D, p, s, d, a)	$\ulcorner a@(l_1, s, l_2) \Rightarrow (l_1, d, l_2) \urcorner$	$\mathcal{O}(B)$
Shift(D, p, c, a)	$\ulcorner a@(l_1, i, l_2) \Rightarrow (l_1, i+c, l_2) \urcorner$	$\mathcal{O}(B \log |N_p|)$

Table 2: Simple Communication Primitives over Domain D and Their Costs

specific target machine. From a compiler's point of view, each communication primitive has a unique pattern characteristic that the compiler can identify symbolically, and issue a call to this primitive when a match with a spatial reference pattern is found. Note that a composition of these primitives can generate many more complex communication patterns. Thus a complex spatial reference pattern may be decomposed to match a composition of communication primitives.

Communication Patterns The data movement of each communication primitive is described by a *communication pattern*

$$\ulcorner a@(\sigma_1, \ldots, \sigma_n) \Rightarrow (\delta_1, \ldots, \delta_n) : \gamma \urcorner.$$

It is interpreted as follows: Let $(i_1, \ldots, i_n)$ range over index domain D. Variables σ_p and δ_p where $1 \leq p \leq n$ are expressions of indices $i_1, \ldots, i_n$, and γ is a boolean predicate defined over domain D.

The communication pattern represents the collection of data movements that bring data pointed to by a from $(\sigma_1, \ldots, \sigma_n)$ to $(\delta_1, \ldots, \delta_n)$ for all the elements in D where γ is true.

Tuple $(\sigma_1, \ldots, \sigma_n)$ is called the *source* expression, and $(\delta_1, \ldots, \delta_n)$ the *destination* expression. There are two special forms of a communication pattern. In the *sender's form*, the source expression consists of the formals $(i_1, \ldots, i_n)$ ranging over domain D. In the *receiver's form*, the destination expression consists of the formals $(i_1, \ldots, i_n)$:

Sender's form: $\ulcorner a@(i_1, \ldots, i_n) \Rightarrow (\delta'_1, \ldots, \delta'_n) : \gamma' \urcorner$,
Receiver's form: $\ulcorner a@(\sigma'_1, \ldots, \sigma'_n) \Rightarrow (i_1, \ldots, i_n) : \gamma'' \urcorner$.

Tuples $(\sigma'_1, \ldots, \sigma'_n)$ and $(\delta'_1, \ldots, \delta'_n)$ are related in the following way. Suppose we can write the source and destination expressions as

$$(\delta'_1, \ldots, \delta'_n) = T_1(i_1, \ldots, i_n)$$
$$(\sigma'_1, \ldots, \sigma'_n) = T_2(i_1, \ldots, i_n)$$

where T_1 and T_2 are well-defined functions. Then T_1 and T_2 must be inverses of each other.

Both of the special forms are needed in synchronizing some of our communication primitives (this point will be elaborated later). When $(\sigma'_1,\ldots,\sigma'_n)$ and $(\delta'_1,\ldots,\delta'_n)$ are linear expressions of the indices, is is possible to determine symbolically the sender's and receiver's forms. But in general a compiler would not be able to do so. In case $(\delta'_1,\ldots,\delta'_n)$ is not computable by the compiler, we allow the user to specify it via the *communication form* construct in which the functions T_1 and T_2 are specified and used in references whenever needed.

2.4 Selecting Communication Routines

We have developed an algorithm for matching reference patterns with communication primitives[11]. The algorithm applies to the reference patterns of a shared-memory program together with a partition strategy selected *a priori*, and generates communication primitives that implement the data movement of the reference patterns. The algorithm works as follows. It first identifies the symbolic characteristic of the reference pattern, e.g. decides whether the data is to be moved from a single point in the domain or from multiple points. It then searches through the list of communication primitives for a matching one. The search is conducted in such a way that if there are multiple matching primitives, the most economical one (based on a communication metric) will be encountered first and will hence be selected. In the case where no matching primitive can be found, the algorithm will break the reference pattern into simpler sub-patterns, and work on each of them recursively. There are many interesting issues in the matching process, such as how to optimize the breakdown of a complex pattern, and how to define a communication metric. Interested readers are referred to [11].

Forced Communication One important issue, however, needs to be pointed out here. The communication routines discussed in Section 2.3 are all defined over regular index domains. By regular, we mean that a domain is either an interval or a Cartesian product of intervals. But reference patterns of a partitioned shared-memory program may have associated predicates, which means the required data movement may only occur in a selected part of a regular domain. For example, consider the following reference pattern

$$\ulcorner a@(2,3) \Rightarrow (i,j) : i > j \urcorner,$$

defined over a two-dimensional spatial domain D. The required data movement is confined in a triangular sub-domain of D, specified by the predicate $i > j$. As far as matching communication routines are concerned, such predicates are ignored, i.e., those processors which do not need data are forced to participate in the aggregate communication. Thus the above reference pattern will be matched with the communication primitive

$$\text{One-All-Broadcast}(D, (2,3), a).$$

As a result, some processors will be getting data they do not need. In the implementation, these extraneous data are discarded as soon as they arrive at the processor in order to free up the buffer space of the processor.

The matching algorithm generates only calls to communication primitives. The issue of where and under what conditions these primitives should be invoked in the target program is not addressed. The remainder of this paper is devoted to these issues.

2.5 Message Aggregation

In most cases, a sub-domain of elements will be mapped to each processor as the result of partitioning an index domain. Due to such partitioning, the actual code for communication would be more complicated than what is shown above. For instance, suppose in the above example the index domain D is partitioned over a two-dimensional network of processors, such that a processor (x,y) is responsible for a sub-domain $E = [I_l(x,y)..I_u(x,y)] \times [J_l(x,y)..J_u(x,y)]$. The parameters to the communication routine must contain this domain information, in addition to the information related to data allocation within a processor and how the abstract machine is embedded in the physical network. For instance, the indices $(2,3)$ must be translated to the node address of the processor network. The pointer to the data, in some cases, is to a local buffer instead of the array itself. (In general, there are also other housekeeping chores such as loading and unloading buffers, discarding unwanted data, etc.) Thus the actual code for the above example would be of the form

$\langle$pre-comm statements$\rangle$;
One-All-Broadcast(E, idx_to_pid$(2,3)$, BUF_a);
$\langle$post-comm statements$\rangle$;

In the rest of this paper, to keep the presentation of the key ideas clear, aggregations are not shown explicitly in the target program with communication calls.

3 Synchronizing Communication Primitives

For the purpose of discussing message synchronization, communication primitives can be classified into two groups: Group A consists of primitives that are implemented by pairs of send and receive commands, such as Copy, Shift, and Single-Send-Receive. To implement a primitive in this group both the sender's and the receiver's forms of a reference pattern are needed. The synchronization issue for such a primitive is to make sure that the parameters to the send and receive commands are correctly set up so that they are matched one-to-one when the primitive is invoked. Group B consists of primitives that are implemented by building message combining trees among a pre-defined set of processors (such as a row or a column), for example Spread, Reduce, One-All-Broadcast and All-All-Broadcast. The synchronization issue for a Group B primitive is to make sure that the primitive is invoked under the same condition on all the participating processors, so that they will all reach whatever communication commands that implement the primitive. The actual time a processor reaches the communication commands however, may differ from processor to processor on an asynchronous multiprocessor like the iPSC/2, since there is no global clock. We illustrate each case with examples.

3.1 Synchronizing Group A Primitives

For a Group A primitive, the critical issue is to derive both the sender's form and the receiver's form of the communication pattern corresponding to the communication primitive. Due to our selection, every primitive in Group A corresponds to a communication pattern that can be symbolically transformed into both sender's and receiver's forms by a compiler. We show the synchronization process through an example.

Example Given the following shared-memory program,

$$\text{for } (t : [0..n])$$
$$\text{forall } ((i,j) : [1..n] \times [1..n])$$
$$a(i,j,t) = \text{if } (t > 1) \rightarrow b(i+1, j-2, t);$$
$$\text{else } \rightarrow a(i, j, t-1);$$

One spatial reference pattern derived is

$$\ulcorner b@(i+1, j-2) \Rightarrow (i,j) : t > 1 \urcorner,$$

and is matched with a Uniform-Shift$(E, (-1, 2), b)$, where $E = [1..n] \times [1..n]$. The target program would look like

$$\text{Program for processor } (x, y):$$
$$\text{for } (t : [0..n]) \ \{$$
$$\quad \text{if } (t > 1)$$
$$\quad\quad \text{Uniform-Shift}(E, (-1, 2), b);$$
$$\quad \text{forall } ((i,j) : [I_l(x,y)..I_u(x,y)] \times [J_l(x,y)..J_u(x,y)])$$
$$\quad\quad \text{if } (t > 1)$$
$$\quad\quad\quad a[i][j] = b[i+1][j-2];$$
$$\}$$

The aggregate communication routine Uniform-Shift$(E, (-1, 2), b)$ is actually implemented by the following pair of send and receive commands[2] in every processor participating in the aggregate communication.

$$\text{send}((-1, 2), b);$$
$$\text{receive}((1, -2), b).$$

---

[2]ignoring the issues of the address translation and message aggregation for the moment.

Notice that the send statement is derived from the sender's form of the reference pattern while the receive statement is derived from the receiver's form. Since the source program contains the receiver's form already, the compiler only needs to derive the sender's form

$$\ulcorner b@(i,j) \Rightarrow (i-1, j+2) : t > 1 \urcorner.$$

The derivation involves a matrix inversion. Under the condition that the matrix is full rank (which is met by all Uniform-Shift cases), the inversion can be performed symbolically, and can be derived automatically.

3.2 Synchronizing Group B Primitives

The implementation of a Group B primitive relies on building dynamic broadcasting (or reduction) trees among a pre-defined set of processors. Take one-all-broadcast as an example. In the first step, the processor which holds the source data sends the data to one of its neighbors; in the second step, the two processors send the data to two new neighboring processors; in the third step, four processors send to another four processors; and so on. If there are n processors, the broadcasting can be done in $\lceil \log n \rceil$ steps. Efficient algorithms for synchronizing and coordinating messages to implement a broadcasting or a reduction on hypercube machines have been developed (e.g. [7, 8]). The implementation of a Group B routine assumes a set of participating processors specified by domain parameter D and uses a pre-determined structure on these processors to accomplish the communication.

As we mentioned in Section 2.4, certain predicates in a reference pattern are ignored in the process of matching communication routines. The major issue in synchronizing group B communication routines is to determine exactly the type of predicates that should be ignored, i.e. the domain parameter D contains all the participating processors. For each and every one of such participating processors, whether forced or not, a call to the communication routine must be issued.

A Boolean predicate P of a reference pattern is said to be *space-invariant* with respect to a domain partition strategy if the value of P is invariant with respect to the values of the spatial indices, otherwise, it is said to be *space-variant*. For example, suppose indices (i, j, t) are defined over domain $D_1 \times D_2 \times D_3$ where D_1 and D_2 are partitioned. Then predicate $i > j$ is space-variant since for different values of i and j, $i > j$ can have different values. On the other hand, predicate $t > 1$ is a space-invariant predicate.

When a space-invariant predicate is in conjunction with a space-variant predicate, as in $(t > 1)$ and $(i > j)$, it is lifted outside of the call to the communication routine while the space-variant predicate is ignored. Since the space-invariant predicate will evaluate to the same value for all participating processors, all, or none, of the processors will participate in the communication, as shown in the following example:

Example From the shared-memory program

for $(t : [0..n])$

$$\text{forall } ((i,j) : [1..n] \times [1..n])$$
$$a(i,j,t) = \text{if } (t > 1) \text{ and } (i > j) \;\rightarrow\; b(3,j,t);$$
$$\text{else} \;\rightarrow\; a(i,j,t-1);$$

the compiler derives a spatial reference pattern

$$\ulcorner b@(3,j) \Rightarrow (i,j) : t > 1 \text{ and } i > j \urcorner,$$

which is then matched with a Spread($E, 1, 3, b$), where $E = [1..n] \times [1..n]$, by ignoring the predicate $i > j$. The corresponding target code looks like

Program for processor (x, y) :
for $(t : [0..n])$ {
  if $(t > 1)$ {
    Spread($E, 1, 3, b$);
    ⟨discard data if forced⟩;
  }
  forall $((i,j) : [I_l(x,y)..I_u(x,y)] \times [J_l(x,y)..J_u(x,y)])$
    if $((t > 1) \;\&\&\; (i > j))$
      $a[i][j] = b[3][j];$
}

It is worth noting that the data sent to any processor that is forced to participate are discarded as soon as they arrive to free up the buffer space at the processor.

3.3 Computing the Inverse of a Reference Pattern

Synchronizing Group A primitives depends on computing the inverse of a reference pattern. In case the inverse is not computable at compile-time, our current solution is to use a Group B primitive instead. Such a primitive requires every member in a well-defined subset of the network of processors (such as a column) to participate, including those who do not really need the data. Since every processor is able to identify its position in the network, synchronization can be easily achieved in this case.

However, this simple solution may incur high performance cost in some cases. For example, suppose the reference pattern (over domain $D = [1..n] \times [1..n]$)

$$\ulcorner a@(2,j) \Rightarrow (c(i,j), j) \urcorner$$

contains an indirect reference $c(i,j)$ whose value cannot be determined at compile-time. Our pattern matching algorithm would match it with a Spread, but a Copy would suffice if $c(i,j)$ was known to be constant at compile-time.

Asynchronous Communication One alternative approach is to generate a Request-Receive pair which interrupts the processor holding the requested value. The target program looks like

> Program for processor p :
> if $(i = 2)$ {
> ⟨Send a request to processor idx_to_pid$(c(i,j),j)$⟩;
> ⟨Wait for an answer from processor idx_to_pid$(c(i,j),j)$⟩;
> }

The Request-Receive pair works as follows: Whenever there is a request coming to a processor, an interrupt handler will send out the requested data if it is ready, otherwise it will queue the request and send out the value when it becomes available. The overhead of interrupt handling and queue management may be reduced if a separate communication co-processor is available in the hardware. In practice, message granularity in this approach is fine enough so that it incurs unacceptably high overhead on machines like the iPSC/2. In addition, asynchronous communication makes this approach far more error-prone. A working mechanism for asynchronous communication on this class of machines may incur additional system overhead.

User Directives Another alternative is to allow the user to provide enough information to generate efficient communication. It turns out that all that is needed is a pair of functions which are inverses of each other for specifying the sender's form and the receiver's form of a given reference pattern. Using the same example shown above, the user can say

> Communication Forms:
> $T(i,j) = (c(i,j), j) = \{(i \text{ div } j, j)\}$
> $T\_inv(i,j) = \text{if } (i <= (n \text{ div } j))$
> $\rightarrow \{(k,j) \mid i * j <= k < \min(n+1, (i+1) * j)\};$

The inverse T_inv can then be used to generate a send-receive pair for efficient communication. The corresponding target code will look like

> Program for processor p :
> if $(i = 2)$
> ⟨Send msg to processor idx_to_pid$(T(i,j))$⟩;
> if $(p \in \{\text{idx\_to\_pid}(T\_inv(i,j))\})$
> ⟨Receive msg from processor idx_to_pid$(2,j)$⟩;

We think this approach is the best and we will support this in the future.

4 Scheduling Communication Primitives

In this section, we consider the problem of the location where a communication primitive should appear in the target program. We first introduce the notions of *maximum granularity*, *computation segment* and *communication segment*. We then define *communication window*, specifying the range in which a communication primitive can legally appear. We then discuss the various trade-offs in choosing the best placement for a call to the communication routine.

4.1 Computation Segments

Assume that all the loop nests in a partitioned shared-memory program are in the canonical form as defined in Section 2. Given an n-level loop nest defined over domain $D = D_1 \times D_2 \cdots \times D_n$, then the first k levels are for loops while the inner loops from level $k+1$ to n are forall loops. For the purpose of our discussion, we assume, in addition, that the inner forall loops are distributed over the array assignment statements in the body of the loop nest. Such loop distribution will not be done actually to generate the target code, in other words, we perform loop distribution over the array assignment statements now and then perform the inverse operation after we have determined the placement of the communication calls.

We use the following notation

$$S(a, E, i_1, \ldots, i_k)$$

to denote the inner loop nest from level $k+1$ to n over an assignment statement of array a and call it a *computation segment* for a, where $E = D_{k+1} \times \cdots \times D_n$, and $(i_1, \ldots, i_k)$ are the index tuple of the first k for loops. An instance of $(i_1, \ldots, i_k)$ is called a *time-stamp* of a computation segment. An example is shown in Table 3.

Since the iterations of forall in a computation segment are fully independent, no communication has to occur inside each computation segment if the data it needs are fetched before it begins execution. However, between two different computation segments, there might be data dependences, hence communication might be needed. Thus a computation segment represents maximal granularity of the loop nest under consideration.

4.2 Communication Segment

Communication in a partitioned program can be represented in a similar way. Recall that in the canonical form of a partitioned shared memory program, the first k domain coordinates are temporal. Given a reference pattern

$$P: \ulcorner a(i_1, \ldots, i_n) \leftarrow b(\delta_1, \ldots, \delta_n) : \tau \urcorner,$$

where $E = D_{k+1} \times \cdots \times D_n$, and $(\delta_1, \ldots, \delta_k)$ is the time-stamp of the segment. We use the following notation

$$C(b, P, E, \delta_1, \ldots, \delta_k)$$

Comp. Segment	Original Code
$S(b, E, t)$	forall $((i, j) : D_2 \times D_3)$ $\quad b(i, j, t) =$ if $(j = t) \rightarrow$ $\qquad \backslash + \{a(i, x, t-1) \mid 1 \le x \le n\};$ $\quad$ else $\rightarrow 1;$
$S(a, E, t)$	forall $((i, j) : D_2 \times D_3)$ $\quad a(i, j, t) =$ if $(t = 0) \rightarrow 0;$ $\qquad$ else if $(i = b(0, t, t)) \rightarrow a(t, j, t-1);$ $\qquad$ else $\rightarrow b(i, t, t);$

Table 3: Computation segments for the example program

Comm. Segment	Corresponding Code
$C(a, P_1, E, t-1)$	if $(t > 0)$ $\quad$ Reduce$(E, 2, t, a, +);$
$C(b, P_2, E, t)$	if $(t > 0)$ $\quad$ One-All-Broadcast$(E, (0, t), a);$
$C(b, P_4, E, t)$	if $(t > 0)$ $\quad$ Spread$(E, 2, t, b);$

Table 4: Communication segments for the example program

to denote the *communication segment* generated for P, including the calls to primitive routines, statements for loading message buffers, etc.. An example of communication segments is given in Table 4. For simplicity, we will leave out the code for the usual housekeeping activities before and after the call to the communication routines.

Granularity of Segments Consider the case where a processor computes some values and then sends them to other processors. The processor can either compute and send one value at a time or it can compute many values first and then send. The difference is the memory usage (data need to be stored if they don't get sent) and the communication overhead (more frequent, small messages incur more fixed cost such as message startup time and time for the calls to the operating system kernel. With respect to the above example, the inner loop nests can all be broken down to smaller segments. For instance, the following three loop nests are possible decompositions of computation segment $S(b, E, t)$:

forall $(i \in D_2)$
$\quad S(b, D_3, t, i);$

forall $(j \in D_3)$
$\quad S(b, D_2, t, i);$

forall $((i, j) \in D_2 \times D_3)$
$\quad S(b, \text{nil}, t, i, j);$

Segments $S(b, D_3, t, i)$, $S(b, D_2, t, i)$, and $S(b, \text{nil}, t, i, j)$ are all of smaller granularity than $S(b, E, t)$.

Selecting appropriate granularity of computation segments and consequently the size and frequency of message-passing requires cost-driven optimization based on both the target machine parameters and cost estimation of the program. The formulation here provides the framework for doing so. In what follows, we present our method using computation segments and communication segments both at their maximum granularity. The optimization issue can be addressed separately and the following method works for any given granularity.

4.3 Scheduling Communication Segments

The main issue of scheduling is to place a communication segment in the appropriate location in a sequence of computation segments. The potential locations for communication segments are points between the computation segments. However, not every such point is legal. A communication should happen no earlier than the time when the transmitted data is ready and no later than the time when the transmitted data is used. We define the notion of a *communication window* specifying the range in which a communication segment must be placed and can be placed anywhere legally.

Communication Window Given a communication segment, $C(b, P, E, \delta_1, \ldots, \delta_k)$, the *top* of the window is the point immediately after the last of the set of computation segments including $S(b, E, \delta_1, \ldots, \delta_k)$ and those which compute the indirect array references occurring in $\ulcorner\delta_1, \ldots, \delta_n\urcorner$. The *bottom* of the window is the point immediately before the earliest of the set of computation segments in which $a(i_1, \ldots, i_n)$ is used.

For instance, given reference pattern

$$P : \ulcorner a(i, j, t) \leftarrow b(i, c(i, j, t), t-1) \urcorner$$

the top of the communication window for communication segment $C(b, P, E, t-1)$ is the point immediately after computation segments $S(b, E, t-1)$ and $S(c, E, t)$. Since the timestamp of $S(c, E, t)$ is newer, the top is the point right after it.

For the communication segments in Table 4, the compiler would derive the following communication windows:

Comm. Segment	Communication Window	
$C(a, P_1, E, t-1)$	$S(a, E, t-1)$	$S(b, E, t)$
$C(b, P_2, E, t)$	$S(b, E, t)$	$S(a, E, t)$
$C(b, P_4, E, t)$	$S(b, E, t)$	$S(a, E, t)$

A communication window specifies the range within which a communication segment can be inserted between any two computation segments. Notice that a communication window may cross loop iterations, which is the consequence of cross-iteration dependencies.

Issues of Scheduling Given a communication window, what is the best placement of a communication segment? Again, this problem involves trade-offs in communication

```
for (t : D₁) {                        for (t : D₁) {
    S(b, E, t);                           C(a, P₁, E, t − 1);
    C(b, P₂, E, t);                       S(b, E, t);
    C(b, P₄, E, t);                       C(b, P₂, E, t);
    S(a, E, t);                           C(b, P₄, E, t);
    C(a, P₁, E, t);                       S(a, E, t);
}                                     }
```

(a) Simple strategy 1   (b) Simple strategy 2

Figure 5: A partitioned program with explicit communication

cost, storage use, balanced network flow, etc., and needs to be answered by cost-driven optimizations based on a model of target machine characteristics. We describe a scenario here to illustrate the trade-off between processor idling time versus network message traffic.

A processor waiting for a message cannot progress with its own program unless the message is received. So the earlier the message is sent out by the processor which produces the required data, the better. On the other hand, if the production and consumption of the messages are too much off-balance, messages may start to saturate the network. Profiling and estimating computation time, message size, etc., should provide clues for where the communication segment should be placed to maintain a smooth flow of message traffic.

Consequently, we want to put communication segments in places where message aggregation can be performed. However, larger messages also mean larger buffers. For large applications, this could cause a shortage of memory. Again, to balance the issue, cost estimation and profiling are needed.

Simple Strategies Here we propose two very simple default strategies which do not take cost into consideration:

1. Place a communication segment at the top of its communication window.

2. Place a communication segment at the top of its communication window if the top is a computation segment with the same time-stamp; otherwise place it immediately before the first computation segment in the window that has the same time-stamp

Using the first strategy on the program shown in Figure 4, we obtain a schedule shown in Figure 5(a); using the second strategy, the result is shown in Figure 5(b).

The first strategy has an advantage in controlling granularity, since a *strip-mining* can be applied to a computation segment and the adjacent communication segments, while the second strategy is slightly easier to generate code for, since there are no cross-iteration dependencies between computation segments and communication segments.

5 Correctness of Communication Synthesis

One important issue in generating communication is to guarantee that no deadlock is introduced by the compiler. We prove this property of our message generation procedure as follows:

The target code generated by the compiler consists of a host program and a node program. The single node program is in the so-called SPMD (single program multiple data) style. As we discussed in the previous section, the node program consists of a sequence of perfectly nested loop nests, each with a sequence of computation and communication segments as its loop body.

Assume that each computation segment is a single-entry single-exit segment (i.e. there are no **goto** or **break** statements), and is generated by the compiler based on semantics-preserving transformations which do not introduce deadlock. Provided that the source program is correct and all the data a computation segment requires are available, then its execution always terminates. Therefore, we only need to check the behavior of communication segments which ensure the availability of the data required by the computation segments.

We prove that for each loop nest, the communication segments so generated do not introduce deadlocks by induction on the sequence of communication segments.

The induction hypothesis is that up to the $N-1'th$ communication segment, the program is deadlock-free, i.e., all processors have reached the beginning of the Nth communication segment since any computation segments in between them terminates eventually.

Case 1: *The communication segment consists of a group A communication primitive.* Since such a communication primitive is guarded only by space-invariant predicates, all processors will execute the primitive. Since the communication primitive is assumed to terminate, the entire segment terminates.

Case 2: *The communication segment consists of a group B communication primitive.* We assume that the message buffer is large enough to hold the entire data transmitted in a message [3]. (1) Since the **send** and **receive** pair of the primitive is arranged as a non-blocking **send** followed by a blocking **receive** (Section 3.1), every processor will execute a **send** statement first. (2) Due to the assumption on the buffer size, no deadlock due to buffer overflow will occur; therefore every processor entering the communication segment will eventually finish executing the **send** statement, and move on to the **receive** statement. (3) Since the predicates for the **send** and **receive** statements are arranged in such a way that for every message sent out to the network, there is a receiving statement matching it (Section 3.2), every **receive** statement will terminate with received data. Therefore, the Nth communication segment eventually terminates, and so the program also terminates.

---

[3] This assumption can be relaxed if we take buffer size into consideration when generating communication.

6 Concluding Remark

In this paper we considered generating a program with explicit communication commands from a program for shared-memory multiprocessors based on a set of standard data partition strategies. In particular, we discussed the problem of coordinating interprocessor communication. The communication synthesis approach has been implemented in the experimental Crystal compiler for the iPSC/2 and the NCUBE [10]. The compiler takes a Crystal program as input and generates C code with calls to communication primitives as output. All the communication primitives discussed in this paper, except for Affine-Transform, have been implemented on the iPSC/2. The preliminary results we have obtained on a few benchmark programs, including matrix multiplication [3], Gaussian elimination with partial pivoting [4], and a financial application [2], have shown that the performance of the compiler-generated code is within a factor of 1.7 – 2.8 of that of the their corresponding hand-crafted code.

When measured independently, an individual aggregate communication routine is far more efficient than corresponding **send** and **receive** pairs with the current generation of hypercube multiprocessors. As the design of communication network advances, however, the cost function may change over time.

As shown by Chuck Seitz, the communication system of the Mosaic system has extremely low latency for send and receive commands. In addition, the so called worm-hole style routing makes the communication done directly by the router much more competitive than user-programmed multi-phase routines due to their need to access the processor memory. One interesting architectural design question is whether the functionality of the routing system should be broadened to do special aggregate communication, taking advantage of the highly correlated communication patterns and the smart algorithms to do them.

References

[1] David Callahan and Ken Kennedy. Compiling programs for distributed-memory multiprocessors. *The Journal of Supercomputing*, 2(2):151–170, 1988.

[2] Marina Chen, Young-il Choo, Erik DeBenedictis, Jingke Li, and Janet Wu. Speedup of a financial application using the crystal compiler for hypercubes. Technical Report YALEU/DCS/TR-673, Dept. of Computer Science, Yale University, January 1989.

[3] Marina Chen, Young-il Choo, and Jingke Li. Compiling parallel programs by optimizing performance. *The Journal of Supercomputing*, 1(2):171–207, July 1988.

[4] Marina Chen, Young-il Choo, and Jingke Li. Theory and pragmatics of compiling efficient parallel code. Technical Report YALEU/DCS/TR-760, Dept. of Computer Science, Yale University, December 1989.

[5] Ron Cytron. Doacross: Beyond vectorization for multiprocessors. In *Proceedings of the 1986 ICPP*, pages 836–844, 1986.

[6] G. Fox, M. Johnson, G. Lyzenga, S. Otto, J. Salmon, and D. Walker. *Solving Problems on Concurrent Processors*. Prentice Hall, 1988.

[7] Ching-Tien Ho. *Optimal Communication Primitives and Graph Embeddings on Hypercubes*. PhD thesis, Yale University, 1990.

[8] S. Lennart Johnsson. Communication efficient basic linear algebra computations on hypercube architectures. *J. Parallel and Distributed Computation*, 4(2), April 1987.

[9] C. Koelbel and P. Mehrotra. Compiler transformations for non-shared memory machines. In *4th International Conference on Supercomputing*, May 1989.

[10] Jingke Li. *Compiling Crystal for Hypercube Machines*. PhD thesis, Yale University, (Expected Dec. 1990).

[11] Jingke Li and Marina Chen. Generating explicit communication from shared-memory program references. In *Supercomputing 90*, New York, NY, Nov. 1990.

[12] Jingke Li and Marina Chen. Index domain alignment: Minimizing cost of cross-reference between distributed arrays. In *Proceedings of the 3rd Symposium on the Frontiers of Massively Computation*, College Park, Maryland, Oct. 1990.

[13] Michael J. Quinn, Philip J. Hatcher, and J.V. Rosendale. Compiling C* programs for a hypercube multicomputer. In *ACM/SIGPLAN PPEALS 1988*, New Haven, Connecticut, July 1988.

[14] A. Ramanujan and P. Sadayappan. A methodology for parallelizing programs for complex memory multiprocessors. In *Supercomputing 89*, Reno, Nevada, Nov. 1989.

[15] A. Rogers and K. Pingali. Process decomposition through locality of reference. In *SIGPLAN'89 Conference on Programming Language Design and Implementation*, June 1989.

[16] Matthew Rosing and Robert B. Schnabel. An overview of DINO – a new language for numerical computation on distributed memory multiprocessors. Technical Report CU-CS-385-88, University of Colorado, March 1988.

[17] M.J. Wolfe. *Optimizing Supercompilers for Supercomputers*. The MIT Press, Cambridge, MA, 1989.

[18] Hans P. Zima, Heinz J. Bast, and Michael Gerndt. Superb: A tool for semi-automatic SIMD/MIMD parallelization. *Parallel Computing*, 6:1–18, 1988.

22 An Introduction to Static Scheduling for MIMD Architectures

H. Dietz, M. O'Keefe, A. Zaafrani

Abstract

Recently, we have developed a technique whereby a new class of MIMD architectures called "Barrier MIMDs" can use static scheduling to remove over 77% of all synchronizations from traditional MIMD code [18]. The new static scheduling technique combines a VLIW-like code scheduling [8] technique with new relative timing analysis that allows the compiler to determine when synchronization constraints can be met without introducing runtime synchronization barriers. However, the use of the new barrier MIMD hardware is critical to this technique, since it provides a mechanism for maintaining and/or regaining precise timing information whereas conventional MIMD computers merely provide directed synchronization.

In this paper, we review the techniques for Barrier MIMD and discuss the application of the same method to reducing synchronization in conventional, directed-synchronization, MIMD computers. This includes discussions of NOP insertion and timing analysis for directed synchronization. A scheduling algorithm and preliminary experimental results are also presented.

1. Introduction

Runtime synchronization overhead is a critical factor in achieving high speedup using parallel computers. A key advantage of SIMD (Single Instruction stream, Multiple Data stream) architectures is that synchronization is effected statically at compile-time, hence the execution-time cost of synchronization between "processes" is essentially zero. VLIW (Very Long Instruction Word) [8], [5] machines are successful in large part because they preserve this property while providing more flexibility in terms of the operations that can be parallelized. Unfortunately, VLIWs cannot tolerate any asynchrony in their operation; hence, they are incapable of parallel execution of multiple flow-paths, subprogram calls, and variable-execution-time instructions. In a recent paper [6], a new architecture, **Barrier MIMD**, was proposed to extend the static synchronization properties of the SIMD and VLIW class of parallel machines into the MIMD domain.

A Barrier MIMD is a MIMD computer which has specialized hardware implementing a new type of barrier synchronization which aids the compiler in performing static scheduling. If a barrier is placed across a set of processes, then no process can execute past that barrier until all have reached the barrier. Unlike other barrier mechanisms, all processes will resume execution in exact synchrony. Hence, immediately after executing a barrier, the machine can be treated as a VLIW, using static scheduling to eliminate the need for further runtime synchronization.

However, VLIW machines do not allow MIMD code structures (e.g., multiple flow paths) nor even variable-time instructions. In a barrier MIMD machine, static scheduling tracks both minimum and maximum completion times for each processes' code; runtime synchronization is needed *iff* the minimum time for the consumer of an object is less than the maximum time for that object's producer. If the timing constraints cannot be met statically, this implies that the static timing information has become too "fuzzy." Inserting another barrier effectively reduces this fuzziness to zero. Scheduling and barrier placement algorithms for barrier MIMDs have been developed and extensively benchmarked; more than 77% of all synchronizations in the benchmark programs were accomplished without runtime synchronization in a barrier MIMD (see figure 16).

The goal of this paper is to show how the timing analysis and scheduling concepts which were designed for Barrier MIMD machines can be applied to more conventional, directed synchronization, MIMD architectures. While conventional MIMD machines clearly cannot achieve the full benefit obtained by statically scheduling for Barrier MIMD computers, similar timing analysis and scheduling can be applied to achieve a significant reduction in conventional MIMD synchronization.

This work summarizes a code scheduling algorithm for barrier MIMDs, an "optimal" barrier insertion algorithm, extensive scheduling experiments on synthetic benchmarks using the new algorithms, and how these techniques can be applied to conventional MIMD machines.

The structure of the paper is that section 2 introduces the basic concepts of timing analysis and static code scheduling for various types of MIMD computers. Detailed timing analysis and code scheduling algorithms are given for Barrier MIMD machines in section 3; performance determined by thousands of scheduling experiments is discussed in section 4. Section 5 discusses performance differences between different architectures, especially between Barrier MIMD and VLIW architectures. Because Barrier MIMD are the idealized target for such techniques, the work in sections 3, 4, and 5 provides an excellent overview of the general technique as well as bounds on its performance for other MIMD architectures. Finally, section 6 summarizes the contributions of this work and the direction of current research efforts.

2. Timing Analysis for MIMD

As suggested above, the primary new contribution in the current paper is the concept of applying Barrier MIMD analysis and scheduling techniques to more conventional directed-synchronization MIMD computers. The differences in hardware structure correspond to significant differences in the structure of the timing problems. In this section, we briefly review the basic principles behind using timing information in scheduling code for a Barrier MIMD and then give a detailed analysis of the timing information available in directed synchronization MIMDs.

2.1. Synchronization vs. Timing

The traditional view of synchronization is that each consumer of a datum must wait until **after** the producer of that datum has executed. In other words, synchronization is viewed as enforcing an **order of execution**. Figure 1 gives a multiprocess time line showing the use of conventional directed synchronization to insure that the consumer executes after the producer. The directed arc from the producer to the consumer represents the runtime transmission of a synchronization object from the producer to the consumer. Process 0 simply generates this message and continues execution, whereas process 1 cannot proceed past the head of the arc until the message from the producer has arrived. This transmission could take a potentially unbounded amount of time dependent on, for example, routing and traffic through a network; hence, in the traditional view, the only timing information available at compile-time is that the consumer will execute at some time after the producer.

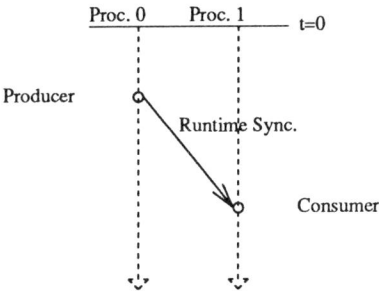

Figure 1: Traditional View of Directed Sync.

However, this traditional view ignores the fact that some timing information is available to the compiler. If compiler analysis attempts to precisely track the minimum and maximum times at which the producer and consumer would execute relative to time t=0, then runtime synchronization may be unnecessary. As shown in figure 2, if the minimum consumer time is greater than the maximum producer time, then no runtime synchronization is required.

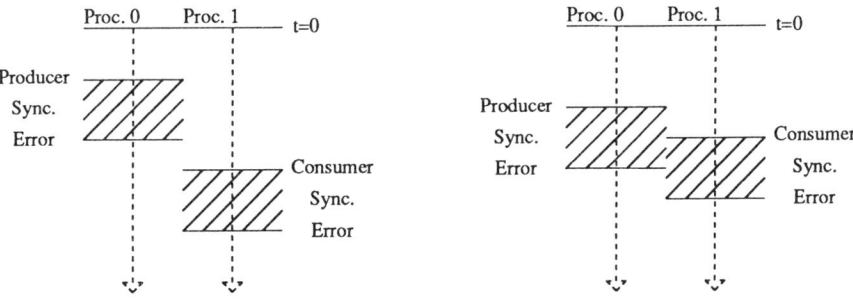

Figure 2: Correct Ordering   **Figure 3:** Potential Race

However, as shown in figure 3, often static timing analysis cannot prove that the maximum time for the producer will always be less than the minimum time for the consumer. In such a case, some action must be taken to enforce the correct timing relationship.

2.2. NOP Insertion

Perhaps the most obvious alternative is to change the code schedule so that some additional instructions are inserted just before the consumer, much as in pipeline scheduling [13] [9]. However, a good code scheduler (such as that presented in section 3) would have taken this into consideration in generating the original schedule, hence there are no additional useful instructions available for use as padding. Instead, one would simply insert enough NOPs (Null OPerations) before the consumer so that the minimum consumer time is greater than the maximum producer time. Sufficient NOPs must be inserted to yield an execution time of at least max(producer) - min(consumer). This is depicted in figure 4.

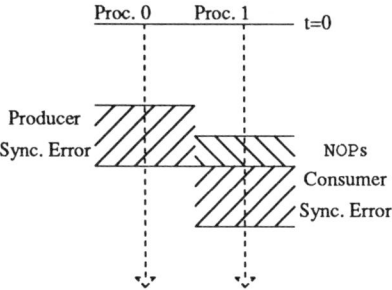

Figure 4: NOP Padding

However, there are two unavoidable disadvantages to using NOP insertion to meet timing constraints:

[1] The NOPs are executed, and delay introduced, even when the particular run does not require the delay. For example, in figure 3 the race condition would not occur in a run where the producer executed at its minimum time and the consumer executed at its maximum, yet NOPs inserted to guard against the worst case would still be executed. In other words, although the worst case performance may be good, best case performance will often suffer the overhead of executing unnecessary NOPs. This is particularly damaging when the difference between average and worst-case timing is large.

[2] Hence, although NOP insertion can enforce a timing relationship, it cannot increase the accuracy with which timing information is known; this leads to fundmental limits on the utility of the technique. As more variable execution time code is executed, the difference between the minimum and maximum time bounds monotonically increases. Hence, NOP insertion becomes increasingly less effective as larger code segments are considered.

Both of these problems are directly solved by using the new Barrier MIMD architecture.

2.3. Barrier Insertion

In essence, a Barrier MIMD scheduler also inserts delays to achieve timing constraints, but the delays (barriers) are structured so that:

[1] Each barrier introduces delay only when needed and only for as long as needed to satisfy the timing constraint in that run; there is no unnecessary delay.

[2] Each barrier eliminates (or at least reduces to a fixed bound) the range between minimum and maximum time in each process participating in the barrier.

Figure 5 shows the primary effect of inserting a barrier to enforce the timing constraint.

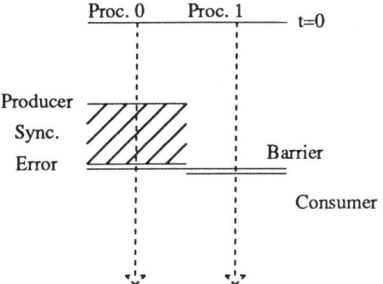

Figure 5: Barrier Inserted

However, inserting a barrier has an important side-effect. Insertion of a barrier not only enforces a timing constraint, but also reduces the difference between minimum and maximum times for the participating processes. This results in an effect unique to the combination of barriers and our timing analysis: inserting one barrier may cause several apparently unrelated timing constraints to be resolved. Consider the producers and consumers of figure 6. When a barrier is inserted to enforce the first timing relationship, the second is also resolved because the narrowing of the range between minimum and maximum times for the second producer and consumer allows the compiler to determine that they are properly ordered.

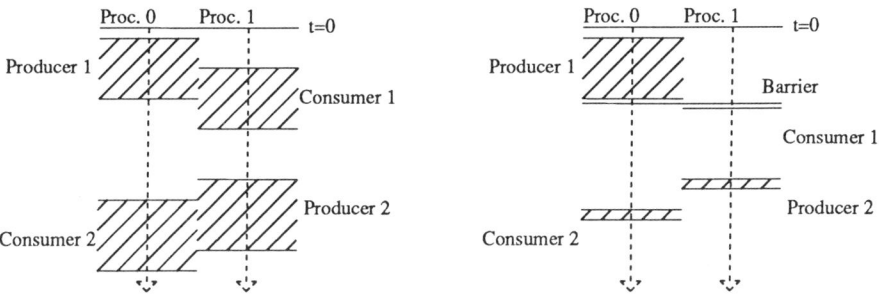

Figure 6: Two Constraints   **Figure 7:** Barrier Side-Effect

According to the studies presented in section 4, this effect satisfies approximately 28% of all timing constraints.

The primary disadvantage in using Barrier MIMD scheduling is that it only applies directly to machines which have hardware implementing this new type of barrier — currently, only the PASM prototype [16]. No doubt, other machines will eventually be built to incorporate this mechanism, e.g., the CARP machine [7]; still, the problem of applying the timing analysis and scheduling to existing MIMD machines remains.

2.4. Directed Synchronization

As discussed in section 2.1, the only synchronization mechanism in many MIMD computers is a directed synchronization primitive which enforces an *after* timing relationship.

Midkiff and Padua [12] and Shaffer [17] have applied a transitive reduction [2] to task graphs to remove redundant directed synchronization in code executing on MIMD architectures. Callahan [4] proposed a similar method for reducing the number of (conventional) barrier synchronizations required in scheduling nested loop constructs. The timing analysis which we propose not only recognizes these redundancies (see figure 8), but also redundancies based purely on timing, without a subsuming synchronization.

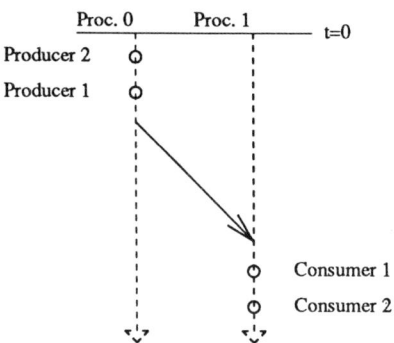

Figure 8: Subsumed Directed Sync.

In terms of timing, if process 0 sends a message to process 1, and process 1 waits for the message to arrive before proceeding, this enforces the timing constraint that the portion of process 1 which occurs after receipt of the message from process 0 also happens after the portion of process 0 which was executed before sending the message. Notice that the synchronization is not symmetric relative to processes 0 and 1; the synchronization is directed from process 0 to process 1.

Figure 9 clarifies this timing relationship. The figure shows that:

- Process 0 executes for between a and b units of time before sending the directed synchronization to process 1
- Process 1 executes for between c and d units of time before it begins waiting for the synchronization message from process 0
- The synchronization message must travel from process 0 to process 1, hence, transmission delay time may vary between e and f (due to network traffic, etc.)

Because the process which sends the directed synchronization does not wait for the receiving process[1], the time at which the first instruction after the synchronization is executed in process 0 is simply (a, b) — there is no delay introduced. However, process 1 might find the message waiting for it or might have to wait for the message to arrive; hence, the time when the first instruction after the synchronization is executed by process 1 is (max(a+e, c), max(b+f, d)).

This yields some interesting properties:

[1] Clearly, unlike using a synchronization barrier, timing for the sending process (process 0) is unaffected by the directed synchronization.

---

[1] In some MIMD computers the process sending a directed synchronization message waits for an acknowledgement from the receiving process. This is modeled as a pair of directed synchronizations, and is discussed in section 2.5 under the title "Simulated Barriers."

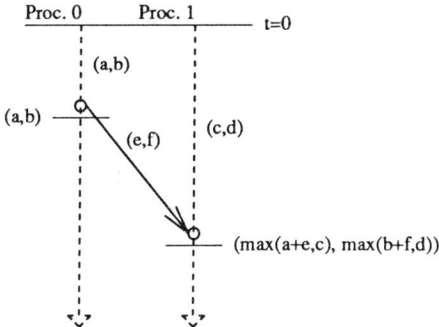

Figure 9: Directed Sync. Timing

[2] The minimum to maximum time range for the receiving process (process 1) can be reduced for some, but not all, values of a, b, c, d, e, and f.

This second point is significant in that it suggests that conventional MIMD architectures might be able to obtain benefits similar to those obtained using timing analysis with the new Barrier MIMD architecture.

There is, however, a fundamental problem with the use of our timing analysis and directed synchronization. Suppose that the consumer process executes a `while` loop, with unbounded execution time, before it consumes the value from the producer. Relative to figure 9, this has the effect of making $d=\infty$[2], but this is turn makes the time for the first consumer process instruction after the synchronization be $(\max(a+e, c), \infty)$. Notice, however, that the situation is *not symmetric*.

If the producer process executes an unbounded `while` loop before sending the synchronization message, then $b=\infty$. Assuming that $d<\infty$, the fact that $b=\infty$ implies that for the worst-case time, the **critical path** to the point where the synchronization message is consumed will be the path of length b+f: the consumer process will have to wait for the synchronization message to arrive. If the critical path *always* includes the message transmission from the producer, i.e., $a+e \geq d$, then the actual values for a and b are immaterial. In other words, if $a+e \geq d$ then we know that, immediately after the synchronization, the consumer process is at time (e,f) relative to the producer process (with no further analysis needed).

First, consider the timing assignments shown in figure 10. A preliminary examination of the timing suggests that the producer occurs at time $(5+3, 7+4) = (8,11)$ and the consumer occurs at time $(\max(5+1, 7), \max(7+3, 8)) + 4 = (11,14)$. Since these times overlap, it appears that an additional synchronization is needed to enforce the ordering, however, the critical path analysis mentioned above proves that the timing is safe. The producer process region before the synchronization is on the critical path in the overlap timing; recognizing this fact, it is easily seen that the producer occurring at time 11 implies that the consumer occurs in the time interval (12,14), hence no timing overlap is possible and no additional synchronization is needed.

Figure 11 demonstrates that this principle can be used to preserve static timing constraints even in the presence of unbounded-time operations such as the afore-mentioned `while` loop. The only difference between figures 10 and 11 is that the producer process region which is on the consumer's critical path has an unbounded maximum time, $(5,\infty)$. This changes nothing, however, because if the

---

[2] Here, we use ∞ to represent an unboundedly large particular number, not literally ∞.

maximum time for the producer is ∞+4, the minimum time for the consumer is ∞+1+4, one time unit later. Hence, no additional synchronization is needed. In fact, we can completely ignore the ∞, instead saying that the producer executes at time (3,4) and the consumer executes between time max(5+1, 7) - 5 + 4 = 6 and time max(∞+3, 8) - ∞ + 4 = 7. Since (3,4) and (6,7) do not overlap, no additional synchronization is needed.

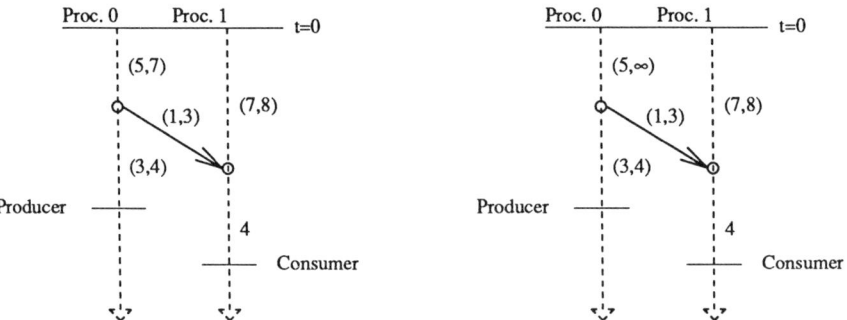

Figure 10: Dir. Sync. Timing   Figure 11: Unbounded Timing

This analysis is vital to using timing in most existing MIMD computers, because most of these machines have processors which must occasionally service interrupts and other unpredictable, variable-delay, events. By enabling this event handling *only on a critical path just before a directed synchronization message is sent*, even infinitely-long delays can be accepted without losing accuracy or precision in static timing analysis.

2.5. Simulated Barriers

Another alternative for existing MIMD computers is to use directed synchronization to simulate the new barrier mechanism. Unfortunately, the simulated barriers have much higher overhead than the Barrier MIMD hardware barriers, and this limits the use of simulated barriers for fine-grain code.

A binary (two-process) barrier can be simulated using two directed synchronizations, as shown in figure 12. In effect, the same critical path timing analysis discussed in the previous section is employed to insure that both the producer and consumer code regions before the simulated barrier are on the final critical path, hence, unbounded execution times in either can be "absorbed." Notice that in order for this to occur, it is necessary that $h \le e+i$, since violating this timing bound could remove the consumer region from being on the critical path for the producer.

Of course, the simulated barrier differs significantly from a Barrier MIMD hardware barrier in that it is not symmetric, has significantly higher overhead, and does not provide exact timing (unless directed synchronization takes a fixed amount of time). In effect, the simulated barrier acts as shown in figure 13.

In figure 13, the barrier is conceptually initiated by process 0 up to e+i units of time *before* synchronization is desired, likewise, process 1 initiates its barrier i units of time before synchronization is achieved. Although this pre-issuing is somewhat awkward to implement, the primary effect is that of creating a barrier which has a timing error of j-i.

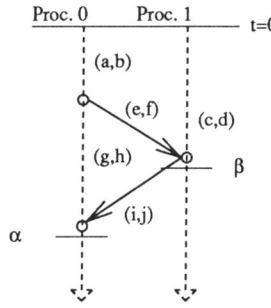
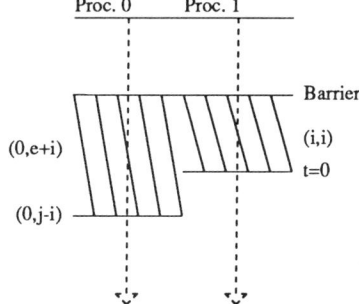

Figure 12: Simulated Barrier   **Figure 13**: Resulting "Barrier"

3. Code Scheduling and Timing Analysis Algorithms

In this section, we describe code scheduling and timing analysis algorithms for Dynamic Barrier MIMDs (DBMs). The appropriate modification for the static barrier MIMD (SBM) is to merge unordered barriers with execution time overlap. Adaptation of these techniques for NOP insertion and directed synchronization is significantly more complex, hence, only a cursory discussion is given in this paper.

Although minimum and maximum times are known for each of the instructions instead of a fixed execution time, it is straightforward to adapt the scheduling heuristics commonly used for fixed-execution-time tasks — and this has been our approach. It is well-known that even for simple or relaxed cases the optimal static scheduling of a partially ordered set of tasks on parallel processors is NP-hard, and hence, computationally intractable [11]. However, several heuristics with bounded worst-case performance degradation (from optimal) have been found to be effective for this problem [10]. In particular, the *critical path* method exhibits good performance at reasonable computational cost.

Some useful terminology is given in section 3.1. Section 3.2 outlines a technique for labeling operations and section 3.3 applies these labels to generate an ordering for list scheduling. Using the list ordering, section 3.4 details the assignment of operations to specific processors. Upon assigning each operation to a processor, it may be necessary to insert a barrier; algorithms for this purpose are given in section 3.5.

3.1. Terminology

Several terms that will be used later in this paper are now defined.

Total Implied Synchronizations:
> The number of edges in the directed acyclic graph (DAG) corresponding to the code generated from a basic block. Each edge is considered to be a producer/consumer synchronization pair.

Barrier Synchronization Fraction:
> The number of barriers in the schedule divided by the *Total Implied Synchronizations*.

Serialized Synchronization Fraction:
> The number of synchronizations satisfied by serialization, i.e., a consumer assigned to the same processor as a producer, divided by the *Total Implied Synchronizations*.

Static Scheduling Fraction:
> The remaining fraction of total implied synchronizations after the barrier and serialized fractions

are removed. This represents the synchronizations that are scheduled away by tracking static timing constraints after a barrier executes, as in the second producer/consumer synchronization of figure 7.

The partial ordering among barriers can be modeled as a directed acyclic graph. This model is developed in separate papers [14], [15] that appear in these proceedings; these papers also describe barrier MIMD hardware design. The two types of barrier MIMD mentioned in this paper, *static barrier MIMD (SBM)* [14] and *dynamic barrier MIMD (DBM)* [15], differ in that the SBM imposes a total order on barrier execution at run-time, while the DBM does not constrain the run-time execution order of the barriers.

3.2. Node Labeling

The scheduling algorithm assumes that the instructions are represented in an instruction DAG $G(N, A)$, where N is the set of n instruction nodes and A is the set of edges representing the precedence (producer/consumer) constraints between instructions. If an edge is directed from node i to node j, node j is said to be a *successor* (or *consumer*) of node i. Similarly, node i is said to be a *predecessor* (or *producer*) of node j.

The DAG is assumed to have one *entry* and one *exit* node; *dummy* exit or entry nodes (with zero execution time) are added as necessary to satisfy this condition. Let $t(i)$ represent the execution time for node (instruction) i, which is assumed to take integral values. For variable-execution-time instructions, $t_{min}(i)$ and $t_{max}(i)$ represent the minimum and maximum execution times, respectively, for node i. For the instruction DAG, the critical path is defined as the longest path from the entry node to the exit node, expressed mathematically as

$$t_{cr} \equiv \max_k \sum_{i \, member \, \phi_k} t(i)$$

where ϕ_k represents the kth path from the entry node to the exit node. Clearly, t_{cr} represents a lower bound on the execution time of the instruction DAG, regardless of the number of processors that execute it. The *height* of node i is defined as the length of the longest path from the exit node to node i where the orientation, or direction, of the edges are reversed, i.e.,

$$h(i) \equiv \max_k \sum_{j \, member \, \pi_k} t(j)$$

where π_k represents the kth path from the exit node to node i.

For the variable-execution-time instructions in the DAG, the *minimum* and *maximum height* for a node i, $h_{min}(i)$ and $h_{max}(i)$, are defined as follows:

$$h_{min}(i) \equiv \max_k \sum_{j \, member \, \pi_k} t_{min}(j) \quad \text{and} \quad h_{max}(i) \equiv \max_k \sum_{j \, member \, \pi_k} t_{max}(j) .$$

The minimum height corresponds to the height for node i assuming all nodes in the DAG take their minimum execution time and similarly, the maximum height corresponds to the height for node i assuming all nodes in the DAG take their maximum execution time.

3.3. Node Ordering

The maximum height and minimum height are computed for all nodes. This can be done in $O(n^2)$ time, since the problem reduces to finding longest paths from the exit node to all other nodes [10] (with edge orientations reversed). The nodes are first sorted into a list in nonincreasing order using the maximum height as the key, and ties between nodes with equal maximum height are broken using the minimum height (largest first) as the key. The complexity of this sort procedure is no worse than $O(n\log_2 n)$ [2].

3.4. Node Assignment

During this phase, the nodes are removed (in order) from the sorted list and assigned to particular processors. Some nodes should be placed in a processor that includes a predecessor (producer) for that node. This *serialization* of the nodes increases efficiency because it reduces the number of processors required and may eliminate a run-time synchronization operation. On the other hand, too much serialization can increase the schedule length. The node assignment algorithm attempts to strike a balance between these two competing aims.

In the following description of the node assignment and barrier insertion algorithms, the current node being scheduled is referred to as node i. The processor to which some node j is assigned is denoted as *Processor(j)*.

[1] The first step in node assignment is to determine the set of processors in which the predecessors of node i, denoted as *Preds(i)*, are scheduled. These are referred to as the *producer processors* for i, or *ProdProc(i)*. Go to step [2].

[2] For each processor in *ProdProc(i)*, determine if no other nodes are scheduled after *Pred(i)* on that processor. If no processor meets this condition, go to step [3]. If only a single producer processor meets this condition, place node i in that processor, and insert a barrier if necessary, as described in the next section. If more than one producer processor meets this condition, assign node i to the producer processor with the largest current maximum time (to possibly avoid inserting a barrier). If all processors in *ProdProc(i)* have the same current maximum time, choose one at random and assign i to it.

[3] Assign node i to a processor such that it is scheduled as early as possible. In case of ties between processors, choose one at random. This helps balance the number of nodes assigned to each processor. Insert a barrier as necessary.

3.5. Barrier Insertion

Two algorithms for barrier insertion are described. The first algorithm is conservative in that it always adds a barrier synchronization when one is necessary, but it may add unnecessary, redundant barriers. The other barrier insertion algorithm is "optimal" in the sense that a barrier is not inserted unless it is absolutely necessary at the time of the insertion. The barrier dag $(B, <_b)$ [14] is constructed incrementally as the nodes are assigned to processors and barriers inserted into the schedule.

The notion of one barrier "dominating" another is useful in constructing the barrier dag [1]. A barrier x *dominates* barrier y, written $x\ dom\ y$, if every path from the initial node of the barrier dag to y goes through x. With this definition, the initial barrier dominates all other barriers in the dag and every barrier dominates itself.

Each edge (u,v) between barriers u and v in a barrier dag contains the minimum and maximum execution time for the code between the barriers.

After consumer node i has been assigned to a processor C, it is necessary to check all producers for i to determine if a barrier is necessary. Suppose that node g is a member of the set *Preds(i)*, the predecessors, or producers, for instruction i, and that it is assigned to processor P.

3.5.1. Conservative Barrier Insertion

To determine if a barrier is needed between instruction nodes i and g, assigned to processors C and P, respectively, the following steps are performed:

[1] Define *LastBar(g)* as the last barrier to execute before node g. Define *NextBar(g)* to be the next barrier to execute after node g. Check for a path between *NextBar(g)* and *LastBar(i)*. Let us call this procedure *PathFind(g,i)*[3]. If a path is found, no barrier is needed; otherwise, continue with step [2].

[2] Find the nearest common dominating barrier for barriers *LastBar(g)* and *LastBar(i)*, written as *CommonDom(g,i)*. Go to step [3].

[3] The length of the longest path, assuming maximum execution times for code regions between barriers, from *CommonDom(g,i)* to *LastBar(g)* is computed. Denote this longest path as $\psi_{max}(CommonDom(g,i), LastBar(g))$, and its length as $l(\psi_{max}(CommonDom(g,i), LastBar(g)))$. Add the maximum time necessary to execute all instructions after *LastBar(g)* up to and including g, denoted as $\delta_{max}(g)$, to this length to yield the maximum time $T_{max}(g)$ to execute node g relative to the common dominating barrier. Go to step [4].

[4] Similarly, the longest path, assuming minimum execution times for code regions, from the common dominator to *LastBar(i)* is computed. Denote this longest path as $\psi_{min}(CommonDom(g,i), LastBar(i))$, and its length as $l(\psi_{min}(CommonDom(g,i), LastBar(i)))$. Let i^- represent the instruction before i on processor C. The minimum time to execute all instructions up to but *not* including i, denoted as $\delta_{min}(i^-)$, is added to this length, yielding the minimum time $T_{min}(i^-)$ to start executing node i relative to the common dominator. Go to step [5].

[5] If $T_{min}(i^-) \geq T_{max}(g)$, then no barrier is needed; otherwise, go to step [6].

[6] A barrier is inserted across processor P somewhere after the producer node g, and across processor C just before node i. To determine where the barrier is placed on P, we compute $l(\psi_{max}(CommonDom(g,i), LastBar(i)))$, and then add in the maximum execution times of all instructions on C after *LastBar(i)* up to node i^-, yielding $T_{max}(i^-)$. If $T_{max}(i^-) \leq T_{max}(g)$, then the barrier is inserted right after the producer node g on processor P. Node i is scheduled right after the barrier just inserted. However, if $T_{max}(i^-) > T_{max}(g)$, and if there is some instruction g^+ after instruction g, such that $T_{max}(i^-)$ falls into the execution time range (assuming maximum times) of g^+, then the barrier is inserted after g^+ on processor P.

This barrier insertion algorithm will sometimes add unnecessary barriers. For example, in the barrier embedding given in figure 14, the conservative insertion algorithm will insert a barrier across processors 0 and 2, after the producer node g and before consumer node i. In the figure, *LastBar(g)* is y and *LastBar(i)* is z. The common dominating barrier for y and z is x. It can be seen that $T_{max}(g) = 9$, while $T_{min}(i^-) = 8$, so it would appear that a barrier is necessary.

However, the longest path from x to z, $\psi_{min}(x,z)$, overlaps with the longest path from x to y, $\psi_{max}(x,y)$, on edge (x,y); recall that different assumptions have been made about the execution time for this edge on the different paths. If this is taken into account, then $\psi_{min}(x,z)$ should be computed, as before, assuming minimum execution times for edges *except* for the edges which

---

[3] This step is similar to the removal of transitive synchronization edges between the producer and consumer employed by Shaffer [17] and others. However, our technique combines scheduling with the transitive reduction step, so that unnecessary transitive edges are never added to the barrier graph.

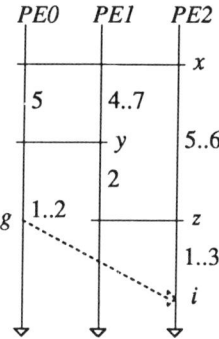

Figure 14: Conservative Barrier Insertion Fails

intersect $\psi_{max}(x,y)$. For these edges, the maximum execution time should be used when computing the longest path. In figure 14, this means that edge (x,y) has value 7, (y,z) has value 2, and the minimum time for i^- is 1, yielding an actual minimum time for node i of 10. Thus, i always executes after g and no barrier is required. In the next section, an optimal barrier insertion algorithm that does not generate these unnecessary barriers is described.

3.5.2. Optimal Barrier Insertion

From the previous example, it is clear that the problem with the conservative insertion algorithm is that it does not take into account the possibility that the longest paths from the common dominator to the producer and consumer nodes may overlap. In such cases, assuming maximum execution times on edges that overlap may increase the minimum execution time for the consumer node just enough to resolve the synchronization statically. (This problem is closely related to the critical path issues discussed in section 2.4 relative to timing analysis for directed synchronization operations.)

Let u be the nearest common dominator for barriers v and w, where v is *LastBar(g)* and w is *LastBar(i)*. Recall that node i is being scheduled, node g is a producer for node i, and it is necessary to determine if a barrier is required between these instructions.

The relationship between the various path lengths can be expressed as

$$l(\psi_{max}(u,v)) \geq l(\psi_{max}^2(u,v)) \geq \cdots \geq l(\psi_{max}^{k-1}(u,v))$$
$$\geq l(\psi_{min}(u,w)) + (\delta_{min}(i^-) - \delta_{max}(g)) \geq l(\psi_{max}^k(u,v))$$

where $\psi_{max}^j(u,v)$, $2 \leq j \leq k$ represents the jth longest path (assuming maximum execution times) from u to v. For each $\psi_{max}^j(u,v)$, find $\psi_{min}^{j*}(u,w)$, the longest path from u to w assuming minimum execution times *except* for edges on the path $\psi_{max}^j(u,v)$, where maximum execution time edges are used. If the condition

$$l(\psi_{max}^j(u,v)) + \delta_{max}(g) \leq l(\psi_{min}^{j*}(u,w)) + \delta_{min}(i^-)$$

is satisfied, consider the next longest path $\psi_{max}^{j+1}(u,v)$ and repeat the process. If the condition is not met, then a barrier must be inserted as described in step [6] of the conservative barrier insertion algorithm, and the scheduling algorithm starts again with the next node in the list.

This process of successively checking the jth longest paths continues until

$$l(\psi_{max}^j(u,v)) + \delta_{max}(g) \leq l(\psi_{min}(u,w)) + \delta_{min}(i^-)$$

is met for the *k*th longest path, proving that the synchronization is satisfied statically and no barrier is required.

4. Scheduling Experiments

The scheduling algorithms discussed in the last section were applied to the synthetic benchmark programs. The effects of varying different parameters that are related to the architecture of the machine and the structure of the synthetic benchmarks have been studied. Architecture parameters that were varied include the number of processors and timing assigned to each instruction; barriers were assumed to always execute immediately upon arrival of the last participating processor. Benchmark parameters included the number of instructions and variables in generated programs. Particular attention has been paid to the different synchronization fractions and how they vary as the parameters change. These results have provided good feedback concerning the performance of the scheduling algorithms.

4.1. Structure of the Synthetic Benchmark Programs

This study focuses on fine-grain scheduling of a single-chip multiprocessor RISC node [7] that employs the barrier mechanism discussed in this paper. Expensive operations such as multiplication and division are implemented as data-dependent code sequences that introduce asynchrony into the chip operation. Memory accesses across a shared bus or interconnection network involve contention that also involves stochastic delays. It is shown that static scheduling may still be used to advantage within this framework.

In this work, we wished to characterize and study the extent to which static scheduling can be employed in barrier MIMDs. In particular, measurements of the number of synchronizations that are satisfied statically, at compile-time, versus the number that require explicit synchronization instructions executed at run-time were desired. To this end, a compiler was developed for a simple language consisting of basic blocks of code with no control flow constructs.

The programs to be scheduled on barrier machines were automatically generated using common instruction execution frequencies [3]. This allowed us to automatically generate a very large number of *synthetic benchmarks* from which summary statistics were obtained. It also made it quite simple to change the various characteristics of generated programs to observe the effects on the statistics of scheduled programs. The drawback, of course, is that it is not possible to take real benchmark programs directly as input. Current efforts include prototype compiler development to generate barrier MIMD code for standard programming language constructs.

4.1.1. Benchmark Instruction Set

The scheduling algorithm takes as input a basic block of instructions. A basic block is a region of code that contains a sequence of consecutive statements. This region should have a single entry point and no embedded control structures [1]. There are nine instructions generated from the synthetic code sequences in the instruction set: four of these nine instructions have variable execution time. For the other operations, it is realistic to assume that they have a constant execution time of one unit. These operations are Or, And, Add, Sub, and Store. Table 1 summarizes the instruction frequencies and execution time ranges.

Instruction	Execution Freq.	Min. Time	Max. Time
Load	—	1	4
Store	—	1	1
Add	45.8%	1	1
Sub	33.9%	1	1
And	8.8%	1	1
Or	5.2%	1	1
Mul	2.9%	16	24
Div	2.2%	24	32
Mod	1.2%	24	32

Table 1: Instruction Frequencies and Execution Time Ranges

Tuple No.	Instruction	Min. Time	Max. Time
0	Load i	1	4
1	Load a	1	4
2	Add 0,1	2	5
3	Store b,2	3	6
4	Load f	1	4
24	Load d	1	4
5	Load j	1	4
12	Load c	1	4
26	And 4,24	2	5
6	Add 4,5	2	5
30	Sub 26,4	3	6
18	Sub 6,0	3	6
22	Add 1,2	2	5
38	Add 12,30	4	7
19	Store i,18	4	7
23	Store a,22	3	6
27	Store h,26	3	6
31	Store e,30	4	7
39	Store g,38	5	8

Table 2: Instructions from Example Synthetic Benchmark

4.1.2. Benchmark Synthesis

A C program was developed to randomly generate the basic blocks according to the statistics mentioned previously. This program requires as input the number of statements, variables, and constants desired in the generated code. It then generates a random sequence of assignment statements satisfying the desired conditions. The frequency of the assignment statements corresponds loosely to the instruction frequency distributions found in [3]. Note that in table 1 the frequencies of load and store are not given. These instructions are provided as necessary during code generation and optimization: the first reference to a variable causes a load for that variable to be generated, and a store is generated when a variable is assigned a value.

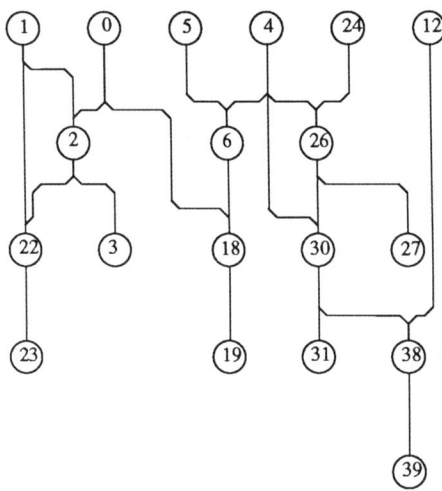

Figure 15: Instruction DAG for Example Synthetic Benchmark

During code generation, the randomly-generated assignment statements are optimized using standard local optimizations, including common subexpression elimination, constant folding and value propagation, and dead code elimination [1]. Hence, the resulting synthetic benchmark does not contain "redundant" parallelism that might skew the results.

An example synthetic benchmark is shown in table 2, and its corresponding DAG (Directed Acyclic Graph) is shown in figure 15. In table 2, the leftmost column represents the tuple number. Each tuple is incrementally assigned a number as it is produced by the code generator. Many tuples are not represented because they were removed by the optimizer. The two rightmost columns represent the minimum finish time and maximum finish time assuming unlimited parallelism. These columns will help in ordering the tuples as will be explained in section 4. In the instruction DAG, the instructions are represented as nodes while edges represent the precedence constraints between instructions. This DAG is important to both code optimization and the scheduling algorithm.

4.2. Experimental Results

At least one hundred synthetic benchmarks were generated for each set of parameters; over the course of the study, thousands of benchmarks were generated. Over all these benchmark programs, the results fell into the following ranges:

- The barrier fraction varies from 3% to 23%.
- The serialization fraction varies from 50% to 90%.

- The fraction of barriers statically scheduled away varies from 8% to 40%.

Note that the last fraction represents a feature unique to Barrier MIMD architectures and our timing analysis.

While the NOP insertion and directed synchronization timing-based code scheduling techniques will achieve some fraction of static scheduling removing barriers, as an approximation to the barrier mechanism, they are bounded by the Barrier MIMD performance. In other words, *all of the performance data can be directly applied to general MIMD architectures by simply treating the serialization as the minimum performance and the Barrier MIMD performance (serialization + static scheduling) as the maximum performance.* This leaves a relatively wide bound in many cases, however, this is not surprising in that it reflects the fact that there are many additional issues for directed synchronization machines; for example, performance will depend strongly on the inherent grain size of the code being larger than the typical variation in synchronization message transmission time. Hence, we seek to find bounds on performance for all types of MIMD machines by investigating in detail the performance of Barrier MIMD machines.

Perhaps the best summary of the Barrier MIMD scheduling results is a scatter plot with the serialization fraction on the vertical axis and the statically scheduled fraction on the horizontal axis, as shown in figure 16. The results for more than 2000 of the synthetic benchmarks (each benchmark contained between 65 and 132 synchronizations) are given in the figure, and it can be seen that the "center of mass" of the points lies near the 85% line; hence, on average about 85% of the synchronizations for the benchmarks in the plot are either serialized or statically scheduled away.

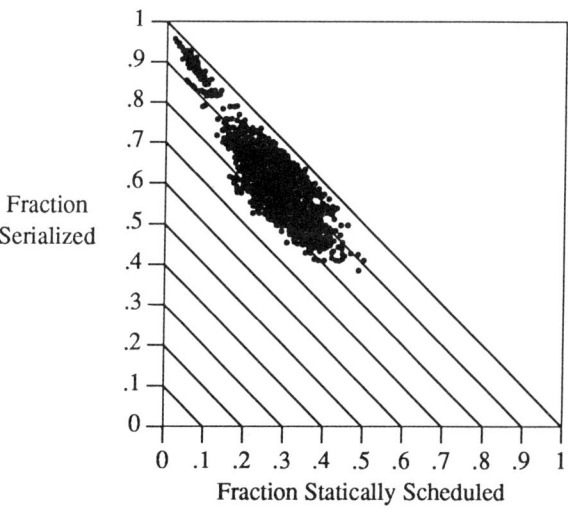

Figure 16: Scatter Plot

5. Architecture Performance Comparisons

Since we have suggested extension of static scheduling from VLIW machines to various types of MIMD architectures, it is useful to examine the relative performance. In this section, we present the results of an experimental comparison between Barrier MIMD and VLIW execution, as well as discussing the performance differences expected for more conventional MIMD architectures.

The experimental evaluation of VLIW versus Barrier MIMD performance was made using the same code scheduling techniques and synthetic benchmarks used in section 4. Figure 17 shows the results.

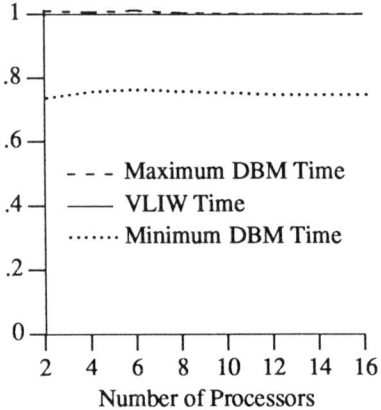

Figure 17: Barrier/VLIW Execution Time

In the VLIW execution mode all instructions were assumed to require their maximum time to execute. No asynchrony was allowed in VLIW execution. As can be seen in the figure, the maximum times for both the barrier MIMD and VLIW were nearly identical. Execution time as displayed in figure 17 has been normalized to VLIW execution time. The barrier machine took slightly longer to complete execution for smaller numbers of processors because more barriers were required due to instruction timing variation.

The minimum barrier MIMD completion time was about 25% lower than the VLIW completion time, and average barrier completion time will fall between the minimum and maximum times, the exact value being determined by the probability distributions of the variable-execution-time instructions. It should be noted that an optimal schedule (completion time equal to the critical path time) was determined for almost all the synthetic benchmarks used in the comparison.

These results suggest that it is important to reduce the maximum execution time for instructions, and this is traditionally done in VLIWs by adding extra hardware for such operations as integer and floating-point multiplies. Also, memory reference delays are reduced by having multiple paths to memory banks and through careful scheduling of memory references to avoid bank conflicts [5].

In considering how more traditional (directed synchronization) MIMD computers will perform, the basic issue is one of grain size. The large timing variations in some MIMD directed synchronization message transmission times make fine-grain parallel code synchronization intensive (or heavily serialized or laden with NOPs). In such cases, the execution time might become significantly longer than for a comparable VLIW; however, if grain size can be made large enough so that the variations in message transmission times are negligible, a directed synchronization MIMD should perform very much like a DBM. We are currently investigating these effects.

6. Conclusions

VLIW architectures have proven to be capable of providing consistently good performance over a larger range of programs than vector processors. However, VLIW architectures cannot achieve efficient parallel execution of while loops, subroutine calls, and variable-execution-time instructions. The new Barrier MIMD hardware, in concert with new relative timing analysis and code scheduling techniques, has shown great potential in reducing synchronization cost while still supporting these code structures, eliminating over 77% of all synchronizations (see figure 16), but current MIMD machines do not support Barrier MIMD operation [14] [15].

In this paper, we have introduced the basic concepts involved in using the new timing analysis and code scheduling for a more general class of MIMD architectures. Detailed algorithms and experimental performance evaluation of the techniques for Barrier MIMD machines are given, further, it is suggested how these techniques can be adapted and approximate performance predicted for more general MIMD architectures.

There is however, far more work to be done. Ongoing work includes the extension of the basic scheduling techniques to more complex code structures (including arbitrary control flow), development of efficient timing analysis and code scheduling techniques for various types of MIMD computers, and construction of prototype compilers for use in experimental evaluation of performance. We are also working toward a complete machine design, the CARP (Compiler-oriented Architecture Research at Purdue) machine [7], that incorporates the Barrier MIMD mechanism as well as various other novel compiler/architecture interactions.

The work described in this paper was supported in part under National Science Foundation grant no. 8624385-CDR.

References

1. Aho, A.V., Sethi, R., and Ullman, J.D., *Compilers: Principles, Techniques, and Tools.* Addison-Wesley, Reading, MA, 1986.
2. Aho, A.V., Hopcroft, J.E., and Ullman, J.D., *The Design and Analysis of Computer Algorithms.* Addison-Wesley, Reading, MA, 1974.
3. Alexander, W.G., and Wortman, D.B., Static and dynamic characteristics of XPL programs. *IEEE Computer*, November 1975, pp. 41-46.
4. Callahan II, C.D., *A Global Approach to the Detection of Parallelism.* Ph.D. Dissertation, Rice University, March 1987.
5. Colwell, R.P., Nix, R.P., O'Donnell, J.J., Papworth, D.B., and Rodman, P.K., A VLIW architecture for a trace scheduling compiler. *IEEE Trans. on Computers*, C-37, 8 (August 1988), 967-979.
6. Dietz, H.G., Schwederski, T., O'Keefe, M.T., and Zaafrani, A., Extending static synchronization beyond VLIW. *IEEE Proc. of Supercomputing 89*, Reno, NV, November 1989, pp. 416-425.
7. Dietz, H.G., Siegel, H.J., Cohen, W.E., O'Keefe, M.T., et al., A compiler-oriented architecture: the CARP machine. *Fourth SIAM Conf. on Parallel Processing for Scientific Computing,* Chicago, IL, December 1989.
8. Ellis, J.R., *Bulldog: A Compiler for VLIW Architectures.* MIT Press, Cambridge, MA, 1985.
9. Gross, T., Code optimization techniques for pipelined architectures. *COMPCON '83*, Spring 1983.

10. Hu, T.C., *Combinatorial Algorithms*. Addison-Wesley, Reading, MA, 1982.
11. Kasahara, H., and Narita, S., Practical multiprocessor scheduling algorithms for efficient parallel processing. *IEEE Trans. on Computers,* C-33, 11 (November 1984), 1023-1029.
12. Midkiff, S.P., and Padua, D.A., Compiler algorithms for synchronization. *IEEE Trans. on Computers*, C-36, 12 (December 1987), 1485-1495.
13. Nisar, A., and Dietz, H.G., Optimal code scheduling for multiple-pipeline processors. *Proc. of 1990 Int'l Conf. on Parallel Processing,* St. Charles, IL, August 1990, pp. II 61-64.
14. O'Keefe, M.T., and Dietz, H.G., Hardware barrier synchronization: static barrier MIMD (SBM). *Proc. of 1990 Int'l Conf. on Parallel Processing,* St. Charles, IL, August 1990, pp. I 35-42.
15. O'Keefe, M.T., and Dietz, H.G., Hardware barrier synchronization: dynamic barrier MIMD (DBM). *Proc. of 1990 Int'l Conf. on Parallel Processing,* St. Charles, IL, August 1990, pp. I 43-46.
16. Schwederski, T., Nation, W.G., Siegel, H.J., and Meyer, D.G., The implementation of the PASM prototype control hierarchy *Proc. of Second Int'l Conf. on Supercomputing,* 1987, pp. I 418-427.
17. Shaffer, P.L., Minimization of interprocessor synchronization in multiprocessors with shared and private memory. *Proc. 1989 Int'l Conf. Parallel Processing,* vol. III, St. Charles, IL, August 1989, pp. III 138-142.
18. Zaafrani, A., Dietz, H.G., and O'Keefe, M.T., Static scheduling for barrier MIMD architectures. *Proc. of 1990 Int'l Conf. on Parallel Processing,* St. Charles, IL, August 1990, pp. II 187-194.

23 Dependence Flow Graphs: an Algebraic Approach to Program Dependencies

K Pingali, M. Beck, R. Johnson, M. Moudgill, P. Stodghill

Abstract

The topic of intermediate languages for optimizing and parallelizing compilers has received much attention lately. In this paper, we argue that any good representation of a program must have two crucial properties: first, it must be a data structure that can be rapidly traversed to determine dependence information, and second this representation must be a program in its own right, with a parallel, local model of execution. In this paper, we illustrate the importance of these points by examining algorithms for a standard optimization — global constant propagation. We discuss the problems in working with current representations. Then, we propose a novel representation called the *dependence flow graph* which has each of the properties mentioned above. We show that this representation leads to a simple algorithm, based on abstract interpretation, for solving the constant propagation problem. Our algorithm is simpler than, and as efficient as, the best known algorithms for this problem. An interesting feature of our representation is that it naturally incorporates the best aspects of many other representations, including continuation-passing style, data and program dependence graphs, static single assignment form and dataflow program graphs.

This research was supported by an NSF Presidential Young Investigator award (NSF grant #CCR-8958543), and by grants from HP, DEC, and IBM.

A version of this paper appears in POPL 91.

1 Introduction

The growing complexity of optimizing and parallelizing compilers has re-focused the attention of the programming languages community on the design of *intermediate program representations*. Some well-known representations are: control flow graphs [2], def-use chains [2], data dependence graphs [14], program dependence graphs and webs [12, 6], program representation graphs [8], static single assignment form [10], continuation-passing style [19], and program graphs [1]. The choice of program representation has a profound effect on the design, asymptotic complexity, and implementation of optimizing and parallelizing transformations. As an analogy, consider Hindu numerals[3], which are more convenient than Roman numerals for performing arithmetic operations, while representing the same information. In this paper, we argue that a good intermediate representation should have the following properties:

- It should be executable. That is, it should be a language with a well-defined, compositional operational semantics. This allows abstract interpretation to be employed when designing algorithms, which facilitates systematic algorithm development and proof of correctness [9].

- It should be possible to view the representation as a data structure that can be traversed efficiently for data dependence information, as required by many compiler transformations [14].

- Loops should be represented explicitly. Some representations replace loops with tail-recursive procedures [3, 11]. In our experience, this transformation is not desirable since many important loop transformations, such as loop interchange, have no natural analog in the context of tail-recursive procedures.

- The storage model should include an updatable, imperative store. The operational semantics of an imperative language is phrased naturally in terms of an updatable store. While it is possible to treat the store functionally (as is done in denotational semantics), such treatments are quite clumsy in dealing with data structures, especially arrays [4].

- The representation should be compact. A new program representation whose size is asymptotically bigger than that of well-accepted representations (such as def-use chains) is unlikely to gain acceptance.

In this paper, we illustrate the importance of these issues by examining a particular optimization — global constant propagation. This optimization is performed by all optimizing compilers and is representative of "scalar" optimizations such as partial redundancy elimination and strength reduction. We discuss the drawbacks of the representations cited

---

[3]Because of an unfortunate instance of aliasing, these are known as Arabic numerals in the West.

above, and demonstrate how a representation that meets our criteria leads to a simple, elegant algorithm based on abstract interpretation. This algorithm is as efficient as the best algorithms that use the other forms, and has an elegant proof of correctness. Our representation, called the *dependence flow graph*, is based on a generalization of the dataflow model of computation, called *dependence-driven execution*. Interestingly enough, many features of previously proposed intermediate representations arise naturally in the context of dependence flow graphs.

In Section 2, we illustrate the drawbacks of previously proposed representations by describing how constant propagation is performed on these representations. In Section 3, we present dependence flow graphs along with a formal, Plotkin-style operational semantics. In Section 4, we present our algorithm for constant propagation on dependence flow graphs, and we indicate a proof of correctness. Finally, in Section 5 we discuss ongoing work.

2 Constant Propagation

In this section, we examine the problem of global constant propagation, a standard analysis performed by optimizing compilers. We define a particularly ambitious class of constants, the *possible-paths constants*, which is discovered by an algorithm due to Wegman and Zadeck [20]. We then consider a number of intermediate forms most commonly used for optimization in imperative language compilers. Finally, we show how previous constant propagation algorithms have been affected by the shortcomings of these underlying representations.

2.1 Problem Description

A *definition* of a variable x is a statement that assigns (or may assign) to x. A *use* of x is an occurrence of x in a statement that reads (or may read) the value of x. We say that a definition of x *reaches* a use of x if execution of the definition may be followed by execution of the use without intervening execution of any other definition of x. As is standard, this definition assumes that conditional branches may go either way [2].

If the right hand side of a definition of x is a constant c, we can sometimes substitute c for a use of x without changing the meaning of the program. For example, in Figure 1(a), the first use of z can be replaced by 1 and the second by 2. This is a simple example of *constant propagation*. If all of the variables on the right hand side of a definition are replaced by constants, then we can evaluate the expression and replace it by a constant. Recursively, this opens up fresh opportunities for constant propagation. For example, in

```
                                                            p := true
            if (p) then                                     if (p) then
                { z := 1; x := z+2 }                            { x := 1 }
            else                                            else
                { z := 2; x := z+1 }                            { x := 2 }
            y := x                                          y := x

                (a) all-paths                                   (b) possible-paths
```

Figure 1: Examples of runtime constants

Figure 1(a), the right hand sides of the two definitions of x can be simplified to the constant 3. The use of x in the last statement is reached by *two* definitions of x. However, since the right hand sides of both definitions are the same constant, we can replace the use of x by 3 without changing the meaning of the program. This motivates the following definition.

An *all-paths constant* is either:

- a constant expression c, or

- an expression e over some set of variables $\{v_1, v_2, \ldots v_n\}$ such that for each v_i, the right hand side of every definition of v_i that reaches e is an all-paths constant c_i.

The class of all-paths constants takes no account of constants in conditionals. However, if the predicate of a conditional can be determined to be constant, then we can ignore the effect of definitions on the side that is never executed. If we modify the definition of all-paths constants to exclude such definitions, the result is the class of *possible-paths constants* [20]. In Figure 1(b), the use of x in the last statement is a possible-paths constant with value 1. Note that this use is not an all-paths constant.

A variety of algorithms for constant propagation have been proposed in the literature [2, 13, 18, 20]. Some of these algorithms are more powerful than others — for example, only the algorithm of Wegman and Zadeck [20] finds possible-paths constants in a single pass. Repeated application of the less powerful algorithms, combined with dead code elimination, will find all possible-paths constants. However, repeated rounds of program transformation and analysis are expensive, and so we seek to discover as many constants as possible in a single pass through the program. As we will see, the choice of program representation plays a critical role in this task.

It is standard to express constant propagation algorithms in the framework due to Kildall [13]. We define a lattice *Lat* shown in Figure 2, consisting of all the constant

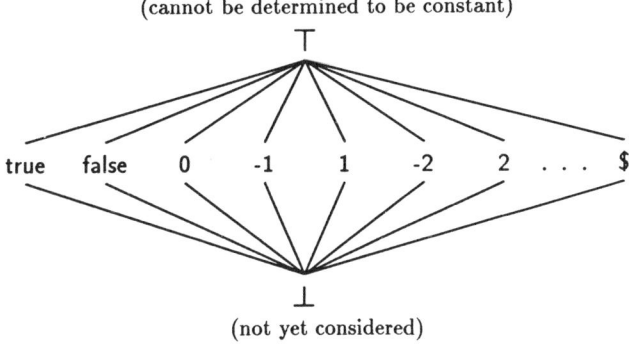

Figure 2: *Lat* — Lattice for constant propagation

values and two distinguished values ⊤ and ⊥. The special constant $ is used only in dependence flow graphs, and plays no part in the algorithms described in this section. Uses of variables are assigned values from *Lat* during constant propagation. Initially, every use of every variable is mapped to ⊥, meaning that we have no information yet about the values that it is assigned at runtime. A use is mapped to ⊤ when the algorithm cannot determine that the use is a constant (*e.g.* if the use is reached by two definitions whose right hand sides are 3 and 4.)[4] At the end of constant propagation, the interpretation of the lattice value assigned to a use of a variable x is as follows:

⊥: This use was never examined during constant propagation; it is dead code.

c: This use of x has the value c in all executions.

⊤: This use of x may have different values in different executions.

To permit evaluation of right hand sides of definitions in the abstract interpretation, it is convenient to extend the usual arithmetic and boolean operators so that they can take

---

[4]Note that the sense of ⊤ and ⊥ in the lattice are reversed with respect to the lattice used by previous researchers [13, 18, 20]. These researchers viewed constant propagation as an all-paths data flow problem; such problems are traditionally formulated so that the desired solution is the *greatest* fixed point of a set of equations. In our framework, we will use abstract interpretation to find constants, and it is more convenient to formulate the desired solution as the *least* fixed point of a set of equations.

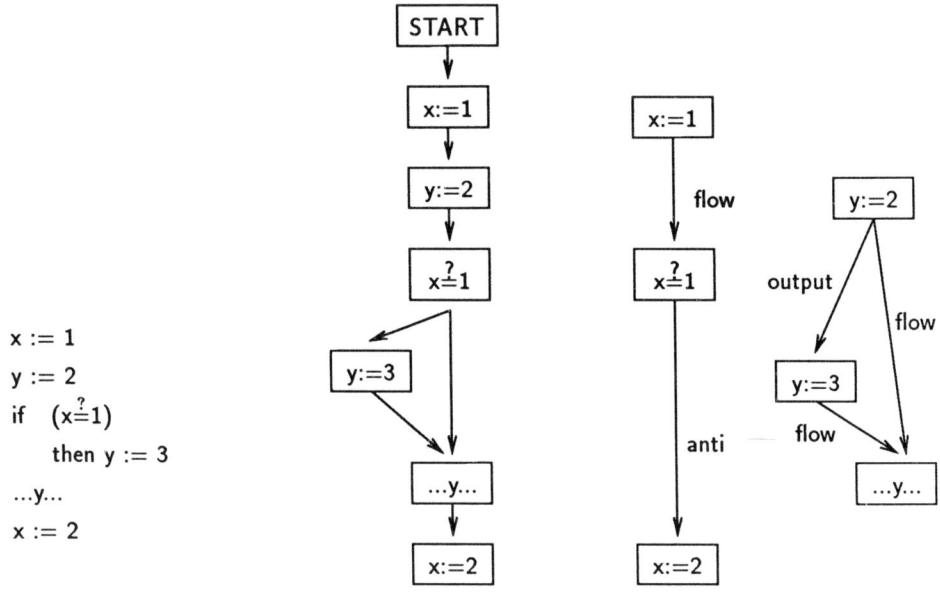

(a) Source Program (b) Control Flow Graph (c) Data Dependence Graph

Figure 3: A Small Program and its Representations

$\bot$ and $\top$ as arguments. For example, the operator v1 + v2 is interpreted as follows:

$$Plus(v_1, v_2) = \begin{cases} \top & \text{if } v_1 = \top \text{ or } v_2 = \top \\ c_1 + c_2 & \text{if } v_1 = c_1 \text{ and } v_2 = c_2 \\ \bot & \text{otherwise} \end{cases}$$

2.2 Control Flow Graphs

Figure 3(b) shows the *control flow graph* [2] for a small imperative program. Nodes are either assignment statements or conditional expressions that affect flow of control, and edges represent possible transfer of control between nodes. An assignment node has a single successor while a conditional node has two successors representing the possible branching of control. In our figures, we follow the convention that the *true* branch of a conditional is always left-most. Algorithms for constructing the control flow graph representation of a program are well-known [2]. Control flow graphs have a simple sequential semantics based on transforming a global imperative store.

A simple algorithm based on abstract interpretation finds possible-paths constants in the control flow graph. At each node, we maintain a vector of values from *Lat*. These vectors have an entry for each variable, and intuitively, they summarize the possible values of variables before the statement is executed. Initially, every entry at every node is set to $\bot$ except at the START node where the entries are set to $\top$. These values are updated monotonically (in the lattice-theoretic sense) as the algorithm proceeds.

The algorithm maintains a worklist of nodes to be processed; initially, this worklist contains all of the nodes immediately following the START node. Nodes are dequeued from the worklist and processed as follows. Let N be a node from the worklist, and let N_{in} be the vector at the input of N.

- If the node is an assignment statement, (say x := e), then the expression e is evaluated, using the values of variables in N_{in}, and a new vector N_{out} is created that is identical to N_{in} except at x where it has the value just computed for e. The vector N_{out} must be propagated to the successor node S of the assignment statement. Let S_{in} be the vector at the successor node. This vector is updated to the join of its value and N_{out}.[5] If this changes the value of S_{in}, then S is added to the worklist.

- If the node is a conditional branch, then the predicate is evaluated. If the value of the predicate is $\top$, then the vector N_{in} is propagated to both successors of the conditional branch. If the value of the predicate is *true* or *false*, then N_{in} is propagated only along the corresponding side of the conditional branch. If the value of the input vector changes at a successor, then the successor is added to the worklist.

We leave it to the reader to verify that this algorithm will find all of the constants in Figure 1. Unfortunately, the asymptotic complexity of this algorithm is poor. If we let V be the number of program variables and N the number of statements, then the algorithm requires $O(NV)$ space and $O(NV^2)$ time. Although the abstract interpretation algorithm on control flow graphs is simple, it is not used in practice because of its high cost.

The inefficiency arises because lattice values must be propagated along control flow paths from definitions of variables to their uses. What is needed is a "sparse" representation that links definitions to the uses they reach, so that we can propagate the values of individual variables to places where they are needed, rather than propagating the values of all variables to all program locations. Def-use chains and their generalization, data dependence graphs, provide such a representation.

2.3 Data Dependence Graphs

Def-use chains are graphs that have the same nodes as control flow graphs, but the edges connect each definition of a variable to all uses reached by that definition. For compilers

---

[5]We cannot simply store N_{out} at S_{in} because S may have other predecessors. If a node has two predecessors, $x := 2$ and $x := 3$, then the entry for x at its input should be $\top$.

that perform wholesale reorganization of programs, a generalization of def-use chains called the *data dependence graph* [14] is commonly used. The data dependence graph for our example is shown in Figure 3(c). Edges in the graph represent dependencies that are classified as *flow* (def-use), *anti* (use-def), or *output* (def-def) dependences.

Note that the data dependence graph is not an executable representation and does not incorporate information about flow of control. For example, in Figure 3(c), execution of the definition y := 3 is not related to the predicate $x \stackrel{?}{=} 1$ in any way. Negating the predicate will change the value of y that is read, but this does not change the dependence edges that sequence operations on y.

The constant propagation algorithm based on def-use chains is similar to the one described earlier for control flow graphs, except that we propagate lattice values from definitions to uses along def-use edges, rather than along control flow paths. At each node, we keep a vector containing values only for those variables that are used by the node. A worklist is kept of nodes to be processed. Initially, every definition whose right hand side is a constant c is placed on this worklist.

To process a definition of the form x := e, the expression e is evaluated, and its value is propagated along def-use edges originating at this node to nodes that use x. Conditional nodes do not need any processing, since there are no def-use chains originating at these nodes. The complexity of this algorithm is linear in the size of the def-use chains of the program.

If we let $E \leq 2N$ be the number of edges in the control flow graph, then a naive representation of def-use chains can be $O(E^2V)$ in size. However, Reif and Lewis have shown that a factored form of def-use chains can be represented in size $O(EV)$ [18]. This yields an algorithm which is a factor of V faster than the one which uses the control flow graph.

Although this algorithm will find all-paths constants as in Figure 1(a), it will not find possible-paths constants as in Figure 1(b). In relying on data dependence information to direct the flow of values, we have lost important connections between data dependence and flow of control. In our control flow algorithm, values were propagated down only one side of a conditional with a constant predicate. This was possible because the control flow path from the definition to the use passed through the conditional. Def-use edges do not flow through conditionals, but reach directly from definitions to uses. Thus, our new algorithm does not find all possible-paths constants, and we conclude that def-use information needs to be augmented with control flow information in some way.

2.4 Control Flow Graphs with Data Dependence Graphs

Most optimizing compilers generate a control flow graph as a first step towards computing the data dependence graph. This suggests the development of "hybrid" algorithms that use both data structures. The constant propagation algorithm described next is adapted from that of Wegman and Zadeck [20].

To find possible-paths constants while still obtaining the efficiency of def-use chains, Wegman and Zadeck refer back to the control flow graph. To keep propagation of values from bypassing conditionals, a boolean *executable* flag is added to each statement, and is initially set to *false*, except for START. The executable flag indicates that the statement may be executed, *i.e.*, that it has not been determined to be dead.

Lattice values flow along def-use chains as before; in addition, information about which nodes may execute flows through the control flow graph. These two flows are not independent since intermediate results of constant propagation may be used to determine that one side of a conditional is never executed. Conversely, a definition does not participate in constant propagation until it is determined that it may be executed. Two worklists keep track of these two flows: the *flow* worklist and the *def* worklist.

The flow worklist is used to propagate the executable flag through the control flow graph. If a non-conditional node N may be executed, then its successors may be executed. Once the predicate of a conditional has been assigned a lattice value, the executable flag can be propagated down one or both sides as appropriate.

The def worklist is used to propagate lattice values along def-use edges as in the previous algorithm. Nodes are placed on a worklist only if their executable flag is *true*; conditionals are placed on the flow worklist and definitions are placed on the def worklist. Initially, the flow worklist contains only START and the def worklist is empty.

Although this algorithm finds the possible-paths constants in Figure 1, it fails to discover the one-sided possible-paths constant in Figure 4(a) since the assignment x := 2 reaches the use of x and is not dead. Wegman and Zadeck suggest transforming every one-sided conditional by inserting a dummy assignment of the form x := x on the else branch. In the transformed program, as in Figure 4(b), only one value is propagated through the conditional if the predicate is constant. When performed on the transformed program, the Wegman-Zadeck algorithm does find the possible-paths constants.

The problem of maintaining two data structures to represent the program's execution semantics and its dependencies is addressed in part by the *program dependence graph*. This graph consists of the data dependence graph augmented with *control dependence* arcs. A more elegant constant propagation algorithm based on the one described in this section can be developed using the program dependence graph. However, program dependence

```
x := 2                          x := 2
p := true                       p := true
if (p) then { x := 1 }          if (p) then { x := 1 }
y := x                                     else { x := x }
                                y := x
```

(a) one-sided   (b) dummy assignment

Figure 4: Transforming a one-sided conditional

graphs inherit many of the problems of the data dependence graph; for example, for constant propagation, we must still perform the program transformation shown in Figure 4. Moreover, they do not have a simple, local execution semantics [8].

2.5 Summary

The control flow graph allows us to formulate a simple algorithm, based on abstract interpretation, that finds possible-paths constants without the need for program transformations. However, its asymptotic complexity is poor. Algorithms that use the various dependence graphs are more complex, and none of them find possible-paths constants without some program transformation. However, the asymptotic complexity of these algorithms is a factor of V better than the algorithm that use control flow graphs.

An ideal program representation for constant propagation would have a local execution semantics from which an abstract interpretation can be easily derived. It would also be a sparse representation of program dependencies, in order to yield an efficient algorithm. Like a Necker cube, this representation will permit two points of view — it can be viewed as a data structure that can be traversed efficiently for dependence information, but it can also be viewed as a precisely defined language with a local operational semantics. The dependence flow graph is just such a representation.

3 Dependence Flow Graphs

Figure 5 shows the dependence flow graph for the imperative language program considered in Figure 3. Dependence flow graphs are a synthesis of ideas from data dependence graphs and the dataflow model of computation. As in the data dependence graph, the dependence flow graph can be viewed as a data structure in which arcs represent de-

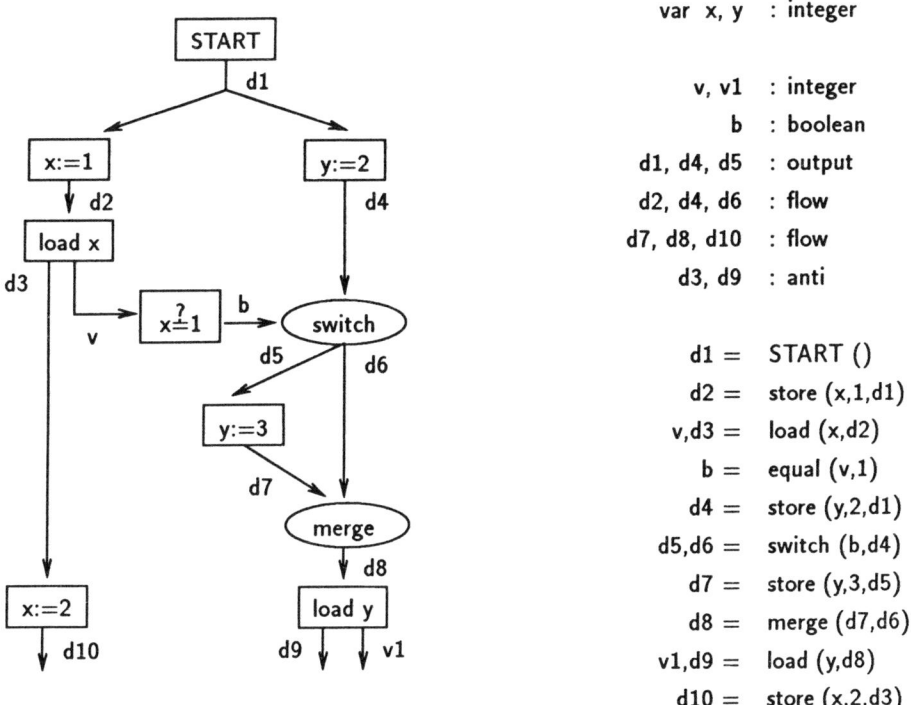

Figure 5: Dependence Flow Graph for a Small Program

pendencies between operations. It is easy to verify that for every dependence arc in the data dependence graph (Figure 3), there is a corresponding path in the dependence flow graph (Figure 5). However, unlike data dependence graphs, dependence flow graphs are *executable*, and the execution semantics, called *dependence-driven execution*, is a generalization of the data-driven execution semantics of dataflow graphs. In dataflow graphs, nodes represent functional operators that communicate with each other by exchanging value-carrying tokens along arcs in the graph. These arcs can be viewed as flow dependencies since they connect a node producing a value, such as an integer or boolean, to nodes that consume this value; we will call such arcs *functional dependencies* in our presentation. In Figure 5, v, v1, and b are functional dependencies.

We extend the dataflow model by adding an imperative (updatable) global store and two operations called load and store which manipulate it. As one would expect, the load operator reads the contents of a storage location and outputs the value as a token. The store operator is the inverse of the load operator — it receives a value on a token and stores it into a memory location. To sequence these operations, we introduce a new kind of arc called an *imperative dependence*. For example, in Figure 5, d2 and d3 are imperative dependencies that sequence operations on location x, corresponding to arcs in the data dependence graph. To preserve the local, token-pushing semantics of dataflow graphs, we make load and store operators produce a special token, $, when they have completed. These tokens flow down imperative dependence arcs to enable operators at the destinations of those arcs. For example, when the x := 1 operator executes, it produces a token carrying $ on line d2. This is said to *satisfy* the dependence d2, thereby *enabling* the load x operator for execution. When the load x operator executes, it produces tokens carrying $ on line d3 and the value 1 on line v. In this way, operations on a given memory location are sequenced, but operations on different locations can execute in parallel.

Imperative dependencies are further classified as *flow*, *anti* and *output* as in data dependence graphs. We classify d2 as a flow dependence and d3 as an anti-dependence. Note that dependence d4 is both a flow and an output dependence, since logically it corresponds to both of the dependence arcs coming out of the definition y := 2 in the data dependence graph. Dependence arcs that sequence operations on location y are intercepted by switch and merge operators, which implement flow of control as discussed below. These operators serve to combine control information with data dependencies, which is exactly what is missing from the representations discussed in Section 2.

To understand dependence flow graphs, it is useful to execute the graph depicted in Figure 5 by pushing tokens. Execution begins when the START operator sends a token carrying $ to the store operations x := 1 and y := 2. Depending on whether the token received on arc b is true or false, the switch operator outputs the token it receives on d4 onto either arc d5 or d6. In our example, the switch routes the token to d5, and the definition y := 3 is executed. The merge operator receives a token on either one (but not both) of its inputs, and simply outputs this token. The reader can verify that a token carrying the value 3 will be generated on arc v1.

In a forthcoming paper, we will describe how dependence flow graphs are constructed, starting from the control-flow graph of a program. This construction can handle unstructured control-flow. Some preliminary ideas are presented in an earlier paper [7]. From an analysis of the construction, we show two facts.

- Dependence flow graphs constructed by our algorithm satisfy Bernstein's conditions: that is, a store operator can never be enabled for execution simultaneously with another store or load operator on the same storage location.

- The dependence flow graph of a program whose control flow graph has E edges and V variables has size $O(EV)$.

Although token-pushing provides useful intuition, we adopt a different style of operational semantics in the formal development. Arcs in the dependence flow graph can be viewed as names that represent a set of single assignment registers or temporaries. Producing a token carrying a value on an arc is similar to storing that value in the corresponding register. Explicit **load** and **store** operators to transfer values between the global store and a set of registers/temporaries have been used in the PL.8 compiler [5] and many Scheme compilers [19]. We develop this point of view in the rest of this section.

3.1 Acyclic Dependence Flow Graphs: Formal Semantics

From a formal perspective, a dependence flow graph is a set of *declarations* followed by a set of *definitions*. Declarations introduce names for locations in the store and for *dependencies*, which can be viewed as names for a set of single assignment registers or temporaries. The body of the dependence flow graph is a set of definitions. A definition is an equation with a left hand side consisting of one or more dependencies, and a right hand side consisting of the application of an operator to dependencies, locations, and constants. The operators and their arity are shown in the left column of Figures 6. A definition is said to be a *source* for dependencies named on the left hand side of the equation and a *sink* for dependencies named on the right hand side. A dependence has exactly one source but can have many sinks.

We now give a Plotkin-style, formal operational semantics for dependence flow graphs [17]. Rather than rewrite programs, as is common in this style of semantics, we will define a state transition semantics in which we rewrite *configurations*. Informally, a configuration represents the state of the computation and a transition represents a step in the computation. In our system, a configuration is a pair consisting of an *environment* and a *store*. To define them, we need the following sets.

- $V = Bool \cup Int \cup \{\$\}$ is the set over which we compute. The metavariables b and c stand for elements of V.

- $Loc = \{L_0, L_1, ...\}$ is an infinite set of global store locations. The metavariable x stands for an element of Loc.

- $Dep = \{d_0, d_1, ...\}$ is an infinite set of dependencies. The metavariables d, v, p, and t stand for elements of Dep.

The environment keeps track of the state of dependencies in the program and the store keeps track of the state of locations used by the program. The environment is a mapping from program dependencies to the set V. For technical reasons, a dependence will be added

$$d = \text{start } ():\quad \frac{d \text{ undefined}}{\langle \rho, \sigma \rangle \to \langle \rho[d \mapsto \$], \sigma \rangle}$$

$$t = \text{op } (t_1, t_2):\quad \frac{t_1, t_2 \text{ defined} \land t \text{ undefined}}{\langle \rho, \sigma \rangle \to \langle \rho[t \mapsto op(\rho[t_1], \rho[t_2])], \sigma \rangle}$$

$$t_{true}, t_{false} = \text{switch } (b, t):\quad \frac{\rho[b] = true \land t \text{ defined} \land t_{true}, t_{false} \text{ undefined}}{\langle \rho, \sigma \rangle \to \langle \rho[t_{true} \mapsto \rho[t]], \sigma \rangle}$$

$$t_{true}, t_{false} = \text{switch } (b, t):\quad \frac{\rho[b] = false \land t \text{ defined} \land t_{true}, t_{false} \text{ undefined}}{\langle \rho, \sigma \rangle \to \langle \rho[t_{false} \mapsto \rho[t]], \sigma \rangle}$$

$$t = \text{merge } (t_1, t_2):\quad \frac{t_1 \text{ defined} \land t, t_2 \text{ undefined}}{\langle \rho, \sigma \rangle \to \langle \rho[t \mapsto \rho[t_1]], \sigma \rangle}$$

$$t = \text{merge } (t_1, t_2):\quad \frac{t_2 \text{ defined} \land t, t_1 \text{ undefined}}{\langle \rho, \sigma \rangle \to \langle \rho[t \mapsto \rho[t_2]], \sigma \rangle}$$

$$v, d_{out} = \text{load } (x, d_{in}):\quad \frac{d_{in}, \sigma[x] \text{ defined} \land v, d_{out} \text{ undefined}}{\langle \rho, \sigma \rangle \to \langle \rho[v \mapsto \sigma[x], d_{out} \mapsto \$], \sigma \rangle}$$

$$d_{out} = \text{store } (x, v, d_{in}):\quad \frac{v, d_{in} \text{ defined} \land d_{out} \text{ undefined}}{\langle \rho, \sigma \rangle \to \langle \rho[d_{out} \mapsto \$], \sigma[x \mapsto \rho[v]] \rangle}$$

Figure 6: Transition Rules for Acyclic DFGs

to the environment only when it is satisfied; therefore, the initial environment is empty. The environment grows monotonically during execution, in the sense that as computation progresses, dependencies are only added to and never deleted from the environment; in addition, the value bound to a functional dependence in the environment never changes. Similarly, the store is a mapping from the set of locations used in the program to the set V; however, locations can be updated arbitrarily. The store, like the environment, is initially empty and a location is added to the store the first time a value is stored to it.

Definition 1

1. *An* environment $\rho : D \to V$ *is a finite function — its domain $D \subset Dep$ is finite.*

2. *A dependence d is said to be* defined *or* satisfied *in ρ if d is in the domain of ρ. Otherwise, it is said to be* undefined *in ρ. The notation $\rho[v \mapsto c]$ represents an environment identical to ρ except for dependence v which is mapped to c.*

$t = \text{loop}\ (t_{in}, t_{back})$:
$$\frac{t_{in}.I \text{ defined} \ \wedge\ t.I.1 \text{ undefined}}{\langle \rho, \sigma \rangle\ \to\ \langle \rho[t.I.1 \mapsto \rho[t_{in}.I]],\ \sigma \rangle}$$

$t = \text{loop}\ (t_{in}, t_{back})$:
$$\frac{t_{back}.I.j \text{ defined} \ \wedge\ t.I.j+1 \text{ undefined}}{\langle \rho, \sigma \rangle\ \to\ \langle \rho[t.I.j+1 \mapsto \rho[t_{back}.I.j]],\ \sigma \rangle}$$

$t, t_{back} = \text{until}\ (b, t_{in})$:
$$\frac{\rho[b.I.j] = \textit{false} \ \wedge\ t_{in}.I.j \text{ defined} \ \wedge\ t_{back}.I.j \text{ undefined}}{\langle \rho, \sigma \rangle\ \to\ \langle \rho[t_{back}.I.j \mapsto \rho[t_{in}.I.j]],\ \sigma \rangle}$$

$t, t_{back} = \text{until}\ (b, t_{in})$:
$$\frac{\rho[b.I.j] = \textit{true} \ \wedge\ t_{in}.I.j \text{ defined} \ \wedge\ t.I \text{ undefined}}{\langle \rho, \sigma \rangle\ \to\ \langle \rho[t.I \mapsto \rho[t_{in}.I.j]],\ \sigma \rangle}$$

Figure 7: Transition Rules for Loop Operators

3. A store $\sigma : L \to V$ is a finite function — its domain $L \subset Loc$ is finite. Just as for dependencies, we can talk about a location x being defined or undefined in a store σ.

4. A configuration is a pair $\langle \rho, \sigma \rangle$ consisting of an environment and a store. The initial configuration has empty environment and store.

Figure 6 shows the transition rules for acyclic dependence flow graphs. The left column consists of definitions and the right column shows a precondition above the line and a transition below the line. If the definition in the left column is present in the dependence flow graph and the precondition on top of the line is satisfied, then the transition shown below the line can be performed.

As an example, consider a definition of the form $t = \text{add}\ (t_1, t_2)$. We would expect this operator to execute when t_1 and t_2 are defined. Once this operator has executed, we want to disable this transition. Therefore, we perform the transition only if t is undefined. The load and store operators are the only operators that access the store. The load operator checks that the contents of location x are defined; this will catch an attempt to read from an uninitialized location. The switch and merge operators implement flow of control. Depending on the boolean value p, the switch operator satisfies either dependence t_T or t_F. The dependence at the output of the merge is satisfied when either of the dependencies at its input is satisfied. Notice that the rules check that at most one input dependence is satisfied.

3.2 Cyclic dependence flow graphs

As far as the input/output behavior of programs goes, loops can be replaced by tail-recursion. However, many loop optimizations, such as loop interchange, have no natural analog in the context of tail-recursion, so we felt it was important to model loops directly using cyclic dependence flow graphs. For this, we need two new operators called loop and until which are used at loop entrance and loop exit respectively. In addition, the transition rules for the operators discussed in Section 3.1 must be altered slightly.

Consider the definition $t = \text{add } (t_1, t_2)$ occurring inside a loop. t represents a different dependence in each iteration; to model this we index t by the iteration number, so that $t.i$ represents the dependence t in the ith loop iteration.[6] $t.1$ is the dependence in the first iteration. This scheme extends naturally for nested loops so that for a two-dimensional loop, $t.i.j$ represents this dependence in iteration i of the outer loop and iteration j of the inner loop. It is sometimes convenient to write this as $t.I$ where I is a (two dimensional) *index vector i.j*. To reflect this intuition, the definition of environments is modified:

Definition 2 *Let Seq be the set of finite sequences of positive integers, including the empty sequence. An* environment $\rho : DS \to V$ *is a finite function — its domain* $DS \subset Dep \times Seq$ *is finite.*

To avoid introducing more notation, we will let the term dependence stand for both an identifier (arc) in the dependence flow graph and its dynamic instance in various iterations, relying on context to make the distinction clear. For any index vector I, the add operator can execute as soon as its operands are available, i.e. as soon as $t_1.I$ and $t_2.I$ are defined. Therefore, the rule for the add becomes:

$$t = \text{add } (t_1, t_2) : \quad \frac{t_1.I, t_2.I \text{ defined } \wedge \quad t.I \text{ undefined}}{\langle \rho, \sigma \rangle \to \langle \rho[t.I \mapsto (\rho[t_1.I] + \rho[t_2.I])], \sigma \rangle}$$

The transition rules for the other operators shown in Figure 6 are extended in a similar manner.

We now discuss the semantics of the loop and exit operators. Figure 8 shows a simple loop and its dependence flow graph. In the first iteration, the statement x := x+1 reads the value of x assigned by the statement x := 1 outside the loop. Therefore, in the dependence flow graph, we must have a dependence from the assignment statement outside the loop to the use within the loop. In subsequent iterations, the statement x := x+1 reads the value of x assigned in the previous iteration. Therefore, in the dependence flow graph,

---

[6]This device is like scalar expansion [15].

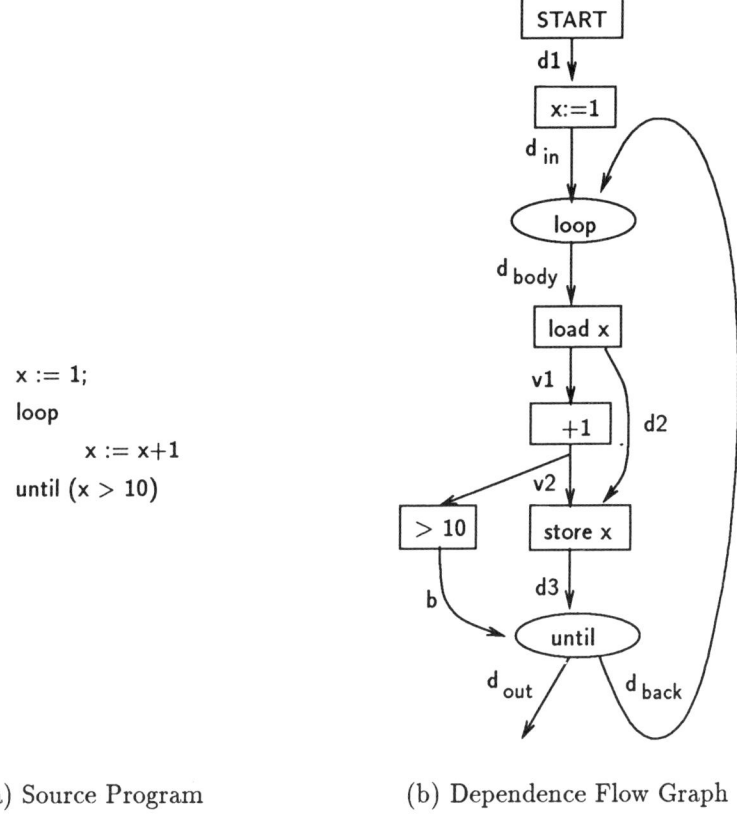

(a) Source Program (b) Dependence Flow Graph

Figure 8: Dependence Flow Graph of a Simple Loop

we must have a dependence from the assignment to x in the ith iteration to the use of x in the $(i+1)^{th}$ iteration. The loop operator (see Figure 7) accomplishes this transfer of dependence from outside the loop into the first iteration and from one iteration to the next. The until operator determines if another iteration of the loop should be executed. In the definition $t, t_{back} = $ until (p, t_{in}), if p is false then another iteration is to be performed, and the dependence t_{back} is satisfied. Otherwise, the loop is to be exited; if this is the $I.j$ iteration of the loop, the dependence $t.I$ outside the loop is satisfied.

3.3 Discussion

The transition system for dependence flow graphs, as described above is deterministic in the sense that it has the *one-step Church-Rosser property*. The proof, which we have omitted for lack of space, rests on the fact that dependence flow graphs, by construction, satisfy Bernstein's conditions. We refer the interested reader to a companion technical report [16].

We can exploit the one-step Church-Rosser property to define a simple interpreter for dependence flow graphs. The interpreter maintains an environment and a store, and keeps a worklist of definitions that may be ready for execution. The initial environment and store are empty, and the worklist is initialized to {START}. While the worklist is not empty, the interpreter dequeues a definition, checks the precondition and performs the transition if the precondition is satisfied. All definitions that are sinks for dependencies sourced by the definition just executed are then enqueued onto the worklist.

The major difference between our representation and conventional dependence graphs is that dependencies, for us, are part of the computational model, and are manipulated by an algebra of operators. Note that load and store, switch and merge, and loop and until are, in an algebraic sense, inverses of each other. Data dependencies are combined with control, and in the next section, we demonstrate how this facilitates the development of optimization algorithms.

4 Constant Propagation on Dependence Flow Graphs

In this section, we demonstrate how global constant propagation can be performed on dependence flow graphs using a simple algorithm based on abstract interpretation. We show that for any program, we can write down a set of equations whose solution corresponds to the possible-paths constants for that program. Next, we show that this solution can be computed efficiently, thereby developing an algorithm that has the same asymptotic complexity as the algorithm due to Wegman and Zadeck [20]. This algorithm can be proved correct by an induction on the length of the computation.

4.1 Equational Characterization of Constants

Figure 9 shows how to write down a set of semantic equations from a dependence flow graph representation of a program. The equations are obtained by replacing the operator in each definition with a function that denotes the abstract interpretation of the operator in Lat. We let $DenOp$ stand for the interpretation of an arithmetic or logical operator op in the domain Lat, as in Section s:constants. The function $DenSw$ stands for the interpretation of switch and is defined as follows:

Syntactic Equation		Semantic Equation	
d	$= \text{START } ()$	d	$= \$$
v	$= \text{op } (v_1, v_2)$	v	$= DenOp(v_1, v_2)$
v_t, v_f	$= \text{switch } (b, v)$	v_t, v_f	$= DenSw(b, v)$
v	$= \text{merge } (v_1, v_2)$	v	$= v_1 \sqcup v_2$
v, d	$= \text{load } (x, d_{in})$	v, d	$= d_{in}, d_{in}$
d	$= \text{store } (x, v, d_{in})$	d	$= \text{if } d_{in} = \bot \text{ then } \bot \text{ else } v$
v	$= \text{loop } (v_{in}, v_{back})$	v	$= v_{in} \sqcup v_{back}$
v, v_{back}	$= \text{until } (b, v_{in})$	v, v_{back}	$= v_{in}, v_{in}$

Figure 9: Abstract Interpretation of Operators

$$DenSw(b, c) = \begin{cases} c, c & \text{if } b = \top \\ c, \bot & \text{if } b = \text{true} \\ \bot, c & \text{if } b = \text{false} \\ \bot, \bot & \text{if } b = \bot \end{cases}$$

This is similar to the standard interpretation of switch, except that it deals with the case when b is $\top$ — if the value of the predicate cannot be determined during constant propagation, then the input value c is propagated to both sides of the switch. Therefore, in the abstract interpretation, both inputs of a merge can be defined. The output of a merge operator is constant only if both inputs are the same constant or if one side of the merge is never executed, and the other side is constant. In the equations, this is stated compactly using the least upper bound operator on Lat.

In the standard semantics, the global store was used to communicate values between the load and store operators. As is the case in all the algorithms discussed in Section 2, the global store plays no role in our constant propagation algorithm. Instead, we take advantage of the fact that there is a flow dependence path in the graph from a store to every load dependent on it. Lattice values are propagated along these paths. The store operator propagates the value of its input to its output, provided that d_{in} is not $\bot$ — that is, if it is possible that this operator may be executed. Therefore, the load operator need only propagate the value of input d_{in} to its outputs.

For any dependence flow graph, we can write down a set of semantic equations over Lat in which the functions on the right hand side are monotonic and continuous. It is a well-known result that such a system of equations has a least solution. Figure 10 shows these values for the program of Figure 5. The possible-paths constants can be read off from the least solution of the semantic equations as follows. Let $C : D \to Lat$ be the least solution. If t is a functional dependence, then, as in Section 2, $C[t] = \bot$ means that the operator that defines t will never be executed, $C[t] = c$ means that if t is ever assigned a value, it is assigned the value c, and $C[t] = \top$ means that the value of t cannot be determined to be constant. The values assigned to imperative dependencies must be interpreted a little differently. Consider dependence d2 in Figure 10. This dependence is given the value 1 by the constant propagation algorithm, but it is given the value $ in the standard interpretation which uses the global store, rather than dependencies, to transmit values between a **store** operation and corresponding **load** operations. If t is an imperative dependence, then $C[t] = \bot$ means that the operator that defines t will never be executed, but if $C[t]$ is any other value, we conclude that this operator may be executed — that is, t may get the value $ in the standard interpretation.

To compute the least solution of the equations efficiently, we run the dependence flow graph interpreter defined in Section 3.3, using the abstract, rather than the standard, interpretation of the operators. This abstract interpreter maintains only an environment, since the store plays no role in constant propagation. In this environment, we keep only a single value associated with each dependence, rather than an indexed family of values, because a dependence is constant only if it is constant in all iterations. Since there are only a finite number of dependencies, we start with an initial environment that maps all dependencies to $\bot$. The worklist of definitions ready for processing is initialized to {START}. While the worklist is non-empty, we remove a definition from the worklist and update the environment using the abstract interpretation rules shown in Figure 9. This update to the environment consists of binding new values to the dependencies whose source is the definition being interpreted.

If the value bound to a dependence changes, we add every definition that is a sink for that dependence to the worklist. Since there can be $O(EV)$ edges in the dependence flow graph and the value propagated along each edge can change at most twice, the complexity of this constant propagation algorithm on dependence flow graphs is $O(EV)$. This is the same asymptotic complexity as that of the algorithm due to Wegman and Zadeck.

This algorithm can be proved correct by a simple induction on the length of the execution sequence. We omit the proof for lack of space and refer the interested reader to the technical report [16].

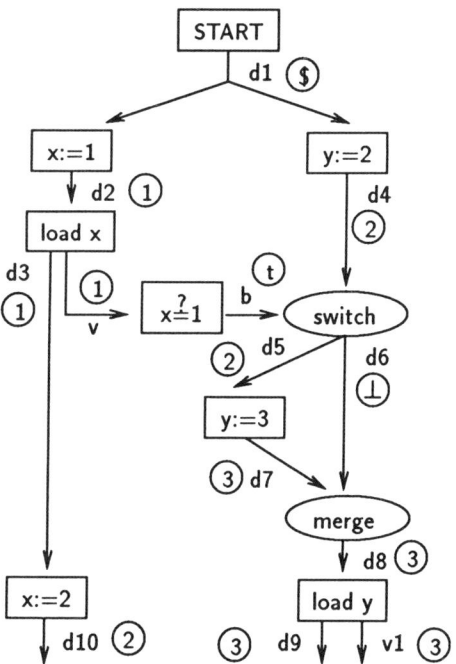

Figure 10: Result of Constant Propagation in Figure 5

5 Conclusions

The ideas presented in this paper form the basis of the Typhoon parallelizing compiler project at Cornell University. We have implemented prototype front-ends that translate programs in FORTRAN and in the dataflow language Id into an intermediate language called Pidgin. Pidgin is a textual form of the dependence flow graph data structure, on which our optimizer is built. The optimizing portion of the compiler is a source-to-source transformer of Pidgin programs.

Much of our future work will focus on loop transformations, scheduling, and code generation for specific architectures. We have extended the definition of dependence flow graphs so that we can represent the dependence information needed to implement loop transformations. Preliminary work on the scheduling of dependence flow graphs has focused on generating code for pipelined RISC architectures such as SPARC; future work will target dataflow architectures, NUMA machines, and VLIW architectures.

References

1. W. B. Ackerman. Efficient implementation of applicative languages. Technical Report TR-323, M.I.T. Laboratory for Computer Science, April 1984.

2. A. V. Aho, R. Sethi, and J. D. Ullman. *Compilers: Principles, Techniques, and Tools.* Addison-Wesley, 1986.

3. Zena Ariola and Arvind. PTAC: A parallel intermediate language. In *Proceedings of the Functional Programming Languages and Computer Architecture*, London, September 1989.

4. Arvind, R. Nikhil, and K. Pingali. I-structures: Data structures for parallel computing. *ACM Transactions on Programming Languages and Systems*, 11, October 1989.

5. M. Auslander and M. Hopkins. An overview of the PL.8 compiler. *Proceedings of the 1982 SIGPLAN Symposium on Compiler Construction*, 17(6):22–31, June 1982.

6. Robert A. Ballance, Arthur B. Maccabe, and Karl J. Ottenstein. The Program Dependence Web: A representation supporting control-, data-, and demand-driven interpretation of imperative languages. *Proceedings of the 1990 SIGPLAN Conference on Programming Language Design and Implementation*, 25(6):257–271, June 1990.

7. Micah Beck and Keshav Pingali. From control flow to dataflow. In *Proceedings of the 1990 International Conference on Parallel Processing*, August 1990.

8. R. Cartwright and M. Felleisen. The semantics of program dependence. *Proceedings of the 1989 SIGPLAN Conference on Programming Language Design and Implementation*, 25(6), June 1989.

9. P. Cousout and R. Cousout. Systematic design of program analysis frameworks. *Proceedings of the 6th ACM Symposium on Principles of Programming Languages*, pages 269–282, January 1979.

10. Ron Cytron, Jeanne Ferrante, Barry K. Rosen, Mark N. Wegman, and F. Kenneth Zadeck. An efficient method of computing static single assignment form. In *Proceedings of the 16th ACM Symposium on Principles of Programming Languages*, pages 25–35, January 1989.

11. K. Ekanadham. Kudos. IBM Yorktown Heights, 1990.

12. J. Ferrante, K. J. Ottenstein, and J. D. Warren. The program dependency graph and its uses in optimization. *ACM Transactions on Programming Languages and Systems*, 9(3):319–349, June 1987.

13. G. A. Kildall. A unified approach to global program optimization. In *Proceedings of the 1st ACM Symposium on Principles of Programming Languages*, pages 194–206, October 1973.

14. D. J. Kuck. *The Structure of Computers and Computations*, volume 1. John Wiley and Sons, New York, 1978.

15. D. Padua and M. Wolfe. Advanced compiler optimization for supercomputers. *Communications of the ACM*, pages 1184–1201, December 1986.

16. Keshav Pingali, Micah Beck, Richard Johnson, Mayan Moudgill, and Paul Stodghill. Dependence Flow Graphs: An algebraic approach to program dependencies. Technical Report TR 90-1152, Cornell University, 1990.

17. Gordon D. Plotkin. A structural approach to operational semantics. Technical Report DAIMI FN-19, Aarhus University, 1981.

18. John H. Reif and H. R. Lewis. Symbolic evaluation and the global value graph. In *Proceedings of the 14th ACM Symposium on Principles of Programming Languages*, pages 104–118, January 1977.

19. G. Steele. RABBIT: A compiler for SCHEME. Technical Report AI memo 474, M.I.T. Laboratory for Artificial Intelligence, May 1978.

20. M. N. Wegman and F. K. Zadeck. Constant propagation with conditional branches. In *Proceedings of the 11th ACM Symposium on Principles of Programming Languages*, pages 291–299, 1984.

Authors' Address: Keshav Pingali
Dept. of Computer Science, Upson Hall
Cornell University
Ithaca, NY 14853
email: pingali@cs.cornell.edu